ARNOLD BENNETT:

The *Evening Standard* Years

'BOOKS AND PERSONS' 1926-1931

ARNOLD BENNETT:

The *Evening Standard* Years

'BOOKS AND PERSONS' 1926-1931

Edited with an Introduction by
ANDREW MYLETT

1974
ARCHON BOOKS

First published 1974 by Chatto & Windus Ltd,
London, and in the United States of America as
an Archon Book, an imprint of The Shoe String
Press, Inc. Hamden, Connecticut 06514

All rights reserved

ISBN 0 208 01444 6

'Books and Persons' 1926–1931
© Dorothy Cheston Bennett and Beaverbrook
Newspapers Ltd.
Introduction, notes and indexes
© 1974 Andrew Mylett

Printed in Great Britain

For Didi

CONTENTS

CONTENTS

CONTENTS

CONTENTS

CONTENTS

CONTENTS

CONTENTS

ACKNOWLEDGMENTS

The publication of this new Arnold Bennett collection was only made possible by the generous co-operation and collaboration of Mrs. Dorothy Cheston Bennett, Mr. Michael Horniman, her literary agent, and, on behalf of Beaverbrook Newspapers Ltd., Mr. Douglas Cobban, of London Express News and Features, Mr. John King, Group Librarian, Mr. A.J.P. Taylor, Honorary Director of the Beaverbrook Library, and Mr. Anthony Hern, Literary Editor of the *Evening Standard*. I am deeply indebted to them all, and thank them once again most sincerely. I am also grateful for the help and advice I have received from my agent, Mr. Richard Simon, and from Sir Rupert Hart-Davis, Mr. Anthony Powell, Professor Walter Allen, Mr. Oliver Warner, Mr. Eric Hiscock, Mr. Richard Bennett, Mr. Henry Adler and Mr. David Batterham. I should like, too, to thank the British Museum Newspaper Library for supplying photocopies of all the *Evening Standard* 'Books and Persons' articles, and the Library of University College, London, for permission to quote two of Arnold Bennett's letters to his agents, J.B. Pinker & Sons. Above all, I thank my wife, for giving and enduring so much more than any work of mine could justify. It is to her I dedicate this book.

The texts of all the 'Books and Persons' articles are reprinted here in their entirety. A few literals have been corrected, the spelling of names standardized, and, for clarity's sake, all book titles italicized. Annotations have been kept to a minimum, allowing the reader, as much as possible, a choice between simply enjoying the articles as articles, just as they originally appeared in the *Evening Standard,* and following up for himself the many autobiographical and literary references, which, if collated here from the complete Bennett *oeuvre* and all surrounding commentaries, would have developed into something of concordance proportions.

All the essential Bennett is to be found – as I now appreciate – in his *Journals* (either Desmond Flower's three-volume edition, Cassell, 1932-3, or Frank Swinnerton's one-volume paperback, Penguin, 1971), his *Letters* (three of four projected volumes having so far been published by O.U.P., 1966-70, all superbly edited by James Hepburn), Reginald Pound's *Arnold Bennett: A Biography* (Heinemann, 1952), Dudley Barker's *Writer By Trade: A View of Arnold Bennett* (Allen & Unwin, 1966), Bennett's own 1917 *Books and Persons* (reprinted in 1968 by Greenwood Press, New York) – and, of course, in the novels themselves, to which these *Evening Standard* articles add such a unique perspective.

A.M.

INTRODUCTION

"I hate to think that anything I write is bad enough, or fragmentary enough, to be lost for ever in the files of a paper," wrote Arnold Bennett in the 27 January 1909 entry of his *Journal*. He had spent two days on the first of a series of articles on novel-writing and the fiction-reading public for his weekly 'Books and Persons' column in *The New Age*, and calculated that within twenty weeks he would have written sufficient for "a striking book." But this, in fact, was one of the very few Bennett projects that was not to see hard covers — at least not as originally conceived, and not until 1917, in a volume of essays suggested and selected by Hugh Walpole one week-end, approved and augmented by Frank Swinnerton, and rounded off by Bennett himself — "softening the crudity of several epithets, and censoring lines here and there which might give offence without helping the sacred cause." It was published by Chatto & Windus (with a grateful dedication "To Hugh Walpole") as *Books and Persons*: Being Comments on a Past Epoch: 1908 - 1911, in July 1917, and sold 3,400 copies in the first five months of publication.

The *New Age* articles from which the selection (one third of the original) was made ran — or, as Bennett so characteristically recalled, "enlivened" the magazine — from 21 March 1908, the year of publication of *The Old Wives' Tale*, to 7 September 1911, the very month in which *Hilda Lessways* was published, appearing above the pseudonym of "Jacob Tonson." Though in a letter Bennett wrote that he only knew of him as "an 18th century publisher," one brief description of Tonson by a contemporary and fellow publisher, John Dunton, recorded in John Nichols' *Literary Anecdotes of the Eighteenth Century*, emphasizes the appropriateness of the pseudonym for Bennett: "a very good judge of persons and authors . . . there is none who does it with more severe exactness or with less partiality, and will flatter nobody."

For the first eighteen months or so, Bennett wrote for nothing — *The New Age*, operating at a loss of over a thousand pounds a year, rarely paid its contributors — but eventually he received a "munificent" guinea a week, as the column did far more than enliven the magazine: it became its most distinguished literary feature, acknowledged as "the most widely read literary causerie of any of our weeklies."

Reviewing the 1917 Chatto collection in *The New Age* itself, the editor, A.R. Orage, wrote that "there neither is, nor has been, in English letters, Mr. Bennett's parallel as a literary causeur. He has all the qualifications for a leading part in this role — an immense store of reading, an eye for contemporary literary happenings, a minute acquaintance with the practical world of publishing, personal relations with authors, a practical experience both of writing and selling, liveliness, audacity, and above all a most readable style. You can read Mr. Bennett's literary criticisms even when you do not agree with a word of them. . . . Disagree as you may please with his judgments, you can seldom dismiss them either as superficial or as idiosyncrasies. There is always something competent, professional, and respectable about them."

"If this column has any interest of originality," Bennett wrote in one of the essays in 1909, "it is that it expresses the point of view of the creative artist as distinguished from that of the critic." And indeed throughout his reviewing career it was as a practitioner, as one who knew so thoroughly and valued so highly the craft of writing, that Bennett could communicate so directly to his readers the excitement and the importance even of the written word. "Jacob Tonson," as John Gross has remarked, "was nothing if not a journalist. He brought his readers news about literature" — and his column Frank Swinnerton has described as "quite different from the literary letters of C.K.S. [Clement Shorter] and Claudius Clear [W. Robertson Nicoll] and the sedate gossips of other bookmen . . . it opened our eyes. The Continent, we found, was rich in authors to be read and judged and perhaps emulated. How exciting that was; and what a challenge to intelligence. . . . His words about Russian writers . . . made his readers examine the meagre representation of Russian novelists standing on their shelves, and long for more." And Bennett/"Tonson" gave them more: most notably Chekhov and Dostoevsky.

His review of the second collection of Chekhov's stories (the first, published in 1903, had already been out of print for several years) was the first true recognition of his genius: "We have no writer, and we never have had one, nor has France, who could mould the material of life, without distorting it, into such complex forms to such an end of beauty." Very soon translations of other Chekhov stories began to appear in *The New Age* itself, and gradually readers and writers (Katherine Mansfield among the first) began to make the same discovery for themselves. Bennett's praise of Dostoevsky, a year later, had an even more immediate and sensational effect. Writing of an early scene in *The Brothers Karamazov* (which he had recently read in a bad and incomplete French translation), "There is nothing in either English or French prose literature to hold a candle to it," he asked: "And now, Mr. Heinemann, when are we going to have a complete Dostoevsky in English?" Six weeks later plans were announced by Heinemann for the publication of all the principal novels of Dostoevsky, to be translated by Constance Garnett. *The Brothers Karamazov* was the first to appear, two years later, in 1912 — thirty-two years after the publication of the original — and the 12 volume edition was completed by 1920.

But if, during his years of writing for *The New Age*, Bennett for the first time made news of literature, in the 1920s and until his death in 1931 he himself was news — and his influence even greater. He became, as Walter Allen has written, "a public figure in a way and of a kind no other English novelist has ever been, not even Dickens."

Once again it was his journalism that accounted for much of his popularity: incredibly he had still not had what could be termed a best-seller (the first publishers of *The Old Wives' Tale*, Chapman & Hall, had allowed it to go out of print within two years), and although *Milestones, The Great Adventure* and other plays had brought him immense success in the theatre, to the public at large he was still best known for his writings in the popular press. A series of articles in the *Daily Express* in 1921, another in *John Bull* the following year, and numerous occasional and controversial pieces elsewhere soon established him as the most prominent journalist — some would say pundit — of the day. As his *Times* obituary was to recognize, he had studied and mastered "the methods of what is now called

xvi

'getting it across'," and with his instinctive love of journalism, and genius for working consciously on different levels, he was in constant demand. His provocative but sympathetic review of *Ulysses* (for which Joyce wrote to thank him) in *Outlook* was boldly advertised on posters proclaiming "Arnold Bennett on *Ulysses*" — "the first time," he wrote, "I have ever seen a *review* as the chief item on a poster."

Then, in October 1923, *Riceyman Steps* was published. It immediately received almost unanimous acclaim — Wells thought it "a great book," Conrad wrote to tell Bennett of his admiration for "the whole achievement" and Hardy, according to his wife, "had not been so interested in a novel for years" — and, unlike any previous Bennett novel, it sold over 30,000 copies in its first three months of publication. The following October it was awarded the Tait Black Novel Prize for 1923 — "the first prize for a book I ever had," Bennett recorded in his *Journal*. At last he had broken through to a wider reading public — though he felt sure "it's all on account of Elsie. What a way of appreciating a book: good God!" "Even barbers delicately mention it to me." "I am suddenly the darling of the public."

In Part III of the book, in a moment of "sublime extravagance," Earlforward summons Elsie to "run out and buy me the *Evening Standard*. . . . Here's a penny." And though she is only able to get a *Star* — the *Standards* "were all sold out" — it was a considerable coincidence that in the same year as the novel was published, 1923, Lord Beaverbrook, a close friend of Bennett's since 1918, actually succeeded in buying the *Evening Standard* (for rather more than Earlforward's penny) from Edward Hulton.

As Minister of Information in 1918, Beaverbrook had invited Bennett to direct British propaganda in France (above all because he so admired the deep understanding of the French psyche which he found in *The Pretty Lady*, a novel that, according to Bennett, "considerably disgusted" his "bourgeois public"). He accepted the invitation, though he refused a salary, and as Beaverbrook recalled in his sixtieth birthday tribute to Bennett, "He showed such remarkable gifts for administration that in the end he rose to Deputy Minister" and "at the end of the war, I recommended [him] for a knighthood." That he was not in fact knighted, Beaverbrook added, "was due to Arnold Bennett himself. He wrote a simple and dignified letter, with no attempt to be brilliant or funny or superior, in which he explained that he would rather that his name did not go forward for this honour."

The friendship between Bennett and Beaverbrook, however, grew steadily deeper with the years, and Reginald Pound has written that "For Arnold Bennett he seems to have been 'the Card' raised to the *n*th power, economically all-conquering, socially masterful, temperamentally intimidating, an ennobled gnome whose ear-to-ear grin proclaimed good-nature and disguised harshness. Lord Beaverbrook's name is written often in the journal pages of the 'twenties; testimony to an intimacy which Bennett relished."

It was only natural, therefore, that when Beaverbrook bought the *Standard* he should ask Bennett's opinion of it, and receive exactly the kind of thoughtful and incisive reply he had hoped for:

INTRODUCTION

24th October 1923

My dear Max,

    re the *Standard*. This is the only evening paper that appeals even a little to educated people, and it ought to be made to appeal a great deal more to them than it does. You can't, in my opinion, get much prestige out of a yellow paper. Hence I wouldn't let it be yellow. . . .

    I should make the *Standard*'s policy positive, not negative. And I should make it less opportunist. You *must* do this if you want prestige. You won't get prestige without burning your boats, nailing colours to the mast, etc. Nobody ever did. I should preserve freedom to be cynical and critical of anybody and everybody. Surely you can afford to do this in *one* paper? I should have the whole paper well written; and especially the news stories — at present they are not interestingly written; they lack brilliance. Books, pictures, theatres and music are none of them well done at present . . . .

    I can see a *Standard* that every well-educated person would *have* to read, if only for pleasure, but it is not the present *Standard* . . . .

    If you think only of circulation you won't get prestige, and if you think only of prestige you won't get circulation; but there is a middle course, with a slight inclination to the right!

Yours, A.B.

Beaverbrook was more than able to repay him for his advice when, a little over eighteen months later, Bennett began work on *Lord Raingo*. Beaverbrook supplied many of the details of Cabinet procedure, recorded at length in Bennett's notebooks and *Journals*, along with a scheme for another novel, based on Beaverbrook's father's dying years — "absolutely brilliant, showing how his own great worldly success had brought about an almost startling change in the old man's ideas and tastes. Its possibilities excited me" — and yet another for "a fine, grim, ruthless novel" about collusion between the parties to a divorce case.

    But it was for *Lord Raingo* that Bennett had most to thank Beaverbrook. "The political part," he could assure his American publisher, George Doran, "was carefully vetted by Beaverbrook," and as Reginald Pound, again, has written, "When Winston Churchill spoke 'very flatteringly' to Bennett about the novel and especially about the accuracy of his description of Cabinet meetings and surroundings — 'you must have been a fly on the wall' — he was also complimenting Lord Beaverbrook." One of Bennett's finest and most personal novels — Frank Swinnerton has said it is "in reality an extraordinarily sincere portrait of Bennett himself in late middle age, and in pain and fear of death" — *Raingo* was in fact bought by Beaverbrook for pre-publication serialization in the *Evening Standard* for £1,100. He spent a further £5,000 on his advertising campaign — large posters all over London asked the question "Who is Lord Raingo?" (Bennett found it "all very vulgar" but hoped it would at least help sell the book) — and when serialization began on 20 September 1926 it aroused an immediate and lasting controversy. Acknowledged, and in some circles condemned, as a roman a clef, in which various members of the War cabinet — Lord Rhondda, Churchill and Lloyd George in particular — were, it was claimed, readily identifiable, the book was published by Cassell early the following month,

xviii

and sold 18,450 copies in the first ten days. "The booming of this novel has been terrific," wrote Bennett in his *Journal*.

In the *Evening Standard* a month later, on 17 November 1926, a bold display headed "Mr. Arnold Bennett on Books" announced that the paper would "begin publication to-morrow of a feature unique in London journalism. Mr. Arnold Bennett, the famous novelist, who years ago earned fame as a literary critic, has consented to resume the role, and will contribute to our columns a weekly causerie of current literary events, discussed with the candour and pungency that mark all his published work. . . ."

Bennett's *Journal* account of the background to the venture is as casual as it is amusing:

> Saturday, 23 October [1926] . . . At 12.15 we drove down to Cherkley to lunch with Max. Max asked me if I would write a weekly article on books under my own name for the *Evening Standard*. I didn't give a definite answer, but what I said and didn't say was not short of a consent . . .

Ten days later:

> Tuesday, 2 November: Beaverbrook and Jean Norton came to lunch. I agreed with Max to do a series of book gossip articles for the *Evening Standard*, beginning next week. Then I rushed off to Wardour films, and spent a final 2¾ hours on *Faust*, finishing it except for passing proofs of titles and choosing some types.

The first article, "Price of Novels Must Come Down," billed as "provocative" in the same November 17 *Standard* announcement, was inevitably picked up on publication and reported in several other newspapers — first, of course, in Beaverbrook's own *Daily Express*. Once again Bennett was making books news, but on this particular occasion he was not at all pleased with the way the news was being handled:

> 18 November 1926
>
> My dear Max,
>
> With reference to the stuff in the *Express* this morning, I hope that care will be taken in future not to give a wrong idea on my stuff. One would get the impression from the *D.E.* that the article was an attack on booksellers. Of course it is not so. The booksellers are mentioned quite incidentally.
>
> Nor do I seek a quarrel with booksellers. Far from it.
>
> Thine, Arnold

By return, Beaverbrook replied:

> 19 November 1926
>
> My dear Arnold,
>
> I am not going to enter into a controversy with you either by letter or word of mouth about anything. If you object to the kind of publicity your articles are getting, I will have it struck out, because I

am keenly anxious that you should not be annoyed by reading a
type of publicity you do not like. . . .

But I would point out to you that both the *Westminster Gazeteer*
and the *Morning Post* in noticing your *Evening Standard* article this
morning select for comment the two points Philpott* stressed i.e. the
excessive price of books and the bad arrangement of booksellers'
windows.

Yours ever, Max

Again, by return, Bennett wrote:

20 November 1926

My dear Max,

Many thanks. I quite see your point of view. I quite understand
Mr. Philpott's difficulty. I quite understand that publicity is a necessary
part of business, and I have no general objection to it.

I know I can rely on you to appreciate the baseness of my motives
in not wishing to quarrel with booksellers. There are at least two realists
in this country — you and me.

. . . All this is as naught to the trouble I shall get into when I begin
to be realistic about the work of my friends. And as I am in personal
relations with nearly all living authors who are worth a damn, and
many who are not worth a damn. . . .

However.

Thine, Arnold

The business settled, a fortnight or so later, Beaverbrook raised a rather
more delicate matter:

December 9, 1926

My dear Arnold,

Would you tell me please what arrangements I made with you about
payment for your articles in the *Evening Standard*.

I cannot remember our conversation on the subject.

Yours ever, Max

Bennett promptly replied with a full "history of the affair":

10 December 1926

My dear Max,

. . . I suggested to you about a year ago, when you told me that you
intended to enlarge the *E.S.* that I should write book articles *under a
pseudonym*.

On the 9th December 1925 you wrote to me thus:

"I also mentioned to Thompson† our conversation about a weekly
article on books. He says he would be glad to take the article over your
signature and pay 'Arnold Bennett' rates. If the article is to be anony-

* H.R.S. Phillpott, then Assistant Editor of the *Express*.

† E.R. Thompson, then Editor of the *Standard*.

mous, he loses the benefit of your name. In such circumstances, he would pay the rates you would expect him to pay W.J. Locke."

I replied that we need not discuss terms as I had offered you the anonymous articles for nothing, and that we would leave the matter to Thompson.

The matter then fell into abeyance for a long time. When I was at Cherkley in the autumn you asked me to write articles under my own name. I said I would think it over.

When you came to this house for lunch, I told you that I had thought it over and that I would write articles under my own name.

Nothing was said by either you or me about payment, and I did not think that anything had to be said, in view of the explicit statement in your letter of the 9th December 1925 as to what Thompson said about payment. . . .

Thine, Arnold

Two letters, both of the same date, were then sent by Beaverbrook to Bennett:

December 15, 1926

My dear Arnold,

Excuse me for the delay in replying to your letter, but I have been filled with anxiety.

I propose to pay you 1/6d. Does this rate seem good in your sight?

Yours ever, Max

And:

December 15, 1926

My dear Arnold,

Here is the last bottle of 1906 champagne I shall be able to send you and I have had to take it out of my own cellar.

My Christmas wishes go with it.

Yours ever, Max

Once more, from Bennett:

16 December 1926

My dear Max,

Sorry to hear that you have been filled with anxiety.

The rate of 1/6d a word will be quite satisfactory to me. It has always been the *Standard* and *Express* rate for me, I have no quarrel with it. But I do not want anybody round your way to go and talk about it, because all other papers pay me 33⅓d per cent more.

Thine ever, Arnold

(It was also, incidentally, agreed when Bennett began his *Evening Standard* articles that he should be entitled to *keep* all books sent for review: Beaverbrook had until then always insisted that his reviewers return them to him for his private library.)

Early in the New Year, Bennett wrote to his agents, J.B. Pinker & Sons:

19 January 1927

Gentlemen,

With reference to my *Evening Standard* articles, I understand that they are being largely cabled to U.S.A. and used there either in whole or in part, in several newspapers. I have had another enquiry for them today from the Herald-Tribune Syndicate. I have given no definite reply. I think it might be worth your while to go into the matter with expedition. The only snag is that the *Evening Standard* might be saying that they had had enough of them, because of the price. I have no doubt that these are easily the highest paid book articles in the world. I get £300* a month for them from the *Evening Standard*, and the length runs from 800 to 1000 words each. . . .

Quite apart from the money and the immense popularity of the articles, Bennett clearly enjoyed writing them — "They get me into trouble, but it is the sort of trouble which I can handle" — and was able to write them with an ease, speed and convenience that both suited and delighted him, as his *Journals* show:

Wednesday, July 20th [1927] By way of holiday today, the day after finishing my novel [*Accident*], I wrote two *Evening Standard* articles, one in the morning, and the other in the afternoon.

Sunday, August 28th [1927] . . . I couldn't concentrate on my own story, so I wrote an *Evening Standard* article on thrillers, etc.

Saturday, October 15th [1927] Madame Komisarjevsky was to arrive at 3.30 to play duets with me. I was fully awake at 3, and so I thought I would just begin my next week's *Evening Standard* article. She came at 4.15. By that time I had nearly finished my article. . . . I finished my *Evening Standard* article before dinner, all by utilising spare moments. This is the secret of doing more work than you can in the time at your disposal.

V.S. Pritchett has called Bennett "the first time-and-motion figure in our literature."

But on at least one occasion he was prepared to write one of his 'Books and Persons' articles at exceptionally short notice:

Wednesday, January 11th [1928] The *Daily News* rang up to say that Hardy was dead, and would I say something. I wouldn't. But I decided that I must get up early tomorrow and write a *Standard* article on Hardy to take the place of the one on Gilbert Murray.†

Thursday, January 12th Rose at 5.50. Began to write an article on

* The equivalent of approximately $1,500.00 at that time.

† Held over for one week as a result.

the late Hardy at 6 and finished it at 8.30. At 9.5 an *Evening Standard*
messenger came to fetch it in a taxi.

The article, "The True Greatness of Thomas Hardy," appeared in the
Evening Standard the same day.

It was at about this time that rumours began to circulate in Fleet Street
that Bennett was considering leaving the *Standard*.

He wrote to his agent:

31st January 1928

Dear Ralph Pinker,

Thanks for yours of yesterday. I too have frequently heard the
rumour that I was leaving the *Evening Standard*. I heard it so often
that I told the editor about it. His reply was that he had heard nothing
of it himself. When I suggested to Beaverbrook some months ago that
they must be getting a bit tired of me, he would not hear of such a
thing. My own opinion is that they must sooner or later get tired of
paying me £3,750 a year for such a short article on such a subject.
I believe, however, that they are very pleased with it.

I have been approached (by Newman Flower) about transferring
the article to another paper at the same price, but I have of course
told him that there is nothing doing. If I leave the *Evening Standard*
of my own accord it will not be to go to another paper, even at twice
the price.

Yours sincerely, Arnold Bennett.

Several weeks later, when asked by Beaverbrook if he had any objection
to his authorizing syndication of the articles in some provincial papers —
the same that were taking David Low's cartoons — Bennett replied most
emphatically that "there can be no doubt, and it is hereby stated formally,
that the serial copyright of my 'Books and Persons' articles in the United
Kingdom belongs to the proprietors of the *Evening Standard*. The said
proprietors are therefore at full liberty to sell the articles for serial use in
provincial newspapers for their own profit."

The articles were in fact so successful that the *Standard's* circulation,
incredibly, rose on book review day. Desmond MacCarthy admitted that he,
like so many people, would "buy on Thursdays the *Evening Standard* for
his sake." Publishers sent their messengers to queue in Shoe Lane for the
early morning edition, and invariably rushed through another printing of
any book he praised — just as booksellers would often order more than a
hundred extra copies on the strength of a favourable Bennett review.

Publishers' advertisements occasionally featured Bennett's name and
review in larger, bolder type than either the title or the author of a book in
which he had found some merit. But as Eric Hiscock (better known today
as "Whitefriar" of *Smith's Trade News* but in 1929 just beginning as "an
advertising-cum-editorial" member of the *Standard* staff) recalls, though
Bennett "knew all about the prevalent quote-with-advertising lark . . . he
encouraged the legend that he went through his copy with a comb to extract
any possible quotes likely to appeal to paying customers" and "alone of all
the book critics (I'd say) . . . was free of the much-talked-about 'booksy

racket'." Even so, knowing that one of Hiscock's duties was to pick up Bennett's "reviewscript" every Monday morning, certain publishers would "lie in wait" for him until late Monday afternoon "then telephone to know whether A.B. was reviewing one of their books. The chances were they would buy advertisement space in the *Standard* the following week if he was, but what they wanted to do more than anything else was lift a handsome quote from the *Standard*, then spend good money advertising it in the top two Sunday sheets, the *Observer* and the *Sunday Times.*"

Certainly no writer either before or since has enjoyed such popularity and celebrity — again Bennett's name and photograph seemed to be in newspapers, on hoardings and public transport posters everywhere ("my physiog on the walls of London, horribly revolting") — and with each week's column he consolidated and confirmed his position as quite the most powerful and important reviewer of books in England. He became compulsory reading.

For many still today Bennett's *Evening Standard* years represent the very highest achievement in modern literary journalism. Dudley Barker has written that "No series of articles in a London newspaper . . . stands out so strongly in newspaper history and public reputation as Bennett's 'Books and Persons' articles." And likewise Reginald Pound has remarked that the success of the series has now "passed into the history of London book-publishing and reviewing."

In his Preface to the 1938 Stonehill sale catalogue of the reviews in manuscript, Sir Hugh Walpole declared that "Bennett was the only man in my literary lifetime who could really make the fortune of a new book in a night." But the familiar list of such best-sellers — *Jew Süss* (which, eighteen months after reviewing so effectively, Bennett wrote "is being overpraised today"), *The Bridge of San Luis Rey, Vivandière, The Story of San Michele,* etc. — seems far less important and impressive today than the extraordinary series of first judgments which Bennett made between 1926 and 1931.

The *Evening Standard* 'Books and Persons' articles really monitored one of the most productive periods in modern literature. Bennett wrote at the time: "I honestly think that we live in a period of quite unusually good authorship, a period which will compare well with any previous period." Lawrence, Joyce, Eliot, Yeats, Shaw, Wells, Galsworthy, Maugham, Huxley, Virginia Woolf, Wyndham Lewis, Dreiser, Faulkner and Hemingway all were writing during this time, which also saw the sudden spate of war books from Graves, Blunden, Mottram, Manning and Remarque in particular.

Bennett was the first English reviewer to recognize Faulkner (on Richard Hughes' recommendation he wrote to his own American publisher in 1929 for copies of *Soldiers' Pay, Mosquitoes* and *The Sound and the Fury*), and one of the earliest champions of Dreiser (having also made the "first printed fuss" about *Sister Carrie*, in *The Academy*, shortly after its publication in 1900, when it received appalling reviews in the United States) and Hemingway ("Short sentences, page after page, admirably marshalled and grouped. Its detachment is perfect"). Lawrence he considered "the strongest novelist writing today," "not yet understood even by the majority of his admirers."

He described himself in one article as "perhaps the most active encourager and chastiser of youthful authors among sexuagenarians," and

xxiv

certainly immediately spotted Graham Greene, Evelyn Waugh, Henry Williamson, Richard Hughes and Ivy Compton-Burnett. With Eliot (whose *Waste Land* he persistently pluralized) he experienced something of a block — "I do like to understand what I am reading" — and admitted to "notorious grave reservations concerning Virginia Woolf."

With a number of eighteenth- and nineteenth-century writers his reservations were even stronger — Richardson, for example: "Life is far longer than it used to be but it is still far too short for *Clarissa*"; Kingsley: "of course he never uses two words if eight or ten will do"; Dickens: "Ninety per cent of Dickens bores me. I can't help it. I won't hide it"; Meredith: "not, in my opinion, a novelist by either birth or inclination"; and Henry James: "It took me years to ascertain that Henry James's work was giving me little pleasure."

His familiar idols, on the other hand, are frequently invoked — "my adored Dostoevsky": "whenever my mind dwells on the greatest achievements in fiction, I think, before any other novel, of *The Brothers Karamazov*"; Balzac: "no novelist since him has really carried the novel further than he carried it"; Stendhal: "my idea of a supremely readable writer"; Chekhov: "greater even than de Maupassant"; Turgenev: "could say more in fewer words than any other novelist that ever lived"; Hawthorne: whose "writing has not been surpassed"; and, of course, George Moore: "in my opinion the greatest living novelist."

Firmly independent of all cliques and academic standards, Bennett achieved a *rapport* with his public that remains as unique as anything else about his 'Books and Persons' articles. Frank Swinnerton has observed so well that "he wrote with a sort of slippered ease; he always talked so that all might join in. He did this in the *Evening Standard*." And who but Bennett could assure his readers so plainly that "I would not mislead you," or, rather more comically, when reviewing Joyce's *Anna Livia Plurabelle*, "it is utterly incomprehensible to me, and it will be to you"?

He wrote his 'Books and Persons' column, he declared, "as a mere student of letters," "on behalf of the great trade union of average intelligent persons," "plain persons such as myself," "the man in the literary street" — "I have no sympathy with the too prevalent writers' tendency to despise the non-writing public," "I am not of the elect and never shall be" — and classed himself variously as "a bookman," "a pseudo-scholar" (he was delighted that E.M. Forster did likewise) and even as "a low-brow" (notably in a reference to "the queen of the high-brows," Virginia Woolf, whose attacks on him both in *Mr. Bennett and Mrs. Brown* and elsewhere, though since quite discredited, had a considerable effect at the time).

Bennett never forgot that "an author does not succeed until he is read," or that most people care so little for literature that they could not "get up any interest in a novel though it were written by God himself." The reviewer, therefore, not the publisher, he insisted, must be "the midwife of new literature." Yet "Many professional critics" seemed to him to "give the impression that literature is the bane of their lives." Still "More subtle is the lying that goes on about what you like and what you don't like. The temptation is tremendous to say that you like what you think you ought to like and don't like what you think you oughtn't to like." "An honest individual opinion, though it may be bad or half bad, is better morally and perhaps artistically, too, than an insincere opinion which coincides with authoritative opinion." "What is the use of pretence?"

Bennett's own first aim was "always to interest the public." Ivor Brown has noted "his power to make a book article not just something put in a corner for the benefit of the bookish," and readers' letters regularly paid tribute to this unique ability: "He has rediscovered the art of reviewing a book in that he does not use it as a mirror to reflect his own erudition, but gently indicates the features that have earned his appreciation. No other living writer can so accurately gauge and enter into the sensibilities of the average man."

The *Saturday Review* wrote: "It is impossible to calculate the effect of good regular literary criticism, such as that of Arnold Bennett every Thursday in the *Evening Standard*, has on taste and on the prospects of the book trade. This feature was an experiment for a popular evening newspaper, of which many at the outset doubted the wisdom, but there can be few now that have not been converted. Perhaps the best proof of its success is the imitation it has received."

And the *New Statesman's* contributor on Current Literature wrote "Nobody who has not tried to do this sort of work knows how difficult it is — not only to write such articles, but to choose the proper book to write about.

"The impression that I have got from reading him, over what is now a considerable stretch of time, is that he has been a most effective influence on the side of the better fiction as against average or inferior fiction. He has a cluster of qualities which fit him admirably to exercise such influence: his immense knowledge of the art of fiction; his intellectual honesty, which is visible in his own novels, and his sympathy both with the point of view of a writer and of a reader.

"He will stick up stoutly for a book, though it must disconcert the average reader, if he perceives in it talent or an interesting or an original intention, on the other hand, he never forgets that the reader also wants to be amused, stirred, carried out of himself as well as to read what he may believe, either on trust or from inspection, to be remarkable."

In turning down an invitation from Eliot to contribute to the *Criterion* in June 1927, Bennett confessed "I am really afraid of doing so. I should have to take so much care over it! My articles, especially those about books, are rather slapdash. I am also handicapped by an intense ignorance. Indeed my life-long regret is that I have no exact knowledge on any subject on earth. I always envy scholars."

Nevertheless, it was his firm belief that "a reviewer must be a journalist before he is a reviewer," and as Ivor Brown, once more, has written, "good journalists know that their readers are usually in a hurry. A havering and wordy introduction will deter them. Cloudiness of thought and style will annoy them. Bennett never havered, was never vague, and never expressed hesitant opinions in a long, tangled sentence." In fact his 'Books and Persons' style was emphatic yet casual, blunt yet thoughtful, conversational yet epigrammatic, and if on occasions slangy — he favoured "sound anti-tosh common sense," which he found so lacking in the writings of "the educated mob," "the big guns" — his sentences and his paragraphs even seem written to suit exactly the speed and flow of a less than three inch wide newspaper column. Like other writers who have suffered a speech impediment throughout their lives, Bennett enjoyed all the more the unbothered comfort of the written word — although almost certainly, as Frank Swinnerton has said, his "painful struggle with speech . . . created the staccato of his emphatic journalism."

He rarely revised, and marked the completion of each 100 words with a small asterisk, entering the final word total in the margin in the minute and immaculate handwriting that was so indicative of his orderliness generally. He was in all ways an ideal journalist — outranking even the greatest of his contemporaries — and as one of his editors recalled, "I could always send Bennett's stuff to the printer exactly as he sent it to us; for it required no sub-editing."

He equally rarely read all of any new book he was reviewing — confessing, even emphasising, in his articles that he tended rather to "read *in*" or "run through" a work, confident that "the reviewer who knows his job can sometimes get the hang of a book in one minute." Inevitably he made mistakes — usually tending to over-benevolence or over-excitement about a new young writer — though "in reality I restrain myself with extraordinary force." And as Samuel Hynes has pointed out, "he was always careful to distinguish the literary artist from the merely popular writer; he never confused his standards."

But literary criticism, he argued, is "not merely a report on a book; it is a report of the reaction of an individuality *to* a book," because "It is not what a man knows that counts in literary criticism, not what he prefers, but what he *is*." And what Arnold Bennett was is plain from the testimonies of the many writers who knew him. Maugham wrote that "He was devoid of envy. He was generous. He was courageous. He always said with perfect frankness what he thought and because it never struck him that he could offend he seldom did"; Swinnerton, that "His integrity was perfect; his humour all-pervading; his magnanimity beyond the dreams of his adverse critics"; Huxley, that he was "One of the most thoroughly 'decent' men I have ever known" and "A first-rate critic of books and men"; Wells, that he was "the best friend I've ever had," "He radiated and evoked affection"; and Walpole, "the one absolutely honest, unprejudiced and wide-seeing critic I know."

He had, of course, his detractors too. Principally, perhaps, Wyndham Lewis, who on one occasion called him "the Hitler of the book racket" and in *Time and Tide* a year after Bennett's death criticized his "Tipster Technique in Literary Criticism" — displaying in the resulting correspondence even more of the "combativeness" that Bennett had so deplored in his not altogether favourable *Evening Standard* review of *The Enemy* five years earlier: "finally he would praise any book put under his nose, whose author, or whose backers, would be liable to write him a 'snooty' letter."

But as Lord Beaverbrook wrote in his obituary article, "Arnold Bennett as I knew him," "In one striking respect he differed from the great tribe of writers — he was absolutely immune from professional jealousy. In fact, in estimating the literary claims of his contemporaries he leaned to the contrary side of generosity. And in another respect he exhibited a compound of qualities which are profoundly unusual. That he had genius few would deny; but his really distinguishing feature was common sense."

Apart from one or two letters and a *Journal* entry, an *Evening Standard*

'Books and Persons' article was in fact the last thing that Bennett wrote during his fatal illness early in 1931. On Monday, January 26 he had seemed to begin to make a recovery from what was then thought to be influenza, and on Sunday, February 1, wrote his next 'Books and Persons' article as usual. But at 12.30 the following day, as he recorded in his *Journal*, he "learnt that the book I had written about yesterday for 'Books and Persons' in the *Evening Standard* was not to be published till the 16th! Terrible. So I had to write another article, on Mrs C.N. Williamson's reminiscences. . . . I began the article at 4.30 and finished it at 6.10. Not bad."

On Tuesday, February 3, he again felt "wretchedly ill," and shortly afterwards was confined to bed with what was now diagnosed as typhoid fever (contracted through drinking water while in France just after Christmas). Reports began to appear in the newspapers that "Mr. Arnold Bennett, who has influenza, did not have a good night, and was not quite so well today" (February 10), then for a while there were "good news" stories that his illness "has taken a turn for the better, and he is now, I hope, on the way to complete recovery" (February 28). But by March 22 *The Times* reported that "Mr. Bennett has been lying ill with influenza for some weeks at his flat in Chiltern Court, Baker Street. On Friday he had a relapse, and his condition was stated to be critical.

"In an effort to obtain complete quiet for her husband, Mrs. Bennett endeavoured to get traffic diverted from Marylebone Road. It was not possible to arrange this, but instead permission was given for straw to be laid in the road for a distance of 150 yards outside the house. Traffic approaching Chiltern Court was slowed down by the police yesterday, and every effort was made to avoid noise, which it was feared would have a bad effect on the patient's heart." On March 24 it was finally announced in the Press that he was in fact suffering from typhoid fever, and on March 25 that "His doctors today carried out a blood transfusion . . . which was entirely successful." But two days later, at ten minutes to nine on the evening of Friday, March 27, he died. He was sixty-three.

Arnold Bennett disliked most introductions to books, finding them "written on a note of ill-advised profuse-at-any-cost laudation which develops in me a mood the very opposite of what is desired." But as the author of more than twenty prefaces and introductions himself — to everything from Low's *Lloyd George & Co* to *The Plays of Noel Coward* (*First Series*) — perhaps he would at least have understood the need today for something to precede the following collection from "the files of a paper."

18 November 1926

"Price of Novels Must Come Down"

Jeremiahs continually lament over the present state of literature; and their burden is that more bad books are published nowadays than ever before. But, of course, they do not phrase it as simply as that. They use a metaphor, of which the key-word is "flood." They never speak of bad literature without comparing it to a flood "poured forth by the Press." (You see, "poured" begins with a "p." and so does "Press," and an explosive alliteration always helps Jeremiahs.)

I agree that more bad books are published nowadays than ever before; but only because more books are published than ever before; more good books also are published nowadays than ever before; the level of production has risen. And who knows a good book from a bad book within a year, or five years, from publication? Very few of us.

Example: Up till quite a short time ago works of reference were referring to *Moby Dick* as negligible, or not referring to it at all. Further, nobody is compelled to read bad books. If bad books are issued, that is the affair of the publishers. Publishers cannot tempt you to pay to enter an enclosed place and then force you to listen to the rendering of a bad book, as cinema managers can tempt you, and then force you to witness a bad film. Readers are free not to read. None can be bored or corrupted against his will.

The trouble in literature is not at the authors' end. It is at the readers' end. The population abuses its liberty not to read. Not enough new books are bought. Indeed, the number of new books bought is almost infinitesimal compared to the population.

Look for a moment at the figures. The population of the British Empire is about 450 millions. A new book that sells 45,000 copies (including Colonial editions) is a terrific success. That is to say, a book is a terrific success if one copy is sold for every ten thousand Imperial subjects. But let us leave out the Empire, as being too vast, and limit ourselves to these islands, with a population of about 45 millions, of whom about half are adult. We then see that the number of copies sold of a terrific success is appreciably less than the five-hundredth part of the potential public.

Visualise a public procession of adults filing past you. On the average 500 individuals would pass you before a purchaser of a terrific success passes you. Grasp this, and if you are convinced of the educational power of books, you will have a sleepless night.

I am by no means the first to notice the appalling discrepancy between the number of potential book-buyers and the number of actual book-buyers. Certain publishers, booksellers, and authors had noticed it, and they have collaborated to form the National Book Council — a body whose objects are the promotion of book-reading and the wider distribution of books, and whose organiser and address are Mr. Maurice Marston,

1

30, Little Russell-street, W.C.1, London.

The National Book Council seeks its ends by administering tonics to educational authorities, the clergy, the film-world, the Press; and by arranging lectures for the stimulation of the general public. Its ends are noble; its methods are sound — so far as they go. I applaud the National Book Council. But I wish its methods to go further. The N.B.C. might, for instance, organise classes for the instruction of booksellers in the art of dressing shop-windows.

Gazing upon the windows of some booksellers, I wonder that they do not hang out a plain sign: "You are requested not to enter this shop." And when some booksellers, after their own fashion, have dressed a window, they are apparently so pleased with it that they leave it untouched for weeks. A departmental store that did not rearrange its windows at least once a week would soon cease to pay a dividend, and its board would have to resign with ignominy.

This is, perhaps, a trifle. What is not a trifle is the price of new books. And in my opinion the price of new books is the chief reason why a new book need sell only 45,000 copies (instead of having to sell 450,000) in order to be a terrific success.

I say nothing of old books or of books not in their first youth, for the circulations of these are notoriously increasing, and shops for the sale of them (with cigarettes and paper-patterns of feminine attire) are multiplying visibly. I speak of new books. And to simplify matters I will speak only of new novels, for the price of biographies, autobiographies, and memoirs (nevertheless a favourite reading of the British public) is too enormous for any discussion.

A good novel (like a bad one) costs 7s.6d. net, a price which in money-value is about the pre-war price, perhaps a bit less. Now a huge number of the lettered feel a strong desire to buy new novels while still new, and they do not buy because they simply cannot afford the price. (Naturally they cannot, for it is as high as the price of a second-rate seat behind a pillar at a musical comedy.) These persons hunger and are not fed. They really do hunger — and the advice offered to them by public uplifters to go forth and buy a copy of *Pride and Prejudice* for a florin only exasperates their appetites and tempers.

Say what you will, new novels (with the latest ideas about the latest life) are more important than old ones, just as new newspapers are more important than old ones.

The price of new novels (as of all new books) must come down. The price of new novels came down with a whack a quarter of a century ago, and it must come down again. I do not suggest that publishers are profiteering on books. I know that they are not. And I know that I am opening up a very large and a very difficult problem. But the work of the National Book Council will be gravely impaired if its popularisation of books is not accompanied, or swiftly followed, by the popularisation of the price of new books. How the latter process is to be carried through I am not qualified to say. But I most seriously commend the affair to the enlightened attention of the National Book Council.

2

25 November 1926

Plain Words to Our Younger Novelists

By a trifling fact, which has no connection with literature, my attention was drawn to Mary Borden's book of stories, *Four o'Clock*. She seems to have reached fame by a novel called *Jane — Our Stranger*, which I have not read.

I admit that, without quite faithfully observing the excellent rule that an author ought never to read other people's books, I do study new fiction less than I might. However, I have read *Four o'Clock* — not because of its sudden notoriety, but because I had heard that the last story in it, *To Meet Jesus Christ*, amounted to a sad lapse from good taste. Well, it does, and Mary Borden will be best forgotten as the author of *To Meet Jesus Christ*. Otherwise, she is a very bright, clever writer who can be read without excessive fatigue.

She has two faults, unhappily too common among young or youngish novelists who devote themselves to the portrayal of smart or high-brow circles. The first is that she describes her circles without any background of the general life. The said circles might be communities which, magically independent of economic law, exist by taking in their own dry-cleaning and running after their own tails.

The second is that she rarely writes natural dialogue. In *Four o'Clock* the characters talk to each other in this style:

"You come of a race of sailors, and had you been a boy would have gone to sea. As it is, you have lived twenty years in London with only the river to look at, to give you dreams." Once when a tourist on a steamer first sighted the Aegean Archipelago and ecstatically declaimed the lines:

"The Isles of Greece! The Isles of Greece!
Where burning Sappho loved and sang,"

another tourist replied with the single word "Rats!" And "Rats!" is the only right answer to the remarks of Mary Borden's personages. In twenty years her dialogue will have become as pathetically comic as that of Douglas Jerrold in *Black-Eyed Susan*.

There are thousands of acres of similar speechifying in the pages of the latest clever fiction. If any of these practitioners would like to learn how to write natural dialogue let them humbly study the first act of *The Last of Mrs. Cheyney*.

Still, Mary Borden may justly boast of writing grammatically. And not all our younger novelists can say as much for themselves. Take, for instance, Mr. Edward Sackville-West, author of *The Ruin*, whom I understand to be the latest orchidaceous efflorescence of modernness. As *The Ruin*, like *Four o'Clock*, is undergoing publicity, I thought I would read it, and I did read it.

Mr. Sackville-West is a cut above Mary Borden. He can sometimes produce emotional effects of beauty (also of what is loosely termed ugliness) which she could not even begin to produce. I should say that he may one day count — though *The Ruin* is perhaps excessively jejune, and has many pages about nothing. But why, so deliciously fresh from school or college, does he flaunt an ignorance of the rules of grammar? Is he above them or below them? Could he not, in future, as a concession to

3

the prejudiced has-beens of literature, contrive to be consistently grammatical?

Further, Mr. Sackville-West is capable of enormities of style. (Possibly this is why he labels his novel "Gothic.") Thus, "He *literally* pulled his eyes away and fixed them upon the piece of cake in his hand." (My italics.) See the orbs somehow gummed on the surface of the cake. The author omitted to describe what the empty sockets looked like.

The above is not mere carping. One must begin at the beginning, and this is the beginning of literary criticism. Why run before you can walk? Why essay a part in a piano quintet before you can play a scale?

I am very interested in young writers — and rather gloomy about them. Nor am I alone in gloominess. I find, when conversation on the subject has grown frank and intimate, that the young themselves are gloomy about their writers. I know that the war killed about 50 per cent. of potential talents. But the other 50 per cent. promise too little, and have performed almost nothing so far.

When I was young I wrote what I thought about literature current then, and I see no reason why advancing age should preclude me from writing what I think about current literature now. The new generation of writers is disappointing; it forces us to defer hope. Perhaps at all times elder writers have said this, but to-day the elder writers who say it are not contradicted by their fiery juniors.

When Kipling published *The Story of the Gadsbys* everybody, old and young, save a few petrified mandarins, agreed that here was a man. Ditto when H.G. Wells published *The Time Machine*. Ditto even when James Joyce published *Portrait of the Artist as a Young Man*.

But to-day? . . . The elders and their immediate successors (such as E.M. Forster and D.H. Lawrence) can and do, when up to their form, knock the stuffing out of the boys and girls. There may be — there must be — one or two semi-exceptions; but not one who has caught and vanquished the general imagination of the educated public. We are concerned, and justifiably so. More can be said about this important matter.

To be continued next week.

2 *December 1926*

Another Criticism of the New School

My remarks last week about the younger novelists have aroused some complaint, and it has been said to be odd that I, for years the champion of the young, should turn and rend them. I will therefore proceed further. What I have already written is nothing compared to what I will now write.

The real champion of the younger school is Mrs. Virginia Woolf. She is almost a senior; but she was the inventor, years ago, of a half-new technique, and she alone, so far as I know, came forward and attacked the old. She has written a small book about me, which through a culpable neglect I have not read. I do, however, remember an article of hers in which she asserted that I and my kind could not create character. This was in answer to an article of mine in which I said that the sound drawing of character was the foundation of good fiction, and in which incidentally I gave my opinion that Mrs. Woolf and her kind could not create character.

I have read two and a half of Mrs. Woolf's books. First, *The Common Reader,* which is an agreeable collection of elegant essays on literary subjects. Second, *Jacob's Room,* which I achieved with great difficulty. Third, *Mrs. Dalloway,* which beat me. I could not finish it, because I could not discover what it was really about, what was its direction, and what Mrs. Woolf intended to demonstrate by it.

To express myself differently, I failed to discern what was its moral basis. As regards character-drawing, Mrs. Woolf (in my opinion) told us ten thousand things about Mrs. Dalloway, but did not show us Mrs. Dalloway. I got from the novel no coherent picture of Mrs. Dalloway. Nor could I see much trace of construction, or ordered movement towards a climax, in either *Jacob's Room* or *Mrs. Dalloway.* Further, I thought that both books seriously lacked vitality.

These three defects, I maintain, are the characteristic defects of the new school of which Mrs. Woolf is the leader. The people in them do not sufficiently live, and hence they cannot claim our sympathy or even our hatred: they leave us indifferent. Logical construction is absent; concentration on the theme (if any) is absent; the interest is dissipated; material is wantonly or clumsily wasted, instead of being employed economically as in the great masterpieces. Problems are neither clearly stated nor clearly solved.

The new practitioners have simply returned to the facile go-as-you-please methods of the eighteenth century, ignoring the important discoveries and innovations of Balzac and later novelists. How different is the new school of fiction from the new school of painting, with its intense regard for logical design!

Lastly, there is absence of vital inspiration. Some novelists appear to have no zest; they loll through their work as though they were taking a stroll in the Park. I admit that I may be wrong on the second count; I may be blind to evidences of a design which is too subtle for my perception. But I do not think that I can be wrong on the first and third counts.

And I admit that some of the younger school write very well. In the novels of Mrs. Woolf some brief passages are so exquisitely done that nothing could be done better. But to be fine for a few minutes is not enough. The chief proof of first-rateness is sustained power.

Among recent novels are to be found admirable specimens of narrative art and character-drawing. They are not, however, specimens of the new method. Rather do they hold fast by tradition. I fancy, for instance, that the Jewish novels of Miss G.B. Stern are as yet much under-esteemed. Then there is Miss Margaret Kennedy's *The Constant Nymph.* It sags in the middle, but it contains nevertheless long stretches of original, richly inspired, highly vitalised stuff.

And finally, I must mention *The Beadle,* of Miss Pauline Smith. The reviews of *The Beadle* — seldom can a first novel have received such praise — do honour to the wakefulness and the insight of reviewers. This novel is simple; it is austere; its field is limited; it is without bravura or ornament of any kind. But its beautiful emotional quality is genuine and marvellously overcomes the reader. *The Beadle* is just about perfect and a masterpiece. The new school of fiction, however, can take no credit for the work, which is as old-fashioned as the moon.

I do not say that a new school of fiction will not arise, and soon. I would not even say that it has not yet arisen. All I say is that even tolerably satisfactory examples of it have not come my way. There may well be satisfactory examples which have escaped my perhaps negligent watchfulness. Also, I would not demand from an example of the new school anything but some fundamental power. In the development of any school of literary creation, the summits of perfection are not usually reached till towards the end.

Further, I cannot see that the Continent is much in advance of this island. I would mention, among the French, only Jouhandeau and de Montherlant as giving a sign of real newness. Among the new Russians, I have been reading Boris Pilniak. He has points, but he is patchy. Apparently he cannot marshal and array his talents to a great end. Incomparably the greatest Continental novelist is Knut Hamsun, and Hamsun belongs to the old brigade.

9 December 1926

Lord Oxford's "Unreadable" Work

Anglers and gamblers are both said to be liars. As to anglers, I can say nothing, having never done any but mackerel-fishing — which is not fishing. But gamblers as a class are certainly liars. And I would class readers as their equals in this branch of depravity.

Nearly all men who are "bookmen" will state, or will give the impressed listener to understand, that they have read what they in fact have not read. The failing is notorious. I have no intention of confessing the immense hidden gaps in my own reading. Truth is dangerous and a boomerang. Even if you aim it at no one in particular it may come back — sometimes after years — and knock you senseless. More subtle is the lying that goes on about what you like in literature and what you don't like. The temptation is tremendous to say that you like what you think you ought to like and don't like what you think you oughtn't to like.

In the past I have often yielded to it (with good results for my prestige among my fellow-readers), but the greying years have almost cured me of the sin. Lately I have been studying biographies and biographical sketches, books of memoirs and essays, and have reached some startling conclusions about my own taste.

And here I must remark that most English biographies are too long, and most English essays too short. The undue length is perhaps due to the perverse desire of the "libraries" to hand out volumes which their subscribers cannot hold in bed, and to the tendency of the reading public to judge literature by its weight and its cubical content. The undue brevity is beyond question due to the practical disappearance of the serious monthly magazines and to the editorial rule of the serious weeklies forbidding any contribution over 2000 words in length. You may write the finest essay ever written of 4000 words and you cannot hope to get it printed unless you yourself start or buy a periodical in which to print it.

Very prominent among autumn books is Lord Oxford's *Fifty Years of*

Parliament. I have a great admiration for Lord Oxford. I much prefer him to his master, that arch-comedian and portentous performer, W.E. Gladstone. He is one of the few living politicians who can be relied on in a crisis to behave like a gentleman. He can turn a phrase neatly and with dignity, and even with majesty.

But I have not read *Fifty Years of Parliament.* I could not. Call it a morass, from which I had to be dragged out by means of ropes and horses. Or call it a marmoreal hemisphere, up whose smooth sides I tried endlessly to climb — only to slip back with resulting sad shininess to my best clothes: it beat me. It has every good quality except readableness. I regard it (apart from the quotations in it) as one of the most unreadable books ever written by an honest and fully-informed man. I would far rather read the monotonous, too stately post-Macaulayese of Lord Birkenhead. Would that Winston Churchill had enlivened with a book the wettest November on record! He is the finest writer in Parliament, if possibly the most dangerous statesman.

To my mind the most agreeable autumn book by a statesman is the late Lord Curzon's *Leaves from a Viceroy's Notebook.* I am conscious of having been (in my heart, if not on paper) unjust to Lord Curzon during his lifetime. I now discover that he knew everything and was an expert on everything; he was unbelievably industrious; he had humour as well as taste, and he was a finished, a charming, a brilliant writer. Lord Curzon was incapable of only one thing — being unreadable. If there are degrees of omniscience, he was more omniscient than Jowett and unquestionably more urbane to the young and the imperfect. I imagine that Lord Curzon's reputation will rise, despite his grandiosity.

One is continually having to revise one's opinions of men. I had always regarded John Wesley as a somewhat eminent religious revivalist, but I learnt the other day from a leading classical scholar of international renown that Wesley was the greatest classical scholar of the eighteenth century.

I should say that the most important recent autobiographical volume is the reprint of E.G. Browne's thirty-three-year-old *A Year Among the Persians.* It has an excellent and excellently brief and sufficiently comprehensive introduction by Sir Edward Denison Ross, the Director of the School of Oriental Studies and the only Englishman who can speak more languages than Mr. Maurice Baring.

A Year Among the Persians, though not too distinguished in style and afflicted with numerous cliches, is readable in a very high degree. It is more readable, for instance, than E.M. Doughty's formidable *Travels in Arabia Deserta.* But I do not agree with the opinion, which I have heard from the lips of authority, that it is a better book than *Arabia Deserta.*

I think that it is not so good a book. Yet I have lacked the grit to grapple with the difficulties and the eccentricities of more than a hundred pages of Doughty, whereas I can gallop through E.G. Browne. Unlike Shakespeare, Doughty made no concession to the weaknesses of mankind. He suffered from spiritual pride — a defect which Browne did not share with him.

To confess: I confess that for me the most attractive autumn autobiographical book is Mr. H.M. Walbrook's *A Playgoer's Wanderings.* Its subject, the stage, prejudiced me against it. I am not a bit partial to the stage.

When my plays were produced and they succeeded, I had a high opinion of the theatre. But when my plays were produced and they failed one after another, I soon reached the conclusion that the British stage had lost its virtue and its interest. Coincidence, of course. Nor is the stage a fool-proof, or a dullard-proof, or a mandarin-proof, or an actress-proof subject.

Who can read Macready? Who can read Frank Archer, brother of William Archer? Who can read dozens of stage memoirs? Nor is Mr. Walbrook, a dramatic critic of long experience, to be ranked among the immortal stylistic autobiographers and anecdotists. He is a competent journalist, and (I doubt not) content with that. Nevertheless, *A Playgoer's Wanderings* has been meat and drink to me. Why? Well, it is unaffected; it is ingenuous; it is straightforward; it is various; it is variegated; and it has the pathetic, touching fragance of departed darlings and dimmed reputations.

16 December 1926

Changes in Christmas Reading

Christmas is now quite otherwise. The British Christmas dinner is eaten in the hotels and restaurants of the world, to deafening bands, and the vogue of mistletoe has diminished. No longer is the friendly Christmas spirit abroad which compelled all the householders on a postman's round to do what they could to send the postman home to his dear wife and children more than half-drunk on Christmas morning. And Christmas numbers are now quite otherwise. Where are the coloured supplements portraying chubby children, and hale old port-drinkers, and thick snow, and simpering virgins in long frocks standing with reluctant feet where the brook and river meet? Terrible maidens, those virgins — in my opinion far more devastating than the knee-showing, cocktail-consuming, smoke-inhaling, sham-jewellery wearing, hard-swearing, painted and powdered damsels of our epoch.

In the days of the simper those virgins were addressed nightly by the poets of three high-brow London evening papers (Occasional Verse the stuff was called, and the poets were known as Occ. poets), and the message of their nine hundred lyrics a year was to the effect that if the virgins smiled in a particular way the Occ. poets would be in bliss for ever, and that if the virgins frowned in a particular way the Occ. poets would be ruined for ever. A somewhat violent conceit; marvellously untrue to life; and where is it now?

And thirdly, Christmas books are quite otherwise. Time was when fairy tales and other illustrated books of fantasy stood in the van of Christmas literature. There are still illustrated seasonal books at Christmas, but they no longer have the prestige of old days. I remember when Andrew Lang's annual volume of fairy stories, in violet, red, pink, yellow, green, or blue, was a great event of December and reviewed with much care and at length as something of general importance and wide interest, and when new editions of such works as *Cranford,* illustrated sugarily by popular artists, were welcomed as a proof that England stood where it did, if not a bit higher. Whereas the Christmas books which to-day ornament my table are such matters as Sir James Crichton-Browne's *Victorian Jottings,* a jumbled but not uninteresting collection, which contains reminiscences of dead men, chiefly authors, and a large number of anecdotes scarcely one of which is quite first-rate: *Wine and Wine Lands of the World,* by Mr. Frank Hedges Butler, full of informed chat concerning distinguished alcohol for expert palates; Julius Meier-Graefe's *The Spanish Journey,* the record of the travels of a connoisseur of pictures — especially El Greco's; Mr. Robert Lynd's *The Little Angel,* a volume of characteristic essays marked by realism, common sense, kindliness, and wit, from which sentimentality and saccharine are totally absent; and two volumes of Mr. Aldous Huxley, *Essays New and Old,* chapters as modern and un-Christmaslike as essays well could be, and *Jesting Pilate,* a travel book in which no effort is made to boost the Empire or to pretend that politics are not just what they are. Any of these books, except, perhaps, the first, would have raised the hair of readers in search of comfort and illusion at Christmas 1900.

And instead of Occ. Verse about fantastically ingenuous and goddess-like girls we have, in the principal volume of new verse of the season, a book which Mr. Humbert Wolfe calls *News of the Devil,* and which contains such mockery of heaven and of the eminent lords of the earth as would have given Andrew Lang and Richard Le Gallienne to think furiously that the end of organised society was at hand. *News of the Devil* has quickly reached a fourth edition — and not a word about goddesses in it. Tennyson in a magical lyric wrote that the long light shakes across the lakes. It does, now, and it has a reddish, terrifying, but theatrical glow.

Children's books seem to be about the same — that is to say, they still apparently have no relation whatever to real life; which is odd, considering that children are nowadays supposed to have no childhood. I look forward to a change in children's books. Some writer will suddenly discover, what everybody else has always known, that of all realists children are the most uncompromising. That writer will have a fearful fight with publishers, who will assert that they alone know what children want; but in the end the writer will win, because in the end writers always do.

Meanwhile, the best children's books, really, are Mr. John Masefield's. Mr. Masefield's famous *One D——d Thing After Another* (Odtaa) was surely composed for the schoolroom. Forty years ago it would have come out as a serial in *The Boy's Own Paper,* a periodical which in the 'eighties, being then a high-brow, I used to glance at with disdain for its lack of serious interest; I preferred even *The Girl's Own Paper,* which taught its girls and one boy how to stencil the walls of rooms and how to manufacture Christmas and birthday presents unlike any other gifts ever given.

Children are changed — thank heaven! They even come into the world differently now (when they come); and their advent is heralded differently. In pre-(Boer) war times the wife always blushingly whispered "something" in the ear of a staggered husband. I remember only a few years ago a play in which a wife (forgetting the century in which she lived) whispered this something to her young spouse. The audience spoilt it all by openly laughing. Rich sign that the earth rolls on. To-day audiences usually know far more than playwrights, and disconcertingly air their knowledge.

23 December 1926

How Time Robs the Reader

By to-morrow night the Christmas book season (which has been a good one) will be over.

Publishers will have sent out their final parcels, and closely estimated their sales and profits (though most of them say they never make a profit). Accountancy clerks will be going to bed earlier. Popular and unpopular authors will have ceased to pester their publishers by telephone inquiries concerning the exact circulation of their books up to the hour of telephoning.

Some authors will be preparing for a merry Christmas in a world where readers have shown a taste for good books. Other authors will be preparing for a gloomy Christmas in a world where readers simply don't know a good book when they see it. Reviewers, an unthanked and misunderstood class, will be preoccupied with hateful questions relating to quarter-day.

The huge book departments of the big stores will be sheeted over, and a copy of *Who's Who* under the sheets will have no more literary importance than "Ephesian's" * rollicking unofficial biography of Lord Birkenhead. Booksellers will have put up their shutters, knowing that when they take them down again they will do so in an atmosphere of slack leisure and hope deferred. Which leisure I trust they will devote to good resolutions towards improved methods of trade.

By the way, my remarks a few weeks ago about the unhelpful aspect of booksellers' windows have raised an immense dust in the trade Press, and the dust has not yet settled. Of course, I have been accused of assertions which I did not make. In particular I did not say that all booksellers dressed their windows badly. I said that some did. At a meeting of the National Book Council some angry person asked whether I thought I was helping the book trade by criticising the booksellers' windows. The answer is Yes. The book trade will certainly not be helped by pursuing the great policy of pretending that things are not what they are, or that the consequences of them will not be what they will be.

To return to the imminent death of the Christmas season. What are the feelings of the faithful, interested reader concerning it? I think they must be something like mine when, the other day, a mighty publisher, with an autumn list as long as the Edgware-road, and far more exciting, insisted on making me a present of nineteen of his principal latest volumes.

I protested: "But I can't possibly read them." He said: "Never mind. I want you to have them." You see, he was born a publisher as a poet is born a poet, and was immensely proud of his literature. So I took them. But if I read eight hours a day for a month I could not get through his great gift. At best I may, actually, read three of the volumes, and even that is doubtful. The rest must be ignored. And those nineteen volumes probably do not represent the nineteenth part of the books which, as a faithful, interested reader, I would like to examine with some care.

Faithful, interested readers — of whom there are many — must certainly have the sensations of despair which I had as they contemplate the

* Pseudonym of C.E. Bechhofer-Roberts.

general output. They would wish to keep themselves up to date, and they simply cannot — whatever the depth of their purses. They are torn this way and that; they make terrific efforts; and after all their efforts they are utterly defeated in their struggle with the Press. Necessarily they are forced at last to the despairing cry: "No! I shall die without having read that — and that — and that — and that," *ad infinitum*.

In fine, innumerable books, which contain meat for them, might just as well never have been written. And ignorance is their portion. Perhaps it is right: for realised ignorance means humility, and humility is the soil of true wisdom.

Time lacks, more even than money lacks, for the faithful, interested reader. Take, for example, only two striking Christmas books, neither of them issued by my afore-mentioned publisher. First *Great Short Stories of the World* (Heinemann). Here are over a thousand pages comprising 178 short stories which extend over all the world, and over thousands of years — 8s. 6d. An extremely remarkable production, at the price of a fair dinner. All the greatest short stories are not in it, but very many of them are, and the number of inferior ones is quite small. But even by this time next year even the bravest reader will almost certainly not have vanquished the whole of that prodigious volume.

Second, *The Oxford Book of Eighteenth Century Verse*, chosen by Mr. David Nichol Smith (727 pages. Price 8s. 6d.). Another vast and yet handy volume. Reading in it to last for months and years. It extends from Addison and Defoe to Wordsworth and Coleridge. It gives in full Christopher Smart's renowned *A Song to David*, which tens of thousands know by name, and only tens by reading. It gives no less than forty citations from Pope, the great typical poet of the eighteenth century, the astounding poisonous little creature of whom some say that he was a poet, and some say that he was not a poet, but none says that he was not a great writer. I always recommend Pope to those who say that they "cannot read poetry." At any rate, everybody ought to be able to read Pope.

I remember one of the most remarkable women of this century (or of the last) once saying to me: "When I try to read poetry I always have to translate it back into prose before I can grasp it." Well, you don't have to translate Pope back into prose before you can grasp him. Mr. Nichol Smith's anthology is also specially valuable in that it provides admirable specimens of a wonderful poet, little read in these days — Dr. Watts. Dr. Watts wrote magnificent lines, and even magnificent stanzas. He wrote the imperishable line about young women's eyes at a party (not given by Mr. Nichol Smith):

And dart delicious danger thence.

Talk about time lacking! The above are two big volumes. Here is a little one in the Christmas exhibition. *The Outline of Sanity*, by G.K. Chesterton (Methuen, 6s.). Only 230 pages; yet so full of matter for reflection and quarrel that you could not finish it up in perusal and discussion in less than about a month.

The Outline of Sanity (which some would christen *The Outline of Insanity*) is Mr. Chesterton's constructive contribution to current politics. The great masses of it are well put together: the details are rather thrown together. I think that it often shows a strange obtuseness to the teachings

11

of history and a similar blindness to the wild ways of the human heart in search of happiness. I think it makes too numerous sacrifices of truth to the flashing turn of phrase. But what a challenging, what a burning, what an amusing, what a frivolous, what a profound little book! Have I read it steadily all through? No. Time lacks.

30 December 1926

Two Great Imaginative Works

At the end of the year I recall that the most important large works of imagination which I have read in 1926 are both American. (They are, of course, novels. A few years ago it seemed as if verse might soon be challenging prose in the field of imagination; but the promise is unfulfilled. Not yet returned are the poetic days when books like *The Excursion, In Memoriam, The Ring and the Book, The Angel in the House,* even *Aurora Leigh,* could and did stand up sturdily against novels by no matter what idol and swell.)

I except from my purview *Clissold,* not because I don't admire *Clissold* — I rate it far, far higher than the generality of critics and readers — but because, though it is a work of imagination, it is less a work of imagination than a sociological testament.

I think that America may be breaking through — both in fiction and in drama. Let us beware of calling American literature vulgar. Wagner was called vulgar once. So was Walt Whitman. Even Eugene O'Neill, while he has, in my opinion, up to now done nothing whatever to justify the immense American pother about him, might, I feel, at any moment throw down to us something notable.

George M. Cohan I regard as quite as good a playwright as most current English playwrights. And the modern play which sticks foremost in my mind is the London failure, *The Show-Off* by an American author whose name, I am ashamed to say, I have forgotten.* And there are more recent American dramatic works which probably count for more than the insular West End of London in its self-sufficiency suspects.

The first of the two works which I began by referring to is Theodore Dreiser's *An American Tragedy.* I read it in the formidable two-volume American edition, but Constable's have published it in one compact volume.

I am not going to recommend *An American Tragedy* to all and sundry dilettante and plain people. It is of tremendous length. It is written abominably, by a man who evidently despises style, elegance, clarity, even grammar. Dreiser simply does not know how to write, never did know, never wanted to know. Dreiser would sneer at Nathaniel Hawthorne, a writer of some of the loveliest English ever printed.

For this and other reasons he is difficult to read. He makes no compromise with the reader. Indeed, to read Dreiser with profit you must take your coat off to it, you must go down on your knees to it, you must up hands and say "I surrender." And Dreiser will spit on you for a start.

But once you have fairly yielded to him he will reward you — yes,

* George Kelly: see also p.74.

12

though his unrelenting grip should squeeze the life out of you. *An American Tragedy* is prodigious. Its characteristics are an absolutely fearless adherence to truth and a terrific imaginative power. Some pages are more exciting than others, but the sheer power is continuous in its spell; it never relaxes; it goes on and on; Dreiser determined to omit nothing at all, until the devastating end.

The story is the same old story that Dreiser has told again and again, the story of the passionate man determined to possess the woman who society and his conscience utterly forbid to him; the background, a panorama of American life. Such stories are bound to be gloomy if honestly told. *An American Tragedy* is saved from depressingness, as every sound, sad tale is saved, by its beauty; but here the beauty is frightening, especially towards the close.

Twenty-six years have passed since I reviewed Dreiser's *Sister Carrie*, with enthusiasm. *Sister Carrie* was marred by sentimentality. Dreiser is an intermittent creator. For ten years after *Sister Carrie* he produced nothing notable. Then *Jennie Gerhardt*; fine. Then *The Financier, The Titan* and *The Genius,* quickly one after another — all long books. Of these *The Financier* is magnificent, the other two unsatisfactory. And now *An American Tragedy* has had an overwhelming popular success in the United States. I doubt whether any English novel so critical, so unsparing, so clumsy, and so sad, could have one quarter of such success in Britain.

My second important large work read this year is Herman Melville's *Pierre,* which ought to be issued separately — at present it can only be had in the standard edition of Melville's works in heaven knows how many volumes. Melville was once famous as the author of those rather second-class (at any rate as bowdlerised for print) South Sea romances, *Typee* and *Omoo.* Then, much later, he became known as the author of *Moby Dick* — a great novel. He may still later become famous as the author of *Pierre.*

Pierre is transcendental, even mystical, in spirit. The basic idea of its plot is entitled to be called unpleasant. It contains superb writing, and also grotesque writing, which its author mistakenly thought to be superb. It is full of lyrical beauty which the veriest sentimentalist could not possibly confuse with ugliness. It is conceived in an heroical, epical vein, and executed (faultily) in the grand manner. It has marked originality. In it the author essays feats which the most advanced novelists of to-day imagine to be quite new.

Melville was an exalted genius. *Pierre,* though long, is shorter than *An American Tragedy;* but it is even more difficult to read. I recommend it exclusively to the adventurous and the fearless. These, if the book does not defeat them, will rise up, after recovering from their exhaustion, and thank me. I intend to pursue my researches into Herman Melville.

I beg to emphasise that both the above novels are American.

BOOKS AND PERSONS : 1927

6 January 1927

Publishers Who Produce Bad Work

The *Publishers' Circular* has issued very punctually its annual analysis of books published. Despite strikes, more books were issued in 1926 than in 1925. Is this matter for pride? Well, I am reminded of the answer of the man who was asked whether words might be immortal. He said: "It depends what words, and in what order?" Similarly, before deciding whether or not to congratulate the country on its output of publishing, we ought to inquire: "What books?" Also "What sales of what books?" No analysis can estimate the moral or artistic value of books issued, and none is ever likely to estimate with accuracy the sales of books. The first is unknowable; the second will never be known.

Novels, of course, head the list. They always do. Fiction is a modern craze. Scott started it with *Waverley,* a novel that to-day not one reader in a hundred would tackle. If I was requested to re-read *Waverley* I should charge fifty guineas for the feat. André Gide tells us that when as a youth he used every quarter to make out a list of books which he would choose to have on a desert island, no novel ever figured in any of the lists. If I had to choose twenty books for a desert island, I doubt if I would include more than one novel; it would be either *The Brothers Karamazov* or *The Charterhouse of Parma* or *The Woodlanders.* Most novels are negligible, and are issued because publishers know by experience that people will read anything to pass the time. But most books in all categories are negligible.

I wish that in future years the excellent *Publishers' Circular* would import certain innovations into its analysis. Why does it class "Poetry" and "Drama" together? What logical connection is there between poetry and drama? How can we learn how many volumes of poetry have been published? Again, what is comprised under the heading "Juvenile"? Does this category include schoolbooks? If not, are schoolbooks scattered about in the categories? Schoolbooks probably have more influence than novels. Surely we ought to have some figures concerning them.

As regards "Religion," it comes next after "Fiction" in number of publications; but "Fiction" counts over 100 per cent. publications more than "Religion." To me the most interesting detail in the whole analysis is that whereas there were 1455 reprints of novels, there were only 90 reprints of religious books. Does this imply that the vogue of books on religion is far briefer even than the vogue of novels? I suppose it must. Food for thought!

I said above that the moral and artistic value of books issued is unknowable to us. So it is; posterity alone will judge our books. We can, however, immediately judge the value of our books considered as physical objects. And this consideration has importance. Most books, and especially most novels, are bad examples of the art and craft of making books. They are badly set up from bad founts of type in a badly designed page, printed on bad paper, badly bound, and enveloped in bad dust-covers — or "jackets," as these gaudy protective pieces of paper are now termed. They offend the

14

eye of taste; they offend an honest partiality for sound workmanship, and when you have read them they look as misshapen as if they had been thrown down in Piccadilly and run over by a motorbus. This is by no means true of all books, but it is damnably true of at least 50 per cent. of books.

The "book-makers" employed by some publishers seem to be marvellously unaware that a page and a title-page can be designed with beauty; that the question of margins is important; that there are beautiful founts of type as well as ugly; that paper can be good or evil; that traditions of fine printing exist; that to produce a beautiful book need cost no more than to produce an ugly book; that book-making is an art and a craft — or should be. If I had generous impulses I should present for the guidance of book-makers copies of the publications of the eighteenth century Baskerville of Birmingham to all publishing firms, so that they might see what a good fount of type and a well-designed page really are.

Lately I visited a small temporary exhibition of modern commercial printing and illustrations in the North Court of the Victoria and Albert Museum. Not all the specimens were successful; but very many were. I saw examples of end-papers and pages and labels and small posters both coloured and plain. If manufacturers of biscuits, hosiery, shipping, and cakes can avail themselves of the latest efforts towards beauty in printing, surely publishers can.

Some publishers, of course, do. As a rule, but not always, it is the younger publishers who do, and the older publishers who don't. Among younger publishers who do, Martin Secker is prominent. Among older publishers who do, Chatto and Windus are prominent. Among older publishers who don't — No! Silence! Discretion!

I must relate an anecdote. A few weeks ago I was interested in the "titling" of a film. I stipulated that I should be an autocrat therein, and I was. After various trials I failed to get the titles done in a style of lettering that I could conscientiously approve. At last I sent to the scribe a copy of the very lovely quarto edition of Terence printed in the original tongue by Charles Whittingham in MDCCCLIV. I said: "Imitate these characters." I think the scribe was a bit taken aback, but he did imitate them, unprotesting. Book-makers are apt to look down on film-makers. Need they?

13 January 1927

A Fine Historical Novel by a German Author

Jew Süss, by Lion Feuchtwanger, a German author previously unknown to me, well translated by Willa and Edwin Muir (published by Martin Secker, 10s.), is a good historical novel dealing with the political and social life of a German State in the eighteenth century.

It will interest people who usually cannot bring themselves to read historical novels, for the reasons that it deals with the whole life of the State, that it is not sentimentalised, that it is outspoken in all matters, and that it has throughout genuine and admirably sustained imaginative power.

In fact, this book is remarkable, full of food for vigorous minds. The picture drawn of existence in a civilised country less than two hundred years ago is terrible. You would think you were in the Middle Ages rather than in the age of Swift and Voltaire. Such a composition of intrigue, corruption, tyranny, injustice, ignorance, cruelty, uncleanliness, and fornication I have seldom, if ever, come across before.

The hero is a Jew (or a reputed Jew), a great, refined rascal, debauchee, and grinder of the faces of the poor. But he is a sympathetic fellow, and his execution by hanging amid circumstances of fantastic terror will move the hearts of the staunchest upholder of morality. The author treats the Jewish community with extraordinary insight and fairness; he may be a Jew himself.

The finest passage in the book is the lyrical, synthetic description of the general life of Jews in the period. If anybody who hesitates to embark on the long novel will read pages 163, 164, and 165, he will be able to judge at once whether the sort of thing Feuchtwanger writes is the sort of thing he can read with appreciation and profit.

I myself hesitated to begin the book, because I have been too often deceived and let down by historical novels, whose authors as a rule do not fully know their subjects, and who consciously or unconsciously falsify what knowledge they have summarily acquired. Feuchtwanger must have immersed himself in his period with the thoroughness and the impartiality of an historical student. He does not shirk difficulties.

He has none of that hankering after the tawdry picturesque which makes 99 per cent. of historical novels such fearful reading. He writes naturally. He accepts human nature (as it was then — a different nature from ours). He seldom shows indignation (an emotion which no novelist understanding and therefore pardoning human nature ought to show). Even in his pages on the lasciviousness of men and the amazing acquiescences of women — Heavens! What a sex were German women in the eighteenth century! — he keeps his head excellently and sins neither by audacity nor by timidity.

If the book has faults — and no doubt books do have faults — they are, first, that the author has a slight tendency to exalt his characters unduly and beyond the bounds of truth; and, second, that sometimes he is apt to bury the interest of the individuals in the too abstract interest of the community.

The fourth section of the book often resembles an historical treatise more than a novel, with the result that the lyrical level of the work falls somewhat, and the reader gets too little of the tonic of dialogue. In the fifth and last section, however, Feuchtwanger pulls himself together, remembers that he is a novelist dealing primarily with separate human beings, and concludes his tale in complete triumph.

I have a minor quarrel with the publishers on the point of book-making. There are no page-titles of any sort, and, though the sections have titles, the chapters have not, neither are they numbered. For the lack of means to identify the chapters, of course, the author is to blame. (He may have been copying Balzac, who in the later editions of his novels developed the naughty habit of suppressing all divisions and titles.) But the publishers should at least have printed the titles of sections at the tops of the pages.

As the book stands, it is impossible to turn back to passages for re-reading without a long time-wasting search that is assisted by no clue. The omission of helpful page-titles is too common in contemporary publishing.

16

I have not directed attention to this book merely because it is a very fine novel, though a very fine novel is rare enough to be always worthy of mention, but because it is a very fine example of a particular kind of novel — the kind with a large panoramic background to the individual interest. There are few examples of this kind of novel in English literature, and I want many more of them. There are more in French, by Balzac and by Zola. There are even better examples in Russian, by Tolstoy.

The English novel, when it is realistic, treats of the relations of male individuals and female individuals, and usually attempts little or no social synthesis. It is the tale of the eternal triangle or the eternal pentagon. Its scope is narrow, its curiosity about life is circumscribed.

One of the chief characteristics of the modern age is an extended curiosity. This curiosity is very inadequately reflected in our novels. *Jew Süss* is a splendid story, but it is also a complete picture of a complex social organism from top to bottom. It entertains, it enthrals, and simultaneously it teaches; it enlarges the field of knowledge. To the ordinary reader it brings home, far better than any history could do, the realities of the eighteenth century, and enables him — nay, compels him — by partly unconscious comparison with the realities of to-day, to perceive the strange rapidity of the evolution of mankind.

20 January 1927

The Reviewer's Yearning for Originality

I am told that a concerted effort is to be made by publishers, or by a group of publishers, to obtain more attention for books in provincial daily papers. This is good. There are intelligent men and women in the provinces who never read a modern book, and who never set eyes on one unless they happen to go into a Boots' establishment to buy razor-blades or a bunch of orange-sticks.

There are large towns which have not a single shop devoted exclusively to the sale of books. (These remarks do not apply to Scotland.) There are provincial dailies which give a hundred reports of football matches to one report of a book. Their editors say they have no space for books. So that the new and beautiful idea of persuading them to give a whole page a week to books seems likely to meet with a certain opposition.

A weekly book-page may help to foster the general interest in books but it will not help very much unless it is readable. Now most provincial reviewing is not, to speak with courtesy, acutely readable. London reviewing is rather better. Reviewers do not always understand that the first duty of a reviewer is to be interesting. Let him be knowledgeable if he can; let him be just if he cares; let him have taste if God has so willed. Everything helps. But unless he is interesting he is a failure with his public. A reviewer must be a journalist before he is a reviewer.

However, I do not blame reviewers. I have been a reviewer myself. I once reviewed one thousand books in three years. The first article I insinuated into a London daily was a review. And it appears to me that I am still (in a manner) reviewing. I have even reviewed for *The Manchester Guardian*! Glorious day! For in the matter of reviewing *The Manchester*

Guardian is a twin summit with *The Times Literary Supplement.* So that I know about reviewing. And although I have suffered from reviewers, I would always defend them against the charges of the laity.

The wonder is not that book reviews are as dull as they usually are, but that they are as bright as they usually are. For you will kindly remember that during a large part of their time reviewers have to occupy themselves with dull books. What can you say about a dull book except that it is dull?

Further, during a large part of their time reviewers must con books of which the authors have all been consciously or unconsciously engaged in imitating one another. Think of the terrible narcotic effect on reviewers. Talk about reviewers being unwilling to recognise originality! Why, no hart ever panted after a water-brook as a reviewer yearns for originality in a book. There are crises in a reviewer's career when the advent of an original work may save him from the madhouse.

I will say this: that English reviews are better than American. And they are more readable. Far more room is given to books in American dailies than in English. The strange thing is that, despite the marvellous flatness of their book-pages, book sales in America should prosper and wax as they undoubtedly do. The handsome and spacious book-supplements of various dailies could surely be conquered by none but highly trained athletes of reading.

Exceptions occur. The best bookish article in America (and perhaps in America and England), in *The New York Bookman* signed "Simon Pure," is as exciting as a historical work by G.K. Chesterton. But then *The New York Bookman* is not a daily, and "Simon Pure" is probably not 100 per cent. American.*

There are also Messrs. Mencken and Nathan, of *The American Mercury,* and elsewhere. These illustrious warriors are very readable. They are also violent, impudent, farcical, grotesque, and intellectually unscrupulous. It is impossible that writers who "go on" with a pen as they do could reliably distinguish a good book or a good play from a bad one. True, taste in literature would have prevented their rabid performances.

But they have done good by their remarkable castigations of the public attitude towards literature. I do not wish them dead. I read them with gusto. They make me laugh as much as a "musical absurdity" at the Coliseum. Indeed, their proper place is the music-hall.

To return. I would particularly defend reviewers in their occasional practice of not reading through the books upon which they pronounce verdicts. Why, in the name of sense, should they read every page? It is often perfectly unnecessary. The reviewer who knows his job can sometimes get the hang of a book in one minute.

For example. I opened the other day Miss Roma Lister's *Further Reminiscences Occult and Social* (Hutchinson, one guinea net, illustrated), and the first bit I read was this: "A German by birth, Walpurga Lady Paget was wrapt in a mantle of the highest culture, *having been until her marriage lady-in-waiting and friend to Victoria, Crown Princess of Prussia.*" (My italics.) Here is an unmistakable clue to one important aspect of Miss Roma Lister's character as a writer and a student of human affairs.

---

* In fact Frank Swinnerton.

18

Her book is interesting to anyone who possesses the craft of reading. It gives genuine information about modern Rome; and tells spiritualistic stories which are diverting, and indeed enthralling, even if you accept them with reserve — as I do. The photographs are amusing and have historical value. But I maintain that three lines of the work furnish quite sufficient basis for a review. Guided by this clue, the competent reviewer could come to a fair conclusion about the book in less time than he could eat his breakfast. For myself I gave much more time than that to it, because it attracted me.

I ought to add that for the moment Miss Lister's book is unobtainable, but those who desire it will soon be able to get it — in a slightly shortened form.

27 January 1927

A Candid Opinion on Henry James

On two occasions in my maturer life have I blushed. The first occasion was when, sitting in the stalls of a theatre, someone lightly touched my shoulder from the row behind, and, turning, I heard a remembered voice say: "You don't know me, Mr. Bennett, but I know you." This was Ellen Terry. The second was when, in the coffee-room of a club to which we both belonged, a stoutish man accosted me and said: "You won't recall me. I'm Henry James. May I join you upstairs later?"

Yes, I did fairly blush — I suppose because I was flattered. Such is the mysterious influence of immense artistic prestige on my blood vessels. Not that I quite believed that Ellen Terry really thought I shouldn't know her, or that Henry James really thought I shouldn't recall him. As regards Henry James, he did join me upstairs later. The first thing he said was: "For me this room is full of ghosts." And he went on to talk in highly-finished phrases of James Payn and other lions, and of asses in lions' skins. He was at once sardonic and gloomy; and marvellously courteous to the boy — for, although about fifty, I felt like a boy in his presence. It seemed to me that the mournful light of the setting sun was in his eyes; he was certainly in bad health.

And now another book has been written upon Henry James, this time by Professor Pelham Edgar (*Henry James, Man and Author*). It resembles most American books about books; it is painstaking, thorough, ingenious, infrequently illuminating — and not succulent. Reading it, you have the terrible suspicion that the author does not entirely understand what he is talking about. I don't assert that he doesn't, but I am not securely convinced that he does.

Artistic prestige has an influence not only on my blood-vessels but on my critical faculty. It took me years to ascertain that Henry James's work was giving me little pleasure. I first had a glimpse of the distressing fact when *What Maisie Knew* began to appear serially in *The New Review* ages ago, somewhere in the Ninth Dynasty.

By the one thousand persons (including myself) in England who are genuinely interested in the art of literature this serial was anticipated with a religious eagerness. I could not get on with it. My fault, of course.

19

Impossible to credit that anything of Henry James's was not great!

But when I was immovably bogged in the middle of *The Golden Bowl* and again in the middle of *The Ambassadors* (supposed, both of them, to mark the very summit of Henry James's achievement) I grew bolder with myself. In each case I asked myself: "What the dickens is this novel about, and where does it think it's going to?" Question unanswerable! I gave up.

To-day I have no recollection whatever of any characters or any events in either novel. And I will venture to say that I have honestly enjoyed, and been held by, only two of James's novels — *In the Cage* and *The Other House*. The former is very short and the latter is not interminable.

I am willing to admit, for the sake of argument, that Henry James knew more about the technique of the novel than any other novelist (save Turgenev). He was fond of saying that a novel, to be artistically satisfactory, must be "organised," and he "organised" his own with unique and in-human elaboration. I will also admit, without any reserve, that his style, though unduly mannered, is very distinguished, and that he said what he so subtly meant with unsurpassed accuracy. I will admit that he knew everything about writing novels — except how to keep my attention.

My doubt is whether he had actually much to say, in a creative sense, that needed saying. I think that he knew a lot about the life of one sort of people, the sort who are what is called cultured, and who do themselves very well both physically and intellectually, and very little indeed about life in general. I think that in the fastidiousness of his taste he rather repudiated life.

He was a man without a country. He never married. He never, so far as is commonly known, had a love-affair worthy of name. And I would bet a fiver that he never went into a public-house and had a pint of beer — or even half-a-pint. He was naive, innocent, and ignorant of fundamental things to the last. He possessed taste, but his taste lacked robustness. He had the most delicate perceptions; but he perceived things with insufficient emotion. He was mortally afraid of being vulgar, and even of being carried away. My notion is that most first-rate creative artists simply do not know what vulgarity is. They go right on, and if it happens to them to be vulgar in the stress of emotion, well, it happens to them — and they are forgiven.

Henry James's short stories have received high praise. I think they are the thinnest of all his work, and essentially commonplace in essence. As for his recollections, such as *The American Scene,* and *A Small Boy and Others,* I think they push uncompromising unreadableness further than it was ever pushed before. His letters are a disturbing revelation of the man.

I offer these views with respect and with reserve; because I am harried by doubts. My eye may have a blind spot for the alleged supreme excellencies of Henry James. But, if so, the eyes of a vast number of other people no plainer than myself are similarly afflicted. I extol him as a literary critic. He was perhaps the first important English-writing critic to deflate the balloon of Gustave Flaubert. His essays on the younger English novelists are masterly, and packed close with vitamines. I have read them twice, and may read them again. But never shall I set out afresh into the arid desert of *The Golden Bowl.* No!

3 February 1927

Do Our Young Writers Lack Faith?

A month or two ago I made some remarks about the apparent inferiority and paucity of young creative writers in this age. These remarks have caused — shall I say? — complications in my existence; the complications continue. If you praise you are safe and a grand fellow. I praised two American novels, and the good tidings were cabled to New York. I praised Pauline Smith's novel *The Beadle,* and the benevolent message was flashed in an instant to Capetown. But when you suggest that all novels are not the greatest novels ever written, and that the younger generation may just conceivably not be quite equal to the older, trouble is yours, and you learn that you are a back number, a one-eyed man, a blind man, actuated by jealousy and victimised by senility or G.P.I.

The curious thing is that nobody has yet denied that the younger generation indeed is inferior to the older. Divergence of opinion occurs only when the explanation of the inferiority begins to be discussed. The argument of the youths and their supporters is that the war is responsible. I willingly admit, and have admitted before, that the war may be to an appreciable extent responsible.

But, then, how comes it that a similar phenomenon does not obtain in France? French youth suffered at least as much as British youth by the war. Yet the younger generation (of novelists, if not of poets) has made a very considerable mark on French literature. There are a good half-dozen quite young novelists in France whose books count. They may not be the equals of Balzac or de Maupassant, or even Bourget, but the lettered public cannot properly ignore them, and, in fact, does not ignore them. Their novels are bought and they are read; they are talked about; they are not like the older novels, and they lead to literary feuds. Can you imagine any young English novel leading to a literary feud? Wells's novels do, but not the novels of our youths.

Again, the war has occasionally made novelists. I should say that A. P. Herbert's *The Secret Battle* is among the best young novels of the period. I would not venture to call it a classic, but it is certainly written with classic restraint and something of classic beauty. It depicts terrible scenes, and, while sticking to truth, deprives them of any offence against beauty. It could not have been written but for the war. If anybody, old or young, urges that a sensitive artist could not pass through the horrors of the war and emerge with a fine book, the reply is that A. P. Herbert did. The mischief with A. P. Herbert is that he seems to have abandoned the novel form.

Further, what has happened to the young women? They, at any rate, did not witness the worst horrors of the war. And many of them now at writing age were still at school when the war ended. Where are the rising young women novelists and poets? Edith Sitwell, a poetess of intense originality, was writing before the war. Pauline Smith, a genuine novelist, was writing sketches in Scottish newspapers before the war. There is Margaret Kennedy, who is a post-war product. She has written one fair and one fine novel. Her next will be examined with the liveliest curiosity. In her place, while writing it, I fear, I should have been too self-conscious to write my best.

My view is that if the war is the cause of the slump in creation, it is only the indirect cause. The young writers seem to lack faith. Perhaps the war has depressed all faiths. The young writers are too much occupied with theories about work, and not enough occupied with work. Apparently they are wondering whether work is worth while. The writers who compose masterpieces have no mind for theories; theories are dust in their mouths. They do not think; they act — and take the consequences. Critics may explain them, but their own explanations of themselves are absurdly unconvincing. Moreover, they work all the time and produce enormously. Through thick and thin they go on producing. Young writers of this calibre may exist among us in caves, but they have not emerged to dazzle our eyes.

I was talking the other day to a novelist who produced a brilliant book a year or two ago. I said to him, "What's the new novel about?" He replied, "I'm not writing one; I haven't any ideas." Fancy a novelist of achievement not having ideas for a novel! The age of unfaith! Consider the case of William Gerhardi. He wrote one excellent novel, *Futility,* and a second novel which glints here and there with genius, *The Polyglots.* No sign of a third novel. The age of unfaith! When a novelist tells you that he has no ideas for his next novel you cannot answer him. You cannot instruct him to go out and get ideas. Creative ideas are not to be fetched. They come.

Just after the war a fine parterre of young poets burst into blossom. How many of them have stayed the course, brief though it is? The best of the survivors are Edmund Blunden and Sacheverell Sitwell. I warmly admire both of them. But where are the others? They seem to have tucked their heads under their folded wings and gone to sleep. Humbert Wolfe arrived a little later. Indeed, he is still on the way hither. He is rounding Byron Corner.

Part of the explanation of the uncreativeness of the epoch may be sought elsewhere. I hesitate to use the word "idleness." But there you are — I have said it. Numbers of young persons are walking about and stating that when they have sufficiently reflected they will write a novel, or that they may write a novel. They are waiting, in a masterly sloth. There have always been such dreamy philanderers with literature, but I think that there are many more of them to-day than aforetime. They have never acquired the saving habit of industry, and heaven knows if they ever will.

Idleness is the curse of this epoch. It is not confined to the members of trade unions. You can see it airing itself on golf courses on Saturday mornings and returning to town from country houses at noon on Mondays. The potential creators of literature are, I opine, stricken with the same disease as workmen and employers. Why, if a versifier publishes a fifty-page volume of verse he thinks he has done a year's work.

10 February 1927

"The Twelve Finest Novels All Russian"

In the matter of Russian fiction I am supposed by the unenlightened to have a bee in my bonnet. But I have no bee in my bonnet. I have been asserting for 20 years that the twelve finest novels are all Russian, and as time passes I find an increasing number of people to agree with me; I have little doubt that the number of people will continue to increase. So that I hope to be excused if I say, as I do say, that the appearance of an English translation of a novel by Lyeskov (or Leskov) is an important event in the literary year.

Lyeskov was writing contemporarily with Tolstoy and others of the great masters, and — so far as one can judge by one's own impressions and the opinions of the learned, such as Mr. Maurice Baring — he was the equal of these great masters. Some years ago there came out a volume of Lyeskov's short stories entitled *The Sentry*. This book contained one or two absolute masterpieces. I showed it to friends; I gave it to friends; but without much result. I do not believe that it had any success worth mentioning.

Later appeared *Cathedral Folk*, which was by no means so good as *The Sentry*, and which forced me to admit that Lyeskov, like Balzac, Scott, Dickens, Milton, and Shakespeare, was a very uneven writer. Great writers ought not to be uneven; but they are. A writer who is at once prolific and not uneven is never great.

Now I am reassured about Lyeskov by the publication of *The Enchanted Wanderer*, translated by A. G. Paschkoff (Jarrolds, 7s. 6d. net). *The Enchanted Wanderer* is a masterpiece — of humour, pathos, romance, and adventure. No novelist ever had a finer narrative gift than Lyeskov. Even if he was not obviously a genius, his mere technical skill would make him remarkable in the evolution of the art of fiction.

The strange thing is that Russian fiction never did evolve. Barely a hundred years old, it began right off with masterpieces of Pushkin's in the 1820's and masterpieces of Gogol in the 1830's, and went on with masterpieces until 1904, when Chekhov died. True, since then there has been naught but brilliant second-raters, but no other country has approached the sustained record of Russia in really first-class novels and stories.

Why Lyeskov, who from the outset was very popular in Russia, has not sooner reached European renown I do not clearly understand. Mr. Maurice Baring, in his *Outline of Russian Literature* (Home University Library, 2s. 6d.), which all should read, attributes it to misdoings of Russian criticism, which apparently was prejudiced by the fact that Lyeskov tilted impartially at both Russian Liberals and Russian Die-hards.

The explanation does not seem to me to be quite adequate. I should be inclined to say that pundits and other high-brows failed to take Lyeskov at a true valuation because of his persistent habit of mixing profound seriousness with light-hearted fun. You can laugh at every page of *The Enchanted Wanderer*. Nevertheless, the book is full, in its implications, of the most mordant social criticism. Lyeskov is as shattering as Chekhov himself, who, I imagine, did as much as any writer to hasten the Russian revolution.

Anybody with a passion for horses ought to read *The Enchanted Wanderer*. No novelist has written more exquisitely and comprehendingly of steeds.

A few words as to translation. The translation of this new book, like the work of Lyeskov himself, is uneven. I know nothing of A.G. Paschkoff, except that he is less familiar with the English language than with the Russian. In the passages of dialogue he varies from the good to the excellent.

But there are many descriptive sentences which could not possibly have been written by a man thoroughly at home with the English idiom. The translation gives the impression — perhaps false — of having been written by a linguistic Russian and revised by an Englishman who was somewhat negligent in the business of revision.

I have recently come up against two terrible examples of the wrong way to translate. The first was in Goldoni's play, *The Father of a Family,* which I saw performed in the theatre of the new organisation calling itself The Playroom Six, at 6, New Compton-street, Soho.

Goldoni was a great dramatist. He was also a charming and amusing dramatist. And he certainly modernised the comedy form. I specially like him for his unrivalled productiveness. Few authors could hope to write a good comedy all complete every three weeks for a year together, as Goldoni is said to have done. (His *Memoirs,* translated by John Black and published by Knopf, 10s. 6d. net, make excellent reading.)

I looked forward to *The Father of a Family.* When I witnessed it I could descry the existence of an admirable play behind the thick veil of the translation, but the translation was worse than bad — it was grotesque. It could hardly have been done by anybody who had ever before written English, or who was not writing English as a foreign tongue. Moreover, I suspect also that the translation was not made direct from the Italian, but from the Italian via the French. Discretion doubtless prevented the management from giving the name of the translator.

The second example was in *The Memoirs of the Marquise de Keroubec* (published by Geoffrey Bles, 7s. 6d. net). These reminiscences of Revolutionary and Napoleonic times must certainly be very piquant in the original French. In the too-original English — well, I could not believe my eyes as I read: and it is a mystery to me how so interesting a young publisher as Mr. Bles could have passed the translation for publication.

One cannot too plainly and fiercely assert that in a good translator the first positive requirement is a thorough knowledge, and a sure taste and large experience in the literary use, of the language into which he is translating, not of the language from which he is translating. Herein is an explanation of the excellence of the translations by Mr. Scott Moncrieff and Mr. Arthur Waley.

17 February 1927

Author's 34 Years Over a Novel

At last I have read Olive Schreiner's novel, *From Man to Man* (Benns). In addition to being a long book, it is certainly a full book, and the work of a very full mind. And to a marked degree it is propagandist literature. In these days, when the social conscience is so lively, sensitive and inconvenient, every serious novelist must be a propagandist of something; otherwise his novels will not "rank."

Olive Schreiner always ranged herself with the Left wing of critical and constructive thought. She was a vehement and ever furious reformer. It is to be observed that, with the exception of Kipling, who began as a reactionary and is now perhaps more uncompromisingly reactionary than ever, our major imaginative writers disclose a passion for reform. Look at Wells, Shaw, Galsworthy. Consider E.M. Forster's *A Passage to India.* And, in verse, consider Siegfried Sassoon, the Sitwells, Humbert Wolfe. All of them are against the *status quo.* Whereas the representatives of the Die-Hard creed make but a flickering and ineffectual show.

I think that *From Man to Man* carries propaganda to excess. True, it is far less propagandist than *Clissold,* but then *Clissold* is clearly, by the very spirit of its conception, a propagandist work. It is a political-social testament. The same cannot be said of *From Man to Man,* which is primarily a South African domestic story of two sisters, of whom the elder, Rebekah (the heroine), suffers desolation at the hands of a too temperamental husband, and defeats the dog, and the younger, Baby-Bertie, drops somewhat casually into prostitution.

The propaganda, though excellent of its kind, is not in the least essential to the story. A hundred pages might be cut out of the book, still leaving the story intact. When the two chief propagandists open their mouths they talk just like Olive Schreiner writes: which fact does not make for convincingness. And neither of them has humour nor gaiety. Only the wicked ones are allowed by their creator to be gay. All the same, Rebekah is a big character; she is drawn, and successfully drawn, on the Valkyrie scale. Pity she is a shade too good, tremendous and sublime for any husband's daily food!

Impossible to conceal that I have been a little, indeed more than a little, disappointed with *From Man to Man.* I had both heard and read rapturous praise of it. Such unmeasured laudation might well have prejudiced me against the book had I not had an intense, almost lifelong, admiration for Olive Schreiner. I read *The Story of an African Farm* in 1889. It is one of the three novels that had kept me up all night. (*Evan Harrington* is another.) Some passages in it are inferior to the rest, but, taken as a whole, it is a mighty affair.

Disagreeing with the majority, I thought *Trooper Peter Halkett* extremely fine. As for the *Dreams (The sunlight lay across my bed),* I shall never forget the impression they made on me when they appeared in *The New Review.* Nothing like them before in English literature! Nor have they been even tolerably imitated. Yes, I was handsomely prepared and apparelled to be ecstatic about *From Man to Man.* One hundred pages, and the thrill didn't come. Two hundred, three hundred, four hundred pages. No thrill! I felt cheated — but solemnly cheated. I respected, I admired, but I wanted to admire much more.

To pass an adverse verdict on the book is not to pass an adverse verdict on the author. Because the book was never finished, and probably the completed parts were not finally revised. The most difficult chapters were not even sketched out. Yet *From Man to Man* was begun in 1873, and the author was still working at it in 1907.

Now, no novelist can write a satisfactory, coherant novel in 34 years. The odd four years alone would be rather long. A novel whose composition spreads over 34 years is a novel written by two authors, if not three. And the authors do not and cannot see their work whole. Perspective is lost. The critical faculty is blurred. The work is bound to go wrong somewhere. This particular work seems in the latter half of it to be vitiated by a curious sentimentality.

But the gravest fault of the book, in my opinion, lies in the conception of the heroine. No woman so big, and politically so constructive, could possibly have continued throughout life to give her main attention to children and domesticity and the sacrificial diplomacy demanded by endless conjugal misfortune. Her genius, in fulfilling itself, would have forced her to put these matters in their proper secondary place. Neither the Karoo nor Capetown could have confined her scope. She would have compelled the attention of the whole Anglo-Saxon literary world — as Olive Schreiner did. Rebekah is consistently too prodigious for her environment.

Her grand protest to the light husband takes the form of a letter which she sits up all night to compose. This letter is the equivalent of a book, and a remarkable book. It is, I calculated, 20,000 words long. Rebekah, though the author says she wore no stays, couldn't have written that book in a night. One feels, while reading on and on and on — and every intelligent reader must feel — that one is being asked to believe the impossible. Count Fosco himself couldn't have written that book in a night, nor in two nights. (See *The Woman in White*.) Balzac couldn't have done it.

If the night had consisted of ten hours, and Rebekah had never moved from her chair nor paused for a word, she would have had to write at the rate of one word every two seconds continuously. I admit that this arithmetical criticism is original and disconcerting, but it is also unanswerable. In 1907 the authoress wrote to a friend that the letter was "too long all to have been written in one night." She added, "But that doesn't matter." I differ. Everything matters that weakens the confidence of the reader in the author's regard for truth.

Withal, *From Man to Man* demands, extorts laudation. It is a very considerable book, by a genius who, unfortunately, was not content to be a genius. The unhappy woman was beset by her visions of the imperfectness of this world. In the end these visions overcame the artist in her.

In reference to Mr. Nigel Playfair's letter, stating that the English translation of Goldoni's *Father of a Family*, given by the Playroom Six, is an eighteenth century translation, I can only say that a great deal of the version I *heard* was certainly not eighteenth century phrasing. The modernisation, of course, may have been due to the natural nervousness of some of the players.

24 February 1927

French Audacities: The Art of Proust

The other day I went into a large and beautiful bookshop in Paris. Bookshops, like all other kinds of shops, are more artistically arranged in Paris than in London. Also the necessary British institution of the "dust-jacket" is happily unknown in France, for the French book (except the French Christmas book) has no binding to be protected. On the other hand French books are too often disfigured by the "just out" band, which not only is offensive to the eye but prevents you from opening the book.

I went off with six or seven volumes, which I have since read or read "in." I will mention the name of but one. Of the rest, though there were three good books in the batch, I will now say merely that the freedom of the press to print anything and any word whatever is growing in the Republic. Such rich and complete candour as some of these books display I have never before met with in good modern work openly sponsored by publishers of the highest standing.

Here and there in the later parts of Marcel Proust's complicated and endless epic of fashionable society occurs a page for publishing which a British publisher would come into painful contact with the police; but Proust does at least enfold his audacities in a film of misty phrases. The newer French novelists waste no time in paltering. What they desire to say they say plainly.

Among the six or seven was *Souvenirs sur Marcel Proust*, by Robert Dreyfus (published by Grasset, in green, price 20 francs). Mr. Robert Dreyfus is a well-known and very reputable journalist, and from boyhood he was an intimate friend of Marcel Proust. Mr. Dreyfus had for this book a magnificent subject, and ample and exclusive knowledge of it. He had a magnificent subject because no really original and powerful novelist — of this century at any rate — ever enjoyed such a tremendous world-vogue as Marcel Proust.

Personally I am not an out-and-out Proustian. That is to say, I hesitate to believe that Proust was the greatest novelist that ever lived or ever could live. My admiration for him has got me into trouble with anti-Proustians, and my reserves about him have got me into more serious trouble with Proustians. So that I am compelled to live in a sort of no man's land. (Not that I mind that.)

Proust has enchanted me, and he has bored me. I am, however, convinced that, taken in the mass — and there is indeed mass — he very considerably "counts." I beg further to state that I was an early admirer. I bought *Du côté de chez Swann* in 1913. It lay like any other book on my shelves for years, and then suddenly I began to say with a careful-casual air, to Proustian friends who were inclined to rise a bit above themselves: "I'll show you the first edition of *Swann*," as I might have said: "I'll show you the first folio Shakespeare." Every time the effect has been all that the snob in me could have wished.

Proust had produced his best book in 1913, and his situation in the world did not improve for a long period. The annals of popularity furnish various instances of delay in the appreciation of a book, but there can be few instances of a book having had to wait six years for a boom so universal and so glorious as that which came to *Swann* in 1919, and which still continues, though less gloriously. In 1919, when Proust received the Goncourt Prize, a French critic could write: "The Goncourt Academy has awarded its prize to an author really unknown; he is unknown, and he will remain unknown." Literary critics have erred before; but what devil so often tempts them to risk gratuitously the frightful dangers of prophecy?

All true-blue Proustians will read Mr. Dreyfus's book on their god. And they will find nutritious food in it for their delicate souls; for it contains many hitherto unpublished letters from the pen of the Unparalleled; which letters are characteristic and admirable. The first one, written at seventeen, is a wonderful epistle for a youth. Proust implies in it that it was written "at a gallop." This I doubt. Every phrase in it is elegantly self-conscious.

But Mr. Dreyfus's book does not strike me as very good. It is a curious mixture of the ecstatic disciple and the society journalist. You see ecstatic disciple in the sentences which introduce the afore-mentioned letter: "To-day I glance at its pages with powerful and sweet emotion, while my hand trembles to copy out this masterly analysis by a psychologist aged seventeen." A man who can write sound reminiscences ought to have more control over his hand than that.

And you see the society journalist even in the solemn post-mortem scene: "I went up to the little flat in Rue Hamelin, last refuge of Marcel Proust, to share in the affliction of my friends, the Robert Prousts, and their charming daughter." No doubt she was charming, but why in that place employ that debased and meaningless cliché of an adjective? And again: "If it has happened to me sometimes to speak too familiarly of a friend so illustrious — " Am I captious, or is this kind of thing truly exasperating?

Still, the book has interesting passages. The pictures of student-life at the Lycée Louis-le-Grand are excellently informing to foreigners. And there is a most diverting account of the preliminaries to the founding of a literary review by the students. This review was to exist in only one example, which was to be passed from hand to hand, each member of the group undertaking to read it with all speed.

One member asked permission to take a copy of certain articles in it when all the members had finished reading it. Proust, who was the group secretary, objected, and fully stated his subtle reasons in a formal, quasi-legal document, with threat of resignation. Mr. Dreyfus, also a member of the group, rather strangely does not know whether or not the review ever appeared!

The Proust translations by Mr. Scott Moncrieff (published by Chatto and Windus) are hereby recommended without reserve.

3 March 1927

Ashley Dukes, William Gerhardi, and a Personal Recollection of Frederick Harrison

Plays are now more and more becoming books for reading. I remember the time when only the plays of Sir Arthur Pinero and Henry Arthur Jones were subjected to the ordeal of the printed page. The rest could hardly have withstood print for general perusal. They were too naive, silly, incredible, awful.

Then Bernard Shaw and Oscar Wilde came along and altered all that. Their plays were as good to read as to see — indeed, sometimes far better. Print shows up a play's small defects, but not necessarily the big fatal defects of construction and dramatic quality. Occasionally you may read with pleasure a play that in performance would drive you out of the auditorium into the bar. To-day all manner of plays are published — and sold (for many of them go into second, third and even fifth editions).

I have received two pieces from Ernest Benn, Limited, who are apparently constituting themselves publishers-in-chief to the superior dramatic world, for they have issued more than fifty modern plays within quite a short period. The two new ones are Mr. Ashley Dukes's *One More River,* and Mr. William Gerhardi's *Perfectly Scandalous or The Immortality Lady.*

28

One More River, though a "book," and therefore technically at my mercy, has just been produced. I will say naught about it, beyond modestly mentioning my inability to comprehend why in the sacred name of prose Mr. Dukes wrote it in blank verse. I feel sure that he had a clever motive. Mr. Dukes is a very clever man. He got the late Frederick Harrison to produce at the Haymarket a play with the plot of *The Man with the Load of Mischief.*

Frederick Harrison was the most courteous and charming manager in London, and the most reasonable to work with. But he was extremely difficult to suit with a play. He refused *Milestones.* Some months after the production of that play I was walking down Dean-street one evening on my way to the Haymarket, and I counted fourteen messenger-boys waiting among the crowd at the pit entrance of the Royalty Theatre to retain seats for people who had failed to get reserved seats. Harrison had invited me to see a play at the Haymarket. "You must have the Royal box," said he. He ushered me himself into the Royal box, with one word: *"Peccavi."* I have always regarded this as the summit of fine manners.

I could write whole chapters about Frederick Harrison, whom I adored. Twenty-five years ago he came with H.G. Wells for a week-end to my house in the country. Wells and I were writing a sensational play together.* It unhappily began with a corpse. Wells had the task of describing the play in detail to Harrison, who said with regret at the end of the recital: "No! I'm afraid I can't have a corpse on the Haymarket stage." This was at any rate better than the adverse decision of another manager about a play in which the moral law was flouted: "Certainly not. Seductions are contrary to the policy of my theatre." (He has since modified the policy of his theatre.)

To return. Mr. Gerhardi is a different pair of shoes from Mr. Ashley Dukes. He is a pet of the intelligentsia, and rightly so. His novels contain passages of genius. But he is (artistically) naughty. He has been naughty in *Perfectly Scandalous or The Immortality Lady,* which is not a good play — as you may judge from the wilful foolishness of the title.

It can be read. It contains many good lines, but even 1000 good lines will not inevitably make a good play. Mr. Gerhardi is of the school of Chekhov, which cannot surprise us, seeing that he is of Russian blood, and a very warm admirer of Chekhov. I admit that when I first *read* a play of Chekhov's I could not imagine what it was all about. When I saw it acted I was dazzlingly enlightened on this important point.

Perfectly Scandalous, etc., might conceivably act better than it reads. But I do not for one moment believe that it would. I know what to look for now in the works of the Chekhov school, and I have looked for it in *Perfectly Scandalous,* etc., and not discovered it. Technically Mr. Gerhardi's play is truly awful. The author informs us that the first act plays forty minutes. But the action obviously extends over at least four or five hours, so that long before the curtain falls all convincingness has vanished, and you conclude that the author is just having a lark at your expense, and not a very funny lark. *Perfectly Scandalous,* etc., has no apparent point.

Reading these plays, I thought of Henri Becque's *Souvenirs d'un Auteur*

---

* *The Crime* (1901-2): only a scenario survives.

dramatique, which I bought recently in the new collected edition of Becque's works. The *Souvenirs* are devastating in their ferocity, but they are the honest souvenirs of a first-rate artist who never compromised. Becque is still quite unknown to the British public. Why? In addition to one or two fine one-act pieces, he wrote the two greatest French plays of the nineteenth century — *La Parisienne* and *Les Corbeaux*. The reputation of nineteenth-century French drama is absurdly beyond its merits. There is not one play by the alleged giants of that period which can possibly survive. Becque is not (yet) an alleged giant, but his best plays are the finest French plays since Marivaux and Beaumarchais. They are as good as the best Ibsen.

I shall never forget the terrific impression made on me by *La Parisienne*, given by Antoine at the Théâtre Antoine, and by *Les Corbeaux*, given by Antoine at the Odéon. I suggest to the always enterprising firm of Benns that they should do a volume of Becque, comprising these two plays and a selection from the *Souvenirs*. Anyhow, some firm ought to do it.

I know not whether either of these plays has been produced on the West End stage. I remember no such production. Whether previously done or not, they ought to be produced now, and if they fail at first they ought to be produced again and again. They are world-classics. And one day they will certainly be recognised as such, even on the West End stage.

Les Corbeaux was produced at the Comédie Française and failed. *La Parisienne* was refused by the Comédie Française at first, but years afterwards produced badly, and with no success — before Réjane made its reputation. I cannot count that relenting to the credit of the Comédie Française, which is one of the most grossly commercial and inartistic stages on earth.

10 March 1927

The "Cowardice" of Thackeray

Some weeks ago in this place I made the statement that the twelve finest novels are all Russian. I first offered this affront to Western literary opinion fifteen years ago in New York. All the principal newspapers from New York to San Francisco instantly fell upon it, and much opposition was aroused. I have publicly offered it several times since, and trouble, characterised by vituperation, has always ensued — until the last occasion.

So far as I know, the glove has not yet been picked up: which seems to show that the work of Mr. Edward Garnett (the original introducer) and Mrs. Constance Garnett (translator in chief of Russian novels to the Anglo-Saxon publics) has at length produced some effect on a generation not wholly unwilling to learn. Indeed, my remark has been received with sympathy, and I have been asked for "guidance" on the matter.

Of course there is, really, no such dozen as "the twelve finest novels." I spoke "in a manner of speaking." It is impossible to say, for instance, that *The Charterhouse of Parma* is a finer novel than *Pride and Prejudice*, or vice versa. Or that *Resurrection* is a finer novel than *The Woodlanders*, or vice versa. When a work reaches a certain pitch of fineness, nothing

30

human can with propriety be raised above it. It exists in splendour, and there it is, safe from any comparisons. You deeply enjoy it, you laud it, and you are content with that.

The Russians, however, have this advantage over the rest of the world: that though in breadth of interest and in artistic discipline they fall a little short of the greatest non-Russian achievements, they handsomely excel in the best sort of realism — namely, the realism which is combined with a comprehending charity of judgment. Also, in the main, their creations are more heroical in scale.

No Russian novelist working on a large canvas has yet equalled Balzac in breadth of interest. The curiosity of Chekhov was every whit as inclusive as that of Balzac — perhaps even more inclusive. But Chekhov never worked on a large canvas. Balzac wrote a novel one of whose chief themes is the French law of bankruptcy, and he made it enthralling. He, at any rate, saw life whole, even if he saw it over-romantically. (I will be courageous, and say outright over-sentimentally.)

The Russians were too absorbed in individual psychology to have time or inclination to worry about the large social problems from which Balzac never shrank. Moreover, in their excuse, it may be argued that the tragi-comic censorship effectively prevented a frank handling of large social problems by Russian writers. There are vast tracts of phenomena affecting the life of human beings which are merely left out of some of the top-notch masterpieces of Russia. I do not remember a single landscape worth mentioning in all Dostoevsky, though there are many in Chekhov and some quite superlative ones in Tolstoy and Gogol, who in their turn had a blind eye, or a blinded eye, for other entrancing aspects of existence.

As for artistic discipline, Russian novelists are unquestionably deficient in it. They appear to despise form — except Turgenev, who could assuredly have taught even Henry James how to "organise" a novel; I reckon that Turgenev could say more in fewer words than any other novelist that ever lived. The Russians as a rule are far too prodigal of words, and far too excited about the particular page which they happen to be writing, to the neglect of the main outline of the work. The consequences are some-times very exasperating to the impatient.

Russian realism stands unique. Probably because it does not occur to a Russian novelist not to be realistic. The unrealists are an enigma to him (and rightly). "Here are the facts," he seems to say. "Why hide them?" But Russian realism is never crude.

Zola was a realist; he gave a complete picture of an entire epoch; he strove to be impartial; his novels are epical. Unfortunately he lacked taste. He is frequently crude. His mind, high though it was, turned too often naturally to the obscene. Worse than this, he lacked sympathy. If he ex-plained the weakness of human nature, he did so with a certain chill, disillusioned hostility towards human nature. The Russians are more generally sympathetic. They are not frightened by any manifestation of humanity, as, for example, Thackeray was.

Again and again in *Vanity Fair* you may see Thackeray approaching a difficulty whose solution will demand honesty and bravery, and you ask yourself: "How is he going to get through this?" Well, he doesn't get through it. He curves away from it, or he stops dead. He is a coward.

31

Perhaps his cowardice springs from a good motive — the fear of disgusting you with human nature. But he is a coward all the same. He half-develops situations which at the critical moment he dares not to grapple with.

The Russians have no qualms about disgusting you with human nature, for they are not themselves disgusted with it. They understand; they forgive; they love. They compel you to do the same. There is a Christ-like quality in the finest Russian fiction.

Next week I will try to enumerate the twelve Russian novels which I would place at the head of the world's fiction.

17 March 1927

The Twelve Finest Novels

Those twelve finest novels in the world, all Russian!

Details. Twenty-five years ago I would have begun with Turgenev; but in those days Dostoevsky had not been adequately or even decently translated. Now, whenever my mind dwells on the greatest achievements in fiction, I think, before any other novel, of *The Brothers Karamazov.* I read this first in French, and though the translation was mediocre in quality and most grossly mutilated, I came immediately to a very definite conclusion about the book.

I had never met with anything so vast and comprehensive in scale, so consistently powerful, so profound, so beautiful, so tragic, so moral, so philosophical in intention and execution, so convincing, so enthralling. Later, I read it twice in the complete English translation, and my estimate of it was thereby only raised.

I am willing to concede arguments to the effect that Einstein is endowed with the most prodigious intellect in the history of the race, that Shakespeare stands alone, and that Abraham Lincoln stands alone; but I implacably affirm that a greater novel (in our modern sense of the word "novel") than *The Brothers Karamazov* has yet to be written. It will be written — I doubt not, for I have a dogmatic belief in progress.

Further, I rate, *The Idiot* little lower than *The Brothers. The Idiot* is lovely; its closing pages are the summit of simple majesty. A still lovelier book, and a much shorter, is *The House of the Dead. The House of the Dead* is chiefly a record of experiences. If you choose you may decline to class it as a novel. It is, in my opinion, the most celestial restorative of damaged faith in human nature that any artist ever produced. The most successful and touching demonstration of the truth that man is not vile.

Fourthly, *Crime and Punishment,* the best-known of the four, a novel which cannot possibly be omitted from the dozen. The objectors to Dostoevsky say that he was an epileptic. Well, he was. And what of it? They say also that he was morbid. This I deny. He was an imperfect person; he made a mess of his life; he suffered terrible trials; he was continuously hard up for a hundred roubles. But none of these things made him morbid; his outlook upon the world was always sane, undistorted, and kindly. He loved men.

Now Tolstoy. He wrote three terrific novels: *Anna Karenina* and *War and Peace* when he was young, and *Resurrection* when he had passed the climacteric. All three took Europe and America by the neck, and they have never in the slightest degree relaxed their hold on the imagination of the Western world — *Anna Karenina* by its pathos, *War and Peace* by its sweeping grandeur, *Resurrection* by its overpowering moral lesson, and all by their sheer mighty force.

You cannot get away from these books. They force themselves instantly into any general discussion of the novel. Everybody who has read them remembers them, and admits their sway; and those who haven't read them must either pretend to have read them or submit to being thrown out of the argument with contumely.

The mind of Tolstoy is harder, less sympathetic, less exquisitely compassionate than that of Dostoevsky. But his regard for truth was not inferior; the general level of his creative power was perhaps slightly higher — at any rate, his methods of presentation are more readily effective, because less subtle and indirect; also he had a better sense of form, and far more discipline, than Dostoevsky. After a course of Dostoevsky you may be inclined to think that Tolstoy is relatively commonplace, banal, vulgar, material. But go back to Tolstoy, and you will once more be his helpless and contented victim.

I have now already mentioned seven books. Exclude any one of them from the dozen and what non-Russian work could you have the effrontery to put in its place? I cannot guess, unless it be a Stendhal. Would you dare to oust any one of them in favour of Dickens?

Turgenev. He no longer has the vogue of twenty-five years ago among the British intelligentsia. Russians never admired him as they admired Dostoevsky and Tolstoy, or even Gogol. I think that as a rule the compatriots of a writer are his best judges. (The exception to the rule is America, which for quite irrelevant reasons seriously underrates Poe and Whitman, and which respects Hawthorne for his secondary qualities. No finer prose than Hawthorne's was written in the nineteenth century. George Moore first made me see this, by quotations.)

I accept the verdict of Russia on Turgenev, but I imagine that it may be somewhat vitiated by a political or social prejudice. Still, no Russian would contend that Turgenev was not among the world's greatest. He cannot so powerfully move me as Dostoevsky and Tolstoy, but he was certainly a more finished artist than either of his contemporaries. Everything that he did shows a superb perfection — even in English. What form, what control of the vehicle, what grace, what tenderness!

I would name *Torrents of Spring* (better entitled *Spring Floods*), *Virgin Soil, On the Eve,* and *Fathers and Children.* They are all short. The longest, *Virgin Soil,* is, I fancy, shorter than the shortest Tolstoy or Dostoevsky, except *The House of the Dead. Torrents of Spring* is youthful — the most romantic expression of young love. *Virgin Soil* and *Fathers and Children* mark an epoch in the sociological development of the novel. *On the Eve* is the quietest, most insinuating, most beautiful thing ever done.

All these books are classics. They do not take you by the neck. They steal around you, envelop you; they impregnate you.

Gogol. He wrote one novel (unless *Taras Bulba* is long enough to count as a novel) — and even that he left very far from finished — *Dead*

Souls. Despite the indignities which it has suffered in various translations (not the latest English translation), and at the hands of misguided individuals who had the impudence to finish it, *Dead Souls* has taken its place in all Europe as a comic, ironic masterpiece of the first order.

It is a rollicking and murderous satire, and must have directly or indirectly influenced all later novelists who have castigated their country because they loved it — yes, down the decades of a century as far as Sinclair Lewis! *Dead Souls* is gorgeous reading. It is the greatest lark imaginable, and withal deadly. Nothing better of its kind exists. (I do not, however, rank it as Gogol's very best. I would give that place to his long-short story, *The Overcoat*.)

That makes twelve.

24 March 1927

Sinclair Lewis Assails Sham Religion

I have been reading some of the latest in novels. For instance, Mr. J.B. Priestley's *Adam in Moonshine* (Heinemann). Mr. Priestley, as all authors know, is a considerable literary critic. I see lots of reason why literary critics should write novels. In so doing they often give themselves away, generous fellows. Mr. Priestley is too clever to give himself away. And yet he does — by disclosing that he attaches too much importance to fancy, and not enough to imagination. *Adam* ("a fable") is neat in narrative, a welter of facile fancy, and touchingly innocent of character-drawing. There are houses where you dine with refinement, and at the end of the repast feel like telling your host that you want to go out to get something to eat.

Again, *Latter-day Symphony*, by Romer Wilson (Nonesuch Press). I have been told, frequently, that she wrote a superlative novel, *The Death of Society*. I hope it isn't like *Latter-day Symphony*, in either style or matter. A specimen of the writing: "Lord Edward handed him a beautiful glass of clouded yellow wine. A cherry and a small purple strawberry knocked their heads together in it." Now that sort of facile fancifulness irritates me, or would irritate me were I not a philosopher. I could teach even a member of the British Academy to write like that.

Latter-day Symphony is about a Chelsea crowd of drunken fornicators. I don't in the least mind novelists writing about drunken fornicators, who certainly ought to be written about. But I recognise no human nature in the book. One of the heroes says to the heroine: "A flame shot through my flesh when you touched me. It was exquisite, but I can't endure that without rapture."

Now, I have lived much in and around Chelsea, but I have never met any drunken fornicator who ever talked so, and I don't believe that any human being ever talked so, except for fun or because he was an incurable ass. The publishers describe the book as "hectic," and the author describes it as a "novelette." The writing is careful, ingenious, and pretentious. But not careful enough. There is a mistake of grammar on page 4.

May I recommend *Grammar for Grown-ups*, by Charles C. Boyd (Allen and Unwin), to high-brow novelists? Though perhaps a little bit over-facetious, it costs but a florin, and is packed with really useful tips for the unwary who strive delicately to run before they can toddle.

A very different book from either of the above novels is *The Time of Man*, by Elizabeth Madox Roberts (Cape, 7s. 6d.). I read it in the American edition, which, out of a noble enthusiasm, was sent to me by Mr. George Doran, who is *not* the American publisher of the book. I should call this gesture unique in the annals of publishing, but perhaps it isn't.

Elizabeth Roberts is an original writer. Though *The Time of Man* shows influences, as it ought, especially if it is a first novel, it has a clear individuality which distinguishes it at once from all other novels. It is the story of Ellen Chesser, daughter of a farm-hand gipsy kind of person some-where in the agricultural wilds of what has been called — but not by God Himself — God's own country. It is a wonderful and an imperfect novel.

The style, American, is excellent. The descriptions are most delectable, the psychology searching, the detail plenteous, exact, and skilfully handled. I read half of it with pleasure — I will say more, with delight. I grew enthusiastic.

But after many pages I began to feel uneasily that the affair was not moving. True, it went on and on, but it did not dramatically move. The second half is inferior to the first. When she is static, the author is fine. When she tries to be dynamic, when she nerves herself to come to the point, she is less satisfactory. The worst page in the book is that in which she introduces the key-phrase for her central idea — "the time of man." Nevertheless, I commend her heartily to the connoisseur and the seeker after a new and sound talent.

And now I must mention a striking case of the born novelist. Sinclair Lewis's new novel, *Elmer Gantry* (Jonathan Cape, 7s. 6d.), is published this day. Sinclair Lewis may be loquacious, with a tendency to slapdash — he is! — but he is a master of narrative. You may curse him, but you will read him.

There are at least three qualities in him that I really admire. The first is his strange narrative gift, which is such that when you have finished a chapter and want to go to bed, you don't go because you suspect that the next chapter will be as interesting as the one you have just read, and the desire to convert suspicion into certainty is stronger than the desire to sleep. The mysterious gift deserves analysis, but this column is not the place for analysing.

The second quality is his instinctive predilection for wide and mighty subjects. Of Sinclair Lewis's three big novels, *Babbitt* (which added a type to our view of human nature) deals with Business, *Arrowsmith* deals with Science, and the latest deals with Religion. The third quality is his fearless fondness for indicting his native land. Sinclair Lewis's indictments of Western civilisation are terrible; they are absolutely desolating. (Yet such is the power of a narrative gift that he is a best-seller, despite his iconoclasms.)

In *Elmer Gantry* the sarcasms, the irony, the satire, the general ferocity of his treatment of shams in the vast American machinery for saving souls must be read to be believed. Yes, he has courage. (It was unnecessary to print on the back of the cover: "This novel has not been serialised." No-body could imagine it in the pages of, for instance, *The Saturday Evening Post*!)

Another attraction of *Elmer Gantry* is that it is not written in English. "Prexy," "the whole cheese," "Abernit," "buttinsky," "welsh on," "gink," "lambasting": these specimens of a foreign tongue, with some others, all occur on one half-page. But it is written. Masterpieces may, after all, be written in languages other than English. I do not assert that *Elmer Gantry* is a masterpiece; but I do assert that it is about ten times as readable as some scores of masterpieces with which I am acquainted.

31 March 1927

The Angry Mr. Mencken: "Lacks Balance, Sense of Justice and Evidence – But Has Done Good"

The centenaries of Newton and Beethoven are now safely over. They were probably the most important centenaries since Shakespeare's, and they are not likely to be rivalled for a long time to come. Still, all centenaries are dangerous to one's peace of mind, as they give rise to a stream of twaddle, the sight and sound of which make one feel awkward, constrained, and lower one's estimate of human nature. Reading some of the tributes to Beethoven, I had some of the terrible qualms of humiliation and self-consciousness which visit me when I have to cross arms and join hands and sing *Auld Lang Syne*.

Newton was better handled. In some papers he was really adequately handled. Einstein himself wrote about Newton. (*Manchester Guardian,* of course – it would be!) This was the least Einstein could do, seeing that he has knocked Newton off his perch. I could desire to assist at the centenary of Einstein, but heaven will no doubt decide against me. In the meantime I wish urgently to know more about Einstein than I do. Here I am, violent but grey-haired, endowed with a fair sanity and general intelligence, and a passion for knowledge – and after all these years I understand little more of the relativity theory than a clever hall-porter. And I have yet to meet a man (not an expert) who understands more than I do of the relativity theory.

Incomprehension of the relativity theory is perhaps the most widespread human characteristic of the age. How comes this about? I cannot say. One hears that without a knowledge of the higher mathematics nobody can grasp the relativity theory. To which my reply is: Stuff! Newton's theory is full of higher mathematics, but I can grasp the fundamentals of it. I shall need much persuading that a theory which re-states the physical universe must remain for ever a perfect mystery to the plain man. Plain men are not so plain as all that.

All the above is introductory to two words concerning Mr. J.W.N. Sullivan's slim volume, *Aspects of Science (Second Series)* (Collins, 12s. 6d.). This book was not sent to me; I bought it. It contains an essay, *A Sketch of Einstein's Theory*, which is worth reading, an essay which did throw for me a few fresh gleams on Einstein's theory. It has not entirely enlightened me, but it did some useful damage to the walls of my ignorance.

Mr. Sullivan is the best expounder (or *vulgarisateur*) of the scientific attitude that I have met with. He seems to have a double mind – the mind of science and the mind of art. He possesses imagination, and he uses it scientifically, as of course artists should always do — but usually don't. His book is really valuable to the plain man, and it is written with distinction.

I wish that the scientific attitude towards things was more generally and more attractively inculcated, not only to the plain man, but to artists and publicists in general. For myself, I derive benefit from a weekly perusal of *Nature,* which was prescribed for me about a year ago by H. G. Wells. You won't understand half of it at all," he said, "but you will understand bits here and there, and every bit you understand will help you." He was right. I didn't and don't understand half of it, or a quarter of it; but I would not now be without it. As a corrective of the sentimental fool which resides in all of us, it has a genuine usefulness.

Mr. H.L. Mencken, that bright and renowned publicist of the United States, provides a striking, deplorable example of the strictly unscientific attitude in his *Notes on Democracy* (Jonathan Cape, 6s.). This little book is amusing, readable, and very capably written — in its dashing, crude way. But it demonstrates nothing whatever beyond the fact that Mr. Mencken is angry with America and determined to have a row.

He lacks balance, a sense of justice, a sense of evidence, and all intellectual scruple. Yet he is moved by a few excellent ideals. He has done good. But how much more good he would have done had he been trained to regard social phenomena without the eyeglasses of emotional prejudice! There is some soul of goodness in this playboy of the far-Western world. Had there not been, Sinclair Lewis could not have dedicated his new novel thus "To H.L. Mencken, with profound admiration."

The second volume of Mr. Frederic Irving Taylor's epic, *Azal and Edras* (Selwyn and Blount, 6s.), is at last out. The first was published in 1923. Good modern epics ought to be noticed. They are very rare. (Maurice Hewlett wrote one.) Also they have in a peculiar degree, as regards their structure, a scientific aspect. I would say that, after the inspiration, structure is the most important quality in an epic. Histologically considered, *Azal and Edras* seems to me to be excellent; but one cannot be sure until the third volume has appeared. Mr. Taylor's epic is a parable of the late war. The third volume will climb up to the League of Nations!

Two real poets, Edith Sitwell and the late T.W.H. Crosland, have given enthusiastic praise to the first volume of *Azal and Edras.* It was evidence of Miss Sitwell's justifiable claim to be an upholder of the classical English tradition that she should so warmly appreciate an epic which in style goes right back to Milton. Crosland mixed up a number of Milton's lines with a number of Mr. Taylor's, and challenged you to say which were which. But I think it is fairly easy to do so.

While I do not rate Mr. Taylor's verse quite so high as did Crosland or Miss Sitwell, I do admire it. And I admire the author's courage in setting out to compose this epic, which the lettered will certainly read with a few real thrills. There are inexperienced persons who have the face to tell you that a short story is harder to write than a novel. And there are similar nincompoops who will tell you that a sonnet is harder to write than a epic. It merely is not so. Of all forms of literary composition the epic presents the greatest difficulties. Of course a good sonnet is harder to write than a bad epic. But then it is harder to jump over a brook than to drop down a well.

In my view, critical pundits to the contrary notwithstanding, good verse is immensely more difficult to write than good prose, because it simply has to be much more scientifically organised. I once had a versificatory period. A colleague said that I could not write a poem. (I had previously written some verse.) I said I could. I spent several most exhausting days in intensely concentrated labour, and produced six quatrains. "Is this a poem?" I asked my friend. "Yes," said he. "It is. But could you write another?" At any rate I never did. I understood that my life could not be satisfactorily conducted on the lines of poetry.

7 April 1927

How Libraries Can Form Public Taste: A Popular "County" Novelist

Glad tidings appeared the other day in the *Times Literary Supplement*. They were as follows: "Applications are invited for the post of Librarian (full time) for the County Library Scheme under the Education Authority. Experience of similar Library work desirable. Salary £150 by £10 to £250," etc.

The Education Authority making this remarkable offer is that of the County of Roxburgh. I doubt whether Roxburgh is as big as Yorkshire, but it is an entire county, and probably proud of its status as such; and a wage of something under £3 a week seems to me, with my inflated Southern ideas, to be just a trifle on the pinching side for a man of experience whose whole-time job will be to control, execute and generally manage the official enterprise of supplying printed and bound matter to the inhabitants of an entire county. I am informed that the jolly dustmen who remove my dust earn more. Certainly a competent chauffeur would not look at such a salary.

It is desirable that the sought-for librarian should be able to read, write, count up to a hundred and fifty, organise, talk to citizens firmly yet persuasively, catalogue, know the difference between a book and a bull's foot, assess the relative values of authors, chaffer with publishers, and sign his august name with a flourish. Also, in his spare time, he should scan reviews, or even books themselves, and have a mind capable of making quick decisions which will affect the intellectual life of tens of thousands of individual aspirants to knowledge or aesthetic pleasure.

Indeed, his influence, if not his direct power, will be enormous; his responsibilities to the Education Authority or heaven will be heavy, and therefore he will be a personage. Less than three pounds a week! . . . I trust that he may find leisure at the end of his day's work for mankind to ponder how best he can maintain the dignity of his position on less than three pounds a week.

However, it is not my business nor my intention to criticise either directly or by ironic implications the economic policy of the Roxburgh Education Authority. How they contrive it I don't know, but Scotsmen do get educated, whereas Englishmen do not. The Roxburgh Education

Authority doubtless knows just what it is about, and what qualifications can be obtained in Scotland for less than three pounds a week. Besides, there is a clear promise that the salary shall rise in the course of a decade to the grandiose figure of nearly five pounds a week. Still —

The foregoing is merely the flighty prologue to an assertion that public libraries and their librarians constitute a more important factor in the national life than we are apt in our unimaginativeness to suppose. If Blücher (with Wellington's aid) won the battle of Waterloo on the playing-fields of Eton, we are entitled to say that the battle for sound literary taste must be won in the public libraries. Education Authorities are mighty, and they rule their librarians with rods, but the librarians in the last resort are mightier, and the unassuming, independent ukase of a librarian receiving less than three pounds a week may bestow or withhold what is called in Glasgow dailies "mental pabulum" whose withholding or bestowal might well change the curve of thought of immense communities. This is not fantastic, but true.

Hence I consider that the panjandrums of literary criticism might sometimes be better employed in examining and criticising the performances of public libraries than in examining and criticising dull books whose sole merit (doubtful) is that they employ printers and binders and help publishers and booksellers to buy flesh-meat once a week at least. The performances (occasionally the incredible antics) of public libraries deserve the closest impartial attention, which attention they seldom receive. The price of freedom is eternal vigilance: this maxim applies nowhere more forcefully than in public libraries.

I am by no means an opponent of censorship in public libraries. Censorship must obviously exist. I do not use the word in the narrow sense of censorship of the obscene. I mean a censorship far more comprehensive than that, a censorship which amounts to encouragement of the good and to discouragement of the bad. Public literary taste will not form itself — or, if it does, it will form itself unsatisfactorily. It needs a wise nurture, which can only be achieved by public librarians experienced and enlightened in literature and with opportunities to read and reflect.

One of the chief aids, if not the chief aid, to good librarianship is the correcting fear of publicity. At present most librarians, with their authorities, are allowed to work in the dark. A town says proudly that it possesses a public library with so many volumes, of which so many circulate so many times a year. This phenomenon may be good or it may be bad. All depends on what volumes circulate, and in what order. My suspicion is that in most public libraries none but the most benighted, perfunctory attempt is made towards the deliberate formation of public literary taste.

On the other hand, I know that some public libraries are well managed. Perhaps, in order to avoid the invidious, I ought not to mention names. Nevertheless, being without scruple, I will mention two at haphazard. Norwich is excellently managed. Halifax is excellently managed. The *Publishers' Circular* recently printed a tabular statement of the principal novels in stock and lent out at Halifax. Thirty-eight authors' names are given; there is not one which it is possible not to respect, and there are many, in very active circulation, of brilliant merit. I was glad to notice that one of the most popular authors, and one whose entire stock is nearly always, "out," is a county novelist, Halliwell Sutcliffe. It is evident that a sound literary taste is judiciously fostered by the Halifax Authority and Librarians.

14 April 1927

Bad Writing: Mr. Churchill as Historian: Modern Stylists

I have been reading Mr. G.P. Gooch's *Recent Revelations of European Diplomacy* (Longmans, 7s. 6d. — not a dear book as prices now go). The subject is a great one. Mr. Gooch reviews the apologetic war-literature of Germany, Austria, Russia, France, Great Britain, the United States, Belgium, and less glorious countries. His views thereon are sound: by which, of course, I only mean that I hold similar views. He speaks his mind with candour, but never allows indignation to impair his admirable composure. On the whole the picture presented, or indicated, of the pre-war diplomatic mind is extremely sinister; and unfortunately there is so far little to show that the post-war diplomatic mind is less puerile, mean, unscrupulous, mendacious, and dangerous to human life than the pre-war.

Mr. Gooch has produced a useful guide to a vast quantity of printed matter. It would have been still more useful than in fact it is had it been more interestingly written. Mr. Gooch is really learned, and he has the defect of many pundits: allusiveness. A pundit has the right to be allusive when writing for pundits of his own circle; but when writing for the rest of us, he has only the right to assume that we never knew much and that we remember almost nothing. Further, Mr. Gooch has apparently no sense of light and shade in writing. His pages are uniformly grey. You may read a page, and, because of this greyness, ask yourself unanswerably at the foot of the page: "What have I been reading about?"

Again, Mr. Gooch does not always write clearly, no doubt because he does not always think clearly. And generally, as regards his style, taken sentence by sentence, I must say that it is unworthy of his learning and of his high political commonsense. Indeed it is still jejune. He has not yet conquered his youthful fear of using the same word twice for the same thing. "What Barrère had *accomplished* with the Consulta, he endeavoured to *achieve* with the Hofburg." Also he has insufficiently buried Macaulay. "The neglect of his warnings was speedily followed by the realisation of his fears." This kind of writing, at this date, irritates the lettered.

Further, Mr. Gooch is afflicted by the fatal word "If" at the beginning of two correlated sentences. His excellent little book, *Political Thought in England*, from which I learnt a lot in the early part of the war, begins thus: "If the sixteenth century was the era of theological controversy, the seventeenth century was above all the age of political discussion." (Note "controversy" and "discussion," "era" and "age.") There is no "if" about it. The thing is not conditional, nor suppositional; it simply and unquestionably was so.

Macaulay was a terrible "if-er," and the sins of his successors are heavy on his head. Macaulay's style will scarcely bear close examination. He can be read with gusto; he had a wonderful dramatic sense of light and shade;

40

he is not unduly allusive; you always know precisely what he is talking about. But his writing is as doubtful as his intellectual integrity. He dealt in clichés, which are septic matter and likely to induce decay wherever they are found.

In Macaulay people are "prone to believe." (Did Macaulay ever consider the meaning of the word "prone"?) They do not go to prison, but are "flung" there. Their spirit is "cowed." (Why cowed?) They are not well-born; they "spring from an illustrious house." And, worst of all, states and parties are "torn by internal dissensions," or "torn by internecine strife." Macaulay was, I think, among the first to use "torn" in this picturesque sense, and I can never forgive him for the tedious mannerism, which persists horribly to this day in the writings of the grandiose third-rate. Nevertheless, he had genius enough to redeem the revolting crudity of his defects.

Not so with John Richard Green, the historian who first discovered the English "people," and whom I was brought up to adore. I think that Green was a really bad writer (besides being a sad sentimentalist). He wallowed in clichés and in single words whose fascination he could not withstand. In Green, "nobles" are "lawless" and "dissolute," and when neither they are "greedy and cruel." Taxation is "crushing"; so is despotism. Resistance is "stubborn." Obstacles are not merely placed; they are "thrown." Men are not persuaded or influenced; they are "swayed." And so on endlessly.

It is disturbing, too, to see things "running" all over the pages of Green. " 'Eye for eye' ran the rough code." ". . . ran the English proverb." Why all this athleticism? The trouble with Green was that he thought not in separate words but in ready-made phrases, the sort of phrases which in a really up-to-date department store you can probably buy on the same floor as you buy your ready-made pyjamas.

Our great lightning historian, Winston Churchill, though he does not write as well as he did 20 years ago, still writes better than Green. I agree with Charles Masterman that he is developing a regrettable tendency to rhetoric, or eloquence. He *will* write for effect, and he has neither the leisure nor the natural ability to do that. Gibbon wrote for effect; but Gibbon did nothing except write; he had an astounding natural ability, and he employed it with a virtuosity which no writer has ever surpassed. Gibbon will stand detailed examination. Winston Churchill will not. I would like to examine in detail a Churchillian page, but who would be interested, except scribes? However, Churchill, accurate or inaccurate, is magnificently readable; he is nearly as readable as Macaulay. And he can hold an enormous work together.

We have to-day two genuinely original stylists, D.H. Lawrence, the novelist, who at his best is quite first-rate, and T.E. Lawrence, author of *Revolt in the Desert*. As I am not dealing with novelists, I cannot now discuss D.H. And I have no room to discuss T.E. I will say only that I should like to know where and how the ex-Colonel learnt to use a pen. He is a better writer than Winston Churchill. He is one of the best English prose writers living, but, like Schubert and Wagner, he does not always know when to stop. He thinks in separate words. Seemingly he has passed unscathed through a world hurtling with clichés.

21 April 1927

Einstein for the Tired Business Man

A few weeks ago on this page I remarked upon the general incomprehension of Einstein's theory of relativity, and the strangeness of the widely propagated notion that an average intelligent man could not grasp the essentials of a theory which is supposed to re-state the order of the physical universe. I received sympathetic letters from readers in the same case as myself. I went about among my brilliant friends asking: "Do you understand relativity?" "Do *you*?" "or *you*?" Nobody could say Yes. On behalf of the great trade union of average intelligent persons, I felt humiliated. I decided that I would go into the relativity affair myself. I now report to the trade union.

I was informed that the best popular exposition of relativity was Bertrand Russell's *The A B C of Relativity* (Kegan Paul, 4s. 6d.). I bought it and read it. Quite a short book, 231 pages. It is disfigured by misprints, which seems odd for a scientific work. It begins ingratiatingly. You think, thrilled: "I am about to be enlightened." The promise is not fulfilled. The strain on the intelligence increases as the book proceeds, and towards the end occur pages which are incomprehensible. Having finished the perusal, you say: "Now what *is* Einstein's theory?" You cannot satisfactorily reply.

Bertrand Russell is brave; he has not shirked difficulties; he once more shows that he has a mind of amazing acuteness. But he has only fractionally succeeded with me. He frequently verges on metaphysics, which (like myself) he despises, and sometimes his mind, with all its acuteness, seems to work with an ingenuity which to me is childish. Moreover the book is not written with his usual elegant clarity. And further, he now and then makes slips which impair one's confidence in his intellectual processes. Thus he writes: "All motion is relative, and there is no difference between the two statements, 'The earth rotates once a day,' and 'The heavens revolve about the earth once a day.' The two mean exactly the same thing, just as it means the same thing if I say that a certain length is 'six feet or two years.' " Surely something is temporarily the matter with a mind capable of seriously putting forward an illustrative comparison so inept. I could give other examples from the book.

Next Messrs. Collins, animated by my praise of J.W.N. Sullivan's *Aspects of Science*, sent me another book of his, *Three Men Discuss Relativity*. The three men of the title are a Mathematical Physicist, a Philosopher, and an Ordinary Intelligent Person. "The very thing," thought I. "I am the third fellow." The author limits his aim. He says that his object is not to present the theory of relativity, but to show what the theory is about. The book is disfigured by misprints, which seems odd for a scientific work.

J.W.N. Sullivan succeeds in his limited aim. He begins beautifully. He has elegance. But he does not succeed throughout in being comprehensible. The book demands tremendous concentration, and this quite apart from the equations, of which there are many, and which are perhaps the most comprehensible things in the book.

Then I received *From Kant to Einstein*, by Hervey de Montmorency

(Heffer, Cambridge). This is a very little book. It is disfigured by misprints, which seems odd for a scientific work. It is not schematic. Indeed, it is no more than a series of notes. These notes, however, are illuminating, and they would have been more illuminating had the author given a glossary of definitions of scientific words and phrases which he employs. Such words and phrases may be the current coin of the intercourse of men of science, but some of them would have meant nothing to me had I not previously read Russell and Sullivan. Nevertheless, I think that Montmorency would be more helpful than either Russell or Sullivan to the tired business giant determined to improve his mind of an evening. I must add that I have been, and am, a warm admirer of Russell and Sullivan, and grateful to Montmorency, whose name is new to me.

Here are some of the conclusions which I, the ordinary intelligent person, have reached about Einstein's Theory.

1. It is a very modest theory. It deals only with the physical relations of things, and with certain of their attributes. It does not touch the constitution of things, nor does it consider the organic.

2. There is nothing new in it. But Einstein has taken the ideas of others, and worked them out with a completeness and a logical ingenuity and force which are positively frightening to the ordinary intelligence.

3. The inquirer into the theory will receive no sudden enlightenment; there is no key-statement to flood the receptive mind with the radiance of a great new idea.

4. Einstein's aim has been to state some of the laws which govern the relations of things in the simplest, barest possible way — so that the formulæ of the said laws shall be equally true for all observers, wherever they are and however they are moving. *He is a simplifier.*

5. The theory does not imply that everything is relative. On the contrary the theory admits an absolute — and quite properly leaves it alone.

6. The geometry of Euclid is not superseded. On the contrary the whole business springs from the celebrated (or notorious) 47th proposition of Euclid, Book 1.

7. The theory, generally speaking, substitutes curved lines for straight lines as the natural path for moving bodies. Einstein argues that space is curved. Here I suspect that he is not expressing himself very happily. A space may be confined within curved limits. A space may be occupied by bodies that move in curves. But surely space itself cannot be curved.

8. "Space-time" is the chief recurrent phrase in the theory. There is absolutely nothing new in the idea of space-time. We have always defined the situation of bodies by measurements in three dimensions, plus a time-observation. To my intelligence it is merely playing with the words to call "time" a fourth dimension. Higher mathematics can postulate four dimensions, even forty dimensions, and can work out sums in them. But my mind cannot picture more than three dimensions, and no mind can picture more than three.

9. The theory does not destroy former theories of space and time. You may stick to your old theories. I propose to do so.

10. The theory does away with the theory of gravitation. It maintains that bodies move along natural paths by reason of forces within themselves, and not by attraction exerted by other bodies. This is just a theory which it supersedes.

11. One of the main snags in the theory of a moving universe is the alleged fact that light can have only one velocity — 300,000 kilometres a second. If you are in a touring car and throw a stone in the direction of the car's motion the velocity of the stone (friction apart) will be the velocity of the stone from your hand plus the velocity of the car. But light (it is said) will not behave like a stone. If you could throw it from your hand in the car, the velocity of the car would have no effect on the total velocity of the light. Thus, if the sun could be projected towards you at a velocity of 300,000 kilometres a second, it would hit you in the eye at precisely the same instant as its ray reached your eye. Which seems to me to be very fishy.

12. The theory has an unfortunate tendency to become metaphysical — in spots.

13. The theory does nothing whatever to answer the old central enigma about the movement of matter. Namely. If matter is continuous in space, how can it move? If matter is discontinuous in space, how is motion communicated from one bit of matter to another?

14. One day Einstein will be superseded. Later, the genius who has superseded him will be superseded by somebody else. In the meantime he and his expounders make enthralling reading. I have been as excited by these brief and superficial studies as I ever was by an ode of Wordsworth's or a novel of Hardy's.

28 April 1927

An Artist Turned Author — Mr. Wyndham Lewis

Mr. Wyndham Lewis's new periodical, *The Enemy* (nearly 200 large pages, and very cheap at 2s. 6d.) has been out for some weeks, but it is not an affair to be disposed of in an armchair in half an hour. It is as long as an average book, and about 90 per cent. of it really is a book, or part of a book — *The Revolutionary Simpleton,* by an author named Wyndham Lewis (not the diverting Wyndham Lewis of the daily Press*). There are pictures, chiefly by Mr. Wyndham Lewis, including an excellent portrait of Mr. Wyndham Lewis, by Mr. Wyndham Lewis.

Mr. Wyndham Lewis made a name, and earned much hatred and some admiration, as a painter. The examples of da Vinci and Rossetti notwithstanding, I mistrust an artist who cannot definitely choose between two mediums. It seems to me that an artist capable of doing anything in a first-rate manner will be so obsessed by that one thing that he cannot be bothered with another thing. I do not presume to assess Mr. Wyndham Lewis's paintings. Some of them I admired while they repelled me.

As a writer Mr. Wyndham Lewis has considerable gifts, with a slightly amateurish technique. But he is always going and never arriving. The fact seems to be that he lacks the ability to marshal and fully utilise the distinguished faculties which are undoubtedly his. *Tarr* had good chapters — chapters that were worth writing. It was, however, in the somewhat Teutonic lump, doughy, and at last unreadable. I mean for me. His

*D.B. Wyndham Lewis, founder of the *Daily Express* "Beachcomber" column.

apophthegms are striking. His treatise, *The Art of Being Ruled,* is striking. His Shakespearean book, *The Lion and the Fox,* is said to be striking. In *The Enemy* there is part of a striking essay on James Joyce — which leaves you nowhere.

I would like to be able to state what Mr. Wyndham Lewis is mainly "after," but I cannot, because I have not been able to find out. One of his minor purposes is to disembowel his enemies, who are numerous, for the simple reason that he wants them to be numerous. He would be less tiresome if he were more urbane.

Withal, *The Enemy* is not to be despised. It can appeal to only the few; but the few, if they have patience, will be able to get a meal out of it, despite its occasional pettiness, its preoccupation with quite unimportant persons, its clumsinesses of style, and its typographical affectations.

Among the other contributors are Mr. J.W.N. Sullivan (who is satisfying on Beethoven), and Mr. T.S. Eliot, who writes a sentence more illuminating than all the 160 pages of Mr. Wyndham Lewis. Namely: "We await . . . the great genius who shall triumphantly succeed in believing *something.*" We do. Doubt is our spiritual curse in these days.

I welcome *The Enemy.* It is to be a quarterly — if heaven wills. We have two other quarterlies of literary distinction, *The Criterion* and *The Calendar.* We want more. And we want some monthlies. (But who is to pay for them? There are about forty literary monthlies in France, where the financial resources of literature are smaller than in Britain.) The attitude of our standard intellectual monthlies towards the newest manifestations in literature and the arts is generally either comically pedagogic, or inimical, or strictly non-committal, or panicky. And our popular magazines have no attitude towards new literature and the arts other than that which can be expressed by photographs. Personally I read *La Nouvelle Revue Française* and the seasonal *Commerce* (not a bit "commerce" in the mercantile sense). I prefer the former. André Gide is the arch-priest of it.

The most remarkable book published in France last year was, to my mind, Gide's *Si le grain ne meurt.* In England I have heard it called dull (not in France); but it very securely held me. Neither Mudies nor W.H. Smith and Son., nor the *Times* Book Club, nor those benefactors Boots would tolerate it were it translated. It is now unobtainable in France. I mention it because it is to be the subject of a great experiment. A popular edition of it, rigorously expurgated, will be published at the equivalent of about sixpence, and a quarter of a million copies will be printed. Enterprise! The expurgations will by no means deprive the book of a very high interestingness.

I have never read André Gide without wishing that we had in Britain more novelists with his bias towards philosophy. I used to say that ideas are the curse of art. I still say so — unless ideas are made the very theme, and not merely the decoration, of the work. A novel entitled *Neighbours* (Holden and Co., 7s. 6d.), by Claude Houghton, was recommended to me by Robert Nichols, whose passion for ideas equals Mr. Wyndham Lewis's passion for enemies. *Neighbours* is a novel about ideas concerning life. It is full of dialogue, and good dialogue. It has beautiful moments. It is original. When I finished it I felt grateful to Robert Nichols for the introduction.

I must mention that the perspicuous will be able to foresee the end of the book. Some people don't like to be able to do that. I do. I think one ought to be prepared for the end of a book as one ought to be prepared for death. I had not before heard of Mr. Claude Houghton, and I know not if *Neighbours* is his first book. It may be, but if it is he must have written a good deal privately. There is naught of the stammering tongue in *Neighbours*.

5 May 1927

Wanted – A Popular Magazine for the Thinking Public

In a recent article, speaking of our popular magazines, I remarked upon their absence of any attitude (save such as can be expressed by photographs) towards the latest manifestations of literature, art, etc. Since then I have been looking afresh at our popular magazines, British and American. There are an enormous number of them, and they seem to be multiplying nearly as fast as automobiles. Indeed, I should say that a new one enters the market, with a powerful determination to win the market, far more frequently than a new brand of automobile. I like this. I am all for competition, and the devil take the hindmost. I have come to two conclusions about the popular magazine.

The first is that I disagree with the commonly accepted theory that American magazines are better than British. Americans are larger; they are perhaps better printed on shinier paper; they have more seductive covers, they certainly have more specious advertisements. But I see nothing to choose between British and American in the fundamental quality of their letterpress and their illustrations. Indeed the star items of their literary sides are often written by the same star-pens. The big noise in the one is precisely the big noise in the other.

My second conclusion is that they are very well done within the limits which they voluntarily impose on themselves. I would go so far as to say that their literature is immensely better than the literature of the one or two high-brow or refined monthlies which look down upon them with a too bland disdain. There is hardly an imaginative writer of the front rank who does not contribute on a considerable scale to the popular magazines. There is hardly an imaginative writer of the front rank who *does* contribute to the high-brow or refined magazines.

The reason for this state of affairs is obvious. The remuneration offered by the popular magazines enables imaginative writers of the front rank to roll majestically along in six-cylinder cars. If the editors of popular magazines ceased to compete for the possibly immortal words of genius, front-rankers would have to descend to 7 h.p. runabouts, and their wives and daughters would get their frocks elsewhere than in Paris.

My criticism of British popular magazines – I will say nothing of American – goes beyond the fact that they have no attitude worth discussion towards the latest manifestations of literature and the arts. It is that, whether in literature and the arts, or anything else, they seem to have no aim except the diversion of their enormous publics. They give their readers nothing to bite on. I think that they are under-estimating the brains of their publics, just as the film kings did, and to a large extent still do, and just as the theatre people did and still do. One would surmise that they are unaware of the fact which other folks are aware of, and which is becoming daily more visible — namely, that the public taste is steadily on the up-grade, and at the same time widening out.

I want another popular magazine — I want several — which will cater seriously for the big public's increasing desire for knowledge. Publishers of books and booklets are catering, with success, for this appetite. Why should not editors of magazines cater for it?

The Home University Library series has been a striking popular success. Its volumes are written by serious experts for serious people, they have a very satisfactory sale, and the sale continues.

The circulation in monthly parts of Wells's *The Outline of History* has had a circulation rivalling that of the popular magazines. For about a couple of years it did indeed amount to a popular magazine whose subject was history scientifically treated.

And now Messrs. Benn have begun a sixpenny series of serious booklets. They are not bound in cloth, but they are excellently printed on good paper. They, too, are written, without any sentimental or cheapening compromise, by serious experts for serious readers. I have seen the first six volumes, and of the six I have read two, Professor Edmund G. Gardner's *Italian Literature* and Mr. D.C. Somervell's *A History of England.* Both are simply admirable — in spirit, in selective skill, in breadth and in style. They are about as good as anything of similar scope could be.

In reading them I discovered that I have known nothing of Italian Literature, and very little about English history. Imagine a readable, picturesque conspectus of English history, abreast of the latest researches and inspired by a scientific temper, in about eighty pages, for sixpence! It wanted some doing, and Mr. Somervell and Messrs. Benn have done it, and I can scarcely conceive that their enterprise will not have the abundant success which it deserves.

My notion is that there should be a magazine which would treat the big public as the big public is now being treated by Mr. Somervell, Professor Gardner, Sir Oliver Lodge and others, and Messrs. Benn. The editor of the magazine will say in effect to his readers: "I have faith in you. I am convinced that you have brains, that you have a serious side, that you want knowledge, that you don't want to be unduly flattered, that your taste is robust, and that, in sum, intellectually speaking, you are out for the goods if the goods are presented to you in common-sense, comprehensible manner. Here are the goods. This magazine is not a Christmas cracker, nor a box of chocolates, nor a milk-diet. It is the goods."

In my belief the public is waiting for such a magazine. In my belief it would sell. I should need some heavy arguments to persuade me that if such a magazine could give in its first number, as the main item, say, the whole of Mr. Somervell's *History of England,* or something else comparable to that, it would have a startling success.

12 May 1927

Assessing Worth by Weight: Unwieldy Volumes
"A Confounded Nuisance"

Yesterday morning I went down to my kitchen with a pile of books in my arms and asked for the domestic scales. The queen of that region no doubt thought that I wanted to weigh the books before despatching them to my enemies by parcel post. Not so. I wanted merely to weigh them. Having weighed them I measured the cubical content of the volumes. And having measured the cubical contents, I next estimated with some careful arithmetic the number of words in each.

Here are the results. Lawrence's *Revolt in the Desert* weighs 2lb. 4oz., has a content of 92.5 cubic inches, and comprises 150,000 words. One would have thought, after this, that Winston Churchill's *The World Crisis* (one specimen volume thereof) would weigh about half an ounce, and its content be about 100 square yards. The actual figures are: weight 1lb. 12oz., content 100 cubic inches (by a strange coincidence exactly the same number of cubic inches as of linear inches in the wheel base of a Ford motor car), and number of words 112,000.

Then a volume of Macaulay's *History of England,* weight 4lb., content 113.5 cubic inches, and number of words 260,000. It is a terrifying thought that the set of six Macaulay volumes weighs close upon a couple of stone. But perhaps not a surprising thought. Then a volume of Macaulay's *Essays* (in the Temple Classics Series): weight 5oz., content 17 cubic inches, number of words 120,000! Finally Dostoevsky's *The Brothers Karamazov* (in Mrs. Garnett's translation, published by Heinemann): weight 1lb. 8oz., content 54.5 cubic inches, number of words 360,000.

All the above volumes are printed in clear, legible type on opaque paper. And they are all stitched (more or less), and bound in cloth, except the Temple Classics volume, which is bound in leather.

The object of my researches was to shed light on the question: To what extent are new literary works or grave literary works larger and heavier than not-new or not-grave literary works? The reader can compare the figures for himself. I will only point out that the Dostoevsky volume contains far more words than the Lawrence and the Churchill volumes combined, weighs just under one-third of what they weigh, and comprises little more than a quarter of their cubic inches.

A comparison of the Macaulay *Essays* with a volume of the Macaulay *History* is quite spectacular. The volume of essays weighs less than a twelfth of the volume of the *History,* comprises less than a sixth of its cubic inches, but contains nearly half its number of words.

In both these cases the disparity is enormous.

The frivolous may consider the foregoing remarks dull. Perhaps they are. I will now try to be interesting. Why should I have to hold a bulky four pounds of paper and print in my hands in order to read a volume of Macaulay's *History,* when I can suspend an equally legible volume of his *Essays* easily between finger and thumb? Are physical strain, aching wrists, general anguish, and feats of balancing supposed to be an aid to intellectual comprehension? Is it logical that I should be able to read Dostoevsky's masterpiece comfortably in bed while Lawrence's masterpiece and Churchill's brilliance (the one much less than half and the other much less than a third of the matter in Dostoevsky) are impossible as bed-books?

Ought not all readable books to be readable in bed? Here are three questions. The answer to the first is: No reason; to the second: No; to the third: Yes. I will add a fourth and broader question: Are not heavy and unwieldy books a confounded nuisance? To which the answer is in the affirmative.

Why then should Macaulay, and especially Lawrence and Churchill, be deliberately handicapped by a format both heavy and unwieldy? The reply (of the publishers) would be, first, that the public refuses to take new works or grave works seriously unless they are also heavy and unwieldy. And, second, that the public refuses to pay a remunerative price for books which are not heavy and unwieldy. In other words, the public assesses a work of literature by its physical weight and bulk.

I believe these answers to be correct. I believe that the popular division of new literature into "serious books" and "fiction" is due to the fact that novels are produced in a handy form, and incidentally at a low price. I feel almost sure that if I myself published a novel weighing 1cwt. 24lb. at three guineas it would get two-column reviews in every daily paper, and be the subject of incessant and urgent demand at the leading libraries; and nobody would dare to call it, or even think it, a pot-boiler.

What is to be done? The affair is obviously one for the National Book Council and the Publishers' Association. A campaign is needed for the education of the excellent, fuzzy-minded public. Such a campaign ought to be undertaken. The said public is capable of being educated. It must be educated. As things are, if Mr. Lloyd George published the whole truth about himself in an expensively produced and easily legible pocket or bed-volume that weighed 6oz., and cost two guineas, the issue would fail as badly as an L.C.C. loan and be sold off as remainder.

But I insist on foreseeing the day when the public will absolutely refuse to touch any volume weighing over 6oz., even were it written by John Galsworthy and Steve Donoghue in collaboration — and given away. Anyhow, the present position is fraudulent, monstrous, and silly. It amounts to an intolerable weight (in two senses) tied round the neck of seekers after knowledge.

19 May 1927

A Criticism of the Art Critic

A couple of books are before me which have, once more, raised in my mind the question: "Are picture galleries really of value to the public?" They are certainly of real value to me and a few other people of my questing disposition. The Tate, for instance, is a godsend, because I can walk thither by the river's brink. I am continually walking thither.

The Tate has some of the worst, and a few of the best, pictures publicly exhibited in London. The best are in the Blake Room, the worst are in the Chantrey Bequest Room. According to my observation, the worst draw rather more attention than the best. This disturbs me, has a tendency to undermine my faith in mankind. And I am disturbed also by the dull, sluggish, impenetrable faces of the strollers in the galleries. Do the galleries, established and maintained at such expense, favourably influence the souls behind the faces? Would it not be more effective to establish and maintain a theatre for the good of the souls behind those faces? (I am a little inclined to think it would.)

At any rate, I feel fairly sure of one thing: namely, that the picture galleries are of more value to the public than they used to be now. The change is due to the introduction into them of literature. The literature is spoken, and takes the form of lectures. These lectures are excellent. I have frequently listened to them at the Tate, the National Gallery, and the Victoria and Albert Museum. They are popular without being silly.

I sympathise with the lecturers (who I hope are handsomely paid), on account of the apparently quite unresponsive stolidity of the listeners. I wonder why the young women who listen so closely to the expository young men nearly always have thick ankles and clumsy shoes? Surely the sweet influence of art ought to reduce ankles and refine footgear? Nevertheless I am optimistic about the results of the lectures. They must do good, because they couldn't not do good. As with books, so with pictures, public taste has to be formed. Art is mainly useless without wise art criticism. The lectures constitute wise art criticism. And the listeners are not, cannot be, as unresponsive to stimulus as they seem.

I wish that we had more art-criticism (popular without being silly) in certain newspapers and periodicals. I remember the epoch when D.S. MacColl (Keeper of the Wallace Collection) and Walter Sickert, A.R.A., and (in a lower category) the late Joseph Pennell wrote art-criticism for the general public. I have been young, and now am almost old, and of course my natural tendency is to assume that this epoch has deteriorated from that epoch.

I must allow for the prejudice of age. I do allow for it, and, having allowed for it, I still believe that in the matter of art-criticism the present epoch really has a little deteriorated from the epoch of my youth. There are, of course, a few truly interpretative and helpful art-critics. But there are far more whose articles are futile, and worse than futile. I commend the matter to the attention of all our powerful editors. The right kind of art-criticism would be read. If, for example, the lectures which I have heard in public galleries were printed, they would assuredly be enjoyed, would add to the popular interest of the Press, and would increase the number of visitors to galleries.

Not only is much newspaper art-criticism ineffectual, but so-called "art-books" are bad. They are bad because they are written by persons who are evidently incapable of emotion before a picture, persons who would be better employed in describing cricket matches. (Not that the best cricket reporters are incapable of emotion before cricket; they are not. That is what makes them produce such good reading about cricket.) But there indeed are a few good books on art. I now come to the two volumes mentioned above.

The first is *The Approach to Painting,* by Thomas Bodkin (Bell, 7s. 6d.). Mr. Bodkin's illustrated book is well planned. In the first part he describes the various ways of approaching painting, and in the second part, putting his principles into practice, he approaches twenty-one individual well-known pictures, by artists from Giotto to Manet. It matters not who you are, you are bound to be stimulated by this book — if you have any interest at all in painting — for the simple reason that its author plainly lives in a state of continuous excitement about the art of painting. Also he knows painting from the inside.

I quote: "Every picture contains effects which can only have come by the quick seizure of unexpected opportunities, by the glad acceptance of happy accidents, by the adroit handling of unforeseen developments, or the wise employment of those personal mannerisms which invariably develop during years of experimental practice."

Now, the man who wrote that must have done more than look at pictures. He must have painted them. He understands the creative processes: an assertion which can be made of few critics of art and few critics of literature. He writes admirably; he has a wide and detailed historical knowledge of his subject, which knowledge does not encumber his style; and he is always interesting. He does help.

The other book is Mr. Clive Bell's *Landmarks in Nineteenth Century Painting* (Chatto, 10s. 6d., illustrated). This is a different kind of book. It does not display the same inside knowledge as Mr. Bodkin's. It is more concerned with theories about the evolution of painting, and with the personalities of painters; and less concerned with fundamental principles. It is more wayward, and sometimes less convincing. It is immensely provocative and amusing, for Clive Bell is a considerable performer with a pen. In earlier years he was much influenced by one of the greatest European experts in painting, an Englishman, Roger Fry. He appears now to have grown out of Roger Fry: which is a good thing. These two books are fine enough to atone for two hundred mediocre treatises on art. Read them, please — and then go to a gallery.

26 May 1927

French Novelist Who Studies English Life

I went into a Paris bookshop to look round, and picking up *Thérèse Desqueyroux*, by François Mauriac (Grasset, 12 francs), I asked the vendor in a confidential, trusting tone: "Is this good?" "Monsieur," was the pained reply, expressing shock at such a question, "he is our foremost novelist (*C'est notre premier romancier*)." This shows how far François Mauriac has advanced in prestige during the last few years. So, of course, I bought his latest novel. By the way, it is very short, less than 250 pages, less than 40,000 words; ten of it would be needed to match the bulk of an average novel by that admired writer, Charles Dickens.

Mauriac is young, and is said to be an ardent Roman Catholic. Some time ago I was strongly advised to read his *Le Désert de l'Amour*. I read half of it, and stopped. Not because it was not highly skilled stuff, with some emotion in it, but because I thought there was in the book too much of the technician, the self-conscious "born-novelist," too elegantly doing his job.

51

I was then told that *Le Baiser au Lépreux* was a better book than *Le Désert de l'Amour,* but I would not get it. I always beware of the determined admirer who says to you, when you show disappointment with a book of his favourite, "Yes, A is not very good, but B is the real stuff, quite different; you must read B." Various admirers of Dickens have persuaded me at one time or another to begin some twenty novels of Dickens, none of which I have ever been able to finish.

Thérèse Desqueyroux is a better novel than *Le Désert de l'Amour.* Indeed, I finished it, and enjoyed the book. It is a curious and original story of the *"landes"* district — curious and original in both subject and treatment. Thérèse makes an attempt to poison her husband, Bernard, a country squire of the heavy, honest, totally unimaginative type. Yes, she is a murderess by intention, and yet quite a nice, even, superior creature, with fine instincts and impulses. You are invited to assist at the analysis not of a monster, but of a human woman.

After reading this book you might well suppose that anybody and everybody is capable of planning murder. Thérèse gets into the hands of justice, but the bill against her is thrown out. The larger part of the story is occupied with her sensations in the train as, after this, she goes back home to Bernard. Knowing her guilt, Bernard still receives her, for the sake of the unspotted name of the family. I will not tell you the end, which is most satisfactorily true.

The book is an exceedingly odd one; it is quite disconcerting. In the first half of the story you are often afraid lest the author is going to get himself into a mess and going to get himself out of it by some sentimental falsity. But as he proceeds he gains your confidence, and the confidence is not misplaced. He is superficially original, but he is also fundamentally original. He does something wonderful without the exasperating air of saying to you: "Now watch me. I am about to do something wonderful . . . You see, I have now done something wonderful!"

Thérèse Desqueyroux, if you read it, will certainly stick in your mind. It has a few slight faults. The mere narrative is now and then clumsy, confusing. And the author does not in the least clear up the problem, which so often presents itself in novels dealing with a highly intelligent wife who turns against a blockhead of a husband: "Why did this so-gifted woman not see plainly from the moment she met him the utter unsuitability of the so-antipathetic fellow?"

Another volume which I bought in the same shop was Abel Hermant's *Les Bargain Sisters,* a collection of long and short stories. Abel Hermant is an example of a rare type, the novelist who had the reputation of being merely fashionable, whereas, in fact, he is a great deal more. I know several pronounced French high-brows who put Hermant pretty high. I put him high myself. He is a fecund and an uneven writer. What is specially interesting in him is that he occasionally does stories of English life. Evidently he takes England for a most romantic place, as indeed it is.

I remember that when Balzac wanted to emphasise the romantic strangeness of one of his strangest and most mysterious women, he said that she was born in Lancashire, Lancashire being for Balzac a region drenched in the exotic. For Abel Hermant England is exotic. That he adores English life, as he assuredly does, is a compliment, for he is not facile in his approvals.

52

He has observed us with a French and a fastidious eye. He puts a new light on the English character and social system. He reveals aspects of them which will perhaps surprise the English reader. Of course, he is often very subtly wrong. But never mind! His misapprehensions have value; he is an honest novelist, and a beautiful writer.

And is he, after all, more wrong than many English novelists, and some good ones? Take Disraeli, who is now coming out in the splendour of a new uniform edition (but what I want is a pocket edition bound in limp leather, that will withstand the wear of railway trains and the tear of hotel chambermaids and the friction of sandy beaches). When I read Disraeli I seem to be always saying to myself: "He has somehow got it all distorted." Disraeli, however, was a bit of a novelist. Though he saw things askew, he did see them for himself. He does illuminate. And he had a tremendous and grandiose verve. Also he could do the purple passage — whole pages at a time — as well as the exquisite and (in his novel) unreadable Walter Pater, and better than Oscar Wilde. What he lacked was taste. Or rather his taste was oriental. By "oriental" here I do not mean Chinese or Japanese, whose taste is far finer than ours; but rather Byzantine. Disraeli had, too, the Byzantine indifference to sex.

2 June 1927

"Pharisaical" Anglo-Saxon Mind that Hates the Truth

Some curious additions have recently been published in the *Intimate Journal* of Amiel. I suppose that to the present generation of book-lovers Amiel is little but a name, and to some individuals who fancy themselves as connoisseurs scarcely even a name. Indeed, only the fear of insulting the omniscience of my juniors prevents me from explaining who Amiel was. In my heyday, if ever I had one, Amiel the religionist was a major subject of conversation in drawing-rooms and other places where they palaver in a literary style. So was Matthew Arnold. Now, neither of these former idols is mentioned.

It is probably true that Matthew Arnold put Amiel on the map in England, as Edmond Scherer did in France. Whether Matthew Arnold influenced Edmond Scherer in the matter, or vice versa, I cannot remember. However, Arnold had more success with his campaign in England than Scherer had in France. The French never appreciated Amiel, and I am not disinclined to agree with them. French reviewers especially were hostile to him — perhaps not because he was dull, but because he was honest. The big guns of French criticism used to combine to assassinate his renown; but Scherer was a courageous and ingenious defender.

For myself, I am slightly against Amiel because he bored me, by reason of what I deemed to be his morbidity. Moreover, I did not regard his subject matter (which was Amiel) as of first-rate interest. Nor did I, nor do I, regard Matthew Arnold as a first-rate literary critic. I prefer him as a critic of manners. He was a first-rate poet, greater than many of us realise, and I would sacrifice the whole of his prose for ten of his best poems. 'Rugby

53

Chapel,' 'Dover Beach,' 'Calais Sands' are by me unforgettable, and because of their effect on me I would forgive the author of them all the irritating passages in his correspondence.

The additions to Amiel's journal consist almost exclusively of self-analytical revelations concerning his adventure in Love, which adventure started somewhat late. The adventurer was nearly forty, and he took too seriously what a younger man would have forgotten in a fortnight. The interesting thing is that the French critics, and especially the big guns, have assumed a hostile attitude towards Amiel the amorist just as they did towards Amiel the religionist. (Odd!) The unhappy lover could not do right for them.

English criticism, so far as I have observed, has shown singularly little interest in these disclosures, which thirty years ago would have aroused an enormous din — and incidentally would, without doubt, have ruined Amiel, with Matthew Arnold and everybody else in this country. If the new extracts are faithfully translated into English they will assuredly have a considerable success of curiosity, which is a kind of success that no real admirer of Amiel would desire for him.

I cannot imagine why French criticism indulges in irony at Amiel's expense. But I can very well imagine why English readers, while reading with eagerness Amiel's detailed account of his reactions to the earnest lady formerly so famous under the delicate pseudonym of "Philine," will publicly condemn them with equal eagerness. The reason is that the Anglo-Saxon mind, in addition to being hypocritical, Pharisaical, and intellectually dishonest in certain matters, hates to learn the full truth about the men it admires. It knows well enough what human nature is, and will privately admit, with some benevolence, what human nature is; but — never above a whisper!

Britain is the land of fine biographies — biographies, however, which would be still finer if they did not, as a rule, omit whole aspects of the lives portrayed. As sure as a biography appears which strives sincerely after all the truth, there is a row about it. At first the biographer suffers at the hands of the infuriated educated mob; then, when the facts have been admitted, the subject of the biography gets his turn of manhandling. People will obstinately confuse two quite different questions.

The poetry of Shelley the angel is to this day under-estimated because of his messy marriages. If Byron had read the lessons in church instead of. . . his poetry would stand as high in England as it stands in the rest of the world. Nearly 40,000 children were illegitimately born in England during the last recorded year, and nobody lay awake at night thinking about it; but when the awful revelation was made that Wordsworth the saint begot one illegitimate child in France, the appalled Wordsworthian public immediately put a sinister construction upon 'She dwelt among the untrodden ways,' and even the stock of the ode on 'Intimations of Immortality' dropped twenty points, and has never recovered.

This wistful clinging of the educated mob to the theory that great men are perfect, and if they aren't they ought to be, is not limited to the rich field of sex. The public has a broad and inclusive mind. Anthony Trollope published an *Autobiography*. Its interestingness is intense, and its honesty almost ideal. It entirely omits the sex question. It does, however, make plain that Trollope, the venal fellow, had a certain regard for money. Well, it did him very serious harm. Heaven knows why, but it did. Perhaps the public held that its favourite ought to have conducted his life as though economic laws did not exist. Only within the last dozen years has Trollope emerged from the disrepute into which by his own deliberate act he thrust himself. (And yet Trollope is supposed to have understood the English character!)

And when unsatisfactory disclosures reach a posthumous publication which the author neither anticipated nor wished for, the public will condemn the author just the same. The public objects, anyhow, to knowing the truth. It loves to guess, but not to know. Or, if it is to know, it must know unofficially, under the rose, and not officially. How powerful must be the desire in authors for self-revelation! One would have thought it was easy enough not to write.

To return for an instant to Amiel. I fear that personally I have a complex which inhibits me from enjoying the kind of thing he wrote. Speaking impersonally, I should say that he is recommendable.

9 June 1927

Artistic Parasites: Authors' Stage Rights

"Francis Grierson" is dead at the age of nearly eighty. He was over sixty in 1910, when I used to meet him in Florence, where he and I were then living. But he did not look sixty, though he was too full-bodied and had an unhealthy appearance. Grierson (a pseudonym*) was one of those writers who have a considerable reputation among a few people. He had two reputations, as an improviser on the piano and as an essayist. I never heard him play, but, since he was a favourite performer at nearly all the Courts of Europe, I am inclined to think that he must have been second-rate on the piano.

Some of his essays were first-rate. I remember reading a volume of them, *The Valley of Shadows,* with pleasure. He had lived in many places, including, in late years, Los Angeles, where he probably felt the lack of sympathetic society. For he was a sensitive and a highly cultivated man. He had taste. He really did know a great deal about the arts, politics, and the way the human mind works. He had the historic sense to a degree which I have rarely, if ever, seen equalled.

Here is a note I wrote at the time (10/4/1910): "Grierson came after lunch. Long talks and tea. He was very fine on the subject of weather and the artistic temperament. Then we went out to buy seats for *ll Rea Lear* to-night at the Pergola Theatre. Grierson began to notice the armorial bearings over doorways, and presently I could see nothing else but these, and I thought how much wiser I should be to sketch a few fine doorways instead of fiddling about with more ambitious things. He said that in front of some of this old stuff he sometimes put himself into the life of the time to such a degree that it became painful."

Here is another note (14/4/1910): "After dining together, the Dutchman Grierson and I walked home through narrow streets of palaces. It was strange to see a cinematograph theatre flaming in the base of one of these

* Understandably: his real name was Benjamin Henry Jesse Francis Shepard.

stone precipices. I said we must go through the Gothic Piazza Peruzzi. The Dutchman said: 'You know it's the *quartier des filles.*' I was not surprised. It was. They were a sinister-looking lot, but they suited the architecture. Plenty of young men talking in groups here and there. *Grierson was much moved by the historic sense.*"

But perhaps the most characteristic thing about Francis Grierson was his attitude towards money. He was evidently poor then, and it is stated that he died in poverty. To me he seemed to be ashamed of earning money by his pen and even of being interested in money. Nevertheless, he did not explain how, in his opinion, an artist or a writer, if he neglected finance, might without humiliation contrive to pay his bills and balance his budget. Of course he did not explain because he could not explain. He was fully capable of thinking the problem out, but he had an inhibition against thinking it out. In this he superficially resembled those grumbling, girding painters, musicians, writers, and dilettanti — quite a large class — who have far less brains than he had, and whose reasoning about money, if their mental processes can be called reasoning, is fatally affected by cerebral sloth, general incapacity, and a revolting artistic snobbishness.

These parasites on society cannot, or apparently will not, understand that the first duty of, for instance, a poet is not to write poetry, but to keep himself in decency, and his wife and children if he has them, to discharge his current obligations, and to provide for old age. I met an Austrian poet the other day who assured me — and I believe him — that he never showed his poems to anybody. A rule of artistic life which struck me as being contrary to common sense and natural instinct, though not socially improper. This poet was old. Many poets insist on reading their verse to you. Most of them want you to read them. Which means that they want you to buy their books. Which means that they have something to sell. Which means that they are merchants. Why, then, boggle at the mercantile aspects of an artistic career?

No artist can rightly be only an artist. When he has finished his day's work of sincere creation he must be a merchant. Therefore he ought to learn how to be a merchant efficiently — that is to say, how to sell his goods in the largest possible numbers and at the highest possible price consistent with honesty. Artists yearn to be appreciated. The best proof of appreciation is the receipt of cheques, notes, or coin. If people genuinely appreciate a thing they will pay money for it to the extent of their means. If not, not. A comfortable earned income should be a matter of pride to an artist. (It is.) Artists who affect to contemn a comfortable income, when they can't make it, are nincompoops in addition to being liars.

I dare say, and I regret, that numerous artistic creators will smile coldly at the recent news from the United States concerning authors. But it is great news all the same. The famous theatrical firm of Shubert Brothers (Jake and Lee), which controls wholly or partially 850 theatres in America, has been defeated by the American Dramatists' Guild. The Dramatists' Guild said that no theatrical manager who refused to sign its standard contract for play-production should do business with any of its members.

The Shuberts said that, unlike lesser managers, they could get along without the Dramatists' Guild. But they couldn't, because the Guild included nearly all dramatists whose work the general public will pay money to see. The Shuberts actually brought an action against the Guild on the ground that it was an illegal monopoly in restraint of trade. The Shuberts did not fight the case out. They came to terms and signed the standard agreement, which is a very fair one. My contention is that the Guild's victory is an event which is honourable to artists and which will have a favourable influence upon the artistic development of the drama in America. My contention is further that anybody who thinks otherwise is a woolly thinker.

American dramatists now stand on the same firm ground as French dramatists. In Britain dramatists have not so far had the gumption to combine in sufficient strength to enforce all-round justice from the theatrical managers. The Authors' Society tried for years to arrange a satisfactory standard contract with the theatrical managers. The society failed on account of our notorious British individualism. Art suffers.

16 June 1927

"Those Sitwells," Robert Graves, Humbert Wolfe

A certain youngish poet, with whom I am on terms of intimacy, but whom I had not seen for a year or two, came to see me, and his opening words as he entered the room were as follows: "Oh, Bennett! Oh, hell!" Not that he had any special grievance. He was merely expressing his general attitude towards life.

At the moment his attitude is mine also. I have allowed books to accumulate around me, and I cannot cope with them, because there are far, far too many. So that I am ready to wish that printing had never been invented, that even writing had never been invented, and that all literary creative artists had been victimised by that infant mortality the thought of which afflicts the minds of earnest sociologists. My curiosity about new books is unappeasable and divine; I want to read everything that has any air of being both original and interesting, whether it is fashionable or unfashionable (though I prefer the unfashionable); but an all-wise providence has made the days too brief, and the seasons also.

Some readers seem to be able to read absolutely everything that one ought to have read in order to keep one's end up at dinner. There is a lady whom I meet almost weekly. One evening I calculated that she had read in the week seventeen books, totalling a million and a half words. It is a rapid reader who can average more than 15,000 words an hour (250 words a minute). So that she must have spent 14 hours a day over books. Quite a feat, considering that she also runs a house, goes to theatres, concerts, and cinemas, plays bridge, entertains and is entertained, and loves her husband passionately! The suspicious might conceivably suspect her veracity, but I am not suspicious, and I know that marvellous people do exist.

For unmarvellous people, such as myself and a few others, the problem of keeping level with the latest interesting publications is a real one; it is also an insoluble one. When some struggling young author sends me a book, or her mother sends me the book, and says she feels sure I will read it and write her privately my honest opinion of it, I take a holy pleasure in selling

57

the book instantly, unopened, to a receiver of stolen goods, disguised as a bookseller. But often and often I part with new books, either by sale or otherwise, with regret, saying to them: "I believe you are interesting. But good-bye! I must reconcile myself to the fate of going down to my grave without ever having read you. My loss!" I am serious. Thousands of determined and catholic readers will comprehend me and sympathise with me.

The above is less an apology than an explanation. Moreover, sloth and incapacity notwithstanding, I have read a few books lately, in verse and in prose. I will take the verse first, because Shakespeare wrote two hundred per cent. more verse than prose. Those Sitwells. A man bluntly asked me last week, evidently accepting me as a leading authority on Sitwells: "Are they charlatans or the real thing?" I replied: "They have really original minds." He asked: "But do they express their minds?" I replied: "Yes. To the elect. But I am not always of the elect." Sacheverell Sitwell has just published *The Cyder Feast and other Poems* (Duckworth, 7s. 6d.). Twenty-five of these poems were written in the month of February last. A poem a day, with Sundays off (except one). An amazing output, comparable to Turner's output of water-colours. This is indeed a poet.

I have for years maintained that Sacheverell Sitwell is one of the most original poets of his generation. I think so to-day. His mind is not only original, but lovely. He never writes anything of which you could positively assert that it was not distinguished. He experiences sensations, and he gets effects, which, so far as my knowledge goes, nobody ever experienced or got before. I derive a most exciting pleasure from his work.

But when somebody comes along and says that he cannot understand Sacheverell Sitwell, I sympathise with that somebody. There is a certain amount of Sacheverell Sitwell that I do not understand, or only half understand. In studying his obscurer pieces, I seem to be having gleams of a beautiful sunlit vision described in fragments through the foliage of a wood. Nor has the intervening foliage yet been in the least degree stricken by autumn winds. I should say that Sacheverell Sitwell has composed many elaborate poems in less time than is required to read them.

Now Edith Sitwell. *Rustic Elegies* (also Duckworth). With an exquisite photograph of the authoress by way of frontispiece. Edith Sitwell, too, was once obscure. She is so no longer. Clarity is hers. The first poem in this volume, 'Elegy on Dead Fashion,' is enchanting. It may or may not be this, that, and the other, but enchanting it assuredly is. Edith Sitwell has a quality, doubtless of sex, which the masculine Sitwells have not. I think that she still has the old tendency to be over-facile in rhymes. My notion is that when she can't find a rhyme she invents a word. "Fazoon" (p. 53, to rhyme with rigadoon) is not in Webster nor in the *New English Dictionary*. Some readers may resent her occasional larkishness with words. I don't. The audacious punning in the phrase "pas de Calais" (same page) charmed me.

Robert Graves has published his *Poems 1914-1926* (Heinemann) collected (and sifted in collection) from eight previously published volumes. This book has deeply impressed me. The effect is greater than the sum of the effects of the previous volumes. Robert Graves is not a minor poet, but a major. Incidentally, his technical achievement is great. If Robert Bridges, the Poet Laureate, knows more about English versification than

Robert Graves he is the only poet in Britain who does. Here is a genius at once grave and bright — and always perfectly clear. (Why the notes to the magnificent ironic poem *The Marmosite's Miscellany*? I know not. I once had to ask T. S. Eliot whether the notes of his renowned poem *The Wastelands* were a skit on such notes or meant seriously. He said that they were meant seriously. Why?) This book is a *book*. It is entirely satisfactory. And without reserve I recommend it.

There remains, of my verse-reading, Humbert Wolfe's *Requiem* (Benns, 6s.), which has already had a large sale and caused much controversy in the world of feet and rhyme. I must read this again, for I have not understood a great deal of it, and of what I have understood much is not, in my present opinion, on the same plane of accomplishment and emotional authenticity as the satiric *News of the Devil*, which I read with gusto. However, I am not of those who have the face to expect an author to excite them with every book he publishes. Readers have their ups and downs.

23 June 1927

A Woman's Political Romance and a Striking First Novel

Last week I discussed some recent reading in verse. I will now mention some new fiction, for which I then had no room. I must begin by saying that — as regards fiction — I exist in a state of excited suspense — waiting, in hope and in apprehension, for *Gallions Reach*, the first novel of H.M. Tomlinson. Tomlinson, as some have been for years aware, is a great prose writer. He is, to use a convenient but of course misleading description, an English Conrad. I have been hearing about this novel for a long time, and at last I hear that it is being printed. It is certain to contain exceedingly fine work. It may be an exceedingly fine novel. None can tell. For those to whom English literature matters, the moment is anxious.

While impatiently attending Tomlinson I have read a bunch of novels. I must say, despite my notorious grave reservations concerning Virginia Woolf, that the most original of the bunch is *To the Lighthouse* (Hogarth Press). It is the best book of hers that I know. Her character drawing has improved. Mrs. Ramsay almost amounts to a complete person. Unfortunately she goes and dies, and her decease cuts the book in two. Also there are some pleasing records of interesting sensations outside the range of the ordinary novelist. The scheme of the story is rather wilful — designed seemingly, but perhaps not really, to exhibit virtuosity. A group of people plan to sail in a small boat to a lighthouse. At the end some of them reach the lighthouse in a small boat. That is the externality of the plot.

The middle part, entitled "Time Passes," shows a novel device to give the reader the impression of the passing of time — a sort of cataloguing of intermediate events. In my opinion it does not succeed. It is a short cut, but a short cut that does not get you anywhere. To convey the idea of the passage of a considerable length of time is an extremely difficult business, and I doubt if it can be accomplished by means of a device, except the device of simply saying "Time passes," and leaving the effort of imagination of the reader. Apart from this honest shirking of the difficulty, there is no alternative but to convey the impression very gradually, without any direct insistence — in the manner of life itself.

I have heard a good deal about the wonders of Mrs. Woolf's style. She sometimes discovers a truly brilliant simile. She often chooses her adjectives and adverbs with beautiful felicity. But there is more in style than this. The form of her sentences is rather tryingly monotonous, and the distance between her nominatives and her verbs is steadily increasing. Still, *To the Lighthouse* has stuff in it strong enough to withstand quite a lot of adverse criticism.

Second novels are a better test of a writer than first novels, especially when, as in the present case, one has not read the first novels. I have two. Mrs. Amabel Williams-Ellis's *The Wall of Glass* (Cape). A social-political novel. Mrs. Williams-Ellis knows her worlds as well as the daughter of Mr. St. Loe Strachey ought to know them. She is a careful, minute, and accurate observer, and she feels passionately, beneath a shell of primness, about her material. She writes well, and, what is more, she writes with intelligence. She has breadth.

But to my mind she has seriously impaired the value of this particular book by a fault very common among writers who know their subject. She has diffused the interest far too much. The opening of *The Wall of Glass* is as bewildering as the opening of *War and Peace,* which is saying a great deal. Mrs. Williams-Ellis introduces too many characters at once. And further, she fails to give the reader any guide *at first* as to the relative importance of the characters. This guiding must be done at the start, or it is useless. The reader is benighted in a labyrinth of a thousand intrigues and a million people (more or less). The fault is technical, and has nothing to do with fundamental power. When Mrs. Williams-Ellis has overcome it she will probably produce a novel more effective.

With *Lolly Willowes,* Sylvia Townsend Warner made some stir in the lettered world. Its successor is *Mr. Fortune's Maggot* (Chattos). A fantastical, moral, philosophical tale of the South Seas. Original and rightly malicious humour. A sharp, surprising wit. A coherent beginning, and a coherent end. Some authentic pathos, but a lack of power. It is a book of which every page has definite quality, but which, considered as a whole, is unsatisfying. After all I had heard of *Lolly Willowes* I was disappointed. Moreover, the author has been very naughty. There is not a single chapter division in the entire book of 250 pages. Why not? It may be all very well to imitate the methods of Balzac, but where is the point of imitating one of his most exasperating idiosyncrasies?

The most striking new novel (probably a first novel, too) that has lately come under my eyes is *Sun and Moon,* by Vincent Gowen (Duckworths). The subject itself is both very striking and fresh: the history of two English children brought up by a widowed father who marries several Chinese wives (together) and keeps a concubine or so in the house. The two English children, having been reared chiefly on Chinese principles, accept the domestic polity of their home as perfectly natural. The author escapes being offensive to British susceptibilities by a simple, natural candour. The characters are very well drawn, the plot is excellently managed, and the general picture thoroughly convincing, while it startles. The chief fault of the book is the woodenness of the dialogue: a matter of phrasing only; in essence the things said are true enough. This novel has solid quality and is quite out of the common.

I have been accused of admiring Russian novels because they are Russian. Unjust! I have read quantities of mediocre Russian novels. Two of them are Vieressaev's *The Deadlock* (Faber and Gwyer), and Shmelov's *The Sun of the Dead* (Dents). (Good translations.) The subject matter of both — the Bolshevist régime — is terrific, and the novels are meant to be terrific, but are not. Probably the authors have suffered too much to write with the necessary form and restraint. On the other hand, Maxim Gorky's novel, *Decadence* (Cassells), is very fine indeed; perhaps his best novel. His latest short stories, *The Story of a Novel* (Jarrolds), are on a lower plane.

30 June 1927

The Wilde Vogue "Over" — His Comedies in the Same Class as *Caste* : Gerhardi's new *Pretty Creatures*

Oscar Wilde's play, *The Florentine Tragedy,* has been given again in London — at the Arts Theatre Club. It is in blank verse, and very poor blank verse. And according to my recollection it is a very poor play. I will go further and say that it has no value whatever. I think that Wilde's popular vogue is over. In the wide sense of the word he had no popular vogue except a post-humous one. The notion that he received large sums of money for his plays is not based on facts. He made a few thousand pounds out of *The Importance of Being Earnest,* but the other plays, very inferior, did not do much.

Somerset Maugham and Frederick Lonsdale have achieved far more popularity with a single play than Wilde achieved with all his plays put together. There is as brilliant an originality in the first act of Lonsdale's *Spring Cleaning* as in any act of Wilde's; and more power and veracity in the first act of Maugham's *Home and Beauty* than in any act of Wilde's. Moreover Wilde has to his credit nothing non-theatrical comparable to Maugham's great (yes, great) novel, *Of Human Bondage.*

The Importance of Being Earnest is Wilde's best work. I admired it intensely for many years. I shall not forget my sensations at its first performance. I said again and again that it was the finest comedy in English since Sheridan. But when I saw the revival at the Haymarket a year or two ago — what a mournful disillusion! What a perturbation of conscience for my critical blindness. I am now inclined to class Wilde with Robertson as a writer of comedies; certainly I would not put him higher than the author of *Caste.*

Wilde's real popularity came after his death, and it was, I imagine, due largely to causes unconnected with artistic merit. (But you never know.) His books, practically all his books, had an immense sale. At which I was glad, for Wilde, even if he was not a first-rate writer, had given keen pleasure to simpletons such as my younger self; and he was a first-rate figure. If you would realise the European figure he made, read André Gide's slim volume, *Oscar Wilde. In Memoriam. (Souvenirs)* (published by the Mercure de France). It displays Wilde at his very best.

Wilde is outmoded: which will annoy his ghost, if ghosts there are, more than anything else could. His reputation among the lettered could not possibly survive such a critical examination, as, for instance, Frank Swinnerton addressed to the reputation of R.L. Stevenson — thereby reducing Stevenson's reputation to about 10 per cent. of its former size.* Certainly 10 per cent. of Wilde's reputation would not emerge from the cold and fearful inquisition. Wilde's style lacked the elements of permanence. Even his greater forerunner and exemplar in preciosity, Walter Pater, has gone under. But whether Pater will rise again I will not prophesy. I seriously question if he will.

Only first-rate styles can survive their mannerisms. Tired of small works, I recently resumed my acquaintance with *The Decline and Fall of the Roman Empire.* It is fantastically mannered. But it lives. It is still as exciting as a sensational serial. I perceived anew the powerful influence of Gibbon on his successors. Particularly on Macaulay. You can find traces of Gibbon even in G. M. Trevelyan's pleasing new *History of England* — which is having a wondrous and well-deserved sale. But the Gibbon tradition has now nearly expired. The next considerable historian will write quite differently.

He is likely to write more in the fashion of Sinclair Lewis, whose style, especially in *Elmer Gantry,* has been severely criticised by the mandarins. With characteristic courage I said to a super-highbrow the other day that I greatly admired the style of *Elmer Gantry,* with its freedoms and its very vivacious idiomatic slang. To my surprise the super-highbrow heartily agreed with me. I admire the style of William Gerhardi's new volume of stories, *Pretty Creatures* (Benn, 6s.), though I cannot understand why the publishers describe it as "a considerable volume," seeing that it comprises less than 200 small pages of large type. Here is a style individual, original, enfranchised. It has the merit of relying more on verbs than on adjectives and adverbs. Here, and in *Elmer Gantry,* and sundry other places, are the germs of the style of the future. Incidentally there is admirable fiction in *Pretty Creatures.* The third story in it, *A Bad End,* can stand up by itself in any modern company.

To return to Wilde. Last week I received the following letter: "This morning I asked at — [a famous and historic circulating library] — for Wilde's *Salome*, as it was listed in their French catalogue for this year, and I was told that it had been withdrawn from circulation. I naturally inquired why a work almost classic, and by an author so esteemed all over Europe, should be so treated in this country, and I was informed that it was probably due to the action of the police."

Of course I disagree with the writer's estimate of Wilde's position, and I jib at the statement that the police had anything to do with the suppression of *Salome.* (I could find a more convincing reason.) But the matter deserves publicity. It is one more illustration of the truth of the proverb that the price of a satisfactory circulating library is eternal

* *R.L. Stevenson: A Critical Study* (1914).

vigilance. Can you conceive an important library banning an innocuous old-world trifle like *Salome?* Well, you must. There are superstitions about certain books as about other things. And I have noticed that at seasons of the sun's eclipse superstitions and oddities are apt to be more rampant than usual. *The Spook Sonata* is being played. Last week, I am told, an evening party was given at which two psychic bus-conductors were the star performers. And last Sunday I saw an advertisement of a free pamphlet which purports to show that the major events of world-history are some-how foretold by the Great Pyramid. And I learn that the Second Advent is upon us, and that a vast amphitheatre has been built, and now exists, on the shore of Sydney Harbour (Sydney, of all places) expressly for the official reception of the Messiah, who will reach it on foot across the shark-infested waves.

7 July 1927

A Protest from Young Authors – And Some More Plain Speaking for Them

On Friday last I received, by the hands of a famous dramatist, a solemn message from young authors protesting against my harsh treatment of young authors. On Monday I got a letter from an author of my own generation saying with a certain acidity that I ought to write about unknown authors instead of wasting articles on such celebrities as Oscar Wilde. All which is unjust, in the customary human manner. For a quarter of a century now I have been searching for unknown authors who ought to be known. I have found a few, and have made them known, but for the rest – well, the best thing that can happen to the majority of unknown authors is that they should remain unknown. As for young authors, I have passed more than a quarter of a century in being too kind to them. And seeing also that they are nearly always too kind to one another, they get quite as much kindness as is good for their characters.

At any rate, I do deal with young authors: which is more than can be said for the great literary critics whom we peruse on Sundays – and some-times Thursdays. These dignitaries too often select for their texts some very new edition of some very old work which nobody reads and nobody ever will read. And I know why they do it, too. I believe that I have drawn attention to more young and unknown authors in the last six months in these columns than the mandarins have deigned to notice (above their signatures) in the last six years.

At this point I am reminded of a pleasing fancy of the late Carl Spitteler's, as follows:-

The Superior Newspaper.

"To X.Y.Z., author. Owing to lack of space we are sorry we cannot print your *Merlin*."

"To Dr. A.B.C., critic. We accept with great pleasure your highly interesting and scholarly paper on a rough posthumous draft of X.Y.Z's *Merlin*, in his own handwriting, and hope to hear from you again."

This is extracted from a very good book of essays and fragments, clumsily entitled *Laughing Truths,* by the late Carl Spitteler, translated by James F. Muirhead (Putnams). I enjoyed it, though I had never heard of Carl Spitteler till last month. For me he was an unknown author. A Swiss, he died three years ago, at the age of seventy-nine.

To return to young authors. I shall continue to be harsh to them whenever I feel like it. Their tender age shall not protect them, nor should it. Nor have I noticed that the young show any inclination to be benevolent towards authors stricken in years. Quite the contrary. I will now mention two more young authors. Conrad Aiken, I gather, is a young idol of the young. I have read his new novel, *Blue Skies* (Howe). It is a relation of a voyage across the Atlantic in a liner. It is very capably done. It is all true. Mr. Aiken is like George Washington: he never tells a lie. But I can see nothing whatever in *Blue Skies.* Its unimportance is perfect, without a flaw. Mr. Aiken has intention, but his intention is as pathetic as a sunblind in a London street.

If young writers are to turn travel or any other experiences into fiction, I wish to heaven that for a change they could contrive to say something worth saying, and to say it with distinction. I commend to their perusal a couple of old books of travel which I have just read. First, John Macdonald's *Travels in Various Parts of Europe and Africa,* edited by John Beresford (Routledge). Macdonald was an eighteenth century footman, and his book is really a great lark and a model of genuine writing. The man's British phlegm in front of the staggering spectacle of the East is magnificent. No auto-psychoanalysis! No embroideries! He curtly tells you what he saw, and he leaves it at that.

Second: *The Life and Works of Alfred Aloysius Horn, an old Visiter,* compiled by Ethelreda Lewis and prefaced by John Galsworthy (Cape). Another of these accursed old authors. He was seventy-three when he wrote and talked. If you had mentioned the word "style" to him he would probably have laughed. But he had it. Read this, concerning the murder of albatrosses: "Believe me, ma'am, when a lad that's seen nothing bigger than the gulls and herons of Lancashire first beholds that great white apparition of beauty men call Albatross sailing the southern elements, he'll not be the one to drain it of breath. Six feet of wafting snow —" If any of the young authors whom I am accused of contemning can describe what he sees in this grand fashion, let him swim into my ken.

My other new author is Dorothy Edwards, responsible for *Rhapsody* (Wishart). A short book of short stories. Dorothy Edwards has little feeling for elegance, but she has something original to say, and she says it, if not with distinction, without nonsense and without verbiage. She is an original and subtle and intriguing talent. I feel kindly towards her.

I observe that Marjorie Bowen, the author of many historical novels, has published a volume of modern short stories, *Dark Ann* (John Lane). I know that these stories are good, because the publishers have given me precise information to that effect by post. They say: "The emotional and spiritual adventures are enriched by the beauty of the author's style and methods of workmanship." (More in the same vein.) I like a publisher who is thoughtful enough to tell me what I ought to think of his publications. Why read, when publishers have read for you?

A Vast Literary Market Neglected

An extraordinarily interesting letter has appeared in the Press from a resident in Calcutta. Mr. Gupta (for that is his name) complains of the price of English books in India and suggests the formation of an "Empire Book Marketing Board". An original notion! I doubt whether the authority which directs the new advertising of Empire goods would have thought of it. Canadian or Australian apples for Britain, yes of course. But English books — are they being recommended to the Empire publics on the hoardings of Montreal, Melbourne, Capetown, Calcutta? Without any acquaintance with the facts I reply positively in the negative.

And I am not sorry that the answer should be in the negative, because Empire advertising up to date seems to me to be of the most futile, inefficient and amateurish sort. Government departments (and their protegés) don't know how to advertise. Certainly one department has proved that it does not know how to advertise books. As for other Empire products, the official posters about them (pretentious without being artistic) would not help to sell an apple even if it was guaranteed to have come from the Garden of Eden and the Garden of Eden was guaranteed to be in a British colony. And the other day, in a busy thoroughfare, I noticed an Empire Advertising Board, from which the posters had been snatched away, waiting forlorn for new posters. Common commercial advertisers would hardly waste valuable space-days in this manner.

If the Government, waking out of its customary coma, really desires to advertise Empire goods, it would employ its departmental energy more effectively by advertising the Colonial exhibits at the Imperial Institute and organising conducted tours therein. A visit to the display of Empire at the I.I. makes a really exciting experience. It thrilled me, whose enthusiasm for the much misused words "Empire" and "Imperial" is marked by restraint. It made the Empire a reality for me, and filled me with a desire to purchase commodities far and wide throughout the said Empire. This, however, has no connection with literature.

Now Mr. Gupta says that India is a poor country: which it unquestionably is. Indeed I imagine that poverty is one of its main characteristics — much more spectacular than, for example, its Oriental picturesqueness. He says also that India pullulates with young persons who are being educated through the medium of the English language. It appears that there are more students in the University of Calcutta alone than in all the universities of England, Scotland and Ireland put together. The fantastic total for this present year is 19,372.

All these young men know English, for they cannot begin their university education till they do know English. Their minds receive the stamp of English tradition. Everything is done to stimulate their interest in and their admiration for British ideals — except supplying them with modern English books cheap. Naturally, therefore, they want to buy modern English books.

But they cannot afford to buy modern English books, and no organisation exists for helping them to buy modern English books. They can only borrow them — and that with much difficulty and delay. Mr. Gupta says that at a certain local lending library H.G. Wells's *The Outline of History* is already booked for two or three months in advance, and that while waiting their turn for it subscribers will not take out any other book lest in so doing they might be prejudicing their claim to *The Outline of History*. Similarly with other books and other authors, and with other Indian universities. This condition of affairs is not pleasing, and something ought surely to be done about it.

Mr. Gupta remarks that 7s. 6d. for an average new English book is too dear for penurious India. My information is that seven-and-sixpenny books are sold in India at 4½ rupees, which is about 6s. 9d. But I admit that 6s. 9d. would be too dear. The (relatively) cheap Colonial editions of new English books are put on the Indian market, and special cheap editions of Anglo-Indian novels are sold at about 5s. 8d. Still, even 5s. 8d. is too dear. Moreover, I doubt if the Indian student pines for Anglo-Indian novels; he probably desires sterner stuff than the sentimentality out of which such novels are too often concocted. Even Anglo-Indian novels sell twice as well in Australia as in India.

The one branch of literature in which India excels as a buyer is the Medical. India buys more medical books than any other portion of the Empire; she buys as many as Great Britain buys.

The above facts add considerably to the force of Mr. Gupta's argument, but he did not mention them in his letter to *The Nation*.

It seems to me that the National Book Council, which I understand to be flourishing, could advantageously extend its activities far enough to include India. Some English books might do harm in India (though not more harm than they do in Britain); but more would do good. Books are the great colonisers, the great penetrators, the great spreaders of ideas. Men like the Secretary for India doubtless feel this in their leisure moments; but could even the mighty arm of the Secretary for India beat down the prodigious departmental practical disbelief in the influence of the best English literature on populations? Has any British Government ever carried out a sustained large-scale literary campaign on behalf of anything whatever? I doubt. That is to say, I don't doubt in the least. The National Book Council is the indicated organisation for getting publishers and authors together for the making and marketing in India of new English books at prices which the ardent Indian can afford to pay.

21 July 1927

Holiday Reading — And Some Famous Names

A journalist of the first importance, and of mature years, said to me the other day when he went for a holiday he usually took with him novels that he had read before, and read them again. He mentioned no titles, but I believe that he confined himself to English novels. The remark made me realise how heterodox I am in these grave matters. I can read certain English poems over again. But if I went away with only English novels I should feel that I was terribly cut off from the great world. In the frightful, but fortunately rare, ordeal of a holiday, I insist on having foreign novels as an aid to keeping my reason.

I have read the following novels three times, and I may well read them again: Balzac's *Cousin Bette* and *The Curé of Tours*, Zola's *Nana*, Charles Louis Philippe's *Bubu de Montparnasse*, de Maupassant's *Pierre and Jean*, Dostoevsky's *The Brothers Karamazov*. These titles occur to me at once. There are other foreign novels which I may have read twice or thrice. And, among English novels, I have read some Hardy and some George Moore twice. But as for English novels in general, even the masterpieces are rendered insular for me by our racial sentimentality and prudery, and few of them indeed would I read again except for a cash payment.

Our pre-nineteenth century novels, like those of other countries, are too old-fashioned to be enjoyable. The novel as we know it only began in 1830, when Balzac began *The Human Comedy* series. Defoe? Defoe was wonderful — for his time. I have not read *Robinson Crusoe* since boyhood's omnivorous, gluttonous days, and I doubt if I shall re-open it. The other Defoe novels, such as *Moll Flanders* and *Roxana,* are too bald and bony to be attractive reading. They are neither sentimental nor prudish, but they have the aridity of reporting. They leave too much out. They lack warmth.

Richardson? No. Richardson is 75 per cent. boring. Life is far longer than it used to be, but it is still far too short for *Clarissa.* Smollett? Certainly not. Too rough-and-tumble. Amusing only in spots. Fielding? Yes. His three principal novels have the wide-world quality, and *Tom Jones* is not much superior to the other two.

Sterne? Yes, I might get through *Tristram Shandy* once more; but it is too individual and capricious an expression of its author to count seriously as a picture of any world. Swift? Well, *Gulliver's Travels* is mighty stuff, but not in our sense a novel. For that it is too fantastic, and its aim too exclusively and ferociously satiric. Goldsmith? Not primarily a novelist; but *The Vicar of Wakefield,* innocent of all construction though it be, is a pleasing enough piece of sentimentality.

Scott I will not now read. He was an original force; he brought something that was almost new into the novel. He changed the novel. He deserved his immense vogue. But his importance has now dwindled to the historic. The trouble with Scott is that he had the country-gentleman mind, which is admirable in its proper sphere, but unsuited to a creative artist. If he knew anything about women (which I doubt) he took care to keep the knowledge out of his novels. His ingenuousness is touching, but it is also tiresome. And he was long-winded as nobody ever was since the interminable author of *The Grand Cyrus.* I once read *Waverley,* because I was determined to read it — being in those days young and strong and obstinate. But during the last pages I was still asking myself: "When is this book going to begin?" Yet there are people of my age who, I am informed, read all Scott every year. Their scant spare time must be given almost exclusively to snatching hasty meals and getting a wink of sleep. I admit that about two-thirds of *The Heart of Midlothian* is extremely powerful; but the remaining third declines and falls off like the Roman Empire — only much less excitingly.

Maria Edgeworth? Certainly not. She merely cannot be read. Fanny

Burney? Bright in parts. Unreadable in the mass. But what could you expect from the astounding foolishness of a young woman who ruined her whole life in order to be a functionary and slave at the dullest court since the court of the singular Spaniard who built the Escurial? The poor thing had no sense and no sense of proportion. She had a sharp eye for the minor comicalities of existence. But the full equipment of the first-rate novelist she did not possess. More, she had, I imagine, no conception of what the full equipment must be.

Jane Austen? I feel that I am approaching dangerous ground. The reputation of Jane Austen is surrounded by cohorts of defenders who are ready to do murder for their sacred cause. They are nearly all fanatics. They will not listen. If anybody "went for" Jane, anything might happen to him. He would assuredly be called on to resign from his clubs. I do not want to resign from my clubs. I would sooner perjure myself. On the other hand I do not want to "go for" Jane. I like Jane. I have read several Janes more than once. And in the reading of Jane's novels there happens to be that which can only happen in the work of a considerable author. I mean that first you prefer one novel, then you prefer another novel, and so on. Time was when I convinced myself that *Persuasion* was her masterpiece, with *Emma* a good second. Now I am inclined to join the populace and put *Pride and Prejudice* in the front, with *Mansfield Park* a good second.

But listening to the more passionate Janeites (and among them are some truly redoubtable persons), one receives the impression that in their view Jane and Shakespeare are the only two English authors who rightly count, and that Shakespeare is joined with her chiefly as a concession to the opinion of centuries. I do not subscribe to this heated notion. I do not even agree that Jane was a great novelist. She was a great little novelist. She is marvellous, intoxicating: she has unique wit, vast quantities of common sense, a most agreeable sense of proportion, much narrative skill. And she is always readable.

But her world is a tiny world, and even of that tiny world she ignores, consciously or unconsciously, the fundamental factors. She did not know enough of the world to be a great novelist. She had not the ambition to be a great novelist. She knew her place; her present "fans" do not know her place, and their antics would without doubt have excited Jane's lethal irony. I should say that either Emily or Charlotte Brontë was a bigger novelist than Jane. The hallowed name of Brontë brings me into the Victorian era of fiction, concerning which I will, if I still survive, enrage the earnest orthodox next week.

28 July 1927

Candour About the Great Victorian Novelists

Last week I threatened remarks on Victorian novelists. The moment has come. First I wish to correct an apparent misapprehension. I have no bias against the Victorians. I am a Victorian myself. I spent the twenty-four most impressive years of my life under influences which were mainly, if not exclusively, Victorian. I am a faithful admirer of the Victorian age. I think it one of the greatest, perhaps the greatest, age in English history. I am a faithful admirer of its finest poets, men of science, philosophers, historians. I think that some of them are still under-rated. Tennyson, for instance, Matthew Arnold, Huxley, Carlyle, and Stubbs. Tennyson is now under-rated. Matthew Arnold was never put high enough, nor Huxley, nor Stubbs.

I also admire the finest Victorian novelists. And the fact that I upbraid them is no proof that I do not regard them as very considerable persons. I am capable of upbraiding Shakespeare. If I deal chiefly with novelists, the reason is that fiction happens to be my specialty. Of late I have largely occupied myself, in print, with modern novelists. But that does not prevent me from highly appreciating other kinds of modern work. I may mention Dr. and Mrs. Beard's *Rise of American Civilisation* (Cape), and Miss Mayo's *Mother India* (Cape, too), in my opinion books which are likely to be as influential, and valuable, as any novels written or to be written between 1907 and 1947.

Dickens. Dickens was a great creative genius. I admit it, while saying plainly that since I was less of a boy than I am to-day I have never been able to read a novel of Dickens from beginning to end. With one exception, *A Tale of Two Cities*, which I undertook to read and write about for a monetary consideration.* The task was desolating. My objections to Dickens are that he had a common mind and an inferior style, and that his novels are very patchy. And how should they not be patchy, seeing that he so often wrote against time?

His plots are childish, his sentimentality is nauseating. That he had a kind heart and a democratic passion for justice is quite beside the point. Many hundredth-rate novelists have had kind hearts and a passion for just-ice. On the other hand he was a superlatively successful creator of comic characters, and nobody but a genius could have written his best scenes of comedy. These scenes are rich; they are full of the juice of English humour. But in order to get at them, what a price you must pay in tedium! I will not pay the price. The purse of my patience is too shallow. Why should I spend my time on Dickens when I can derive a pleasure almost unmixed from reading Thomas Hardy or George Moore?

Thackeray. Now, Thackeray was very naughty. He had more education and more taste than Dickens. Dickens did not sin against the light. Thackeray did. *Vanity Fair* is a great novel. Yes, I think it is. But the com-promises between falsity and truth which disfigure it, the evasions, the omissions, the shirkings of difficulties — these things are unworthy of any serious artist, much more of a great artist. The man knew what he was doing, and he did it deliberately. He wanted to be loved more than he wanted a clear artistic conscience. And he was cursed by a certain smugness.

As for his other chief works, *Pendennis* can assuredly be read. *Barry Lyndon* is perhaps his most satisfactory book. *Esmond* is a tour de force. After reading it I had to go away to recuperate; but I did read it. *The Newcomes* cannot be read. *The Virginians* — the thought of its dullness and deadness appals the spirit. Thackeray created brilliantly a few unsympa-thetic characters. But he was a Snowdon compared to Dickens's Ben Nevis.

* *Daily Express,* 27 September 1926.

The Himalayas are not English.

The Brontës. I will leave out Anne, who was a mere sister. I would rank both Emily and Charlotte as bigger people than Thackeray. They had a fundamental power fully equal to Thackeray's. And in addition they had a sense of beauty which heaven denied to him, and a sense of the romantic quality of life which he could not approach. When I think of the Valkyrie Charlotte being nervous and tongue-tied in the presence of a prim warrior like Thackeray, with his fondness for armistices, I at once try to think of something else. I regard *Wuthering Heights* as the summit of feminine attainment in fiction. *La Princesse de Clèves* is marvellously distinguished, but seems slight after the colossal affair of Emily. *Wuthering Heights,* by its beauty, grandeur and romance holds me as no novel by Scott could.

As for Charlotte, *Jane Eyre, Vilette,* and *Shirley* are all fine, extremely fine, and the first two come as near to Emily's lonely masterpiece as any work by any woman ever did. If the word genius is applicable to any writers it is applicable to Emily and Charlotte. What fire! What loveliness! What creative force! What invention! What style! Had destiny given them a fair chance, instead of installing them in an ecclesiastical drawing-room whose windows overlooked a country churchyard, what could they not have accomplished! Their trouble was that they knew not enough of the world. Charlotte learnt more of it than Emily; but both were inadequately furnished with external inspiration. They lacked perspective, and the fault was heaven's, not theirs. Miraculous creatures, however, they were. The other major Victorians must stand over for seven days.

4 August 1927

More About the Great Victorian Novelists

I must now finish the chief Victorian novelists left over from last week. The Brontës ended my previous article.

George Eliot. The excellent and somewhat formidable creature, after basking — she and her ghost between them — in a prodigious popularity for many years, is now an exile among the Neglected. (But she may well one day be received again with bay-leaves and triumphal arches.) I have an idea that her temporary fate is the result of her most imposing books, *Romola* and *Daniel Deronda*. She had built big houses, and she said to herself that she would build bigger and still bigger. But these were houses of the dead. Indeed, the inhabitants of the two tremendous edifices never came to life. They were born whole, born mature, but born dead.

Thus all the learning and the historical imagination and the philosophy and the invention which went to the making of the monuments were thrown away. Happily their author never learnt the sad fact; for both books had immense sales in their time. They are probably still bought, but my information about human nature prevents me from believing that they are still read.

The earlier books are a different matter. George Eliot began late and she began well. No woman novelist has had a better equipment for the grand enterprise of fiction. She was highly educated; she had a fine mind, which she both refined and broadened by study; her knowledge enabled her to correct her notions of the present by reference to the past: and throughout the years of ardent preparation she managed to preserve intact her sense of humour.

She was nearly forty when *Scenes of Clerical Life* appeared and was half-drowned in merited praise. You can enjoy even to-day *Scenes of Clerical Life*, but only on one condition. You must abandon relatives and friends, and all ties, and all other interests, and yield yourself totally and utterly to the preliminary long-windedness of the author. If you can accomplish this feat of renunciation you will not arrive at the close of her first volume of fiction without being convinced that you have read something.

She then wrote three really admirable novels: *Adam Bede, The Mill on the Floss,* and *Silas Marner.* What the faults of these books are I really don't know. They have form, creative power, pathos, humour, honesty, beauty, style, and a definite point of view. Some of the characters have become typical. They are solid works. Nothing flimsy about them. The themes are handled with thoroughness. What else do you want?

Then, after she had failed to learn the stiff lesson of *Romola,* artistic ambition overweened in the unhappy lady, and she wrote *Middlemarch.* I read a lot of *Middlemarch* not long ago, and I assert that solid it is not. Chapter after chapter starts splendidly, sinks into clever dialogue, and passes away into nothing at all, without having advanced the story one inch. Then she failed to learn the equally stiff lesson of *Middlemarch,* and went and did *Daniel Deronda.* It was a pity. For *Daniel Deronda* seems to have fallen down on *Adam Bede* and crushed the lovely thing deep into the earth.

But *Adam Bede* will be disinterred. I think it was *Adam Bede* that the impulsive Charles Reade pronounced to be "the finest thing since Shakespeare." A wild verdict. But Reade knew a book when he saw it. (And, by the way, he also wrote two superb historical novels, one long, one short: *The Cloister and the Hearth,* and *Peg Woffington.* I read the latter recently. It survived brilliantly. So did I. I am afraid to come to grips with *The Cloister and the Hearth* again, lest a horrid disillusion might darken the afternoon of my existence.) My admiration for George Eliot has been rising of late years.

There is a small but influential cult for Lord Beaconsfield. The rites of the cult are performed in private; but I have assisted at them — without actual initiation. I like Beaconsfield because he was such a grandiose adventurer, not merely in politics, but with a pen. He wrote *Vivian Grey* at eighteen, and the reader of it would guess the author's age in the first eighteen pages. As a boy I took the sketches in *Ixion* for matchless satire. I have read most of the mature novels. The trouble with Beaconsfield as an artist is that he was a statesman who diverted himself with fiction instead of being a novelist who diverted himself with politics. He created an empress, but I doubt if he created anybody else.

A fellow of terrific energy, variety, shameless flatteries, and bluff, he composed novels as he might have composed symphonies had the idea occurred to him. He revelled in his own gifts. Too often, as you read, you are inclined to complain "This Oriental artificer is not writing a novel, he is just larking around." The animadversion would be just.

His best things are his worst: glorious fustian such as the descriptions *de luxe* in *Lothair*. Every few pages he gets drunk, wonders where the devil he is, and pulls himself together like a gentleman. Withal, he had moral passions and political vision, together with an informed sympathy for the underdog. The sermons implied or direct in his novels are sound enough. None of his books is consistently good, and none consistently bad. I think that *Lothair* and *Sybil* are the most satisfactory to read *in*. Among the best is *Endymion*: perhaps that was why it failed.

Another secret cult has taken possession of Captain Marryat, who must be mentioned among Victorian novelists. His worst books have an individual quality. His best are fun as gorgeous as you will find.

Lastly Trollope. Trollope is on the crest of the wave. He has been in some danger of classification as the greatest of the Victorians. He is not that. He had neither genius nor style. But he was a worker and a realist and a non-sentimentalist, and he knew what life is. His pictures of Victorian manners are far more exact and various and complete than those of either Thackeray or Dickens. There was no nonsense about him. Unfortunately when he had once begun a novel he drove right on, up hill and down dale like a Roman road, and no doubts or hesitations or artistic scruples would stop him or even slacken his speed. Four miles an hour, no more and no less, the whole time.

This is no way to write a first-rate novel. He did not write one. His dullness and his clumsiness are frequently extreme, his demands on the reader's forbearance are ruthless. His novels, will not, I am convinced, survive. But for the present he insists on being read. He cannot be ignored. Possibly in fifty years our unimaginative posterity will be saying of us: "How could they read such tedious drabness?" Never mind!

I have not discussed him who is conceivably the greatest of the Victorians. Of course I mean Thomas Hardy. He lives, and is thereby spared the infliction.

11 August 1927

A Playwright on the Theatre: Some High-Brow Successes: London's Meagre Hope of a Renaissance: "Paris is Worse"

A brilliant example of a book which might have been wholly good but through slackness is merely half good is Nicolas Evreinoff's *The Theatre in Life*, edited and translated by Alexander Nazaroff, with some pleasing illustrations by B. Aronson (Harraps, 12s.6d.). Evreinoff is known as a playwright in Paris; he was played in New York eleven years ago. With luck he may reach the London West End stage eleven years hence.

I see from an Introduction to the book by Oliver Sayler that Evreinoff has been circus performer, actor, playwright, stage-manager, flute-player, musical composer, painter, psychologist, law-graduate, Government official, archaeologist, teacher, traveller, historian, and even novelist. "And a tyro at none of these occupations." It may be. But he is certainly a tyro at writing a book about the theatre. I have read the volume through, and I do not know what Evreinoff's main idea concerning the theatre, the new theatre and the newest theatre, really amounts to.

He talks about "the theatre for oneself," in which you play plays composed by yourself for yourself and for none else. He gives three schemes for such plays; two of them are very poor, indeed (I think) impossible, and one is fair. In an imaginary conversation between Schopenhauer, Tolstoy, Wilde, Bergson and others, he makes Schopenhauer speak thus: "I will admit this: according to your idea, the 'plays' of 'the theatre for oneself' should be created by spontaneous effort, as it were, by divine inspiration; all such works of art possess the great quality of being pure and sincere and fragments of our creative enthusiasm . . . They are free from the alloy of analysis or of deliberate tendency . . . However insignificant, they may have a stronger appeal and be more convincing than the greatest works of art executed through years of sustained effort." All of which seems to me to be much more like Evreinoff himself talking than Arthur Schopenhauer talking. Anyhow, in this speech lies, half-formed, the idea which is the kernel of Evreinoff's book.

That there is anything in it — except for children — I doubt. Such improvised and trifling plays as are proposed would be totally insignificant, and at the best could only serve as hints for genuine plays. I certainly do not see any appreciable minority of our populations deliberately concocting and playing such plays for their own diversion. Western populations have a sense of humour, doubtless deplorable, which would stop them indulging in such pranks.

The book, like many Russian books with a thesis, diminishes as it goes on to nothing at all. The central idea, if idea it may rightly be called, is not worked out; what ought to be the culminating chapters are thin and almost negligible.

Still, *The Theatre in Life* is well worth reading, if only for the first half of it, in which the author shows, in very considerable detail, how large a part of the life of men and other animals is made up of the pleasure of play-acting and the pleasure of watching existence as though existence were a show. Here Evreinoff is dealing with preliminaries; he has not yet come to the hard tussle with the difficulties of his theme; and he is decidedly good; he is even inspiring. After reading these chapters I was conscious of a certain faint renascence in me of the long-dead desire to write plays. It is ingenious of him to suggest that the restful value of "a change of scene" lies in the fact that we cease for a time to be actors and become spectators of the great world-play.

Evreinoff appears to be full of hope for the immediate future of the stage. I mean the ordinary stage, not the "theatre for oneself." I am glad. But I do not at present share his hope. Some months ago in Paris I saw his best-known play, called in French *The Comedy of Happiness,* produced by Dullin, probably the best French producer, and acted by Dullin, one of the best French actors. Evreinoff's play is like his book in this — it begins admirably, maintains itself for a while precariously, and then fizzles out in weakness and confusion. Its lesson is the practical auto-suggestive utility of acting in life. But the lesson does not convince.

The success on the summit of Montmartre of *The Comedy of Happiness* has been brought forward in support of the argument that the French stage is being born again. This notion is becoming prevalent. It was even mentioned to me by an American popular lecturer on European literatures. I cannot accept it. There have been successful plays of the "art" theatres in Paris during the last year. Evreinoff's is one.

The second is Mr. Sutton Vane's *Outward Bound*. Well, we know what *Outward Bound* is — a first-rate dramatic idea mishandled. An excellent, though badly written, opening act. A bad second act. A worse third act. And not a trace of original treatment in the whole play. Besides *Outward Bound* is not French, and *The Comedy of Happiness* is not French.

The third high-brow success is a play called *Maya*, by Simon Gantillon, which has enjoyed great "acceptance" in the Champs Elysées. I assert that if *Maya* had not dealt realistically with the life of prostitutes of the lowest class in Marseilles it would not have run a month. It has absolutely no freshness, and it is without dramatic quality. M. Benjamin Crémieux, a very sane and very enlightened critic, called it "hardly more than a scenario." I would not call it even a scenario. I could not sit still through it. I witnessed it in the company of a well-known French author and well-known English author, and we were all three bored in quite the grand manner.

So much for the new birth of the French stage. The best modern French play is Marcel Achard's *Malbrouck s'en va t'en guerre*; but this is a play of fancy, having the slenderest relation to life. It is, however, a gem.

And in London, is there any sign of a new birth? I think not. One or two plays are to be seen with moments of very diverting brilliance and some dramatic "criticism of life." But of originality — naught!

The Russian ballet *The Cat* had striking originality, and it was beautiful and dramatic. One had only to see it in order to perceive that there is nothing in the regular London stage to come within a hundred miles of it. And Paris is no better. Paris is worse.

As for America, George Kelly wrote *The Show-Off*, which failed here, but which I admired with enthusiasm. The trouble is that George Kelly seems now to be imitating George Kelly. We shall soon be in a position to decide for ourselves whether Sidney Howard (author of *The Silver Cord*) is worthy of his quickly-rising reputation. Readers are requested not to name to me the name of Eugene O'Neill, for I regard his plays as ponderous, pretentious and preposterous. I dislike being pessimistic about the stage or about anything; but I dislike still more hiding my head in the sand in order not to see the frightening face of truth. I had better not say any more lest Hubert Griffith* should summon me for trespass.

18 August 1927

Why Read to the Bitter End? — A Woman's Much-Discussed First Novel

Lately the readers of various newspapers have been assailing dramatic

*Drama critic for the *Standard* at the time.

critics — a sort of holiday diversion, I suppose. God knows that literary criticism is nonchalant enough, and that dramatic criticism, with one or two grateful and comforting exceptions, is even more nonchalant. Nevertheless, in the tussles, the dramatic critics won easily. Seldom have I read indictments more exquisitely inane, absurd and silly. Literary critics have not so far come under fire. I will now expose myself to attack.

Quite a number of times during recent weeks I have been reproached by friends, enemies, and the superiorly indifferent for having ignored Miss Rosamond Lehmann's novel, *Dusty Answer* (Chatto, 7s. 6d.). Men and women, mainly young, have pointed out to me that Miss Lehmann is a young novelist, and *Dusty Answer* a first novel of remarkable properties and qualities, and that therefore my obvious duty, as perhaps the most active encourager and chastiser of youthful authors among sexagenarians, was to deal with the said work.

My reply was that *Dusty Answer,* being the most discussed and the best belauded first novel by a woman since *The Constant Nymph,* had no need of my attention. If I liked it my praise would not help it; if I disliked it my blame would not harm it; and merely to proclaim its existence would be a waste of space, seeing that the whole Anglo-Saxon world is aware of its existence. I stood firm. But I could not get away from *Dusty Answer,* which seems "literally" (as they say) to pervade London and all the politer provinces. In the end *Dusty Answer* broke down my resistance. It somehow insinuated itself into my hands. My surrender to it was probably due to the fact that I was sick of being asked "Have you read *Dusty Answer?*"

In my opinion *Dusty Answer* is a good novel: by which I mean that it is thoroughly well done. It is honest, accurate in observation, sympathetic, successful in its characterisation, agreeably written, sufficiently picturesque, and on the whole convincing. Some of its tableaux of the life of student girls at Cambridge reach excellence; they really inform. Its themes are youth, love and work. Throughout it one is conscious of the writer saying in her creative mind: "I will see things for myself, not as others have seen things before me." All of which is satisfactory and praiseworthy.

And yet I can perceive little or no originality in the work, and no genuine distinction. I have learnt from it nothing about "modern youth" that I did not know before. The enigma of modern youth has not been solved for me. Not that I believe for a moment in the existence of any enigma of youth special to these wondrous latter days. My belief is that youth to-day is no more enigmatic than youth was a quarter of a century ago or fifty years ago. Nor have I ever talked with a youth of either sex who even attempted to persuade me of the contrary.

I meet to-day youths who know what they want, and youths who don't know what they want; and thus it has ever been. A sad lot of yearning nonsense has been and is being talked about modern youth, chiefly by the elderly of a sentimental turn. To her credit, Miss Lehmann, anyhow, does not talk nonsense. She may be pedestrian; she may stick in the plain; but she walks straight. If she has a positive fault it lies in her over-indulgence in passages of dialogue which are totally unimportant and futile. I would say that *Dusty Answer* is all performance, with no promise.

The burden of this article is not my estimate of Miss Lehmann's novel, but the fact that I have not read it! I have read *in* it. I calculate that I may have read in all a hundred pages of it, which would be rather less than a third of the whole. At this point Miss Lehmann and her numerous admirers might excusably sit up and protest: "A nice thing! He doesn't read the book through, and yet presumes to pass a verdict on it!"

But why not? I should be considerably startled if further perusal led me to modify my judgment. I reckon that I have possessed myself of the author's mind, of her attitude towards life, and of her narrative method. These matters I find interesting, but not enthralling. I left the book with respect, and even liking, but without regret. Some books are not read through because they are unreadable. *Dusty Answer* is not among these. I could have read it and still escaped ennui. I abandoned it from a private assurance that I had appeased my curiosity concerning it, got from it all that it could give me.

Not to read through a detective novel or an adventure novel is proof that it has failed with you; for the main thing in it is the "story," the procession of events. But few novels depend first for their interest on the mere narrative. In the great majority of cases what holds you in a fine novel is not the story, but the originality and interestingness of the author's mind and vision, which reveal themselves on every page, and of whose ceaseless activity you would not willingly miss a single manifestation. The story of *Hamlet* is perhaps no better than the story of *East Lynne;* but this does not prevent *Hamlet* from being on the whole perhaps a more interesting work than Mrs. Henry Wood's masterpiece of sentimentality.

Of course, if for any reason you desire complete knowledge of a work, you must read it from beginning to end; but if your sole object is your own pleasure and betterment you are justified in reading no more of it than you feel like reading. Indeed it would — I think — be a true saying of most books that you can derive more satisfaction from a part of them than from the whole, because the effect of them, far from being cumulative, may decrease as the pages turn. Few books improve as they proceed.

Many readers, and experienced and expert readers, make a point of conscientiously finishing whatever they have begun. But I am in the other camp. I maintain that there is not sufficient reason for such a rule, and that the literary life of most readers would be enlarged and enriched if they read less of more books. In a material sense authors would benefit, far more copies of their books would be sold. Their pride would suffer; but it would suffer deservedly, for the business of an imaginative author is to *make* you read his every page. Besides, the pride of an author is always suffering, and it is good for his soul that this should be so. I am entitled to speak as an author. And I speak.

25 August 1927

The Season Reviewed: Wells, Miss Mayo and Miss Waddell: The Genius of Blake

As this is the last Thursday in August, and as according to report the August holiday is about to begin, the moment seems proper for referring to the general character of the past literary season.

In regard to imaginative literature, I do not esteem the season very highly; there has been some distinguished poetry, but very little distinguished prose — that is, fiction. Of course unforgettable works may have been published in the early part of the year, but by the end of the season we have usually forgotten their very titles. It is always the books arriving late in the season that receive laudation. Last come, best served.

In the non-imaginative or semi-imaginative section, however, the season has been rendered memorable by at least two books which have made deep dents in the smooth surface of the Anglo-Saxon world's complacency. The first and finest is Dr. and Mrs. Beard's historical study of the United States, which I have mentioned before. This long, solid, judicial, judicious, grimly humorous and original work has probably excited more passion in America than in Britain — as is right. No one who reads it can escape the disturbing experience of a rather violent revolution among the contents of his mind. American history, like American literary studies, rarely reaches the European standard. But the Beards will hold their own comfortably in any European society of the philosophical-learned. They count. They set a new standard.

The second work is Miss Katherine Mayo's *Mother India,* which also I have previously mentioned. A shocking book, in the honourable sense. It has received, and withstood, very fierce criticism. It has even divided hitherto united families and other groups of persons. It was bound excessively to annoy large numbers of interested people, chiefly Hindu, and it has done so. Some of these have tried to get it suppressed, wholly or partially. But a book so completely documented is insuppressible. Nor is its indictment answerable. The one charge that could possibly succeed against Miss Mayo is that her perspective is here and there just a bit awry.

In the matter of dents, one of the major indentations has been achieved by H. G. Wells in *Meanwhile,* a book which brilliantly combines fiction with a political tract. What disagreeable, disconcerting and gay truth in this appalling mixture! The young, I gather from certain reviews, have a considerable "down" on H.G. Wells. That will not alter the fact that there is nobody else on this earth who could begin to do what he does. An exasperating man for the complacent and the ineffective.

I must mention Miss Helen Waddell's *The Wandering Scholars* (Constable, one guinea) as a book quite outstanding in the season. It is not often that works of scholarship can justifiably be called "jolly." But this one is very jolly. I picked it up in one of those periods which are only too frequent in my existence — a period of waiting for a friend who was late for an appointment. It held me. *The Wandering Scholars* re-creates the Dark Ages, and in so doing deprives them of their traditional sinister adjective. The Dark Ages may have been dirty, but with the wandering scholars flitting brightly around, they could not have been dark. Miss Waddell is incredibly learned, but intensely readable. And she is a wonderful translator. She has enriched us.

Reprints have given lustre to the season. The collected edition of Robert Graves's poems was an eye-opener for a lot of readers, including myself. And then Blake. Happily the recent Blake centenary celebrations have passed off, despite many fireworks, without any serious casualty.

The articles upon him have been on the whole excellent. I am not an authority on Blake — or on anything except unimportant subjects such as what literature bores me and what doesn't. Few men can both read and write professionally. I write. But two great epochal days in my life were concerned with Blake.

The first was the day on which I made acquaintance with his *Songs of the Seasons*. It seemed to me that here I had encountered the very essence and supremacy of verse. If I am asked what I understand by poetry I always recite:

> O thou with dewy locks, who lookest down
> Through the clear windows of the morning, turn
> Thine angel eyes upon our western isle,
> Which in full choir hails thy approach, O Spring!

And so on.

The second day was that on which by pure hazard I read some extremely profound proverbs in a French magazine — pages of them. I asked myself: "Who is this tremendous French writer whom I am now meeting for the first time?" But the pages were a translation of Blake's *The Marriage of Heaven and Hell* — a work which I had never read, having ignorantly classed it many years ago among the *Prophetic Books,* which at that time were supposed to be incomprehensible save by lunatics.

After having read it in English about six times, and also enlarged my poor general knowledge of Blake, I decided for myself that *The Marriage of Heaven and Hell* is Blake's masterpiece, and one of the greatest short poetical philosophical works ever written by anybody. It is indeed a very short book, but it cuts as deep as any.

Read Mr. Max Plowman's admirable essay on it at the end of the facsimile reprint in colour and gold published by Dents (one guinea). This reprint, by the way, is very beautiful, and the publishers deserve the highest credit therefor. It is a slim quarto of few pages, and the price may seem excessive, but really the book is cheap. As a gift book in these coming months it will not and cannot possibly be surpassed. Blake is now being lifted towards his right place in the hierarchy of English poets and draughts-men, but he is not yet quite there. I like to think of this transcendent genius working quietly and unappreciated as a draughtsman, engraver and printer, perfectly content, in the society of his marvellous wife, who helped him in the craftsmanship to the best of her ability. The divine woman marred sundry copies of his books by her imperfect sense of colour, but what matter? No creative artist ever had a more consummate helpmeet.

1 September 1927

Mr. H.M. Tomlinson's First Novel:
First-Rate Writing, But Imperfect Construction:
The Love-Interest in Fiction

To-day is published H.M. Tomlinson's first novel, *Gallions Reach: A Romance* (Heinemann, 7s. 6d.). Mr. Tomlinson has long been a traveller, and the enthusiasts for literature whose opinion gradually makes reputations have long recognised him as a great writer. It has even been asserted that he is the greatest English prose writer now writing. I will neither contradict nor support this claim; but I will go so far as to say that there are pages in his books as fine as anything done within the present century, which is going quite a considerable distance.

The enthusiasts have looked forward to *Gallions Reach* with the very keenest interest. The romance begins with a kind of prologue on a ship entering, via Gallions Reach, the port of London. Colet, the hero, is a child. A certain sentimentality here in the treatment of the romance of the grand entry. Next Colet is an important clerk in a ship-owner's office. He is alone in London, but his solitude is slightly mitigated by the friendship of a girl named Helen, whom we see with Colet at a Soho restaurant and in her rooms. Perriam, the ship-owner, is a harsh and unsympathetic gentleman, and Colet, by a physically unprovoked assault, knocks down the oppressor of the poor and kills him. Legally, perhaps, the deed amounts to murder; on the most favourable construction it is manslaughter.

Colet gets away in a ship eastward bound. There is a shipwreck. There is a lot of perilous travel in the Orient. There is a fabulous discovery of tin. There are other wonders. In the end Colet decides that he must return to London and place himself at the disposition of the law. On this decision the story closes — still in the East. Colet's final words are: "There's no fun for us unless we obey the order we know."

Everything in the novel is admirably done — the East-end scenes just as well as the maritime scenes and the Orient scenes. In all latitudes and longitudes the author seems to be equally at home. Romance is achieved on nearly every page. The writing is rarely lower than first-rate, and often it is simply masterly. The effects aimed at are realised. The East-end and the East are rendered about as well as they ever have been rendered. The characterisation, given the limits which Mr. Tomlinson has obviously set himself, is thoroughly satisfactory, thoroughly convincing. In landscape and seascape Mr. Tomlinson has no superior; here he keeps level with his best. And, not least important, he displays in this book an adequate narrative skill. Briefly, *Gallions Reach* is a demonstration that its author possesses the gifts of a novelist.

The average reader, however, will ask as he reaches the final page: "Yes. This is all very fine and true and so on, but what about that girl Helen? And what about that murder or manslaughter?" Justifiable questions, in my opinion. Especially the question about the girl. There is no love-interest in the story. Mr. Tomlinson is possibly in revolt against the generally accepted sentimental theory that love is the greatest interest in life, and that therefore you must have a love-interest in a proper novel. Apparently he is not, as a novelist, very interested in love. And he is and has always been "against the Government" — whether aesthetic or political. The fact that nearly all novels have a love-interest is nothing to him. If he said that the conscience-interest or the work-interest is often more important in life than any love-interest, I should agree with him. And if he said that there is no artistic reason why a novel should have a love-interest I should agree with him.

I would even venture the assertion that, speaking broadly, no theme in fiction is treated with less insight and regard for truth than the theme of love. Sometimes in my novel-reading I have ejaculated: "Stay me with flagons. Comfort me with apples, for I am sick of love." In many novels, where the love-interest is not the main interest, the love-interest is clumsily and insincerely tacked on in order to comply with custom. Rarely, in such novels, is the love-interest a fundamental part of the scheme — as it is, for instance, in Zola's *L'Œuvre* or in J. Kessel's new Irish story *Mary de Cork*. (The latter, by the way, published by the Librairie Gallimard, Paris, is a quite first-rate small piece of fiction.)

But if I have correctly divined Mr. Tomlinson's attitude, why does he mislead the reader by introducing the attractive Helen for no visible purpose? Helen serves no end. She is material wasted. And why is the conscience-interest not fully exploited? The book is really about conscience; but at the close of the tale conscience has only just actively manifested itself. Tremendous experiences lie before Colet when he reaches London and the police, but the author stops short of them. He deliberately arouses a high curiosity and then shuts up. The book might fairly be compared to a canvas in which the excitingness of the composition is confined to the left hand, with hardly anything to balance it on the right hand. The book is admirably executed, but it has been imperfectly conceived and constructed. Either it should have been longer or Mr. Tomlinson should write a sequel to it. It is not a whole novel. That it proves Mr. Tomlinson to be capable of writing a whole novel makes it all the more disappointing.

There remains the problem of the influence of Joseph Conrad upon Mr. Tomlinson. I should say that the Conrad influence is pretty plain on the face of *Gallions Reach*. I do not murmur at this. I merely note. Every artist is, and must be, influenced by somebody, and the influence of Conrad cannot but make for nobility. The main interest of most of Conrad's novels is a conscience-interest. His heroes have a way of sinning against their own codes, and then redeeming themselves at terrific cost. Mr. Tomlinson's Colet is just such a hero in just such a fix. Withal, the critic who would deny to Mr. Tomlinson genuine originality, genuine individuality, and great and authentic emotional power, ought to leave literature and devote his critical faculties to greyhound racing or finding losers on the Turf.

8 September 1927

The Art of the Crime Story: Conan Doyle, A.E.W. Mason, And Some Others

An author who has written and published fifty novels wrote to me the other day and suggested that instead of spending my appraising activities on the young I should criticise the work of living writers who have produced at least fifty novels. It was urged upon me that these veterans yearn to be seriously handled before the pen slips from their ageing hands. There are a number of them — more than you might think. Mr. G.B. Burgin, for instance, who has done eighty novels! I declined the suggestion.

The work would be too delicate. And why should I seriously disturb the tranquillity of these experienced practitioners so set in their ways? No end would be served thereby.

Nevertheless, my mind was jerked out of its rut. Fate sent me at this juncture one or two mystery novels. In the ordinary way I should not have read them, or, if I had read them I should have kept silent about them. For years past I have been disastrously disappointed with my adventures among mystery fiction. I think that even Poe is overpraised as a mystery novelist, for the reason that the interest of his tales is too exclusively limited to detection. I want more than mere detective ratiocination in my mystery stories. I want love, romances, and all sorts of things besides.

The creator of Lecoq wrote two fine crimes novels, and a number of very dull ones. One of the best crime novels that ever held me in a vice of curiosity was Anna Katharine Green's *The Leavenworth Case*. But that was thirty or forty years ago. What should I think of it to-day? Never will I try to read it again, for I am capable of sentimentality — thank heaven! The finest of all mystery novels is in my opinion *The Mystery of the Yellow Room*, which I regard as a masterpiece of its kind. The solution of it turns on one single moment of misapprehension, a moment which requires, and which gets, the very nicest skill for the success of its effect on the reader.

Then of course there is Conan Doyle, whose early work really thrilled me. (I gladly admit it.) But Sir Arthur never (so far as I know) wrote a full-length crime novel. He excels in the short story, which demands far less power and invention and ingenuity than a novel, for the maintenance of interest at full strength throughout. Chiefly I admire Sir Arthur for his Dr. Watson. Dr. Watson is an authentic human creation. Sherlock Holmes himself is not.

The plenteous generation of mystery-mongers which has followed Sir Arthur's youth I have found for the most part unreadable. Again and again I have hopefully started on their concoctions — and have been beaten off. The great Sax Rohmer is beyond me. I cannot read even the widely esteemed artificer of *The Man in the Brown Suit*. These writers do not excite curiosity in their first chapters. I cannot wait. My flesh is weak.

Two of the crime novels recently read by me are *The Curse of the Reckaviles*, by Walter E. Masterman (of whom I had not previously heard) (Methuens, 3s. 6d.), and *No Other Tiger*, by A.E.W. Mason (Hodder and Stoughton, 7s. 6d.). (The latter was reviewed in these columns last week, but I may be permitted to refer to it again.) *The Curse of the Reckaviles* must count among the most disconcerting novels, artistically considered, in my life as a reader. It does hold the attention through every page. It does state a mystery: it does solve that mystery, right at the end, on lines which (I think) no reader could possibly foresee; and the mystery is solved in a perfectly convincing way. This is an achievement, and a rare one, and worthy of public gratitude. Mr. Masterman possesses a pleasing, ingenuous knack of narrative.

Yet he is apparently the most artless writer alive! His characterisation is extremely jejune, and much of his motivation is no better. His young detective, besides never once talking as a detective would and must talk, is the biggest and stupidest fool in all the imagined annals of Scotland Yard.

And Mr. Masterman's writing! His clichés, of which there are at least five on every page! They must be read to be believed. In Mr. Masterman's chapters organs "peal," people "adjourn" from one place to another, people have "strange forebodings," attention is "riveted," the night is "far spent," the end is "bitter," "all" is "bustle and excitement," "accents" are "faltering," babies are "tiny mites," tears take the form of "a bitter flood," people are "much in request," people are "consumed with impatience." Villains "hiss," and what is worse, they hiss "Thou hast found me, oh mine enemy!" Men are "moulded like one of the old Greek gods." A funeral is the "last sad ceremony."

And so on, and so on. And, for a superlative stroke, when the heroine-wife was developing into the heroine-mother, she "shyly took up a piece of work" — "a little garment." "What are you working at?" asks the husband. "Her face sank down over her work, and a crimson flush like a sunset dyed her neck." She "whispered" in reply: "Can't you guess? I could not tell you . . . ." Well, well! I say it is disconcerting. But you don't care. You read on.

Mr. A.E.W. Mason's affair is immensely more sophisticated and better achieved; and *No Other Tiger* is as excellent a thriller as you could desire. When in the Secret Service Mr. Mason must have had wild and marvellous adventures himself, in outlying parts of the earth. He knows the earth, and he knows the world and men and women and the structure of society. He can mingle the Occident with the Orient. He can draw diverse characters. His pen is alert and bold. He is interested in words. He can keep a sentence together. His plot has genuine novelty. His solution is at once convincing and startling. And quite as well as Mr. Masterman or the Ancient Mariner he squeezes you in his steely grip continuously from one end of the book to the other. When I finished *No Other Tiger* I took breath and said to myself: "This time you have not been let down."

It was immediately after reading these two earthly works that I took up *Journal of Katherine Mansfield*, edited by J. Middleton Murry (Constable). What a terrifying difference! Katherine Mansfield lived on another planet. She had a strange, exotic mind. She was tortured by her conceptions of the Art of literature. By temperament she was destined to infelicity, and she did not miss it. I think that she wrote a few good short stories, but I cannot rank her in a class by herself, as Mr. Middleton Murry does, and as quite a few other critics do. Nor do I agree with Mr. Middleton Murry that she was not influenced by Chekhov. If she had not been a fervent admirer of Chekhov she would never have written as she did. Still, her *Journal* is a highly curious document, unlike any other document in this genre. Much of it is exceedingly interesting. Some of it isn't.

15 September 1927

Magazine Sales: What the Public Wants: Love, Beauty, Adventure, Heroism

I suppose it must be some 35 years ago. I was a lawyer's clerk and I sat in

a room with another lawyer's clerk: a family man who "engrossed" documents, being paid for his work by the piece — so much for every folio of
72 words. He was most formidably industrious and earned quite a good
income. At that time I had the book-collecting mania, and made a habit
of buying a book every day. Every day I brought into the room at least one
book, old or new, English, French or Latin. My earnest colleague never
once showed the slightest interest in these volumes, never opened one,
never touched one, never asked a question about one. So far as I know
he never read anything except possibly a halfpenny daily paper and
Tit-Bits.

But one day he returned from lunch with a blue brochure, which he
exhibited with pride. It was a copy of the just-out first issue of *The
Strand Magazine*. The man had shown a flair. His interest in imaginative
literature had been awakened. He became a reader.

I always regarded this day not only as the natal day of the popular
illustrated magazine, but as a positively dramatic tribute to the correctness
of the psychological insight of George Newnes, and to the remarkable skill
of Mr. Greenhough Smith in bringing to full fruition George Newnes's idea.
(Mr. Greenhough Smith still edits the *Strand Magazine*.) The number of
popular illustrated magazines grew. It is still growing. To-day the biggest
bookstalls have difficulty in finding room to display the month's output
of popular illustrated magazines so gloriously coloured with girls' cheeks
and the firm chins of handsome youths and the names of best-sellers. You
might think that illustrated popular magazines dominated the printed field.

But they don't. The world of newsagents is disturbed and even alarmed
about these magazines. Though some of them sell triumphantly, their
general sale has fallen. The reading public is increasing. The sale of the
magazines, taken on the average, is declining. I am disclosing no secret.
The trade-press discusses the declension openly, and newsagents contribute
to the said Press their views of the causes of it. I have as yet seen no hint
that one of the causes of the decline of sales is a decline in the excellence
of contents. And I don't believe it is. I would say that never were the
contents better, more varied, more ingeniously appealing, than they are
to-day. No — nor more costly to the purses of proprietors.

One of the chief causes is clear enough. You can see it for yourself.
Wander round the coasts of Britain in these months when the populace
has leisure to read and probably reads more than in any other season, and
look at the bookstalls and the newsagents' shops, and you will perceive
everywhere the same phenomena: cheap, cloth-bound editions of well-
known novels and copies of popular illustrated magazines struggling against
one another for space and attention.

Look at the occupants of the millions of deck-chairs leased out at
twopence apiece to visitors by canny seaside corporations, and you will
see, first (of course) girls addressing picture-postcards to distant darlings;
second, people reading illustrated dailies; third, people reading cheap,
cloth-bound editions of novels, and fourth, people reading popular illustrated magazines.

A book has prestige not possessed by a magazine. (In the early days
the magazine was very frequently called "the book.") People think that
somehow the contents of a book are superior to the contents of a magazine.

(It is not so.) Again, the choice of books is infinitely wider than the choice of magazines. I have counted more than fifty different titles in a single shop.

Further, books are as cheap as magazines. Indeed they are often cheaper. In the marts crowded with perambulators and parents and those about to marry, where you can buy a pearl necklace for sixpence, a necktie for sixpence, a saucepan for sixpence and a fountain-pen for sixpence, you can also buy a novel world-famous and bound in cloth for sixpence — dust-jacket and all.

These editions have enormous sales, and the publishers of them, having learnt something from George Newnes, are exceedingly clever. In the 1880's Cassells started a National Library comprising such works as Johnson's *Rasselas* and Bacon's *Essays*. These works sold well, but their sales must have been infinitesimal compared with the sales of these latter days, when publishers have discovered that you could not give away copies of Johnson and Bacon to the vast masses of the newly "lettered" public. The new public wants love, beauty, luxury, adventure, thrills, heroism, simply and perhaps crudely presented, in its literature; and it gets the same. Any publisher will tell you that though the circulation of new books may not be rising, the demand for very cheap editions of not-new books rises and broadens every year. (Any established popular author will confirm the happy tidings of the publisher.)

There may be a way out for the magazines, a path to glory. But before the true path could be indicated it would be necessary to examine certain other causes which are prejudicing the prosperity of the magazines. I do not believe that the cheap book is the principal cause. The magazine has in my opinion more serious rivals in the great business of inciting the public — us — to commit murder. (For need I say that our chief purpose in reading magazines is not to enlarge our minds and to save our souls, but to kill time?) The subject indeed is immense. I will return to it.

22 September 1927

Newspapers and Wireless as Enemies of the Magazine

Last week I dealt with one important cause of the admitted decline in the sale of magazines — namely, the competition of very cheap editions of modern novels and other books. Another chief cause is the competition of broadcasting.

Now broadcasting, according to report, is the enemy of all other forms of entertainment, diversion, and instruction. Theatrical managers, music-hall managers, cinema-managers, concert-givers, book-publishers, clergymen, lecturers, all complain of the insidious newcomer,* which is cannibal in that it eats up its fellow-creatures. The newspaper alone seems not to suffer from the depredatory excursions of this young leviathan. I am not the person, nor is this the place, to inquire into the reasons for the immunity of the daily Press. I will only remark that newspaper-managers

*British broadcasting began on 14 November 1922.

are exceedingly alert and astute people.

The purchase and perusal of magazines may be postponed daily for a month, and at the end of the month more magazines hopefully appear. You are not bound to study them. To study them you must read; often you must wear spectacles; you must sit up; you must turn over many pages; you must have a good light. Whereas to enjoy broadcasting you need do nothing but exist. No effort is demanded. You may be likened to the blissful legendary being who lies at the foot of a fruit tree, opens his mouth, and allows the ripe fruit to fall thereinto. I am told that there are peculiarly constituted beings who while reading can listen-in to jazz, Beethoven's Ninth Symphony, or a discourse on Persian poetry. But such individuals are rare. The majority of us are incapable of listening-in while doing anything else. Thus every hour given to wireless is an hour taken away from other diversions, including especially the magazines.

But the arch-enemy of the magazine is the newspaper itself. In my youth the popular newspaper was a newspaper and nothing more. It was one article of mental diet. It is now a complete mental diet. It is still a newspaper, and even more of a newspaper than of old. But it is also everything else. It prints not only novels, but short stories. It prints essays. It has its humorous section. It gives you far more pictures in a month than any magazine gives you in two years. It treats of biography, history, geography, philosophy, science, education.

No writer is too proud to write for it, and it easily induces many of the greatest authorities on all these subjects to discuss them in its innumerable columns. It caters for women in such detail and with such fullness as to beat even fashion and housekeeping magazines on their own ground. Without counting the advertisements (which are in themselves a most rich and exciting entertainment), it provides daily as much printed matter as any monthly magazine, and more varied than any magazine. You may read the news at breakfast, the magazine stuff in the afternoon, and the fiction at even-tide, and still have enough reading left over for a sleepless hour in the night. Also, the newspaper, with large pages and no exasperating wire-stitching, is physically far easier to handle and read than a popular magazine.

I would say that the newspaper, taken as a whole, is the most compelling and brilliant and deservedly successful phenomenon in modern literature. It may have faults; it certainly has; but unreadableness is not among them, and lack of variety is not among them. It obviously must hit the magazine very hard. Nobody is to blame. Merely the terrestrial ball is rolling on, pursuant of the mightly scheme of evolution.

Unless I now plainly deny it, commentators in the Press will be saying at the end of the week that I have predicted the imminent demise of British magazines. I have not. I do not wish to exaggerate. I would not even go as far in pessimism as the "trade" apparently does. I think that British magazines are still strong, and they will continue to be strong. All I assert is that many of them have been losing circulation, and that all of them are being severely tried by non-magazine competition. I do not care at present to suggest a remedy. Remedies will doubtless be discovered.

I look across the Atlantic, but even in that great republic of magazine-readers, there has been, according to my latest first-hand information, a certain decline in magazines sales and a corresponding increase in book sales. The cases, however, are not parallel. The big American magazine is primarily an advertising medium. The literary matter of popular American magazines (some of which, by the way, are "dumped" into Britain at ruination prices) is assuredly not better than the literary matter of popular British magazines. But what counts over there is advertisements: which Americans love and trust with a confiding affection surpassing the love of women. There are tongue-tied American hobbledehoys who seriously believe that after an advertised short course of lessons they will become socially charming and capable of holding the attention of dinner-tables by aplomb and bright converse. (Perhaps they will — you never know.)

Withal the literary matter is carefully looked after by American magazine editors, and in a way that is not in the least British. A few weeks ago I got a letter from the editor of an important American magazine asking my advice about the treatment of "sex" in his periodical. Similar letters had evidently been sent to some other authors. No editor of a British magazine ever approached me for advice about the treatment of "sex," or about anything else.

And I received also a letter from the general editor of an extremely powerful and wealthy firm of magazine-publishers. This letter (which was only a circular letter and began "Dear Author") stated with precision the editorial requirements in fiction. It ended with these memorable words: *"We'll be watching the mails for an envelope from you."* Touching! Touching! The great editor watching his mails for my envelope! Nobody could possibly imagine any British magazine-editor wistfully watching his mails for the author's business envelope. Personally, I have no business envelope.

Perhaps there lies hidden here the germ of an idea for the remedy so urgently desired.

29 September 1927

Where English Fiction Surpasses French

The unexpected has happened. The impossible has happened. And from the whole French-reading world of Europe and the Americas will go up a tender sigh of relief. The enormous work of Marcel Proust, the work which occupied almost the whole of his creative life, the work which has enjoyed a planetary vogue surpassing that of any other modern novel among the intelligentsia, is concluded and published; and Mr. Scott Moncrieff, our arch-translator from foreign tongues, and Messrs. Chatto and Windus, Proust's English publishers, now know the immensity of the task which lies before them.

The work is not as long as *Clarissa*, but it is terrific. The first part is entitled *A la recherche du temps perdu* (which Mr. Scott Moncrieff courageously translates *Remembrance of Things Past*), and the second *Le Temps retrouvé* (which Mr. Scott Moncrieff has not yet translated, and which I courageously will not).

I have just read the closing pages, not without emotion. A year or two ago, I was permitted, in an essay contributed to a volume published in homage to Proust*, to make some very serious reservations about his work.

* *Marcel Proust : An English Tribute*, edited by Scott Moncrieff (1923).

I find now that I must maintain those reservations. Some of the later work I have read with difficulty, and some I have quite failed to read. Though I have no doubt whatever that the novel contains within its vast borders several small masterpieces, I question whether it is a masterpiece in its entirety. My chief objection to it is that the author's curiosity is so narrow. He will not even glance at whole regions of the human spectacle.

An eminent French critic said to me long ago: "The difference between modern English fiction and modern French is that the English is so much more complete. You can walk all round an English character in fiction. A French character seems to be in only two dimensions." Or words to that effect. I would apply this criticism to the work of Proust.

The French stay at home, where they know where they are. The English, both as men and as artists, are always rushing off in search of discomfort, ordeals, and obdurate material to conquer. The recently published *Letters of Gertrude Bell* (Benn, 2 vols., 2 guineas) occurs to my mind. Here was a young woman who had in England everything that a young woman could decently demand. She had even an admirable literary style, a sense of character, and a faculty of witty observation, which would have enabled her to write excellent novels about the upper middle-class. But no! She must needs wander forth in search of hardships and strangenesses. The British passion for discovery forced her eastwards. Go she must, and subdue Asiatic deserts, chiefs, and kings. Obviously, no matter how sincerely they were devoted to her, she must have been a polite rod for the backs of distinguished Orientals, for she was a masterful person and an arbitrary.

What she did was worth doing. Her "letters" have a continuous sensational interest. But a Frenchwoman, or a Frenchman either, would with bland Latin cynicism ask: "What possessed the odd, inquisitive creature? Had she not Belgrave-square and Hyde Park?"

She often used a caustic pen. She remarks, for instance: "There is little satisfaction to be got out of reviewers, whether they praise or blame." How sardonic, and how true! I must mention a most graphic description of her in Bagdad, by Mrs. Harold Nicolson, inserted in the second volume.

Or take a new novel, *Our Mr. Dormer* (Chattos), by R.H. Mottram, author of the justly esteemed *Spanish Farm Trilogy*. This is the simple tale of a little bank clerk who lived and died. But it is more. It is a dramatic conspectus of the whole of the nineteenth century. A really original, sound, and comprehensive work of fiction, not long, yet exhaustive. The chapter of the Jubilee fire has an impressive bigness. Mr. Mottram scarcely leaves a small East Anglian town, but he is as full of enterprise as Gertrude Bell herself, adventuring into all sorts of mysteries sociological, historical, municipal, sartorial, criminal, which Marcel Proust would not have moved a foot to see.

To return to Proust. At the finish of his book he frankly describes the feelings of the creator of a large work of imagination, in terms which are bound to move the heart of any author who has had a similar temerity. Thus:

"To give an idea of what it is, one must make comparisons drawn from the most elevated and various of the arts; for the writer, who moreover would have to show each character in opposing lights so as to give the work solidity, must prepare his book minutely, with continual regroupings of forces, as for an offensive, must endure it like a fatigue, must accept it like a rule, construct it like a church, follow it like a régime, vanquish it like an obstacle, win it like a friendship, over-nourish it like a baby, create it like a world, without leaving on one side those mysteries which probably can be explained only in other worlds, and of which the presentiment is what moves us most deeply in life and in Art. And in those large works are to be found parts which there was time only to sketch, and which would doubtless never have been finished, on account of the amplitude of the architect's plan. How many great cathedrals remain uncompleted? . . ."

And this (certainly autobiographical) detail — is it not touching? "The idea of death lodged itself in me as does a love. Not that I loved death, I detested it. But after having reflected upon it from time to time as one reflects upon a woman whom one has not yet begun to love, the thought of it adhered so completely to the deepest stratum of my mind that I could not occupy myself with anything without that thing encountering first the idea of death; and even if I reflected upon nothing at all and remained in perfect repose, the idea of death kept me company as continuously as the idea of myself."

The translations are my own, and I apologise for their fallacious infelicities.

6 October 1927

Why a Serial is Harder to Write than a Short Story

Serial fiction is now more than ever an important part of the daily paper, which cuts in and bids against the weekly and the monthly for attractive names and even for attractive tales. More pens than ever before are concocting or trying to concoct serials. Hence *How to write serial fiction*, by Michael Joseph and Marten Cumberland (Hutchinson, 6s.), ought to be interesting. It is. It will interest not only the literary-ambitious, but also the common reader with a sane curiosity about the going round of hidden wheels. The common reader in particular will be pleased to learn from the book what he wants in his serials, or what editors have decided he wants or ought to want.

The most diverting section of the book (one-fourth of the whole volume) is the chapter entitled "Serials I have written by Twelve Famous Serial Writers." I had very much heard of Arthur Applin, May Christie, May Edginton, Valentine, Louis Tracy, and Douglas Walshe. Berta Ruck, too, is a name familiar to me, and I observed with regret that this arch-serialist is not among the twelve. But so fame-tight are the various compartments which divide the world, and such is the blindness of man to phenomena which he is not accustomed to look at — I have no recollection of having previously heard or seen the names of John Chancellor, Jefferson Farjeon, Sydney Horler, John Hunter, Andrew Wood, or T. C. Bridges: all apparently stars of magnitude in their firmament.

I particularly like May Edginton, who has individuality and writes with force. "Serial writing is a business," she begins her contribution; and I would add: "All writing worth reading is a business." Miss Edginton, describing one of her serials, says: "It was a dangerous story to write . . . However I was content to write it and to sell it, not very advantageously . . . I knew I had a cast-iron film plot." A sound reason, which I applaud. Grave novelists may writhe at the reason; but I doubt whether there is a grave and readable novelist alive who in his deep and secret and wicked heart (where pretences cannot exist) would not feel responsive to the sinister whispering of such a reason. Shakespeare would. Shakespeare, in addition to being something of an artist, was a practical man, to whom writing plays was a business. I wish I had space to discuss Miss Edginton's very sensible propositions at length.

Messrs. Joseph and Cumberland, authors of this technical handbook, are full of wisdom. For instance, they say that purely humorous serials are extremely difficult to market. I have made this discovery for myself, and re-made it. I once wrote a serial called *The Card*, and laughed aloud as I wrote. But the thing was turned down and turned down. Ultimately, if a deceitful memory can for once be trusted, it appeared in *The Times* weekly edition. I know I only got £150 for the serial rights of it.

But Messrs. Joseph and Cumberland, while they describe the demands of the serial market in much accurate detail, do not, to my mind, give adequate instruction in the method of meeting the market. They insist heavily on subject and form, to the neglect of fundamental matters, and I think that they disclose their weakness in the strange statement that it is more difficult to write a short story than a serial. I join issue flatly. They might as well have said that it was more difficult for Wordsworth to write a sonnet than *The Prelude*. (See what a sad mess W. W. made of *The Prelude*, and see the perfection of his finest sonnets!) I admit that it is more difficult to write a good short story than a good first instalment of a serial. Any idiot can write a good first instalment, just as any idiot can write a good first act. Messrs. Joseph and Cumberland deal plenteously and sagaciously with the first instalment. They would have been better advised to deal plenteously and sagaciously with the tenth instalment. That is where the big trouble becomes acute. A serial is harder to write than a short story because it demands far more sustained imaginative power. Messrs. Joseph and Cumberland lay no stress on the supreme importance of imaginative power (which is quite a different affair from invention or fancy). The maintenance of imaginative power is indeed the big trouble, compared to which all merely technical troubles are naught. Why does nearly every serial sag in the middle? Because the author is imaginatively too weak to hold it up.

I can recall only one newspaper serial which never sagged — but only because it had a "cast-iron" plan. The author had the masterly idea of imperilling the virtue of the heroine — victim of villainous machinations — at the end of every second instalment. It was touch and go thrice a week. Readers could hardly live through every second night, hoping, fearing hoping. When the serial was nearing its close, the editor sent for the author and positively commanded him to draw out the agony indefinitely, which he honourably did. I believe that serial ran for about two years. In the end the heroine arrived immaculate at the altar, and 75 per cent. of the readers had a shameful feeling of disappointment.

The way of the serialist is full of pitfalls. Here is a specimen given by Messrs. Joseph and Cumberland. An editor summoned his serialist and said to him: "I see that next Wednesday you have in your story a particularly dramatic murder. Rather nasty, too." The serialist ably defended the murder. "Quite," replied the editor, "it is perfectly plausible, but that is not my point. The fact is, next Wednesday is Princess Mary's birthday, and I cannot have anything of an unpleasant nature appearing on that date in my columns." I have enjoyed *How to write serial fiction.*

A higher-brow work about fiction is *Scheherazade, or the Future of the English Novel*, by John Carruthers (Kegan Paul, 2s. 6d.). But it is less interesting than Messrs. Joseph and Cumberland's. I am unacquainted with the previous work of Mr. John Carruthers. (He seems to be a novelist himself.) Some of his *obiter dicta* are amazingly wrongheaded. Also the book, though tiny, is confused. Mr. Carruthers says that the novel of the future will be inspired by "the conception of organism." Let us hope so. I would that Mr. Carruthers' book has been one-tenth as much inspired by the concept of organism as the novels of, say, Eden Phillpotts. Still, Mr. Carruthers makes a few good points. As that if a novelist's work is to be significant he must be a man of strong and comprehensive beliefs, whereas the new men of to-day apparently believe in nothing, and use their gifts not creatively but to destroy. Again, he points out that novelists are "hopeless and obsolete" in their knowledge of science, and that "the most advanced in appearance and in their own estimations are in fact the most backward." True!

And he is almost right about the unsatisfactoriness of novels written from the point of view of one character. "The pattern in only one aspect is false; the true pattern combines different aspects . . . no one of which must be sacrificed to any other . . ." Five-sixths true. I have sinned myself, but I admit the high percentage of truth in the assertion. I wish that Mr. Carruthers had taken more care over his essay, which lacks not only pattern but style. And I wish that he had clearly summarised his conclusions. For it has not been vouchsafed to me precisely what his conclusions are.

13 October 1927

More Reading Done in England than in France

Feeling the need of an entr'acte in the tremendous drama of re-reading Gibbon's *Decline and Fall*, I rang down the curtain on the death of Julian, and went to the bar — the bar being a good foreign bookshop. I asked for a Dumas. (I mean the elder Dumas. Thirty years ago, the younger Dumas was smothering his father; to-day he is as dead as Lytton, while his father enjoys a second time on earth.) I got *Le Comte de Monte Cristo* (six volumes — like Gibbon) because I could not get the work I wanted. *Monte Cristo* is very good indeed, up to the escape; but it would be much better if it were shortened by one-half, as might easily be done. One often feels that Dumas was often influenced by the fact that his contracts were for payment by the line. By the way, Dumas' *Mémoires*, though he evidently had no passion for exactitude, contain magnificent stuff, and a one-volume edition of them, cut down to about 30 per cent. of the original matter, ought to be both valuable and popular in English.

To return. I did not obtain the Dumas I wanted, for the reason that it was out of print. This melancholy news really grieved me. Was it conceivable that the famous blue edition of Dumas at a franc apiece (now five francs) was no longer kept complete, even as regards some of its major items? This question answered, I asked another: Are the French fond of literature? And I was bound to reply that, as compared with the British, the French are not fond of literature. Such an answer seems at first perhaps too startling to be true. But I think it is true. And I have found many confirmations of its truth. In the first place, if Dumas were English he would certainly never be out of print. More, there would be several editions of him. There is, so far as I know, only one current edition of Dumas in French.

In the second place, to take a wider view of the situation, the French pay much less for their books than the British. They are a rich nation, but if a Frenchman were asked to pay English prices for his books, he would simply cease to pay.

In the third place, French authors are miserably remunerated. Few of them can live, or expect to live, on their earnings. This is the best test of a rich nation's bookishness.

In the third place, there is far less reviewing in France than in Britain: which is a proof that there is far less popular interest in books. Various English papers have a daily book-column, or columns, or page; no French. Further, French reviewing is frequently venal: that is to say, it is paid for by the interested parties and amounts to nothing but a disguised advertisement. Then, the French maintain no serious and scholarly weekly paper entirely devoted to books. They have nothing at all comparable to *The Times Literary Supplement*. Certainly they have *Les Nouvelles Littéraires*, a weekly got up to look like a daily paper, and lively and stimulating enough; but not nearly in the same class as the *Lit. Supp.*

In the fourth place, the French have very few circulating libraries, and no important ones. The French would merely shrug their Gallic shoulders if an ordinary commercial business ran an immense circulating library as an adjunct and helper of its staple trade; as is done, with success, in Britain.

In the fifth place, the French middle and lower-middle class in the provinces simply do not read books. This I have observed again and again. The same classes in England do read. They may not read Shakespeare, Dante, and Homer, but they read something in covers.

In the sixth place, the production of cheap editions, and good cheap editions, and good cheap editions of great catholicity, is vastly larger and better in Britain than in France. The Everyman Library has no rival in France. And as for the famous Temple Classics, no French publisher has ever come within a thousand miles of it.

In the seventh place, the British public demands, and gets, far, far more than the French in the way of biography, memoirs, history, manuals of all kinds, and works of reference of all kinds: for which it pays cheerfully. There is, at any rate within my knowledge, no good up-to-date encyclopaedia in French. And I would say the same for dictionaries, including word-dictionaries. Where is the French equivalent of the *Dictionary of National Biography*? Where is there a genuinely comprehensive French word-dictionary? I know of none. The dictionary of the French Academy is merely comic. (Two or three years ago it excluded from its pages, on political grounds, the word "defeatist"!) There are French word-dictionaries which have begun excellently and grandly, and then foundered in misery, for lack of public interest. Their first volumes are apt to include "A. to G.," and their second and last "H. to Z."! The only fairly decent French dictionary for common use that I am familiar with is the little *Larousse*. It is a handy enough tome, but without any serious pretensions. The selection of English word-dictionaries is quite considerable. And in addition we have the finest and most complete word-dictionary in the world.

In the eighth place, the general machinery for the distribution and supply of books, bad enough in Britain, is much worse in France. There are plenty of towns in France with forty appetising cake-shops, and not a bookshop worth a billberry. Upon ordering a modern book in a French city of universal renown it has happened to me to see an expression on the face of the shopman which said: "Well, you *may* get it — in the course of the year."

Being intensely and characteristically British, I hate to think that my own country is not the very pattern of slackness, inefficiency, ignorance and stupidity. But obvious facts, now that I have steadily faced them, compel me to the conclusion that our inferiority-complex in relation to France about the things of the mind is grotesque.

I admit that in France there is a very small lettered class which probably has a finer and surer taste in books, and a more redoubtable love for books, than any such class in Britain. You can detect it in the continuous demand for special and limited editions. This for our chastening! I admit also that French authors are on the whole less money-grubbing than English. But this is only because in France there is no money for authors to grub.

20 October 1927

A Woman Novelist's Much-Discussed Story of Religious Mania

Two volumes, respectively by Mrs. or Miss Ray Strachey (I am quite sure the author is a woman: I have not seen her name on a title-page before) and Professor Julian Huxley, have reached me together. They make a most curiously contrasting pair, and between them illustrate in a dramatic manner the reassuring fact that civilisation does move.

Mrs. Strachey's book is a novel, *Shaken by the Wind* (Faber and Gwyer, 7s. 6d.). The author calls it "a story of fanaticism." She would have been more exact to call it a story of religious mania. The scene is chiefly laid in Delaware, U.S.A., in the first half of the nineteenth century. Mrs. Strachey has got hold of a wonderful theme; and, within limitations, she has handled it well. The tale is probably based on some real happenings. All the characters, except about two, have the type of mind (now happily becoming as rare as, for instance, the Sibthorpia plant) which believes in a deity omnipotent, omniscient, and omnipresent — but not unknowable. This type of mind knows the will of its God with absolute certainty, and can and does on nearly all occasions state positively what that Being wants and does not want. Further, it can "wrestle" with its God, and emerge alive and very active from the formidable encounter.

In my youth I was personally acquainted with various specimens of this type, and from my own imperfect knowledge I would say that Mrs. Strachey understands it profoundly; indeed she understands it in a rather original manner, and her irony concerning it is immanent and very subtle. One's knowledge of the curiosities of human nature is appreciably increased as one reads.

The story grows compacter and weightier and more impressive from the point where the majority of the characters are gathered together into a community withdrawn from the world. The whole business is absurd, silly, and mad: but it is convincing. Thenceforward the extraordinary richness of the subject blossoms out in fresh forms on every page. Erotomania, as not seldom, goes with religious mania, and truly astounding scenes follow one after another in an ascending scale of piquancy, culminating in the birth of a Messiah (with a joke by one of the more malicious personages about the possibility of there being a competition in Messiahs). And you cannot put your hand on any passage and say: "*Here* the narration slips off the edge of the precipice into the gulf of the preposterous." Because the narration never does slip off the edge of the precipice. I hate the word "inevitability" (that cliché of reviewers hampered by a too restricted vocabulary of praise), but the sequence of events in *Shaken by the Wind* has some of the quality of inevitability.

The novel has caused, and is causing, a lot of very favourable talk among people who reckon they know the difference between a book and a bathbun. It well deserves praise. But in my opinion it is over-praised. The writing has no distinction whatever, and even bad grammar abounds in it (not that I would give too much importance to grammar; we are all sinners against the light).

Again, Mrs. Strachey's narrative method is very loose and ramshackle. She seems to despise dialogue, which is a great help in the maintenance of interest, and yet she will use it where there is no need for it, while eschewing it where it is blazingly necessary. Further, she seems to be not always able to feel the difference between a major scene and a minor scene. Thus (on page 155) an interview of crucial importance between Rufus, the arch prophet, and Thomas, an amateur ditto, is described anyhow in a negligent paragraph without a single phrase of dialogue. Also she is frequently not attentive to details the persuasive realism of which would have added considerably to her general effect; and she several times appears to get quite lost in a sort of spreading delta of the streams of narrative. Lastly she betrays, in the management of equivocal situations, that verbal clumsiness which is the mark of the courageous woman-writer.

In sum, I would say that the theme has given more to the author than the author has given to the theme. Withal, Mrs. Strachey has comprehended the theme. And her character-drawing is excellent.

Professor Julian Huxley's book is one of a series under the general title, *What I Believe*, and other authors in the series are Father Ronald Knox (*The Belief of Catholics*) and Miss Maud Royden (*I Believe in God*). Professor Huxley calls his volume *Religion Without Revelation* (Benn,

8s. 6d.). What a difference between the crude, hot certainties of nine-teenth century Delaware, and the cautious, dignified and respectful attitude of the author of *Religion Without Revelation*! I think that possibly dogmatists may have much to learn from men of science about decorum and humility in presence of the conception of a supreme being. The book is discursive, especially at the beginning, and would have lost much by compression.

In the matter of the aforesaid conception, even Professor Huxley has a certain slight tendency toward dogma. He says in one sentence that he is agnostic and in the next that he is "not merely an agnostic." According to the way my brain works you either are an agnostic or you are not. If you are "not merely an agnostic" then you cease to be an agnostic.

Professor Huxley gives an excellent and fair account of the present situation in regard to creeds, and there are two brilliant chapters dealing with comparative religion. He utters wise words about belief — wise, but hard for the sentimental. Thus: "I hold . . . that neither faith nor agnosticism is in itself the better way, but that each has its right occasions . . . In fact, I hold that beliefs are essential tools of the human mind — no more than tools, but no less than essential." Here he is applying to the unknowable the "working hypothesis" method of the scientific inquirer. But perhaps if he had employed the phrase "working hypothesis" he might have given offence. And he has obviously striven not to give offence. *Religion Without Revelation* has real value.

27 October 1927

Margaret Kennedy's New Novel about the Dilettante Class: "The Writing is Nearly Faultless, But —"

Margaret Kennedy's new novel, *Red Sky at Morning* (Heinemann, 7s. 6d.), is this day published, and the publication is an event of genuine importance for a very large number of regular readers, that ardent tribe who insist upon keeping an eye on things, who take the printing-press seriously, who take themselves seriously, and without whose perennial interest imaginative literature and the makers thereof would soon be in rather a poor way. Yet *Red Sky at Morning* is only the third novel of a young author whose first novel produced no impression on the public mind.

All to-day's curiosity and discussions are concerned with the writer of one sole book, *The Constant Nymph*, a novel which most of us much admired, a few adversely criticised, but nobody disdained. After several years the principal characters in *The Constant Nymph* — and especially the nymph herself — still radiantly live in the general memory. Which is a great deal to say for any novel.

Miss Kennedy's prestige had to face an ordeal when the book was trans-mogrified into a popular play. Not that I would damn the play without reserve! The first act was brilliant; it *was* the book, though perhaps imperfectly comprehensible to non-readers of the book. But the second act was bad: the third was worse: and both were well calculated to kill any desire of a non-reader to become a reader. Nevertheless the prestige of

Miss Kennedy has survived the ordeal intact. And to-day everyone will be wanting to know what everyone else thinks of the successor to *The Constant Nymph*. An enviable position for a young novelist; but a position, too, of extreme delicacy.

All the characters in the new novel, with about three exceptions, belong to the dilettante class. The exceptions are a young country clergyman, the dame of a country house, and the dame's plain-faced daughter, who expressed in inferior literature what — had her features been different — she might have expressed more effectively in children and the revulsions of a husband or so.

The dilettante class — already large and, I fear, increasing — is terrible. Its members are idle, they are uncreative; they rarely earn a living; they suffer from the worst of all vices, self-pity and spiritual pride, they have an infallible taste for the latest third-rate in all the arts, with every succeeding fashion they display anew the originality of sheep; they talk too much; they are parasitic. I would not be too hard on them, for we are all God's creatures; but they do generally strike one as uppish, snobbish, tedious and futile.

I do not disapprove of them as material for a novel. Indeed I like objectionable characters in a novel, provided the author shows adequate appreciation of their objectionableness. Miss Kennedy's ironic strokes, though admirable enough, are perhaps too few and too gentle. With the result that *Red Sky at Morning* superficially resembles a mere fashionable, shop-finished novel about dilettantes: which it is not.

Further, there is to my mind too much dialogue in this book. The damnable slickness of dilettante chatter about life and the dailiness of the day is excellently reproduced: but at too great length, and without due regard for the dramatic welfare of the theme. Even when a character is alone the author will divide him into two beings, A and B, and allow the pair to indulge in back-chat.

Often, the reader cannot without going back be sure what character in a dialogue is speaking what lines. The author herself seems now and then to get lost in the talk. There is a disconcerting discrepancy in the conversation on pp. 162-163. The over-prevalence of dialogue was bound to enfeeble the narrative interest; and it does.

But the interest is still more seriously prejudiced by the fact that the six or eight leading characters are of nearly equal importance, and that at the beginning of the book the reader is misled as to their relative values in the scheme of the story. Novels must have central figures, in order that the interest may be centralised. The interest of *Red Sky at Morning* is too diffused. The main theme does not emerge clear. Every novel should have a main theme that can be stated in ten words. The theme of *The Constant Nymph* was stated in three words — in the title. I could not state the main theme of *Red Sky at Morning* in a thousand words, because I am not sure what it is. I have not managed to discern, in the profusion of episodes, the author's general direction, or even tendency. Nor am I sure which of the characters are hero and heroine.

And theme or no theme, hero and heroine or no hero and no heroine, there is hardly a thrill of excitement until about two-thirds of the way through the book — at the point where the startling betrothal of Emily is announced, with a hint of a possible sinister reason for it. The emotional mood of expectancy is maintained for only a few pages. Though excellent small situations abound, there is no really dominating situation, of either tragedy or comedy.

These criticisms are grave, especially when one admires the talent of an author as much as I admire that of Miss Kennedy. I can and do say that the writing of the book is as near faultless as makes no matter, that very great pains have obviously been given to the work, that the character-drawing is convincing, that the action, taken episode by episode is convincing, that every page has distinction of attitude and of thought, that some scenes recall the exquisite and touching piquancy of some scenes in *The Constant Nymph*, that some characters — such as William and Emily — are of the Sanger blood, and that a pleasing humour and wit pervade the entire affair. All very well! Yes! But I have been disappointed. My fault! I expected Miss Kennedy to produce two very considerable novels one after the other. I ought to have known better. From the third onwards Beethoven's more important symphonies are the odd numbers. Miss Kennedy's will, I hope, be the even numbers. Her second was certainly important. Her third is not an Eroica. Her fourth must be.

3 November 1927

Some Personal Memories of Conrad: "Cad" as a New Word: His "Twilight"

Three years since Joseph Conrad died. And now arrives his *Life and Letters*, edited by G. Jean Aubry (Heinemann, 2 vols., 2 guineas). I have long maintained that English biographies are too long. The present work is in two volumes, over 700 pages in all — large pages, closely-printed pages. At first sight of the vast edifice one is intimidated and resentful. The actual biography, however, is quite short: only about 170 pages. The rest is letters — which you need not read unless you happen to be interested in letters exciting and distinguished and written by a great man.

The index to the work is admirable: but the table of contents and the chapter divisions are imperfect. The table of contents of Vol. 1 gives no clue whatever to the contents of half that volume. And a new chapter ought certainly to begin on page 173. The bibliography at the end of the second volume is not a bibliography of Conrad, but a bibliography of the extensive and varied sources of M. Aubry's biography. A bibliography of Conrad, accessible to the general public, is much needed. Mr. T.J. Wise ought to see to this, and to copyright his labours, so that they may not be stolen by piratical and parasitical Americans and others.

M. Aubry is probably better known to the lettered world in Paris than in London. He has already made a name as a musical critic. He now stands forth in England as the author of a very important biography very well done. M. Aubry was an old and intimate friend of Conrad's. He has not allowed this most valuable friendship to excuse him from exhaustive research. His industry has obviously been remarkable, and so far as I can judge his accuracy is impeccable. He understands what a creative artist is.

He writes well, and he writes concisely. Would that all our biographies of great men, and especially statesmen, could be confined to 170 pages. What a saving of time and temper!

For myself I do not see how this biography can ever be superseded. So long as the novel-form persists Conrad will be read, and so long as Conrad is read this biography will have to be read. It is a prime source, and nothing can possibly disestablish it. So that M. Aubry is to be congratulated upon his debut in the crowded world of English literature.

I first met Conrad about 28 years ago (I pretend to neither accuracy nor industry, but I am sure that the meeting occurred towards the end of the last century), at the house of H. G. Wells. Even then, from the way he talked, one could perceive at once and all the time that creative writing for him was not a literary pursuit, but a sanguinary war, in which victories were won at an enormous cost. His working days were terrible. The most suitable epitaph for the artist in him would be that which Francis Adams wrote for his own life as a whole:

> Bury me with clenched hands
> And with eyes open wide,
> For in storm and struggle I lived,
> And in struggle and storm I died.

At that period Conrad's command of colloquial spoken English was rather imperfect. Even towards the end of his life he could not utter ten words of English without betraying by his accent a foreign origin. Then, he was still more spectacularly a foreigner. Nor did he really understand English literature, which nevertheless he read eagerly and admired much. I remember his dramatic declaration that Milton was not first-rate. (I will not be sure, and I do not wish to traduce a friend; but my recollection is that H. G. Wells supported him in this deplorable position.) It would have been too onerous a business for me to defend *Paradise Lost,* but I did raise my poor shield over those unsurpassed masterpieces, *Lycidas* and *Comus.* No! Conrad would have none of Milton. He called Milton "woolly." I never mentioned Milton to him again.

But a still stronger, and a more fantastic, instance of the gaps in his knowledge and comprehension of English occurred when we were discussing some trifling literary scandal. Somebody — I forget whom, but it was no doubt Henley — had referred to R. L. Stevenson as "a man of three letters." (There are writers who cannot keep off the classics.) Conrad took me aside and said "Of course, I know the Latin reference, but Stevenson was never a thief. What English word is meant? Is it 'pig?' "

I said: "The word has not been printed, but I think it must be 'cad.' "

" 'Cad'?" he said. "What is that? I have never heard the word."

At first I could not believe this, but he positively assured me that he really never had heard the word "cad." He had already written one first novel in English. True, it was dotted with locutions which, while more or less correct, no Englishman would have enjoyed.

I remember another meeting, accidental, in the office of the late J.B. Pinker, his agent and mine. He was very melancholy. He needed, but did not want, a change. I suggested some new form of activity — I forget what. He shook his head sadly. "*Non!*" he replied in French. "*Le pli est pris.*" To translate this as "The crease is formed" would be ineffective. One could only render it: "I'm in the groove and can't get out." This brief remark affected me as much as a phrase in the letter which accompanied his gift to me of a copy of *The Rover*. *"Twilight lies already on these pages."* It did.

My last meeting, also accidental, with Conrad was at the house of a mutual friend, Mme. Alvar. I had not seen him for some years, and for a few minutes he failed to recognise me. Then he suddenly came across the room to me and gripped my shoulders with both hands. His dark eyes were burning into mine, his broad shoulders shaking. "My dearrr Bennett," he said, in his earnest, formidable voice. "You have been my faithful friend for 25 years, and I do not recognise you! Forgive me." Believe me, I was profoundly touched, and could scarcely speak to him.

10 November 1927

Two English Humorists, and Mr. Osbert Sitwell's Poisoned Chalice

Punch ought to be a critic of national and domestic life. And I should think it is, to a certain extent. Its misfortune is that it has no serious competitor. Its defects are that its political cartoons present no interest whatever, that its draughtsmanship is not on the whole good enough for its great tradition, that it has too many jokes about children and the minor domesticities, and that it gives a general effect of smallness by trying to deal with too many things. Why, for example, should it handle plays and books — unless indeed it handled them in a humorous way: which usually it does not?

On the other hand, it publishes absolutely first-rate comic and serio-comic verse (for instance, A.P. Herbert's), quite as good as Calverley's or J.K. Stephen's — indeed occasionally, in my opinion, better. Some of the captions under moderately funny drawings are extremely funny. Its weekly scattered collection of misprints and press-bloomers, with the curt comments on them, make for joy; and some of its "sketches without words" live in the memory and deserve to do so. Who could forget "The Boy who breathed on the glass at the British Museum", or could even think of it without a smile of thanksgiving to the artist? Yes, on balance, one could not *not* see *Punch*.

Nevertheless I regret, and shall always regret — till it alters itself, and it won't alter itself, being too prosperous — that *Punch* is not more down-right, more ruthless, less careful, less urbane, less infernally prim, and wider and ruder in its grasp of British existence. I do not wish it to be like *La Vie Parisienne*, which has only one topic and which, despite some brilliant drawings, is tedious. But I would have it learn a bit from the ferocity of *Le Rire*, and one or two German weeklies. And I would not in the least mind if *Punch* papas and mammas had to have an argument now and then as to the advisability of leaving the esteemed periodical on the drawing-room table.

Further, I would have it in colours. Why Continental weeklies can be printed from end to end in colour, and why even French dailies can give illustrations in colour, while the same thing cannot be achieved in Britain, is a mystery. Newspaper proprietors have striven to explain the mystery to me, but they have failed.

I was moved to consider the case of *Punch* by the perusal of books by two of its principal literary contributors: A.P. Herbert and E.V. Knox. Mr. Herbert's *Misleading Cases* (Methuens, 5s.) is more than a legal satire; it is a general satire on certain aspects of English life. It is very good: restrained, effective, rich, elegant, and subtle. Twenty-one "cases" are "reported" and not one is not excellent. But the book, in continuous reading, gives an impression of monotony. It is on a high level, but it is all the same. Also it ignores entirely several fertile fields for destructive satire.

Mr. Herbert, to judge by his (unanswerable) letters to *The Times*, is in politics a reactionary. Reactionaries are very useful persons, and without them we should soon rush headlong to the devil. Yet, were Mr. Herbert not hampered by *Punch* habits of thought and expression, he might perhaps react with a greater elasticity and resilience. Otherwise said, he walks too delicately, and he insufficiently strays from high-roads.

Awful Occasions (Methuens, 5s.) is a shining example of Mr. E.V. Knox's talent, though it contains one or two items too slight to deserve reprinting. Mr. Knox's prose is as good as Mr. Herbert's. It has several of the characteristics of Mr. Herbert's. Indeed, so strong is the *Punch* influence, there are passages in it which nobody not a Home Office expert could from internal evidence positively swear had not been written by Mr. Herbert. (And similarly of Mr. Herbert's book and Mr. Knox.) Mr. Knox occasionally has a disconcerting tang which makes me yearn for more tangs. *Bluebells*, for instance, is a fundamental criticism of the modern love of nature, as it is a criticism of all Mr. Wells's prophetic novels. It lifts the veil of the future and shows hell forming faintly but clearly in the middle distance. It is divertingly witty, but its essential humour frightens you if you try to stand up to it.

In Mr. Osbert Sitwell's *England Reclaimed* (Duckworth, 7s. 6d.) you meet a satirist of a different type. Mr. Sitwell is not a contributor to *Punch,* and he is not likely to be. He accepts nothing without the strictest and most hostile examination. He is a fundamental objector, with the bellicose, haughty and ruthless spirit of a Renaissance prince. His artistic existence is a crusade. He can be at once bitter and courtly. He will hand you the poisoned chalice, watch you fall in agony, contemplate your corpse with a bland smile, and go out calmly for a constitutional! He is that sort of man. In technique Messrs. Herbert and Knox have nothing to learn from him. On the contrary he may have something to learn of perfection from them. His book contains some poetry, much fine verse, and some prose divided to resemble verse.

He is often unfair, and seldom judicial. He adores England, and hates it with love. He is English, yet his mind is not English; his mind has no nationality. He is totally unlike anybody not named Sitwell. He sets out to anger England, succeeds, and is satisfied. The title of the book may mislead the hasty, for Mr. Sitwell has the good gift of using words as if they had never been used before. A more descriptive title for plain readers would have been *The England that is gone or going redeemed from oblivion.*

Some of the pieces combine beauty and a simple, lethal sarcasm with strange felicity. On p. 29 is a short poem which begins with a lovely descriptive passage. It ends,

> Then the Family would come down,
> Like so many cats after the birds, she always said.
> The snowflakes would sway down,
> And thud,
>   thud,
>   thud,
> would sound the falling pheasants.

For myself I can savour the *Punch* school, and I can savour Mr. Osbert Sitwell. He fulfils a necessary moral function in our life. He exasperates. We need to be exasperated. We are not exasperated enough. You may resent Mr. Sitwell as much as you please, but you cannot ignore him. His darts stick and rankle.

17 November 1927

Life and the Novel: Witty Author Laughs at the "Big Guns" and the Public

I now announce a jolly book, by Mr. E.M. Forster, author of those justly famous novels *Howards End* and *A Passage to India* (and other good novels). When I saw the title of Mr. Forster's new book, *Aspects of the Novel* (Edward Arnold, 7s.6d.), and saw also on the title-page that Mr. Forster is a Fellow of King's, Cambridge, and read in the introductory note that the volume comprises The Clark Lectures "under the auspices of Trinity College, Cambridge," I was seriously apprehensive of ennui. The title is ill-chosen and forbidding; the subject rouses terrible apprehensions; and the mere word "lecture" affrights me. I once listened to a college lecture at Cambridge — or was it Oxford? — and went to sleep. I once read a book on the English novel, the late Professor Walter Raleigh's — and went to sleep. And *Aspects* seems to suggest the laborious composition of some University literary professor, in (say) Omaha or Nebraska, who tries to make up by earnestness what he lacks in pep.

Mr. Frank Swinnerton is reported to have been engaged (perhaps an engagement not quite amounting to a betrothal) for years upon a work on the English novel. I have been pining for that work; it is certain to be good. But if it is better than Mr. Forster's it will be good with a profane adverb. Mr. Forster has to a considerable extent assuaged my longing for the thesis of Mr. Swinnerton.

Mr. Forster is probably less like a lecturer than any lecturer ever was before. Had I been privileged to hear his remarks I should not have gone to sleep. He is colloquial, and glories in being so. He is larkish, witty, humorous, epigrammatic, full of sly fun. He laughs at himself, you (the public), the big guns, the entire art of fiction. He takes the side of Wells in the great quarrel of Wells v. Henry James. In asserting that the big English novels stand on a lower plane than the big Continental novels, the only examples of big Continental novels which he cites in support of his contention are

100

Russian novels. He praises me handsomely, and then knocks me out with three homicidal words.* All these things, and many others, endear him to me.

But what more than anything endears me to him is his eager admission that he is only a "pseudo-scholar," and his defence of pseudo-scholars: "We are a very large and quite powerful class, eminent in Church and State, we control the education of the Empire, we lend to the Press such distinctions as it consents to receive, and we are a welcome asset at dinner-parties." Good! I have hitherto tried to conceal the fact that I am only a pseudo-scholar. I will try no more. I state exultantly that I am a pseudo-scholar.

Withal, Mr. Forster profoundly knows what he is talking about; he knows in a manner and with an understanding possible only to a creative artist and impossible to any real scholar, because no real scholar can be also a creative artist. Nobody intelligent enough to be interested in the higher manifestations of the art and craft of fiction could read his book without both pleasure and profit — to say nothing of the mere almost continuous amusement which accompanies the lecturing.

Mr. Forster has an enlightening way of explaining the differences between real people and characters in novels. He points out that of the five principal human experiences — birth, eating, sleeping, loving and dying, three are inadequately treated — birth, eating and sleeping. "When a baby arrives in a novel it usually has the air of having been posted." (Not true of Tolstoy.) He says that food in fiction is mainly social, whereas in life it is mainly nutritive. Sleep and dreams are handled perfunctorily in the novel. Dreams "are introduced with a purpose, and that purpose is not the character's life as a whole, but that part of it he lives while awake. He is never conceived as a creature a third of whose life is spent in darkness." (This seems to me to be a rather fundamental criticism of all novels without exception.)

He shows that love has far less importance in life than in fiction, and he furnishes reasons for this. Incidentally he says, truly: "The constant sensitiveness of characters for each other — even in writers called robust like Fielding — is remarkable, and has no parallel in life except among people who have plenty of leisure." I think that Mr. Forster is the first person to note this important difference between life and fiction.

Read him, too, on the two sorts of life which we live concurrently, the life in time and the life by values. "I only saw her for five minutes, but it was worth it." There you have the two sorts of life compared in a sentence. Then he displays the difference between a "story" and a "novel." A "story" relates one event after another, without any connection between them except their sequence in time. A "novel" has to include life by values as well. And now we come to the question of plot. "A plot is a narrative of events," like a story, but, "with the emphasis on causality." " 'The king died and then the queen died' is a story. 'The king died and then the queen died of grief' is a plot." It would be difficult to be at once more illuminating and more succinct.

* Writing of the "memorable" *Old Wives' Tale*, Forster decides "it misses greatness."

On the difference between "flat" characters and "round" Mr. Forster is equally brilliant. Dickens's characters are nearly all flat. Mrs. Bertram, in *Mansfield Park*, is generally flat, but sometimes round. All complex novels must have some flat characters (that is, characters who are identified by a single characteristic or small group of characteristics), otherwise they would never end. "The test of a round character is whether it is capable of surprising in a convincing way. If it never surprises, it is flat. If it does not convince, it is flat pretending to be round."

I say that I never met this kind of perspicacity in literary criticism before. I could quote scores of examples of similar startling excellence; and a very notable one about the spirit of "prophecy" in fiction.

Mr. Forster twice calls his work "ramshackly." Here and there it is a bit ramshackly, as in the pages on Defoe and in the brief speculations on the future of the novel. But speaking generally, it has order and it has comprehensiveness. What I miss in it is a discussion of "creative power." There is only one short reference to this tremendous topic, on p. 107. Mr. Forster puts it in the very centre of the whole problem. What does creative power depend on? Not on truth, because novels can be true without any breath of life, whereas novels quivering with life can be quite strikingly false (Balzac's, for instance). Well, what *does* it depend on, spring from? One day, Mr. Forster might attempt to answer this perhaps unanswerable question.

24 November 1927

A Strange Work on Art and a "Dazzling" Novel

This is an age of handbooks, and the handbooks are yearly getting shorter. There are handbooks and handbooks. The title of the latest series to reach me is alluring: *Mental Handicaps*. The man who thought of this series must be a genius and invaluable to publishers. The title of the particular volume which has engaged my eager attention is *Mental Handicaps in Art*, by Theo. B. Hyslop, M.D., C.M., M.P.C.(Hon.), M.R.C.P.E., F.R.S.E., etc., etc., (Baillière Tindal and Cox, 3s.6d.). The booklet comprises 120 sparsely charactered pages.

A foreword by Arthur Thomson, M.B., F.R.C.S., LL.D., D.C.L., ends on page xvii. Mr. Thomson is professor of anatomy. The core of his introduction seems to be in this sentence: "It is a common experience, in these days, that the human figure is often represented in stone or graphic form by a type of artist whose virtues are extolled by a certain class of critic. What is their aim, what is their ideal? Their efforts are characterised by a lack of that sense of fitness which is an essential feature of Nature." Etc., etc.

It is a pity that Professor Thomson does not give instances. He is too vague. The impression he leaves is simply that he is talking about something which he does not like. I fancy that, were El Greco a living painter, he would object to El Greco. Still, El Greco after three centuries is more highly esteemed to-day than ever.

Then comes a preface by the author himself. Dr. Hyslop, in addition to being an author, is a physician, a painter ("his canvases have adorned the walls of the Royal Academy"), an orchestral conductor and a musical critic. I will assume that he is an A1 doctor, a fine painter, an inspiring conductor, and a penetrating musical critic. But I am not quite sure that he can write.

The core of his preface seems to be in this sentence: "It is sadly to be feared that some individual members of our great Empire are, either through indifference to their own judgments or from proneness to be affected by alien subversive interests, thereby subscribing to a trend which the great tribunal of time might perchance label as one of degeneracy." I do not know what this means. I do not, for example, know how one can "subscribe" to a "trend"? And I cannot see why Professor Thomson and Dr. Hyslop should drag in Nature, Time, and the Empire.

One would have supposed that after the Foreword and the Preface, preliminaries would be done with. Not at all. The booklet itself begins thus: "The object of this small book is to endeavour to draw the attention of students to some of the mental pitfalls which bestrew their paths," etc., etc. To which I would incidentally reply that the object of the booklet is not to endeavour; it is to draw attention. Also that pitfalls cannot "bestrew" a path.

The entire booklet is written in this style. And simultaneously in several other styles. Thus Rembrandt is described as the "artist-king." Thus, of a number of artists from Inigo Jones to Turner, it is said that "*although of lowly extraction*, they achieved distinction by sheer industry and hard work." (My italics.) Did they now! And what is the distinction between industry and hard work?

Dr. Hyslop has specialised in idiocy, lunacy, and the "borderland" between the insane and the sane. He does not plainly say so, but I suspect his general conclusion to be that the leaders and followers of modern movements in art are off their nuts. He uses a boss word, "paranoic." It would be more comprehensible to say "subject to delusions." But "Paranoic" is a boss word, and well conveys that sense of pitying disdain which assuredly animates Dr. Hyslop in regard to modern art. He may be right. Who can tell? Anyhow, his criticisms would apply with much force to a play called *Hamlet* — a sad example of unhealthy decadence no doubt due to the ravages of paranoia in its diseased author. One phrase in Dr. Hyslop's booklet I have understood and agree with: "The higher the nervous organisation, and the finer the intellectual or emotional temperament, the less the tolerance of alcohol."

I have read better handbooks than *Mental Handicaps in Art*, as to which I neither assert nor deny that it is just tosh. Dr. Hyslop has himself written another handbook: *Mental Handicaps in Golf*. This is probably better than the one under review. I can conceive that Dr. Hyslop is somewhat more convincing on golf than on art.

A novel entitled *Jew Süss* was published some months ago. Its author, Dr. Feuchtwanger, is about to visit this city. He will undoubtedly be lionised. His book has had an enormous sale in English. Everybody who respects himself has read it, and about 95 per cent. of its readers admire it extremely. It has just been banned from the public libraries of Glasgow. (Rather late in the day.) I would like to know whether Dr. Hyslop diagnoses paranoia in the author — or in the Glasgow Public Libraries

Committee. A nice question, meet to be seriously considered by the distinguished alienist.

And I have just read two novels (if novels they can sanely be called) which I fear must be the decadent fruits of paranoia. The first is *Tarka the Otter*, by Henry Williamson (Putnam, 7s.6d.). Instead of dealing with mankind, Mr. Williamson deals with otters, fish and other aquatic and amphibious beings. His knowledge of them and his imaginative sympathy with them are really astonishing. But is not this preoccupation with beasts and fish a sure symptom of paranoia? *Tarka the Otter* has been very highly praised by some of the finest literary critics in our depraved land. For example, by Edward Garnett. I agree that it is marvellous. And the writing of it is marvellous. Indeed, to my mind, the writing of it is too marvellous. I consider it to be over-written, marked by a certain preciosity. The author has searched too often and too long for the utterly right word. But I have no other criticism.

The second novel is *The Bridge of San Luis Rey*, by Thornton Wilder (Longmans, 7s.6d.). I had never heard of Mr. Wilder, but I find that he has previously published *The Cabala. The Bridge of San Luis Rey* deals, I regret to say, with life in the early eighteenth century in such mad places as Lima. And a strange and hot decadent lot the characters indeed are! Paranoics, nearly every one of them, and their creator a paranoic, according to what I can gather of the definitions of Dr. Hyslop. A horrid qualm seizes me — I am a paranoic myself. In my opinion *The Bridge of San Luis Rey* is an absolutely first-rate work. It dazzled me by its accomplishment. The writing, simple, straight, *juste*, and powerful, has not been surpassed in the present epoch. The author does not search for the right word. He calls; it comes. Here is a sample of the writing: "She saw that the people of this world moved about in an armour of egotism, drunk with self-gazing, athirst for compliments, hearing little of what was said to them, unmoved by the accidents which befell their closest friends, in dread of all appeals that might interrupt their long communion with their own desires."

1 December 1927

The American Mind and the British

In my opinion it is easier to write books than to sell them. Other authors may disagree with me, but publishers will certainly agree. In fact, to hear some publishers talk, you might be excused for thinking that they, and not the authors, deserve the chief credit for the literary successes, both artistic and commerical, of the present age. If Shakespeare had lived to-day, his publisher would doubtless refer self-complacently to "my *Hamlet*." His theatre-manager would certainly do so.

In America selling books is a business, whereas in Britain it is too often a superior, lordly, and distinguished profession. In America men of business explore the possibilities of markets for books. About two years ago a group of explorers came to the conclusion that there were quantities of potential readers in outlying parts of the greatest republic who were not being adequately catered for. (It should be remembered that in America there are no circulating libraries and no "chain" retail shops where you can buy a piece of court-plaster and borrow a book at the same time — and almost at the same counter.) Then the Book of the Month Club came into being.

The Book of the Month Club is now about eighteen months old, and has a membership of some 45,000. The members pay no subscription. They merely sign a form to the effect that they will buy a selected book once a month at a price not exceeding three dollars. They are not even asked to pay in advance for their volumes. The book is sent, and in 99 cases out of 100 the money for it is sent in return. Americans are a trustful race, and their confidence in one another is justified by results.

In Britain we are more cautious. In Britain department stores will not accept even cheques as cash from strangers. Goods are not despatched until cheques have been cleared. Why not? I have never noticed, in commercial transactions, that Americans are more dependable than Britons. The reason for excessive caution probably is that British houses have not really thought the matter out in percentages.

The selected monthly book of the Book of the Month Club is chosen by a committee of authors, presided over by Professor Canby, who started the (American) *Saturday Review* some years ago. The decision of the authors "goes": by which I mean that the business management has to accept it and does accept it. The committee also prepares a list of ten or a dozen "honourable mention" books, and the club managers say to the members: "Now, if you don't care for our selected book of the month, you can have instead any one of the ten or a dozen other books." Also if a member doesn't like the look of a volume actually received he is at liberty to exchange it.

The club does not undersell the booksellers but it gets special terms from publishers, as any retail buyer would who gave an order for 45,000 copies. All the work of delivering the books is done by the club itself. On the whole good or goodish books are chosen, and no unmitigated trash is chosen. The sales of the selected book jump at once by 45,000 copies, and I am told that the general sales thereof are also much stimulated. Thus is the book market nursed and exploited in America, and perhaps the idea is just worth the consideration of that excellent British concern, the National Book Council.

Of course, there is a snag in the enterprise; it lies hidden within the job of selection. The committee of authors may be relied upon to choose meritorious books. But the committee cannot read all new books. Hence new books have to go through a preliminary sieve. The human nature of this preliminary sieve has not been disclosed. I fear that now and then a good book by a comparatively unknown author (just the man who ought to be encouraged) must fail to pass through the sieve. A pity. But where is the remedy?

Few original schemes can exist alone for long, and it is well that this should be so. The Book of the Month Club has a younger rival in America, the Literary Guild. Less than a year old. Membership, 20,000. The Literary Guild gets its money in advance — 18 dollars a year. No cash, no book. It employs canvassers to enrol members. It buys its books unbound, and binds them in its own binding. Also it undersells the booksellers, thus producing friction between booksellers and publishers. But in its most important characteristic it resembles the Book of the Month Club — its selected books are chosen by a committee of authors.

Two things remain to be said about these organisations. Both were established, and are financially run, by groups of advertising agents. And neither of them has yet shown a profit, which statement probably means that both of them have shown a loss. At least one of them may expire unless better terms can be had from publishers. The attitude of publishers towards them is lukewarm. The attitude of booksellers is fiercely hostile. The attitude to authors is very friendly. But authors are a venal lot. Unlike publishers and booksellers, authors think first of personal gain.

Being an author, I see much good in these schemes, and I wish them prosperity — on the condition that somehow or other they make their peace with the booksellers. But objections have been raised to them by the unbiassed. It is said that they gratify indolent minds — those who are not sufficiently interested in books to choose for themselves, the sort of people who would lie under a tree and wait for the fruit to fall into their mouths. I do not regard this as an objection, for indolent minds may develop into, or produce, active minds. And it is said also that the schemes encourage snobbishness ("I belong to the B.M. Club," or "I belong to the Literary Guild," with an air of spiritual pride!). It may be so.

I doubt if such schemes would succeed in this individualistic island, whose citizens obstinately insist on thinking and choosing for themselves — within limits, naturally. In America you have to think like other people or emigrate. American life is standardised, and it is becoming more standardised every year. You can see that in American hotels. All American hotels are now alike, so much so that when you are inside you cannot be sure which one you are inside. They all have comfortable beds, and easy chairs that are not easy, and a thousand other traits in common. As with American hotels, so to a large extent with American minds. Once you are inside one . . . . Still, they do try hard to sell books in America. And they succeed. And let us remember that until it is sold a book does not effectively exist.

8 December 1927

Elegant Mr. Swinnerton and Mr. Aldous Huxley, Realist

Two books by Frank Swinnerton and Aldous Huxley respectively make me think about the relations between literature, journalism, life and other large affairs. The Jupiter of a very considerable daily paper who was re-organising his literary staff said to me some time ago: "I want a man who can take up a definite attitude before any book."* (This demand showed the born director of a newspaper.) Such men exist, but are extremely rare, and the last thing that most of them want to do is to confine themselves

*Beaverbrook, of course. He wrote to Bennett on 18 March 1927: "I must select a young man, vigorous and a good writer. He must be prepared to take up a position on every book — good or bad."

to taking up an attitude before any book. They usually prefer the business of taking up an attitude before any manifestation of life itself. Their curiosity and power of judgment transcend literature. When you have a genuine attitude, you are bound to be interesting about anything and everything. Examples of writers with an attitude are G. K. Chesterton, Robert Lynd, Hilaire Belloc, and the two younger men above named.

And note how the form and subjects of their work have been conditioned by journalistic and commercial considerations. An editor demands an essay of a certain length, and often he demands it on a certain subject. He applies to a man who knows the job of article-writing. Call this man a hack, if you like — I don't mind. The hack either looks around for a subject or he accepts a subject suggested. He says to himself: "Well, I'm a professional, and I can do this thing." He does it in a workmanlike way. If he had not been invited to do it, and paid for doing it, it would never have been done. In this way, many of the finest essays — beautiful short masterpieces, by especially Chesterton, Lynd and Belloc — have come into being. Influence of journalism on the art of literature!

My belief is that nearly all first-rate novelists, if circumstances forced them to be journalists, would be first-rate journalists — on account of their attitude. At the persuasive call of a modern editor Disraeli might have become even a greater journalist than he was a novelist. Indeed he was a very great journalist; only, he put his journalism into his fiction. *Coningsby* is full of the most brilliant and amusing political articles, which have about as much to do with the story as the descriptions of Paris have to do with the story in Balzac's *The Girl with the Golden Eyes*. The same, though less so, with *Endymion*, which I have just had in "The Bradenham Edition" (Peter Davies, 10s.6d.), with a very Guedallan prefatory adornment by Philip Guedalla.

The Bradenham edition is handsome and imposing. It is too imposing. It is almost exactly the size of a volume of the *Dictionary of National Biography*. Why should a novel be as unwieldy as a work of reference? This book cannot be held in one hand for reading. It could not be read in bed without employing a system of cranes. Why do publishers insist on ignoring the important fact that a book exists to be read in comfort, nor merely to be beheld with pride on a shelf?

The volume has another fault. It possesses neither table of contents nor page-titles. At the end of it is an unfinished novel, *Falconet* (rather diverting), but you can only discover where *Falconet* begins by turning over pages till you come to its title-page. Are these matters trifles? Certainly not. They seriously impair the amenities of perusal and are unpardonable.

To return. The essays in Frank Swinnerton's book, *Tokefield Papers* (Secker, 7s.6d.), have mainly appeared in two well-known magazines. Odd? Not at all. The phenomenon simply demonstrates that the editors of those periodicals are alive. Swinnerton has an extraordinary natural gift of elegance. None can handle a sentence with more skill. Devilishly adroit, he can get himself out of any compositional scrape without re-casting his phrase. Sometimes I wish he were less dexterous. But his attitude is maintained throughout. He is a realist concerning human nature, harsh, slightly cruel, yet kindly and always urbane. He amounts to a tonic, and should be taken at least twice a year. His urbanity and his moderation of statement are formidable. Witness his book on R.L. Stevenson. He has not

107

destroyed Stevenson, but Stevenson's renown emerged from that ruthless examination as from a railway accident. *Tokefield Papers* is Swinnerton's seventeenth volume, not counting at least one anonymous work never yet publicly acknowledged.* The time has now arrived for him to come forward with a novel on a bigger scale, and with a heavier weight of emotion. than anything he has yet attempted.

Aldous Huxley's book is entitled *Proper Studies* (Chattos, 7s.6d.). A strange case, Aldous Huxley's, about which I have my own ideas. The chief of them is that his best work is poetical, *Leda*, to wit, with the prose-poems in the Leda volume. I hold that as a novelist Aldous Huxley is still finding himself. I do not think his early novels and stories are satisfactory: for this reason, that they deal with types rather than with individuals. *Antic Hay* excited the youth of the present epoch, but for myself I failed to discover what it was about. *Barren Leaves* was better, but not vastly better. Only in the stories in *Two or Three Graces* did I at last meet here and there living individual creatures that I could walk round and observe with convinced satisfaction from different points of view. I have serious hopes of the novelist of *Two or Three Graces*.

Proper Studies is sociological philosophy; but it does not constitute, nor pretend to constitute, a system. It exhibits the scholar, the man of tremendous reading, the best educated of all our novelists, old or young. Aldous Huxley has even read the 2000 pages of Pareto's *Sociologia Generale*. His learning, never flaunted, intimidates plain persons such as myself. He is our sole rival of the late Whewell.

Like Swinnerton, he is a realist. He has his grandfather's grave regard for facts, and bland disregard of unproved assumptions. He rings a coin on the counter, and doesn't trouble to tell you that it is counterfeit. Names do not affright him, not even Descartes and Helvetius. He is brilliantly illuminating on religion, democracy, dogma, ideals. There is a lot of hard, clear, destructive thinking in this volume, something to bite on. And it is not without a charming ornamentation.

I can barely mention Miss Eleanor Brougham's *Comments and Queries* (The Bodley Head, 5s. net). Short historical essays, some of which I had read in periodicals. Not in the street of the aforementioned authors; but agreeable, showing a historical sense and a sense of romance; respectably written. And there are passages and quotations in this little, ingenuous book which excite feelings like those inspired by the memory of a figure beautiful, beloved, intelligent and kindly, too soon rapt away, whose imagined wraith shines through the gloom and points us to the skies.

15 December 1927

Adventures in the Literature of Youth — And the Discovery of a Classic

The Christmas season. Children's books. I don't think that children are half so mysterious as grown-ups; but they are fairly mysterious. What

* *Women* (1918).

108

literature do they really both respect and enjoy? I never did read myself, and I was never with children who read, the orthodox children's books of that pliocene period — except, of course, the serials in *The Boy's Own Paper* and *The Girl's Own Paper*, which I think we read because the magazines came into the house every month looking like fresh fruit. Enjoy those serials? Yes. Respect them? No.

I had keener enjoyment in, and greater respect for, the serials in bound volumes of *Sharpe's Magazine* — "Frank Fairleigh", "Lewis Arundel", etc. These introduced one to the great adult world of the day or the day previous. And the books which held me as a boy were *The Successful Merchant* (? by Samuel Budgett*), Smiles's *Self-Help* (an ingenuous work of vast influence, equally for good and for evil), Grace Aguilar's *The Days of Bruce*, and the intensely exciting narratives of Flavius Josephus. I read some Trollope and some Victor Hugo; but no Scott, Thackeray, George Eliot, and very little Dickens. As soon as I left school I began to buy Cassell's National Library, because I thought it was the correct thing to do. I can recall only one item in it, *Undine*, that held me, and even this barely got pass marks as a maintainer of interest.

If I have not received the Victoria Cross, the fact is but another proof that injustice reigns. For I had the astounding courage as a "young youth" to order from a friendly bookseller of a conspiratorial turn of mind Zola's *The Soil*. How the rumours of Zola's daring and originality had penetrated into the central fastnesses of the Five Towns I cannot imagine. The culpably careless bookseller neglected my detailed instructions about delivery, and coming home one Saturday I found my Zola lying, unswathed, on the dining-room sideboard, where new arrivals were always put. My heart ceased to beat. Two minutes later, and my father would have seen the thing first, and there would have been seventy and seven devils to pay. I snatched it away into secrecy, under my waistcoat. *The Soil* did not by any means reach the height of my expectations, because it was not beautiful. (*Nana* is.) The one beautiful book that I remember was Hans Christian Andersen. A thrill in that, a thrill which still vibrates in me!

It was not till I was amply adult that I even heard of Mrs. Ewing, author of *A Flat Iron for a Farthing, Jackanapes*, and many other stories. For close on forty years I kept hearing that Mrs. Ewing was "good", without ever reading her. The other day I observed in the Press that Messrs. Bell (her original publishers) were issuing a uniform edition of Mrs. Ewing's tales (2s. each), and I sent for four volumes of them, and opened them with apprehension . . . Well, you know, Juliana Horatia Ewing is indeed good, very good. She started young as an author (20), and she died young (44). For nearly half a century after her death her books have survived, and during the last few days I have appreciated more than ever the truth of George Moore's assertion that a good book cannot be killed. Print a good book in an edition of one copy, and cast that copy into the deathly wastes of the Sahara, and it will somehow survive.

Juliana came of literary stock. (Her mother's pen was immensely productive, though I shall probably never read anything by the once-esteemed

* Actually *The Successful Merchant: Sketches of the Life of Mr. Samuel Budgett, Late of Kingswood Hill* by William Arthur (1852).

Margaret Gatty.) You can see that she was "used to books". Take *Jackanapes*, with its quotations from Shakespeare, Byron, George Herbert. She was a religious woman. When she used the word "GOD", as she frequently did, she always printed it in capitals. She was a grave writer. She showed faith in the intelligence and the seriousness of children. You might think that children would be frightened off. But the proof that they have not been frightened off lies in the appearance of the new edition. I should not be surprised to learn that after 45 years Mrs. Ewing has a larger sale than Ruskin or Carlyle. Her continued popularity demonstrates in a most charming and persuasive manner that there is something radically sound after all in the alleged-to-be-decadent British race.

She writes with genuine distinction. She has style. Consider the use of the italicised word in: "The old postman waiting for them, *rigid* with salutation, at the four cross-roads." She has a very pleasing imaginative wit. Speaking of the legend of Bonaparte, she says: "The Grey Goose [on the village green] thought he was a Fox, and that all the men in England were going out in red coats to hunt him."

She has an illuminating worldly wisdom. Thus: "One thing the supreme-ly afflicted are entitled in their sorrow — to be obeyed — and yet it is the last kindness that people commonly will do them." Did anyone else ever say that before her — or since? And this: "There is a heritage of heroic ex-ample and noble obligation, not reckoned in the Wealth of Nations, but essential to a nation's life; the contempt of which, in any people, may, not slowly, mean even its commercial fall. Very sweet are the uses of prosper-ity . . . . But, there be things . . . "the good of" which and "the use of" which are beyond all calculation of worldly goods . . . : things such as Love and Honour, and the Soul of Man, which cannot be bought with a price, and which do not die with death." I conceive that Rudyard Kipling must have read Mrs. Ewing when he was young, and I wish I had.

Jackanapes is the very simple story of a boy who became a soldier and sacrificed his life to save the life of a man much less valuable than himself. A story which must have been told a thousand times, but never better. It is naught; yet it is everything, because it is beautiful, heroic, witty, charged with delicate and authentic sentiment, and absolutely free from the corrod-ing vice of sentimentality. And *Jackanapes* is a long story, quite a long one, out of many, also long.

I know that numerous readers will exclaim upon me: "What! You have just discovered Mrs. Ewing! She is a classic, and has been familiar to us from our youth up." I can't help it. I had to proclaim my own personal discovery. Mrs. Ewing is assuredly a classic.

22 December 1927

A "Beautiful" Novel: *Encyclopaedia Curzonica*: Why Not More Biographies of the Living?

The earth has its mysteries, and one of them is that St. John Ervine, the author of a really fine novel like *The Wayward Man* (Collins, 7s.6d.), should only publish a novel once in seven years. I cannot understand his infecundity, but I can deplore it. I have heard that *The Wayward Man* is having a good sale. It ought to have a very good sale for a very long time. This book is a *book*. It has none of the characteristics of a stunt work. St. John Ervine does not assault you. He takes you by the buttonhole or the button, and seems to say: "Just listen and have patience. I've got a few interesting things to tell you about Robert Dunwoody, the Ulsterman, and his mother." His spell is deliberate, but powerful and sure. Another of earth's mysteries is that a writer who can be so skittishly challenging in his journalism should produce a novel so informed with the pure classical spirit of restraint. I do not propose to discuss *The Wayward Man*, but I will not let Christmas pass without recommending it as something unusually good and beautiful.

The mystery which really concerns me today is the announcement that the official biography of Lord Curzon will be in three volumes. Why? Why not thirteen and call it the *Encyclopaedia Curzonica*? Lord Curzon, if not a great, was a very remarkable man, of miraculous energy and thoroughness and quite considerable achievement; also he wrote admirably on many subjects. I certainly do not agree with Geoffrey West's pronouncement that he was "in his way one of the stupidest men who ever set foot in India." But is any man important enough for a three-volume biography? (Even Disraeli was not, though he got it.)

The three Curzon volumes will be big volumes, heavy volumes, unwieldy volumes. And, except subscribers to circulating libraries, probably few will read them. The British craze for prodigious biographies is exceeding the bounds of reason. I would not suggest the enactment of a sumptuary law limiting the length of biographies, but I should hesitate to oppose it. These vast and comprehensive compilations can appeal only to specialists and to idlers. What is worse, they gravely hinder the production of shorter and cheaper biographies which appeal to the plain man, because such shorter biographies must be based on the big ones and the authors of the big ones might justifiably object to the process of basing. Thus the intricate lines of the undoubtedly interesting and valuable life of Lord Curzon will in all probability remain for ever unknown to the plain man.

I am inclined to think that if the first official biography of Lord Curzon had been compressed down to the length of a novel, 100,000 words, and published at the price of a novel, 7s. 6d., it might have had as large a sale as a very successful novel, say 50,000 copies, and that the authors and publishers might have made as much out of it as the authors and publishers of a very successful novel. The author at any rate might have got over £4500 as his modest share of the booty.

Of course the specialists, the historians, would have had to go to the original sources for information about an infinity of details. But what of that? Let them. Our fashionable biographies are not, and ought not to be, primarily prepared for the benefit of the erudite votaries of Clio.

Another point. Why do we have to wait until after the funeral service for reliable summaries of knowledge about our leading men? Impartial biographies of the living would do genuine service to the public. Some are published, but too few. The trouble is that biographies of the living are generally conceived in a sentimental and highly misleading spirit of adulation. They need not be. Honesty, while difficult, is by no means impossible.

111

ARNOLD BENNETT: THE EVENING STANDARD YEARS

My thoughts have been drawn to this subject by a new biographical series — *Representative Women* — edited by Francis Birrell and published by Gerald Howe Limited at 3s. 6d. each. Francis Birrell shows himself to be no ordinary editor. Three volumes have come before me: *Elizabeth Chudleigh (Duchess of Kingston)* by Beatrice Curtis Brown, *Aphra Behn* by V. Sackville-West (Mrs. Harold Nicolson) and *Mrs. Annie Besant* by Geoffrey West. The first I have not yet read. The second is a very agreeable and useful floriated essay on a woman of whom public ignorance is intense. The third is a quite model short biography of a living person. One of its virtues is that it will exacerbate a number of cranks.

Mr. West has a rich subject in this powerful, gifted, and strange individuality, who by the way was until recently one of the greatest orators of the time. She began her career — I was unaware of this piquant fact — as the wife of a country clergyman and had two children by him. Then an appeal for guidance to the famous Pusey, who made himself ridiculous! Then Bradlaugh! In the 'eighties and even in the early 'nineties (said W. T. Stead) "it was considered hardly correct to allude to her except in the most distant manner, as if she inhabited another and improper world." Then Blavatsky and theosophy! (A deadly blow for Bradlaugh.) I once read, for the purpose of collecting material for a novel, Mrs. Besant's theosophical work, *The Ancient Wisdom*. It is a bad book. An orator she was, but certainly not a writer. However, she possessed the quality of perfect assurance of the rightness of whatever position she happened to adopt.

Then the Orient! For a long time she was the worshipped queen of the masses in India. During the war the Indian Government interned her, and the agitation for her release was stupendous. "Who would have thought," said an indignant high official, "that there would have been such a fuss about one old woman?" The British Empire and the welfare of civilisation had to give way. Mrs. Besant was released — and unconditionally. She stood at the summit of her amazing renown. Yet within a short period she was being howled down, hooted and hissed by natives at their public meetings.

But perhaps her greatest moment came later when she had discovered or invented a Messiah — Krishnamurti, and the handsome youth spoke to a throng of 6000 people with a "voice not heard on earth for 2000 years." The Messianic words have been reported, and they are excessively platitudinous.

Converts to theosophy come and converts go; sometimes they go faster than they come; but Mrs. Besant survives, a monument, an institution, a topless tower of semi-fanatical idealism. Geoffrey West's verdict on her is a just one. You will find it on p. 88 of his book, which is a book not to be missed by those who are interested in the major curiosities of human nature.

29 December 1927

Literature of the Year: "Not Much of it Has Stuck In My Mind, But —"

The other day a young reader wrote to the editor of this paper asking advice about the choice of books (apparently English books were wanted) of established reputation. Such advice can be given, and in detail: but I doubt if any two advisers would agree in their counsel, and no counsel would give very satisfactory results. The fact is, you can't help people. You can only help them to help themselves. There are many short manuals of English literature, and a few good ones. Let the tyro read one. Then let him get catalogues, from a bookseller, of one or two series of cheap reprints, such as the Everyman Library, the Temple Classics and the World's Classics. And then let his fancy choose. All the books in these series are cheap, and nearly all of them are worth reading — by the right reader. The tyro may make mistakes. He will. But it is his business to make mistakes.

When a homing pigeon is released from its basket it rises and surveys all the earth within its range of vision, and probably sees nothing that answers directly to the call of its soul. It tries an experiment, is disappointed, returns, tries again; and so on till it gets a clue; the rest is as easy as sliding down a slope.

The tyro is like that pigeon. What more can one say, except to urge him to keep his head cool as he comes to the full realisation of the vast and varied mass of really fine literature which English writers have produced in less than six hundred years? Nobody can read everything, or the hundreth part of everything. And the man who sets out to read everything will know nothing worth knowing, because his task will have cut him off from life itself.

The mere mass of literature is enough to daunt the most intrepid. Last week I went into one of the largest bookshops in London, and I was positively intimidated by the physical spectacle of literature in bulk. There were dreadful sights: such as a mountain of four hundred copies of one book, giving a sinister impression of wholesaleness which was repugnant — as the book happened not to be one of my own. The whole world seemed to be buying books. I did not get what I wanted. I found what I wanted. I called plaintively to one flying handmaiden after other: "Can you attend to me?" They all replied in tender, soothing accents: "One moment, sir." But the moment never came. I departed, my money in my pocket. I might well have put the desired books in my pocket. Only two things prevented me from doing so: the fear of detectives and my absurd conscience. Almost certainly there were no detectives. And I knew that the limited company which owned the store was paying dividends of over twenty per cent. And have not persons accounting themselves my friends stolen books from me? I reckon to lose a dozen books a year through borrowers who are thieves in that they forget to return. Still, I went away with the certainty that the public does buy books: which is something.

For myself, at the end of half a century of struggle, I have given up the appalling enterprise of "keeping abreast." Now, when I am asked:

"Have you read ——? Do you mean to say you haven't read ——?" I reply stoutly: "No, I haven't. And I don't want to, and I never will. And that's that. And I don't care." And there are other things than books, too. I have run till I am breathless after music, and after painting, and after architecture. So I take holidays from being in the movement. During which holidays, which sometimes continue for months at a stretch, I totally refuse to go to concerts, or I refuse to go to picture-galleries, or I refuse to look at buildings. I just lie down and, glancing up now and then from a book, sardonically watch the strugglers struggling. Then I arise and start again, and, refreshed, I can often outstrip the exhausted, earnest simpletons who have forgotten to loaf and invite their souls. This is a good plan.

Our fathers have told us that a little learning is a dangerous thing. But my children, bodily and spiritual, shall relate that I told them that too much learning is a poison to the possessor and a nuisance to his fellows. And further, my attitude to those who continually stuff themselves with the masterpieces of the past is decidedly inimical; it is even contemptuous. And when they question me, and discover gaps in my reading, I assault them, saying: "Do you know Binstead's *Gal's Gossip*? Do you know Grossmith's *Diary of a Nobody*?" And they say they do not know these works, excusing themselves on the ground that these works are unmentioned in the manuals and encyclopaedias. And I say: "Then you simply aren't alive." And I leave them for dead on the field of battle.

The British Museum is a great place; it is perhaps the greatest place in the world. But who would make it his residence, fix his bed there, eat his oranges and brown bread there? Some people read on such lines that they might as well be living night and day in a museum. I enjoy going into museums. I am always popping in and out of them. But I must have still more frequent adventures in the foolish, wise, vain invaluable world. Most of these adventures are unprofitable, or not directly profitable. However, I have had them, and none has been utterly futile because they have saved me from feeling "apart." When I look back at the literature of the year I discover that not much of it has stuck in my mind. Nevertheless, if I had the year to live again I would not in this respect live it differently. I have had contacts. I have been among the things that are. And this is my New Year's thought.

Knowledge For All in a "Terrific" Ten Dollar Work

I have just encountered what seems to me to be a quite new sort of work of reference. I confess to a mild passion for works of reference. Not that I refer to them very frequently, having a natural gift for ignorance. The first I ever bought (apart from common dictionaries, etc.) was Louis Moreri's *Great Historical Dictionary or Curious Mixture of Sacred and Profane History* (French). Magnificent folios, bound in full red morocco, and weighing tons. Auction price, 1890, about 2s. 6d. Yes, this is not a misprint. Alas! I sold the work, partly because of the cost of transporting it from lodging to lodging, and partly because it is not really amusing.

Next I got Pierre Bayle's *Historical and Critical Dictionary*, third edition, Rotterdam, 1720. Four superb folios in full yellow calf. Price, some eight shillings. Bayle is always readable, and sometimes he is a great lark. He must have been one of the first men, if not the first, to run successfully a periodical devoted to literary criticism: *News of the Republic of Letters*; of which I once got a bound volume for a shilling. His Dictionary, which was largely intended to correct and improve upon Moreri's, makes admirable browsing. Bayle knew an immense amount, and probably nothing accurately. But he had sense. Also he was the real founder of eighteenth century scepticism. Of course, his Dictionary went straight on to the Index, on to all the Indexes. Hence its sale and influence were enormous. He was a fellow friendly to his readers. He would say (textual): "I am sure that the public will be glad to have these letters. *That is why* I am going to add them." And he adds the letters in a note.

The Dictionary contains far more notes than text. I have beheld it for nearly thirty years, and I still consult it about twice a year, and it will be the last book I shall sell. Nor would I sell the vast *Larousse Encyclopaedia* in seventeen colossal volumes, chiefly because it gives lavish musical extracts from all the principal operas. Selling standard works is a mistake. I regret having sold the French *Universal Biography* in over eighty volumes.

English modern works of reference are better than French. I regard the *New English Dictionary* as the grandest of all achievements in reference (except *Whitaker*). I have been buying it in parts for nearly forty years, and am still buying it. The longest sensational serial ever written! As for *The Dictionary of National Biography*, it is like the Bible — an uneven work. I have never owned the *Encyclopaedia Britannica*, because I brought myself up on *Chambers'*, which is the best thing extant of its size. The new edition thereof is one of my latest toys.

But who would guess that the work I consult most often (twice or thrice daily) is Funk and Wagnall's one volume *Practical Standard Dictionary?* And why should this be? Because it gives not only words but names of people and geographical names under a single alphabet. And shall I omit to mention Haydn's *Dictionary of Dates*, of which a new edition is urgently required? I must cease these referential reminiscences

115

and *obiter dicta*, adding only that the gentlemanly ideal of bliss in reference is to be able successfully to "look up" any important fact whatever in one's own library. This bliss, I maintain, is mine.

To come to the new work. *Introduction to the History of Science*, by George Sarton. (*Science* — "systematised positive knowledge.") Twenty-six volumes. Something over 9,000,000 words. But only one volume is yet published — at Baltimore. (I now at least understand why Baltimore is called "the electric city.") It is the 376th publication of the Carnegie Institution. Eight hundred and thirty-nine stately pages. Ten dollars. Besides the ten dollars, I spent about a month in obtaining my copy. (The publishers are the Williams and Wilkins Company, Baltimore, U.S.A.) Mr. Sarton has imagination. He blandly describes the whole affair as a "sketch." "A full-fledged history [of science], realising completely the promise of my sketch, will be the work of another generation." But will it, ever? I like Mr. Sarton. He has written the whole of the first volume (from Homer to Omar Khayyam) himself. He intends to write seven more volumes himself, and parts of two others. I hope he is young. "It is clear," says he, "that when [the work] is completed, supposing it to have been done as well as contemporary knowledge permitted, we shall have a fairly good notion of the progress of human civilisation." Well, we shall — those few of us who are here to have it. In any case, a bumptious and self-complacent posterity will have it.

The scheme of the work is original, and it is intended to accomplish what has never been accomplished before. It is divided into three series. The first is a chronological series of sections, of half a century each, baptised by the name of the chief fount of knowledge of the half century dealt with. Thus: "Galen." Each section is divided into sub-sections. The first sub-section gives the general scientific history of the period, and must be read. The other sub-sections give corrective details in limitless amplitude, and are not for reading but for reference.

The second series, to be in eight volumes, surveys the contributions to science of different types of civilisation — as, Moslem, Jewish, Chinese, Hindu, Mediaeval. Eight volumes. The third series surveys the evolution of the different sciences — physical, biological, anthropological, mathematical, etc.

The first volume may or may not be good. I think it is very good. And I assert with confidence that it is very readable. Nay, if you have the faculty of browsing, it will enthral you. Among other trifles it gives you the history of astronomy, of geography, of medicine, of theoretical music, of mathematics, up to the eleventh century.

Not till I had pored over this terrific work did I know that the notes of the musical scale were designated by Guido of Arezzo (who died in 1050) from the first syllables of the first six lines of a hymn to John the Baptist. (Let us remember that in those days music was held to be an integral part of science.)

Mr. Sarton writes clearly, avoiding eloquence and all frills. His learning frightens me, but apparently not him: for he carries the burden of it with the utmost equanimity. When his volume arrived I was reading, concurrently, Dostoevsky, Gibbon, and Captain Marryat. It seduced me from all three of them. Anybody who is interested in knowledge and has ten dollars to burn, now knows how to burn them.

The True Greatness of Thomas Hardy

When I last saw him, in London, Hardy was nearly eighty, a spare man, very young and active indeed for his age, who chatted and chattered away quite cheerfully and — thank heaven! — quite ordinarily. He talked about anything, and of nothing long. He had authority, but did not show it, perhaps scarcely felt it. When in the street you passed Swinburne's tremendous head balanced on Swinburne's trifling body, you knew at once and for sure that you had seen greatness. But if I had not been introduced to Thomas Hardy and known beforehand that I was to meet Thomas Hardy I certainly should not have been aware that I was in the presence of greatness. I liked him to be thus. I remember thinking: "This man is all right." No nonsense about him. No pose. No secret but apparent pre-occupation with the fact that he was the biggest living thing in English literature.

Neither was he rustic, rural, nor of a hermit style. It is often forgotten that Hardy in his youth had lived in London for years, had later had contacts of all kinds, was the darling of universities. Throughout his life he had contacts which he never unreasonably avoided. True, he did not seek them. He was the mountain to which all Mahomets came.

I can recall little that he said. What I do recall is that coatless and hatless on a windy and bleak day he went out on to the balcony of Sir James Barrie's flat in the Adelphi and stood there for ages, gazing and gossiping around, while I shivered and trembled lest both of us might catch our deaths of a chill. He felt no cold. Yet he was taking prizes at the Royal Institute of British Architects years before I was born.

For at least twenty-five years every great man just dead has been saluted as "the last of the great Victorians," the implication being that the day of giants was at last definitely over and done. Hardy was one of the last. But even he was not the last, for there still remains George Moore. You may say that George Moore is not a Victorian. He is, however, just as much or as little a Victorian as Hardy was. Room for an extreme variousness in that spacious epoch! Would anybody say that Swinburne was not a Victorian? Our notions of Victorianism have to be enlarged.

In his youth, forty years ago, George Moore wrote very adverse criticism of such of Hardy's novels as had then been published. The criticism stands. I did not see any answer to it at the time, and I do not see any answer now. In those novels, passionately admired by a few in the 'eighties and still passionately admired, there is crude and sentimental melodrama which would have ruined a French writer, for instance, in the esteem of Frenchmen of taste. Such passages in Hardy's work cannot be defended.

And they need not be defended. England is one country and France is another. Shakespeare was guilty of all manner of sins a single one of which, had Racine committed it, would have destroyed Racine's good name. In this island we are more robust. What interests us with Hardy, as with Shakespeare, is not his defects but his positive qualities, which qualities, I fear, have never been fully perceived by George Moore. What matters is not the short passages where Hardy's aesthetic taste and invention and creative power failed him, but the long and innumerable passages where invention, creative power, and the finest taste are combined in the highest degree. There were times when Hardy wrote as beautifully as Nathaniel Hawthorne himself. (I mention Hawthorne because George Moore has asserted, and I would not dissent, that Hawthorne's writing has not been surpassed.) There were times when he showed a sustained power which has not, in my opinion, been surpassed by anybody anywhere.

But Hardy created a wayward God, and the explanation of Hardy's occasional artistic casualties is that this God was as revengeful as any Hebrew Jah-veh. Hence Hardy now and then had to pay for his caprice in God-making. Fantasy runs through all Hardy's fiction. It is seldom absent. His best books are those in which he contrived to subdue it to a lovely pattern. All his novels have a lovely pattern in places. Even *Desperate Remedies,* his first, has it. And certain stories, such as *The Well-Beloved* and *The Romantic Adventures of a Milkmaid* — stories which have been indulgently smiled at and never widely appreciated at anything like their real value — have it constantly and dazzlingly. To my mind the supreme example of total success is *The Woodlanders,* and after that *The Life and Death of the Mayor of Casterbridge. Tess of the D'Urbervilles* is terribly uneven, with marvellous pages. *Jude the Obscure* never had a chance with the British public, which is incapable of distinguishing between subject and treatment, and whose definition of beauty is too limited.

I consider that none of Hardy's novels ranks with *The Dynasts,* a work which for range, power, insight, historic sense, fundamental realism, pity, and consistent beauty comes second to nothing in European literature. You cannot compare it with Tolstoy's *War and Peace,* the only other book to which it might be comparable. But if you could so compare it you would have to give it the palm for wide sweep, the eagle vision, and the creation of ideal beauty out of terrible events. Also, it is not marred by prejudice. *War and Peace* is.

As to Hardy's poetry, I feel diffident. That he was a true poet and a fine poet and a poet by vocation I would admit and affirm. But a great poet — as he has been adjudged by more than one sound critic! I cannot see it for myself. He seems to me to resemble A.E. Housman in this, that he keeps on writing the same poem over and over again. . . . The relic under this green sod was once a pretty girl. This room was once inhabited by individuals like you and me. This furniture was polished by their use. They are gone. We shall go. They loved; they lost. She loved; he didn't. He loved; she didn't. They met, and never met again. Once they had bliss. Destiny is comic, and it hurts. We must endure it till we die. . . . In short, an obsession, with the transience and the futility and the cruelty of things. A subject for great poetry. Yes! A subject for one great poem, but not for volumes. Other and greater subjects exist. Moreover, Hardy's style in verse was surely a very grave disadvantage to him. If he was a great poet, what sort of poets were Matthew Arnold, Wordsworth and Shelley?

But I am inclined to think that how great a *writer* he was, some of us yet but imperfectly comprehend.

19 January 1928

Professor Gilbert Murray's "Light-Giving Brilliance"

Like the majority of citizens I know no Greek. Unlike the majority of citizens I am continually annoyed and engloomed by my ignorance of Greek. Starting with a prejudice against classical education, due perhaps to the public antics of pedagogic persons whom a classical education had obviously left narrow-minded and therefore uncivilised, I gradually came to understand that Greek literature had not been overpraised. And this in spite of obstacles put in my way by translators.

How Keats contrived to be inspired by Chapman's Homer passes my comprehension. True, the title of his sonnet is: 'On *first* looking into Chapman's Homer.' If he had waited till the tenth look Keats might never have written that sonnet. I maintain that Chapman's Homer is unreadable, and that Pope's Homer is little better. I maintain that Homer can only be read in English in prose. But I also maintain that Homer in English prose makes magnificent reading, unique reading.

Similarly I would say that Jowett's translation of Plato is a vicious translation — inaccurate, misleading, shirking difficulties, and not stylistic. (I know that in this animadversion scholars would support me.) Nor do I think that Professor Gilbert Murray's translations of Greek plays are utterly satisfactory. How do I find the audacity thus to criticise the professor's work? By comparing it with literal translations. And by reading such books as Professor Gilbert Murray's own *Euripides and his Age,* which is a fine little work. Professor Murray's translations are delightful dramatic pieces, full of fancy; but in my opinion, by adding to the Greek he has taken away from the Greek. I have sometimes wondered what the shades of the Greek tragedians would say about the Professor could his translations be literally translated back into Greek for their consideration.

Nevertheless, though stage performances of Greek plays usually send me to sleep — so far off and incredible is the motivation of them, I murmur about the original author on reading such a thing as for instance *The Trojan Woman:* "This fellow knew how to do it." And I murmur on reading some of the dialogues of Plato: "This fellow knew exactly how to do it." And the same of the dialogues of Lucian. And of Homer: "This fellow knew the whole job." And of Aristotle: "This is the only fellow who ever really could do it." And when I first set eyes on the Acropolis at Athens I said out loud — no mere murmuring: "These fellows could do it."

Yes, to this day, the Greeks have never been beaten, and very rarely equalled. And I can conceive that if I knew Greek as well as I know French (but no Englishman on earth knows Greek half as well as thousands of Englishmen know French) I should be as puffed up about it as any pundit and as disdainful of other literatures and civilisations than the Greek.

The above dithyrambic vehemences have been occasioned by reading Professor Gilbert Murray's *The Classical Tradition in Poetry* (Oxford University Press, 12s. 6d.). If I have seemed to belittle the life-work of the Professor, appearances are misleading. He may be, in the literary sense, a little bit on the prim side, but perhaps I myself am not sufficiently on the prim side, and anyhow, the Professor has been and is a great civilising influence on the present age. I immensely admire his taste, his moral bases, and his achievement. And he emphatically is not narrow-minded. His sympathetic vision can and does embrace many varied manifestations of life, including the modern; he constantly shows this by his allusions and his comparisons.

The main lesson of the book, for me, is the continuance of tradition. One is familiar with the phrase "Greek influence," but if you want to feel the weight of the phrase read the Professor's chapter, full of detail, on the Greek influence upon such writers as Shakespeare and Milton — especially Milton. The illustrative quotations and other proofs are quite startling; indeed they are exciting. And, says Professor Murray, in comment: "It is one of the very feeblest of critical errors to suppose that there is a thing called 'originality,' which consists in having no models." Homer must have had models, and his models had models, and no doubt the first model was a gesture of the arms, an expletive, and a kicking of legs in the air.

In connection with this matter, I enjoy Professor Murray on certain theoretical exaggerations of new movements in the arts: "Modern critics seem to hate the thought of 'imitation' or 'representation.' They are in love with the idea of 'self-expression,' self-assertion, the revelation of personality and the like. . . .The truth seems to be that, whatever you do, you will inevitably reveal your personality, but that if your work is good, it will be an interesting personality, and if not, not. Therefore, you can safely concentrate on doing the work as well as possible and let your personality look after itself." And again: "Poetry is the opposite of egotism." And again: "You cannot enter into the kingdom of poetry except by losing yourself." Wisdom, deep wisdom! I had an impulse to go forth to the post office and telegraph these important tidings to a dozen poets and bright prosers of my acquaintance, but lethargy and considerations of expense intervened.

Upon occasion Professor Murray's fancy is extremely brilliant. The best example of his light-giving brilliance is his expansion of the remark: "In good poetry no single statement bears its face value. It means indefinitely more," likening the reader to a Siberian exile who has picked up a torn fragment of an old railway timetable. I can recall nothing of the kind as good. He is excellent, too, in his demolition "of the absurd theory that the poet sees and understands the world as a whole." Substitute "banker" for "poet," and you would be much nearer the truth. And he has made a new definition of beauty: "Beauty is that which when seen is loved." Of course, it isn't really a definition, because beauty is indefinable, but it goes about as far as a definition of beauty can.

Here is a book I can recommend. I would like a reprint of it soon at two half-crowns instead of five. Does the Oxford University Press expect a man to pay as much for a book which might influence his whole mental and emotional life as he pays for a stall at a musical comedy? It is a quiet book, though with agitating pages, as I have shown. It must be read with sustained attention, when the brain is not fatigued. And it may be called dangerous to complacency. Its final words are: "He who seeks the spiritual kingdom must take his life in his hands." But, varying the metaphor, I would describe the book as a meal both appetising and nourishing. It is not free from trifling slips. There are three references to myself, and as the highest living authority on the subject I am in a position to state that each of them factually errs.

26 *January* 1928

How Tolstoy "Cross-Examined" Bernard Shaw

Many people say behind my back, and some to my face, that I have a bee in my bonnet. Fortunate indeed is the man with only one bee in his bonnet. There are people who go about with hives for headgear. But as regards my bee, said to be Russian! Six years ago Bernard Shaw wrote a letter to the Press, and this letter was endorsed by such diverse persons as the editor of *The Fortnightly Review*, the *Sunday Express*, and *The Observer*, Sir Arthur Conan Doyle, Sir Hall Caine, Anthony Hope, H.G. Wells, W.W. Jacobs, two Ambassadors, Marie Stopes, Jermoe K. Jerome, Sir Oliver Lodge, the headmaster of Eton, the director of the London Library, and Henry Arthur Jones. (Dozens of other glittering names.) The object of the letter was to interest the British public in a projected English translation of certain Russian works — to wit, those of Tolstoy. No such overwhelming battery of variegated great guns was ever brought up in support of an enterprise for popularising the books of any English author. I say no more about bees.

Well, six years have passed; 1928 is the Tolstoy centenary year; and the Tolstoy Society now exists for the especial purpose of helping to sell a Centenary edition of Tolstoy's works; translated by Mr. and Mrs. Aylmer Maude and to be published by the Oxford University Press. Viscountess Grey is the president of the society. I was invited to be a vice-president but I refused, my real reason for the act of renunciation being the fear lest my name might prejudice the affair in the eyes of Englishmen who abhor enthusiasts. I am entirely outside the society, but I recommend it to the enlightened. You can join it. If you do you will get 10 per cent. off the published price of the volumes. Its secretary is Miss L.E. Elliott, Ladywell House, Great Baddow, Chelmsford.

The Tolstoy translations of Mr. and Mrs. Aylmer Maude that I have seen are in my opinion incomparably the best English translations. Indeed they put a new complexion upon Tolstoy. Tolstoy himself preferred them to any others. Publication will begin in August next. Twenty-one volumes will be issued, in three yearly instalments of seven each, at the published price of nine guineas the set. (Perhaps a further fourteen volumes will be issued later — that depends on you.) The price is low for the value. I express the hope — more, I pray heaven! — that the books will not be bulky nor heavy. They are either bed-books or nothing.

The number of sets is limited to one thousand. The society officially states that "the edition may quickly attain a rarity value." For several reasons it may well be necessary to limit the edition. Nevertheless that word "rarity" affronts me. Also it reminds me of a pamphlet by Sir Ernest Benn, recently published by Benns. Sir Ernest is against rarity in books. So am I. He says: "My trade, like many other trades, is obsessed with the notion that wealth can be made out of scarcity, but it cannot." This pamphlet is very interesting and very disconcerting.

Sir Ernest estimates that thirty books are written for every one published; and that two out of every three published are failures. Hence ninety books are written for every successful book published. Further, 12,000 books are published yearly, and there are 11,000 booksellers. If every bookseller employs two assistants, it follows that on the average three men are occupied for nearly a whole year in selling one book. Says Sir Ernest: "I can think of no human service . . . which is rendered to the community at such a frightful cost." Nor can I. Again, whereas the nation spends 315 millions per annum on drink and 180 millions on tobacco, it spends six millions on books. The number of books published has only doubled itself in nearly fifty years. Sir Ernest sees a potential market for books to the amount of 450 millions per annum. Naturally this potential market will not become actual by making books a rarity.

I trust, therefore, that when the limited edition of Tolstoy is sold out, as it will be, a cheaper edition, utterly unlimited, will be offered to this potential market by the Tolstoy Society. Only thus will the society fully justify its existence and its labours.

I should now like to write an essay on Tolstoy, but as it would fill the rest of the paper and probably have to be continued to-morrow, I shall forbear. I will say merely that I have been disturbed in my private mind by the opinion, implied if not definitely expressed by Mr. E.M. Forster in his book, *Aspects of the Novel,* that Tolstoy is the greatest of the Russian novelists. A few weeks ago I said what I thought of Mr. Forster's book, and I will not deny that his opinion intimidates me, while it surprises. I give it weight. I have always been the champion of Dostoevsky — at any rate since Dostoevsky reached England. I am still convinced that *The Brothers Karamazov* is the finest novel ever written. I am convinced that it has a heroical quality and an emotional power and a large spirit of sympathetic charitableness that Tolstoy could never compass.

Not long since I re-read *Anna Karenina,* and found it marvellously true, but hard — hard. Now and then it rather bored me. I regard Tolstoy as too didactic — and cantankerously didactic — for an absolutely supreme artist. He was for ever too harshly teaching somebody something. I think that he suffered from spiritual pride — possibly the worst human vice, except self-pity. Also he was beyond question wrong-headed on all manner of subjects. Dostoevsky was seldom or never wrong-headed. And Dostoevsky was a sinner in a world of sinners, and knew it.

But of course Tolstoy had a simply terrific creative energy — more terrific even than Balzac's. An author who could produce *War and Peace* at under forty and *Resurrection* at over seventy is entitled to be called unique. And on consideration, though I continue to maintain the primacy of *The Brothers Karamazov* among all novels, I am, at the present writing, less sure that Dostoevsky was a greater artist than Tolstoy — taking them all in all.

The other day I talked to a friend who had met Tolstoy at Tolstoy's house at Yasnaya Poliana. The capricious author of *What is Art?* was aged and ill in bed. He had just finished reading Shaw's *Man and Superman,* and nothing would do but he must dictate to my friend an English letter to Shaw about *Man and Superman,* cross-examining Shaw and pointing out where and how often Shaw had failed to express the truth that was in him or ought to have been in him. I thought that that was very characteristic of Tolstoy. My friend said that what chiefly struck him about Tolstoy was the fact that he gave at once a feeling of intimacy, and that this intimacy was based on an instant understanding and comprehension of the stranger. "His understanding," said my friend, "seemed to envelope me." Which narration somehow helped me to see Tolstoy more clearly. Yes, Tolstoy understood. But he was a contradiction of the proverb that to understand all is to pardon all. He gives me the unfortunate impression that if anything untoward had happened in heaven he would have felt himself ready and able at a moment's notice to direct the universe.

2 February 1928

The Weakness and Greatness of *Tess*:
Famous Pictures that Help to Interpret Hardy's Genius

The mists of doubt are apt to rise and obscure the reputation of a supposedly great writer as soon as he is dead. You say to yourself: "Was the immense fuss justified? Or was he after all just a second-rater like many other admirable second-raters?"

Meredith has been dead nearly twenty years, and those mists have not yet cleared away. But they will. I was moved to take up a novel of Hardy's. I chose *Tess*, with apprehension, because I regarded it as the most vulnerable of his mature novels. It made his name with the large public, and therefore is suspect with the small public. Uneven it is; sentimental it occasionally is; maladroit it often is. But I had not gone far in it before I began to be convinced afresh that I was in the presence of greatness; and the conviction deepened as I went on. It has, not realistic truth, but ideal truth, which is the more stable and satisfying of the two.

At first there is uncertainty about the character of Tess. Considering her origins, could such a young woman have existed? Would not the refined Angel Clare have been repelled by her mere manners? Could she have lived contentedly with the other dairymaids, and yet have experienced the high sensations which Hardy attributes to her? As the story proceeds the answers to these questions formulate themselves satisfactorily. You think more and more of the influence of her aristocratic ancestors. You learn, half-way through the novel, that her achievements at school were sufficiently striking to mark her out for a career of a teacher. You perceive that she has a mind, and an original mind, and in the result your misgivings are quite dispelled.

Of course, she is made to use a vocabulary such as no rustic wench could possibly have used. Again and again the mere language renders you uneasy. But then you realise that all the characters express themselves, verbally, in an unrealistic way — and not least Angel Clare. You recall that Shakespeare makes Hamlet and Macbeth talk as no princes could ever have talked. And you are gradually reconciled to what is a superficial, instinctive if not intentional, and effective falsity. Every work of art must be conceived and executed within a convention. And the Hardy dialogue is only part of the general Hardy convention.

You may question the authenticity of Angel Clare. Could there have been, actually, such a man? But when Hardy sends him on a visit to his own home, and shows Mr. and Mrs. Clare and the two high-minded, narrow-minded priggish brothers, and the whole entourage fits together around Angel, corroborating the truth of him, you are reconciled to the strangeness of Angel also. More than reconciled. You are aware that he is right. These matters, and many other similar matters in the book, are, however, less important than the unifying impression of the book in its entirety. It is a simple book. Yes. But the characteristics of the greatest art are simplicity and repose. *Tess* has these characteristics intensely. Great art allays spiritual unrest; it tranquillizes the sound. And thus does *Tess*.

My experience is that great pictures help you to comprehend the aims, the spirit, and the self-set limitations of the writers of great books. Whenever I am sick of books (as occurs), and worried about the art and craft of writing and the inadequacy of themes and the treatment thereof, I go out and walk through parks and streets of shops to the National Gallery. Sometimes I visit the Tate, and, more rarely, the Wallace Collection. But the National Gallery is the supreme place for moral refreshment, not surpassed by the Prado at Madrid or even the Kunsthistorisches Museum at Vienna. I think that there are more absolute masterpieces to the square yard in the National Gallery than anywhere in Europe.

True, it is a disconcerting place. You see a picture on one wall one morning and the next morning it is gone and has to be looked for. All good pictures are magical, but the pictures at the National Gallery have a most uncanny habit of wandering about the dark and deserted rooms at night and choosing new homes for themselves. I have followed one of my favourite pictures, that triumph of realistic idealism Masaccio's *Blue Madonna* (which the late Arthur Clutton-Brock used to maintain was the finest picture at Trafalgar-square), all over the building. (It is, for the moment, well hung.) Assimilate the Masaccio, or Mantegna's *Agony in the Garden*, and they will help you to assimilate the masterpieces of Hardy.

Or, for another and perhaps a more suitable example, behold any of the classical pictures of Nicolas Poussin. Gods and demi-gods and mortals never lived as Poussin portrays them, in such colourings, in such lovely attitudes combining themselves together in perfect combinations; yet their idealism is based on a fundamental realism of truth to nature and godhead and humanity. You are obliged to say to yourself: "All things are not always like that. But, though rarely, some things are sometimes like that; and that everything might always be like that is not beyond my imagination." You are uplifted, inspired and encouraged by the vision of the possibilities of life. The same with great books. The same with Hardy, who took a dairy-farm and made it at moments the beautiful paradise that all dairy-farms might be.

The difficult business in a man's secret life is to maintain the balance between the idealism of an artistic creation and the realism of the daily world. The one is as necessary as the other to a full existence. You cannot, in the ardour of the search for ideal truth, repudiate the magnificent commonplace world. Some do, and they lose the world in addition to losing their own souls.

Hardy did not; as you could see at once from his conversation.

Nevertheless he chiefly confined his interest and curiosity to quite a small portion of the earth and its denizens. He knew a lot more of the world than the London publisher who has recently stated on a dust-jacket that the scene of a novel about Mexico is laid in South America; but he certainly did with apparent contentment limit the inquiries of his creative mind. Which may or may not be a defect.

The grand example of an artist who founded the highest idealism on the wildest realistic contacts with earth was Goethe, who stands alone in this respect. *Faust* is the proof. A mountain of a work! No, not a mountain — a range of mountains! Goethe spent considerably more than half a century in writing it; he preserved its unity; and embedded in its endless idealism all the realisms of a long and variously active life.

9 February 1928

Meredith Centenary:
The Novelist Who Never Learned to Tell a Story

George Meredith was born a hundred years ago, and has been dead nearly nineteen years. We have had opportunity, therefore, to make up our minds about him. But a writer's posterity, occupied with its own affairs, is apt, like a millionaire, to keep the suppliant waiting in ante-rooms, and apparently we have not yet decided to receive Meredith. All that can be said with certainty is that at present we do not even read him. That is to say, he is read only by those few whose passionate interest in what they believe to be good keeps the flame of renown alive through ages of general neglect.

There are misconceptions concerning Meredith. People say that he was the son of an ordinary tailor. So he was. But he was the grandson of a most extraordinary tailor, a character, a figure in a large town, a diner-out and a sportsman; a fellow of the grand manner. George Meredith took after the grandfather. Also his aunts were the mistresses of opulent homes. Also he made many distinguished and educated friends who understood how to combine high thinking with material comfort. Thus, though he had the bad habit of being poor, his pictures of leisured and luxurious life are probably not the fanciful inventions which some of us once supposed them to be. He knew what he was writing of when he collected his characters, intellectual or smart or both, in a country house where wine and philosophy were appreciated with equal expertise.

He was a fine sight for any beholder. A born comedian, he loved in later years to play the part of a great man, and he played it perhaps to exaggeration but with a sense of style. He had the evil temper of a tyrant; I am willing to attribute this to ill-health, despite which he lived very long.

He was not, in my opinion, a novelist by either birth or inclination. The first business of a novelist is to tell a story, and Meredith never learnt it. (Hardy did.) He halts his stories in order to give a performance — of otiose psychological analysis or unnecessary description. He wanders vaguely around. He gets lost. Even when going straight he often goes too slowly. So that the reader says impatiently to himself: "Yes. This is brilliant and

125

sound stuff, but it irritates me, and I almost wish I hadn't begun the thing. Still, having begun it, I'll struggle with it till I finish it or it finishes me." More than one of Meredith's novels has finished me.

Worse, Meredith wrote obscurely — not always, but frequently. Now obscurity of writing can be due to nothing but obscurity of thought. Oscar Wilde said that Meredith had mastered everything except language. This was an understatement. He had not mastered thought. And, worser and worser, he had not mastered construction — the prime constituent of a work of art. None of his novels is really well constructed, except *Beauchamp's Career* and *Evan Harrington.* These two works, and no others, hold you. No! It is not that they hold you. There are indeed others which hold you, but by your exasperated neck. *Beauchamp's Career* and *Evan Harrington* persuade you, draw you easily forward in their wake. The heavenly powers watched over the author as he wrote them, saying: "Just twice we will make you better than you are."

Meredith began with verse and ended with verse. I suspect that he preferred verse to prose, and felt himself more at home in verse. To mere narrative he was assuredly at heart indifferent. His fundamental desire was not to narrate, but to be lyrically static, or static in the comic vein. (By comic I of course do not mean farcical.) He is at his best in ecstasy, and in the comic exposure of weak characters. And when he slips into one of these moods he sends the story to the devil. He knows he can do what he chooses with you then, and naughtily makes you pay for two pages of perfection by inflicting on you twenty pages of face-scratching, trackless jungle. I exaggerate, but the truth is in me.

The popular judgment on Meredith is that his two best books are *The Ordeal of Richard Feverel* and *The Egoist.* With one reservation I concur in this judgment. His literary career, which stretched over sixty years, can be divided into two parts. *Feverel* opens the first part and *The Egoist* the second. Twenty years separate them (1859-1879). He had written two prose things before *Feverel* — *Farina*, which is a short and tedious pastiche, and *The Shaving of Shagpat*, which is a longer and less tedious pastiche aiming to outdo the Oriental extravagance of *The Thousand and One Nights.*

Then came *Feverel.* It has the fine Meredithian characteristics: rapture and high comedy. The chapter, "A Diversion played on a Penny Whistle," one of the most celebrated passages in English fiction, is as wondrous and faultless to me to-day as it was when I first read it forty years ago. Odd how this scene recalls the shepherd's piping in *Tristan,* Act III. (But it preceded *Tristan* by several years.) There is, amid the ecstasy, the same touch of realism in both. Meredith: "The self-satisfied sheep-boy delivers a last complacent squint down the length of his penny-whistle." Wagner, having caused his sheep-boy to hit on a pleasing phrase, makes him repeat the phrase again and again with a naive self-complacency.

But *Feverel* has also the less satisfactory Meredithian characteristics. The author gets lost in the maze of his tale; and the motivation goes to bits. Why did Richard leave Lucy? Every admirer finds a different reason, but nobody finds a good one and Meredith never gives a clear one. You have another example of these inexplicable separations in *Diana of the Crossways.* But Diana was a clever fool, while Lucy had the wisdom of simplicity.

126

Feverel waited nineteen years for a second edition. By that time Meredith was well sick of the British public, and he determined to write solely at his own sweet wilfulness. *The Egoist* was the first result. Despite its faults of technique, no finer and richer comedy than this novel exists in English. The next book, *The Tragic Comedians,* is dense and heavy. The last three novels, of his autumn and old age, are disfigured by too much of Meredith's own sweet wilfulness. Utterly occidental, they yet show the oriental extravagance of the writer of *The Shaving of Shagpat.*

Of all Meredith's novels I like best *Evan Harrington.* It has few faults and a hundred virtues. It is solid, restrained, shapely, and of an ample and continuous inspiration. Nothing unduly stands out in it. Perhaps that is why it has made less noise in the world than great but inferior books. It was written next after *Feverel,* when Meredith was thirty-three. A marvellous achievement for so young a writer. When I first read *Evan Harrington* I began it after supper and finished it just in time for breakfast — without one moment of exasperation. This is praise.

No space left for my idiosyncratic and doubtless inexpert ideas about Meredith's poetry. Some of the best of it is sanely bitter.

16 February 1928

Some Consequences of Tolstoy's Vanity:
Wanted, A Translators' Trade Union

By reason of the forthcoming centenary edition of Tolstoy's works in the Aylmer Maude translation, Tolstoy will soon again be prominently before the English literary world. I am moved to write more about him, apropos of something that was written by Mr. Bernard Shaw half a dozen years ago. Mr. Shaw pointed out that Tolstoy had "invited all publishers in all countries to take the fullest advantage of the absence of international copyright between Russia and other countries by publishing his writings in such translations as they could procure without any reference to his moral or legal rights." Tolstoy's aim, of course, was to get the largest possible sale for his works throughout the world.

This strange invitation to the whole earth is a striking example of Tolstoy's wrong-headedness. The immediate result of it was that all kinds of publishers clutched at a few of his more celebrated or more notorious books and had them translated helter-skelter. Serious publishers, publishers who really care about the contents of the volumes which carry their imprint, paid good money for good translations, only to find their versions in competition with inferior versions produced anyhow at the cheapest rates. And the competition was real, for the public is not always discriminating. The name of Tolstoy on a title-page was enough for most people, who recked not of translators. Serious publishers, if they did not actually lose money, could not make money. And even serious publishers have to live. No publishers indeed made any money worth talking about.

And Tolstoy himself suffered. He suffered in prestige from the incompetent, misleading translations, from which also the public suffered — though perhaps without being fully aware of it. And he suffered because his lesser known works were not translated at all. In the case of a non-copyright author a publisher can rarely undertake a collected edition. In every popular collected edition some volumes sell much better than others, and best-sellers compensate for the worst-sellers. If the publisher cannot hope to make a pretty handsome profit out of the best-sellers he will leave the worst-sellers alone. Thus everybody suffered: Tolstoy, the publishers, the sweated translators, and the public. And, not unimportant, literature suffered. Here one sees how economics are inseparable from art.

Tolstoy was to blame not merely for muddled and uninformed thinking. He was to blame for a certain egregiousness, conceit or vanity which his action implied. It was as if he had said: "The circulation of my works is a supremely urgent matter for the earth. I am a man of means. The financial returns from my books will not affect my way of life. Therefore in order to force my ideas on the world in which I consider myself so important, I will defy the ordinary laws of commerce and will advocate a course which, if it were widely followed, would be prejudicial to the majority of book-writers and book-producers."

In my opinion this was not right. Beyond doubt it lays bare the intense secret egotism of Tolstoy's character. Tolstoy ought to have chosen a serious publisher in every country and given to him the valuable imprimatur of his exclusive approval in return for a royalty. If in his quality of a Russian noble he was above royalty-taking, he might have given his royalties to charity. But he assuredly ought to have demanded and accepted royalties.

So doing, he would have diminished the number of translations by discouraging bad translations — not merely of his own, but of other men's works. Here I am reminded of a foreign book, H.L. Mencken's *Prejudices. Sixth Series* (Cape, 7s. 6d.), which is mainly made up of some of the finest and most exciting modern journalism I have seen. Mr. Mencken, speaking of eugenists, says: "They succumb to the modern craze for mass-production. Because a hundred policemen, or garbage men, or bootleggers are manifestly better than one, they conclude absurdly that a hundred Beethovens would be better than one. But this is not true."

I would say the same of translators. We do not want a hundred translations — or even a hundred good ones — of Tolstoy or anybody else. Each would help to kill all the rest, like bulbs too thickly planted in a flower-bed. I see from the recently issued *English Catalogue of Books for 1927*, edited by Mr. James Stewart (published by *The Publishers' Circular*), that even last year three different translators were at work on Tolstoy. Among the Tolstoy items is a version of *Resurrection* in 250 small pages. What kind of a version can this be? It may be cheap (sixpence), but positively it can only give an inadequate notion of what *Resurrection* really is.

I see also, in the same mine of facts, that during 1927 one translated book was issued for every day of the year, Sundays included. I wonder how many of these were faithful and dignified renderings of their originals. I personally know of some that were not. Every bad translation does harm.

By the way, I must not leave *The English Catalogue* without noting that the industrious and praiseworthy editor still sticks to his naughty scheme of joining "Poetry" to "Drama", under one head. I have not yet thought of any justification for this strange mingling.

I am strongly in favour of translations — subject to the strict avoidance of competing translations. I would like to see two new institutions: a sort of college of qualified translators capable of keeping translations at a fair level of literary decency and honesty; and a trade union of qualified translators to maintain the wages of translators at a subsistence level. All readers widely experienced in these fields know that over fifty per cent. of new translations are deplorable. They are not translations but assassinations — either brutal or negligent. The first qualification of a translator into English should be that he can write correct and seemly English. Few apparently can. The second qualification is that he can speak fluently and idiomatically the language out of which he is translating. Not one translator in a hundred, perhaps not one in a thousand, possesses the two qualifications. I receive quite a number of letters from would-be translators of me. They all assert (usually in imperfect English) that they have a thorough knowledge of English; but I cannot recall a single one of them who took the trouble to assert that he was an experienced and accomplished writer of his own language.

23 February 1928

New Authors Discovered:
A "Genuinely Interesting" French Novelist

Not long since I saw an advertisement of a novel, *The Honourable Picnic*, by Thomas Raucat. I have not read it, but I have just read the French novel, *L'Honorable Partie de Campagne*, by Thomas Raucat (Gallimard, Paris, 12 francs), of which I assume the English book to be a translation. By the way, I hope that the translation of the book itself is better than the translation of the title. And yet I could not offhand suggest a more adroit translation of the title. But then translating is not my job. Further by the way, there is at least one passage in the original which could not safely cross the Channel, and which I am quite sure, while not knowing, that the English translator has prudently discarded. He could afford to do so, for he had a winning hand without it.

This book was quietly but firmly recommended to me by one of the flying squadron of adventurous tasters who make reconnaissances on behalf of my lethargic self. I now in turn can quietly but firmly recommend it. Indeed it is a deeply diverting book, and well written, and well worthy of the success which it has had and is having in France. The author's notion is to give a picture of modern Japanese manners through the mouths of Japanese characters who take part in an excursion to a Japanese country hotel. The characters are men of business, work-girls, geishas, bourgeois, and so on. Each does a chapter. It is the best picture of Japanese manners that I have seen — notably better than that in a novel called *Kimono*, which appeared some years ago and caused discussion.

Japan is a terrible country — terrible by reason of the cast-iron conventions which hold its society together. It had a general election last Monday. Its Parliament is less than forty years old. It is more Western than the Europe which it has too sedulously copied; but it remains fantastically Oriental. In polite Japanese circles — and all Japanese circles are polite — everything is "honourable," both persons and things; even a warm bath is "honourable." "Honourable" is the key-word of all social relations. Socially, every Japanese is walking on a tight-rope over the Niagara of solecism all the time. There can be no relief for him, night or day.

The story is a criticism of Japan, but it is also a criticism of Europe. What matters, however, is its sedate, coy, malicious, ricocheting humour. Not mirthful, it consciously creates abundant mirth.

I wish it was perfect. It isn't. The author has severely handicapped himself by a complicated and unconvincing machinery of narration. Much more technical skill than he possesses would be required to weld together into a tight-fitting coherence the contributions of eight imagined different tale-tellers. The book sags. The earlier parts are in the main superior to the latter, though the penultimate chapter, written by a geisha, is one of the best. This chapter is truly illuminating about the daily life and ideals of a geisha. It gives you to understand; and it is tremendously proper — super-"honourable."

Thomas Raucat is that rarity — a genuinely interesting new author. Is he or is he not a man to follow? I was arguing the question with a French writer not long since, and he kept cautious attitude. "Yes," said he. "Raucat's book is certainly very good. But perhaps it is the fruit of one striking personal experience. Raucat may never write another half as good. Anybody with a competent pen can write one good book if he has been struck hard enough."

A few days later I sighted and captured a new book by Thomas Raucat: *Loin des Blondes* — which I would facetiously translate: *Far From the Palefaces.* (Same publisher and price.) "Ah!" I said to myself. "I shall know now what to think about Raucat's potentialities." But I still don't know. *Loin des Blondes* is a series of travel-sketches — chiefly Oriental. Somewhat in the style of Paul Morand (author of *Open All Night*), but better; and yet not quite good enough. (Morand has been over-praised.) One of the most elaborate chapters, "A Night in Shanghai," amounts to little more than nothing at all. Nevertheless the slim tome will serve to pass an hour without aesthetic humiliation.

Another genuinely interesting new author is Julien Green, said to be perfectly French but of American origin on one side. All I know of the man himself is that on the telephone he speaks perfect idiomatic English: which is a feat on a French telephone. His first novel has been published in English under the title *Avarice House.* I have read his second novel, *Adrienne Mesurat.* It is fine, and held me throughout. Julien Green shows none of that intention, so common among both French and English young high-brow authors, to be unreadable and incomprehensible at any cost. I have also read his third novel (short), *Le Voyageur sur la Terre* (Nouvelle Revue Francaise). It is a very strange story of madness, but still what I should call "sound". At the end of it one asks: "Why?" Julien Green is beyond doubt a man to follow. Also he is eminently translatable.

Lastly there is a new German novelist, Stefan Zweig. A book of his, *Conflicts: Three Tales,* has just been published by Allen and Unwin (7s. 6d.). The translation, being by Eden and Cedar Paul, is competent, though I have read better translations by this experienced pair. I had never heard of Zweig, and the book gives no syllable of biographical information about him. The publishers merely say of him: "The man whom Romain

Rolland, Maxim Gorky and equally discerning critics have recognised as one of the great story-tellers and psychologists of our day." Zweig may be all that; but for my part I say that it is the duty of the sponsors of a new foreign author to furnish English readers with a few facts about him. Age; origin; output; etc. Opinions concerning him we can form for ourselves.

The third tale in the book, *Episode in Early Life*, touches on a subject which has been treated with marvellous delicacy and realism by Marcel Proust, and with staggering directness by André Gide (in his finest book, *Si le grain ne meurt*): homosexuality. It may offend some sensible readers, but it cannot outrage any sensible reader. It is done with considerable tact. In any case, it would, in my view, be protected from anathema by the moral prestige of the publishers, a highly serious firm. This story is perhaps slightly marred by passages of that tedious sententious semi-sentimentality in description which is characteristic of good German literature, and which you may observe in Thomas Mann's masterpiece and even in the autobiography of Goethe. It contains, however, really wonderful pages of lyricism about Elizabethan drama. I have not yet decided whether I can wholly agree with Rolland and Gorky as to Zweig. But the book is more than respectable. It has sparks of the divine fire.

1 March 1928

The "Monstrous Conceit" of Some Modernists

Some schoolmasters, according to the latest serious stage spectacle, seem to consider it a crime to be young, and quite a grave crime to be a young poet. I sometimes feel this way myself. When I catch myself at it I administer reproof to myself: "You are making a noise like a back-number." For one month there had been lying on my desk Miss Laura Riding's book, *Contemporaries and Snobs* (Cape, 7s. 6d.). For three weeks I shied at that book, though I liked the title. I knew it was a book about modernist poetry, and so I made up my mind that it must be silly. Then I girded my loins and read the thing.

Well, it isn't silly. Miss Riding possesses intellectual power; also some intelligence. Also various defects. I shall not attempt to state her theory of modernist poetry. In order to do so, I should have to read the book again, and I would not read it again for £100. The book is metaphysics. I think it might interest Mr. Bertrand Russell, who probably alone in England is capable of grappling with it effectively. Miss Riding's notion is that modernist poetry is a search for the absolute and that Gertrude Stein is its chief prophet. All metaphysics is a search for the absolute; but the best metaphysicians are aware that the search must be ultimately futile.

Miss Riding certainly does give a semi-coherent account of what Gertrude Stein is after. Gertrude Stein has been after it for more than twenty years, and I affirm that she is now no nearer her goal than she was in 1906. I should merely smile at Gertrude Stein, who has been the cause of more chatter among literary coteries, sects and schismatics than any author within living memory, were it not that she is championed by Edith Sitwell. Edith Sitwell is a real and an original artist, and I respect her views, even

131

if I totally disagree with them.

When I think of what Edith Sitwell thinks of Gertrude Stein, the horrid thought arises in me: "I may be wrong about Gertrude Stein." Then I read bits of Gertrude Stein, and am reassured. This bit, for instance:

"Everything is the same except composition and as the composition is different and always going to be different everything is not the same. . . . Romanticism is then when everything being alike everything is naturally simply different, and romanticism." Upon which Miss Riding comments: "We may draw from this a definition of classicism: it is the sameness of the differentness of composition."

Upon which I must comment: "On what mad principle does heaven distribute the sense of humour? These formidable pioneers are the very people who need it, and it has been denied to them." *Contemporaries and Snobs* does not contain the thousandth part of one per cent. of humour. At the end of the book Miss Riding gives a list of her works. Two are published. A third, done in collaboration with Robert Graves, is also published. Three are "forthcoming." Miss Riding's *First Poems* are "forthcoming"! Incidentally, I should love to know what Miss Riding thinks of the admirable but sadly un-modernist poetry of her collaborator.

In addition to suffering acutely from a total absence of humour, these pioneers suffer from the sense of being all alone, and utterly right, in an utterly wrong world of letters. They rejoice too richly and too contemptuously in their apartness. Which is a roundabout way of saying that they are monstrous conceited persons. But their worst fault is that they cannot write in a comprehensible fashion. When you have to read a paragraph seven times to get the hang of it, and even then don't quite get the hang of it, one conclusion is sure: the author cannot write. The great philosophers, metaphysicians, critics can always be understood in once. Consider T.H. Huxley, Matthew Arnold, Hume, Lessing, Bertrand Russell, Aristotle. They say clearly what they mean. Studying them, you are not driven to brandy to tranquillize your exasperated nerves. They can write.

Here I must interject a reference to a new volume, *The Tower* (Macmillans, 6s.), by one of the greatest living poets, W.B. Yeats — the man who thirty years ago wrote:

> No man nor woman has lover otherwise
> Than in brief longing and deceiving hope
> And bodily tenderness; and he who longs
> For happier love but finds unhappiness,
> And falls among the dreams the drowsy gods
> Breathe on the burnished mirror of the world
> And then smooth out with ivory hands and sigh.

There is nothing as lovely as that in *The Tower*, but it is all finewrought stuff, and pellucid. The book is beautifully produced, like nearly all Senator Yeats's books.

To return, Miss Riding is terribly hard reading. But this vice of inefficient writing is wider spread than I had thought. A new edition has just appeared of Professor A.N. Whitehead's *Science and the Modern World* (Cambridge University Press, 8s. 6d.). I bought it, partly because for years I have been forming the idea, while knowing little of him, that

Professor Whitehead is a great man, and partly because the book has been most enthusiastically praised by men such as Julian Huxley, Bertrand Russell, and J.W.N. Sullivan — Viscount Haldane states that he has read it three times! Could I resist the bait?

Now I can answer the question why Professor Whitehead, being great, has yet made so little impression upon general omnivorous readers. *Science and the Modern World* is certainly a wonderfully original volume, and the breadth of the author's culture is certainly, as Bertrand Russell says, "astonishing." But Professor Whitehead is hard to read. In other words, he cannot (what I call) write. He fumbles. He over-charges his sentences. He makes his transitions rather clumsily. Some of his paragraphs lour darkly and illegibly like a tempestuous sky. He is capable of dashing his reader by using a word such as "universality" immediately after a word such as "university." He is even capable of using the same word in two different senses in the same line. All which phenomena must be painful to his admirers. I recommend the work — to those who are ready to pay as high a price for their enjoyment as a dog will pay for the marrow of an adamantine bone.

My idea of a supremely readable writer is Stendhal, and I respectfully bring him to the notice of both Miss Riding and Professor Whithead. Stendal just wrote plainly what he had to write. He let each simple sentence stand up by itself. He never began sentences with phrases such as "Be that as it may——." Messrs. Chatto and Windus have published a new volume of their English edition of Stendal — the famous treatise *On Love* (7s. 6d.). It is well translated by Vyvyan Holland. Glancing through it, you don't say: "I won't read any more just now." You say: "I must just read one more page."

8 March 1928

A Passionately Hunted Narrative Poem:
An Indictment that Has Frightened America:
Two Pounds of Dostoevsky

By the alert lettered élite the most discussed and most desired book of the day is Mr. James Laver's *A Stitch in Time: or Pride Prevents a Fall* (Nonesuch Press). A narrative poem written in Popeian rhymed couplets, and apparently a pastiche of *The Rape of the Lock*, with a modern Belinda for heroine. The anecdote related is to the effect that Belinda, rising in a hurry and rather late even for her (4 p.m.), discovered a rent in her green chemise and mended it with pink cotton. She then went to a tête-à-tête tea in a young man's flat, endangered her virtue, and only preserved it in the nick of time by imaginatively realising that no decent-minded girl could possibly permit herself to expose to the male view a green under-garment darned in pink.

This is the sort of story that to-day appeals strongly to the alert lettered élite. The thing has a fundamental and fatal fault. It does not convince. Belinda would never have mended green with pink; she would have done no mending at all. She would have put on another garment, seeing that according to the narrator, who should know, she had lots of them.

133

By the élite of the élite the poem has been derided, not because of its fluffy naughtiness, but because the Popeian rhymed couplet is so easy to write. For myself I see here no ground for derision. No doubt the Popeian rhymed couplet is easy to write, but it is not easy to write as well as Mr. James Laver writes it. The trifle is really accomplished. Though I would by no means class it with its great exemplar, I would certainly say that it is neater than Pope, who, contrary to general report, was often somewhat untidy. Mr. Laver has achieved some pleasing effects. Thus, of "the battery of kisses" that assailed Belinda:-

> The first went wide, the second fell more near,
> The third exploded just beneath her ear,
> The fourth, a lock of hair blows right away,
> And then, with paralysing ricochet,
> Along her brow and cheek rebounds and skips.
> The fifth lands full on her protesting lips,
> And shakes the fortress to its finger tips.

And many good single lines. For instance:

> Assumed a vice, although she had it not.

I heard much talk of this bit of confectionery before I succeeded in getting possession of it, for it is being passionately hunted by collectors and, the edition being limited, the price has risen — by 400 per cent. — and is still rising.

Why the Nonesuch Press should describe itself as a "press" I do not understand. It does not print its own books. However, *A Stitch in Time* is beautifully printed. But oddly designed. It is a quarto disguised as a folio, stands within a fraction of a foot high, and has to be shelved with high antique tomes like the *Plato* of Henry Stephen. Holders are hereby advised to sell. Belinda didn't fall, but the price of her very probably will.

It was a sinister coincidence that brought to me simultaneously with *A Stitch in Time* Judge Ben Lindsey's *The Revolt of Modern Youth* (Brentano, 10s. 6d.). Before I saw it I thought that *The Revolt of Modern Youth* was about literature. It is about something more important: life. Judge Lindsey (who writes with a slangy freedom that would be the ruin of any English judge) presides over the celebrated "Juvenile and Family Court" of Denver, U.S.A., and his book shows in horrifying detail the consequences of playing Belinda's pranks when the parents of Belinda blindly adhere to the usual parental conventions of upbringing.

Judge Lindsey is on the side of the erring children every time. And I am on the side of Judge Lindsey every time. He puts forward a tremendous indictment of respectable parenthood. His facts concerning the prevalence of adolescent immorality in Denver are scarcely credible, but the Judge makes you believe them, and *The Revolt of Modern Youth* has frightened all America. It ought to be widely and carefully read in Britain. Parents should read it with humility. Clergymen, priests, and Nonconformist ministers should study it, having first forgotten all that they have ever learnt about the mentality and the instincts of the young of both sexes. It has no relation to literature. It is a most formidable document. The serious reader of it will not have to make notes while reading — he will remember.

Another scarce and seemingly new book is Mr. Ludwig Lewisohn's

(American) novel, *The Case of Mr. Crump* (published by Titus, Paris, edition limited to 500 copies, price unknown to me). Though agreeably and even luxuriously printed, it is heavy and unwieldy and begins to fall to pieces at a glance. I have heard that for reasons turning on the law of libel the book will not be published in U.S.A. I suspect it of being too true to life, or to one life. Mr. Lewisohn has unquestionable talent. He writes well. He has imagination and some power, he tries to be unprejudiced, and he carries you on, though uncomfortably, from page to large page. His only grave literary defect is that he cannot successfully manage dialogue and therefore too frequently avoids it, with desolating results. But what an old-fashioned work, in its persistent squalor, sordidness and naive, unnecessary, high-minded indulgence in not-nice words! Thirty or more years ago I should have ardently admired it as the revolt of modern youth against Anglo-Saxon primness. To-day I regard it as I regard a Victorian wool-mat. It is full of printer's errors. It is also another of those carelessly produced volumes which give no clue whatever to the pages on which new chapters start.

It will not have escaped the regular reader of this page that my career is devoted to a campaign against needlessly unwieldy books and uncharted books. (Twice above I have had to animadvert upon unwieldiness.) I regret to say that Messrs. Routledge (to whom the lettered owe so much) have just sent me one: *Dostoevsky, the Man and his Work*, by Julius Meier-Graefe, adroitly translated by Herbert H. Marks (25s.). This volume measures 10 inches by 6½ by 1¾, contains 113 cubic inches of paper, and weighs nearly two pounds. I object to holding such a volume, for whose dimensions there is no apparent excuse. Further, the book has no list of contents and no index, and the chapters have no titles. How can one find one's way about in this jungle?

The subject of the work has a strong attraction for me, and I greatly admire the author — as what reader does not? — for his masterly biography of the painter Van Gogh. But quite apart from its mere physical pro-digiosity, I must condemn this *Dostoevsky* on various counts. It is too long for its matter; it is windy; it is too often dithyrambic — almost hysterically so; its descriptions of the novels are fantastically over-detailed. Here and there occur fine pages worthy of Mr. Meier-Graefe. Among other illustrations are two very interesting reproductions of Dostoevsky's MS. of *The Possessed.* They are epileptic. If they went to the printers they must have filled madhouses with compositors. My adored Dostoevsky! . . .

15 March 1928

Handicaps in the Theatre: The Producer Difficulty: Mr. Noel Coward's Versatility — And an Annoyed Preface

The characteristics of the literary, dramatic, musical, and artistic critics of *The Manchester Guardian* — a formidable band — is a determination not to lose their heads. Mr. Ivor Brown, principal dramatic critic of *The Manchester Guardian*, has written a book called *Parties of the Play* (Benns, 8s. 6d.), in which the relation and interplay of author, actor, producer, and public are discussed. Mr. Brown keeps his head therein. It is a sane book. There may perhaps be a little too much of the allusive and elegant fantasy of phrasing which the editor of the *M.G.* probably encourages. But there is balance, that enemy of interestingness — and Mr. Brown has defeated the enemy while respecting him. If Mr. Brown had only nailed a slogan to his mast, or been violent, impudent, unfair, or cursed or canonised, everybody would read *Parties of the Play*. Everybody may. Everybody should; for everybody is to-day preoccupied about the theatre.

High-brows by force of habit still condemn the British theatre; but you see them more and more at first nights. Says Mr. Brown: "The art of the theatre in England is in a more lively state of health than most critics would admit. There is a greater stream of intelligent activity going into the theatre . . . than there has been for centuries . . . The enormous expansion, the ambitions and the quality of amateur acting are further symptoms of a theatrical renaissance."

These statements are certainly true. The last sentence is as important as any.

Of the four parties to the play, the actor is handicapped by the fact that he seldom takes the trouble to make himself clearly audible, the public is handicapped by the same fact, the author is seriously handicapped by the ignorance and the indifference of managers; and the producer is cock of the walk. The best English producers are full of good ideas and intentions; but they lack thoroughness, which they might learn, if they chose, in New York or from the presentation of American plays in London.

Mr. Brown puts his finger on the producer difficulty thus: "A theatre in which the producer was absolute sovereign would be more easily and accurately directed if you could scrap the fickle creature man and create your spectacle by the manipulation of Robots." Yes! The theatre is pre-eminently a *human* machine, and the fault of the arch-producer is that he is apt to forget this. Considering that Mr. Brown has, I suppose, had little experience of actual rehearsals, he is surprisingly wise about producing.

I remember two very well-known actresses coming to me at a rehearsal with the news that they would leave the cast if something "different" didn't happen at once. I took aside the producer and said to him: "Praise is what is required." The producer answered: "I see what you mean." The next day the senior of the two actresses, who had no notion of the nature of my remarks to the producer, came to me beaming, and said: "We're so grateful to you. It's all right now." This is a story with a moral for arch-producers. I cannot here discuss, I can merely indicate, Mr. Brown's urbane, subtle volume.

Mr. Noel Coward has had the wit to publish his two latest failures, *Home Chat* and *Sirocco*, together with his British-banned but not American-banned play, *This Was a Man*, in one volume (Secker, 7s. 6d.). He has introduced them with a Preface attacking the·Middle Class. In my opinion creative artists would be better advised not to write annoyed prefaces. What is the matter with the Middle Class anyhow? It is the backbone of every theatrical audience, and is mainly responsible for all Mr. Coward's numerous successes. *Home Chat* and *Sirocco* did not fail because they are bad plays; far from being bad plays they are out of sight superior to nineteen new plays in every twenty shown to London, New York, Berlin or Paris. They failed partly because they are original in feeling, partly because a certain quite common type of mind resents a too brilliant success in the young, and partly because Mr. Coward loves to make opposition vocal on a first night. Not only should dramatists never write annoyed prefaces; they should never appear before the curtain — except with a revolver. Mr. Coward does not know this, but he knows everything else about the theatre, and assuredly more about the theatre than any other man in England.

Mr. Ivor Brown's education in the theatre is still incomplete, and will remain so until he has seen Noel Coward directing rehearsals of pieces which he has written, instructing the orchestra about the music which he has composed for the said pieces, enlightening the singers about singing the said music, showing the dancers how to dance the dances which he has invented, giving highly technical tips to the actors and actresses — and doing it all with a genuine and accepted authority. A phenomenon which must be witnessed to be believed.

A technical and very specialised book about the theatre (which should nevertheless interest the majority of "intelligent patrons of the stage") is *Correspondence between Richard Strauss and Hugo von Hofmannsthal, 1907-1918*, translated by Paul England (Secker, 18s.). The letters comprised in this volume show in detail the progress of the grand collaboration which resulted in that enchanting operatic masterpiece, *Der Rosenkavalier* and other goodish works.

These letters are extraordinarily honest and direct. Writes Hofmannsthal to Strauss, in the earliest stages of their partnership: "I must insist before all else on the fact that I am writing for myself and not for you . . . although, of course, your music is a most beautiful addition to whatever I do . . ." Yet in appearance, demeanour, and conversation Hofmannsthal is a very modest man. Strauss had the sense to accept the ultimatum, and Hofmannsthal had the sense not to insist too much on it. Four years later Hofmannsthal was addressing his partner as "my alter ego." Indeed, the letters are packed with solid sense.

To continue with the stage. I daresay that a hundred times as many people have seen the undistinguished *Cavalleria Rusticana* as have seen the distinguished *Der Rosenkavalier*. And not one in a hundred of them knows or cares that the "book" of it is founded on a very fine short story by Giovanni Verga, who wrote, in addition to a very fine novel, many very fine short stories, some about peasants and some about wanton fine ladies. I recall reading the story *Cavalleria Rusticana* in English thirty years ago, and being considerably impressed. It has been issued, with other stories, in a new and lively and curiously untidy translation by D.H. Lawrence (Cape 6s.). And another volume of Verga's short stories (but still shorter ones) entitled *Little Novels of Italy*, also translated by D.H. Lawrence, has been reissued at 3s. 6d. (Secker).

Lastly, to conclude with the stage, I must mention James Agate's excited and exciting biography of *Rachel* (Howe, 3s. 6d.), which is beyond question the best life in English of the greatest tragic actress (and one of the greatest *grandes amoureuses*) that the world has known. Mr. Agate's biography is briefer than Lord Ronaldshay's biography of Curzon, and better written. It tells, as far as a man can tell in 92 pages, the whole truth about Rachel, which truth only began to be told even in France a few years ago. I protest, however, musically, against his phrase: "Meyerbeer, Donizetti, Bellini and all the brainless crew." None of the three composers deserved such derision. None was brainless. All had power, originality and distinction, and all achieved beauty; some of the music of all of them still gives pleasure to those who have ears to hear.

All the aforementioned books are handsomely worth reading.

22 March 1928

The Best and Worst of George Moore: Wanted – A New Translation of Ibsen: A Woman Novelist to be Watched

There are books which you never forget. And you don't know quite why. The everlasting result may be due to the book itself, or it may be due partly to the book and partly to the mood in which you encountered it. Three such books, for me, are Spencer's *Introduction to the Study of Sociology*, which may be as second-rate as some people say, but which aroused the latent common sense and sense of justice in my mind and gave me a new habit of thought; Samuel Butler's *Notebooks*; and George Moore's *Confessions of a Young Man*.

I find on research that I have what appears to be, but probably isn't, the first edition of the *Confessions*, with a mediocre portrait signed "W.S." (? William Strang). I once possessed the second edition, with a far more interesting portrait by a French artist. When I was about as young as Mr. Moore was when he wrote it, I read the *Confessions* without taking breath. In spite of the fact that Mr. Moore had previously written a number of books (including one of his masterpieces, *A Mummer's Wife*, which opens in the Five Towns and which first opened my shut eyes to the extraordinary romantic quality of that sinister district), the *Confessions* is one of the youngest books ever written. It is a wild, wilful, naughtily challenging book, written with the really remarkable narrative skill which came to full maturity in *Esther Waters*. It describes artistic Paris, as artistic Paris was never described before and has never been described since. It is a book for creative artists and for those who are not afraid of life and all life. It angers some excellent persons; but it excited in me a pure, unreserved enthusiasm – enthusiasm which remains integral to this day.

It has now been republished in Heinemann's Travellers' Library, at 3s. 6d. – cheap! – and I cannot let its appearance pass without acclaim. As it is a short book a number of Mr. Moore's essays have been added to it. Also there are three preliminary pieces. First, a dedication to Jacques Blanche, written with a pardonable affectation in French – I say affectation because M. Blanche speaks English as well as Mr. Moore speaks English. (By the way, M. Blanche has recently re-issued in a revised and definitive edition the novel which he printed anonymously some years ago, *Les Cloches de Saint-Amarain*, published by Emile-Paul, Paris). Second, the Preface proper. And third a Note, introducing the new edition.

The Preface shows Mr. Moore's style at nearly its best. It was evidently composed in a justifiable mood of self-satisfaction. For instance, he says: "The first eulogies written in England, I might almost say in any language,

138

of Manet, Degas, Whistler, Pissarro [the last name is spelt 'Pissaro' — Mr. Moore could always write but could seldom spell], are in this book of Confessions, and whosoever reads will find himself unable to deny that time has vindicated all of them splendidly." Time has. Time has vindicated the entire book, which in forty years has scarcely aged by one day.

I have not re-read it right through; but so far as I have read in it, Mr. Moore has not altered the work, as he has altered — and in my judgment seriously impaired — various other of his books. Mr. Moore's weakness is that he cannot leave a book alone. Those who wish to get the best out of George Moore are hereby solemnly advised to read the early books in the early editions thereof, with all their ingenuous crudities.

The great and wholesome influence of George Moore on modern English fiction has not yet been adequately appreciated — hardly even noticed. But it exists. Like Fielding, like Scott, like Dickens, George Moore brought something into English fiction which was not there before. That something is Gallic — a candour, a wider and more courageous search for beauty, and a more logical detachment in the selection of material. I know nothing in modern English fiction to compare with *Esther Waters* in the technical craft of selection.

In this week of the Ibsen centenary I am reminded of another emotional experience which ranks in my memory with any experience resulting from the perusal of a book. Namely, a performance of *Hedda Gabler*, in the last century, in some theatre now destroyed, and with an actor in the part of Judge Brack whose name I cannot recall. But I can recall the name of the actress who played Hedda — Elizabeth Robins, novelist. Elizabeth Robins was not among the first practical Ibsen pioneers: Janet Achurch, Charles Charrington, Edmund Gosse, J.T. Grein, and William Archer: but she put an Ibsen character, and the romantic beauty of a great play, over the foot-lights, in a manner which I have not seen surpassed. Unforgettable! You may centenarize Ibsen with banners and flags and special articles that wave adjectivally in the controversial breeze, as much as you like. Ibsen, however, is not yet appreciated in this country. Ibsen's chances were scotched by one of his most devoted admirers, William Archer. I liked and greatly respected William Archer; he did a lot of good, but his translation of Ibsen's plays is dreadful. None but those who have assisted at Ibsen re-hearsals in English can realise the utter "unsayableness" of Archer's lines. The *sine qua non* of the popular success of Ibsen in Britain is a new trans-lation of him by someone with some sense of dialogue.

And I will name one more emotional experience: the reading of André Gide's first novel *L'Immoraliste*. In 1903 I picked up for about a couple of francs in a book-box on the Seine quays, a copy of the first edition (1902, limited to 300 copies and finely printed) of this wonderful book, and comprehended the same evening that I had encountered a new author of original and genuine importance. And now the publishers who call them-selves "Le Capitole" (Paris) have issued in Gide's honour one of those massive memorial volumes which are fashionable in France but unknown here: a book of studies, documents, biographical pieces, bibliography, portraits and other illustrations — all signed with distinction. It is a very composite work, and must be possessed by the faithful, though possibly only André Gide himself will read it all through. It costs about a pound in London.

I will add in parenthesis that the cheap French edition of Gide's latest and finest novel, *Si le grain ne meurt*, is seriously expurgated. It had to be. Only the three-volume edition is complete. As, however, the novel is all good, the popular edition is all good, and well worth having.

George Moore's *Confessions* are of course autobiography, doubtless arranged and "stylised" for an artistic end, like his extremely amusing and malicious *Hail and Farewell* trilogy. Had he been writing the *Confessions* today he would perhaps have made a novel of them. More novels, especially early novels, than you would suspect are in fact reminscences. I feel nearly sure that Elizabeth Madox Roberts' *My Heart and My Flesh* (Cape, 7s. 6d.) is to a large extent reminiscent. Miss Roberts is American, and the author of *The Time of Man*. I mentioned her last year as a novelist to be watched. She writes admirably. *My Heart and My Flesh*, which contains terrible things, somewhat lacks both power and form. But it has beauty, and should not be missed. Mr. Cape (may his shadow never grow less!) has also published a slight volume of Miss Roberts' poems about childhood. *Under the Tree* (3s. 6d.). I should call them charming, honest, authentic; but prettyish and a little monotonous. Still, I would not give the book away, neither sell it to a dealer.

29 March 1928

Are American Short Stories Better than English?
The Genius of Pauline Smith: Truthfulness in Fiction

For some time past I have been hearing of the wonder of the short stories of the American writer, Barry Benefield, and now at last by the combined enterprise of Mr. Edward J. O'Brien, specialist in short stories, and the publishers (Allen and Unwin), a volume of his work is offered to the British public: *Short Turns* (7s. 6d.). Mr. O'Brien contributes a brief preface to the book, and this preface makes plain to me why I so often disagree with his judgments about short stories. It appears that in the last dozen years Mr. O'Brien has read some 12,000 American short stories — without counting multitudinous English short stories. My position is that nobody could read 12,000 American short stories in twelve years and keep his head.

Mr. O'Brien sums up Mr. Benefield thus: "His peculiar distinction is to sublimate the finest essences of life out of the most dusty material, and so to glorify our clay." To which I would reply that either this sentence is mere verbiage or, if it means anything, it applies equally to nearly all good imaginative writers, and is not peculiar to Mr. Benefield in the slightest degree.

As for Mr. Benefield, he is certainly better than the average contriver of shop-finished short stories for the glossy pages of American magazines. He writes cleverly and clearly, though without distinction. One of his faults is the continual employment of a sort of jargon of over-emphasis. As for instance: "The big woman threw both hands over her mouth to force back the screaming curses that mobbed her lips. Her seething mind coined curses and laid them . . ." etc. A manner which to me is both tedious and exacerbating; assuredly it is not first-rate. I do wish that these modish purveyors would study with humility the work of the inventor and master of the modern short story, de Maupassant, who realised from the start, and never forgot, that over-emphasis is the enemy of forcefulness. Mr. Benefield always begins by annoying you.

Still, though he hardly succeeds in hiding under a layer of cynicism that secret sentimentality which is his fault-in-chief, he does sometimes get somewhere. He has been visited by excellent ideas for short stories, and he handles the ideas adequately, now and then brilliantly. *White Silk Tights* is good. About half-way through it the author really draws a character (the unfaithful husband), and achieves some genuine pathos. The story *Daughters of Joy* (second cousin, once removed, and on the wrong side of the blanket, of de Maupassant's *La Maison Tellier*) is showier than *White Silk Tights*, but it is too ingenuously concocted to be convincing, and at the end of it you say to yourself: "Yes, all very well; but did these things happen?" Artfulness is there, but not the artfulness which conceals artfulness.

If I were the examiner, and Mr. Benefield the examinee, I would give him a pass; but not honours.

It is a commonplace of English newspaper criticism, and of American editors, that American short stories are better than English. I doubt it. I will go further, and say that I positively deny it. Mr. O'Brien asserts that in the last ten years four distinguished writers of short stories have appeared in U.S.A.: Sherwood Anderson, Manuel Komroff, Ernest Hemingway, and Barry Benefield. Anderson I know and am dubious about. Komroff I have never heard of. Hemingway is very adroit and smart, too slick, and rather narrow in range. He has been influenced by Paul Morand and Henri de Montherlant. Morand is not at all a good model. Montherlant, on the other hand, is an authentic artist, and Benefield and Hemingway could not come within ten miles of him. By the way, a translation of de Montherlant's admirable if occasionally "precious" Spanish novel *Les Bestiaires* has recently appeared under the title of *The Bull-Fighters* (Cape, 7s. 6d.).

There are, however, in my opinion, much better short story writers in America than Anderson, Hemingway and Benefield. One of them is Joseph Hergesheimer, whose *The Sprig of Verbena* is a lovely thing. But for the very best short stories you must explore that decrepit isle, Britain. No writer in America has approached Kipling. None has approached H.G. Wells. I question whether any American writer has approached A.E. Coppard, a volume of whose tales has just been reissued in The Travellers' Library (a series which seems to be published jointly by Heinemann and Cape).

Further. In the matter of short story writers the principal discovery of the age has been Pauline Smith, the author of *The Little Karoo*, and of a novel, *The Beadle*. Pauline Smith's finest story, *The Pain* (in *The Little Karoo* volume), is a masterpiece — and I do not use this word lightly. When it first appeared in *The Adelphi* review letters about it were received from the uttermost parts of the earth. If the United States can produce a story fifty per cent. as good I should very much like to see the thing. I must say, in justice to Mr. O'Brien, that *The Pain* did not escape his detective glance. Miss Smith's acceptance by the public was said to be handicapped by two factors — all her work is about South Africa, and all her work is uncompromisingly tragic. Yet she came through. Publishers, I hear, are now competing for her next book. But I should be surprised to learn that magazine editors are competing for it.

I would think as soon of trying to teach my grandmother to suck eggs as trying to teach magazine-editors, and especially American magazine-editors, their own business. Nevertheless I hear in my heart a still, small whispering of a suspicion that they may just possibly have something to learn from the public attitude towards Miss Smith's work. The magazine-editor, with his hand (theoretically) on the pulse of the public, insists on having stories with a happy — or at worst a not-gloomy — ending, and he insists also on some sentimentalisation of the truth concerning life. My idea is that public taste has moved faster than the magazine-editor is aware of. And precisely as the average theatre-manager notoriously lags behind his public, so, I contend, the magazine-editor lags behind his public.

In my view there is a large demand, and a better market, for truthfulness in fiction than editors assume. I think that if a popular magazine regularly printed, say, one story in six that resembled life much more closely than the other five, that magazine would at once excite remark and improve its circulation. A very considerable section of the public is eagerly on the look-out for truth, and this section, warned by experience, consistently ignores the popular magazine.

Of course, a magazine-editor, being just as naive as the rest of us, will take anything, even a tragic ending, signed with a prodigious name, provided it is not too expensive for him. Why then should he refuse similar work from the less illustrious? Prodigious names have little or no *permanent* effect on circulation. It is the general run of the contents that sells a magazine and keeps on selling it. Hence the contents should in some degree cater for all widespread varieties of taste. At present the contents fail to do this. I have friends among magazine-editors in two hemispheres; I like them; I understand some of their difficulties. But our amicable relations do not blind me to their wrong-headedness in the affair of short stories. The majority of them, for example, still hold that it is harder to write a good short story than a good serial. It isn't. I am not arguing with them.

5 April 1928

My Reply to George Jean Nathan

This article is about myself. Its aim is to show what a grand, peace-breaking fellow I am. In the new number of *The American Mercury* (published in London by Knopf, 2s. 6d.) George Jean Nathan, the *Mercury*'s principal contributor, after the editor H.L. Mencken, says in his usual stately Johnsonese that the unfairness of English literary critics towards American books is so excessively irritating that unless something is done about it quickly, something will come about which "will bode ill for international amity." He refers to "the arbitrary snootiness, condescension and downright animosity of England and the English to almost all American literary endeavour." Again: "Hardly an American book can be published in England without calling forth in English newspapers and periodicals a violent nose-fingering and derision." Again, of the English reviewer's fell work: "Snide and dirty deal."

And lastly. "On all sides are writers and critics like Arnold Bennett and Chesterton and a hundred lesser men who lose no opportunity to deride and insult American writers, denying them fair criticism. . ." etc., etc.

Well! Early in the present century I wrote an article on American fiction for *Harper's Magazine. Harper's* withheld it for years — possibly because it was too friendly towards their native writers. They at length, taking advantage of the advertisement of my presence in U.S.A., printed it in another of their periodicals, *The North American Review.* Shortly afterwards an American novelist whom I had praised thus addressed me: "Mr. Bennett, for years I had received no recognition in America, and I had absolutely decided to give up literature and find another calling. But your article gave me hope, and I determined to try again." Later, I met him by chance in a London street and he told me that he had "come through" — solely by reason of the encouragement of an English critic. This is an example of my arbitrary "snooting"!

Take Theodore Dreiser. More than a quarter of a century ago I reviewed *Sister Carrie* for *The Academy.* I had never heard of Dreiser. Nobody had. I praised his book with enthusiasm. My article crossed the Atlantic, and, I was told, laid the foundation of his fame in America. At any rate Dreiser was extremely grateful to me. I have been preaching Dreiser ever since. In 1926 I wrote (here): "At the end of the year 1926 I recall that the most important large works of imagination which I have read in 1926 are both American." The two books were Dreiser's *An American Tragedy*; and *Pierre.* The author of *Pierre* is Herman Melville — but how many American critics would know this off-hand? Of late years Melville has enjoyed a boom. One of the beginnings of that boom was a solemn decision by Frank Swinnerton and myself that the finest of all sea-stories was *Moby Dick* and that the fact should be proclaimed. It was proclaimed. No doubt a "dirty deal."

I have consistently praised Sinclair Lewis. I have letters from him attesting his deep satisfaction thereat. Of *Elmer Gantry* I wrote (here) that it was a "big" novel. And I warmly defended his style against ridiculous current jibes — chiefly American. I think this treatment must be a "snide."

When James Branch Cabell got into difficulties with American morality-mongers I wrote, for American publication, that I was uncompromisingly on his side and against his enemies. Probably an "insult."

A year or two ago Elizabeth Madox Roberts was unknown. I had never heard of her when I came across her first novel, *The Time of Man,* of which I wrote (here): "It is a wonderful and an imperfect novel. The style, American, is excellent. The descriptions are most delectable, the psychology searching, the detail plenteous, exact and skilfully handled." Also the other day I drew attention to her second novel. This may be "nose-fingering."

I was loud in my acclaim of Thornton Wilder in England. I wrote, here: "In my opinion, *The Bridge of San Luis Rey* is an absolutely first-rate work. It dazzled me by its accomplishment. The writing, simple, straight, *juste,* and powerful, has not been surpassed in the present epoch." I have been told, with what truth I know not, but both in the Press and privately, that my verdict, transmitted to New York, was partly responsible for Mr. Thornton Wilder's immense success in America. It was certainly so for his immense success in England. An instance, I daresay, of my British "condescension."

I rarely mention an American book that I do not treat in the manner exemplified above.

The truth is that time after time the vogue for American authors has been started by derisive, condescending, sniding and hostile English critics. I have said in the past, and I say again, that English critics are on the whole better than American critics (just as English short story writers are on the whole better than American). They have a keener flair and far more courage. Until a few years ago American literary high-brows disdained American authors. This is notorious. I have heard with my own ears two of America's greatest writers, Poe and Whitman, sniffed at in the drawing-rooms of Boston. What American critic has said, as George Moore has said, and as I, copying him, have said, that in Hawthorne America has one of the loveliest stylists in modern English literature? It is nearly 20 years since I wrote in the highest snooty terms of the stories of Ambrose Bierce. I should like to see any American appreciation of them as "snooty" as mine.

Nor have I confined my dirty dealing to American imaginative writers. About six months ago I wrote, here: "If I deal chiefly with novelists the reason is that fiction happens to be my speciality. Of late I have largely occupied myself, in print, with modern novelists. But that does not prevent me from highly appreciating other kinds of modern authors. I may mention Dr. and Mrs. Beard, whose *Rise of American Civilisation* and Miss Mayo's *Mother India* are in my opinion likely to be as influential and valuable as any novels written or to be written between 1907 and 1947." Odious arbitrary handling by me of three authors, all American.

Nor have I pursued with my fervent animosity only American authors. I have included American journalists. I have said that American leading articles in daily papers were better than English. And I wrote (here) of the editor of *The American Mercury* itself, that he had written "some of the finest and most exciting modern journalism I have ever seen." A pity that I could not have referred similarly to H.L. Mencken's principal contributor! If I had, G.J. Nathan, being passably human, might just conceivably have chattered in a different vein about English critics.

There is not the slightest fear of English criticism of American books fostering any anti-English feeling in the United States. For one thing, neither the American public nor any other public is so passionately interested in literature as to render such a phenomenon at all possible. The suggestion is mere malicious bosh. But there is a fear that deliberate excitations to international ill-will such as G.J. Nathan's may not be without some sinister effect.

If Mr. Nathan can answer my article let him try; but in order to avoid international misrepresentation let him persuade his editor to reprint my article in full in the issue in which he attempts the reply. However, I know, and he knows, that he cannot make a good answer. I did once say, here, that G.J. Nathan's proper place was the music-hall. His outburst confirms me in this pleasant notion, for so far as I am concerned he has either given a marvellous performance of talking through his hat, or he is deliberately dishonest. He can choose between the two alternatives; but choose he must.

. . . . I will stop. I want to wake Mr. Nathan up, but, in the phrase of the *de*vine Dorothy, there is no need to wake a sleeping man with a mallet.

12 April 1928

A Critic *Can* Be a Novelist:
E.M. Forster's Startling Ghost Story in the Wells Manner

Can critics? That is: Are literary critics capable of producing the kind of creative work which they criticize? And can imaginative writers do good criticism? History answers these questions with: "Yes, sometimes." Without going far back into history, you may choose Wordsworth, a great poet and a fine literary critic (though few know his criticisms). Matthew Arnold, a greater poet than we yet appreciate and a great literary critic, is probably the best nineteenth century example of the creator-critic. And probably the best twentieth century example is E.M. Forster, who has given us three very fine novels, and whose recent book *Aspects of the Novel* (discussed by me some months ago) contains as sound and as brilliant literary criticism as any we have lately had from any author exclusively critical.

Mr. Forster, after his divagation into criticism, has now returned to creation. His new volume of short stories, *The Eternal Moment* (Sidgwick and Jackson, 5s.), can only fortify his reputation as an imaginative writer. It comprises remarkable things, and one quite startling thing — *The Machine Stops*. This tale, of the far future, is in the vein of H.G. Wells when he is fantastic. I think that if H.G. Wells had not written *When the Sleeper Awakes* and *Tales of Space and Time*, etc., etc., it would never have occurred to E.M. Forster to write *The Machine Stops*. Mr. Forster has done the fantastic before; but never with such complete success. Indeed, Mr. Wells might have been content to sign *The Machine Stops*.

It is original; it is full of imaginative invention; it hangs together; it is terrible (but with a hopeful close); it is really impressive in a very high degree. It ought not to be missed. If the majority of readers who like this sort of story are not enthusiastic about *The Machine Stops*, then I will enter a retreat for critics who have prophesied falsely, and in future write nothing but reviews of new editions of seventeenth century versifiers whom nobody except their editors has ever heard of. The title of the book itself is the title of the last story, and one may surmise therefore that this story is the author's favourite. If so, I disagree with the verdict of the author, though *The Eternal Moment* is fine and extremely subtle. The whole small volume (half a dozen tales) is excellent. Talk about American short story writers . . .!

James Agate is chiefly a critic — dramatic. He has just published an excellent life of Rachel; and now he publishes his third novel, *Gemel in London* (Chapman and Hall, 7s. 6d.). In the matter of titles, apparently it did not occur to Mr. Agate, when he decided upon his title, that in *Gemel In London* there are five vowel sounds, two pairs and one odd, all short and all unimpressive; that the three words of it neither convey a clear idea nor excite curiosity; and that therefore the title is a poor one. Bad technique.

The good qualities of the book are many. It is very observant. Its descriptive passages are effective. It is tireless. And it is sprightly. Indeed it is never not sprightly and never not readable. But at the end of fifty pages, even of thirty, you want an entr'acte, so that you can go into the foyer and listen to some dull person with an elephantine mind or no mind worth mentioning. Mr. Agate's continuous sprightliness fatigues.

The bad qualities of the book are also many. Quite apart from his sprightliness — half Meredithian, half Stevensonian — Mr. Agate has a mannerism of narration which dates from the 'forties or 'fifties of the last century. One example will show what it is. Speaking of a pair of characters, the author says: "But now evening has invited them to move on, and we will pursue and overhear." This mannerism was diverting when Dickens employed it, but to-day it is tiresome, because not natural to the age.

Again, Mr. Agate does not draw his characters convincingly. The girl Lintie is a stock figure — an imitation of an imitation of an imitation. Gemel — the hero who comes to London to worship a musical critic, Mark Rubicon, worships him, and leaves London — prints no image on the memory. Rubicon himself, the doggy, untidy, blusterous, untidy, insolent, untidy, and golden-hearted Titan, is an imitation of an imitation, and he is by no means distinctively a musical critic; he might just as well have been a cricket critic — perhaps better.

Thirdly, Mr. Agate is maladroit in narrative. He hates sequence, and he loves a disgression as much as he loves a periphrasis. No doubt he could describe very wittily what "plot" is, but he cannot make a plot. He scorns "story." Chapter XIV is simply and exclusively a lecture delivered by a Rubicon to an Amateur Dramatic Society. It does not help the tale, nor does it enlighten any of the characters. It is just a wayward lark. It may be a good lark; but in the efficient novel to-day there is no room for mere larks. The book is not organised.

Rubicon once wrote a novel. "Is it a good novel?" Gemel asked him, and Rubicon replied: "It's good everything else. I loathe writing novels." True word spoken in jest! Rubicon defends the writing of novels by critics; his defence is not good. For myself, I see no reason why a writer who is a critic should not produce a sound novel. But while he is writing the novel he must be a novelist — that is, a story-teller. *Gemel in London* is diverting; it is diverting everywhere. Open it anywhere and you will be amused and possibly edified. The author calls it a novel. It isn't. I don't seriously object to it not being a novel. I do seriously object to it not being a coherent whole.

James Agate is a lover of the French language, and often indulges in French quotations. And why not? This reminds me that a fortnight ago I wrote in my article as follows: "Of course a magazine-editor, being just as naive as the rest of us. . ." And readers have complained about "naive." They learnedly inform me that the word editor is masculine, and that the proper French adjective is "naif," not "naive." How true! The information does not surprise. What surprises me is that readers, before trying to correct me, do not make sure that they know what they are talking about.

My articles are written in English, not French. Good dictionaries and grammars are cheap, and any good English dictionary will tell these naive complainers that "naive" is an English adjective, and any grammar will tell them that the English adjective is "invariable" and does not "agree" with its noun. "Naive" has been good classical English for centuries. Dryden uses it, and he is not the first. I mention the matter because for years past the fussy-naive have been cavilling at my use of the word "naive." Sometimes they cavil anonymously, sometimes insolently, and always superiorly. At last the worm has turned.

19 April 1928

A Novelist of Genius

It has been written by somebody young, I am told, that there is only a single English novelist living who counts: D.H. Lawrence. But there may be others. Indeed there are. William Gerhardi counts. In my opinion Gerhardi has genius. Like the accouchement of a political duchess, the appearance of his new novel, *Jazz and Jasper* (Duckworth, 7s. 6d.), is an interesting event.

But it is now time that Gerhardi grew up, and *Jazz and Jasper* is not quite adult. It is chiefly adolescent — sixth-form. Gerhardi is still too preoccupied with the physics of love: a good topic, but a bad subject, which is apt to become tedious, especially in a satirical fantasy like the present book. Gerhardi's Russian and semi-Russian women, while drawn with brilliance and truth, are much less interesting than he imagines: and also their interminable promiscuities lack the quality of being typical of life.

Withal, in describing them, the author has his moment of beauty. This is beautiful: "When an object like Eva shows no visible sign of containing a subject, but appeals beyond all analysis, it means that the divine spirit has found in her a happy home." On the whole, however, the Gerhardi Evas exasperate.

Further, the story is not organised. Either the author cannot construct, or he disdains to construct. Many pages in the first half of the novel are wearisome, because the mere mechanics of the narration are excessively clumsy. The latter half, dealing with the gradual disintegration and disappearance of the earth, is better. Though often frivolous, it impresses. The satire is continually, not continuously, gorgeous. As, for instance, when Dickin (the hero), having hinted that he has Imperial Russian blood in his veins, is asked by the Press whether he claims the empty throne of the Tsars, and is thrown out of a night-club by an angry authentic Grand Duke. Interviewed by a pressman about the affair, Dickin replies, for publication: "I feel — I say it earnestly — that we who love Russia should know how to merge our petty differences in a common devotion to a holy cause." All this ridiculous episode is masterly.

The real hero of the book is not Dickin but Lord Ottercove, the newspaper Napoleon, "the big drum in the jazz band of our civilisation," whose saving grace was that he "suffered from an inferiority complex in the presence of Lord Beaverbrook." Ottercove is handled with profound subtlety, and with a ruthlessness which yet somehow shows both appreciation and affection. The disintegration and vanishing of Ottercove, with his novelist-friend Sprott ("a writer of talent but a merchant of genius"), till naught but the glowing ends of their two big fat cigars survive (to be transformed into the twin stars Castor and Pollux), is very rich; and it is touching.

Gerhardi has all the gifts of a major novelist except, apparently, the gift of marshalling and controlling his gifts. He should acquire this. He should also acquire the trifling accomplishment of correct English composition. The Russian in him slips and stumbles among English slang. "You never let it on," for "You never let on," discloses a disturbing ignorance. "Acclivious" is not English. "Neither of them could understand each other" is not English. "Neither knew a word of the other's language and made love with the aid of a dictionary" is neither English nor sense. And so on and so on.

In essentials William Gerhardi's style is admirable.

While you are reading it you get too used to the wild, casual and brilliant originality of a book like *Jazz and Jasper*. It is the after-taste that is valuable. And for myself I doubt if I fully savoured the after-taste till I was reading, a few days later, Aluizio Azevedo's *A Brazilian Tenement*, translated from the Portuguese by Harry W. Brown (Cassells, 7s. 6d.). You would expect strangeness and exotics from such a novel. But you will not get them. Azevedo, I gather, is very important in and to Brazil. I think that the work of these newer authors in countries where literature does not abundantly flourish is usually about fifty years behind the times. The early novels of Blasco Ibanez (before he became totally negligible) are painfully sedulous imitations of the less crude work of Zola. Azevedo belongs to the same school. There is not half an ounce of originality or fantasy in the whole of *A Brazilian Tenement*. But it is a sound book and was worth translating. It lights a lamp over the obscure lives of common people in Rio.

I am sometimes reproached for giving attention to foreign literature, while native literature is so urgent. But I am determined to give attention to foreign literature. Why not? Though Britain is a small island, the world exists. What can he know of English literature who only English literature knows? Here is another foreign book: *As they seemed to me*, by Ugo Ojetti, translated (well) by Henry Furst (Methuens, 6s.). Ojetti is a Fascist journalist, and a fine journalist. You may not think he is a fine journalist till you are far into the book, but in the end he will win you. He should be read.

The book consists chiefly of sketches, more or less personal, of Continental authors, composers, statesmen, philosophers: Maeterlinck, Barrès, Matilde Serao, Mommsen, Puccini, Gorky, Zola, Einstein, d'Annunzio, Valéry, Pierre Louys, Mussolini. They are all very subtly observed and all good. Many are very good, and a few superb. Some time ago I gave high praise to the American journalism of H.L. Mencken. I will give equally high praise to Ojetti's Italian journalism, though the contrasts between the two are tremendous. Nordic and Latin at their extremes, these two!

Ojetti recounts a word of advice given by Mussolini to the violent among his adherents: "You must cure yourself of my failing." There is something wistful, appealing, pathetic in this remark. And speaking of

Mussolini, Ojetti adds a remark of his own, tersely pregnant: "His doubts he keeps to himself."

As they seemed to me is disfigured by an introduction from the flowing pen of d'Annunzio. D'Annunzio at his most preposterous! I have admired d'Annunzio in my time. But could he be re-read with satisfaction? It is at least doubtful. I think that Verlaine must have had d'Annunzio in his prospective brain when he wrote the line which contains the wisest counsel ever given to exuberant authors: "Take eloquence and wring its neck."

Two notable translations from the French have recently appeared: André Gide's *The Counterfeiters* (Knopf, 7s. 6d.), which the author describes as his "first novel," though he has been publishing novels for a quarter of a century: and *Thérèse*, by François Mauriac (Secker, 6s.). I referred to both these novels on their original appearance in French last year. François Mauriac is not in the same class with a master like André Gide, but he is a serious writer, very much in the movement, and he has excited considerable interest.

26 April 1928

Disappointing Novel by Lady Oxford

The appearance of a novel by the Countess of Oxford is a social event, and as such ought to interest the student of society, if not the student of letters. It certainly will.

As a mere student of letters I am a little disappointed in *Octavia* (Cassells, 7s. 6d.). I have found some literary interest in Lady Oxford's autobiographical compositions. The autobiographer in her, though often guilty of almost incredible lapses from good taste, can describe persons and things seen, with gusto and genuine dramatic power. She shows a grasp of character. She can make a phrase. She possesses indeed an individual and occasionally quite distinguished style. But *Octavia* has no more distinction, verve or originality than its author's sermonising essays.

It is a hunting novel. Octavia, when at the age of seventeen she first goes hunting, on a strange horse, jumps everything and by her horsemanship excites the enthusiasm of the greatest experts. In the ancient days (of forty years since) a heroine and a hero were brought close together by a missing of the last train. To-day, in hunting circles, there are no trains, there are only automobiles, for long distances, and nothing but a fog can put an automobile out of action.

Thanks to fog, Octavia and her Greville, meeting for the first time, find themselves forced to spend a night alone together in a country house. Heroine asks hero to play a Bach fugue. Hero plays, after refusing to play. Heroine falls asleep, Hero picks up heroine and carries her to bed. That is how romance begins in the Octavian modern world. It ends with an authentic honeymoon preceded by a false one.

The rest is venery which is unlikely to misplace in our affections the venery of Surtees or even of Tolstoy.

Intimidated by the fame of the author, and whipped into perseverance

149

by a formidable conscientiousness which is natural to me, I read every page of *Octavia* in the hope of discovering somewhere in it some taste or savour or bouquet of the celebrated Chateau Margot cup; but I discovered absolutely naught of the kind. All that I can say in favour of the book is that it has been composed with obvious care. I should have preferred less care, and more of the characteristic headlongness, more of the bright temperament whose notion of a joke nearly half a century ago was to ride a horse into the ancestral hall and bring down a crystal chandelier. All is sober, grey, unglinting, guarded.

And yet, despite care, the writing of *Octavia* is not seldom lamentable. Thus: "Frictions that are *smuggled* and not *fought out* are wont to re-appear." New sort of versatile frictions! Again: "While wiping her face *with a towel* . . ." In the grand, free hunting shires do young women wipe their faces with hearthrugs — or their noses with broken bottles? (My reference is to a notorious French slang phrase.) The book is turgid with what, had an unknown author committed it, would be called padding.

Worse than this, the people in it do not live: they hardly exist. They are novelistically conventional, and are constantly doing and saying things that people never do or say, and never could — no matter how many days a week they hunted. Worse than all, the book is dull. It can be read, for I have read it; but its dullness is terrifying.

I do not exaggerate; I am not being swept away by the resentment of a reader who has suffered too much. There may be duller novels: I cannot say, for I have not read every novel. I honestly and sympathetically regret *Octavia*. At any rate Lady Oxford can safely say that she has rarely been dull before.

My recent article, apropos of Mr. G.J. Nathan's absurdities about the reception of American books in England, has brought in various letters about the reception of English books in England. Chief among these letters is one from Mr. Fowler Wright, the author of a novel called *Deluge*, which he published himself because he failed to persuade anybody else to publish it. The book was ignored by most London papers (but not by the *Evening Standard*). After an interval, five leading periodicals, having somehow heard interesting things of the book, sent for copies. (They had already received review copies and lost them.) Booksellers would not stock the book. Scarcely 2000 copies have been sold in England, of which only 50 were taken by retail booksellers. There is nothing unusual in all this. A sale of 2000 copies is quite good for a first novel by an unknown author. But read on.

On the strength of certain English reviews of this English book sundry American publishers read the work and then approached Mr. Fowler Wright. He made a contract with an American firm for a first edition of 100,000 copies, of which over 70,000 were sold before publication including 40,000 to the American Book of the Month Club. Immediately after publication, American booksellers, even in Los Angeles, were recommending the book to their customers, while English booksellers were telling their customers, who enquired about it, that they had never heard of it. A hugely important American editor said to Mr. Fowler Wright: "You won't trouble about the English market when you see what we can do for you." I wonder. I wonder whether Mr. Thornton Wilder, the

American author of *The Bridge of San Luis Rey*, of which one London bookseller alone is reported to have sold 3000 copies, does not trouble about the British market. The matter is all very complicated.

But it is still more complicated than this. The other day I received the following communication from a friend, a writer herself and the wife of an English writer: "When I was in America in 1920, I went into a large and famous bookshop in Fifth Avenue and asked to be shown some *American* novels. I mentioned that I'd read Edith Wharton, Ernest Poole, etc., etc. The assistant looked astonished at my request, but led me to a large table covered with novels. I discovered that every one of those novels was the American edition of an English novel.

"I then protested and said again 'American novels.' The assistant searched for several minutes and then handed me with great pride *The Moon and Sixpence*, by Somerset Maugham. Having just read *Jennie Gerhardt*, I thought I'd ask for novels by Dreiser, but the assistant in a most superior manner assured me that Theodore Dreiser did not write novels, but only essays. When I insisted that he should look up a list, he did so, and had to confess that Dreiser did apparently write novels but he regretted that they did not 'carry' any."

Apparently, therefore, one of the very best American authors, not to mention others, receives, or did until recently receive, less attention from American booksellers than he receives from English booksellers. The London bookshop is perhaps not perfect; but there is certainly no London bookshop where an enquiring customer would be informed that Theodore Dreiser was not a novelist.

Forty opposing conclusions might be drawn from the letters of my two correspondents.

3 May 1928

Some Good Detective Stories:
A Superlative Work Waiting for the Right Publisher:
Mary Webb's Novels, And a Further Attempt at Resuscitation

A friend said to me not long since: "Why don't you follow Shakespeare in taking old plots and treating them afresh in your own way?" (Not that I had been crying aloud for a plot!) I said: "For instance?" He said: "Well, *The Moonstone*." Thus I came to read *The Moonstone*, chiefly to find out just what my friend considered a good plot worth rehandling.

The Moonstone has recently been republished by the Oxford University Press in the World's Classics Series with an introduction by T.S. Eliot. Mr. Eliot is an American with no discoverable trace of Americanism. He is a high-brow critic, austere and penetrating, who sometimes awes me. He is also a poet, whose chief poem is held by the esoteric to be a landmark in English literature (only I don't think it is). The spectacle of Mr. Eliot dealing with Wilkie Collins promised piquancy, but the promise is not fulfilled. His Introduction is merely sound, convincing and admirable. Nothing to shock in it. His exposition of the interactions between Wilkie Collins and Charles Dickens is new and has much interest. He describes *The*

Moonstone as "the first, the longest, and the best of modern English detective novels." (Are there any old English detective stories?) I am inclined to agree.

The tale is told with the author's customary clumsy machinery; but it holds you continuously. It is far better than *The Woman in White*, which I have twice failed to re-read. It is well written. It has humour, and plenty of invention, and some satisfactory if exaggerated character-drawing. I cannot endorse the certificate of excellence which Mr. Eliot gives to the portrait of the arch-detective, Sergeant Cuff. There are a number of things in this portrait which call for explanation, but which I fear cannot be explained.

I enjoyed *The Moonstone*. It is extremely earth-to-earth (by which I mean *terre-à-terre*), even more so than Mr. Watson's narrations about Sherlock Holmes; but for what it is it finely succeeds. It succeeded in interrupting for several days my perusal of a really superlative work, the Napoleonic *Mémoires* of Madame de Rémusat, an author of first-rate merit who is not in *Chambers' Encyclopaedia*. A publisher who issued these *Mémoires* in English in portable form would probably have his reward.

Another recently republished detective book is M.P. Shiel's *Prince Zaleski* (Secker, 3s. 6d.). I read, and was excited by, *Prince Zaleski* when it first appeared (in, I think, John Lane's Keynotes Library) thirty-three years ago. I never hoped to see it again, and I am glad to have seen it again. Mr. Shiel is a scholar, a linguist, and an inventor. He overwrites, in the heavily decorated manner of the 'nineties, but he writes well, and he has a rich sense of words and a pretty feeling for the curve of a sentence. Though not a first-class stylist, he is a stylist: which is something — in detective fiction.

He has published a number of books, of which in my opinion the best is *The Purple Cloud*. If he has not adequately impressed himself on the consciousness of the public, the reason is that he seems not to be able to hold a book together. Herein is the defect of *The Purple Cloud*. That mortal enemy of the author of a long book, centrifugal force, is always shooting him off at tangents. *Prince Zaleski*, however, is a short book — or rather it is a trilogy of three short stories, and centrifugal force does not get a chance in it.

Sherlock Holmes made his first appearance some years before the Prince. But the Prince derives more from Poe than from Sir Arthur Conan Doyle. The Prince sits in a room of some horrific, crumbling Castle of Otranto, listens quietly to the recital of a mystery, and then proceeds to ratiocinate thereupon, with the result that the mystery is solved in about an hour — and the Prince meantime has not moved from his faded chair nor interviewed any of the sinners or the sinned against, and has certainly not inspected the scenes of crime. It is all very wonderful — while it lasts. The first story is the most satisfactory.

The book has worn surprisingly well. It is superior to most work of later mystery-mongers, but I doubt if it will appeal powerfully to readers without a taste for words and a taste for exact ratiocination. In any case, it cannot challenge the French masterpieces of detective fiction — Gaboriau's *The Crime of Orcival* and Gaston Leroux's *The Mystery of the Yellow Room*. The latter sticks in my mind as the most dazzlingly brilliant detective story I have ever read.

The resuscitation of books out of a state of suspended vitality is a fine game. Mr. Stanley Baldwin has just been playing at it — with the novels of the late Mary Webb. I receive with polite reserve the pronouncements of Prime Ministers about imaginative literature. As a rule, either their taste has been distorted by terrible experiences in public schools, and resembles a bicycle after it has been run over by a motor-lorry, or they have been too busy conscientiously misguiding the destiny of fifty million human beings properly to nourish their taste.

It was once related to me that H.H. Asquith, a great and a magnanimous man, could recite backward from memory the fantastic catalogue of our Poets Laureate. That damaged him with me, and when I read in a newspaper that on his famous journey to meet King Edward in Spain or somewhere he was observed to be carrying a copy of Marcelle Tinayre's fashionable, feeble-sentimental novel, *The House of Sin* — that finished him with me as a connoisseur of current literature. (What would you?)

But Mr. Stanley Baldwin has made no mistake about Mary Webb. I have read only one of her novels, *Precious Bane* — and I admit that I should not have read even that had it not been forced upon me with violence by an enthusiast for the distinguished unappreciated. *Precious Bane*, however, can scarcely count among those of Mary Webb's novels which are in a state of suspended vitality. It has been reprinted every year since its original publication. The latest edition of it (in the Travellers' Library: Cape) has a very charming format. Mary Webb had power; she could create beauty; and she is truthful concerning human nature. All I would say against her is that her writing is somewhat mannered. If Mr. Baldwin's remark has a sequel in the shape of a uniform edition of the Webb novels he may go down to posterity.

And now I in my turn will attempt a resuscitation. Mr. G.F. Bradby's *The Lanchester Tradition* is a pre-war public-school story. Booksellers inform me that it is out of print. This may or may not be true. It was issued by Smith Elder and Co., a firm deceased but a historic and a sound firm. Mr. Bradby has published other books, not novels. *The Lanchester Tradition* is dissimilar from other public-school yarns in this, that it deals mainly with the teaching staff and scarcely at all with the boys. Its theme is indeed the internal politics of a big school. The critical events are true enough to the irony of life, and exquisitely absurd. Mr. Bradby has a humour shy as a faun; you get glimpses of the animal flitting across the ends of glades of seriousness. He understands character and has few illusions. He seeks not after emotion. He writes well. At present it is no use my recommending *The Lanchester Tradition* to readers. I am recommending it to publishers.

Lastly I must record that A.P. Herbert's impressive war-novel, *The Secret Battle,* has been resuscitated by means of a new edition with a pleasing introduction by the most discussed personality in England — the Chancellor of the Exchequer* (Methuens). It is nine years old. Good books do come through.

* Winston Churchill.

10 May 1928

A Diary Full of Plums

I feel as if I had at last got some authentic news out of Bolshevik Russia. It is a feeling new to me; for hitherto I have found the tidings brought by travellers very unconvincing — even those of the special private envoy of American bankers (whose results, though marked by an earnest desire to be unprejudiced, showed little insight and had no body).

My bulletin is "Ognyov's" *The Diary of a Communist Schoolboy*, well translated by Alexander Worth (Gollancz, 7s. 6d). "Ognyov" is only one of the pseudonyms of the writer, whose real name is Rozanov. His age is 36, and he was in Russia as late as 1921. His remarkable book is a novel — at any rate it is fiction. But it has all the characteristics of fundamental truth to life. I am persuaded that it tallies with the facts — and with all the main facts — of school-psychology in Russia to-day.

The youthful diarist is made a real person. And he must have been a person very trying to his teachers. When one teacher referred to the pupils as "children," the diarist violently took offence at such an opprobrious epithet. He was not going to permit the children to be called children, not he!

If a political crisis arose in the management of the school, this is what happened: "The bell was rung for a general meeting. Everybody dropped his books there and then; those asking questions in labs dashed off in the middle of a sentence. The skworkers [teaching staff] were flabbergasted." At the meeting a pupil said: "Personally I consider that presidents at meetings are simply a bourgeois prejudice."

But the old Russia has evidently survived. Here it is: "The Dalton Plan has been introduced here. Once a month tasks are given out on each subject, and we have to work them out independently. The teacher only tells you what books to consult, but you can't get these books anywhere, and to buy them is, of course, out of the question." Which reads just like Chekhov of the 'nineties.

And this is most subtly right: "Sylvia isn't quite such a fool and intellectual as I thought she was. She dislikes dancing and wears a propeller-bow, because her mother makes her do it. Yesterday I advised her not to pay any attention to her mother, but she said she loved her and therefore obeyed her. This is something I can't understand — how one can wear a bow against one's convictions." The perfect doctrinaire! It is all sadly comic and comically sad. I have not picked plums out of the book. Or, if I have, the book is simply all plums. It is what I call an important book. But unlike some important books it is continuously interesting.

Ognyov's book depicts a developing social organism. Mr. Fowler Wright's *The Island of Captain Sparrow* (also Gollancz, 7s. 6d.) depicts a social organism in debasement and decrepitude. The island is one of your hitherto-overlooked islands — in the Northern Pacific. Perhaps not wholly unconnected with H.G. Wells's *The Island of Dr. Moreau*. It contains towards the end a scene easily surpassing in horror any scene in the earlier island, which nevertheless was compact of horrors. Indeed I have never read anything as frightful as that scene with the rebel giant-cassowaries. I ought to warn readers that my own stomach is more robust than most.

Mr. Fowler Wright has been compared to H.G. Wells. I would not put him on the Wellsian plane at all. But he has genuine originality of outlook and invention, and, like Dumas, just when you think he is going to be tedious, his pen is refreshed by a new inspiration. The writing of the story is uneven; at its best it is quite good.

I am glad that I read this book, though I should probably not have read it had not its author been also the author of *The Deluge*, the novel (already referred to by me) which has had such contrasting receptions in Britain and in the United States. Mr. Fowler Wright, by reason of his strange and exciting experiences as a writer, is now prominently in the public eye. I should say that he will do better and better in the future.

Another romance about a Pacific island — not overlooked, but as it were mislaid — is André Maurois' *Voyage au pays des Articoles* (Gallimard, Paris, 9 francs). As this book will undoubtedly soon appear in English, I will not discuss it in detail now. I will say only that it is a very slight and bright story excellently well done, and that it "reads itself." The Articoles are authors and other kinds of artists who are kept in order, for the common good, by the "Béo's" (Boeotians) of the island. I recommend this amusing work, which, without being profound, should give all artists to think.

M. Maurois, by the way, has been the target of wholesale accusations of plagiarism in the dignified pages of the *Mercure de France*. Seeing that he occupies quite a special place in the current literature in Britain, that no other French author is so widely read here, and that few are so highly esteemed, the lettered British public cannot be indifferent to the "affaire." The matter has been before the French public for over two months, and it is still before the public. M. Maurois has replied twice, at length; but more briefly than his accuser, a M. Auriant, whose name I am unfamiliar with. I have examined the case with some care, and if it were tried by a jury and I were on the jury, I should vote unhesitatingly for M. Maurois.

In the early part of *Voyage au pays des Articoles* M. Maurois mentions the book of a modern adventurous navigator named Gerbault, who achieved notoriety a while ago. M. Auriant asserts that M. Maurois has plagiarised from M. Gerbault. Among the instances of plagiarism, M. Auriant gives the epithet "vicious waves" and the argument that the voyagers must have been nearing the land because birds were seen. Well, "vicious" applied to small waves yapping against a small boat is almost a cliché. Readers of sea yarns must have met with it dozens of times. As for the second instance, it simply is not worth discussing.

M. Auriant also attacks Maurois' Shelley book and his Disraeli book. Take the former. He alleges that much of the material was abstracted from Dowden's work on Shelley. Some of the material was certainly based on Dowden's. And why not? M. Maurois made no pretence of original research, though he did some original research. If M. Maurois used Dowden, Dowden certainly used earlier biographers. You might as well accuse Shakespeare of being a plagiarist. And indeed Shakespeare was one of the biggest plagiarists that ever lived. (So was Handel.) Whatever his sources, M. Maurois in his studies of Shelley and Disraeli unquestionably produced books of brilliant originality. Incidentally he made some of Dowden's material readable, which Dowden never did.

155

I am assured on good authority that M. Auriant is entirely honest and unprejudiced. I accept the assurance. Did I not accept it I should venture the theory that his attack (which is far from adroit) was due partly to a desire to give voice to a widespread literary jealousy of M. Maurois' immense success, and partly to the fact that years ago M. Maurois changed his name from something less pleasing to French ears than Maurois.* Sir Edmund Gosse has strongly and indignantly expressed his disagreement with M. Auriant. I also strongly disagree with M. Auriant; but I am incapable of moral indignation.

M. Maurois' recent lectures (in English) at Trinity College, Cambridge, showed that he thoroughly understands the biographer's job.

17 May 1928

A Shining Biography

I am in favour of biographies of novelists, or biographies of anybody, being written by novelists. Novelists have the art of narrative (possessed by few biographers), and, when they are talking about the work of novelists, they know what they are talking about.

Mr. Hugh Walpole has just produced, in the celebrated or notorious *English Men of Letters* series a life of Anthony Trollope (Macmillans). It has zest. It is readable. And amid the calamities of tedium formerly produced in the same series by literary mandarins such as Leslie Stephen, Henry James, Canon Ainger, and John Morley (their dead victims being respectively Johnson, Hawthorne, Lamb and Burke) it shines like a radiant deed on the night's Plutonian shore. (Recently I read Sir Hall Caine's Life of Coleridge, published in the *Great Writers* series some thousand years ago. It is a good book. If you thought that the author of *The Manxman* did not understand literature, you were wrong.)

Mr. Walpole has more than zest and readableness; he has knowledge. He is a real bookman, and, differing from most bookmen, he reads books instead of gazing at them adoringly on shelves. He has read all or nearly all of Trollope. To read all Trollope is itself a career. He appreciates the romantic quality of his subject.

Trollope's life was extraordinarily romantic, full of what they call in morning papers astonishing "gestures." His youth had a terrible melancholy. It is not known whether his first novel sold a single copy. It is known that his second novel sold only 140 copies. From this state he emerged quickly into a best-seller. He got into the Post Office without examination and without knowing the multiplication table (for his education had been perpetrated at a public school). He failed as an official in London, and then went to Ireland and blazed gloriously as an official.

He was idle, and his activities were unorganised, until he reached the age of 26. Then he suddenly became the most industrious and the best organised novelist in the history of the world. He would start work just before Balzac would be going to bed, and in the matter of productiveness beat Balzac all to bits. He gave the entire proceeds of one book as a present to his publisher: a gesture utterly unique. He wrote a volume about South

* He was born Emile Herzog.

Africa which won the praise of no less an authority than Sarah Gertrude Millin (whose South African novels have the stuff of truth in them).

Mr. Walpole's book is very short; a goodish proportion of it is given to quotations and to Mr. Walpole's individual preferences. "Here personal feeling must of course count." Further, so far as one can judge, and according to the author's candid admission, it contains little original research and is based chiefly on Trollope's inspiring *Autobiography* (which by its un-British frankness laid his reputation to sleep for over thirty years) and on Mr. Michael Sadleir's biography.

The best passages in Mr. Walpole's book are his admirable appreciations of the little-known novels (such as *The Way We Live Now*), and his by-the-way remarks. His description of Trollope — "a man of heart and sentiment but no nonsense" — is excellent. And there is something profound in this: "All novels of the first-class show victories over professional technique won by creative passion."

Mr. Walpole has frightful defects. He writes nearly, but not quite, as untidily or clumsily as his great subject. He persistently spells the name of the priceless Archdeacon "Grantley" instead of "Grantly" as it appeared in *The Warden* and as Trollope himself spelt it when he happened to think about spelling. But Mr. Walpole evidently has a perverse fondness for the letter 'e'. He writes 'judgement' instead of 'judgment.' Spelling is settled by custom, and despite the opinion of the magisterial Fowler (author of *Modern English Usage*), 'judgement' has long ago been sentenced to death by custom. Lastly Mr. Walpole misspells the glorious name of Jane Austen's "Elizabeth Bennett." A man capable of this appalling deed would be capable of assassinating his grandmother.

The autobiography of George Arliss, *On the Stage* (Murray), agreeably reminds one of Anthony Trollope. George Arliss is America's most popular actor. Of course he is British, like Charles Chaplin, Mary Pickford, and Armour. By Armour — I must inform the unlettered — I do not mean the indefatigable Chicago packer, but America's open golf-champion, a greater man than Hagen (not the villain of Götterdämmerung).

There is heart and sentiment in George Arliss, and no nonsense. Never have I heard any other actor talk so much common sense to the minute as I have heard from George Arliss — I mean *viva voce*. His book interested me by its simplicity and plainness. He has gleams of dry humour — as for instance about David Belasco: and he is kindly and just to Mrs. Patrick Campbell, whose personality the London theatrical world has up to now deeply misunderstood.

George Arliss is the sort of man who takes his coat off and gets to work. He is not the sort of man who sits up at night talking about himself, other folk's scandals, himself, the true inwardness of dramatic art, himself, and the ingredients of recondite cocktails. His immense and solid success is due partly to histrionic gifts and partly to the gift of self-organisation.

An obscure American poet once said "Lives of great men all remind us we may make our lives sublime" (or words to that effect). * I would rather

* Longfellow ('A Psalm of Life'): "Lives of great men all remind us/We can make our lives sublime."

157

say: "Lives of great men all remind us we can make our lives sublime only if we organise and discipline our mental and physical outfit." It does not quite scan, but it is better sense.

A fair example of lack of self-organisation is the late Isadora Duncan. She was a great artist, about whom artists would rave. She had really rare genius, and in a way she impressed herself upon the entire dancing world. But somehow she never quite acquired either the prestige or the felicity which ought to have been hers.

Isadora's autobiography unconsciously reveals the reasons for the subtle failure. In the first seven lines of the book she strikes the Isadora note: "If people ask me when I began to dance I reply, 'In my mother's womb, probably as a result of the oysters and champagne — the food of Aphrodite.'" (Her mother would take no food except oysters and champagne at the time.)

The book is constructed of two materials (which coalesce well), the life of her dancing, and the life of her senses. Its candour is staggering — but not repellent nor ugly. However, I am not reviewing the book (title, *My Life*, publisher, Gollancz), for the reason that it will not be published till to-morrow. I am merely referring to it, because it cannot keep itself out of this article. I would not call it quite first-rate autobiography. It is too loose for that. But it is a strange and a resistless book.

A third kind of artist was Mary Cholmondeley, whose *Diana Tempest* and *Red Pottage* I used to think were the authentic article — and quite probably they are. She had something of Jane Austen's temperament. Mr. Percy Lubbock has written a brief biography of her — *Mary Cholmondeley, a Sketch from Memory* (Cape, 3s. 6d). The right sort of biography of this esteemed lady would have met a felt want. But I doubt if Mr. Lubbock's is the right sort. It contains too much of Mr. Lubbock's musing and too little factual toughness to bite your teeth on. It is excessively sentimental. It is full of lucubrations like this: "The daughter of her race she was indeed to the core of her being. She belonged, she never ceased to belong, to her stock, her county, her England. . ." To which the only polite rejoinder is Tut-tut.

24 May 1928

Reading Without Finishing

It is the fashion to say that the late Edmund Gosse wrote one very fine book. This fashion is justified. He did write one very fine book, *Father and Son* — a biography of the father combined with an autobiography of the son. It may or may not be a masterpiece. I am inclined to think it is. If hard uncompromising truth and a decent human sympathy put down with skill and some distinction can make a book live, this book will live.

I doubt whether anything else by Edmund Gosse will live. His verse is graceful, refined, sensitive and negligible. His literary criticism is first-rate journalism, but if it is first-rate criticism — then there is no word left for Matthew Arnold's. His scholarship was uneven; and if, as has been said by his intimates, his errors annoyed him, he must have suffered frequent annoyance. He has been charged with maliciousness, but I enjoyed his urbane malice, which was an agreeable piquant seasoning to the solid dish which he offered to the public. He has also been charged with a habit of interfering somewhat high-handedly in affairs which did not concern him. On this charge he was beyond question guilty.

But what matter? He had a quality which must inalienably endear him to bookmen. He was passionately interested in literature. Many professional critics give me the impression that literature is the bane of their lives. In the occasional conversations which I had with Edmund Gosse, he always showed that he had a divine curiosity about books, and that he lost no opportunity of satisfying that curiosity. Further, and more important, he came out again and again on the side of the angels, by which I mean of the young. He was superlative on young French authors.

What I most envied in him was his achievement in keeping abreast of publishing activities. Mr. Logan Pearsall Smith is credited with reading seven or eight hours a day. Edmund Gosse apparently read twenty-seven or twenty-eight hours a day. He kept level with things. I cannot. Not only is the mass of books enormous, but the mass of books worth reading is enormous. It defeats me. My tables are always covered with books which I am reading but cannot immediately finish, because I am not Edmund Gosse. Here are the names of some of them lying at hand.

First and chief, *Blue Trousers,* translated by Arthur Waley from the Chinese of Lady Murasaki (Allen & Unwin, 10s. 6d.). This is the fourth volume of the *Tale of Genji* novel. I think it is the best. It is simply marvellous in beauty and truth, and so modern, both in feeling and technique, that it might have been written yesterday. *Travels in Tartary, Tibet and China,* by those early nineteenth-century ecclesiastical explorers, Huc and Gabet (2 vols., Routledge), in the fine translation of William Hazlitt, with a wonderful introduction by a French scholar, Professor Paul Pelliot. I have always heard of this work as being one of the most alluring travel-books ever written. I think it is. To read it is like seeing the scenes described. The edition is admirable. Sir Denison Ross is the editor.

In another category — *But Gentlemen Marry Brunettes,* by Anita Loos (Brentano, 7s. 6d). I am an admirer of Anita Loos. She is an original humourist. Her two books, however, are monotonous. They take you out of yourself, but they lose you. Much the same is to be said — assuredly not of Sinclair Lewis's fiction as a whole — but of his latest Babbitt manifestation (short), *The Man Who Knew Coolidge* (Cape, 7s. 6d.). It, indeed, is rather a manifestation than a novel. Ironic to the point of cruelty! It ought to be taken in small doses. But I must handle Sinclair Lewis delicately. He has immense creative power.

People have been telling me for a long time of the American writer, Thomas Beer. His novel, *The Road to Heaven* (Knopf), though it savours of Dorothy Richardson modernised by whiffs of James Joyce, has imaginative originality. It is excellently written.

Finally, three volumes of American short stories. A few weeks since I said I knew nothing of Manuel Komroff. Now I do. His *The Grace of Lambs* (Cape, 7s. 6d.) is a collection of tales in the Russian style. Exotic, to us, in subject. . . Chekhov still stands. . . . So does Kipling. The lauded Ernest Hemingway has published *Men Without Women* (Cape). Fourteen quite short stories. I read all of them. I call them goodish, which is rather less than good. The best, *Fifty Grand*, is about a woman, who never appears. Miss Willa Cather's *My Mortal Enemy* (Heinemann) consists of one sole short story. It reaches the level of praiseworthiness, but I doubt whether it is worthy of this American author's high reputation — or whether any of her work is.

The above confession of reading without finishing reminds me (not, I admit, that I needed reminding) that "in another place" "Alpha of the Plough" has been defending Edward Dowden and censuring myself — apropos of the accusations of plagiarism against André Maurois which I recently discussed. Alpha of the Plough (a pseudonym which now fails to hide the personality of one of our most illustrious journalists*) — Alpha (for short) says: (1) That I once wrote, "Not that I have read Dowden, or ever shall." (2) That the other week I wrote that Maurois (in his book on Shelley) had made "Dowden's material readable, which Dowden did not." (3) How do I know whether Dowden is readable or not if I have not read Dowden? (4) How do I know that Maurois has used Dowden's material if I have not read Dowden?

To take the last point first. Alpha knows nothing about the Maurois controversy. I do. I have read the whole of it — some scores of pages in the *Mercure de France*. If Alpha will read it he will see how I came to know that Maurois has used Dowden's material.

As regards the other points. (1) I agree that I said I had not read Dowden and never would. But Alpha is too literal. I, of course, did not mean that I had read nothing of Dowden. Alpha could not reasonably suppose that I would decry an author of whose work I was totally ignorant. I obviously meant that I had not *read* Dowden. But I have dipped into him. Indeed, my ignorance of Dowden is not the lovely perfect sphere that one could walk all round and not discover a single flaw in it. I had read the whole of Dowden's shorter book on Shakespeare, and I had cast critical glances on his books on Shelley and on Browning, and on some of his essays. Similarly, I have examined, for instance, Burnet's *History of His Own Time*, though I have not "read" Burnet. (2) and (3) By these experiences I know that Dowden is not readable — whereas Burnet emphatically is.

Is Alpha aware of the Oxford Dictionary definition of readable: "interestingly written"? When a man says, "I cannot read So-and-so," what he means, and must mean, is that he *has* read some of So-and-so, and could not comfortably continue. Alpha enjoys Dowden. I don't. I call Dowden dull, not readable — for me. Tastes differ. Alpha has characterised Dostoevsky's novels as "muck." At this point, if I were a classical scholar, I should quote Latin.

31 May 1928

A Critic of 20th Century Literature

It is a useful and amusing, but a dangerous thing to write a general survey

---

* A.G. Gardiner, who wrote for the *Star* under his "Alpha" pseudonym.

of modern literature — especially imaginative literature. Mr. A.C. Ward (deputy-principal of the City Literary Institute) has performed this feat in *Twentieth Century Literature: The Age of Interrogation* (Methuens, 5s. net — cheap). I am glad to learn by the way that the City is literary: a pleasant fact which I knew not, nor suspected. The City has Companies of Painters and of Musicians, also of Tallow-chandlers; but no Company of poets, novelists or critics — unless these categories of strange persons are to be found on the roll of the Company of Scriveners — which I doubt.

I do not think that Mr. Ward justifies his title. The present age is of course an age of interrogation: but so, equally, were other ages. Mr. Ward says of the Victorian age that the Voice of Authority was accepted in religion, in politics, in literature, and family life. Perhaps in family life: but if the Voice was accepted in religion, politics and literature, how came all those great interrogators, Carlyle, Huxley, Darwin, Ruskin, Dickens, Charles Reade, and that rebel Swinburne, to make the deep mark they did?

I should say that the Victorian age was quite as revolutionary as ours, and that its sword-brandishing, murderous prophets received no more vituperation than ours. All ages worth a tinned apricot have interrogated furiously. And indeed it is the everlasting business of literature to interrogate. Even gentle ironic Jane made question-marks on the British social organism.

Mr. Ward writes with skill; and he is fairly comprehensive. He deals with fiction, drama, verse, essays, literary criticism, biography, travel, and he wanders about in these flower-enamelled landscapes with a certain topographical ease. He has got as much as he could get into a couple of hundred pages, but I wish he had doubled the number of pages and got in a hundred per cent. more stuff.

Fiction is his chief topic. He has given most space to what are sometimes called "The Big Four," without saying anything new about any of them. (In the matter of Joseph Conrad he appears to me to be quite at sea.) He ought in my opinion to have dismissed the Big Four far more summarily, and dealt more fully with the more exciting younger scriveners. The elders are fixed, and only meet to be shied at.

On the younger he delivers some very weird verdicts. He says that Dorothy Richardson's heroine Miriam is "an entirely uninteresting young woman." I disagree. I would rather maintain that the first thousand pages or so written by Miss Richardson concerning Miriam had real interest; they were most certainly unlike anything published before, and they have had their effect on other writers. After a thousand pages — say the end of the fourth volume — I admit that I fell by the hard wayside while Miriam strode ruthlessly on and is now long since out of sight. But Miss Richardson was a pioneer.

Then Mr. Ward gives only a few lines to the immense portent of James Joyce, who positively cannot be dismissed as Mr. Ward dismisses him. James Joyce is damnably unequal and exasperating, and he is capable of unsurpassed tedium. Still, he has done things as good as anybody ever did. Proust at his best is not better than James Joyce at his best. He is an originator. His influence is considerable. And will be.

Nor do I think that Mr. Ward's treatment of D.H. Lawrence and

E.M. Forster comes within a hundred miles of adequacy. He really ought not to put off novelists of their importance with a dozen condescending lines apiece. Lastly, Mr. Ward makes no mention of R.H. Mottram, author of *The Spanish Farm* and *The English Miss*. For myself I regard R.H. Mottram as the most interesting novelist of his years in Britain to-day. And he is not a promising author; he is an author who has achieved large and mature work.

In the section of poetry Mr. Ward is less at home, and his standards are more awry. His verdicts on Chesterton, Masefield, Noyes, Flecker, Rupert Brooke and Belloc astonished me by their curiousness. He overpraises most of these poets, though not Belloc, who is the best of them when in the vein.

In the section of drama he is — well, odd. For instance he says: "There are no standards of literary judgment applicable to Barrie." Barrie is a genius, but he has upon occasion been rather naughty, and why he alone should be exempt from the application of literary standards I cannot conceive. Barrie's worst enemies are his hysterical admirers — of whom I admit that Mr. Ward is not one. And Mr. Ward says not a word about C.K. Munro, the most promising dramatist of the last twenty years. If C.K. Munro had the faculty of self-criticism he would probably stand first in the modern theatre. He is deficient in that faculty, but to ignore him is a masterpiece of casual neglect.

In the section of essays and criticism, Mr. Ward is piebald — there is no other word so descriptive of him here. He says good things — and then he characterises Mr. Percy Lubbock's prose as "of unique loveliness"! Great Heavens and Scott! Mr. Percy Lubbock uses a nice pen, but in the affair of loveliness, Lawrence, Chesterton, Belloc, Wells can write him clean off his feet. The worst is that Mr. Ward quotes a twelve-line passage of Mr. Percy Lubbock's unique loveliness, and thereby gives the whole show away. Loveliness has other textures than smooth, and other tints than purple.

Withal, I gladly record that I have perused *Twentieth Century Literature* with sustained interest. I find many faults in it; but then all bookmen could and would find many faults with any similar book. Mr. Ward has done something that was worth doing. And his index is good. What I now demand is a book on Edwardian and Georgian literature with the name of Frank Swinnerton on the title-page. Such a book would be fun.

Last week I said that "Alpha of the Plough" had characterised Dostoevsky's fiction as "muck." Alpha has denied the accusation. He is right. I wrote without being able to refer to a file. I was wrong, and I apologise. The explanation — there is no justification — runs thus. Months ago I wrote here contrasting certain Russian writers, including Dostoevsky, with Thackeray, to the latter's disadvantage. I asserted, what could easily be proved, that Thackeray would not face difficult situations. (I had no thought of difficult sexual situations at all.) Alpha defended Thackeray, and my recollection was that he had used the word "muck" in reference to Dostoevsky. He used it in reference to James Joyce. I should have been less resentful if he had used it about Dostoevsky, because Dostoevsky cannot be even temporarily harmed, whereas James Joyce can.

Here is a novelist who brought new methods into the composition of a novel, and who has done strictly first-rate work. And Alpha dismisses him as muck! It is precisely this kind of criticism which militates against literary evolution in Britain. About Dostoevsky I am apologetic to Alpha, but he none the less remains in my sight a sinful creature.

7 June 1928

A New Venture in Criticism

In my opinion the main business of literary critics is to stimulate interest in good books and check interest in bad books. As to the measure of their achievement in this great matter I will not say what I think; I might be too realistic. Now Desmond MacCarthy, one of our most eminent and certainly one of our finest literary critics, has just begun the publication of a monthly periodical, *Life and Letters* (price 1s.), under his own editorship. I regard the appearance of *Life and Letters* as a literary event; it has "news" value. Therefore I call attention to it. First numbers are notoriously very difficult to produce, and I will not judge the editor by his first number. It is good, but subsequent numbers ought to be better, and no doubt will be.

Does the first number carry out the critic's main business? To a certain extent it does. The most original thing in it is the section entitled "Reader's Reports" (over twenty pages of them). These appreciations or depreciations of new books are modelled on the reports of "publishers' readers" to publishers. Plain, straightforward affairs, making no attempt to exhibit the learning or the literary elegance or the ingenuity of the reporter! Intended simply to give a fair general notion of what the books actually are and how they will affect the general reader! These are excellent, all except the section devoted to detective novels: which assuredly will not attract the sort of public which *Life and Letters* aims to attract.

There is an illuminating essay on *Hamlet*, by George Santayana, written twenty years ago, and much less gaseous and elusive than some of his later work. Also a sound and witty depreciation by the editor of the later essays in biography of Emil Ludwig. Also a short, early, common-sense essay on "The Science of Fiction," by Thomas Hardy, which demonstrates that Hardy was among the few creative artists who understand roughly what they are doing.

The star-turn of the number is by Max Beerbohm — "Two Glimpses of Andrew Lang." The piece — it is a "piece" — suffers from inadequacy of subject. Fifty per cent. of young readers are likely to ask impatiently: "Who the devil was Andrew Lang after all?" I well remember in the 'nineties seeing the once-mighty feline Andrew correcting proofs in Gatti's Restaurant. I was tremendously thrilled. But I should deem it not worth while to try to communicate my historic thrill to others to-day, when Andrew Lang is as extinct as Churton Collins, who, also in the 'nineties, was supposed by us ingenuous youthful ones to be the supreme incarnation of bookish omniscience, over-topping even George Saintsbury. *Eheu fugaces*, as Horace exclaimed, little guessing that he had hit on a sentimental phrase which was to serve dozens of generations of European quotation-mongers! I do not quite see the appositeness of the title *Life and Letters*. Life generally is too big for Letters. *Letters and Literary Life* would have been more accurately descriptive.

I will suggest a contributor to Desmond MacCarthy; namely the anonymous author of the remarkable leading article on "Rossetti" in the *Times Literary Supplement* a few weeks ago. Who he is I have no idea, but he is a stimulator.

If literary critics faithfully performed their business of stimulating interest in good books, D.H. Lawrence's new book, *The Woman Who Rode Away and other Stories* (Secker 7s. 6d), would have had ten times the reception it has had — though it has been well enough received. This volume is the best Lawrence I have read for years. I am inclined to say that it is the best Lawrence I have ever read. D.H. Lawrence has his faults. He can be very morbid; he is obsessed by the sexual relation; he can be formidably unreadable; nearly all his books have long passages of tiresomeness. But he is the strongest novelist writing to-day. *The Woman Who Rode Away* is first-rate, every page of it. Ten stories of varying length, and all of them characterised by superb creative power, and by a fundamental originality of observation! There are whole pages together where every sentence gives new light on human nature and, reading them, you know that you are face to face with a rough, demonic giant. A page or two of Laurentian morbidity here and there, but no more!

Of course the book is all about men and women, and their mutual attractions and repulsions: of course it discloses an obsession — "Beyond all race is the problem of man and woman." But what freshness! What force! What a series of small masterpieces! What breezes blowing through it from the inclement north whence the creative "Aeolus unlocks his windy brood." Curious that Lawrence should disdain all elegance, should throw the stuff down on the paper anyhow, repetitive, ungainly, wasteful, indeed with a nonchalance which I suspect to be assumed and defiant.

The publishing people responsible for the new fashion of "omnibus" volumes of short stories by distinguished writers deserve all the immense credit which is due to stimulators of interest in good books. We have had a Hardy; we have had a Chekhov; and now we have *The Stories of Robert Louis Stevenson* (Gollancz, 7s. 6d.). The latest volume, like the others, is a miracle of cheapness. 1120 large pages, on good opaque paper, stoutly and nicely bound, for the price of a common novel. And all, or nearly all, of it copyright stuff.

The best of Stevenson is here. It will be remembered — or it will not be — that Frank Swinnerton, in the critical study of Stevenson which did so much permanent damage to Stevenson's reputation, excepted the short stories from his animadversions. He was right. I have re-read a lot of stories in this volume with real pleasure. My recollections were that the best of Stevenson was in — not *New Arabian Nights*, but *More New Arabian Nights*, otherwise styled *The Dynamiters*. One story in this group, a tale of the Mormons, entitled *The Destroying Angel*, had stuck in my mind for thirty years or more as the very prince of thrillers and shockers. I turned to it again with apprehensive eagerness after half a lifetime. And I rejoice to report that it has lived well up to its secret prestige in my private mind. Stevenson had his mannerisms — I mean less his mannerisms of style than of construction and development — but he was a consummate expert in his own perhaps narrow field. Emphatically the stories can still be read, though a few of them are enfeebled by a sad Scottish sentimentality.

Talking about mannerisms I must mention Mr. Ernest Bramah, whose latest Kai Lung volume, *Kai Lung unrolls his mat* (Richards, 7s. 6d), has been before the public for a month past. Mr. Ernest Bramah has renown. He has been vigorously praised by critics of good judgment and a delicate taste. I cannot count myself among the laudators. Mr. Bramah's mannerism — one large omnipresent mannerism of phrasing — frets me, so that I always draw away from close contact with his mind. He is full of invention and ingenuity, and he has a sense of fun. He cannot be ignored. But for me his name is Dr. Fell. My loss!

14 June 1928

A Few Words to Publishers

It appears that Alfred Neumann's *The Deuce* (translated by Huntley Paterson, published by Heinemann, 7s. 6d.) is to be seen, in the original, in every German house one enters. I certainly saw it in every bookshop I entered in Berlin eight months ago. To translate this historical novel into English was a seemly and a useful act, for in our withdrawn isle we ought surely for our betterment to know something about a book which has made a furore and a fortune in the most bookish country in Europe.

I have been wondering whether any English book of the harsh serious-ness of *The Deuce* (meaning *Der Teufel*) will or could ever be found in every English home one enters. Certainly not under present conditions of book distribution by publishers and booksellers.

A dozen days ago the Associated Booksellers of Great Britain and Ireland, assembled at Edinburgh in annual conference, were discussing the Report of a joint committee of Publishers and Booksellers. The result of the pow-wow was vague. Apparently the bookish trade is in a pretty bad way, but hope springs, because booksellers are at last becoming aware of the fact that their chief aim in life ought to be, not to extract the final halfpenny of discount out of publishers, but to sell books. I have before now censured the methods of booksellers, but publishers are perhaps equally to blame for a state of affairs in which the very existence of new books for sale is jealously guarded as a sinister secret from the general public.

The matter is large, delicate and complicated, and I shall not try to deal with it here. But I don't mind asking a few questions (to which I expect no reply). Why are the preliminary publicity paragraphs which publishers circulate so ingeniously uninforming, so sterotyped in matter, so loose in composition? Why do publishers so seldom furnish interesting biographical information about their authors? Why in particular do they invariably conceal the birthplace of their authors? Supposing an author to have been born in Bradford — authors have been born in Bradford — why do publishers not spread the bright tidings in Bradford, specialise in Bradford, make a bid for big sales in Bradford, force the citizens of Bradford to say unto one another: "An author first saw the light in this our city. Let us therefore as good citizens read and criticise him, and decide whether or no he is an author worthy of his august birthplace."

And why do editors of newspapers, especially provincial newspapers, experience such difficulty in obtaining photographs of authors? Why are not photographs of authors offered to editors? Photographs of authors make excellent publicity. Why are so many important books published on Thursdays and Fridays? Editors more and more regard the issue of certain books as news, and would like to review the books on the day of publication, but lack of space prevents them from reviewing a dozen volumes on a single day or on two days. Thus books get left. What would happen in the theatre if important first nights were confined to Thursdays and Fridays? Theatrical managers arrange not to clash. Why not publishers?

Lastly, do publishers in their heart of hearts really want to encourage the sale of their merchandise — or to impede it? All these questions, save the last, touch merely the fringe of the problem.

The Deuce is a novel about the age of Louis XI of France. *Quentin Durward* is also a novel about Louis XI. Two historical novels could hardly differ from one another more profoundly than these two. The author of the former stresses the brutal and bestial vices of the period. He rejoices in them. Scott looked the other way and held his nose. *Quentin Durward*, though brilliant, is a shockingly careless piece of work; not welded but chucked together. With all his gifts Scott was too proud, and too interested in estate values and beauties, to be a truly professional novelist. He insisted on being first a gentleman. Perhaps a pardonable caprice. Alfred Neumann is a professional and proud of it. His novel shows that "German thoroughness" at which we island amateurs smile with a too facile superiority.

Yet on the whole I prefer *Quentin Durward* to *The Deuce*. Neither of them is true to life. Almost all historical novels are false to life. They give you the impression that past ages were all romance, intrigue, dash and colour. Well, they simply could not have been. And my private view is that past ages were immeasurably less romantic, dashing, coloured, intriguing than our own. For the average man living in them past ages were dull, drab, and less dangerous than crossing Piccadilly Circus is to us. And even the exceptional man could not possibly have lived at the sustained height of nervous tension to which historical novelists always sentence their heroes and villains.

The dialogue of *The Deuce* is composed in a terrible jargon, patently false to any possible form of human life. Here is a piece typical of thousands of lines of back-chat:

"But if you are hoping to strike a bargain and, in exchange for the white body of your wife, to throw the grey head of the Cardinal into the jaws of the King, allow me to inform you that it will need a far greater effort than you have already made to read my cards. . . ." (Oh, that "white"!)

I can more calmly suffer the conversational verbiage of Scott than this. Alfred Neumann has "got up" his period. But he has not yet got up human nature nor the human tongue. And as a novelist he owes nearly everything to Scott. Withal, the characters of Louis and his devil-barber are imposingly drawn. There are effective scenes. There is also much tedium. The book is scarcely in the same class with *Jew Süss*, but it is of the Feuchtwanger school.

In her new volume, *Black Sparta* (Cape, 7s. 6d.), Mrs. Naomi Mitcheson shows much more valour than either Neumann or Scott. There are twelve stories in the volume, all Greek, and the period of the least antique of them is nearly four hundred years before Christ! This kind of thing wants some doing. Mrs. Mitcheson is very cunning in her method. She builds a substructure of landscape, sun, and the behaviour of animals, running water and plants, none of which phenomena has changed since B.C.

> There are eternal colours that haunt all Aprils
> Back through a million years.

Thus she reassures you, making you feel that the B.C. world was not, after all, so B.C. as you feared. And when she comes to her characters she neatly and honestly emphasises the indubitable fact that B.C. people were human in a thousand small things as we are. Nevertheless she does not blink Greek manners, certain of which, if practised by Greeks to-day in Britain, would land Greeks with ignominy in British jails.

Apparently she knows her epochs, but she has the wit not to render her learning formidable, as Flaubert did. If anything she is *too* readable, and makes *too* little demand upon the reader's brain. The stories are slight. They lack power. They please, without exciting. Otherwise they are difficult to find fault with. The story about Pindar writing a poem can fairly be called a distinguished achievement. Mrs. Mitcheson is assuredly developing, and *Black Sparta* at its best is better than, for instance, *Cloud Cuckoo Land*. The book contains a number of original poems, from one of which the above quotation is taken.

21 June 1928

The Censor in the Library

For unknown authors, especially foreign authors, publishers, as I have more than once previously urged in these columns, ought to furnish some testimonial matter. Who is Valeriu Marcu? What is his literary history? His output? Marcu has written a book on an extremely important subject — *Lenin* (Gollancz, one guinea — a large tome) — and his English publishers give not a word about him! By this omission they diminish their publicity, and they leave critics in the dark. They do not even say whether Mr. Dickes' translation is from the German or from the original Russian.

There is a quotation from Novalis at the beginning of the book: "We search everywhere for the absolute [or abstract] and always we find only the concrete." To which I would reply: "I have searched everywhere in Marcu for the concrete and always I have found the abstract." One of the chief objects of a biographer should be to present a picture of his man. Marcu never gets within sight of this object. He is vague, wordy, windy, and has a monstrous passion for metaphors. Thus: "He was living in a panic. He implored his friends to act, as a drowning man might cry for help to a steamer majestically ploughing by." Not bad, but: "This usually tedious writer, whose collected Works were as necessary for their own day as its daily bread . . . but are to-day like the remains of a meal . . . wrote now in utmost haste letters of which the sentences are impregnable barricades."

You would be wrong to think that Marcu couldn't continue such a bizarre procession of metaphors. In the very next sentence the impregnable barricades have become "harmonies with the ring of the Marseillaise." Literally there are thousands of metaphors in the 400 pages, and about 2 per cent. of them are good metaphors.

The mere existence of these serried, jostling metaphors is a proof that the author is incapable of writing a good biography — or a good anything. He has no sense of actuality. He tries to render everything in terms of something else, because, without being aware of the fact, he dare not trust to the faculty of direct vision. It is a pity that so vast and solid a theme as Lenin should have been frittered away by incompetence and an unfit temperament.

The Romans created gods out of their emperors. The Russian nation turned the dead Lenin into a god more authentic than all the Roman emperors put together. The publishers by simply printing the name Lenin on the jacket of the book in larger characters than any dust-jacket ever had before (1⅜ inches by 8¾ inches) have succeeded far better than their author in conveying to the reader an idea of the size of Lenin.

The book is not wholly bad. A blurred image of grandeur does indeed emerge from it. But it demands from the reader a quality of doughtiness which is rare in the reading race. The author has tried to be impartial (though he has scarcely succeeded). He does occasionally impart bits of clear information, but not often. And occasionally he quotes Lenin with brilliant effect. For instance, in the Dictator's reply to accusations of Bolshevik stupidity: "There are stupidities and stupidities. If the Bolsheviks do something silly, it is of the order of 'twice two makes five.' If their opponents do something silly, it is of the order of 'twice two makes stearine candles.' " The mind of the realistic statesman is here revealed. The world still awaits an adequate biography of Lenin. When the book comes it will be what I call a book.

A more "actual" biography, more concrete, far more readable than *Lenin,* is Mr. Sewell Stokes's fragmentary *Isadora Duncan, an intimate portrait* (Brentano's, 6s., with a few very interesting illustrations). Mr. Stokes attempts no epic, nor is he in any sense an inspired writer. Much of what he writes is trifling. Some of it is quite bad. "A bottle of champagne, golden-necked and amorous." How amorous? "The food, superbly cooked, sizzled beautifully on our plates." Also he uses the word "indescribable." No author ought to describe anything as indescribable. To do so is to admit that he does not know his job.

But he is never afraid of disclosing the weaknesses of his heroine. And he certainly does in the end achieve a credible, lifelike picture of a woman who was half a great genius and half a great fool.

The most valuable pages are those giving the scene in which Isadora talks about her project for an autobiography. "Look what they've done to poor Duse. Have you read her biography? Why, they've made the poor darling a saint. And she never pretended to be that. Poor Duse! . . . The greatest actress in the world dies and they just smother her with whitewash. . . . Look at Ellen Terry's book — it was so *dull.* But, then, Ellen Terry's the sweetest, kindest woman living, and I expect when she wrote her book she was thinking of her children. But I've no children and no husband to think of, so I could write the truth. . . . It would be worth doing. Because I'd leave *nothing* out."

Well, in *My Life* Isadora did leave almost nothing out — and the result is that the big circulating Libraries, who began by saying that they would supply it freely on demand, have (with one glorious exception) ended by banning it in practice. The Libraries appear to have given three answers to subscribers (1) There were no copies in. (2) There were only a few copies in and these few were bespoken. (3) The book was not at all a nice book to have about.

One subscriber, who pointed out that he had subscribed for an "unrestricted service," did by pertinacity obtain the book, but only as an exceptional favour — and with the dust-jacket turned inside out! . . . Island, thy name is indeed Britain!

I gravely question whether the Libraries do themselves anything but harm by these antics. The reason for their conduct cannot be a nice regard for the morals of their subscribers, for they sometimes lend with the blindest freedom novels containing passages which really are pornographic in both intention and effect. And Isadora Duncan's autobiography is most positively not pornographic. It is a remarkably fine book. Isadora loved where she listed: but there was not a drachm of pruriency in her whole nature.

Some of the Libraries are apparently under the delusion that the nineteenth century has not yet come to an end. They have forgotten to alter their calendars. We all do that, but not quite to the same extent. There may be a few subscribers to circulating Libraries who desire moral guidance in addition to a supply of books. If such subscribers would be good enough to express their wish on the subscription forms, the Libraries would know where they stood, and the other 95 per cent. of subscribers would be spared a deal of annoyance and the expletive use of a deal of bad language. I recommend this idea to the attention of library managers.

28 June 1928

The Craft of Writing and Printing

This is the season of tennis, where in the more enterprising West-end squares of London and elsewhere you can see the second greatest English pastime being played by young and middle-aged persons of whom the majority have obviously not learned how to use their feet nor understood the grand principles of the game. Yet in some ways they take the game quite seriously and perspire much more than they need. Only it has not occurred to them to have a few elementary lessons from an expert.

Similarly you can go to concerts of earnest persons who really do enjoy music and yet have no notion of the shape of a symphony and could not for their lives tell you whether a given passage was being performed on an oboe or a bassoon. Nevertheless handbooks exist, a perusal of which would enlighten them on these and many other points.

Similarly you can see persons in picture-galleries who know twice nought about the development of painting, whereas handbooks exist . . .

etc., etc. All these people get less fun out of their pleasure than they quite easily might. And, tackled, they could offer no excuse for their joy-reducing ignorance.

I regret to say that the great confraternity of ardent book-readers comprises a large proportion of persons who must be put into the same category. Lots of them, I admit, have acquired some knowledge of the history of literature and the biography of authors. But of the principles which underlie the composition of the line-by-line *stuff* of literature they comprehend hardly the A.B.C. They will talk about liking an author's style — and they merely don't know what they are talking about. They resemble the music-amateurs, who remark with touching complacency: "I don't know anything about music, but I know what I like."

I would not be too exacting, and certainly I would not be pedantic. A reader may appreciate "The quality of mercy is not strained" without being sure of the precise difference between an adjective and an adverb. But a distant acquaintance with the rules of grammar does help literary appreciation. I confess to a cynical annoyance when I hear an enthusiast say: "Between you and I, my opinion is that Conrad's style is a bit over-praised." I have a fearful temptation (which I resist) to ask the man: "Can you tell me why you say 'Between you and I,' while you wouldn't dream of saying 'Between I and you'?" However, I will let grammar go. There are profounder things than grammar in the line-by-line stuff of literature.

What some of these things are the curious may discover in a volume recently published: *English Prose Style*, by Herbert Read (Bell and Sons, 9s.). This book, though it might have been more entrancingly written, is a good book. And I hereby solemnly assert that 95 per cent. of book-readers will enjoy their reading much more keenly after studying it than they did before. The author suggests that his book is rather for writers than for readers. I disagree. Beyond doubt it is a book for writers, but it is also, and equally, a book for readers. I would even say that readers need it more than writers.

Mr. Read divides his work into two parts. First, Composition, and second (what he somewhat technically calls) Rhetoric. In the first place he deals with the line-by-line stuff in detail — words, epithets, metaphors, the form of a sentence, the form of a paragraph, and the general arrangement of matter. In the second he deals with such elements of style as imagery, (what he calls) intelligence and personality, tradition, narrative, and so on. His pages are full of meat, perhaps a trifle tough now and then, but always succulent for those who are prepared to masticate conscientiously. To my mind he at times barely escapes vagueness — and yet I don't know. Perhaps he does escape it, but only by a near shave!

Anyhow, he shows a fine and a disciplined passion for his subject. His dicta on style are sound. Here is one: "The vitality of writing corresponds in some inexorable way to its contemporaneity, and is nourished not so much by the study of examples as by the act of living, from which it takes an accent of reality. The history of a word is entirely irrelevant in prose style; its face-value in current usage is the only criterion."

No wonder he warns us that the just assessment of words and phrases in style is "perhaps peculiarly difficult for those who confine themselves to the reading of classical models." Something like half the book consists of short and long quotations from good writers admirably chosen to

170

illustrate and reinforce the author's arguments. *English Prose Style* meets a want which is insufficiently felt.

The short passage of wisdom just quoted reminds me of another informing book recently published, Messrs. Oliver Simon and Julius Rodenberg's *Printing of To-day* (Peter Davies, Ltd., one guinea). This book is a magnificent quarto, very well printed and produced, with over a hundred and twenty specimens of British and foreign post-war typography; and though a guinea approaches the price of a stall at the opera, the book is really cheap at a guinea. Those who, in addition to appreciating literature, can appreciate the beauty of books as physical objects will enjoy *Printing of To-day* and will probably learn a lot from it.

In the general preface to the volume by Aldous Huxley occurs the following: "Machines exist; let us then exploit them to create beauty — a modern beauty, while we are about it. For we live in the twentieth century; let us frankly admit it, and not pretend that we live in the fifteenth. The work of the backward-looking handprinters may be excellent in its way; but its way is not the contemporary way. Their books are often beautiful, but with a borrowed beauty expressive of nothing in the world in which we happen to live." (Note the similarity of feeling between this and Herbert Read's declaration about style.)

Here, indeed, is "one" for William Morris and his weirdly archaic Kelmscott Press publications. Beautiful tomes, no doubt, but unreadable! Nevertheless, Morris (whose highest adjective of praise for anything was "jolly") did do some good by directing attention to the interest of books as artistic physical objects.

Oliver Simon's Introduction dealing with modern English printing is excellent. He says roundly that machine-printing can be as good as handprinting, and so it can — and is. At all events, machine-printing is practically the only printing in Britain to-day, and we must, can, and do make the best of it. The mischief with modern English printing is that so much of it is in "period" type. Racially we have a passion for periods, as you may perceive in almost any "artistic" drawing-room. Mr. Simon says that there are almost no new types worth talking about. All the good ones are reproductions or imitations of old types.

Which implies that modern printing is considerably in advance of modern typefounding. Which in turn implies that, since modern typography is in effect under the control of two companies, the Linotype Corporation and the Monotype Corporation, it behoves these grandiose joint monopolists to set artists to design a beautiful type recognisably modern. Such a type would assuredly receive from typographic amateurs a welcome comparable to that of, say, Sophie Tucker on the music-hall stage or the latest centurion-cricketer at Lord's.

The Continental section of *Modern Printing* is good, but the United States section is inadequate. As a rule, the "making" of modern American books is not as good as the English ditto (though Americans would perhaps not agree). There have, however, been some fine experiments in U.S.A. The specimen page of the most distinguished American printer, Bruce Rogers, is ill-chosen, for the reason that its spacing is horridly unsatisfactory.

I recommend *Printing of To-day* to all those who (like myself) can discover as much pleasure in a fine page as in a fine cigar. The "publicity" of its publishers has been imperfectly done. If I had not been of an adventurous temperament and had not gone forth and courageously demanded the book at a bookshop and bought it with my own money, I should never have seen it, and the majority of the enlightened and eager bookish readers of this paper might never have heard of it.

5 *July 1928*

The Agonies of Conrad

"The Nonesuch Press" has published *Letters from Joseph Conrad,* with an introduction by Edward Garnett (925 numbered copies, 25s.). It was a righteous act on the part of the Nonesuch.

Some time ago I remarked here that the Nonesuch, while calling itself a Press, was not really a Press, seeing that it did not print its own publications. In its latest catalogue of announcements the Nonesuch, admitting however that I had not been guilty of "serious" misapprehension, corrects me. The Nonesuch has indeed a small press, whose main function is to produce experimental pages, and on which have been printed at least two complete books and at least one catalogue. The name "press" is therefore not technically a misnomer: but it is practically a misnomer, since the great majority of the Nonesuch books are not printed on the Nonesuch Press.

The present Conrad is printed, admirably, by R. and R. Clark of Edinburgh. It happily shows, by its sobriety, that the notions of the Nonesuch about the art of printing are developing in the right direction. Some previous publications have been characterised by preciosity, if not by dandyism. Notably, the Nonesuch edition of Congreve's plays, which somehow gave me a sensation similar to that aroused by the sight of a too finicky and pale necktie on the neck of a young blood in Bond-street.

I bought this edition some years ago; and, much preferring the classic Congreve printed by John Baskerville at Birmingham (blessed among cities) in 1761, I gave my Nonesuch away to a bookish friend, who politely accepted it without a murmur, though, as I learnt later, he already possessed the Baskerville edition.

The three volumes of the latter must count among the loveliest in all the annals of English printing. I said to myself at the time that a firm which had christened itself the Nonesuch (a word presumably meaning "unrivalled") exhibited a certain nerve in entering into competition — and so unsuccessfully — with a really great printer.

However, my wish is not to belittle the Nonesuch, but rather to belaud it. The Nonesuch has unquestionably stimulated public interest in fine books. Also its editing is very sound and very careful. Also it has not disdained the large public. Its complete Blake (published to celebrate the Blake centenary — nearly 1200 beautiful pages for five half-crowns) makes about the best value in cheap editions ever offered.

Also, as I see from its announcements, the Nonesuch has some majestic and high-spirited plans for the future. I anticipate that its promised *Don Quixote,* with coloured illustrations by Mr. McKnight Kauffer, will draw money out of my private pocket.

172

Mr. McKnight Kauffer's Underground Railway posters have changed the face of London streets for a lot of people, including me; and the man who can "stylise" every-day metropolitan scenes is the man to illustrate Cervantes to my taste. The popular success of those posters proves that popular taste is on the up-grade. In the matter of artistic book-production it is assuredly on the up-grade. Hence, though something of an expert in apologetics, I do not apologise for publishing the above remarks in a daily paper of large circulation.

The 330 pages of the Conrad letters makes a mouthful — indeed quite a long meal (sharply seasoned savouries not omitted). They chiefly consist of Conrad's pell-mell outpourings about his work, his moods, and his views on the work of other writers. The correspondence is intensely, if unconsciously, egotistic.

Some will say that they feel able to struggle along in this vale of tears without reading the pell-mell outpourings of even a great writer about himself. They may. But others will find nourishing food in the book.

Except the *Correspondence* of Gustav Flaubert, it is the best and completest revelation of an imaginative creator (and the loftiest inspiration for a young author) that I know of.

I have maintained for many years that the work of literary creation is the hardest, the most exhausting, the most desolating, known to man. This book supports my contention. The agonising way Conrad suffered in accouchement . . . well, its terrors simply can't be exaggerated! A creature who went through what Conrad went through in the long process of giving birth to a masterpiece — or a failure — need have no fear of hell.

This book has tedious pages, and in particular those in which he criticizes in detail works with which the reader cannot reasonably be expected to be familiar. But on the other hand far more pages have the excitements of a beautiful landscape seen under a thunderstorm. Conrad is at his best when he is depressed, furious and "stuck." Thus he described a well-known editor as a "malefactor."

"Console him," he writes to Edward Garnett, "by the remark that he shall not have J.C. in his page at that price [£10 a thousand words] or at any other conceivable price. Strengthen his faint soul by pointing out that the thing [an essay] is low down and commonplace enough to please the divine mediocrity of the only god he knows — his public. Tell him these wholesome and fortifying truths in order that his constitution should be braced up for the extraction of Five Guineas."

When he gets angry with a laudatory critic for ranking one of his own (Conrad's) stories with a story by the god-like Turgenev, his infuriated strain runs like this:

"It is enough to make me wonder whether the man has sense and judgment enough to come in when it rains. Has ever the Shade of a great artist been more amazingly, more gratuitously insulted? Couldn't someone speak to him quietly and suggest he should go behind a counter and weigh out margarine by the sixpennyworth?"

It must have been on one of his bad days that Bernard Shaw encountered him. "G.B.S. towed by Wells came to see me reluctantly and I nearly bit him."

As a critic, though he had his hours of just and penetrating vision, Conrad was far too apt to fall into wild extremes. Like all Poles, he detested certain Russians. Mentioning *Anna Karenina* he says: "Of the thing itself I think but little."

The Brothers Karamazov he sets down as "An impossible lump of valuable matter. Terrifically bad and impressive and exasperating . . . . Too Russian for me. I understand the Russians have just discovered him. I wish them joy."

About his own work he is scathing. Most of us regard *The End of the Tether* as not quite the worst story in the world. Conrad calls it "heart-breaking bosh." *Nostromo*, which has generally been classed as a masterpiece, he classes as "an imbecile sort of story." Not that he meant that. He didn't really mean hundreds of his impassioned utterances.

In praise of his friends and those sympathetic towards him he was quite Oriental.

But not a bit Oriental in his reasoned praise of Edward Garnett as a critic of imaginative literature! Here, in this reiterated laudation you see Conrad at his best as a judge. It is to be remembered that all the letters in the volume (save a few to members of Garnett's family) are addressed to Edward Garnett. Few literary critics have received a more magnificent compliment. And Edward Garnett deserved the compliment.

By the perusal of a jejune and very imperfect novel, *An Outcast of the Islands*, Edward Garnett divined instantly the potential greatness and grandeur of Conrad. His perceptions are profound. I will also call them "uncanny," though I detest the word. He has been right again and again. I doubt if I have ever known him wrong. He has made the literary prestige of at least three firms of publishers. And he it was who first singled out Mr. Williamson's *Tarka the Otter*, which has just received the Hawthornden prize.

Personally I doubt if *Tarka the Otter* is the sort of book that ought to be "crowned," but it is vastly superior with all its preciosity and queerness and over-writing to some other books that have received the Hawthornden prize. It has really fine qualities. Mr. Williamson owes a lot to Edward Garnett. So do we all.

12 July 1928

73 – And a Writer of Real Romance

"Aloysius Horn" as his editress, Mrs. Ethelreda Lewis, calls him,* made a very considerable success, especially in America, with his first book of adventure, *The Ivory Coast in the Earlies*. It had a preface by John Galsworthy, it was praised by lots of people, including me, and it sold like evening papers on the day of a classic horse-race.

But there was always a current of criticism adverse to it. The critic of *The Manchester Guardian*, a man of fine taste and particularly qualified to deal with adventure in literature, was decidedly sardonic, and the chief implication of his article was that "Aloysius Horn" had contrived to "get away with it."

The adverse current still continues. I have reflected upon the whole matter in a spirit judicial and detached, with the result that I definitely

---

* His real name was Alfred Aloysius Smith.

range myself on the side of Aloysius Horn and against his detractors. My opinion is that he and Mrs. Lewis between them delivered the genuine goods, and that there can be no question of them having "got away" with a spurious article.

Aloysius Horn, at the age of 73, is undoubtedly a bit of a card — you can see that in his portrait — but he is a truly remarkable writer with a wondrous gift of phrase. He has real romance in him, and he can, and does, communicate romance to the reader.

The second volume of *Life and Works, Harold the Webbed,* introduced by William McFee (another authority on adventure) and edited by Mrs. Lewis (Cape, 7s. 6d.), is before the public. It has already been favourably reviewed in this paper, but I take the liberty of referring to one aspect of it.

Mrs. Lewis has had a difficult job, perhaps an impossible job. The story itself is short, too short to make a fair-sized volume, and Mrs. Lewis wanted, actually, to convey an impression of the card's extraordinary individuality. She has therefore inserted after every chapter a "conversation" with the card.

The conversations are excellently rendered, and they do give a brilliant impression of the card's individuality. The total effect, however, is not quite satisfactory.

Mrs. Lewis adopted a similar method in the first Horn book. There the effect was more satisfactory because the narrative portion of the work had less unity and hence suffered less from the interpolations.

In this second book the narrative portion forms a complete story, and it does beyond question suffer from the interpolations, admirable though they are. *Harold the Webbed* does not produce one total effect: it produces two separate effects, each fine, but each marring the other.

Aloysius Horn's disquisitions to his editress are largely sociological. He has an authentic feeling for the poor, and a pleasing bias against mere theologians and fanatics. "The Redeemer said, 'Suffer little children to come unto Me.' That's plain enough. It's children He wants. He's not asking for Unitarians and other fancy religioners to be brought. Arguing their case, and so on. Learned talk tires in the ultimate. No love about it. (Excuse me, I know you're a Protestant)."

As a literary artist Aloysius Horn is self-conscious enough (an artist ought to be self-conscious); and he can smile at himself (as few artists can). "All those little black boats full of knowledge of the sea . . . . And swimming down on 'em like swans scorning a water-hen the galleons of Spain. All the sheen of the Adriatic upon them. Blue water of foreign parts (better get that down in case I forget it again: 'All the sheen of the Adriatic upon them'). You can use it to touch up a descriptive passage of Caesar's fleet if I get a bit tired of the high lights."

What phrasing! These brief extracts (scores could be, and have been, quoted just as striking) ought really to create in the hearts of those who have not yet read Aloysius Horn an inexorable determination to read him.

Aloysius Horn comes near to being a master of narrative — that form or kind of literature in which Mr. Herbert Read (author of *English Prose Style*) temerariously asserts that we English are deficient. I thought I had met with another near-master of narrative in Mr. Robert Byron, who has written *The Station* (Duckworth, 18s., interestingly illustrated with new photographs).

The Station is a very thorough description of a very thorough visit to Mount Athos, the lofty retreat whose chief charm for some strange-minded persons seems to be that no female of either man or beast or fowl (female nocturnal insects are apparently not banned) has ever been permitted to enter therein.

The opening of *The Station* reveals a travel-writer of sly, urbane wit and all inclusive observation, with a sense of style and a refreshing vocabulary. The body of the book, however, is less satisfactory.

Mr. Byron's aim was "to picture Athos in every aspect as the composite and living memorial of a great civilisation." He has not quite succeeded in presenting a "picture" because of his inability to handle large masses of detail. He fights a continuous battle with rebellious unwieldy detail, and if he is not beaten he certainly is not victorious. His book is less a composition than a medley.

Still, *The Station* has value, and it is readable enough — if you can resign yourself to go at the author's pace, which is slow. Also it shares a merit with the work of Swift in that its innumerable moral implications are never more than implications. You feel them without perceiving them. Mr. Byron has an attitude towards existence.

In this matter of moral implications, I will mention Eden Phillpotts's new volume of verse, *Goodwill* (Watts, 2s. 6d.). Here the moral aim of the author is boldly explicit. He does not hide it; he displays it. The "goodwill" of the title is the goodwill which ought to prevail — but rarely does — between artists and men of science.

Eden Phillpotts preaches the necessity of cultivating that goodwill in order to expedite the progress of civilisation. He certainly has the right to take the pulpit. No imaginative writer to-day, not even H.G. Wells, has shown in practice a deeper appreciation of scientific principle in the largest sense than Phillpotts. His novels (not yet generally assessed at their true worth) are inspired, vitalised, and shaped by a scientific conception of existence.

This small book is stark serious. It must be taken seriously or not taken at all. The preface states the theme plainly and succinctly. "Art does ill to nourish the implicit aversion from science which we find a common instinct of the artistic mind . . . . Similarly science might well recognise more vividly the profound influences of art on human life, pay it deeper respect and seek to understand it. Art and science complement each other, and between them surely hold the keys of human hope."

And it is so. And the sooner both artists and men of science seize this truth with goodwill *and imagination*, the better. "While cast in shape of verse," says Eden Phillpotts, "these thoughts do not pretend to poetry." They may not pretend, but they sometimes achieve.

19 July 1928

I Read a "Thriller" — And Startle My Friends

I had never read a novel of Edgar Wallace's; nor have I ever seen one of his dramas (though it is not very easy nowadays to go to a

West End theatre without seeing one).

I have asked friend after friend and acquaintance after acquaintance: "Have you read Edgar Wallace?" and the answer was always negative, until last week I put the question to Frank Swinnerton.

The general attitude was: "Have I read Edgar Wallace? Good heavens! What do you take me for?"

Nearly all bookish people are snobs, and especially the more enlightened among them. They are apt to assume that if a writer has an immense circulation, if he is enjoyed by plain persons, and if he can fill several theatres at once, he cannot possibly be worth reading and merits only indifference and disdain.

For myself, though undeniably a bookish person, I came many years ago to the conclusion that there is little to choose between certain popular authors haughtily neglected by the elect and certain authors a knowledge of whose work is considered to be absolutely necessary to the equipment of self-respecting diners-out.

I was much younger than I am when, for instance, I got into trouble for asserting that the late Marie Corelli was quite as good, and quite as true to life, as the late Mrs. Humphry Ward. (Beyond doubt, she was far more readable.) I was laughed at, scolded, upbraided for my disregard of the dignity of letters.

But to-day few serious critics would maintain that artistically Mrs. Humphry Ward's novels are a brass button better than Marie Corelli's. Both lots are equally dead, and they are equally dead because they are equally false in their crude sentimentalisation of the spectacle of human existence.

Well, I saw a new novel by Edgar Wallace in my daily list of publications, and I said proudly to myself: "I will read that novel." I said also to various friends: "I am going to read Edgar Wallace." They were startled. They strolled around saying: "He is going to read Edgar Wallace. What next?"

Such is our literary snobbishness — for their ignorance of Edgar Wallace's books was as complete as the deadness of Marie Corelli and Mrs. Humphry Ward, I seemed to be receiving adieux on the seashore.

Two of Edgar Wallace's novels have lately been published. One is *The Orator*. I read the other one, *The Gunner* (Long, 7s. 6d.). In stating that, having read *The Gunner*, I wouldn't mind reading *The Orator*, I disclose my view of this writer.

I much prefer him to the celebrated Agatha Christie (whose books I can begin, but not finish), and the ingenious author of *The Cask* * which beat me off with great loss before I was half way through it).

In *The Gunner* something sinister and exciting is continually afoot. The amount of incident to the page is prodigious, and to the chapter is incalculable. Often, when you think that the author's inventive powers must be exhausted, he will suddenly change the scene — and in the middle of a chapter, too! — and start anew as fresh as if he had risen up from twelve hours dreamless sleep.

True, only one character, that of the detective — "the Sparrow" — is really drawn (the detective is a genuine master of back-chat); but in the turmoil of a thousand escapes and other sensations you have no breath to demand character-drawing.

* Freeman Wills Crofts: see also p.413.

True, Edgar Wallace does not spare improbabilities, gross improbabilities; but he has the wit not to insist on them. In two lines, he has staged and forgotten them, and so have you forgotten them.

When Mrs. Humphry Ward, in *Helbeck of Bannisdale* wanted to make her two lovers miss the last train home, she took pages and endless trouble to give verisimilitude to the age-worn device — and failed. Edgar Wallace would have been content to say: "They missed the last train home," and left the thing at that.

Considered as a whole, his highly complex picture of "underground" London is at least as convincing as, say, Lady Oxford's picture of hunting circles in *Octavia*, and no more odd. He is more picturesque than Lady Oxford, and than most novelists. And he might carry picturesqueness even further without exceeding the limits of realism.

A few weeks ago in America a shot "gunner" lay in state in a dinner-jacket in a silver coffin, with an imitation rose at his head lit by an occulting electric light, and at his feet a slot in which the faithful could put money for flowers if they felt like it.

Edgar Wallace at his loftiest does not rise to such a height of gorgeous picturesqueness.

Evidently he writes very rapidly (as Scott did), and corrects only in proof (as Scott did). And a few slips have survived the proof-reading. Thus he calls a lady "Lila" on one page and "Millie" on another. Peccadillo! His style is sometimes quite good, but sometimes it is the style of a man in a hurry.

It was certainly sinful of him to describe coffee as "the delicious beverage," and to write "she shrugged milky shoulders," and to write "his face went grey." (I have never seen a face go grey, except in illness.)

To compensate, he is generous with bits of queer information. For example: "There is quite a brisk trade in blank cheque forms and certain sources from which they can be obtained." Who would have guessed it? By the way, Edgar Wallace's grammar, usually perfect, seems rather doubtful here. But anyhow his grammar is out of sight superior to Jane Austen's. I have been re-reading *Mansfield Park*, which is studded with bad grammar.

High-brows are requested to note: I make no claim for Edgar Wallace, except (I) that I read *The Gunner* as Barrie's hero read *The Chaplain of the Fleet*, without fatigue; and (2) that there is no nonsense about him and above all no padding in his work. (2) endears him to me.

The Gunner may conceivably be forgotten before *Mansfield Park*. Indeed, I think it will be. For Edgar Wallace has a very grave defect and I will not hide it. He is content with society as it is. He parades no subversive opinions. He is "correct."

Now it is well known that all novelists who have depicted contemporary society, and who have lived, abound in subversive opinions.

Look at Defoe, Swift, and Fielding. Feel their lash. Remember the whips and scorpions of Dickens, and the effort of even the Agag-footed Thackeray to destroy utterly the popular convention of the romantical hero. And Hardy's terrible rough-hewing of the divinity that shapes our ends. And Wells's innumerable overthrowings of the entire social structure.

It may be counted a maxim that good modern literature is never made out of correct sentiments. If there are exceptions to this rule they must be extremely few. Withal, I am judging Edgar Wallace by one novel, and he has written as many as Alexandre Dumas himself, though not as many plays as Dumas wrote.

Perhaps I am unfair to Edgar Wallace. Perhaps in earlier years he has chastised society with intent to be immortal.

26 July 1928

Two Good New Authors in One Week

The greatest and proudest pleasure of every literary critic (unless the critic has arrived at the age of boredom — many arrive at it before forty) is to find an unsung author in whom he honestly believes there is the stuff of life.

Some critics are so convinced of the inferiority of the new to the old that they never do find a new author worth singing about. Some others find about one a week.

For myself I feel sure, in the light of history, that future generations will rightly reverse at least eighty per cent. of the verdicts of the present generation.

Hence I feel sure, also, that our best new authors will escape my questing gaze. Either I shall miss them entirely (it being an impossible task to examine personally even the fiftieth part of the total output of current publications); or, chancing to see them, I shall fail to recognise them for what they are.

And the major tragedy of my critical existence is the continual thought that I am ignorantly not praising young men and women who deserve appreciation and are hungering for it.

I receive letters from authors whom perhaps posterity will consider great — and I ignore them. What else can one do? One must reconcile oneself to being an instrument of injustice. Happily I am so constituted that I can bear with stoic fortitude the injustices which other people have to suffer.

To-day I tremble, for I must announce not one author, but two authors, who I think have in them the stuff of life, and for whom (if they possess the solid character which is essential to the production of first-rate art) the next twenty years hold brilliant potentialities. Two good new authors in one week — it is a strong dose! But I can't help it. A belief is a belief!

The first new talent is H.A. Manhood, author of *Nightseed* (Cape, 7s. 6d.). A volume of sixteen short stories. Large numbers of readers, if they begin to read them, certainly will not like these tales. They are very outspoken, and rather free in the matter of inconvenient words. Also Mr. Manhood is addicted to unusual words, words with which I for one doubtless ought to be familiar but am not.

Within a dozen pages I met the following: bedeguar, bullace, brangle, sorning, rummer, pretzel; and I could site scores of others.

Further, Mr. Manhood sees life very gloomily, though not bitterly. He loves horror and disaster, and he seems to love little else.

Some of the stories are merely frightful, heart-breaking. One of the best,

Misery Cottage, is composed of decay, stultification, adder-poisoning, incest and a couple of suicides. An appalling dish to set before a decent circulating library subscriber!

Still further, Mr. Manhood, so far, is deficient in inventiveness.

The main quality in an imaginative author is the quality of imagination, the power to see his characters with intense and persuasive force — a force which compels the reader to see them too. But this main quality alone is not enough. The author must be able to invent interesting and truly illustrative incidents to carry out his theme.

Mr. Manhood fails here, not wholly, but partially. His invention, when he has any, is often too maladroit — I will not go so far as to say clumsy.

I have stated as shortly as I can the case against Mr. Manhood. The case for Mr. Manhood is that he observes life afresh, with originality, that he has a style as to whose fundamental excellence there can hardly be two opinions, that he has a genuine, an appealing, a touching sense of beauty, and that his imaginative power is sometimes simply tremendous.

Yes, he can see, and he can make you see. Apparently he is young and inexperienced — in letters if not in life. He has a lot to learn, but he can learn. His defects are curable, by self-training and the efflux of time. Meanwhile he has emphatically done something.

Read the book. I would not guarantee that you will like it. I would rather guarantee that you won't. But I guarantee that it will shake you out of the rut of indifference.

The second new talent is Richard Pyke, author of *Lives and Deaths of Roland Greer* (Sanderson, 7s. 6d.). A novel, whose chief business is the statement and analysis of family relations — the relationship between Roland and his mother and between Roland and his brother Daniel.

This business is extremely well done; many pages are so good, so fresh, so original, and so charged with emotional quality that they could scarcely be better. The game of draughts at the end of Part I is noble and really moving; it and other scenes also show a remarkable power of sympathetic imagination.

Mr. Pyke, if this is his first book, as I conceive it to be, might one day produce a work closely coinciding with my idea of a masterpiece — provided only that he is capable of acquiring his craft and disciplining his faculties.

Mr. Manhood has at least grasped the truth that the first job of the novelist is to tell a story; his trouble is, not that he has no story to tell, but that he has not the full skill to tell it. Mr. Pyke seemingly is not yet aware that a novel must be a story. A great deal of his book is a treatise on the psychology of the Greer family, without anything recognisable as a sequence of events.

It is sound stuff, but it does not sweep the reader on. At the close of the first part one asks what has definitely and clearly happened, and the answer is "Naught."

Further, he is so preoccupied with mind-states that he forgets that mind-states ought to have some physical dress. The characters worry one another incessantly in rooms, of which rooms we know nothing.

The hero is a pianist and composer, but we hear no word of his training, his professors, his practising, his artistic growth, his composing, and a mere sentence or two as to his concerts. His sisters, who have rôles not unimportant in the opening chapters, are allowed to vanish from the story without explanation.

As for his faculties, the literary faculty gets the bit between its teeth, running wildly after metaphor and simile with painful results, and indulging in verbal tricks, such as the three identical beginnings of the three parts of the book, which are deplorably naive.

The imaginative faculty again and again defies its proprietor, and nowhere more calamitiously than in the final scene of Roland's suicide.

I don't object to suicide in a novel, but I object to being bathed in blood for no reason. Here Mr. Pyke's unruly demon has outraged the general decency of nature.

Such ill-conditioned excesses may be, and probably are, the mark of an exceptionally strong creative talent at an early stage of development. But Mr. Pyke will do well to make arrangements as quickly as possible to be master in his own house.

I look forward to his next book with eagerness. His first is a fiery sign on the horizon.

2 August 1928

A Marvellous Woman Novelist

"Colette" is the best woman-novelist in France. She has more finesse and more genius than any other woman-novelist I know of in the world. But her field of action is very restricted. It comprises love, and loves — almost exclusively her own; she does not conceal this fact — and it comprises nothing else.

Within her field, however, she is marvellous — cynical, gentle, capricious, ingenuous, sophisticated and entirely graceful and delicious. Nobody like her! Her interest is in the sentimental hearts and the unruly bodies of women and men; she cares naught for the social structure, politics, theologies. But how intense, beautiful, and just is her searching interest!

Her new novel, *La Naissance du Jour* (Flammarion, 12 francs) is not really a novel. It would have been better, I think, without its puerile plot, without any plot. It ought to have dropped the mask of a novel and called itself frankly: *My Farewell to Love*. Colette recognises that the years have been passing.

It is a short and lovely book, delicately daring, a curious mixture of naiveté and immense experience, full of original observation and of tender melancholy.

The novel is one to be read — by those English who can read it. The Englishman who can read it may flatter himself that he has some acquaintance with French. Colette's style was never easy, and it is growing more difficult. It is now overcharged, and wilfully overcharged. Simplified and lightened, it would be greatly improved.

Colette has two methods of baffling the would-be foreign reader. First, she indulges herself unduly in colloquial idioms and even in the idioms of slang. Second, she indulges herself in strange, unusual words. Her brilliant novel, *Chéri*, was an example of the first method. It could not possibly be well understood by anyone who was unable to talk colloquial and slang French. And no dictionary would help the struggler.

La Naissance du Jour is an example of the second method. It abounds in words that nobody has ever heard of, though its idioms are comparatively easy. Many of the words have not yet reached our French-English dictionaries and never will.

In this connection I must say that English people explicitly or implicitly exaggerate their familiarity with the French tongue. The phrase, used of an Englishman, "He speaks French like a native," is preposterous. There are not a hundred Englishmen on the face of the earth who could speak a hundred words of French without giving away their Englishness to a Frenchman.

I remember talking to one of the finest and most famous linguists in Britain. He said to me: "I regard French as the hardest of all languages. When I read French I seldom find a page that doesn't contain words or phrases that I can't translate." I was glad to hear such a confession from such an expert. It comforted me. And I have further comfort in this: that nineteen times out of twenty when I have asked a Frenchman the meaning of a word unintelligible to me he has answered: "I don't know."

Still, Colette remains a very distinguished author — I would say a unique author. Let me add that for the foreigner her easiest book, *L'Envers du Music-Hall* (Flammarion), a series of brief sketches of the existence of music-hall performers, is among her best. It cannot fail to please.

The trilogy (sometimes picturesquely called by booksellers' assistants and others "triology") is becoming quite a feature of English fiction. A vast double trilogy of novels has just been brought to a dignified conclusion. Others are completed; and still others are on the way.

But the devices of a succession of novels dealing with one set of characters, or with one set and their descendants, is not an English invention. Balzac did it first and best — considerably best — and no novelist since him has really carried the novel further than he carried it. This strange and lone prodigy still awaits a rival, despite the fact that his romantic sentimentality is now finding him out.

Zola did it on a larger scale, and more logically than Balzac, but not so well. Zola is at present undervalued. At least four of the Rougon-Macquart novels are tremendous affairs, *Germinal, L'Assommoir, L'Œuvre* and *Nana.* I have read *Nana* three times, to say which is to praise. *L'Œuvre* is to my mind the finest battle-piece (the battle being between the artist in a man and the lover in a man) ever accomplished. Romain Rolland did it on a big scale in *Jean Christophe,* but *Jean Christophe* is very unequal; also it sprawls.

And to-day Roger Martin du Gard is doing it comprehensively and thoroughly in *Les Thibault.* Five volumes of *Les Thibault* have appeared, the last two recently; two more are announced, and heaven knows how many others are beneath the horizon. English novelists, however, need feel no humiliation; the volumes are comparatively short. Zola or John Galsworthy or R.H. Mottram might well have put the published five between two covers.

Du Gard is a writer who counts — and who will count more. He is immensely superior, for instance, to such a fashionable and yet able and not negligible author as François Mauriac.

Du Gard would hate to be fashionable. He rolls up his sleeves, gets to work, works intensely with a single eye to honest perfection, never exaggerates, never searches after effects — and leaves the rest to Time. I think that Time will not disappoint his faith.

The first book of du Gard's that I read, about 15 or 20 years ago was *Jean Barois*. It is a novel in dialogue, most distinguished, very readable and entirely successful.

In my opinion his later books are less impressive. The Thibault series appears to me somewhat to lack form and concision. But it should emphatically be read. The two latest volumes are *La Consultation* and *La Sorellina*. The former is chiefly medical in substance. Never was medicine more exhaustively handled, or with a more poetic transmutation of the stuff of professional life into poetry. I hereby solemnly recommend all five volumes.

Another French trilogist is Jules Romains, who years ago wrote a short novel highly original in conception, *Morte de Quelqu'un*. Since then he has produced all sorts of novels, prose, verse, and plays (including *Knock*, which was all fine except the last act — bad enough to ruin any play).

The trilogy has the general title *Psyche*. Two volumes are published: *Lucienne* and *Le Dieu des Corps*. The latter is just out. It is a rather physical novel, written with a pure mind. Not everybody will be able to tolerate it.

These are the most important new French novels that I have met with. But I must mention with satisfaction a book that is not fiction: Julien Benda's *La Trahison des Clercs*.

Although not a new publication, it still has a large sale and causes a lot of lively discussion. It is a political survey of the post-war world — and let not this description of it frighten the timid, for it makes first-rate reading.

I do not like to agree with Mr. Benda's theory that nations and classes, instead of drawing together, are drawing further apart. But he is very persuasive. I cannot understand why *La Trahison des Clercs* has not aroused interest in Britain. It assuredly ought to be translated — but with more literary decency than marks certain recent deplorable translations from the French.

9 August 1928

My Brilliant but Bewildering "Niece"

The publication of her strange book, *The Strange Necessity* (Cape, 10s. 6d.), makes a proper occasion for considering the case of my brilliant "niece," Rebecca West (it is she who claims the relationship). *

Miss West has done two novels. Differing from certain critics whose judgment demands respect, I do not think that *The Return of the Soldier* is good. It seems to me to be fatally vitiated by conventional characterisation,

---

* In the book, Rebecca West refers to the four "uncles" of her earlier days — Shaw, Bennett, Galsworthy and Wells.

by sentimentality, and by bad writing. It is "literary." It never convinces me. On the other hand it is well constructed.

The first half of *The Judge* is better, much better; but the second half is a failure. It reads as if the author had said to herself: "I can't think how the deuce to finish this book, but finish it I will — somehow."

Strange that a book can be so good and so bad! There are, however, earlier and greater examples. For instance, *The Heart of Midlothian*, which suffers from the same complaint as *The Judge* — namely, a broken back.

But Miss West is far more of a journalist than a novelist. At her best, especially in short articles, she has no superior, and few equals. She is courageous, brutal, acid, very witty and extremely independent. She is widely read and widely experienced. She has a broad taste for life. She has delicate sensibilities. Above all, she has an agile and acrobatic mind, clever and resourceful enough to enable her to emerge without discredit from the innumerable glorious scrapes which it gets her into — political, sociological, philosophical, metaphysical, even aesthetic.

That disorderly mind of hers ranges like a tigress over the whole spectacle of mankind, and recoils before nothing in the immense panorama.

One third of her new volume is reviews of books, which reviews are more remarkable for lively readableness than for insight and sympathetic understanding. The bulk of the volume consists of one long essay, "The Strange Necessity."

"Why does art matter? And why does it matter so much? What is this strange necessity?" Such are the questions which she poses, and tries and dazzlingly fails to answer. I didn't expect her to answer them, for they have never been satisfactorily answered and never will be. (Genuine creative artists are rarely interested in them.)

But I expected her to be less unsuccessful than in fact she is. She succeeds only in being bewildering. Take any page, every page, and it is certainly great fun, but the separate pages, whose numbering might be rearranged without anybody noticing it, amass themselves into enormities of tedium.

If she had a conscious direction in composing the wild work, she has managed to hide nearly all trace of it. She dashes from notion to notion, from fancy to fancy, from author to author, from city to city, from moral to moral. You cannot catch up with her. She sometimes contrives to be in two places at once. She has an idea. Down with it on paper! She has another idea. Down with it on paper! Sequence be hanged! She out-Shaws Shaw in wilfulness. And she has not Shaw's fundamental sobriety nor his style.

She must, at any cost, "perform." She must be odd. She has, for example, a deep and righteous admiration for George Moore. She richly praises him. Yet she has to dance jigs around him. His fiction she describes as "incompetent novels that suggested round-hand crawling over the pages of an exercise-book."

She says that he "wrote poetry that sounded like an angry woman working a sewing-machine that was out of order." Is this amusing, or is it ridiculous? George Moore never wrote poetry; he has shown what he thinks of his verse by suppressing it. But it would not be easy to devise a more preposterous description of his verse than my niece's.

The essay is infested from end to end by this sort of mere irresponsible silliness.

As for Miss West's conclusions about art and the necessity thereof, I don't know what they are. Here is a sentence which may or may not be a conclusion: "We have strong grounds for suspecting that art is at least in part a way of collecting information about the universe." Her more precise definitions are worse than this. Now and then in her hit-or-miss variety show she hits, with startling effect. Not often.

Miss West has been writing for quite a long time. Her gifts are enviable and indisputable. But she has not learnt how to use them. In other words, she does not know how to live. And unless and until she sets her mind in order she won't know.

In principle I am not favourable to literary godfathership: the sponsoring by famous names of books signed with less famous names. I think that a book, however good, delicate, modest, it may be, should take its chance in the rough general mêlée of the market-place. Moreover, the owners of famous names are sometimes erratic in their judgments and apt to be too benevolent.

But there may be exceptions. It certainly would not have occurred to me to read Radclyffe Hall's *The Well of Loneliness* (Cape, 15s., a large and long novel) had I not been attracted by a line in the publisher's advertisement: "With a commentary by Havelock Ellis" — Havelock Ellis being a name which means much to me. I knew nothing of the author's previous work, nor of the subject of this new one.

I ought to have guessed its subject. It is Havelock Ellis, the essayist, to whom I am indebted for the enlargement of my outlook, but Havelock Ellis, in addition to being a very valuable philosophical essayist, counts among the greatest European authorities upon the vagaries or aberrations of nature in the matter of sexual characteristics.

The Well of Loneliness is the story of one of the victims of one of Nature's caprices. Havelock Ellis stands by it. He praises it for its fictional quality, its notable psychological and sociological significance, and its complete absence of offence. I cannot disagree with him.

Uncertain in touch at first, this novel is in the main fine. Disfigured by loose writing and marred by loose construction, it nevertheless does hold you. It is honest, convincing, and extremely courageous. What it amounts to is a cry for unprejudiced social recognition of the victims. The cry attains genuine tragic poignancy. The future may hide highly strange things, and therefore conservative prophecy is dangerous; nevertheless, I must say that I do not think the cry will be effectively heard.

Nature has no prejudices, but human nature is less broadminded, and human nature, with its deep instinct for the protection of society, can put up a powerful defence of its own limitations. *The Well of Loneliness* is not a novel for those who prefer not to see life steadily and see it whole.

The appearance of a collected edition of the works of the late Mary Webb (Cape, 5s. per volume) is a very satisfactory phenomenon, and quite as thought provoking as it is satisfactory. For there would not have been any collected edition of Mary Webb had we not a Prime Minister with some taste for and in literature, and had he not happened to read a novel of Mary Webb's, and had he not happened to praise it in a speech.

That single speech by a politician did more for Mary Webb's fame than years of praise by enthusiastic critics, public and private. (The lettered may say that Britain is a strange country, but it is not stranger than other countries.)

The first volume of the collected edition, *Gone to Earth*, has a preface by John Buchan, who puts his hand on the weakness of the author's style. Mr. Baldwin himself is doing a preface for *Precious Bane*: a gesture which reflects equal credit on the benevolence of the Prime Minister and the enterprise of the publisher.

16 August 1928

Books Not For Daughters

Since I last discussed, a few weeks ago, the question of censorship by lending libraries I have had plenty of proof, both oral and by correspondence, that the matter is one of general and rather acute interest. The representative of a large lending library called to see me about it. He was very polite, but he left me in no doubt as to his opinion of my opinions. He spoke to me thus:

"I don't want to put it too bluntly, but you are quite wrong. Now I will tell you what happens. A lady arrives in our library and she chooses, say, this autobiography of Isadora Duncan that has caused all the fuss recently. Well, she comes again in a day or two and asks to see the managing director.

"The managing director is a busy man, but the lady is an important customer, and she absolutely insists on seeing him and she does see him, and he has to treat her with the utmost tact.

"She shows him the book, and she is angry. He says to her soothingly, 'Now, madam, I understand you have a complaint to make about this book. What exactly is it? We are anxious to satisfy our subscribers in every possible way.'

"'Complaint!' she cries. 'I should just think I had a complaint to make! I took this book home quite innocently. I knew nothing of it. But as you circulated it, I naturally thought it was all right. I noticed that my young daughter seemed to be very absorbed in it, and so I thought I would glance at it myself. I did look at it myself.

"'Really, Mr. ——! Really! I did imagine that I might have confidence in your judgment and taste. I could scarcely look my daughter in the face. Of course, I couldn't for a moment blame her. Your library is supposed to be perfectly respectable; it is supposed to be for the use of people with nice feelings and some sense of decency. Really, Mr. ——, if I am to be subjected to these terrible risks I must cease my subscription at once and try some other library where more care is exercised!'"

"Well," my visitor went on, "what is one to do? The lady considered that she had a genuine grievance, a very serious grievance. What was the managing director to say to her? We can't afford to lose customers. He could only apologise and promise that he would exercise more care in the future.

"No object in arguing, was there? We are a commercial concern, and our business has to be conducted on strictly commercial lines . . . .

"And I must just say this," the library representative added, "you made a suggestion in one of your articles to the effect that we might warn our subscribers about certain books. But in practice this cannot be done. How can we ask our young ladies to tell customers that such-and-such a book is improper?

"Customers would instantly question our young ladies: 'How do *you* know it's improper? Have you read it?' Not a pretty stiuation for our young ladies! There are things you simply can't do in a commercial house. We had no alternative but to withdraw the book entirely from circulation, and this was what we did."

I was full of sympathy for the managers of this lending library. I could not deny for a moment that circumstances had placed them in an extremely difficult position. Lending libraries are not "out" for the broadening of popular taste nor for the education of matrons, nor for the evolution of ideas, nor for anything whatever except the declaring of dividends from monetary profits made by lending and the sale of books.

But there is another side to the affair. And this other side is well presented in a few sentences from a letter which I have received from a London police-magistrate.

"It seems to me," writes the police-magistrate, "that the library should say so if it is of the opinion that the work is indecent, and face the consequences. If a book is unfit for decent reading, why are not the police invoked? The average subscriber denies the library's right to say what is suitable reading for him."

The average subscriber, and even the unusually broadminded subscriber, has indeed a very strong case. The lending library makes a legal contract with him by which in return for a cash payment it undertakes to lend to him current books in a continuous supply. In some cases the library specially undertakes to render an "unrestricted" service of books.

No lending library says in its legal contract that it will only provide for the subscriber such books as may be approved by mothers fearful for the perfect innocence of their young daughters. If it did it would speedily be compelled to put its shutters up.

The notion that the supply of books lent must be confined to volumes suitable for the perusal of young girls was utterly exploded years and years ago. And yet library-directors and mothers will persist in going on just as if the notion had never received the slightest damage.

What in the name of sense would be said if a father walking along a fashionable shopping street with a son aged eighteen were to go into a shop and protest:

"Look here, you are making such a display in one of your windows as is more than likely to put ideas into my boy's head which will destroy the innocence that I am carefully preserving in him. If you don't empty the window immediately I shall at once give instructions that no member of my family shall patronise your establishment"?

It would be said that the anxious father was ripe for a lunatic asylum; and it would be justly said.

And, after all, the matron whose reasoning I have narrated was not a bit logical. In her house is the family copy of Shakespeare expurgated for the use of young daughters? Has *Measure for Measure* or *Troilus and Cressida*

187

been cut out of it with maternal scissors? And has, for another example, the thirteenth chapter of Samuel II (containing one of the best-told and most touching love-stories in literature) been removed from the sacred volume by the same instrument? I doubt it.

Let young girls and male adolescents be brought up according to the consciences of their parents, by all means. But do not let their bringing up interfere with the reading of intelligent people. And do not let it penalise authors who have something to say and know how to say it. And let it be remembered that books proscribed by the libraries are almost always written by reputable writers and published by reputable publishers and sold by reputable booksellers.

Let it be also remembered that in not one case in a hundred do the police find any reason for intruding into the matter.

There are a dozen ways out of the difficulty for libraries. Here is one. They might stick a red seal on certain books; and they might exhibit a notice thus: "Red Seal. We express no opinion upon works marked with a red seal except that possibly some parents may regard them as unsuitable for perusal by their children or themselves."

Thus no parent could complain that she or he had been misled.

I anticipate that there would be quite a rush for the red-sealed volumes. Lending libraries may lose a customer now and then by broad-mindedness, but they lose at least as many customers, and they antagonise far more customers, by adjusting their policy to the pernicketiness of anxious parents.

23 August 1928

Something the Luxury Hotels Forget

The summer season of luxury hotels, grand hotels, family hotels, residential hotels, boarding-houses and furnished rooms is now beginning to close. One can review one's experiences. For myself, I draw two chief conclusions.

Namely, first, that physical luxury is still increasing in establishments of all grades — except in regard to the provision of noiselessness, and especially nocturnal noiselessness.

In the most expensive *de luxe* establishments you may find a flower floating in the carefully-warmed water of your finger-bowl, while the arrangements for silence in your bedroom are either non-existent or futile.

Yet silence might be effectively provided at far less cost than various luxuries which work no good at all to anybody whatever. And a comfortable bed is not the sole condition preliminary to sleep.

Second, that nothing, even in the more palatial palaces, is done for the luxury of the mind. Hotel-owners might perhaps be pardoned for assuming that clients who play golf all day and gamble half the night have no minds worth consideration. But the assumption, though pardonable, cannot be justified. Hotel-owners ought to know that we all have minds.

I say nothing of pleasure hotels (outside London); the matter is too delicate for my rough pen. I will confine myself to Continental hotels. Now, the large majority of Continental hotels are organised to cater for Anglo-Saxon tastes. Nearly all the employees can speak a language which sometimes resembles English, and the eccentricities of the Anglo-Saxon races are well understood and thoughtfully attended to.

Nevertheless, if an Anglo-Saxon asked for the *Racing Calendar* or some golfing annual in a Continental hotel he would be regarded as exceeding the normal Anglo-Saxon madness. Indeed, you seldom see any book which is not private property in a Continental hotel.

In a few Italian hotels collections (called libraries) of unreadable and dead English books are occasionally to be discovered by the persistent. In America I remember that the Tremont at Boston (Mass.) had not only a real library but a printed catalogue thereof. But Boston is not a pleasure-resort; nor were the Tremont breakfasts anything like equal to its books.

I would not go so far as to ask a Continental hotel to include a general library in its luxuries. I think, however, that a request for a small reference library would not be unreasonable. Almost everybody pleasuring on the Continent has a desire at one moment or another to "look up" something of interest to himself. He may desperately "want to know" some simple ordinary fact (such as the right spelling or pronunciation of a word; or the date of a birth, death, or battle).

Well, he can't do it. On all sides his efforts are met with a blank and unscalable wall. Not an English dictionary nor an English almanac is to be found in a whole town full of necklaces, melons, lingerie, cocktails and aspirin. The searcher after knowledge is completely baffled.

This should not be. This is a scandal, and a scandal that could be easily and cheaply remedied. But will hotel-owners remedy it? They will not – at present. They are so puffed up at being able to advertise "250 bedrooms, 250 bathrooms" that they cannot bother about such odd trifles as books of reference.

Possibly when they have raised themselves to the high condition of being able to advertise "250 bedrooms, 500 bathrooms" they may, looking for new worlds to conquer, turn to the provision of informative literature. Not before.

Hence the only course for the tourist is to travel with his own reference library. I do not suggest that he should add to the vast expense of excess luggage by wandering around with the *Encyclopaedia Britannica*, the *New English Dictionary*, and the *Dictionary of National Biography*. No. I am not an extremist.

What I do suggest is that some enterprising publisher should issue a work of general reference in one volume. Why not? A quite interesting compendium of information is published annually to assist the sale of a certain soap. It is not just what I want, but it shows something of what can be done. Some years ago Jacks (a Scottish firm, of course) published a very useful and cheap encyclopaedia in one volume. But it is too bulky for travellers. Also I want more than an encyclopaedia. The volume of which I dream does not exist.

Its physical attributes are important. It must have a limp but stout leather binding which will stand the vicissitudes of travel as stoically as a sleeping-car conductor. It must not be large, but it may be thick. Indeed, thickness will give it stoicism. Take as a basis of calculation Bellows' larger *English-French Dictionary*. It measures 7 ins. by 4¾ ins. – about the right convenient size. Bellows is thin, only 11/16th in., and it contains 700 pages. The imagined volume, therefore, might well contain 1500 pages and still be less than 1½ ins. thick.

As regards the mechanics of the page, a comprehensive system of abbreviations must be employed, such as the extraordinarily ingenious one which has been perfected for the well-known *Michelin Guide*.

As to its contents, although I would entitle it *The Traveller's Cyclopaedia*, it need and should not give special information about travel, seeing that travellers provide this for themselves according to destination — and if they don't, let them suffer for their wanton negligence; for they deserve no sympathy! My volume would be merely a general compendium for the use of people who happen to be away from home.

It positively must contain four features. First, a dictionary and encyclopaedia arranged under one alphabet, after the manner of Funk and Wagnall's *Comprehensive Dictionary*. Second, a world-atlas. Third, a manual of health with remedies (in English and French) for common complaints. Fourth, a collection of statistics and "records" of all sorts and for all tastes.

With these four solid dishes it would be possible at any rate to stay the worst pangs of hunger and knowledge. If there was room to spare, other features might be devised on the rich inspiration of say, *Whitaker's Almanack*.

The Traveller's Cyclopaedia could not be cheap. I doubt whether it could be done for less than a pound, because it would have to be thoroughly well done in every aspect — editing, paper, printing, stitching, binding.

And why not a pound? A pound is less than the cost of a cabin occupied for a couple of hours on a Channel steamer, much less than the average cost of a new hat, incomparably less than the average cost of a chair at any gaming-table, and quite decidedly less than the average cost of any new biography of nobody in particular in two volumes.

The affair would involve the laying-down of capital by the publisher, but are not publishers brought into the world by heaven in order to lay down capital? My conviction is that the book would sell, with a sale steadily increasing as its merits got about. My conviction is that there is money in the idea, which idea, with characteristic nobility of soul, I make a present of to the publishers of Edinburgh, Glasgow and London.

30 August 1928

Mussolini Writes a "Serial"

Less than twenty years ago Signore Benito Mussolini was a provincial working journalist in Italian-speaking Austrian territory, but he only did journalism in time left over from being secretary to the local Socialist organisation and from giving French lessons. His journalism consisted in helping to edit *Il Popolo*, and in writing, himself, the weekly supplement to *Il Popolo*.

For this supplement he wrote, very fast, at night, after long days of hard and varied labour, a serial entitled *Claudia Particella*. Which serial had a considerable success, inasmuch as it unquestionably increased the sale of the paper. Of few serials can it be asserted positively that they increase sales.

Impossible not to admire the energy and the ability of such a man! Difficult not to wonder whether, still young, and even more energetic than he was at twenty-five, he does not sometimes regret, from the height of an extremely anxious and dangerous glory, the democratic obscurity of his situation in 1909!

An English translation (bad) of *Claudia Particella* has recently been issued in America as *The Cardinal's Mistress*; and I have read it — in proof form.

I have heard nothing of a British edition, but a British edition ought to be published, because *The Cardinal's Mistress* is an interesting pheno-menon and incites one to thought. It is a historical novel (seventeenth century), not good and not bad, not worse than hundreds of other his-torical novels, and better than hundreds.

A single quotation will give the measure of the book: "Claudia was leaning slightly over one side of the bark and had immersed her hand in the water to enjoy its freshness. Beneath her silken robe was visible the provocative outline of her body, and her white face gleamed beneath her black tresses. Her half-closed eyes understood the sorcery of poisonous passions."

One smiles. But read this: "Bounding from the other man like a grey-hound from his keeper's leash . . . he sprung through a second and a third room . . . . No living mortal was to be seen in either of them. He called upon his lady's name, at first gently, then more loudly, and then with an accent of despairing emphasis; but no answer was returned. He wrung his hands, tore his hair, and stamped on the earth with desperation. At length a feeble glimmer of light . . . crevice in the wainscoting . . . concealed door. He rushed at the door . . . forced his way almost headlong into a small oratory, where a female figure which had been kneeling in agonised supplication . . . now sunk at length on the floor. He hastily raised her from the ground and, joy of joys, it was she whom he sought to save. He pressed her to his bosom."

Is the second quotation essentially any better than the first, less untrue, less conventional, less tawdry? The second is from *Quentin Durward*.

Of course, I do not want to rank Mussolini as a novelist level with Scott. But the same faults can be charged against both of them. Both are large employers of clichés, and though Scott founded a school of fiction and influenced all Europe, he used the clichés of his predecessors. Neither gives anything like a true or a full picture of the age he describes.

Both threw their novels together anyhow, and faked or omitted the more difficult scenes. (As to this last, see *Quentin Durward* especially.) Both concocted cliché characters — is Di Vernon more authentic than La Particella? — and made them behave as real people never do behave. . . . I had better not say too much.

Is not the fact remarkable that Mussolini, overworked and not a novelist by natural inclination, should be able to compose a historical novel which is quite credible, according to accepted standards, and which captivated multitudes of readers? And if really sound, realistic historical novels exist, where are they? Is there a single historical novel which could be ranked artistically with a first-rate novel of contemporary life? If not, why not?

I have recently failed to re-read Victor Hugo's *Notre Dame de Paris* and *Les Misérables*, and Dumas's *The Queen's Necklace* (but I achieved the six volumes of *Monte Cristo* with satisfaction).

Is the historical fiction of Thackeray still alive? I think not. The historical fiction of Flaubert is certainly not alive. Balzac's *Catherine de Medici* is heavy, but can be read. I am not forgetting *War and Peace*. I exclude it because Tolstoy was too near its period for it to be properly termed a historical novel.

Of late we have been celebrating Stanley Weyman, and I used to think that *A Gentleman of France* was the genuine stuff. I don't now. The latest German fashionable historical novel, Neumann's *The Deuce*, is as old-fashioned as the moon, and realistic only in the sinister narrow sense. It is a work far inferior to *Jew Süss*, which itself is being overpraised to-day.

When I reflect upon my perusals in English historical fiction, I find that the only novel which has maintained its place in my mind as a fairly complete artistic success is Charles Reade's *Peg Woffington* — rather a short book.

In my view the first-rate historical novel conceived on an extensive scale has yet to be written. In historical fiction there is far more scope for a pioneer than in modern fiction, which has been very thoroughly exploited. Perhaps the required article may be on the way.

Naomi Mitcheson has already given inklings of a new departure. When I read Helen Waddell's wonderful *Wandering Scholars*, I exclaimed to myself: "What a novelist wasted on erudition! She is really interested in mankind and sees it steadily and whole and with a sense of humour. And in addition to knowledge she has the narrative gift!"

Truth to human nature is the chief lack in historical fiction. The majority of historical novels are no nearer to human nature than, say, Wagner's *Ring*. There is more truth in one pretty good novel of modern life than in a whole year's output of historical swashbuckling, hair-tearing, fustian eloquence, hissing crime and deathless passion.

Take, for instance, a novel such as Helen Ashton's *Far Enough* (Benn, 7s. 6d.). I merely choose it because I happen to have read it. Not a great book. Not the book of the year, though certainly better than most.

The scene is laid in Jamaica, and Jamaican climate, scenery and society are set down with an uncommon and convincing sober realism. More important, the characters are individualised, they are not cliché types; neither are they super-human nor sub-human. They live. Which is something. You say as you read: "This woman knows what she is writing about, and she can write."

The novel has a fault. Too many past events are narrated by means of dialogue, and the movement of the story is not clear, definite and sustained. Here it fails where, I admit, the less tedious historical novel does succeed. But as a whole *Far Enough* is incomparably superior in interest, truth, and humanity to 999 historical novels out of 1000.

Why should this be? Why should even the better historical novelists be content to imitate imitations of imitations of imitations, whereas the better novelists of modern life go straight to life? Was human nature in the periods which we call historical utterly different from modern human nature? It was not. It was only slightly different. I suggest that some young author not yet sure of his path should look into this affair.

6 September 1928

German Lesson in Historical Romance

No sooner had I written last week's article about the relative inferiority of historical novels — as compared with novels of modern life — than I received an English translation from the German of Jacob Wasserman's *The Triumph of Youth* (Allen and Unwin, 7s. 6d.). The book has none of the characteristic defects of the historical novel, and so I am rather confounded.

The publishers have accepted my reiterated advice to publishers generally and have printed a biographical note about the foreign author. But the note is too brief and too vague and has the disadvantage of being written by the author himself. Further, the publishers do not give the date of the original German publication, nor the titles of the novels by Wasserman previously translated into English. Moreover, we have here an example of the present craze for introductions and prefaces carried to the very edge of the ridiculous. "With a prefatory note by Emil Ludwig," says the book-cover. Well, the prefatory note by the famous Ludwig consists of these words: "I consider Jacob Wasserman to be one of the greatest authors of our time." And it consists of nothing else. Were these fourteen words worth advertising?

I am inclined to agree with Ludwig's *obiter dictum* thus too pompously displayed. Wasserman is now nearly sixty. He must have been writing a long time. And whether *The Triumph of Youth* is an early or a late work I have no idea. It is, however, a remarkable book, and I read it with an admiration which increased as I slowly penetrated into the story. The story, in which no dates are vouchsafed, is of the dark age in the Germany of the Holy Roman Empire, when imagined evil spirits thickly populated the air and lurked in the bodies of citizens, and witchcraft was the sin of sins, and the suspicion of witchcraft was enough to condemn the suspected to torture and extermination by incandescence. A horrible age. An age of dirt, darkness, cold, superstition, madness, hysteria, cruelty, and affrighting stuffiness moral and spiritual. It reminds you of H.G. Wells's Rampole Island. It reminds you, too, of the first hysterical years of the Great War, when to be suspected of the witchcraft of pro-Germanism was equivalent to ruin, and when one of the greatest War Secretaries that Britain ever had, with the evidence of his greatness overwhelmingly demonstrated in practice, was cast with ignominy out of the War Office, like a devil by incantations out of a human body.*

There was a Prince-Bishop maniacal against witchcraft. There was his Confessor, who terrorised him by a savagery more ruthless than his own. There was the Bishop's sister-in-law, a light, conscienceless woman fool of a woman. And there was her son, the Baron Ernest, the youthful teller of tales to children. All these characters are magnificently drawn, with rare

* Lord Haldane.

and original psychological insight. Thus the different reserves of the Bishop and his nephew. The Bishop's: "His face revealed nothing, even when he desired to express some inner emotion, because his inner life was too impoverished and nothing could reach the surface." The youth's: "He never showed any trace of sadness or of care. The radiant dreaminess of his nature enveloped his entire personality like a glittering garment which it was impossible to penetrate with a view to understanding his inner life." The book is full of this kind of thing, full of subtle perceptions concerning not only individuals but masses.

The youth is inevitably suspected of witchcraft. If not possessed of a devil, how could he captivate, entrance and subjugate whole countrysides? He is arrested by his uncle, imprisoned, sentenced to death, and saved in the last hours by a vast uprising of the children his admirers. Tallulah Bankhead herself never had fans like these impassioned infants, and there were tens and tens of thousands of them. They invaded and occupied the streets of the entire city, intimidated soldiery, stormed the gaol, and set their hero free — to tell them a story. What particularly and astonishingly satisfies me in this book is its atmosphere of naturalness. Everything is terrible, but nothing is forced, and beauty disengages itself from the asphyxiating horror. The people are not aware that they are living in the dark age. They hate their age: they are unhappy and unfortunate in it: but their age is as ordinary to them as ours to us. They have no idea that any other age could be different from theirs. Herein is the supreme excellence of a historical fiction. Jacob Wasserman is indeed an uncommon fellow. He has at once imagination, insight, a fine sense of form, and marked dramatic power.
sense of form, and marked dramatic power.

While ranking the book very high, I wish not to mislead possible readers. The work has not been conceived on a large scale. I estimate it to be under 40,000 words in length — half that of an average novel, and less than a quarter that of a large scale historical novel. It is an episode, superbly exploited in detail; but still an episode.

And it has to be read with an unusual intentness of concentration. This is, I am sure, the fault not of the author but of the translator. The name of the traitor has been prudently withheld by the publishers. There may be two of him. At the first glance the translation has an air of distinction. But in truth it is inept, clumsy, inaccurate, and exasperating. It bears slight but unmistakable traces here and there of an American origin. Many of its locutions might have been, and almost certainly were, concocted by one of those foreigners of whom their compatriots say that "he speaks English like a native." The translation, in brief, is deplorable: it is an offence and an obstruction. But the book has substantially survived the translation.

If Jacob Wasserman has written a long novel on the grand scale, and it has been tolerably translated, I want to know what it is. My remarks last week about the state of the English historical novel, past and present, have caused a certain amount of protest. They were intended to do so. I should like a great row and shindy about the English historical novel. And if there are any modern English historical novels comparable to Wasserman's book, I am most desirous of reading them. The English novel of modern life (including of course the American) has made immense progress since —

since George Moore began to write. The English historical novel has not, in my opinion, kept up with it. So far as I know only one English historical novel in the last dozen years has to any extent excited the people who know a book from a bonbon — Naomi Mitcheson's *The Conquered*, and I could find a lot of fault with that. The *genre* historical novel is comatose in English. It is a fine *genre*, an important *genre*, a *genre* worthy of very serious attention from both creative artists and critics. Let the spotlight be centred on it for a time.

13 September 1928

"Tips" for the Book Collector

I have never dealt with book-collectors in this column. Some of them are criminals; some others of them, too simple-minded, are swindled by criminals; but the vast and growing mass of them appear to be honourable and intelligent citizens who, if they seldom read books (as indeed is usually the case), do at any rate buy and cherish books. Which is something in a material age. Therefore I will refer to book-collecting. And my reason for doing so is an article by Oliver Brett in the current issue of *Life and Letters*, and a new book entitled *First Editions by Modern Authors and How to Tell Them* (Elkin Mathews and Marrot, 3s.), by H.S. Boutell. (Why "tell," and what does Mr. Boutell want to tell these first editions? He tells them nothing.)

Mr. Brett's article — too short, like many articles in *Life and Letters* — is nevertheless a lively affair, and thought-provoking. His main thesis is that, speaking generally, modern first editions are not as rare as they are supposed to be. He believes that many copies of them are in the possession of non-collectors, who neglect them and have no idea of the value. I agree. His secondary thesis is that the commercial value of first editions depends on their intrinsic literary value. This is true, but the proposition should be modified. A bad book by an author who has written absolutely first-rate books will always have commercial value. For instance, the two volumes of George Moore's verse, *Flowers of Passion* and *Pagan Poems*, which are entirely without literary value. Very many years ago I procured these thin volumes for a trifle, being then, as to-day, the most convinced "fan" of George Moore on this round earth. In an insane fit of generosity I gave them away. The two of them are now worth together £50.

It surprises me that the alert Mr. Brett should make no mention ot *Flatland*, a rare book, a fine and an original book (in the vein of H.G. Wells, but preceding Wells). Its first edition is collected, but not enough. Its price will rise. It was published in 1884 by Seeley & Co., at 2s. 6d., and has a strangely designed cover and a strange sketch at the end. If it has not been republished, it ought to be.

I am pained to see in Mr. Brett's article, and in *Life and Letters,* an error of grammar. And I am even more pained to see in it a mistake of fact. The error concerns myself, and though I hate to be personal, I must correct it. Mr. Brett credits me with the authorship of *Sidney Yorke's*

Friend, a novel published in the Chatterbox Library — about the time of the Ninth Dynasty. This work is continually being attributed to me. I have even seen it in secondhand catalogues as a rare item of mine. It may be rare; but I never wrote it, unless I wrote it in a trance and sold it to the Chatterbox Library in a trance and received nothing for it.* I have not read it nor seen it. It may be great stuff. I hope it is.

So far as my experience goes, collectors of modern stuff are not very wideawake. Books of mine of which thousands of copies exist are the object of constant search, whereas certain scarce booklets, of which only a hundred were printed, are never or hardly ever asked for, in England. Being of course a purely commercial author, I foreseeingly retained some of these booklets. One day the all-acquiring Dr. Rosenbach came along and bought a few of them at a price far exceeding the cost of the entire edition. I did not tell him that I had yet a few more up my sleeve. There has never been any enquiry for the rarest of all my books, printed in an edition of three copies. I possess one; I know the possessor of the second; but of the whereabouts of the third I am ignorant and propose to remain ignorant. And of a still rarer item (a pamphlet) I believe that only one copy has survived. I have it. I am conceitedly holding it, like certain Russian stock, for the rise. When ardent and admirable persons say to me: "I have a complete collection of first editions of all your work," I privately smile because I know they haven't. Nobody has, least of all myself — but then I lost interest in first editions years ago.

Instead of buying books I sell them. I am vaguely aware that up and down my bookcases are many modern first editions worth money. I let them lie, seeing in them the potential capital to provide an old-age pension. The other day I came across a first edition of Proust's *Du côté de chez Swann* which I purchased on publication. Enough of this author — meaning me, not Proust.

I venture to say that the modern first-edition market is an acutely ticklish proposition, at least as ticklish as the Stock Exchange gamble. Nobody can succeed in it without a genuine taste and a sound judgment in literature. In second-hand catalogues I see items marked at fantastic prices, which prices are absolutely sure to fall heavily, for the reason that the author concerned, despite his immediate reputation, is in reality tenth-rate. I shall name no names.

Mr. Boutell's book is extremely odd. It is a collection of replies from publishers, English and American, to the question: "How do you distinguish the first editions of your publications?" Most of them give comprehensible answers. Many admit that, though they have a rule, they don't always stick to it. One or two, candid but naughty, reply, in effect: "We don't distinguish." And these last are publishers doing an immense business. To my mind the worst fault of English publishers is their frequent omission to put any date at all on their books. *First Editions by Modern Authors and How to Tell Them* will be useful to tyros, but will add little to the awareness of experienced collectors. It is fairly complete, not quite

---

* F.J. Harvey Darton subsequently wrote to the Editor of the *Standard* admitting he was responsible for "this false attribution" in his "little book on Mr. Bennett's work" (*Arnold Bennett*, 1915), and adding that he had since found the author "to be a *Miss* E.A. Bennett, who lived in Staffordshire."

complete. For instance, there is no word about the American publisher Crosby Gaige. Now Crosby Gaige makes a practice of rare editions. Nearly all of them are literature or near-literature, and all of them are finely printed, some by Bruce Rogers, who is perhaps the finest printer working to-day. The merchandise of no living publisher is more likely to rise in value than that of Crosby Gaige.

Book-collectors deserve more attention than they get from authors and publishers. After all, ingenuous creatures, they do radiate an interest in books. I see no reason why British publishers should not follow the French practice of issuing limited editions concurrently with the first ordinary edition of a book. Such limited editions provide innocent pleasure for collectors and money for authors and publishers. I take the first French book that comes to hand: Bernard Grasset's *Remarques sur l'Action* (Paris, Gallimard, 6frs.). The first edition of the small book consists (according to a plain detailed statement therein) of 3,571 copies, of which 3,000 are ordinary copies, 465 are not for sale ("hors commerce"), and the rest are special copies. The special copies are not all alike. Thus there are three copies on old Japanese paper, 12 on Imperial Japanese paper, 20 on another paper, and so on: all numbered. This is certainly a good scheme.

By the way, I have for months been intending to call attention to *Remarques sur l'Action*. Its author is the well-known publisher, and he has written a witty, caustic, and rather original book. Here are a few of his "remarks." "Activity is the daughter of sensibility; great actions spring from the heart." "When a man of action writes his memoirs, he has ceased to understand his epoch." "The man of action is interested only in what can be changed." "To measure one's words is not necessarily to soften the expression of them, it is to have foreseen and accepted their extreme consequences." "One creates only with the substance of oneself."

20 September 1928

The English "Old Girl" and "Good Sport"

Count Hermann Keyserling, author of *The Travel Diary of a Philosopher* (a book which by reason partly of its solemnity, partly of its semi-incomprehensible vagueness, and partly of its solid second-rateness has become temporarily world-famous as a masterpiece) has of late years made a social progress so triumphant through London, New York and other capitals that even a critic whose business should be limited to literature feels himself somehow forced at least to take note of it.

London received the Count not without awe. He entered New York, always the readiest of cities to cast itself down and place its eager neck under the tyrannic heel of notoriety — he entered New York as a conqueror, the Alexander of the talkie-movie age, and as a conqueror majestically left it — prone.

Such a phenomenon has real sociological interest, especially when coupled, as it was in America, with an immense and prolonged sale of the Alexandrine books. For obviously not one in a hundred of the kneeling "fans" could have even begun to understand what the Count thought he was driving at in the said works. A supreme example, indeed, of the will-to-be-in-the-movement.

The Count styles himself a philosopher, and a philosopher he is — in the modern sense which connotes the teacher of a code of morals. But, though I have often been asked what the Count's philosophy amounts to, I have never been able to answer the question. Nor have I ever heard the question plainly and succinctly answered. I suggest that the Count might write a book entitled *What I Meant*.

A translation (by Marcus Samuel) of the Count's latest book has just been published under the title *Europe* (Cape, one guinea). The original German title is *Das Spektrum Europas*, which Mr. Samuel in a note rather oddly translates *The Spectro-analysis of Europe*.

The book deals with all the principal European countries, including England. The publisher says of it that it is "in a far more concrete vein [than *The Travel Diary*], it is simpler, and it is more lightly written, with frequent flashes of humour and even strokes of satire. It has been called the spiritual Baedeker of Europe."

Surely it was dangerous to bring in Baedeker, whose productions are among the most perfect and most intelligible things in all the literary history of mankind!

The Count himself perhaps gave the word to the publishers. He writes "Whosoever is untouched by the divine grace of self-irony, with him I can and will have nothing in common. I can have nothing to do with those who are in deathly earnest, who are unapt for laughter, with those, altogether too numerous, who are at once both profound and stupid. They are the ones who are really capable of true psychological seriousness."

Which is an excellent profession. Nevertheless, in summing up his own book the Count writes: "After the first swift draft I thought the book out carefully, chapter by chapter; I have not the impression that I have not been just, utterly just, to every people."

Here is an instance of the humourless arrogance which characterises the whole book. Unless, of course, it is a sample of the Count's newly-acquired humour. And perhaps the following is another sample: "I believe also in a hierarchy of human values. Strength and beauty are higher, in the absolute sense, than weakness and ugliness; superiority is higher too in the absolute sense, than inferiority . . . ."

If the passage is intended to be funny, the intention is too artfully hidden; if "meant serious," then it is prodigious with an unsurpassable prodigiosity.

I have discovered satire in the book, but no humour. One man's humour, however, is not always another's. My personal impression about the Count's alleged flashes of humour is that one day, and not long ago, a guardian angel murmured to him that hitherto he had omitted to be humorous in his writings, and that thereupon he resolved: "True, I have been forgetting humour. But I can be anything, and I will be humorous." And he was.

The point remains: *Can* Alexanders be humorous? I think that Alexanders can be humorous in action. Thus when the Count's great forerunner, being ill, had received Parmenio's warning letter that his physician had decided to poison him, he welcomed the physician carrying a potion and, showing him the letter, began immediately to drink the potion, and "looked merrily" at the physician. Lo, a humorist in the grand manner! But the Count is not a man of action. He is a prophet over the face of the globe.

With all this there are pages in the Count's new book where the antipathy which it arouses (and which its author expects and exults in) gets restive and gallops away, and sympathy takes its place.

For example, in the chapter on England. The Count would doubtless say, as a philosopher, a Baltic aristocrat, and a German, that the English are incapable of judging themselves. Nevertheless in our child-like ingenuousness we do reckon to have a certain competence in this matter. And some of us therefore will venture to say, with due respect to the intellectual Alexander, that he has written down a few things here and there not entirely bereft of insight.

Naturally he is frequently inept, in a Teutonic style; for he has no more tact than humour. Thus, of Englishwomen, he asks: "How can a woman develop sensual charm when she is fundamentally known as 'old girl,' and when the highest praise she can win is that she is a 'good sport'?"

Does he really understand an Englishman's English, or is he merely being imitatively silly?

Or again: "The ablest English colonial administrator responsible for the most far-sighted measures, rarely thinks of anything but food, drink, sport, and, if he is young, of flirtations." There is quite a lot of this sad stuff in the English chapter, and in all the chapters.

But, to balance, the Count fairly well succeeds in the hard task of explaining why the Continental peoples regard England as a nation of children.

He is distinctly good on the English conception of loyalty. He is still better on English respect for the self-respect of others. He rightly, in my opinion, puts English intellectuality lower than Continental. Then he adds: "But nowhere else can fine and profound souls be found in equal numbers." Indeed, it becomes plain that he admires the English national character more than any other. In my naive English innocence, this pleases me.

The best passage in the volume is a long quotation from Jung on the influence of the negro and the Indian characters upon American character. The lucid and modest profundity of this excerpt sinks Count Keyserling to his proper level.

27 September 1928

The Curse of the Stage

St. John Ervine, who has gone to America in order to tell Americans what they ought to think of American plays, has just published a book called *How to write a Play* (Allen & Unwin, 5s. net).

He says that the title is "purely catch-penny." It is. He says that neither he nor anyone else can explain satisfactorily how a play ought to be written. True.

He says that the two principal existing textbooks on the subject, Professor Baker's *Dramatic Technique* and William Archer's *Play-making*, are derided by every dramatist of his acquaintance. True, I imagine. I am a dramatist of Ervine's acquaintance. He says that both Bernard Shaw and Maugham have declared those two books to be actually harmful to would-be dramatists. No doubt.

He says that Professor Baker's most famous and most successful pupil, Eugene O'Neill, has broken nearly all his teacher's rules. Obviously. He says that in *The Merchant of Venice* Shakespeare broke every known rule of dramatic technique. Yes, he did; but *The Merchant of Venice* is really a very bad play indeed. He shows up some of the amazingly crude technical defects of *Hamlet*.

Further, he mentions the case of the author of a fairly recent book called *How to succeed in Literature* (or some such title) who a few months later committed suicide because he had been unable to succeed in literature. He reminds us that William Archer, after seeing Bernard Shaw's first play, advised Shaw to abandon playwriting for the reason that clearly he had no dramatic talent.

He admits that he, St. John Ervine, though he is a successful playwright and a successful critic, and did once indeed manage a theatre for a considerable period, is "almost completely ignorant of the technical business of the stage and has a difficulty even in distinguishing between the Prompt and the O.P. sides."

In short, his main theses are that only unimportant details of technique can be taught, that technique is a matter to be ignored, and that the one person capable of teaching a young dramatist his job is the young dramatist himself.

Nevertheless Ervine has composed and put forth this book with the catchpenny title, and it is easily the best book on the subject that I have ever met with. (I say this, though I myself have twice in books dealt professionally and technically with the subject.)

It is a very good book, admirably written, rich with experience, bold, lively, amusing, and full of inspiring and informing commonsense. Even Henry Arthur Jones at 77, Arthur Pinero at 73, Bernard Shaw at 72, Noel Coward at 17 (or whatever his age may be), and Sardou in heaven, might read this book — certainly with pleasure, and probably not without profit.

Its chief virtue is that it will force the young dramatist to think hard for himself. One of its minor virtues is that the author illustrates his points by downright criticism of plays, not minding whether the authors thereof are living or dead.

His practice has always been to say just what comes into his head and chance the consequences — I trust that he will continue the practice in New York. Thus he takes hold of a piece which for years was spoken of with awe by London high-brows and which when produced fell deservedly dead — Mr. G.D. Gribble's *The Masque of Venice*; and he remarks with warm brevity that it "reveals no signs that its author has the faintest conception of what drama is."

On his bracing return to this flaccid clime Mr. St. John Ervine ought to start an English *American Mercury*, and write the whole of it himself. We need a tonic. America needs one.

On one branch of this august subject — stage dialogue — St. John Ervine does in fact give detailed instruction, and very convincingly. He demonstrates the wrong-headedness of Noel Coward's theory (and practice) that stage characters ought to talk as people actually do talk.

The conclusion of his argument is that the dramatist's aim should be not to *reproduce* everyday language but to *represent* everyday language. Few dramatists do either. Frederick Lonsdale is the best of the representers; nobody else, I think, can approach him. St. John Ervine's chapter on dialogue is a very satisfying affair.

The book suffers from the lack of both a table of contents and an index. Also from a far more serious lack — the lack of a chapter on "the last act." Herein the author has missed a unique opportunity of showing his gifts. He could have treated the last-act problem most brilliantly and most effectively.

The last-act problem has always been the curse of the stage. The last act of *Hamlet*, like the last act of *The Importance of Being Earnest*, is a sad mess. Of all the present-century English comedies I have seen — I confess I have seen as few as possible — I can remember only three with good last acts: *Arms and the Man, The Admirable Crichton* and *Dear Brutus.*

The third example is the best. A terrific feather in the cap of Barrie to have devised two thoroughly sound last acts! Of nearly all successful comedies it may be truthfully said that the first act is fine, the second fair, and the third fudge.

I commend the last-act theme to St. John Ervine. And I will give him also the title of two other books which it is his duty to write: *How to sell a play when you have written it,* and *How to produce a play when you have sold it.*

There are said to be about 50,000 aspiring dramatists in Britain. They would all of them (except Edgar Wallace) buy the book of the first title, and quite half of them would buy the second.

So far as I can gather, the latest visible dramatist in America, where play-writing seems to be the subject of a regular university course, is a certain Paul Green. His plays have apparently not yet reached the ordinary public, even in New York so avid of novelty; but I have been hearing of him favourably for some time, and I have now received five of his volumes, of which one, *Wide Fields* (cotton fields), consists of short stories — very good, good and goodish. Only one of the volumes of plays, *In the Valley, and other Carolina plays,* is published in England (Samuel French, Ltd. — a strictly limited edition).

I cannot discuss Paul Green now. I will only say that in my opinion he has something new to say, and to have said it, so far, in a manner defiant of his teachers, Professor Barrett Clark and Professor Koch. Paul Green will be heard of, and he deserves to be heard of.

4 October 1928

Books to Save from the Burning

The Master of Balliol caused quite a lot of talk last week by an *obiter dictum* uttered (possibly not with the full sense of responsibility proper to the holder of that fearsome office) to the Library Association. He is reported to have said that he felt that "if he could retain the Bible and Shakespeare,

Plato's *Republic* and Kant's *Critique of Pure Reason*, all the rest [of books] might be burned."

He was probably being sprightly. But ought the Master of Balliol, especially when addressing the Library Association from the presidential chair, to permit himself to be sprightly? There are things that simply are not done.

Of the four books which he would consent to save from a fatal incandescence the first two must be allowed.

The very daring, such as myself, might say that both of them have parts extremely inferior to other parts. Also that if either of them was issued as literature to-day for the first time, Sir William Joynson-Hicks would suppress it in no time as a menace to the purity of home life in this great country. Nobody, however, would deny their absolute supremacy and indispensableness.

But the other two? The *Critique* I have only looked at, not read. This fact should not, according to the modern critical code, prevent me from assessing a book. But it does. I will merely say that, though I have looked at Mont Blanc, nothing will induce me to climb it, even if I could. I suspect that I should vote for the survival of Newton's *Principia* rather than Kant's *Critique*.

And Plato's *Republic*. Well, I have read the *Republic* and I venture the opinion that it is lovely, wrong-headed, very unequal, and a very mischievous performance.

I will remark further that the Master of Balliol would have shown a more delicate taste not to mention it, seeing that the chief English version of it, by the most notorious of his august predecessors, is probably the most incompetent and most dishonest translation into English that ever won the esteem of the simple.

Withal, Mr. Lindsay's speech to librarians was full of strong and bold sense. He said, for instance:

"We must be on our guard . . . lest we should think the main thing was done when we got books into a well-ordered library. Nothing could be falser . . . . The library is an instrument, but it is only an instrument. In the use of the instrument . . . there is a great field for the activities and the personality of the librarian as the person who can help . . . the reader to a knowledge of standards and of values . . . . If public libraries are to take advantage of their opportunities in adult education present notions of what size of staff a public library requires will have to be completely revised."

This is unpleasantly true. Public libraries are either insufficiently used or misused, or (sometimes) not used. Just as 80 per cent. of the heat of a coal fire is wasted, so is 80 per cent. of the value of a public library wasted. And the reason is the inadequacy of the staff.

One hears that public libraries do not spend enough on books. I would reply that if they spent less on books and more on an educated staff, far better results would be obtained. It is not books that lack in the libraries; it is the key to their effective employment. That key is the individualities and the attainments of librarians and their staffs.

In this connection, the National Book Council — an ingenious organisation which seems to be steadily growing — has set up a scheme for bringing to the notice of potential readers precise and informing news about new books.

Vendors of such things as wine, cigars, frocks, hats, furniture, woo the prospective purchaser. Booksellers rarely woo. To buy books is a difficult affair. To get gratis reliable and impartial information about new books on subjects specially interesting to oneself has been an impossible affair. The N.B.C. has now instituted a system of *Reader's Guides*, published four times a year.

The procedure for the thirster after literature is marvellously simple. He calls at a bookseller's and asks for a registration card. Or, if (as may happen) there is no bookseller at all within a thousand miles or so, he sends a post-card to the secretary (3, Henrietta-street, W.C.2) and asks for the said card.

The card displays twelve divisions of literature, sub-divided into one hundred categories. Thus under "Sports and Pastimes" there are five categories. Under "Fiction," four. Under "Sociology," twelve. He marks on the card the category or categories in which he is interested. He writes his name and address. He affixes a halfpenny stamp. He posts to a bookseller.

Thereafter he will receive from his bookseller, free, four times a year a detailed Guide to all the principal new publications in his chosen categories. If he knows no bookseller (as may happen), he posts to the secretary and the secretary will forward the card to a bookseller.

Nor is this all. If he orders a book by post, he need not send cash. The bookseller will take the risk of "opening an account" with him. I believe that the scheme is succeeding. It is financed as regards the printing of the Guides by publishers, and as regards the distribution of the Guides by booksellers.

I gather from a minute study of the Guides that nearly all the leading general publishers are already in the scheme. It is praiseworthy and pro-mises well for the commonweal. Hence I spread the tidings of it with pleasure.

To return to the Master of Balliol. He wisely said that voluntary efforts, now very considerable, for the furtherance of knowledge of the com-parative values of books must be helped by the State; but that the inde-pendence of voluntary efforts must not be thereby imperilled. In other words, he demands assistance without control. I hope he may get it; but I have doubts.

I shudder at the thought of State interference in the popularisation of literature. I would sooner do without State help than receive it at the price of any control.

This reminds me of a striking and yet moderately-worded article on "Literary Taboos," in the current number of *Life and Letters*, by Desmond MacCarthy. Mr. MacCarthy instances the case of Havelock Ellis's *Studies in the Psychology of Sex*, a book recognised everywhere in Europe as a first-rate scientific work, indeed the chief work on the subject.

Havelock Ellis's publisher found himself in prison for publishing "a cer-tain lewd, bawdy, scandalous and obscene libel," etc. And the ineffable Recorder of the Central Criminal Court said: "It is impossible for anybody with a head on his shoulders to open the book without seeing that it is a pretence and a sham . . . merely entered into for the purpose of selling this obscene publication."

Such is State interference.

11 October 1928

Turning Over the Autumn Leaves

The "Autumn Books" supplements to the sometimes-intellectual weeklies are now appearing. It seems to me that the National Book Council (which is the offspring of the publishers and the booksellers) and the editors of these organs might advantageously get together and try to do something about these highly unsatisfactory supplements.

They are intended to furnish appetising particulars of the season's fruits to those interested in literature. They don't. Only the advertisements in them are attractive — and by no means all the advertisements. Beyond the advertisements they contain merely one or two reviews of more or less new books, and a long list of autumn publications.

The list is a deplorable example of inefficient publicity. It is divided into two categories, and herein is its sole virtue. It is not complete. Who makes the selection, and upon what principles, I have no notion. The contents of the different sections are not even arranged in alphabetical order.

Nothing is printed to show whether a work is a new book or a new edition of an old book. Nothing is printed to show whether a work is original English or a translation into English.

Nothing is printed to show whether publication has already occurred or has still to occur. The lists comprise books which have been before the public for weeks. These are serious defects, and they might and should be remedied.

In fiction, among the new English novels and short stories promised are works by Oliver Onions (*The Painted Face*), A.E. Coppard (*Silver Circus*) Henry Williamson (*The Pathway*), Rebecca West (no title), Frank Swinnerton (*Sketch of a Sinner*), Ford Madox Ford (*A little less than Gods*), Harold Acton (*Humdrum*), and R.H. Mottram (*Ten Years Ago*).

Among authors translated are Pushkin (*The Captain's Daughter* — already out), Knut Hamsun (*The Women at the Pump* — already out, and fine), Pirandello (*The Old and the Young*), Thomas Mann (*Death in Venice*), Romain Rolland (*Mother and Son*), Johan Bojer (*The New Temple*), Gogol (*Mirgorod*), and Stendhal (*Armance*).

All these books deserve the attention of the enlightened-curious. Not all the enlightened are curious.

The season so far as it had proceeded strikes me as unusually distinguished. Aldous Huxley, the most destructive force in the younger fiction, and a tonic, hostile and audacious witness of the age, has appeared at full length. "Anonymous" (whose identity is amply revealed by internal evidence) has issued an autobiographical novel, *Memoirs of a Fox-hunting Man*, of real importance. Written with a certain sporting negligence of composition, it has much originality and much beauty, and is certainly right past the comprehension of nineteen M.F.H.'s out of twenty.

Many honest open-air fellows who buy this first prose work of Siegfried Sassoon's on its title will assuredly want their money back.

A genuinely new humorist has presented himself in the person of Evelyn Waugh, whose *Decline and Fall* is an uncompromising and brilliantly malicious satire, which in my opinion comes near to being quite first-rate

— especially in its third part dealing with the prison system. I say without reserve that this novel delighted me.

Much has been said about Norah Hoult's *Poor Women* — short stories. All these tales state a problem, and none of them resolves its problem. Nevertheless, Norah Hoult is a realist; she writes what she has to write like a woman and not, thank heaven, like a man; she convinces you; she will count.

Much has also been said about *The Gypsy* (why two y's?), by W.B. Trites — an American author who can no longer be young. Too much has been said. I should not call it "genius" or "great." Also it has only the dimensions of a long short story. But it is a good, sordid, beautiful, tragic affair, and ought to be read.

I count as fiction *The Life of Moses* by Edmond Fleg (translated from the French). Impressive! Yes, you have to insinuate yourself into it, but when you have done so, impressive it assuredly is.

Chief among translations are the two opening volumes of the very satisfactory "Centenary edition" of Tolstoy — *Twenty-three Tales* and *Plays*. The translations are unequalled. The format is excellent; but I could have spared the frontispieces.

Another important tome is Richard Aldington's translation of Julien Benda's *The Great Betrayal (La Trahison des Clercs)*, which I mentioned some time ago. Mr. Aldington has to some extent avoided the Frenchman's overcharged and intricate sesquipedalianism. The courageous should face this book.

Among collected editions, which have been fashionable this year, the most intriguing, to me, is *The Collected Poems of D.H. Lawrence* (Secker, one guinea the pair). This edition, which is handsome, meets a felt want. Lawrence the poet has met with insufficient appreciation. His short introduction is full of valuable biographical material.

The season has at any rate already produced one volume of extreme loveliness, and if between now and Christmas the season produces anything more lovely, I shall be astonished. *The Poems of Nizami* described by Laurence Binyon (The Studio, 30s.).

Despite the hosannas (broadcast and otherwise) of Sir Denison Ross about Persian poetry, I am not yet a convinced admirer of the same, and I doubt if Laurence Binyon is either.

The paramount interest of the book, however, lies in the sixteen marvellous coloured reproductions of Persian paintings from a Nizami MS. in the British Museum. I suppose that if I tried hard I might succeed in exaggerating the beauty of these illustrations, but I doubt it. With his customary high competence and restraint Laurence Binyon discourses on the manuscript, on Persian painting, on the painters of these pictures, on the poet, and on the five poems.

The book is printed in London by Herbert Reiach (Limited), and in it are very properly given the names of the individual engravers, the photographer, and the general supervisor. The amateur of fine books might well buy one copy of this one for himself and another to give away. As a Christmas present it is not going to be beaten. It is a folio, 18 in. by 10 in., and extraordinarily cheap.

Another large and stately illustrated volume published by The Studio is

Modern Book Production (price unknown to me). The reproductions of pages show that the general curve of bookmaking is toward the skies, though there have been grave setbacks, as we know.

Finally I must mention, in the way of beauty, the enchanting limited signed edition (published in England by Hodder and Stoughton, 250 copies) of Philip Guedalla's *Bonnet and Shawl*. This edition is printed in America by William Rudge, and it is a masterpiece of typography. The binding is not equal to the printing.

18 October 1928

Cheaper Books Not Wanted

I said it seventeen years ago, and I say it again: America is a wonderful place. Things occur there that couldn't occur in Britain; and here is one.

Edna St. Vincent Millay is a poet renowned in America. For five years she had published no volume of poems (why?), until the other day. The new volume is *The Buck in the Snow* (Harpers, New York). Less than 70 pages. Twenty-one poems, all short. Rate of production: 4 poems per annum. Price of the ordinary first edition: 2 dollars; said to be quickly rising.

The cheaper limited edition, 479 copies, at 25 dollars, was subscribed for more than twice over. The dearer limited edition, printed on vellum, 31 copies for sale at 50 dollars (£10) apiece, was subscribed for more than four times over. It is the cause of the phenomenon.

The publishers appointed a committee of three to draw the names of the thirty-one booksellers who were to have the privilege of buying one copy each. The Committee consisted of the editor of *The Publishers' Weekly*, the executive secretary of the National Association of Booksellers, and the President of that Association.

I assert that such an event could not happen in this isle. I wish it could. Our interest in verse has never gone so far and probably never will. If people tell me that the affair is financial, I reply that national interest in books can only be demonstrated in terms of finance. No book effectively exists until it is read, and it cannot be read until it is bought or borrowed for a monetary consideration.

Personally, I think that in Britain we have better poets than Miss Millay. But she can take pride in Thomas Hardy's *obiter dictum* that there are two, and two only, great things in the United States, and that Miss Millay's poetry was one of them.

We in Britain have other methods of encouraging the public interest in books. Here is a British phenomenon. Recently a new novel was published in exactly the style of the ordinary 7s. 6d. novel; but its price was fixed at 3s. 6d. — as an experiment.

A similar experiment was made in England about twenty years ago, but it was not limited to one book. It failed. Booksellers would not encourage it.

To-day's venture has not been encouraged by the booksellers. The subscription for the novel was no larger than it would have been had the book been offered at more than twice 3s. 6d.

One of the very largest booksellers in the country, if not the largest, actually objected to the reduced price. He preferred dear books: that is, he did not want books to be popularised in the only way in which they can be popularised. He said: *"I am here to supply a demand – not to create it."* So there you are.

Nevertheless, there are many thousands of readers in Britain (and I have heard from many scores of them) who are debarred from reading new books because they simply have not the money to pay for them.

Books are dear in Britain – relatively dearer than in America. They might be cheaper, but they will certainly not be cheaper until publishers and booksellers join in a co-operative effort to make them cheaper. Such a movement, if intelligently and courageously led and carried out, would result in larger profits for both publishers and booksellers.

A few weeks ago I was in a bookshop in Chambéry. Chambéry is a small town and an old town, and the main street thereof has scarcely been altered since Rousseau walked under its arcades. It is just the sort of town whose English counterpart would have no shop for new books. But this bookshop was a very good bookshop.

I asked for four books, and they were all in stock, and the total cost of the four was 9s. Similar books in Britain would have cost over £2. Britons spend far more than Frenchmen on books, but they get fewer books for their money. If Frenchmen had to pay as much for books as we pay they would give up reading.

Take a book like R.A. Scott-James's *The Making of Literature* (Secker, 15s.). In France the price of such a book would be at most the French equivalent of half-a-crown. How many Britons who would enjoy *The Making of Literature* can pay 15s. for it? Only a small percentage.

It is a good and a profitable book. Mr. Scott-James is perhaps a bit prim in deportment – I wish he had some of the impishness of E.M. Forster – but he has fully thought out his theme; he possesses wide knowledge; he has come to conclusions; he says what he means with distinction; he is a realist.

His sub-title is: "Some principles of criticism examined in the light of ancient and modern theory." He is the first person, in my imperfect reading, to make clear the difference between the creative artist and the critic. He decides that the critic is one sort of creative artist. I think he is right.

He takes a number of literary critics – from Aristotle to Percy Lubbock and Virginia Woolf – and he shows with excellent acumen just how far they are to be trusted. He is especially light-giving on Aristotle, Ste. Beuve and Matthew Arnold.

And this is wise: "The critic must have some knowledge of that tract of life from which the creative writer starts . . . . He must have an understanding of life itself . . . . If the book be a play or a novel, he must know not a little about human nature, the raw material upon which the theme is built. The trouble with most of our book-critics is their pathetic ignorance of life."

About prices, let me be clear. I am not so simple as to imagine that if Mr. Scott-James's book had been published at half-a-crown, it would have had a large sale. It would not; but the reason would be, not that the relatively impecunious would not like to have it, but that book-traders have not yet taught them to expect cheap books. The process of teaching would take time. The new demand would have to be created — by advertisement and use.

A curious book about a (non-existent) book is J.D. Beresford's *Writing Aloud* (Collins, 6s.). It displays at length a novelist's procedure and methods in composition. It ought to be attractive to the pen-profession. It would have been much more attractive if it had been written about an actual book — say, *The House in Demetrius Road*.

Mr. Beresford refers to the *Journal* which André Gide kept of the writing of his novel, *The Counterfeiters*. Gide's *Journal* is a very different affair from Mr. Beresford's. As you read it you can compare it with the novel, the story of whose composition it tells. Still, *Writing Aloud* is a new thing in English.

1 November 1928 *

My Advice to Novelists

Lately I have been reading some very long books. A question arising in my mind is: Are long books read, or are they skipped? In the Standard edition *Our Mutual Friend* comprises 1000 pages. It was probably read, partly because a lot of it is masterfully readable, but more because in the Dickensian epoch days were longer, the average man's difficulty being to fill out the day — not to squeeze into it all that he wanted to do.

I have read, in an American edition, Jacob Wassermann's *The World's Illusion* — nearly 800 pages. Though too long, this novel dealing with contemporary life from Argentina to Moscow is important. I shall discuss it when an English edition is available: which I believe will be soon.

I have read (most of) von Guenther's much-heralded historical novel *Cagliostro* — over 600 pages, too long, but in the main readable enough by those who like their historical novels to be boisterous, picaresque, conventionally characterised, and dotted with ebullient exclamations such as "Sapristi!" and "Maledetto!"

I have read Aldous Huxley's *Point Counter Point* — over 600 pages; not too long, save by a few pages here and there; full of meat (some of it raw), but not well-proportioned; the account of the first night of the story takes over 200 pages.

And lastly I have read Henry Williamson's *The Pathway* (Cape, 7s.6d.) — over 400 pages of smallish type; by no means so long as the others, yet more definitely too long than the others.

One had anticipated *The Pathway* with unusual interest, because Henry Williamson wrote *Tarka the Otter*. It is a better novel than *Tarka*; it has chapters which are marvellous; it is written (even over-written); it must be read. But Mr. Williamson has still to learn a few things about the novelist's supreme job of being continuously interesting. He is a bit

* The 25 October 1928 'Books and Persons,' which dealt with book censorship, was held over because legal proceedings had been instituted regarding *The Well of Loneliness*. It eventually appeared, in revised form, on 29 November 1928.

too ruthless with the reader.

A man of immense technical experience in writing suggested to me the other day that authors frequently get flat because, in the desire to be industrious, they go on with their work after the divine (or devilish) afflatus has weakened through inspirational fatigue.

I think this is true. A good rule for novelists is forcibly to stop the day's work while the impulse to proceed is still powerful. If this rule were observed we should have shorter and more concentrated books, and better books.

The hero of *The Pathway* is an author. All three of the principal male characters in *Point Counter Point* are authors. One of the latter trio says: "I am not a congenital novelist." Some autobiographical touch here, I imagine! If a congenital novelist is a novelist who is more interested in characters than in ideas. Mr. Huxley certainly was not a congenital novelist until he wrote *Two or Three Graces.*

Point Counter Point, though bursting with ideas, shows that he is gradually becoming a congenital novelist; for some of the personages are very fully and convincingly drawn.

Mr. Williamson is without doubt a congenital novelist, though perhaps excessively (for an artist) preoccupied with the spiritual consequences of the war. His interest in his characters, all their surroundings, their dogs, their domestic rituals, is passionate; it is terrific. He leaves nothing out, and when he is at the top of his form he fits everything into its right place, and makes pictures which — I should say — have in their line never been surpassed.

The opening scenes in the Ogilvie household on the Devon coast are masterly. All the dialogue is absolutely lifelike. Also in landscape, the movement of water, the passage of birds, the oppression of nights, Mr. Williamson is a creator of loveliness.

But before page 100 one sees signs that his talents are getting beyond his control. Too much of this kind of thing:

"The invisible player touched the notes in darkness, out of which stole the glimmer and mystery of moonlight in an unearthly waterfall. A Spirit glimmered in the pool, a Spirit of the celestial stars, and then the Spirit fled . . ."

A kind of thing that will not survive examination!

The hero writes a novel. "No plot," said Mrs. Ogilvie, the wisest person in the book. The criticism applies to the book itself, which lacks movement; or if movement it has, it lacks direction.

The final tragedy is not made plain. I don't mind the hero with all his fine qualities of soul and his sensitiveness being an infernal nuisance to his fellow-creatures, cruel in his uncompromising idealism, and spiritually conceited. But I do mind the obscurity of his motivation. At the crucial point the author has, in my opinion, funked his big scene.

The Pathway is a novel richly worth quarrelling with. The author's gifts are authentic and dazzling. He has yet to show himself the master of them.

It is quite a long time since I read anything by Joseph Hergesheimer, author of *The Three Black Pennies* — and of better books. Now I have read *Quiet Cities* (Knopf, 7s.6d.). The volume contains ten sketches or stories. They have no titles, and there is no table of contents. So that you cannot find your way about the book. Why should this be so? Is it due to naughtiness or negligence?

The book is very good. I am inclined to say that Mr. Hergesheimer is the most subtle author in America. He takes as much pains as Rudyard Kipling. More. Too much pains. A note says that he re-wrote one of his early stories twenty times, and some parts of it a hundred times! Certain pages in the present volume have evidently been altered and altered and altered, with the result that the author's original matter is buried.

Sometimes you cannot be sure, without minute re-examination, which of two or more personages is being described, or even which is speaking. But what vast and minute knowledge, what opulence of local colour, what imagination, what sense of beauty, what power, in these reconstitutions of the past American cities! Mr. Hergesheimer makes America seem as old as Britain itself.

I think that the best of the ten sketches is the fifth, dealing chiefly with New Orleans before Louisiana became part of the United States. It is more nearly a story than any of the others. All is fine and entirely satisfactory in these thirty pages. Two of the old Pennies are the chief characters in it. The brothers Penny, with the wife of the elder and her sister Mariquita, the prismatic life of the community, the tragedy, the horror — how wonderfully are all these people and matters rendered!

The author is equally good, though hardly as picturesque, about Pittsburg and Albany. Mr. Hergesheimer writes as though he had behind him a tradition, a civilisation, of hundreds of years. He creates America afresh, shows it in a new light.

He ought to be translated into French. The acutest French critics would appreciate him more delicately than he will ever be appreciated in America or England. I am conscious of an impulse to read or re-read the whole of Hergesheimer's output. Of course, I shall conquer the impulse. Life is short. Books are long and many.

8 November 1928

A Woman's High-Brow Lark

You cannot keep your end up at a London dinner-party in these weeks unless you have read Mrs. Virginia Woolf's *Orlando* (Hogarth Press, 9s.).

For about a fortnight I succeeded in not reading it — partly from obstinacy and partly from a natural desire for altercation at table about what ought not to be read. Then I saw that Hugh Walpole had described it as "another masterpiece," and that Desmond MacCarthy had given it very high praise.

I have a great opinion of the literary opinions of these two critics. So I bought the book and read it. I now know exactly what I think of it, and I can predict the most formidable rumpuses at future parties.

It is a very odd volume. It has a preface, in which Mrs. Woolf names the names of 53 people who have helped her with it. It has, too, an index. I admit some justification for the preface, but none for the index.

Further, the novel, which is a play of fancy, a wild fantasia, a romance, a high-brow lark, is illustrated with ordinary realistic photographs, including several of Vita Sackville-West (a Hawthornden prizewinner), to whom the book is dedicated. The portraits of Miss Sackville-West are labelled "Orlando."

This is the oddest of all the book's oddities, and I commend it to the attention of Mr. H.M. Paull who has just published a rather comprehensive volume entitled *Literary Ethics: a Study in the growth of the literary conscience* (Butterworth, 15s.).

Mr. Paull has a chapter on "Actual Persons in Fiction and Drama." True, the numerous instances which Mr. Paull cites were not done with the consent of the "actual persons" concerned. Mrs. Woolf's obviously was.

Orlando at the end of the book has achieved an age of some four centuries. Which reminds one of the Wandering Jew and the Flying Dutchman. Half-way through the story he changes into a woman — and "stays put." Which reminds one of *Séraphita,* the dullest book that Balzac ever wrote.

I surmise that Orlando is intended to be the incarnation of something or other — say, the mustang spirit of the joy of life, but this is not quite clear to me.

The first chapter is goodish. It contains vivacious descriptions of spectacular matters — such as a big frost, royal courts, and the love-making of Orlando and a Muscovite girl in furs and in the open air amid the fiercest frost since the ice-age. Mrs. Woolf almost convinces us of the possibility of this surely very difficult dalliance.

The second chapter shows a startling decline and fall-off. Fanciful embroidery, wordy, and naught else!

The succeeding chapters are still more tedious in their romp of fancy. Mrs. Woolf does not seem to have understood that fancy must have something to play on. She has left out the basic substance. For example, Orlando, both as man and as woman, is said to have had many lovers, but details are given of only one love.

I shall no doubt be told that I have missed the magic of the work. The magic is precisely what I indeed have missed.

The writing is good at the beginning, but it goes to pieces; it even skids into bad grammar (e.g., on p.262). Mrs. Woolf has accomplished some of the most beautiful writing of the modern age, including paragraphs that Nathaniel Hawthorne himself might have signed. *Orlando*, however, has nothing anywhere near as good as her best.

The theme is a great one. But it is a theme for a Victor Hugo, not for Mrs. Woolf, who, while sometimes excelling in fancy and in delicate realistic observation, has never yet shown the mighty imaginative power which the theme clearly demands. Her best novel, *To the Lighthouse*, raised my hopes of her. *Orlando* has dashed them, and they lie in irridescent fragments at my feet.

Mrs. Woolf's publishing firm, the Hogarth Press, has just issued a critical work, *The Structure of the Novel* (3s.6d.), by Edwin Muir. In dealing with the later developments of English fiction, Mr. Muir names James Joyce, Mrs. Woolf and (to a less extent) Aldous Huxley as the only important innovating novelists.

I would concede him the first and the last, but I have horrid doubts about the middle term. In particular I have failed to perceive any genuine originality in the method of *Mrs. Dalloway*. If originality there is, it fails in its object of presenting a character.

Nevertheless, Mr. Muir has written, and admirably written, a very clear analysis of various fictional methods. His is a far better book than Mr. Percy Lubbock's *The Craft of Fiction*; but it suffers from the same defect: ignorance, relative or complete, of the actual creative processes of the artist. (Mr. E.M. Forster's *Aspects of the Novel* is free of the defect. On every page of it the artist feels the mind of a fellow-artist.)

I do not know to whom most of these books about the technique of imaginative writing can appeal.

The lay reader usually gives them a miss. The artist, whom they render impatient, learns nothing from them — perhaps not because they have nothing to teach, but because the things they might teach cannot be taught. The artist knows or feels that fundamental imaginative power alone counts. The analytic critic seems to be interested only in machinery.

Here is Mr. Edwin Muir discussing the modern novel, and he makes but passing reference to D.H. Lawrence, and no reference at all to R.H. Mottram, the two novelists who more than any of their contemporaries, continually disclose genuine originality, the two real British geniuses of the new age!

Just a week ago appeared Mr. Mottram's *Ten Years Ago* (Chatto, 5s.), a sort of "pendant" to *The Spanish Farm Trilogy*. There are no other war sketches comparable in freshness and power to these seeming trifles.

Another book (very short) a knowledge of which is necessary to lively conduct at dinner-parties is *The Angel that Troubled the Waters* (Longmans, 6s.), by Thornton Wilder, author of the triumphant *Bridge of San Luis Rey*.

A series of sixteen brief dialogues, mainly religious in mood. A very youthful work. The last six are the best, and of the last six perhaps the best are *The Flight into Egypt* (in which the ass talks) and *The Sea shall give up its Dead*.

The stage-directions which close the latter are characteristic: "The three panic-stricken souls reach the surface of the sea. The extensive business of Domesday is over in a twinkling, and the souls divested of all identification have tumbled like falling stars, into the blaze of unicity. Soon nothing exists in space but the great unwinking eye, meditating a new creation."

But the finest thing in the book is the Foreword — a perfect piece of witty and wise writing. Something here for Mr. Muir and others:
"The training for literature must be acquired by the artist alone, through the passionate assimilation of a few masterpieces written from a spirit somewhat like his own, and of a few masterpieces written from a spirit not at all like his own.... The technical process of literature should be acquired almost unconsciously on the tide of a great enthusiasm ... even syntax, even sentence-construction ... even spelling."

I feel an obligation to Mr. Wilder for having resuscitated from Coleridge that rare and elegant word "unicity."

Writing As a Living — And Why Not?

Authors are very prominent in these days: which is in itself a phenomenon not wholly evil. Scarcely a day passes but what prominent authors are asked by important newspapers, simply because they are prominent authors, to give their views upon matters on which their views are not worth a bilberry, and unfortunately many of them accede to the request.

If a prominent author enters a restaurant or a theatre people are sure to put their heads together and murmur: "Look! There's so and so." They will even point fingers at the fellow defenceless against their impolite curiosity. Whereas the Governor of the Bank of England, or the head of a great trust or mercantile concern, or an illustrious barrister would pass unnoticed anywhere.

People want to know even what authors eat and drink and how they dress. If a prominent author uses his handkerchief in a public place he will read of the event next day in the press. Such items are "news," and paragraphists earn their living and keep wife and children in comfort by supplying them.

Advertisements of books occupy more and more space in newspapers. And the number of books published seems, according to my experience, to be growing. Every week I read official catalogues of every book published (except technical manuals); they are so numerous that I can examine at the most not more than 5 per cent. of the actual books. Of that 5 per cent. I read possibly 5 per cent, and of the new books I read and would like to write about I cannot deal with one-third.

Lastly, more and more books are published about the technical or professional side of authorship. In late weeks I have discussed several, and today comes another one: Mr. A.S. Collins's *The Profession of Letters* (Routledge, 12s. 6d.).

Some time ago Mr. Collins published a book treating of authorship between 1726 and 1780. This book was interesting and sound. The second volume, which continues the story from 1780 to 1832, is equally interesting and sound. It "reads itself." Its pages will attract anybody who cares to learn — and which of us doesn't? — how other human beings have organised or disorganised their lives — especially in a financial sense.

The 1780 to 1832 period was a golden age of authorship. In it authorship developed into a regular profession, of which the chief professors were Scott and Southey. Scott said he would employ literature as a stick but not as a crutch. In the end, however, literature was much more of a crutch than a stick to him.

Southey was apparently the first un-Bohemian professional man of letters. He set out to live by his pen, and he did live by his pen — and very successfully and happily. Scott would have done the same if he had confined himself to literature and kept out of commercial responsibilities and the absorbing business of being a country gentleman.

Authors were well paid in those days — as well paid, relatively to the value of money, as they are to-day. Poets got large sums, larger than

213

any modern poet has got since Tennyson died.

Mr. Collins quotes with approval a well-known passage from Hilaire Belloc's *The Cruise of the Nona,* in which Mr. Belloc asserts (1) that literature was "never meant to be a trade"; and (2) that "a man is no more meant to live by writing than he is meant to live by conversation, or by dressing, or by walking about and seeing the world"; and (3) that there is "no relation between the function of letters and the economic effect of letters"; and (4) that "the relationship between the excellence or the usefulness of a piece of literature and the number of those who will buy it in a particular form is not a causal relationship, it is a purely capricious one"; also (5) that literature is "the hardest and the most capricious and, indeed, the most abominable of trades."

With all these five high sounding *obiter dicta* I disagree. The first two signify naught. "A man is no more meant to live by writing," etc. . . . Who "meant" him not to live by writing? Nature? A deity? Are tens of thousands of excellent citizens at this moment sinning against nature or against a higher power? Obviously lots of persons were "meant" to live by writing. Mr. Belloc was. Working in conditions imposed by commercial considerations, he has lived and he has produced a few admirable books. Would he have done better had he been endowed with ten, twenty, or fifty thousand a year?

Shakespeare worked under similar conditions. And after having achieved in those conditions the greatest things in the history of the world, and after having made all the money he needed, Shakespeare retired and wrote, so far as we know, not another word.

Dickens and Thackerary and Trollope made of literature a trade. Did they or did they not produce masterpieces? Would they have accomplished more or better if they had been heirs of all the Rothschilds? Were they unnatural, were they godless? Thomas Hardy told one of his publishers that unless he could make money by novels he would return to architecture.

The vice of creative artists is sloth, and this should not surprise us, since, although writing is not the "most abominable" of all trades, it is assuredly the hardest. The best safeguard against sloth is the urgent want of money. The urgent want of money has been responsible for more fine literature than all the wealth of modern times.

With due respect for Mr Belloc, I call entirely absurd his statement that there is no relation between the function of letters and the economic effect of letters. There may not be a perfect relation, but there is some relation and a considerable relation. The aim of the artist is and should be to please others while pleasing himself. Authors who have succeeded in this aim have generally succeeded in making money. * Other things being equal, good work brings in more money than less good work.

And the biggest money-makers in literature do not "prostitute" themselves. They are as a rule sincere, and they do the best they can. All classes of mentality are entitled to have books which give them pleasure, and authors are entitled to appeal to whatever class suits them.

That the rewards of literature are sometimes incommensurate with the effort of writing is notorious. But the same is true of all other trades. A

* Bennett himself earned approximately £22,000 in 1928.

214

man may fashion beautiful furniture or he may keep a shop stacked with good stuff at fair prices, and yet go bankrupt. Even the sublime genius of company-promoters is frequently unrecompensed.

Some authors complain of injustice or misfortune in the struggle for life. Coleridge did. But Coleridge could never have earned a living at any trade; he lacked the character to do so. He was born a great poet, but he was born a great failure in life.

Lastly, many authors have so strong a bent for letters that to invite them to earn a business living by day and keep only their evenings for literary composition, unhampered by commercial considerations, would be preposterous. Hence they must live not only for literature but by it. Living by literature they must make it a trade. Literature for literature's sake is a silly and unsocial idea, invented by grumblers and idlers.

22 November 1928

Being New at Any Cost

I have been reading, or reading *in* some good books — old ones — English and foreign, and comparing them with some new books. First, *The Complete Works of Jane Austen,* with a satisfactory introduction by J.C. Squire (Heinemann, 8s. 6d.). This volume, not too bulky, is value for money. It contains over 1400 pages, and comprises four full-length novels and one shorter novel (*Persuasion*).

I am not an extreme "Janeite"; I do not feel convinced that Jane Austen was the only estimable author who ever lived. But the general level of these novels is very high. *Northanger Abbey* is the least fine; even *Sense and Sensibility* (Jane's first book) is its superior. I concede to the Janeites that their goddess at her best has never been beaten in the field of pure comedy. Continual richness! Also blunt plain speaking when the same is called for! She loved her social system — but had no (or few) illusions about it.

Second, Kenneth Grahame's *The Golden Age* (Bodley Head, 7s. 6d.) with drawings by Ernest Shepard which excite not my admiration. *The Golden Age* is a destructive masterpiece, but I do not regard it as the author's best book, which in my opinion is *The Wind in the Willows.* Although people rarely speak of *The Wind in the Willows* — most people have never heard of it — it has some past, and it certainly has a future.

Third, *Mirgorod*; translated from the Russian of Gogol by Constance Garnett (Chatto, 7s. 6d.). This collection of stories contains the famous *Taras Bulba.* The rest of the volume I had not previously read.

The whole book is masterly. Anybody who can appreciate broad, satiric, benevolent humour will enjoy *The Tale of how Ivan Ivanovitch Quarrelled with Ivan Nokiforovitch,* and nobody who dislikes quiet, desolating tragedy should read the last three pages.

Prince Mirsky says in the introduction to another just-published Russian book that "in England at least Gogol is regarded as no more than an amusing humorist." Prince, how misguided you are! This isle is not populated by idiots, and none but an idiot could regard Gogol as only a humorist. Gogol can be heartrending.

The other Russian book is Lermontov's *A Hero of our Time*, translated by Reginald Merton (Allen, 7s. 6d.). This is a landmark in the annals of Russian fiction; it had considerable influence on Chekhov, and much of it is as good as Chekhov, if very different. Indeed, though the construction is episodic and extraordinarily loose, many scenes are as good as can be found anywhere. This is saying a great deal, and I say it. It has the sobriety, the power, and the grace of a classic. Further, it is very romantic and picturesque. I had not read it before.

Lermontov was a poet; this is his sole novel. He died at 27. I apprehend that a lot of the implicit social criticism in *A Hero of our Time* must be lost upon anyone, such as myself, not deeply intimate with Russian social history.

No doubt the charm of the author's alleged incomparable style is lost in the translation, which the publishers call "excellent and scholarly." Why write "post-ship" for "mailboat"? Why write, of a boat, "she turned on her side" when the meaning obviously is "she changed her course"? And so on indefinitely. Nevertheless, despite the excellent and scholarly translation, do not miss this book. And if you are not enthusiastic about it, read it again in ten years' time. Its irony is extremely subtle.

One thing that strikes me about all the aforementioned authors is their perception of, and preoccupation with, the basic fact that the first business of a storyteller is to tell a story clearly. They give the reader a fair start, by giving him a vision of either what the characters are or where they are, or both. They do not envelope the poor votary of fiction in a mist which refuses to clear for fifty pages, or a hundred, or at all.

And one thing that strikes me about some of our young authors is that in their contempt for established methods, and their determination to be new at any cost, or from mere amateurishness, they ignore the said basic fact.

As an instance I give Mr. Harold Acton's *Humdrum* (Chatto, 7s. 6d.). To this hour I can only make one positive statement about *Humdrum*, namely that it ends with an orgy. (I am sick of orgies — they are so old-fashioned and tedious.) Over and over again, in the perusal, I was asking myself: "Who is speaking now? Where is she? What in heaven's name am I reading about?" Rarely did I "see" a character.

However, the book has a kind of thesis. And Mr. Acton sometimes shows a healthy interest in words. But the interest is too intermittent. He has the attitudes of a high-brow; he follows the cult of the day. Yet his novel is infested with antique clichés. He even shockingly misuses the word "phenomenal." And he is capable of stylistic enormities, such as "She toyed with the idea as if she was picking at a quail, *drawing the line*, however, at Jack's suggestion," etc.

Another instance is Mr. Louis Marlow's *Mr. Amberthwaite* (Gollancz, 7s. 6d.). This is a better book than *Humdrum*. But still its unnecessary and maladroit demands on the defenceless reader are a little excessive. More than half the time the author, like the reader, is in two senses at sea. When I compare these books with the straightforward, highly accomplished, unpretentious masterpieces previously cited, I ——

You say it is unfair to compare the work of beginners with masterpieces.

But my contention is that the work of beginners ought always to be compared with masterpieces. How else shall you judge them? Only by constant comparison with masterpieces can the sense of proportion be kept.

A new book (by a young author) of a different quality is Phyllis Bentley's *The Partnership* (Benn, 7s. 6d.). A year ago or less I meant to write about Miss Bentley's earlier book, *The Spinner of the Years*; lack of space defeated me.

Miss Bentley does not try to be modern (but she is). She practises the technique of the masters. She is as direct as de Maupassant or Gogol. In *The Partnership* you know where you are and who is who from the beginning. The narration is slightly flat-footed at moments; but Miss Bentley is a fundamentally sound novelist. The character of Lydia is most admirably drawn. A book meet for attention.

29 November 1928

Who Should Select Books for Censorship?

Does reading influence the moral character of the young? That is a question we ought to attempt to answer before we decide whether it is worth while trying, for a moral end, to set limits upon the range of books which children should be permitted to read. Admittedly books do fulfil, at any rate, two purposes — for readers of all ages. They inform; and they give pleasure by exciting the imagination and by arousing the sense of beauty. But do they to an appreciable degree have the effect of improving or debasing the moral character of the young? And, in particular, are they capable of debasing their moral character?

In my own experience I have never met with any proof that books, unaided by home example, actually do so. And I do not believe that they do so. Children, if they are to be influenced, require something more concrete than books — something more concrete even than films. The most that books can accomplish is to *bring out* character, either good or bad. The creation of character is in my opinion beyond their power.

Children have a sturdy secret independence of mind. Give a nice child *The Newgate Calendar* (I hope you won't, for it is a prodigiously dull affair), and he will remain nice. Give a nasty child *The Pilgrim's Progress*, and he will remain nasty. A child will only take from a book what he wants. The rest will slide off his intelligence like water off a duck's back.

A very wise word on this point is to be found in an agreeable and erudite book of literary essays — entitled *Pious Opinions* and published a few years ago — which I have lately re-read: "A child reads on without bothering about anything beyond its comprehension."

And the gently cynical author of *Pious Opinions* is still more explicit. He says: "All education is in the nature of a gamble — or at best a doubtful investment. On the whole, to let children loose in a library is as safe a venture as any other."

Now, the author of *Pious Opinions* is clearly a man of very wide reading, and the library of his assumption will no doubt therefore comprise works such as those of Swift, Rabelais, Swinburne, Gibbon, Lucian, even the composer of the Song of Solomon.

I am in agreement with him. If I had a daughter aged fourteen I would give her the run of all my bookcases, and of anybody else's bookcases, confident that the result, though it might not be strikingly beneficial, would not be in the least pernicious.

As for adolescents, those mysterious and hypersensitive creatures, they strongly resemble children, and I would confer upon them a similar freedom; and so, I think, would the sagacious author of *Pious Opinions*. I feel sure I should do more harm by forbidding any book than by permitting all books.

When I was an adolescent I had a passion for Ouida, then held to be shamelessly immoral. But, looking back, I can assert positively that her novels of gilded vice, self-indulgence, and all manner of roseate unrighteousness never inspired me with the slightest desire to outrage the strict code of my nonconformist parents. *Per contra*, I can recall contemporary earnest students of Smiles's *Self-Help* whose later careers have besmirched the honour of the Five Towns.

As for adults, they strongly resemble children. . . etc. With this slight difference: that every one of them resents every effort to circumscribe his reading for his own good. Every upholder of a literary censorship advocates it for other people, never for himself. Every upholder says: "Of course, no book could possibly harm *me*, but —" Why the would-be censors should put themselves in a class apart I have not yet understood.

If books could exercise a deleterious influence upon moral character, our houses would be burgled nightly, and the population would be decimated by innumerable murders in the street or in bed. For half the most popular novels — together with two-thirds of the most popular plays and three-quarters of the most popular films — present crimes of violence in an exceedingly attractive light. (I say nothing of the thievery, the crude cheating, and the large, comprehensive dishonesty which they make a practice of praising with faint damns.)

Moreover, who shall have the wisdom to choose, and what artfulness shall select, books meet for censorship? If I said, for instance, that Dickens ought to be suppressed, I should probably be cast for ever out of the companionship of the same. And yet I will venture to quote, and to applaud, the following statement by the author of *Pious Opinions*: "Of all writers Dickens is the most immoral in one particular — the irresistible appeal of his worst characters."

Here I am reminded of a magnificent tome (a foot and a half high) containing 152 reproductions of book-pages from early German Presses (*German Incunabula in the British Museum*, admirably introduced by Stanley Morison, and just published by Gollancz at 12 guineas — roughly the price of a ringside-seat at a world-championship prize-fight).

This volume is a lovely and a majestic thing, meet to be pored over for many hours by those who delight in the aesthetic marvels of the finest printing Europe has seen. There are fewer wealthy lovers of typography than of ringside-seats at a prize-fight; but such as there are would spend their money well in buying the book. It is certain to go out of print and up in value.

Why am I reminded of it? Because the pages which it reproduces belong to the golden Gothic age of censorship. Naturally, with the conceit of the posterity of that age, we deride the clumsy Gothic censorships. But ought we to deride? I wonder.

One thing is certain about censorships: that every age has laughed at the age which preceded it, and been the laughing-stock of the age which succeeded it. The opprobrious adjective "Gothic" might properly be applied to all censorships for hundreds of years after the fifteenth century.

Less than a century ago *The Quarterly Review*, as quoted by the author of *Pious Opinions*, said of *Jane Eyre*: "If it was written by a woman it must have been written by one who, for some sufficient reason, has forfeited the society of her own sex."

Less than two centuries ago, Fielding's *Tom Jones* was prosecuted for being immoral. The prosecution failed. "At any rate . . . it taught the police to leave literature alone," joyously remarks the author of *Pious Opinions*, who, by the way, is Sir Chartres Biron.

6 December 1928

People Who are Tired of War Books

Two good war-books have recently been published.

(The other day a friend wrote to me, asking: "Are you ever in at 5.15?" I replied: "Yes. I am generally at home at 5.15; but any man who breaks in on me is likely to be killed." In the same way, when I hear people say that they are tired of reading books about the war, I feel inclined to answer them with a dagger. Nobody except a fighter has the right to be bored by good books about the war.

If millions of brave and tenacious men could fight for over four years, we ought at least to have the decency to read with interest what they write concerning their experiences. If I could do it by persuasion and not by compulsion I would have every man who was safe at school in 1918 read every good book that appears about the war. Good books about the war are the finest possible propaganda for common-sense methods of settling international differences.)

The first of the two recent war-books is Arnold Zweig's *The Case of Sergeant Grischa*. As another hand has already reviewed it in this paper, I will only say now that it has had the closest possible shave of being a masterpiece. It suffers from irrelevant and undigested detail; some of it is confused; the author gives away the emotional instability of his taste by many absurd chapter-titles. But much of it is masterly, and the closing chapters show tremendous force legitimately employed.

The second is Edmund Blunden's *Undertones of War* (Cobden Sanderson, 10s. 6d.). Zweig's method may be described in the phrase which Walter Scott applied to his own: "the big bow-wow" manner. Edmund Blunden's method has nothing in it of the big bow-wow. It is quiet, restrained, unpretentious, subtle.

He paints no large, comprehensive pictures. He tells, with an apparent artlessness which is full of art, merely what happened to himself. He does not seek effects, but is always achieving effects. The intimate horror of war has never been, and never will be, more movingly and modestly rendered than he renders it.

Take his narration of the "accidental tour into enemy country" (pp. 141-143). Take a sentence such as the following: "Men of the next battalion were found in mud up to the armpits, and their fate was not spoken of; those who found them could not get them out."

Edmund Blunden is young. He fought in the trenches for more than two years. He is a poet. Other poets say that by a future generation he will be recognised as Keats is now recognised. I cannot judge, not possessing enough expertise. All I know is that he is a distinguished poet.

All poets write good prose. There is no finer prose than Shakespeare's, who wrote a great deal of prose. Edmund Blunden writes superb prose. The opening chapters of *Undertones of War* are wonderfully written, packed with original observation accurately set down in original phrasing of truly exquisite perfection.

Later on in the book he seems to have become too obsessed by his subject to think about his pen, and the writing, though always very admirable, has fewer marvels for the sensitive, educated palate. This book will be a classic. It cannot *not* be a classic. Literary critics used to talk about "beauty and terror." *Undertones of War* has beauty and terror, together with wit and a disquieting backwash of humour.

The publication of the first English translation — at any rate, I think it is the first — of Stendhal's first novel *Armance* (Chatto, 7s. 6d.) ought to make more stir in the British world of letters than probably it will — especially as the translator is Mr. C.K. Scott Moncrieff, who has a positive genius for this ungrateful and accutely difficult task.

Armance has not been easy to obtain, even in French, except in the expensive collected edition. I never succeeded in buying it in the cheap edition, which was always either out of stock or out of print.

Some say that Stendhal was the greatest psychologist among novelists in any language. I would not deny it. Nor would I assert it, though I think he was. *Armance* was not only his first novel, it was his favourite among his novels. He wrote it at the age of 46. About 26 years passed before it reached a second edition.

I will not recommend it to any save Stendhal enthusiasts. Stendhal is an acquired taste; but the taste once acquired, it makes drunkards of its victims. I have been one of the victims — for now a quarter of a century. I read Mr. Scott Moncrieff's version with intense pleasure.

I can, however, well conceive that the book may bore those who have not been initiated into the cult. It is naive; it is a wildly romantic love-story, and a wildly romantic picture of French Royalist manners 101 years ago. Despite statements to the contrary, it is a novel with a key to it. The heroine, Armance, was drawn from life, and the principal salon depicted is understood to be that of the Duchesse de Broglie. Both the heroine and the hero, Octave, behave with the most sublime, preposterous and ridiculous high-mindedness.

Mr. Scott Moncrieff says that "the main distinction, the impassable gulf between *Armance* and the novels which we read to-day is this: Octave was a gentleman." I should prefer to say that Octave was an aristocrat. No novelist ever "did" aristocrats equal to Stendhal. (See *Scarlet and Black*.)

220

Octave was not always a gentleman. The prime cause of the duel which indirectly led to his death was his behaviour one night at the opera — the behaviour of a cad.

The author says, in a note: "Like Rousseau, poor Octave is fighting against phantoms." Which is only half true. Poor Octave's whole outlook on life was distorted by the quite non-phantom-like reality of the most sinister physical disadvantage from which a man can suffer. This defect the author does not make entirely plain to the reader; from which it follows that the hero does not make the disadvantage plain to the heroine.

Armance is full of faults; but it is full, too, of Stendhal's upright, realistic, romantic and passionate mind. It can be tedious only to those who have not entered into his mind, as into a chapel for "the happy few" (his own phrase).

Anyone who has read and enjoyed Stendhal's enchanting theoretical treatise *On Love* will find in *Armance* the theory put into practice. The famous idea of "crystallisation" is fully illustrated in characters which live and which psychologically carry complete conviction to the reader, no matter how superiorly the reader may smile at their antics of sentiment.

13 December 1928

Devastating Things about the American Mind — From an American

Though I have sinned in that way myself quite a number of times in the last twenty years, I still object to authors writing prefaces, forewords, or introductions to the books of other (living) authors. A book should not be led into the ring like a performing horse at a circus, etc.

Nevertheless, I do take notice of prefaces, etc. The names of certain introducers would inhibit me for ever from opening any book introduced by them. The names of some introducers, on the contrary, fascinate me as a snake is (falsely) reported to fascinate a bird. Two such names are those of T.S. Eliot and Walter de la Mare. They appear almost simultaneously as introducers, and I could resist neither of their wards.

Mr. Eliot prefaces *This American World*, by Edgar Ansel Mowrer (Faber and Gwyer, 7s. 6d.). Mr. Eliot is American, but probably less so than any American now on earth. Henry James and J.S. Sargent were both less American than Mr. Eliot; but they carried their Europeanisation to excess. They were more European than Europeans. To be more royalist than the king implies a lack of tact.

Mr. Eliot is a fine poet — sometimes, if not in that celebrated piece of verse, *The Waste Lands*, at the mention of which the very young bow the head in adoration. He is also a fine critic, if dry and over-dispassionate. There must be something in any book that he ceremonially sponsors.

There is a great deal in *This American World*. Indeed, it is one of the most enlightening and frankest books on American psychology that I have ever read; and, apart from a few too perky brightnesses, it is well written.

I may say that if a European author of reputation had said half as much as Mr. Mowrer says in criticism of the American mind, international

221

complications would quickly have ensued. H.L. Mencken and G. Jean Nathan would have emerged from their wigwams with bludgeons to slay the offender. But Mr. Mowrer, being American, is no doubt safe.

The best things in *This American World* are the comparison of the typical American mind with the child-mind. It is devastating — and as diverting as unanswerable. The next best thing is the chapter on "The Essence of Americanism," in which he makes frightful statements as if they were platitudes. Thus: "*Of course* our personal freedom, in the absolute sense, grows less from year to year. We never did much believe in it." (My italics.)

Be not under a misapprehension. Mr. Mowrer believes in Americanism, and gives good reasons for his belief. He even prophesies that American ideals will ultimately rule the entire world. I think he may be right. Anyhow, if he is, I feel that I can now justifiably ask: "O death, where is thy sting?" This book is original, subtle, acute, excellent — and short.

Of Mr. de la Mare's ward I think less highly. Mr. Odell Shepard, author of *The Joys of Forgetting* (George Allen & Unwin, 7s. 6d.), is an American, an essayist, an organist, a solitary pedestrian, and though nearer forty than fifty years of age, proclaims himself the author of *The Harvest of a Quiet Eye*.

Many years have passed since I read a book called *The Harvest of a Quiet Eye*. It had an immense circulation and I thought it excessively tedious.

Mr. Shepard's essays are good, but they are not very good. And if an essay is not very good it is naught; in fact it is about minus five. Mr. Shepard is not comparable to Lamb, Hazlitt, certain former contributors to *The Pink 'Un*, Max Beerbohm, Robert Lynd, the earlier G.K. Chesterton, or the earlier Hilaire Belloc. He mildly pleases. It is not enough. An essayist should, by incessant sound sense and perfection, either dazzle or excite. Still, Mr. Shepard can be read.

Incidentally, the book contains the longest sentence ever written. It runs to approximately 1500 words. The author wrote it for fun and maliciously. To write it was a feat. To write it well was a brilliant feat. It is written very well.

Speaking of essays and of length, I am reminded of what seems to me to be a new, and a better, kind of biography — a kind which I hope will be imitated. The prototype is *Life and Work of Sir Norman Lockyer* by T. Mary Lockyer and Winifred L. Lockyer (Macmillans, 18s.).

Now, the curse of British biography is, as I have frequently insisted, length — mere length. The present is a volume of 474 pages (including a good index) and less than half of it is given over to the customary biography. The major half of the volume consists of essays by various eminences — such as Sir Richard Gregory (editor of the most authoritative of all weekly papers, *Nature*), on various aspects of Lockyer's life work. (Lockyer himself edited *Nature* for fifty years.) From a statement in the preface the novel plan of the book appears to be Sir Richard Gregory's. If so, he is now doubly a public benefactor.

I read with a special interest Professor Dingle's essay on Lockyer's labours in the matter of "The Sun and Meteorology." I remember the time when Lockyer's theory about sunspots agitated even the non-scientific world. And I remember being told by a student of science who had been enlisted by Lockyer in the cohort of daily observers that a slothful member of the cohort would occasionally take a day off, and then fill in his sheet with imaginary details of observations adroitly arranged to support the Lockyerian theory. This particular thing probably did not happen; but such things do happen, I suppose, even in science.

The book is good. It has enlarged my notions of the physical world. But at the same time it demonstrates once more that men of science know no more about so-called inorganic matter, and the mysterious antics thereof than doctors know about the human body. The merit of the best of them, like the merit of the best of doctors, is that they know they don't know. A few know that they never will know: which is an even greater merit.

The book on the whole shows quite considerable literary accomplishment. . . . If all scientific people wrote as well as T.H. Huxley, what a different world the world of science would be! Too many men of science have never taken the trouble to learn to write. I could prove this unkind remark from the columns of *Nature* itself.

20 December 1928

I Go Buying at the Book Barrows – And Find There are *Still* Bargains to be Had

I would read any book on book-collecting, and I have read *A Primer of Book-Collecting*, by John Winterich (Allen and Unwin, 7s. 6d.). Messrs. Allen and Unwin are among the few publishing firms who give information about their authors; but in the present instance they have fallen away from a good habit. Who is Mr. Winterich? I assume that he is not English, as his book has been "revised and edited for English collectors" by Mr. Raymond Dean.

Well, the book has a certain interest, on account of its subject; but it will never rank among the bibliophilic classics. It is discursive, ill-arranged, and has no index. Its best chapter is entitled "What makes a rare book rare." This chapter has interest.

Mr. Winterich lays insufficient stress on the great fact that the first qualification of a book-collector is keenness. The man who casually sets out to be a book-collector because he has nothing else to do has no more chance of success than the man who sets out to be a poet for the same reason. There are as keen book-collectors to-day as ever there were; but they don't seem to write enough about their glorious mania.

For nearly a hundred years we have had no such enthusiastic bibliographical author as the Rev. Thomas Frognall Dibdin (elder brother of Dibdin, the sea-song writer and pernicketty dramatist*), author of *The Library Companion, or the Old Man's Comfort and the Young Man's Guide*, etc., etc., of *Bibliomania, or Book Madness*, and of the immense *Bibliographical, Antiquarian and Picturesque Tour*. This parson was one of the most inexact writers that ever lived; but he was keen, and he can still be enjoyed by his fellow maniacs.

---

* Actually his nephew. See also p. 238.

Nor does Mr. Winterich clearly define the phrase "book-collector." A book-collector is one who buys rare books, because they are rare, at prices which he deems to be lower than their worth. He is a bargain-hunter. A good book which is not rare has no attraction for a collector, whose chief instinct is the commercial.

These observations will arouse resentment, but the truth is in them. I speak freely because I have been a collector myself. I have even been a bookseller in a small way. And two of my catalogues, sent forth in the 'nineties, are now among the rarest rarities of modern times. I have refused (relatively) vast sums for specimens of them, though their intrinsic value is nil.

It is a common saying today that bargains are no longer to be had. Mr. Winterich ought to have stamped on this saying as being the absolute nonsense which it is. Bargains are always to be had. But few collectors recognise every bargain that comes their way. Or rather they lack the foresight to perceive that a given book which at the moment is commercially worth nothing will in due course become valuable.

I once possessed the nine volumes of the entrancing *Journal* of the brothers de Goncourt. A thieving friend borrowed it from me. I have failed to get another copy. A few weeks ago I saw in the catalogue of a Brussels bookseller a copy of a limited edition of the *Journal,* priced at 10,000 francs. (I let it alone.) But another bibliomaniacal friend (not a thief so far as I know) has shown me a perfect copy of the same edition which he bought for about £4 – a fair price for it when he bought it. He had foresight.

Twenty and thirty years ago people were complaining, as they do to-day, that bargains had ceased to exist. Yet at the period the most astounding bargains in Hardys, Conrads, George Moores and so on were current everywhere.

It is the same at the present hour. I venture to say, for instance, that bargains in Blundens and Siegfried Sassoons are to be picked up all over the place. They may seem not to be bargains; but potential bargains they positively are.

The value of early Blundens and Sassoons has risen even in the past month, owing to the popular success of their recent books in prose. It will rise much higher. To distinguish a potential bargain in its primary stages demands, however, independent and sound literary taste: a gift which few collectors possess. But potential bargains can be had, without the exercise of literary taste, by those who have been endowed by heaven with common sense and a large view of things.

Every book printed before 1501 has value; and none is procurable as a bargain. Every English book printed before 1601 has value, and none is procurable as a bargain. Every English book of verse printed before 1701 has value, and extremely few are procurable as bargains. The collecting potentialities of these centuries are exhausted. But the eighteenth century remains to the prescient.

I predict that the time will soon come when every illustrated book of English verse printed before 1801 will have value. I say also that in the domain of the eighteenth century, hundreds of such bargains are at the moment lying around.

For example, not long ago I saw a copy of Falconer's well-known and not despicable poem *The Shipwreck*, with engravings from pictures by T. Stothard, R.A., bound in full leather, and admirably printed by an unnamed printer. I bought it for its historical interest and as a beautiful object. No bookseller would look twice at it, and few collectors. It cost me 1s. 6d. — about its present worth. But the vogue of the eighteenth century is bound to arrive, and cannot be long delayed. When it has arrived, collectors will go about boasting that they have picked up an illustrated Falconer's *Shipwreck* for a sovereign.

Another untilled field is sixteenth century continental editions of the Greek and Latin classics. (Idle to protest that you can't read them and don't want to read them! If you are a collector you don't read them — you merely gaze and collate.)

In Dibdin's time, fifteenth century editions of the classics fetched far less than they do now; but sixteenth century editions, curiously enough, fetched far more than they do now. In Victoria's reign the latter slumped in a very strange manner, and the market has never recovered.

Bargains abound in sixteenth century classical reprints, and many of them are lovely to behold. An example. I bought a copy of the truly superb folio Plutarch printed in Florence at the celebrated press of Philip Junta in 1517. It cost me about half-a-crown. Why so cheap? The answer is: The incomprehensible vagaries of fashion. Fashion changes.

I found that antique tome on a book barrow in Mile End Road. When young I used to visit every Saturday the book barrows in Mile End Road, Shoreditch and Farringdon Road. On November 3rd, last, after some twenty-five years, I had the caprice to revisit Farringdon Road. I obtained five modern books (one of which was a poetical rarity, and all of which I desired) for six shillings. In ancient days I would have carried five heavy folios under my arm to a suburb. Now, even for octavos, I have to add to the cost of the books the cost of a taxi for transport home.

27 December 1928

No Really First-Rate Detective Stories

This being the season of goodwill and leisure, people indulge themselves in the perusal of imaginary, sanguinary narrations of crime-detection. I have just read a once very celebrated detective novel, Anna Katharine Green's *The Leavenworth Case* (Gollancz, 7s.6d.). I read it on its first appearance *x* years ago. (Mr. Gollancz might have given the date of the original edition, but he does not.)

Dangerous to read again after a long interval a book which once enthralled you! You may be disappointed. (I was, seriously.) The book cannot have changed; therefore you have changed: a phenomenon which disconcerts you. I could remember nothing of *The Leavenworth Case* except that it gave me, as a youth, immense enjoyment. Now, in maturity, I have read it with difficulty; indeed I only got through it by the exercise of a steely determination.

One cause of the trouble was the long-windedness and marked clumsiness of the narrative, especially in its less exciting sections. The other cause was the inflated, maladroit and frequently ungrammatical style, especially in the dialogue, which is plenteous. Thus, for instance, talks one of the two glorious heroines in this American fiction: "It is hard for a delicate girl, reared in the lap of love and luxury, unused to aught but adulation and sincerest regard, to be obliged to assure the world of her innocence. . . ."

The said heroine was unjustly accused of foul murder, and it would have served such a stilted ranter right if she had been unjustly hanged by the neck till she was dead. And since all the characters habitually converse in this astounding and fantastic manner, every one of them ought to have perished in the last chapter — always assuming that the authoress had any sense of poetical justice.

I notice that an exalted person has called the book "one of the best detective stories ever *written*." (My italics.) Which dictum shows what may be the terrible consequences of a classical education.

The story is supposed to be a mystery story. There is, however, little or no mystery, for the reason that the book is soaked in sentimentality. Now in sentimental detective-fiction the elucidation of the enigma must and does invariably depend, not on logic, but on considerations of sentiment.

You can tick off nearly all the Anna Green characters one by one and assert with assurance: "He is nice, and *he* is nice, and she is nice, and *she* is very nice. Hence none of them could possibly have done the fell deed; for the reader would never stand for it."

Only one character, the murdered man's secretary, is not demonstrably nice; and in the early chapters you know for certain that, despite all appearances to the contrary, the secretary and no one else is guilty. And so it falls out.

In some respects *The Leavenworth Case* is good. The plot has originality and is constructed with the completest care. The whole business holds tightly together. The scene which the gouty detective stages for the final revelation of his own superlative perspicacity is really ingenious and effective. The horrid secretary's impassioned confession rises from bombast into something near genuine eloquence.

The secretary, by the way, slipped into assassination because he belonged to the tribe of males who give undue importance to the rôle of women in life, an importance which women themselves rarely allocate to women, save in the Press and on the platform. In the major and minor crises of domestic experience, being realists, women usually come down to brass tacks.

The Leavenworth Case has other merits. But a first-rate detective novel it is not. Nor have I read a single first-rate detective novel published since *The Mystery of the Yellow Room*. Of the present school of idolised mystery-mongers, I think that they are over-praised.

In default of a first-rate detective novel (of which there are perhaps not more than a score in the world), I would recommend a verbatim report of a "big" murder trial, such as those in Messrs. Hodge's series, *Notable British Trials*.

These volumes run to 250 large pages and more. They are of real value to any earnest student of nature who wishes to learn "how the other half lives." Glasgow has conspicuously figured in this series, and I feel that I know more about middle-class life in Glasgow than about any other subject in my curriculum. All the tiny, trifling, revealing details of the domestic day are there in thousands. Turns of speech are there. Psychology is lit up by innumerable gleams. And the interest is nearly continuous.

The latest addition to the series is the *Trial of Eugene Marie Chantrelle* (a Frenchman), edited by A. Duncan Smith. The speech for the defence in this case is a wonderful example of the legal art of making bricks without straw. Chantrelle was obviously guilty; but when his advocate sits down you are aware of grave doubts about his guilt — until the Lord Justice-Clerk gets fairly to work with his summing-up.

The lengthy evidence of the admirable servant girl, Mary Bryne, constitutes as striking a piece of character-drawing as Balzac himself could have achieved.

Mr. Duncan Smith's Introduction is less interesting, though his account of the criminal's last moments has authentic horror in it: "Then the fifth chapter of Second Corinthians was read — *a book being held by Mr. Wilson in front of the pinioned man.*" Mr. Duncan Smith is an addict of platitude: "And so ended the melancholy career of a man whose knowledge, skill and accomplishments, had they been properly directed, would have assured success for him in many positions in life, but whose misdeeds, laid bare by the inflexible hand of justice, eventually brought for him their terrible retribution." Etc.

Such passages might be excused in the mouth of a judge resolved to make an effect in the next day's newspapers. But coming from the pen of a criminological introducer they read like a parody.

The volume ends with thirteen appendices, several of which the profane might call padding. There is a facsimile of the handwriting of the murdered wife. A facsimile of the handwriting of the murderer would have had more interest.

In this connection I must mention Robert Saudek's *Experiments with Handwriting* (Allen and Unwin, 18s.). Who Mr. Saudek is I know not; but he is evidently somebody of importance in the calligraphic world, for the book had been published simultaneously in four countries. Whoever he may be, he intimidates me — by his thoroughness, his comprehensiveness, and his deductive powers.

Not very easy to read, he is very much worth reading. Yield yourself to his elaborate sentences and you will be held. His analytic studies of the writing of various celebrities, such as Lord Grey and Mussolini, are truly impressing. The book is a monument. I wish somebody would publish a handbook designed to teach other celebrities how to write their signatures legibly.

3 January 1929

Give Us Fewer and Better Books

The misdemeanours and crimes of 1928 are now found out, for the *Publishers' Circular and Booksellers' Record* has issued its annual statistical *Newgate Calendar*, from which we may learn that 1928 published an average of ten books a week more than 1927, and an average of seventy books a week more than 1922.

The majority of these acts of publication were misdemeanours; many were crimes; and some were crimes of violence. In other fields of iniquity misdemeanours are decreasing, but this cannot be said of the literary field.

The section of "Poetry and Drama," however, is clearing up its red-light district: 1928 published 87 fewer volumes in this section than 1927. *The Publishers' Circular*, by the way, is still, despite protests, lumping Poetry and Drama together, for no convincing reason. But the editor, for my benefit and therefore for the benefit of the *Evening Standard*, has personally communicated to me the fact that out of the 796 volumes in the section 240 contained single plays or groups of plays. He further kindly gives me his opinion that the decrease in the section is due chiefly to a decline in what is styled "minor poetry." (Poetry is here a misnomer.) Such tidings are cheerful.

In the matter of publishing I am glad to note that, influenced by my animadversions, at least one important firm has entirely ceased to publish its books on the two most crowded days of the week — Thursday and Friday. Certain other firms, obstinate, have continued their practice of issuing a dozen or a score books on one day — that day being always a Thursday or a Friday. It is very naughty of them, and against their own interests.

I will again urge publishers to give more biographical and bibliographical information about their authors, both British and foreign, on the dust-jackets of their books. Also, in the case of new editions, to give the dates of the original editions.

The trade press, whenever I promulgate advice to the trade, invariably blossoms into sarcasm at my expense. My head is bloody, but unbowed.

As to fiction, by far the most considerable department of imaginative literature, 1928 shows an average increase of more than three volumes per week over 1927.

This is bad. I admit that the more novels published the better is the chance of a really original new author slipping unobstructed into publication. But some enthusiastic firms have a perfect rage and craze for novel-production. Indeed, it is impossible to conceive why half the novels published are published at all. They do not remuneratively sell; they have no merit; they are not seriously reviewed, and they give no satisfaction to the handful of courageous but misguided explorers who peruse them.

Fewer books mean a higher level of excellence, and a higher level is what we need, and always shall need.

Withal I think that the level of modern fiction is pretty fair, and the outlook promising. You have only to compare the average novel with the average play to perceive how distinguished, relatively, the average novel is.

I have witnessed, in restless agony, this year and in previous years, a number of plays which were more amateurish, more stupid, more imbecile, more false, than the worst novel ever published in the history of the world. And I have witnessed no new play (I except the revue *This Year of Grace*) comparable in excellence to any one of scores of good or goodish novels. I am resentful, but I do not exaggerate.

Still, though there is a school of thought which predicts the approaching decease of the novel as a literary form, the novel gives no sign of dying. Quite the contrary. It is growing in popularity and in skill. The general level is higher than it was in 1900, or even ten years ago.

The novel is making progress. It has been galvanised by the very important experiments of James Joyce, D.H. Lawrence, R.H. Mottram, and Aldous Huxley: all of whom have brought something new into it. The biggest of these is, or was, James Joyce.

I should say from glimpses I have had of his latest work, that he is now carrying eccentricity to extremes. *Ulysses* was somewhat eccentric; it was assuredly obscene. But it did something that had never been done before. Its influence has far exceeded its circulation, and is everywhere perceptible. For myself, I never write fiction without thinking of Joyce's discoveries. D.H. Lawrence is a genius. Unequal, wayward, obsessed, but a genius. He has enlarged the scope of the novel.

R.H. Mottram is a genius. He writes like a genius. He has individuality, and he knows how to use it. Aldous Huxley may or may not have genius. He has enormous talent, and an intellect and an intelligence perhaps unique among living British novelists. He brings to the English novel what it most lacks: harshness, even brutality. He is the implacable foe of the English novel's worst enemy — sentimentality.

For years he could not create a character. Then he did create a character or so in *Two or Three Graces*. And now *Point Counter Point* is peopled with convincing characters.

With such original and audacious leaders of the young as these four, English fiction, I maintain, is in a healthy way of life, and for its future we are justified in great expectations. American novelists have brilliantly advanced in late years. Two or three of them have shown immense power — and sustained power. But the pioneers of modern Anglo-Saxon fiction are British.

If for no other reason than that nature abhors a vacuum, the novel will not and cannot presently die, nor wane. It is sufficient to ask the question: What could take its place? Is there the slightest glimmer or symptom of anything that could possibly take its place, or the tenth part of its place? The answer is beyond doubt in the negative. The novel lives and thrives because it has proved itself to be endlessly adaptable.

I have been reading Peacock's *Gryll Grange* — the flower of his old age. How alive, how strange, how inordinately peculiar is this story devoted, more than any other established novel, to classical and other learning and to the arts!

The literary form that has had room for achievements so utterly dissimilar as (say) *Gryll Grange, Erewhon, A Storyteller's Holiday* and *Ulysses* is not going to take to its bed and expire the day after to-morrow.

All is not jam for the aforesaid young leaders of fiction. I will not conclude without expressing dissatisfaction with their very imperfect sense of form. Not one of them (save possibly R.H. Mottram) but has flouted the Greek principle that, after inspiration, the chief quality in a creative artist is the sense of form. This principle cannot be flouted with impunity. It is deathless.

10 January 1929

The Most Romantic Figure in the History of Fiction

Balzac is one of the most romantic figures in the history of fiction; to me personally the most romantic of all. An English translation of René Benjamin's *The Prodigious Life of Honoré de Balzac* has just been published under the title *Balzac* (Heinemann, 10s.6d.), and it deserves attention.

Apparently the translation is American; therefore, in the interests of international goodwill, I will say nothing about it, except that I have read it. I read the work in the original French about a year ago. I then thought it fairly good, but not very good. A second reading confirms me in my view.

M. Benjamin is inclined to sentimentalise the prodigiosity of Balzac's career. You can see his tendency in the titles of the three divisions of his book: "The Struggle with Life," "The Triumph of Genius," "The Struggle with Death." Here is over-emphasis. Balzac had not only grandeur; in addition, he was grandiose. M. Benjamin insists too much on both characteristics. He paints the lily.

André Maurois would have accomplished this business much better. Those who call M. Maurois "superficial" are themselves superficial. Everything that he does he does extremely well. I will mention in passing his new novel *Climats* (Bernard Grasset, 12 francs), which in its quiet and subtle way is richly worth perusal. Still, M. Benjamin has not failed with Balzac. He might have made a mess of his tremendous subject; he has not done so. Parts of the book are thrilling, if merely by reason of the splendour of the material.

I should say that no novelist was ever so dominated by the demon of creative work as Balzac. It is generally believed that he died, at fifty, of work. But I doubt if work ever killed anybody. Balzac's death was due rather to his insane methods of work, and to excessive coffee.

When other people went to bed Balzac went to work. He worked all night and drank coffee all night. He told Eva de Hanska that he wrote eighty pages of *The Illustrious Gaudissart* in a night. If he had known how to organise his energy he might just as well have written those eighty pages by daylight. At another period, when ill, defying his doctor, he worked 18 hours at a stretch.

In one year he wrote *The Thirteen, The Marriage Contract, Séraphita, The Lily in the Valley, The Atheist's Mass, The Commission in Lunacy,* and *The Cabinet of Antiques*: all important works, except *Séraphita,*

230

a total failure which cost him "200 nights," and which only fanatics like George Saintsbury or myself could read. When, at the end, his doctor gave him a week to live, he sat up and cried: "A week with fever! There should be time to write a book!"

Balzac, however, was incapable of organising his energy. In practical matters he was a perfect fool. His absurd business schemes were deservedly disastrous. He made quite a lot of money, but was usually hard up. His dentist sent him to prison for an unpaid bill. In common with many authors he was apt to be naughty with publishers. But he was more frank about his misdeeds than most authors. He protested thus against the well-founded complaint of a publisher: "Is inspiration to be ordered like a pair of shoes? Contracts between authors and publishers should be unalterable only so far as the publishers are concerned." Which is sublime!

He was always talking about francs; and his novels are full of francs; so are his letters. He wasted half a fortune in proof-corrections, simply because he was always in a hurry.

He must have been in every way a restless worker. He exclaimed: "This year I have killed two armchairs under me." Which means that either he couldn't sit still or the armchairs were acutely gimcrack.

As a boy he dreamed of success in the worldly sense. After thirty years of struggle he won it, enjoyed it for about three years, and then began to die. He specially wanted social success. He won that, too, though he took no care of himself, was fat, and often dressed fantastically. And he dreamed of success with women. He won that also, several times.

By the way, in M. Benjamin's biography there is a strange silence as to his final relations with Eva de Hanska. New and sinister material about these came to light some ten or fifteen years ago, but M. Benjamin does not mention it.

One thing is to Balzac's credit in the enterprise of daily existence. He never made his wife unhappy — because he never lived with a wife. I have been reading *The Diary of Tolstoy's Wife* (Gollancz, 12s. 6d.). It is tragic. I always suspected that the domestic Tolstoy, even more than the domestic Dostoevsky, must have been insupportable. He was.

Balzac's attitude to his women was different. He adored and worshipped them. And he did not neglect them. Despite his vast creative obsession, his letters to Eva de Hanska were as the sands of the sea, and many of them are marvellous compositions.

As a boy Balzac dreamed also of a new kind of novel. His father, no ordinary man, dismissed fiction as "the opium of the West." Said Balzac (later) to his sister: "But supposing the novel, instead of sending people to sleep, was to wake them up; instead of amusing, was to instruct them . . . . There is a nobler task. For years past haven't I told you I would perform it? To-day I am certain that I will. . . . The physical, psychical, physiological, metaphysical picture of our society. . . . The historian of the nineteenth century won't be a man who will relate accounts of battles. It will be me."

He entirely changed the status of the novel. Nobody before him had ever written novels with the scope of his. And for eighty years afterwards nobody enlarged the scope further. And none even of the present enlargers of the psychology of the novel can draw a character as completely or as powerfully as Balzac. Nor do any of his present imitators approach him in interest.

231

Upton Sinclair has just issued *Boston* (Werner Laurie, 10s.6d.). A terrific theme — Saccho and Vanzetti. 730 close pages. It was Balzac who made that theme possible for a novelist. I have not read the whole of *Boston,* and I shall not. But I am in a position to affirm that Upton Sinclair has not risen to the Balzacian height of the theme.

Balzac created new characters as easily as Dickens, and far more completely. Look at Cerfberr and Christophe's biographical dictionary of the characters of Balzac. It has the convincingness of a dictionary of historical persons. 560 large pages! 2000 entries!

These 2000 fictitious individuals have the very semblance of reality. Balzac often succeeded in persuading himself that they indeed existed. Among the more memorable of them is Bianchon, the great doctor, pupil of the still greater Desplein. On his dying bed Balzac implored his nurse and his mother: "Bianchon! Summon Bianchon! He at any rate will save me!" This is what it is to be passionately a novelist.

In recent years I have re-read much Balzac. I regret to say that some of it dates. *Eugénie Grandet,* the wonder of one's youth, dates. Nor the power even of Balzac could render immortal its romantic sentimentality. But the best of the novels do not date. For instance, *Cousin Bette,* which I always held, and still hold, to be the finest of the lot. Never was achieved a better, more heroical, more ruthless, more touching portrait of a libertine than the portrait of Hulot in this masterpiece.

17 January 1929

I Take Up the Challenge of Detective Fiction Lovers

Life is full of pitfalls, into which even the most innocent may tumble. I said last week that Balzac's death was partly due to coffee. (It was.) I had no wish to hurt anybody's feelings. But the editor of *Grocery* wrote thus to me, on the very day of publication: "I was shocked and deeply grieved to learn that you attribute the premature death of Balzac to the excessive drinking of coffee."

Apparently I have dealt a cruel blow to the grocery trade. The fact is that, like G.K. Chesterton, who is a contributor to *Grocery,* I adore grocers.

A few weeks earlier I said here, of detective fiction, that in my opinion the new school of "mystery-mongers" is over-praised. (It is.)

This remark has caused much more serious trouble than my mean remark on coffee. I have indeed had many spirited protests from passionate admirers of the said school of novelists, and many injunctions to read various supreme modern masterpieces — named by name — and then humbly to reconsider my views in the light thereof. Every correspondent chose a different supreme modern masterpiece.

I was prepared to reconsider; but I had insufficient leisure to peruse all the masterpieces. Hence I obtained advice from an independent and erudite student of detective fiction. He told me to read J.J. Connington's *The Case with Nine Solutions* (Gollancz, 7s.6d.). He said the novel was representative, and among the best of the school. I have read it.

But before reading it I took the precaution of re-reading an older masterpiece of detection — Emile Gaboriau's *L'Affaire Lerouge*. I read this work in English as a youth. I read it again in French in 1910, and now I have read it a third time. It is over sixty years old. You can judge its antiquity by the fact that one of the characters is saved from a nervous breakdown by running into a doctor's and getting himself bled. But the novel still vigorously lives. It held me once more.

The basis of the plot is far older even than the book: substitution of infants soon after birth, in this instance one half-brother for another half-brother! (Gaboriau very persuasively exonerates himself from a possible charge of conventionality.)

The dénouement is delayed because, out of regard for a girl's honour, the accused man would not establish an alibi! What is even worse, the plot depends on two enormous coincidences. The amateur detective — there were amateur detectives before Sherlock Holmes — happens to live in the same house as the assassin! And the examining magistrate happens to be madly in love with the aristocratic girl, who is madly in love with the accused man! A trifle thick, or steep? Yes. And further, the murder is insufficiently motivated.

Nevertheless, the narrative sweeps you swiftly and irresistibly along, because, the coincidences and the one defect of motivation being condoned, it shows a consistent logic, and also it has a continuous powerful human interest, which interest is worked out with extreme thoroughness — perhaps with excessive thoroughness.

The characters are conceived with some originality, and convincingly drawn. The amateur detective, the examining magistrate, the two half-brothers and their astounding patrician father, the noble girl, the expensive wanton, and the dying mother of the assassin, are *created*. You are genuinely concerned about their destinies.

The scene of the discovery of the crime, and the first activities of the amateur detective, are brilliantly presented. All the detective parts are indeed excellent. But in the scheme of the book they are not more important than the human drama; nor are they developed at such length as the human drama. Take away the entire business of detection, and the book would remain a good, sound, old-fashioned emotional novel. Gaboriau was a novelist, not merely a clever amateur detective.

I had set a high standard for Mr. Connington to reach. But of what use is a standard if it is not high? *The Case with Nine Solutions* is based on the mad passion of two men for one woman. It is a murderous work, for four assassinations — three by one man — occur in it within quite a brief period. Three of these homicides are insufficiently motivated, and I am not sure about the fourth. In my experience real people do not go about committing capital crimes with the nonchalance of Charlotte cutting bread-and-butter. The dose of blood is exaggerated. Nor, to-day, would a correct dénouement be delayed because, out of regard for the honour of a girl, an accused man will not establish an alibi.

Still, Mr. Connington has a fairly logical mind, and he has unquestionably developed and resolved his plot with an unusual and satisfying ingenuity. It is agreeable to watch the narrowing down of the nine solutions to one solution.

His opening scene in the fog is very well done; though of course fog in a detective novel is a rather facile device. The clues are marshalled with a truly adroit misleadingness, to which no exception can be taken. And so on.

But I cannot say that I was particularly interested. As early as page 8 Mr. Connington impaired my respect for his knowledge of the world by the strange assumption that in moving a telephone-receiver nearer to you, you also move the telephone-bell nearer to you! A detail, but disquieting. More grave, the series of murders seem to leave all the people implicated or bereaved in a state of unperturbed calm. No excitement even in the great provincial town where these enigmatic murders happen! One must suppose that murders in that neighbourhood were part of the daily round, the common task.

The (innocent) husband of the murdered woman went to his job just as usual the day after the first horrifying crime, and instead of rushing to the police waited for the police to come to him. He was a chemist (not an apothecary), and the police found him sitting before a delicate balance. Again, if there were four sensational violent deaths, there must have been four sensational inquests. Mr. Connington says nothing about any of them. And so on.

But my main adverse criticisms of the story are that the human repercussions of its events are simply not handled; and that only one character has any life, the chief constable of the borough. He lives. The rest do not. The book is inhuman. If a jig-saw puzzle has emotional quality, then *The Case with Nine Solutions* has emotional quality. If not, not.

The story is flat; it has no contours. And the writing is as flat as the story. I do not deny that the thing can be read. It has some attraction, but no attraction of emotion. It has employed the invention of the author, not his imagination. A tragedy is not a tragedy until it moves you. This book has four tragedies, and you do not care twopence.

The mystery-mongers of 1929 ought to understand that detective-novelists are subject to the same great principles as other novelists. One of these principles is that a good novel cannot be made out of puppets. I shall have to try another mystery-monger.

24 January 1929

Idleness and Dawdling

I find that I am not yet out of the wood of my recent article on Balzac. Last week I dealt with one criticism. Now Mr. James Douglas, editor of the *Sunday Express*, has emerged on a weekday with a most scandalous article. In calling the article scandalous I do not refer to its personalities, which, being merely the product of James Douglas's characteristic undisciplined didacticism, are innocuous and even touching. I refer to the anti-work attitude of the article.

I wrote: "It is generally believed that Balzac died, at fifty, of work. But I doubt if work ever killed anybody. Balzac's death was due rather to his insane methods of work, and to excessive coffee."

James Douglas says that people are killed by work. He talks of

234

"work-addicts" who work "right around the clock," their arteries hardened, their blood-pressure high, their heart muscles enfeebled. I have not met one. Nor had I lunatics in mind. No one could work the clock round for more than three days. And in any case literary work never hardened the arteries, nor increased the blood pressure nor enfeebled the muscles of the heart.

James Douglas asserts that Dickens died of work. He did not. Dickens, of a very histrionic temperament, had a passion for exhibiting himself, which passion, together with his desire for money, led him to give incessant readings. He continued to give readings when his health was such that he had to be followed about by a doctor. It was these readings that killed him.

Perhaps the everlasting worry of publishing early instalments of his novels before the novels were anything like finished hastened his demise. The scramble for money, and the totally unnecessary scramble in work, was more strenuous in those days than to-day. But Dickens could have done his work easily enough if he had kept his energy for his work. He didn't. Trollope worked harder than Dickens, and work did not kill Trollope.

If authors die too soon, the reason is that they have not learnt how to live. Provided the body is sensibly treated, idleness of the brain means simply rusting of the brain. Few authors know how to treat their bodies sensibly. Witness the number of them who wake up exhausted and cannot even begin to work till the afternoon: sure proof of an idiotic way of life. For myself I have not worked after dinner for over a quarter of a century. Nor would I.

James Douglas's article is scandalous because it is an apology for idleness and dawdling, the sins of an age which exults in cocktails and bed at 2 a.m. after a wanton waste of four to six hours of eternity; an age whose great schools and universities frown on work. I cite the case of a young man who made a century at cricket, and before he left the field received three offers of assistant-masterships in public schools.

I have just read W.B. Trites' novelette *Ask the Young* (Gollancz, 5s.). A tale of two idling dilettanti which in its first part very amusingly shows the nature of the fruits of sloth. It contains also a brilliant description of the city of Malaga. The second part, however, slips into American domestic sentimentality and stays there until within a few pages of the end, which is good.

I see signs of Mr. Trites becoming the rage of the high-brows; but I doubt his capacity to stay the course. Still, he has said things that wanted saying. He is anti-sloth. He displays the so-called cultured youthful manners of the age as barbaric and the very negation of culture.

I have just read Edith Sitwell's new poem, *Gold Coast Customs* (Duckworth, 5s.). In its intense individuality, its frightening freshness of vision, its verbal difficulties, its implicit bitter ironies, its disdain of the casual, careless reader, it stands by itself. What a horrid picture of barbarism! But the depicted barbarism of the Gold Coast is rivalled by the barbarism of W.B. Trites' pair of cultured dawdling lovers.

I have just read Julian Hall's *Alma Mater, or the Future of Oxford and Cambridge* (already reviewed in this paper). Julian Hall endorses H.G. Wells's phrase about "the waste of seriousness" at our ancient universities. He says that youth is sceptical. He says "The sceptic has no sense of certain activities as having more claim on him than others." A rather profound remark!

And it is to this generation, thus so poignantly characterised by its elders and by itself, that James Douglas scandalously depreciates or deprecates work! The first thing that this generation has to learn, and has not yet been taught, is the difference between work and play and the relative unimportance of the latter.

And I have just read *The Goodman of Paris* (Routledge, 12s.6d., a comely tome), Eileen Power's admirable translation of the late-fourteenth-century French compendium of housewifery, cookery, and conjugal demeanour, *Le Ménagier de Paris*. (There is a grammatical error in the preface.) This hitherto neglected book is delightful. It gives a surprisingly effective and complete picture of domestic ideals, manners and customs in the middle age. It is meet to be read by the discriminating.

The picture, obviously truthful, inspires one with no desire to go back with G.K. Chesterton and live in the middle age. It would certainly affront the wassailers of even the staidest cocktail party; and I admit that the young wife for whom it was composed could not have had a very joyous time if she seriously endeavoured to live up to the goodman's teachings.

Her perfect husband must have been very trying in his demands for all the virtues and all the humilities in his mate. Implying throughout that virtue is its own reward, he indeed fails adequately to motivate the ultra-righteousness which he imposes on the defenceless young thing. And yet sometimes when I view the antics of our sceptical irresponsible youth (and their complying elders) of the present enlightened day, I am inclined to think that a step backward for six months into the era and the austere rule of the Goodman of Paris would not be a wholly evil experience for us all.

About that word "motivate." I used it last week, and I have been vituperated for using it by classical scholars, authors, grave journalists, and members of the learned professions: who throw doubt on its authenticity and condemn it as ugly. It is not uglier than irritate, desecrate, palpitate, procrastinate, or ipecacuanha.

As for its authenticity, I beg to announce to these misguided and imperfectly erudite cavillers that it is a good English word, that it has been in constant use for sixty years at least, that important writers have employed it, likewise contributors to such august periodicals as *The Edinburgh Review, The Contemporary Review,* and the (late) *Athenaeum,* that there is no alternative verb, and that I propose to go on using it. I will not guarantee not to use it next week.

31 January 1929

A Girl as a Master of Realism

At this day there is a breach between the historical novelist and the more enlightened section of the British public, because the British public has educated itself to the point of enjoying realism, while historical novelists have not yet educated themselves to the point of producing realism.

The German historical novel flourishes in both Germany and Britain, for the reason that German authors can convey the sense of the past with realism (or a fair imitation of realism), whereas British authors are still under the immense shadow and prestige of Walter Scott, that great sentimentaliser of human nature who had to be picturesque at any price. (Compare Scott's waxwork heroines with the Ugly Duchess.)

I am not using the word "realism" to signify the sordid. Certainly not! If I were, I should suggest that the fantastic libertine careers of, say, Cardinal Beaton and Archbishop Hamilton might provide rich material for a young novelist who had a taste for "realism" and for Scotland in the sixteenth century. By realism I mean the business of attaining grandeur while not departing from truth to nature.

I can illustrate what I mean and what I don't mean by a reference to a very "modern" work — The Set-up, by Joseph Moncure March, just published by Martin Secker in a limited edition of 2000 copies at 10s. 6d.

Mr. March is now famous or notorious as the author of The Wild Party (out of print), a work which has had a quite considerable success of scandal in London circles regarding themselves as cultured and advanced, where scandal is as welcome as cocktails.

The publisher describes The Set-up as a "narrative poem." But it is never poetry. It is hardly verse. It is prose divided into short lines (frequently of only a single word — and that a monosyllable), rhymed when a rhyme is easy, unrhymed when a rhyme is difficult, and rarely rhythmical. The author has been influenced by Edith Sitwell, but her spirit and her poetry have entirely escaped him.

The story of a crooked American boxing-fight between Pansy, the nigger, and Gray, the sailor, ending with violent death in the subway! Not in the least scandalous; scarcely a reference to women! A magnificent theme, full of heroical possibilities! The work is true to certain aspects of life, but it does not once attain grandeur. Hence it misses what I should define as realism.

There are a score of prize-fight reporters in Fleet Street who could have done the thing as well, or better, if the editorial command had gone forth to them to do it thus.

The book is without importance. It is not untrue, but it is without emotion. Having read it, one is inclined to address Mr. March in terms of a quotation from himself:

> "Don't try to pull no rough stuff,
> See? — "

Now I read last week, on the recommendation of a fellow-critic, a historical novel which seems to me to be realistic in the full and the best sense. It is modestly epical, and it is also in the main true to life. It has realism as well as emotional beauty, together with some grandeur, and the author never falls into the German error of confusing the realistic with the sordid. Vivandière, by Phoebe Fenwick Gaye (Martin Secker, 7s. 6d.). A first novel, I believe; and official information is given that Phoebe Fenwick Gaye is a girl "in her earliest twenties."

Miss Gaye has not been afraid of a tremendous theme: the march of the Napoleonic grande armée to Moscow, its sojourn in the enigmatic and deserted city, and its disastrous retreat thence home to France. She has even crossed the Beresina with her fleeing rabble of starved soldiers.

The retreat as a whole, and the Beresina in particular, has often been done before, both in memoirs and in fiction, with overwhelming effectiveness. Balzac did the Beresina in a few supreme pages of horror. But Miss

Gaye has had the prudence and the discretion to see the affair chiefly as a background to the individual adventures of her heroine Julie, the *vivandière*. It is only when she temporarily abandons this plan, as in the dialogue of horses (p. 124) and the historical disquisition (beginning with Ney and Davout) between pp. 261-267 that her grip of the reader loosens.

The descriptions — as of the scavenging among the dead, the first sight of Moscow, the looting in Moscow, the burning of the Khovansky house, the three frozen-dead Khovansky women in the coach, the bird-haunt — are beautiful, and never forced by heightened phrasing into the bravura of the literary performer. They keep the natural note; they convince; and they please.

Occasionally Miss Gaye uses a colloquial letter from one character to another to achieve indirectly a narrative end. Thus the lack of discipline in the *grande armée* in Moscow is most admirably rendered by means of an officer's letter to a brother officer. And she can be terribly sinister, as in the conversations between jealous wives and their surviving soldier-husbands who, after incredible sufferings of body and mind, have regained the domestic hearth.

As for the story of Julie, it is a love-story, with a tragic close impossible to foresee. Julie was a sinful creature; she willingly loses her innocence under a strange misapprehension; and she commits arson in a fit of rage. But she has the master virtues of cheerfulness and kindliness. And Miss Gaye is determined to maintain her in the reader's full sympathy. Perhaps too determined; for now and then Julie's essential goodness transcends the faulty average of nature — and topples down into sentimentality.

Withal *Vivandière* is indeed a genuine book. It may be immature; it is sometimes. But it has originality, form, coherence, and sustained imaginative power. The writing will appeal to amateurs of style. Phrase after quiet phrase sticks in the memory. "The *investigating* flames" (in Julie's arson). "Villages were deserted when they [soldiers] came up to them, the inhabitants already warned by *the telegraphic thrill of fear.*" *Vivandière* is a novel which one can recommend with some confidence.

I point out to the publishers that as the book has no list of chapters and no running chapter-titles or chapter-numbers, reference back to passages is wantonly made difficult. Why this negligence?

I have offended once more. It is over eighty years since the death of Thomas Frognal Dibdin, the zestful but inaccurate bibliographer, and here is one of his descendants in quite a pet because I referred to Thomas as a book "maniac." Descendants of even third-rate famous men are apt to be too sensitive — and to exaggerate the importance of their forbears. But is Mrs. Violet Dibdin de la Rivière aware that Thomas, before me, applied the word "mania" to his charming foible? Has she read his best-known work, *Bibliomania*? Let her answer Yes or No.

7 February 1929

Slack and Self-Centred Youth

About the idleness and dawdling which I discussed a couple of weeks ago. A young correspondent (who need not have remained anonymous — unless

238

indeed he feared the British Medical Council's passion for seeing self-advertisement in the most innocent printed letter from a doctor) has stated in these columns that he dances and drinks cocktails, but that such activities do not constitute the whole of his daily existence.

I hope he does dance, and I do not object to his drinking cocktails. I did not suggest that the younger generation spends all its time in dancing and drinking. For myself, I dance. And I also drink a cocktail upon occasion. But I have seen specimens of the younger generation gulp down as many as five cocktails quickly in succession.

What I do object to is the regular habit of cocktails (though there are more harmful beverages than a dry cocktail), persistence in late hours, and indulgence (disastrous to sustained work) in "week-ends."

A few days ago I received a circular from a night-club (to which I belong) containing the following words: "At the suggestion of *many* members who have commented upon the difficulty of obtaining entertainment after 2 a.m. ... the Club will remain open, and the Band will in future play until 3 a.m." (My italics).

I ask the plain question: After these 3 a.m. revels, what happens to one's work the next day?

But in the article upon which the correspondent animadverts I was talking about creative writers. Now I will not assert that creative writing is the hardest and most exacting work in the world; but I am convinced that there is no harder or more exacting work.

I speak with some experience, for I have done, and do, other kinds of work than creative writing. I say that business men, for instance, simply do not know what the hardest possible kind of work is. Often I have sat down to work in the very height of good fettle, and at the end of three hours have found myself utterly and completely exhausted.

Men of business can transact business all day, every day. Painters can paint all day, at one picture in the morning, at another in the afternoon, according to the light. Executive musicians can practise their instruments eight or ten hours a day. A chemist can toil in his laboratory for indefinite periods continuously. A creative writer cannot work these hours (except in bursts) and produce his best stuff. He just can't do it. The reason is partly that he is creating out of himself, but more because the required degree of intense concentration is so extreme.

Therefore a creative writer must watch with the closest attention his bodily condition, upon which his mental and imaginative condition depends. If his brain is deranged by alcohol, or if he stops up late and deprives himself of sleep, his work will seriously suffer.

A barrister may stay up and drink and still give a fair or even a brilliant show in court next day. This is not true of a creative writer. If a creative writer maltreats his body one of two results will occur. Either his work will be inferior to his best (and remain so for ever on the printed page), or he will scrap the day's task and do it afresh. The first result is permanently deplorable; the second involves waste. Both results will damage his self-respect.

More than any other sort of worker, the creative writer must make sacrifices to the end of keeping his machinery in thoroughly efficient order. More than any other sort of worker he has to remember that the great goal cannot be reached without a constant subordination of momentary impulses to the main purpose.

I maintain, out of a first-hand knowledge of the facts, that a large proportion of young men (and women), from slackness, from weakness, from a fundamental scepticism, fail to arrange their daily existence in a manner to ensure creative efficiency, that they neglect their machinery, and that the consequences of such neglect are apparent in both the quantity and the quality of their output.

Why are so many books so slight? Why are the ends of so many books inferior to the beginnings? Why do books sag in the middle? Why is the mere writing of them frequently so careless? Because the authors, owing to their way of life, have no margin of strength for a creative crisis.

The creator should always have something up his sleeve for an emergency. Too many young writers live right up to, and beyond, the edge of their creative income. They have no margin.

If you choose to say that I am demanding that creative writers should submit to martyrdom, I shall answer that it is a martyrdom mitigated by subtle and deep satisfactions.

In any case the last thing I should ask of creative writers is that they should cut themselves off from life. One of my complaints against them is their timidity before the spectacle of existence, and in particular their repudiation of plain non-artistic persons. They live too much among themselves, taking in one another's washing, and mooning around under the false pretext of their need for meditative reflection.

Not 10 per cent. of imaginative writers have acquired, by mental exercise and self-discipline, the power to concentrate the mind for a single hour upon any given matter. Many of them retire solitary to a room or to the streets to "think," and they don't think. They allow their minds to wander agreeably at large, like a young woman in an empty cathedral, because they have never mastered their thought-apparatus.

And their taste in humanity is not sufficiently robust. They cannot tolerate this kind of individual, not having grasped the paramount fact that it is the business of a creative writer to tolerate, and to tolerate sympathetically, every kind of individual. How else should he arrive at the knowledge and the compassion necessary for a fair portrayal of the world?

The world is coherent; every section of society affects every other section. A just perspective cannot be obtained without some knowledge of all sections. A breakfast in a semi-detached house in Putney is just as much "life" as a cocktail-bar or a night-club at 2 a.m., or a refined party of high-brows who can talk only about the arts. "Life" is a pretty big affair. Let creative artists sample it extensively. If they have the right organising skill they can well do so without injuring their machinery by any sort of excess.

14 February 1929

The Power Behind Big Book Prices

The Jerome Kern sale of books and manuscripts, recently concluded in

New York,* presented one of the most remarkable phenomena in all the exciting history of book-auctions. Nearly every item showed a rise in value, and many showed a tremendous rise. While prices of shares on the New York Stock Exchange were shooting aloft in a manner to startle the entire world of speculators, the prices of books and manuscripts were outsoaring them, and some rose so high that it seems as if, being out of sight, they could never come down again.

An eighty-page manuscript of Charles Lamb's was sold for £9600 which had been purchased only a short while ago for the odd £600. (In matter this manuscript was by no means of the first interest.) Even the breathless ascension of Margarine Union shares on the London market is a dull trifle compared with this.

A number of other items provided thrills for the bibliomaniac; but the dispassionate and sane observer was probably less moved thereby, because the items were signed with fashionable names, and to follow the fashion, especially in America, is always very expensive. For which reason, the bidding up of a mere four-page letter of Edgar Allan Poe's to £3900 must certainly be accounted the supreme event of this mighty auction. For Poe is still not a fashion in America, and a letter written by Nero after fiddling over incandescent Rome, could hardly have fetched more than the Poe epistle.

I doubt whether the great American book-buying people would be very well acquainted with the name of Poe were it not for the solid and warm esteem in which he has always been held by critics in Britain and France. European opinion has saved more than one American genius from American oblivion.

The price of the Poe epistle has an implication. Prices are affected more by literary prestige than by anything else. It is the best critics who are ultimately responsible for prices at literary auctions. It follows that there are two publics, the large public, which does not know and the small public which does know and is prepared to back its conviction of knowledge in the sole way possible to a financial age.

You say: Well, of course there are two publics – everybody is aware of that. Granted. But everybody does not imaginatively realise it. And the paying of £3900 for a four-page letter of Poe's brings home to the imagination of everybody the fact that the small knowledgeable public does indeed exist and is indeed extremely powerful.

The apotheosis of the Poe item has emphasised for me the real importance of two recent books destined for the small public – books which I have enjoyed and which have humbled me, though neither of them will reach a circulation of a million copies.

The first is W.H. Hadow's *Collected Essays* (Oxford University Press, 15s.). Sir William Hadow, a composer, is best known as a critic of music, and as such only Ernest Newman (in my opinion) can rank with him. Nearly all the book is given to music; but not all the book consists of essays; some of the contents are lectures (three of them delivered in Texas). Lectures, being composed for hearing, lose a little in reading; but these do not lose much. What a solace, to people like myself who yearn after erudition

* At the Andersonian Galleries, January 7-10.

without the least hope of achieving it, to read an erudite work which is at once admirable in form and taste, and lit up by wit and fancy!

No pedantry in this book, no "parade of learning." Its instilling of knowledge, and of criteria of judgment, into the reader is conducted quite painlessly — nay, it produces sensations akin to those of going away for a week's holiday to some urbane paradise of which one has heard, or through which one has passed by night in the train.

Sir William gathers all the other arts together around music. He is extremely clever, and clever enough not to be too clever. He knows, but he also feels — and feels with intense but controlled emotion. I am grateful to him for a hundred passages. He begins right away on page one with six ironic lines about criticism that are a delight to the intelligence. I owe him thanks for authoritatively confirming my long-held suspicion that that solemn composer, Bruckner, who is continually being preached to us, is a mediocrity. I wish he could have condemned Mahler also; he doesn't.

Sir Hubert Parry could have knocked spots off Mahler in any branch of musical composition. But then Parry was a mere Briton. Perhaps the most valuable and influential thing in the book is the appreciation of Parry (whose book *The Art of Music* is, for me, the finest, kindest eye-opener to ignorant amateurs in the English language).

Sir William Hadow dates the modern renascence of English music from 1880, when Parry's *Scenes from Shelley's 'Prometheus Unbound'* was performed at the Gloucester Festival. I do not think that Sir William overpraises Parry, but I think that he is a shade too benevolent towards Brahms.

The volume is marked by one serious omission. It ought to have contained an essay entitled "Are we a musical nation?" with an answer in the negative. *Collected Essays* is a book for everyone with sense enough to attend a good concert, and sensibility enough to enjoy the same; and all concert-goers ought to read it.

The other book is the late Professor W.P. Ker's *Form and Style in Poetry* (Macmillan, 10s. 6d.). For weeks and weeks this volume has been silently accusing me of not reading it. What with detective fiction, the habits of young writers, and other grave affairs, I found no chance to open it till last week. I knew it would impress and charm me; and it did. It has probably more erudition than Sir William Hadow's, and as much enthusiasm, but with slightly less grace. It consists of lectures and notes.

The twenty-four "London lectures" on form and style in poetry are an education. If, having read Milton, for example, you read Ker on Milton, you will return to Milton with the clarified vision of a man who has had a successful operation for cataract. I might be able to convey some notion of the book in ten or a dozen articles. But in one paragraph I cannot.

21 February 1929

New Enfant Terrible of Literature

Last week, determined to buy a new French book, I went into a large bookshop in Paris, opening and shutting the door with extreme rapidity, because of the intense cold — which by comparison made frozen London seem summery. I made the tour of that shop six times, without finding a single new book attractive enough to draw money from my pocket. There were plenty of fine old-fashioned works; but either I possessed them, or I had read them, or I positively intend to die without reading them. (For example, in the third category: Victor Hugo's *Torquemada*.) I noticed that the novel which has just won the Goncourt Prize* was in its hundred and fifteenth thousand, and this fact decided me to deprive myself of it; moreover many years have passed since the Goncourt Prize was given to a good book; its record is worse even than that of our Hawthornden Prize.

Lacking the moral courage to depart without a purchase, I bought an *Anthology of Ronsard and his School*, edited by an excellent critic, Auguste Dorchain, and I am now charmed with this book of 500 small pages; it is highly recommendable. But Ronsard and his school are four centuries away from being modern, and my experience persuaded me that interesting modern French literature had for the month ceased to exist.

Subsequent inquiries and gifts showed me that I was wrong. Two days after my sterile adventure there was published, and I received, an extremely stimulating affair: Paul Léautaud's *Passe-Temps* (Mercure de France, 12 francs). This book is worth not merely 12 francs but 12s. of the spare cash of any lettered person who can read French. I have performed the act known as "revelling" in it.

Léautaud, while a pillar of the staid *Mercure de France*, is nevertheless the terrible infant of French literature. He dedicates his book "To Solitude." He lives alone, hates mankind (not really), and adores animals. He is the declared foe of all solemn and pretentious nonsense, no matter who may sign it. He cares not one fig for any reputation. He is naughty and malicious and witty. He will write down anything that comes into his head. Some of what comes into his head has to be represented by dots. Some that is printed in French could not conceivably be printed in English. Much is grossly and wilfully unjust. But who minds? Not I, at any rate. For at bottom Léautaud is a kindly cynic, and he has taste and the maddest courage. He has published little, and only one novel — scandalously based on the life of his parents.

The present book is made up of sketches (various, including one on the death of Charles Louis Philippe, author of the celebrated, superb and untranslatable *Bubu de Montparnasse*), bons mots, remarks, and anecdotes. There is a delicate account of a young stray dog of the female sex, who became the mistress of Léautaud's study. He says that for three months he wrote nothing, devoting all his evenings to contemplation of the animal. She had a gourmand's passion for books. Léautaud bestowed on her twenty volumes of the (alleged) poetry of the fecund ballad-monger Paul Fort, and at the rate of three a week she ate them all. Not a leaf was left. "Rarely," says he, "has a literary work been so appreciated." Léautaud's *Pastimes* make a morsel than which nothing more diversely diverting is likely to be published for a long time to come.

Two other new books, both novels, were indicated to me as having at once real value and a certain vogue with discerning readers. The first, *Belle de Jour*, being by Joseph Kessel (the author of a very fine short story,

---

* *Maurice* by Constantin Weyer.

Mary of Cork, which I lauded in this place last year), I read at once. It has a singularly repellent theme; it is composed and written with skill; but in my opinion it never attains beauty and it never convinces. I therefore regard it as a failure.

The second novel, *Amour, Terre Inconnue*, which I read immediately after the first, is by a new author, Martin Maurice. Its theme (the eternal triangle + jealousy + masses of physical lore) is very efficiently handled. It convinces, but in my opinion never attains beauty, and I therefore regard it as a failure.

These novels have been warmly praised by competent and severe critics such as Paul Souday of *Le Temps*. They are published by an entirely reputable firm (Gallimard) which during the last ten years has probably put forth more fine literature than any other firm in France. French taste is not (thank goodness!) as squeamish as English taste; and the literature of a country should be judged by its own, not by foreign, standards. Hence I will content myself with saying that the stark outspokenness of both novels would have made Zola's hair stand on end.

In a quite different class is Drieu La Rochelle's *Blèche* (Gallimard, 12 francs), which also was recommended to me. La Rochelle is chiefly a poet and essayist, and has published only one previous novel — not, I believe, of remarkable quality. *Blèche* has remarkable quality, and should be read, though the mere writing is sometimes rather obscure. Nothing could be more commonplace than its theme — the relations of a typewriting girl and her employer. But nothing could be less commonplace than the handling of the theme. The flavour of the book is strange and mournful. The story finishes, as it should finish, in sheer ordinariness. No rending of the reader's heart at the close! *Blèche* held me firmly throughout. It has originality, power, and a consistent beauty.

I wonder what Professor F.C. Green, of Toronto University, thinks or would think of the above modern French novels. Professor Green has just published *French Novelists. Manners and Ideas. From the Renaissance to the Revolution* (Dent, 7s. 6d.). This book, which intimidated me until I "got into" it, is so excellent that its author owes to the Imperial public a sequel dealing with the period from Balzac to Proust.*

The novel in its earlier forms, unlike the drama in its earlier forms, has been utterly outclassed by later developments. I could never, till I read Professor Green, discover much interest in the pastoral novels, the crude satirical novels, the equally crude propagandist novels, etc., etc., of the 16th and 17th centuries in France. For me the first "real" French novel was Prévost's *Manon Lescaut*. It still is. But Professor Green has considerably and agreeably enlightened me on the inwardness of its forerunners. And on the subject of the two greatest and most influential French novels of the 18th century, Rousseau's *La Nouvelle Héloïse* and Bernardin de St. Pierre's *Paul et Virginie*, he is truly magnificent — he is lyrical. I doubt whether any modern novel, and particularly any modern French novel, will rank historically with these prodigiously revolutionary works. Since Balzac, since Zola, the French novel has lost amplitude. The English novel has not. We are muddling through.

---

*In 1931 Green published *French Novelists From the Revolution to Proust.*

28 February 1929

A Good Play Becomes a Better Novel

A few good novels and many bad ones have been turned into bad plays; and one or two good novels have been turned into fair plays. Many bad plays have been turned into worse novels. But a good novel adapted from a good play is a rarity. John van Druten's *Young Woodley* was a good play, and John van Druten's *Young Woodley* (Putnam's, 7s. 6d.) is a better novel.

In the realm of goodness, other things being equal, a novel will be more convincing, more truthful, than a play. The medium of the stage is so clumsy, so limited, and so absurdly difficult to control, that it puts authors at a terrible disadvantage in the effective conveyance of truth and beauty, a disadvantage for which no possible compensating advantages can fully atone. If Shakespeare had lived in a novel-writing age he would have written novels far greater than *Hamlet* is great as a play. He was obviously worried by the restrictions of the stage, but though he often tried to break through them, they were often too much for him.

All modern authors who habitually produce both plays and novels produce better novels than plays. What play of Galsworthy's can rank with *A Man of Property*? Somerset Maugham's *Of Human Bondage* is simply in a different class from even the best of his plays.

John van Druten seems to me to be a pioneer. It was an original scheme to try to turn a good play into a good novel. Van Druten had a sound reason for making the attempt. The Censor had forbidden public performance of the play. Why the Censor forbade it is part of the enigma of the universe. Nobody has ever squared the circle. Nobody has ever explained why the Censor banned *Young Woodley*. However, the Censor, to his credit, admitted error; and a good play, for once, enjoyed vast adventitious publicity. But meanwhile the author had begun to work on the novel; he was right to finish it.

Of course *Young Woodley* (the novel) ought to be judged entirely apart from *Young Woodley* (the play). But this is impossible. "Everyone" saw the play. ("Everyone" is a word of very elastic meaning. In the present case I estimate that "everyone" means about one per cent. of the electorate. Such is popularity in letters!) The play has somehow entered into the general consciousness. Good plays are so few that, having seen one, you cannot get it out of your head. It sticks.

Young Woodley has stuck. You recall it throughout the perusal of the novel. Nearly everywhere the novel easily surpasses the play. You feel that the novelist is at his ease, whereas the dramatist was hampered. The creation of a work of art may be likened to a prize-fight between the artist and truth. The dramatist has to fight in a long overcoat and leggings. No wonder he is so often counted out! The novelist wears only a cotton fig-leaf. Some of the newer novelists wear nothing at all; but Van Druten is a newer novelist and is still decently clad.

His play differed from most good plays in that the first act was the worst. It had atmosphere but little or no drama, and scarcely any subject-connection with the later acts. The play indeed began with a theme which might be described as Puberty and Public Schools. It continued and ended as a simple love-story between a youth and an older woman. The opening of the novel is better than the opening of the play. Per contra, the love-scenes were better in the play than they are in the book. Which is not to the discredit of the author, but to the credit of the players, who even triumphed over imperfect production. It wanted some nerve to carry off a tender and highly dangerous love-scene within a few feet of an enormous window giving on a garden where husbands and other inconvenient persons might stroll past at any moment. The audience must have thought: "What inconceivable idiots are these twain to run this frightful risk!" The actors did provide the necessary nerve. Kathleen O'Regan and Frank Lawton, by their power, delicacy, sincerity, and infinite tact, not only conjured away the enormous window, but safely and brilliantly put over line after line which a momentary clumsiness would have ruined. No page in the novel will quite give you the marvellous sensations given by certain moments in the play.

But, with one other exception, everything else in the novel is better than in the play. The book is more coherent than the play. It is a love-story against a background of the secular public-school tradition as to which the author is justly so ironic; while the play is a pell-mell of two unsatisfactorily related matters which are too nearly equal in importance.

The exception is the character of the villain of the story, the housemaster Simmons. Mrs. Simmons in both the play and the book is admirably drawn. She is neither black nor white, but grey, a mixture of fine and ignoble impulses, often inconsistent, often a fool — in fact resembling most women — and most men. But Mr. Simmons in both the play and the book is all black, consistently ignoble, unimaginative, and cruel to the degree of mere wantonness. Such a man, though he may be found in life, is unsuitable for the rôle in the story to which he is appointed — unsuitable because too abnormal, too extreme. His existence shakes the moral foundation of the tale. Moreover the author has got his knife into him, shows him no mercy, in either play or novel. An author, being their creator, ought to have some natural compassion for all his characters. An author ought to strive after the large-heartedness of God.

Further, the repellent ignobility of Simmons infects the tale with a violent improbability, and the mind of the hearer and the reader with an unanswerable question: Why did such a nice girl as Mrs. Simmons marry such an offensive brute as Simmons? How, even as an inexperienced virgin, could she have been attracted by him? This unanswerable question which rises in the silence of the brain damages the very root of the verisimilitude of the story.

The reader or hearer is continually thinking, if perhaps only subconsciously: "It isn't true; it isn't true; because to begin with she couldn't possibly have married him." And no amount of enjoyment of fine passages, of conviction of minor truths, of laughter at witty phrasing, can make up for the harm done by the exaggeration of Simmons's obtuse malevolence. Within its own convention a story should always seem true. In so far as it does not seem true it fails. Thousands of stories about the sufferings of a kindly and refined woman married to a humourless, thick-headed tyrant have been vitiated by just this same unanswered question: Why in the name of sense did she marry him?

Withal, *Young Woodley* is a good novel, and a new, promising novelist has appeared among us via the stage.

7 March 1929

A Censorship By All Means, But —

"Our desire is to prevent the sale of those obscene prints and other publications which has become of late so alarming."

"There is no country in Europe of which the circulation of such articles is permitted with the same facilities as exist in this country [England] ."

"Men are sent out from London with indecent prints. They periodically visit the different country towns and attend the different fairs, races and markets . . . as a regular trade."

No! These quotations do not apply to the present day, whose decadence from Victorian purity is so often deplored by right-thinking persons. They have been culled by me from the House of Lords debates on the Bill which became the Act under which recent prosecutions of authors and publishers have been instituted. (Hansard. 3rd series. vol. 146.) The date is 1857, the very heart of the pure Victorian era. You may judge from them into what a foul mess of iniquity the Georgian era has sunk, in comparison with the chaste rectitudes of the Victorian!

The House of Lords debates were much more interesting than those in the House of Commons. Indeed, the Upper House was then, as it still is, the main bulwark of British liberty. The protagonists of the debate were Lord Chief Justice Campbell and Lord Lyndhurst. Campbell always hated Lyndhurst; but Lyndhurst, a peer of an acute mind and unsurpassed forensic skill, tore Campbell to pieces in argument, and compelled him to remodel his Bill.

Many passages in the grand shindy were extremely comic. And not the least comic was that in which Campbell fell on W.H. Smith for selling on his railway bookstalls *The Lady with the Camelias*. Campbell considered that Dumas' description of certain flowers was indecent! W.H. Smith was not the man to submit quietly to this kind of charge. He protested, and he won, and was characterised in the Lords as "a truly Christian gentleman." Hear, Hear!

It appears clearly from the debates that the Bill was chiefly directed against prints offered with a pornographic intention, rather than against books. Campbell stated that the Bill was meant "to apply *exclusively* to works written *for the single purpose* of corrupting the morals of youth." Lyndhurst predicted that the Act would be misapplied. We in 1929 can see how correct was his prediction.

Lyndhurst made various sagacious remarks. As that, "It is unwise and imprudent to poke into these questions and agitate the public mind concerning them." Also, "I am satisfied that the law as it stands is abundantly strong enough." Again, "There is not a single volume of that great poet [Dryden] which would not come under the definition [of obscenity] ."

For myself I would go further and say that there is not a single volume of Shakespeare, and very few fine novels, from Thackeray's to Aldous Huxley's, which would not come under the definition. The definition of

247

obscenity is so wide and so loose that hardly any book with any stuff in it could not be attacked under it. According to the law as it stands recent decisions have been perfectly justifiable. And any meddlesome idiot who chose to invoke the law might well obtain the suppression of 50 per cent. of the imaginative literature of the last hundred years.

And yet we are threatened with a further "strengthening" of the law. Why? Because one of the defects of the Anglo-Saxon temperament is a passion for interference with other people's tastes. The results of such interference are sometimes truly astonishing. Thus to-night, after a certain hour, I am allowed by law to buy a copy of the *Evening Standard* from a boy exposed to damp and rheumatism outside a newspaper shop, but I am not allowed to buy the same esteemed sheet within the shop. I submit. The fact is that as a British citizen I have developed law-abidingness into a positive vice.

In one category these interferers are too frequently — I do not say always — ridden by an obvious morbid obsession. The phenomenon is notorious. I have myself seen it peep forth in conversations with some of our leading interferers. I specially except from any charge of morbidity Sir William Joynson-Hicks, whose agreeable personality I admire — and I admire him even more because he is in my opinion the sole prominent full-blooded Tory in Parliament. A full-blooded Tory is a useful thing in the Legislature.

At the same time I do consider that Sir William is seriously over-endowed with the racial passion for interfering. Apparently I am not alone in this view. If he does ascend, against his inclination, to the House of Lords, he will find there opponents who will uncompromisingly oppose — very different from the half-hearted dilettanti of liberty in the Commons. In the Lords he will be less of a public danger.

Am I in favour of a censorship? Of course I am. No country can exist without one. I was asked the other day whether I would permit in Britain the unrestricted circulation of one of the most wonderful and original of modern novels, James Joyce's *Ulysses*. My plain reply was that I would not. It simply would not do. A censorship there must be. But I maintain that any form of censorship does some harm, and that our present censorship does immensely more harm than good. If the law relating to censorship is to be altered, it ought to be weakened, not strengthened. Nevertheless, I would not alter the law. (At the present juncture it might, despite excellent motives, be too easily altered for the worse.) I would leave it alone. I would entrust my liberty to its sane administration and to the tendency of all excessively drastic laws to fall into desuetude through their own inherent absurdity. As a fact the present law fell into partial desuetude from the moment it came into operation, for the reason that to apply it strictly would have meant its instant death from ridicule.

Modern fiction, with which I am particularly concerned, may offer occasional examples of unpermissible sinfulness, but on the whole it is much more "healthy," honest and tonic than Victorian fiction. Anyhow, no amount of interferingness will stop its march. And if current administration makes mistakes, these mistakes will sooner or later correct themselves.

The latest decision, ordering the destruction of Miss Norah James's novel *Sleeveless Errand* as obscene, was expected, and is probably unassailable under the letter of the law. The book is well planned, well written, and (I think) true to one kind of life. It lacks power and beauty. It is an absolutely merciless exposure of neurotics and decadents, and I should say that the effect of it on the young reader would have been to destroy in him or her all immoral and unconventional impulses for ever and ever. But it records realistically the chatter of a familiar type of persons who cannot express themselves at any time on any subject without employing words beginning with "b." It contains more profanity to the page than any other book I ever read. What the prosecution objected to was this excess. The Home Office ought to issue an edict stating arithmetically the percentage of profanity legally permitted to a novelist in dialogue. *Sleeveless Errand* has little importance, except that it reveals a new talent for fiction.

14 March 1929

The Domestic Novel Will Never Die

A woman, an experienced and abandoned reader, lamented to me the other day that the domestic novel was disappearing. I could not agree. At any rate I, who do indeed glance at novels now and then in my spare time, have observed no signs of it. The great majority of novels have been and will be chiefly domestic in matter. And historical novels are becoming more domestic; some of the latest are exclusively domestic. Even Tolstoy in *War and Peace* had to come down to the bedrock of domesticity in the end. To my mind the last hundred pages of that perhaps supreme work, dealing in the main with a very narrow domesticity, are the most poignant in it — and the most effective.

Also we must remember that domesticity has changed itself of late years. There are people who think, in some confused way, that cocktail parties are not domestic, whereas the tea-parties of yore were domestic. I do not follow the process of thought. Again, domesticity is now more scattered. Rents are higher; families have to be content with fewer and smaller rooms; hence they are apt to carry their domesticity abroad — to restaurants, trains-de-luxe, hotels. But domesticity remains domesticity. Can the imagination of man conceive anything more intimately and terribly domestic than a two-berth compartment in a train-de-luxe? I doubt it. Restaurants, cabarets, dance-floors are the setting for all sorts of purely domestic scenes — and don't we know it! Domesticity is inescapable. No novelist can escape it, or would if he could.

Of course I am well aware what the lamenting lady meant. She meant that the old-fashioned domestic novel was disappearing. Naturally it is. The old-fashioned everything is disappearing, and has been disappearing steadily for thousands of years. There was a time when the horse, in Egypt, was regarded as a dangerous innovation and had to conquer exactly the same sort of hostile suspicion which marked our attitude towards the automobile only 30 years ago. As the automobile compared with the horse, so the modern domestic novel compared with the old-fashioned domestic novel covers more ground and does more extensive work. If you would appreciate the difference between the new and the old, contrast, for instance, Lady

Russell's recent novel *Expiation* with the novels which she published in the first decade of the century. Nevertheless *Expiation* is a domestic novel if ever there was one.

But old-fashioned domestic fiction still survives. An excellent example of it is Lorna Rea's *Six Mrs. Greenes* (Heinemann, 7s. 6d.). This book is not a novel. Nor is it a collection of six short stories. It is a collection of six fictional sketches of three generations of the ladies Greene, a couple of each generation. An unequal book — all of it good, but some of it extremely good. The author has succeeded best with the oldest generation and the youngest. The first sketch is perfect. The second — a study of a case of cancer — lacks perfection because it finishes before the end.

The sixth sketch, of the wedding-day of Mrs. Hugh Beckett Greene, in addition to being perfect, is really brilliant. Its modernness could not be surpassed, and yet, strange to relate, there is no trace of what we euphemistically term "vulgarity" anywhere therein. It is "just sweet," and yet, again strange to relate, it never cloys, it is never untrue, never sentimental, never cowardly in avoiding psychological facts. Decency does not triumph over verisimilitude, nor verisimilitude over decency. Both are fully maintained. The thing should be a lesson to some of our cruder modernists in fiction. And we who are inquisitive and hopeful concerning the future of prose works of imagination may look forward with a certain confidence to seeing what Mrs. Rea will make of a novel.

Another author of domestic fiction which counts is the Norwegian Sigrid Undset, who lately received the Nobel Prize. Two of her novels, *The Garland* and *The Mistress of Hussaby* (the former is a sequel to the latter), have reached me. I am not sure whether they are sold in London by the Danish firm of Gyldendal or by Brentanos. But they can be had and they are worth having, despite the American translation, which carries clumsiness to excess. The publishers are reticent as to the identity of the translator, and their reticence is prudent. But they ought to have given some information about the foreign author, of whom we know naught except that she is a Nobel Prize-winner. Why publishers should be thus secretive I cannot understand. I will not, however, cease to gird against such secretiveness.

Sigrid Undset in these novels deals with domestic life in the fourteenth century in Norway. Her treatment is very modern, and would have appalled Walter Scott, if not Wagner. But she is dignified and decent withal. Substitute mead for cocktails and there seems to be little essential difference between domestic life in Norway in the fourteenth century and domestic life in London in the twentieth. I always suspected that the domestic immoralities were no Georgian novelty. Now I know it.

The author, though slow-moving, gets hold of you and keeps hold of you, and fully convinces you of the authenticity of her characters and their deeds. She shows sustained power quite extraordinary in a woman. Also she employs immense historical knowledge without advertising the same. I would I could read her in her own tongue, so that I might have been spared such English dialogue as "I know 'tis not only the evil spirits that are abroad this night!" The non-transliteration of proper names, too, is exasperating. Why write "Eirik" for "Eric," and "Lavrans" for "Laurence," and so on? Patient readers of Sigrid Undset will be rewarded.

Her latest novel is *The Snake Pit* (Knopf, 7s. 6d.)

If you would realise what life can be without domesticity, see M.P. Shiel's *The Purple Cloud* (new edition, Gollancz, 7s.6d.), which is the story of the only survivor of a world-catastrophe. In search of domesticity, the solitary fellow travelled all over the face of a world inhabited solely by corpses; he found it only when he found another survivor, of the female sex. Domesticity then set in, and not too soon. I read this novel with much admiration 28 years ago. I have just read it again. It has worn exceedingly well. The affair is stupendous in conception, and rather more than adequately executed. I call it grandiose, fearsome, and truly distinguished. Three other novels, not so impressive, by Mr. Shiel have also been republished by Gollancz: *The Yellow Peril*, *The Lord of the Sea* and *Cold Steel.*

21 March 1929

Sinclair Lewis, the Master of Rushing Narrative

The novels of Sinclair Lewis have always one admirable quality: they are *about* something. Not merely about certain people. They have a definite, important, and understandable theme, which affects whole classes and even whole nations. Of many novels you say: "It isn't so bad. It can be read. It is good, page by page. But what is it about?" You cannot ask this of a novel by Sinclair Lewis. He does not begin to write a novel until he is obsessed by a theme, and a big theme. ("Obsessed" is the word.)

Most of his principal novels are tremendous, smashing indictments of his native country: and the wonder is that — to the great credit of the United States — books so ruthless and so effective have achieved such immense popularity in America. The theme of *Dodsworth* (Cape, 7s.6d.) is the relative merits of the civilisation of the United States and of Europe and the reactions of the one civilisation to the other.

Sam Dodsworth, an automobile magnate, aged fifty, is the protagonist of the United States; Fran, his wife, aged forty, a grandmother before the end of the story, and an American citizen with some German blood in her, is the protagonist of Europe. She takes her half-unwilling husband to Europe. They see Europe together — and especially London, Paris and Berlin. The main theme of the book is illustrated by a secondary theme, the conjugal relations of Sam and Fran. Fran is immensely inferior to Sam in brains and in character. And the author's picture of her has the cruelty of justice. But Sam is in love with Fran — he is fool enough to forgive two of her adulteries.

This very bright young grandmother is curious, restless, exhaustingly energetic in her search for culture, and she keeps Sam out of the torpor into which, but for her, he would have fallen. Fran is rather better drawn than Sam. She is seen from the outside. Sam is seen from the inside, as a man sees a man, and the picture of him is less clear and less dramatic than hers. Fran is "presented" at once. Sam emerges slowly. In the end, however, he does emerge. The secondary theme is not as well handled as the main theme. Towards the close, while the destinies of the pair are being finally settled, one feels that the book is running along by a previously-acquired momentum and not by an ever-renewed motive force, as it should be.

One cannot say that Sinclair Lewis favours America against Europe — or the contrary. He is, for so impassioned a writer, most meritoriously impartial. Nevertheless, Sam makes some startling points in answer to Europe's accusation against America of materialism. "Not one in ten Europeans," says he, "who do go to America ever goes there to learn, to see what we have . . . . They go just to make money." The same cannot be said of Americans who go to Europe. On the other hand, Sam has a sledge-hammer to pulverise American hustle.

Dodsworth is a tract if you choose (so was *Babbitt*), but it is a tract in the form of a truly first-rate story. It is "good reading." Embark on it, and you are carried away on a swift tide, and you exult in the swirling stream under you. Sinclair Lewis has few equals as a master of rushing narrative — I can't at the moment think of any. He possesses also a wonderful style, in which he employs not only slang, but thousands upon thousands of picturesque and accurately descriptive metaphors and similes. His personages make long, very long, speeches to one another; yet the speeches are never dull — not for one line. Every sentence in them is a tonic.

He is at his best in sustained dithyrambic descriptions of complex senses. The pages (hostile) on the spectacle of New York as seen by Sam on his first return from Europe are simply marvellous. Nearly as good is the dreadful tirade on a sale in an American departmental store. The pictures are unscrupulously exaggerated, but how well they bring out the truth!

The verve of the entire book is overwhelming. One could discover many faults in it. No matter. The faults are reduced to trifles by its general, massive, creative force, by its immense, fecund inspiration, so charged with invention, wit, fancy, and a queer sense of the beauty of common things. You look forward to a new novel by Sinclair Lewis. You don't cry: "I shall have to read that." You say: "I have just got to read it — and at once." For myself, he has not disappointed me yet, and *Dodsworth* is no disappointment. The man is at the height of his power. And now I suppose that the whirligig dervishes of *The American Mercury* will begin to dance around and screech that I am sniffing once more at American literature.

Immediately after reading *Dodsworth* I read Mr. Sturge Moore's *Armour for Aphrodite* (Cayme Press). Mr. Sturge Moore, equally distinguished as a poet and as a critic, is generally regarded as "precious." He could not with any success rebut the charge. If he tried to do so, the very title of his new book would undo him. In his place I would have called the book simply *Liking Literature and the Arts*. In it the author seeks to free the faculty of artistic appreciation from the chains of fashion and of theory. He is against the "overweening exclusiveness of intellect," and in favour of the untrammelled exercise of aesthetic enjoyment. He understands the processes of creative art, what the artist is "after," and what the attitude of the enjoyer ought to be.

Interjected between his chapters are a number of aphorisms, and though some of them are not immediately helpful, others are lamps in a dark world. Here is one of the latter. "Beauty is rarely simple, *and always supposes completeness*." Think it over. Here is another: "To cherish beauty in memory *prompts us to seek it everywhere*." Think it over. Such lamps really do illuminate.

Anything less precious than the work of Sinclair Lewis could not easily be imagined. The preciousness of Sturge Moore's mind could not easily be exaggerated. Sinclair Lewis has a passion for wordly contacts. I doubt whether Sturge Moore would give three cheers for Sinclair Lewis, and I am of opinion that Sinclair Lewis would grow slangily restive under a prolonged dose of Sturge Moore. Nevertheless these two so-separated artists are both revealers of beauty — one on one side of the flawless sphere and the other on the other. Certainly I will not without reserve recommend *Armour for Aphrodite*; for the wrong man might get hold of it and then curse me, and I have an antipathy to maledictions. The book is not everybody's meat; but it is somebody's meat.

28 March 1929

It's Still the Novelist Who Delivers the Goods

America is still a wondrous place as a literary market (and of course in nearly all other ways). It has recently capped its wondrousness by establishing Lytton Strachey's *Elizabeth and Essex* as the best seller of all best-sellers. No novel comes anywhere near *Elizabeth and Essex* in popularity. Its closest rivals are, or lately were, *Sergeant Grischa* and *Joseph and his Brethren*. According to the latest information its sales are just upon triple those of *Sergeant Grischa*. (The figures are the result of counting the actual business done in the various books by one of the leading wholesale book-dealers in New York.) This phenomenon is truly remarkable, if not unique in the history of modern book-selling. Why the vast American public should have chosen *Elizabeth and Essex* for first favourite I cannot imagine. In Britain the book certainly occupies no such dizzy position.

Those ingenious and formidable brothers the Shuberts, who own hundreds of theatres — and somehow make them pay — not long since asked 30,000 of their patrons what had induced them to go to certain plays. Nearly 12,000 replied that they went on the recommendation of their friends; 6,918 were persuaded thither by newspaper advertisements, and 6,884 by theatrical criticisms. Only 1,200 were drawn by the magic of starry names. The other aids to theatre-going were negligible by comparison.

I should say that people buy or borrow books for much the same reasons as they visit plays, except that a name is assuredly more valuable in the book world than in the world of the theatre. It follows that the chief cause of the enormous popularity of *Elizabeth and Essex* was probably gossip among friends and acquaintances. But how did the laudatory gossip originate? That question will never be answered. All one can assert with any safety is that the second-ratedness of the book must have helped its vogue. (For *Elizabeth and Essex* is the least satisfactory of Lytton Strachey's works.)

Britons in their terrible insular conceit will naturally smile at the simplicity of soul which compels multitudes of Americans to read books that the majority of them cannot possibly appreciate. For myself, I would not smile. I would rather admire. Americans do try. They do show a genuine and urgent curiosity. If now and then in their quest of the right cultural thing they bite off more than they can chew, who are we to blame them?

253

They are not indifferent. We are indifferent, and that is the worst of Britons.

I am not surprised to learn that the triumph of *Elizabeth and Essex* over all fiction whatever in the land of hitherto-triumphant novelists is regarded in some quarters as a portent of the long-predicted fall of the novel as a literary form. For myself, I do not regard it as such. I regard it simply as a diverting accident. Many Elizabeths and many Essexes will have to outsoar best-selling novels before the complacency of novelists even begins to be disturbed.

In this age of social criticism, destructive and reconstructive, the novelists can and do deliver the wanted goods. Non-fictional writers rarely deliver the goods. For every non-fictional social writer who really impresses either the big public or the small public, there are at least a dozen novelists whom nobody can neglect. True, the big public are children, children love stories, and the novelists have the great advantage of being story-tellers. But this is not their only advantage. As a rule they write better than the non-fictionists. And in addition to being story-tellers they are critics and moralists. And as critics and moralists they are more effective than their rivals, not merely because they tell stories and write better, but because they know more and understand more about human nature and about social conditions. There is more and better moral sustenance in, for example, a *Dodsworth* than in twenty books by, for example, such a sound and interesting non-fictional writer as André Siegfried, who nevertheless has been very well appreciated in America.

Brains and imagination exist more abundantly in the heads of novelists than in the heads of other writers. This has been the state of affairs for quite a century and a half, and it still is. Until it is altered novelists will continue to hold the field. I see no real sign yet of any alteration. If *Elizabeth and Essex* had been a great book I could conceivably have accepted its success as some sort of sign. But it is not a great book; it is a little, carefully-wrought book on a great subject, and not comparable in either power or scope or insight or beauty to any one of lots of novels published in the last decade. Still, I am glad that it has risen so high in popular esteem, for it is considerably above the average of its kind.

And let not our novelists sit content and self-satisfied. The average novel of to-day may be superior to the average of the past — more true to life, more honest, more serious, composed with a more instructed and conscientious skill. But the average novelist of to-day is just as deficient as his average forerunner in the supreme attribute of imaginative power and the gift of creating beauty out of ugliness.

I read many novels about which I never write a word. I read one the other day without thinking to mention it. But I will mention it. *Sense and Sensuality*, by Sarah Salt (Gollancz, 7s. 6d.). Sarah Salt has a pseudonymic sound. Here is a novel of the latest fashion, gemmed with the fashionable profanity, and aiming to be realistic (as the too-facetious title implies). It is realistic in only a narrow sense. One cannot say that it is badly done, or that it is unreadable, or even dull. But it does not lay forcible hands on the reader, nor does it ever achieve beauty. Finishing it, the reader asks two questions: "Why did Sarah Salt write it, and, what on earth have I gained by reading it?" There is no satisfactory answer to these questions. *Sense and Sensuality* has a specious air of originality. But in ten years it will seem as old-fashioned as a newspaper of its own date. Withal, I would assert that it ranks not lower than the average contemporary sociological or historical work.

And for a specimen of the higher-than-average novel, I will mention *Two Made Their Bed*, by Louis Marlow (Gollancz, 7s. 6d.). I am not reviewing this novel. I say merely that its author has a mind, a mass of social information, an attitude, a judgment and a power of presentment which exceedingly few "serious" non-fictional writers could match. As for his dramatic sense and his sense of beauty, well, they could only be matched among authors of novels. A non-fictional study equal in merit to *Two Made Their Bed* would be noticed at length and with immense respect in all dignified organs of opinion. Nevertheless the name of Louis Marlow will be unfamiliar to many readers. Mr. Marlow has not yet reached general recognition. He will reach it.

4 April 1929

Every Biography Should Have Its Thrill

Many months ago in this column, writing on the subject of biography, I suggested that a short life of Alexander the Great ought to be done. Therefore when I received *Alexander the Great, a Biographical Study*, by E. Iliff Robson (Cape, 7s. 6d.), I felt rather excited. Alexander was tremendous. I would not urge that he was "one of the most remarkable men that ever lived," though he was. There have been so many extremely remarkable men — one may say incredible men — in the brief history of this small planet, that the phrase really means little. There have been hundreds of the most remarkable men that ever lived, and in all walks of life. Still Alexander, leaving out all comparisons, was a tremendous fellow, as soldier, statesman, physical organism, and public performer with a keen sense of the dramatic. And he was, too, very humanly imperfect: a fact which must help his biographer. As a subject he could, I think, hardly be bettered.

I expected great things from Mr. Robson. I have not received them. Mr. Robson evidently knows his theme; he is informed; he is a sound scholar; he seems to be, and no doubt is, impartial; he is not sentimental; he controls his theme, and never allows it to control him; he is a good corrector of legends and other falsities; he sins neither by exaggeration nor by diminution; he never gushes superlatives about his hero; he has all manner of estimable qualities. Also he writes well, if not with any shining distinction. But he managed to cool my sympathies from the start.

His book opens with a Preface, followed by an Introduction. I cannot see the need of both a Preface and an Introduction — particularly to a book of less than three hundred pages. I don't recognise the difference between a Preface and an Introduction. A short book ought to begin without preliminary palavers. The Introduction deals with the philosophy of history, and includes a definition of history. Why? Is not all this out of place? Then the first chapter begins: "The present chapter contains — " Why? Every chapter of every book might begin with the same words: "The present chapter contains — " Then follows more philosophy of history. The actual biography begins on p.35.

I could forgive all these nervous hesitations in making a real commencement if the body of the book had accorded with my notions of what such a biography ought to be. It does not. Mr. Robson seems incapable of doing the biographer's main job. He fails to present a coherent, integral picture of Alexander, or of his epoch, or of any of his spectacular deeds, battles, crises. He tells you lots *about* Alexander without showing you Alexander. His pages are not warm with the humanity of an individual. The subject surely demands some lyricism, and Mr. Robson cannot be lyrical. He is aloof. He walks around holding a balance and weighs facts with chemical nicety. But he would sooner die than be emotional. And when you have finished his book you say to yourself: "Well, I know what Alexander did and didn't do. Indeed I know all about him. But I do not know Alexander."

Hence the work is a disappointment. What Mr. Robson has done is negative. He has blurred for me Plutarch's picture of Alexander. You cannot read twenty pages of the doubtless inaccurate Plutarch without seeing and feeling Alexander himself. Whereas if Mr. Robson's book had had 3000 pages instead of less than 300, the reader would still never have seen and felt Alexander. It would be absurd to blame Mr. Robson because he does not possess the genius of Plutarch, but it is reasonable to blame him for undertaking a book for which he seemingly has not the primary qualification: the power to re-create. A biographer must be re-creative. Mr. Robson is not re-creative — not a bit, not for one line.

I have given some space to this life of Alexander because for me the entire question of biography is important, particularly to-day. The demand for biography is certainly growing. I mean short biographies, biographies of people who have been dead long enough to permit their biographers to be utterly truthful about them. I do not mean the interminable, ponderous, deliberately deceitful biographies of Englishmen and Englishwomen recently deceased, not one in fifty of which is worth one-fiftieth of the price charged for it, and not one of which is weighty save in the avoirdupois of the paper it is printed on, or spacious save in the dimensions of its page. The field for the first kind of biography is enormous, and so far a very large part of it has been totally ignored.

Mr. Robson has shown some originality in his choice of hero, but in my opinion he has failed in the treatment thereof. "Lives of great men all remind us —" wrote the world's nearly-worst poet.* Only the life of no great man will remind us of anything if the great man is not graphically presented in his proper environment, if the story is not rendered picturesquely, if it does not inspire. And what is the use of a biography if it does not inspire, if it does not communicate the sense of romance and the sense of greatness for good or for evil or both? A biography must be more than a collection, even an ordered collection, of facts. It must be a poem and it must be a sermon. It must procure for us a thrill.

A far more successful biography than Mr. Robson's *Alexander* is *The Tempestuous Prince: Hermann Puckler-Muskau*, by E.M. Butler (Longmans, 12s. 6d., illustrated). I could wish that Miss [?] Butler had exercised her evident gifts upon a subject with more popular prestige than this extraordinary feudal nobleman, who, born in the late eighteenth century,

---

* Longfellow, again.

survived till late in the nineteenth, and who was as good a landscape gardener as he was a writer and a lover. But Miss Butler has done well to revive the memory of the man. The surprising thing is that he should have been so soon and so completely forgotten by posterity. Miss Butler does not write any better than Mr. Robson. She probably knows no more of her subject and her period than he of his. But she paints pictures of a man and of a civilisation. She re-creates. She has form, and brightness, and she is not afraid to exult passionately in her second-rate theme. Her book ought to be reissued in handier shape at five shillings.

There is a deal more to be said about popular biography, but I must leave the enthralling matter at any rate until I have read the just-published English translation of André Maurois' book about it. My present view is that English biographers have something to learn from French. I think that the former are still intimidated by the gaunt ideals of the *English Men of Letters* (first) series. The second series is more human.

11 April 1929

There's Still Hope for Biography

Last week I discussed biography, compendious biography, popular biography, biography which should present living pictures of great or of highly reprehensible men set in the frame of their times. I have now read André Maurois' *Aspects of Biography* (Cambridge University Press, 7s. 6d.).

The volume comprises the 1928 Clark Lectures, at Trinity College in English, recomposed by the lecturer in his own tongue, and excellently translated back into English by S.C. Roberts.

Aspects of Biography is dedicated to the ineffable "J.J." — and those who do not know who "J.J." is, those who have not taken the trouble to witness his progresses through the streets of Cambridge, do not deserve to know who he is and will not be told by me.*

I will say only that he is an O.M., an Order which has had one or two narrow shaves of being sullied, but which so far has escaped.

André Maurois followed E.M. Forster in the Clark rostrum — a difficult man to follow; for Forster's *Aspects of the Novel* was a very glorious, humorous, sagacious affair. André Maurois has emerged from the ordeal with the success which one had the right to expect from his brilliant intelligence, an intelligence unsurpassed to-day in the field of letters. Nobody could be cleverer or saner.

The lectures are full of material for quarrels and argumentary duels, but the man who challenged would take his life in his hand. I reckon that André Maurois is one of the chief European authorities on the art-and-science of biography, if not the chief authority. He is a practiser as well as a preacher. He had his detractors both in France and in England; indeed in France he has been the object of a ferocious quasi-political vendetta. (But the scatheless object.) In Britain certain mandarins have charged him with being superficial.

* In fact, Sir J.J. Thomson, then Master of Trinity.

Of course, there are Britannic minds with an ineradicable conviction that what is neither dull nor long must be superficial. If André Maurois is superficial, I am all in favour of superficiality. In my opinion his biographies of Shelley and Disraeli are models of what the short biography should be.

Intensely readable, diverting, amusing, ironic, and re-creative, they have not been seriously impugned for inaccuracy. I don't care what any mandarin, or forty thousand mandarins, may say — I read them with zest. I was sorry to turn the last pages of them. And I feel fairly sure that they present pictures of their subjects as faithful as any we have had or are likely to have. They live.

As for *Aspects of Biography*, it is a pessimistic work. M. Maurois examines biography as a science and as an art: he examines autobiography; and he sees terrible possibilities of error everywhere. He appears to despair of getting at the truth about anybody or anything; but for myself I perceive no reason why we should not get at as much truth in biography as in any other matter. At least a biographer who knows his job, as M. Maurois does, ought to be able to offer a picture in which unavoidable error, by being evenly distributed, does not result in distortion.

M. Maurois quotes that misesteemed writer Herbert Spencer in stating the most dangerous pitfall laid by nature for the biographer: "By leaving out the humdrum part of the life, forming that immensely larger part which it had in common with other lives, and by setting forth only the striking things, [the biographer] produces the impression that it differed from other lives more than it really did. This defect is inevitable."

Well, I admit that the defect is very grave; it is the graver because we all have a tendency to imagine that what we don't know is magnificent (*Omne ignotum pro magnifico,* if I may be excused for declining into a classical tag — my first offence of the kind). But I do not agree that the defect is inevitable. Many novelists contrive to avoid it. Why not biographers? A footnote on every fifth page thus conceived would help to do the trick: "Kindly remember that my hero had to lace his boots and have his breakfast each morning, and was worried and bored, in a manner unworthy of a great man, by innumerable trifles of precisely the same sort as worry and bore the reader."

Doubtless there are other ways of avoiding the defect; but this is one method, and an easy one, of continually reminding an ingenuous world that a great man is great for only about four hours in the twenty-four. Four hours indeed is a high daily average. A minute and a half would be nearer the average of certain great men. The aim of some biographers seems to be to prove that a great man spends his whole time in being great. Such biographers are deceivers as barefaced as the anonymous authors of gravestone inscriptions.

There would at first be an enormous outcry if the full truth were related concerning great men. Truth has a strong and acrid taste. Yet finally the palate gets used to it and will crave for it as for pâté de foie gras or oysters. When a few years ago the remarkable tidings were spread that that very great man Wordsworth had had a sordid and not barren intrigue with a young woman in France, every lettered amateur of truth in Britain smacked his lips with pleasure.

M. Maurois sees a faint hope of salvation for biography in the use of the imaginative technique of the novelist. Assuredly! The biographer ought to possess in some degree the gifts of the novelist. He cannot do a satisfactory portrait without them. He must, in the painting, add imaginative psychological conjecture to the undisputed facts. And why not — so long as he indicates clearly what is fact and what is conjecture? His success with his readers will depend on the convincingness of the conjecture — the power of its secret appeal to common sense and to mankind's experience of human nature.

I regret that the closing sentences of M. Maurois's book should be gloomy, for on the last page but one even his faint hope of fictional devices fades away. He holds that "the future of biography will not be very different from the present." He holds that there is no such thing as progress in literature. "Tennyson is not greater than Homer," etc. The usual complaint! Tennyson may not be greater than Homer. And I have no expectation that in the future finer biographies will be produced than in the past. But the *methods* of literature do progress, and the methods of biography are at this present improving. And M. Maurois himself has done something to improve them.

I anticipate with confidence the time when Victorian methods of biography will have been ridiculed to death.

18 April 1929

Mr. Arnold Bennett Takes a Busman's Holiday

Experience has shown me that of all habits the most difficult to break is the reading habit. Recently I found myself on holiday occupying a house in a foreign land where food is understood but tobacco is not. I could get a good meal without being able to get a good cigar after it. Thus, thanks to the blessings of state enterprise, I had to endure terrible austerities for days. The philosopher in me came triumphant through the ordeal. But, as a proper holiday signifies complete change, I had resolved not to read, and here I was less successful.

Soon I learnt that just as the toper is the slave of alcohol, so was I the slave of books. The toper when he is sane hates alcohol, and similarly I hate reading. The house contained quite a number of books — including more editions of Stevenson, Balzac, Maeterlinck and Wilde than I had ever before seen. The better part of me did not want to read; but I read. In particular the better part of me did not want to read Stevenson; but I read Stevenson. My hand trembled in front of *Treasure Island.* I struggled against the sinister fascination of the tome. It beat me. I had not read *Treasure Island* for decades. It now insinuated itself between my unwilling fingers. I opened and began it. I finished it at one gulp, as the toper a cocktail.

To re-read a story which in the historic past has given you intense pleasure is a dangerous proceeding. It may destroy illusions. In this instance illusions were not destroyed, but they were very seriously damaged. The narrative is most brilliantly handled — except where the doctor takes it up for a chapter or two — but what *is* the book? It is naught but a picturesque anecdote. It has no implications, no undertones, and especially no overtones. You read the lines, but between the lines there is nothing. Considered as a book for boys, the thing is superb. It is, however, a book for boys — *et preterea nihil. Robinson Crusoe* and *The Swiss Family Robinson* are books for boys, and for girls too. But they are much more. They are criticisms of life. Is *Treasure Island*? I doubt it. And I doubt if *Treasure Island* will live.

As for the famous Stevensonian style, is it a style, or is it only a manner? The fellow was an enthusiastic craftsman of words. But he has the air of being a performer in public with them, as one who says: "Watch me, I will give you a bravura display of prestidigitation such as you have not yet beheld." *Treasure Island* diverted me but disappointed me.

Then, frankly admitting myself the slave of habit, I read *Weir of Hermiston. Treasure Island* is an early book. *Weir of Hermiston* is a late work, the last. Stevenson was writing it on the day of his death. On the morning of the day of its original publication (I remember) I hurried to a bookshop and bought it and read it, and was animated by it to transports of enthusiastic appreciation. Well, at this second reading it remains still extremely fine. It had admirably survived from one century into another. It is all alive with implications, undertones, overtones. The character of the Lord-Justice-Clerk is a superlative piece of harsh, beautiful realism. The writing has ceased to be a self-conscious public performance.

But — but — *Weir of Hermiston* is a fragment, a mere threshold of a book. The plot of the whole, as partially revealed to us by Sidney Colvin, sounds satisfactory and powerful enough. But could the author have maintained the pace, stayed the course? Could he have lived up to the full imaginative grandeur of the beginning? It is so easy to start grandly, so difficult to finish. The deciding word about Stevenson has probably not yet been said. The question of his ultimate fate still disturbs me.

But there is a more serious case than that of Stevenson: a world-case — Stevenson is only a British case: I mean Balzac. I do re-read Balzac at intervals, and during the last few years I have been tortured by frightful apprehensions concerning this man, once my hero. I used to regard *The Curé of Tours* as the finest short story ever written. (I now know that the number of finest short stories ever written runs to at least a thousand. Someone has just re-discovered Pushkin's *The Queen of Spades*, which I am ingenuously pleased to say I met with long ago. And I have a new favourite in short-story writers, whom I shall mention to the public at an early date.) I have read *The Curé of Tours* four times. On the second occasion I still thought it the finest short story ever written. On the third I was not sure. On the fourth I was sure — that it isn't. But it is good.

With reluctance and with shame I have been at last forced to admit to myself that neither of those illustrious masterpieces, *Eugénie Grandet* and *Old Goriot*, is in truth a masterpiece or anywhere near being one.

After the trial of *Treasure Island* and *Weir of Hermiston*, I was foolish enough to take down from the shelves of the French house Balzac's long novel known in English as *The Harlot's Progress*, the first part of which is entitled "Esther Happy." Never can I, or would I willingly, forget the exquisite sensations aroused in me by "Esther Happy" thirty-five years ago! What romance, what worldliness, what social learning, what realism, what wit, what subtle malice, what a broad arch the book had — as of the firmament itself! I read the tale night and day. I talked about it. I held defenceless friends spellbound by my impassioned discourses upon it. Balzac was the greatest man that ever, etc., etc.

It was foolish, it was rash, it was foolhardy of me to try *The Harlot's Progress* again; for in doing so I went through agonies of humiliation and disillusion. The opening chapter, of the masked ball at the Paris opera! Fustian! Imposing, but fustian! False, tawdry, excruciatingly sentimental! Not true to any kind of life except the kind of life that Balzac (a simpleton at heart like most artists) incorrectly supposed life to be. The wit — how obvious! The malice — how crude! The social learning — fiddlesticks! The generalisations — facile, and often preposterous! The snobbishness — painful! I was shocked.

Of course I know better now than I knew in the 'nineties. I am wise. My taste is impeccable. Nothing spurious can deceive me. But who shall say that in another ten years I shall not be looking back superiorly on the Me of 1929 as a simpleton?

I feel sure that a lot of Balzac will have to go. But I cannot, will not, believe that a few things, such as for example *Cousin Bette*, will not victoriously survive. I cling to the relics of a faith.

And next you will perhaps ask me what I at present think of *Pelléas and Mélisande*, and Wilde's *The Picture of Dorian Gray* and *The Decay of Lying*. My answer is that I took infinite care not to re-read them. I had learnt my lesson.

25 April 1929

A Story *About* Passion that Lacks Passion

Mr. Herbert Asquith is now in process of becoming a popular novelist. His previous novel, *Young Orland*, had a very considerable sale. Its successor, *Roon* (Hutchinson, 7s. 6d.), is just out. The superficial faults of *Roon* are surprising in the work of an author with an Eton-Balliol tradition behind him. They provide one more example of the evil effect of classical studies upon a writer of English — I have noted many similar examples in my time. If the English language is not safe in the hands of men who have enjoyed (what is supposed to be) the best education that England offers to the fortunate, to whom then can the care of it be entrusted?

Mr. Asquith seems to be content with ready-made phrases such as might be picked up at 6d. a dozen in the bargain-basement of a literary department-store. In his pages groups "melt away," music is "haunting," accents are "halting," and human beings "drift." Indeed the heroine, Roon herself, on one occasion "drifts" upstairs. She might conceivably have drifted downstairs, but how a solid body could drift upstairs, save in a cyclone, I cannot imagine. Roon also "glides" upstairs. She might have glided up an escalator.

Further, Mr. Asquith employs various locutions which cannot be approved as correct. Thus a "walk" is described as a "red-letter day." Even his grammar is not always impeccable. His most annoying trick is the repetition, apparently unintentional, of odd epithets. Thus on page 79 the stairs are called "dusky" and a labrador dog is called "dusky." On the next page the hero's "muffled form" is called "dusky." And on the page after that a punt slides through the "dusky" waters. Dusk is no doubt a romantic phenomenon, but one feels that the twilight business can be overdone. You may say that these things are trifles. They are. Nevertheless a thousand trifles amount to quite a lot. In the present instance they certainly mar the pleasure of reading. Elegance and exactitude have importance in literature, whether classical or merely English. I hope that Mr. Asquith writes Greek or Latin or both better than he writes his native language. If he does not, why Eton and why Balliol?

Roon belongs to a very common type of novel. All the characters in it are well-to-do; and if one of them affronts the risk of penury a relative, not previously mentioned, expires with timely benevolence and leaves a modest but sufficient income to the rash adventurer. They all indulge like anything in week-ends, and their sole preoccupations are their sports, pastimes, passions and ambitions. They all behave with propriety — except when passion sways. The struggle for life is not theirs.

Roon, without loving him, marries the wrong man, Hubert, is then attracted by the right man, Dick, saves his dog from drowning, nurses him after an accident, becomes his mistress, informs Hubert of the situation, asks to be divorced. Hubert refuses a divorce. Then the war enters into the plot. Dick is wounded, and later is killed. Roon's and Hubert's little boy dies under an operation. Roon commits suicide.

Save for the suicide, which is weak and sentimental and unconvincing, the plot is a good one, though as old as fiction itself. Some of the personages are well drawn, in particular Roon, her sister, and her artist father. Senhill, a leading politician, is brilliantly drawn, and the scene in which he addresses a meeting is really fine. On the other hand, Hubert, the wrong man and the wronged husband, is treated by his creator with gross unfairness. The reader will ask: Why was Roon such an idiot as to marry the Pharisaic monster? And, as usual in this brand of plot, the reader will get no answer to his question. The departure of the hero to the war is good, and the war-episodes hardly less good.

The chief defect of the novel, which is *about* a passion, is that it lacks passion. Roon is put forward as a fundamentally decent girl. There could be no excuse for her unfaithfulness but passionate love. This passionate love is not rendered. The narrative suffers from an excessive gentlemanly restraint. The sentence in which is recorded the physical coming-together of Roon and Dick is comic in its calm sobriety.

It is impossible to say upon what plan the author selects or invents incidents for full description. Some incidents are related at extravagant length, while for something like a hundred pages Roon's child, who must have been a very important factor in the psychological equation, vanishes utterly from the tale.

The dialogues, far too sententious, are ill-placed and sadly fail in verisimilitude. Hero never on earth addressed heroine as Dick is made to address Roon. Example: "Primroses will survive when pines crash to the ground. Laura's religion is like some forest flower holding great things in small compass" etc. No wonder the heroine remarked in reply: "I think I'll dry my feet." (They were paddling in a pool.)

Roon merits, perhaps, severer criticism than I have given to it. Withal it displays at intervals authentic talent and some very genuine creative power. I have a hopeful idea that one day Mr. Asquith may write a novel consistently good. If only he could learn his craft and moderate his portentousness . . . .

I would respectfully recommend all novelists afflicted with this dread malady of portentousness to read a book entitled *Travels in Asia and Africa,* by Ibn Battúta (Routledge, 12s. 6d., illustrated). The volume is the latest of the truly diverting series, *Broadway Travellers,* edited by Sir E. Denison Ross and Miss Eileen Power. It has a first-rate informative introduction by Mr. H.A.R. Gibb.

Ibn Battúta was a fourteenth century Moroccan with a resistless taste for wandering travel. He got as far as China, via India. He could not have been more "modern" if he had been born in the twentieth century: in which case he would almost certainly have written unsurpassable picaresque novels. He had a sure taste in the choice of incidents, and he was a finished master of narrative. And there wasn't half an ounce of portentousness in the whole of him. He saw marvels and miracles and terrors and horrors; and his writing never strays from simplicity nor his common sense from the great fact of the oneness of human nature.

The entire book, beautifully translated, has intense interest. The account of the court of the Sultan of Delhi (Chapter VI.) is as exciting as anything of the kind I ever read. Those were "times," with a vengeance. I would rather have been the Sultan than any of his subjects. He was cruel and sanguinary, but he practised the most colossal munificence. The trouble for the twentieth century reader is that he uncomfortably realises every moment where the tons of royal treasure came from. They came from the unrequited sweat of a persecuted peasantry.

2 May 1929

For Any Best-Seller Who Needs a Moral Bath

Inspired to do so by a certain book, I went into the National Gallery the other day, after more than a month's absence from it, and found a new and hardly recognisable National Gallery. This transformation, by the way, is an important piece of news which I have not seen mentioned in any newspaper. The entire plan has been rearranged, and much better arranged. The Bellinis are assembled together, ditto the Poussins, ditto the Titians.

The over-estimated "Ansidei" Madonna of Raphael has been degraded from a position which it ought never to have occupied, being as it is one of those shop-finished affairs to which Raphael was addicted because, like Rubens, he knew that he knew the entire job and enjoyed dazzling his public instead of moving it. Also in the N.G. the impossible has been achieved: the large English room now positively looks distinguished! The explanation of the improvement may be that the worst picture in the Gallery, and one of the worst out of it, has been exiled. I could wish that

Titian's grotesque and smudgy Reception of Charles V. by the Trinity (called "La Gloria") had been sent to join it. But directors and others are afraid of great names.

Which reminds me that on the jacket of the cheap edition of Feuchtwanger's *The Ugly Duchess* (Secker, 3s. 6d.) there is a reproduction of a masterly realistic portrait of this lady by Quentin Matsys, and that a very large multiple-shop firm of booksellers has refused to touch the book on the plea that the jacket is "unrefined," while another large firm, affrighted by the said jacket, is only touching the book with, metaphorically, a pair of tongs. I am able to state that Sir William Joynson-Hicks is a partner in neither firm.

What has all this to do with literature? Something. The book which sent me to the National Gallery was *Introduction to the Method of Leonardo da Vinci*, by Paul Valéry, translated by Thomas McGreevy (Rodker, price unknown to me). This is a collector's, a bibliophile's book, a lovely book, beautifully printed on beautiful paper — edition limited to 875 numbered copies. The translation appears to be quite good; but there is a fantastic slip in the translator's note; and Mr. McGreevy, being on the staff of that terrific Parisian institution, the Ecole Normale Supérieure, ought surely to have known that according to the best French tradition accents are not placed upon capital letters. (In dealing with pedagogues one has perhaps the right to be pedagogic.)

The case of Paul Valéry is among the most curious of modern times. He wrote, but wrote little, for about twenty years — the present short work was written a quarter of a century ago — and then suddenly and inexplicably he achieved wide fame, and before he could turn round he was elected to the French Academy and his presence became necessary to all self-respecting Paris salons! No Academy election during this century has given more satisfaction to the lettered. His rate of production, however, has not increased. I should imagine that all his output added together would hardly reach the length of a common novel. His few poems are beyond my understanding. His prose is exquisite; his thought, marvellously subtle, is also exquisite.

As for the *Introduction to the Method of Leonardo da Vinci*, it is at least as much an introduction to the method of Paul Valéry as to that of da Vinci. Nearly half the book is openly devoted by the author to the author. This half, intensely interesting, is full of wise, pure ideals concerning the art of literature. When any best-seller, French, British or American, feels in need of a moral bath, he should peruse it. He will emerge from the cold and pellucid waters humbled, instructed, and I hope with fresh and exalted resolutions for the future. The book is not easy reading. But it is gloriously worth the effort of reading. And even if you buy and don't read it, it will increase the nobility of any shelf of fine books.

Another French book about a very great man has appeared this week in English: *Beethoven, the Creator*, by Romain Rolland (Gollancz, illustrated, 30s.). The fact that Ernest Newman deigned to translate it is sufficient to put the work in a high class. You are apt to think that da Vinci, in addition to having the completest brain in human mental history, was an artist not to be transcended. Then you think of Beethoven, and you perceive that Beethoven transcended him. To me Beethoven was the loftiest artist that ever lived, in any art. Artur Schnabel's performance of the "33 Variations" (on a theme by a thirty-third-rate composer) at Queen's Hall a few months ago provided one of the major sensations of all my life.

I have my doubts about the authenticity of much of Rolland's ten-volume novel, *Jean Christophe*; but his early little book on Beethoven was unquestionably the real stuff; and this new and far larger work — the first of two or three volumes — is the real stuff. Biographies of famous composers have too often been dreadful. Witness Niecks' *Chopin*. *Beethoven, the Creator* is both distinguished and solid. It may also be indispensable.

I offer two criticisms of it. First, just as the book on da Vinci is largely on Paul Valéry, so this book on Beethoven is largely on Romain Rolland. Too much of "a portrait in a mirror"! ("It was in my mind to say that a portrait should be the image of one spirit received in the mirror of another," — quoted by Charles Morgan.) Second, it suffers from an excess of eloquence. Such as: "But October has come — October that chills the sun, that of the fields and that of the blood. . . . " Surely the first four words would have been enough. Romain Rolland might advantageously have followed Verlaine's poetic advice: "Take eloquence and wring its neck." I consider that Ernest Newman should have taken and wrung its neck on behalf of the author. There are scores of examples of redundant floriated eloquence in the work. Nevertheless, *Beethoven, the Creator* is a book full of illuminated and lofty emotion, and extremely readable. Physically it is too thick and heavy for comfort — perhaps because of the plates, which are very interesting. And the stitchery of the binding has not yet won my confidence.

Julien Green, the Anglo-Saxon author who writes in French, is already well established in England with *Avarice House* and *Adrienne Mésurat*. His new novel *Léviathan* (Plan, 12 francs) has not yet been published in English but soon will be. I have read it in French. The author is developing, and *Léviathan* is his best yet. To my mind it is rather overloaded with psychological analysis, the construction is odd, and the interest weakened by a too equal dispersion between those middle-aged dames Mme. Londe and Mme. Grosgeorges. But the originality of the author's mind is more freely disengaged in this book than in previous ones. And the sombre power of the tragedy is simply tremendous. Mr. Green is assuredly of the lineage of great novelists.

9 May 1929

Early Days in the Museum Reading Room

The Reading Room at the British Museum is the most efficient and complete literary institution on earth. It seats nearly five hundred readers under the second largest dome on earth: which dome might have been the largest on earth had not Panizzi, its conceiver, been an Italian with possibly a secret patriotic regard for the dimensional pre-eminence of the dome of the Pantheon. Mr. G. F. Barwick, superintendent of the Reading Room, has written a first-rate, quiet, characteristically Museumish book about his sacred charge: *The Reading Room of the British Museum* (Benn, 10s. 6d., interestingly illustrated).

This book, which I must note has no Table of Contents, has achieved what no other book ever did. It has made me sentimental. In the earliest 'nineties I obtained a ticket for the Reading Room. And I shall not forget the awe, shyness, and feeling of foolish ignorance with which I first entered the overwhelming fane of Athena. Dishonest, I used to visit the place after an A.B.C. lunch of tea and roll, unscrupulously stealing office-time from my bland employer. Then, as now, I rarely indulged in research — except during a brief period when I helped a little in the compilation of Rupert Simm's vast *Bibliotheca Staffordiensis*, afterwards issued in a limited edition of 200 copies. I went to the Dome not for organised study but to browse, and as I was usually more than content with the 20,000 volumes which could be taken from the lower shelves without formalities, I did not often apply by slip for other books. The General Catalogue made excellent reading. I wondered whether my own name would one day thrillingly appear in the Catalogue. It somehow did. It probably now fills quite a number of columns in one of those gigantic folios. But I have never seen it, for thirty years and more have passed since I last sat under the Dome. And if I were to see it I doubt if I should be thrilled. *Tempus* —— (This growing habit of recondite classical quotation must be broken.)

Human nature does change; and it does improve. In the ancient days, a century ago, before the Dome arched its formidable curve, in the days when readers were half-a-dozen a month (as against many hundreds daily now), every obstacle was put in the way of students. The gentleman in command objected to the excessive labour of a six-hour day. There was no catalogue worth a button. And books had to lie for years before they were allowed to be catalogued at all! Books were refused to readers because the officials desired to preserve them! Red-tape was far more abundant than available books. The rules were fantastic.

But already in the 'nineties human nature had been transformed. You received what you asked for within a few minutes. And the chief-priest in the centre of the circle not merely possessed the convenient attribute of omniscience, but was ever willing to impart his infinite knowledge with perfect urbanity — nay, with eagerness. To-day, though efficiency has doubtless even increased in the establishment, the service is perhaps less speedy. And with forty-six miles of shelves, what could you expect? If an attendant has to walk as far as from London to Leicester in order to supply you, you could hardly hope to receive your demanded volume in less than ten minutes.

Mr. Barwick records some dramatic developments. Thirty years ago the woman-readers were two in ten of the daily average. At present they are four in ten, and Mr. Barwick foresees that they will soon be five in ten. And will it stop there? And there have been developments more dramatic. At the beginning of this century, theology was the favourite subject of research. The favourite subject now is science. *Poetry comes second.* Theology third. I question if the alteration of taste is due to the influx of women. Men, not women, are the great students of poetry.

These vicissitudes at the Museum Reading Room bring me to Mr. E.E.

Kellett's small volume, *The Whirligig of Taste* (The Hogarth Press, 3s.6d.). A book which, considering its subject and its immense scope, is better than I could have hoped for. It is a good book, readable, learned and sound. Despite its scope, which reaches from Homer to Browning and later, it contains only 160 pages. Mr. Kellett demonstrates the folly of calling any book immortal.

He reminds us that Euripides was held to be the supreme Greek dramatist for six hundred years up to 1000 A.D., that he was then degraded to the class of "botchers" and "bunglers" for 900 years, is now put among the twelve great poets of the world, and in 1950 may be a botcher and a bungler again. He also insists that mere accident may make or break reputations, and instances Mary Webb, whose name was lifted out of obscurity in an hour by the Prime Minister. Had Mr. Baldwin not happened to read her and to speak of her, she would have been nobody today.

And also he says: "Everything must be considered with a view to its purpose . . . If a book satisfies a certain number of readers, it is so far good; it attains its end, and there is no other definition of goodness." He also says: "A book *cannot* be written except for its author's contemporaries and compatriots." He admits that both Milton and Macaulay claimed to write for posterity — which, I say, was like their cheek! — but both used the dialect of their time and of their country, and that no two books can be more easily dated than *Paradise Lost* and the *History of England.*

Mr. Kellett in his *Whirligig* is full of sense — and of brightness. He may be the very man appointed by destiny to be the author of that history of English literature which I desiderate and which no literary critic has yet had the wit to write. Indeed there exists no history of English literature. There are many histories of (what we deem to be) *good* English literature. But what should we say of any historian who confined himself to *good* kings, statesmen, soldiers? Is there, for example, any history of Victorian literature which conveys the general *feel* of reading from 1840 to 1870? If there is, I have not heard of it. Was Dickens really the most popular author of his time? How many persons in the 'forties had read a line of Wordsworth or thought tuppence of him? What I ask for, and what the public is entitled to is a *Literary History of the English People.* (But I hope it may be less sentimental and better written than John Richard Green's too famous general *History of the English People.*) Here is an idea for an enterprising publisher. It is not wholly mine. I was helped to it by an article in a French literary weekly from the pen of a professor at the Sorbonne whose name I cannot recall.

16 May 1929

A Man Who is Funny Every Day

The startling has happened. "Beachcomber" has published a book. I had long since given up hope. I have my own views about "Beachcomber", whom I do not know and whose worldly name I do not know.* People whose experience should have taught them better think it miraculous that "Beachcomber" can produce a composition of paragraphs for the *Daily Express* every day of the week. There are lots of men in journalism who produce every day an article which gives them just as much trouble as "Beachcomber's" compositions give "Beachcomber." A daily article is a tie, so is an actor's nightly task; but I will not regard it as a miracle. And, from stylistic evidence, let me surmise, without asserting, that now and then articles assumed to be by "Beachcomber" are in fact written by other gentlemen of the same name.

Then again people exhibit amazement because "Beachcomber" is always funny. Of course he is funny. It is his job to be funny, and he profoundly knows his job. Being funny is a job like another and if you have the gift for it, and the moral gift of sustaining an effort, you can be funny for decades. I could mention a dozen humorists who contrive to be consistently humorous without showing fatigue. "Beachcomber" never makes me laugh; but that is because I never do laugh, except when I see a fat man attempt to sit down on a chair that is not where he imagines it to be. "Beachcomber" makes me smile: which is more genteel on both our parts.

I am a convinced and constant admirer of "Beachcomber's" humour. For me, however, his prime importance in the scheme of the universe springs from his criticism of manners. He is a fearless, fierce and ferocious critic of manners. He knows a very great deal about most things, and he is afraid of nothing. (He will even now and then subtly guy his own paper.) He is a great antiseptic force. Naturally he could not carry off his devastating criticism without the help of humour. But what renders him valuable and impressive is less his humour than the correctiveness beneath it. Not all humorists are social critics. For instance, the wonderful "P.G." is not.

"Beachcomber's" book (his first, so far as I am aware) is *Mr. Thake* (Bles, 7s. 6d.), reprinted and arranged from the *Daily Express*. The subtitle is, *His Life and Letters*. A more accurate description would be, *His travels and gallantries*. The thing splendidly bears republishing. Mr. O. Thake is what is called a creation. And "Beachcomber" was never more daring than when he created this simpleton. For O. Thake is rather like the hero of the brothers Grossmith's classic *Diary of a Nobody*. If I had "Beachcomber's" pluck I should say that *Mr. Thake* is as good as *The Diary of a Nobody*. But I have not. I feel sure that if I said so thousands of devotees of the deathless *Diary* (hundreds of formidable high-brows among them) would write to maintain that *The Diary of a Nobody* is the funniest book ever written or that ever will or could be written, and I should be held up to ridicule.

The similarity of the two heroes may be judged from the following brief passage from *Mr. Thake*. (Mr. Thake is in New York.) "There are also English papers, but naturally, as you will guess, they are some days behind the actual date of the moment. Perhaps I can put it better by saying that the news I read to-day in the *Daily Express* of some days ago, is the news you read in the same paper of the same date, only some days ago.

---

* J.B. Morton, who took over the "Beachcomber" column from its originator, D.B. Wyndham Lewis, in 1924, and still runs it today.

I mean you actually read it some days ago, although to people out here it was — or rather is — to-day's, not in actual date but allowing for transit."

Another fine antiseptic humorous force is A.P. Herbert, whose *Topsy, M.P.* (Benn, 7s. 6d.) is recently out. A.P. Herbert, as you may judge from his political letters to *The Times*, is a Tory. But he is a tremendous assailant of fatuity in all camps. Silliness cannot live in his presence. I do not propose to discuss the book. Only to say that the course of Topsy's development compels the author's fun to be even more seriously destructive than aforetime, and that his vocabulary is as original and his phrasing as perfect as in the earlier works.

Another humorous book of an utterly different and an uncritical kind, a book which is not yet a book but a serial in *Blackwood's*, is *The Story of my Yacht*, by Alexandre Dumas, author of *The Three Musketeers*. These personal memoirs were found in manuscript (and are translated) by Mr. R.S. Garnett; and they have not yet been published in French. We have the first taste of them, and we deserve it, for the English appreciate Dumas better than the French do. The work is extremely diverting, and a masterly example of narrative. It is also a masterly and brazen example of the art of padding. Never was such outrageous discursive padding. Dumas' padding was notorious; he never forgot that he was writing at so much a line. Often, too often, the padding was very tiresome. But in the yacht story you enjoy it all. Stevenson was a great narrator. Dumas was a greater. The brief work, when it comes to volume-publication, will give pleasure.

Last week I demanded from the bookish and the publishing worlds a *Literary History of the English People.* Within forty hours of the publication of the article I received from Messrs. Benn *A Literary History of the English People* by the eminent French critic, J.J. Jusserand (three volumes). This imposing work was originally published in English 35 years ago, but the latest revised edition is only four years old. I admit at once that it is a literary history of the English people. Not, however, quite the sort of book that I had in mind and that I want. For one thing it stops at the Civil War. I want something more modern. Something that begins about fifty years later than Jusserand leaves off. For another thing it lacks, and it was bound to lack, the ten thousand intimate details of reading which I thirst for and which would display the homely reactions of readers to books. I have not read it all, but I have read enough of it to show me that it is a sound and comprehensive affair. It certainly does relate national literature to national life.

Also within forty hours I received from Messrs. Harrap tidings of a book called *The Shaping of English Literature*, by Amy Cruse, stated to show the reader's share in the development of our literature. This very interesting book comes nearer to my desire, but it says very little about popular bad books. Also it stops when Jane Austen starts. I learn that Mrs. Cruse is engaged on another book, *The Englishman and his Books During the Nineteenth Century*. A title which promises well.

23 May 1929

Some Short Stories from a Master Hand

The Count de Gobineau has been dead nearly fifty years. A French citizen, he was really a citizen of the world. He saw many countries, and not only knew them but proved in print and beyond argument that he knew them profoundly. In Paris, a capital with a high percentage of brilliant talkers, he was known as a diplomatist and as a talker. He talked about everything — except his own works, imaginative, poetical, sociological, philological, ethnographical and sculptural. His works therefore remained comparatively obscure. This was his own fault. Any modern British or American author could have told him that if you want your books to be known the indispensable preliminary is to talk about them yourself. I am acquainted with authors who have one sole subject of conversation — their own books.

He was a friend of Wagner's, who "took to" him. Whether Wagner's fancy for him is to be counted, or not counted, in his favour, I will not say. Wagner in the 'seventies was an extremely self-centred person.

Gobineau did not believe that all men, or even all races, are equal before the Lord, and he said so at length. Which rendered him somewhat unpopular among the sentimental. But as he was one of the first champions of "Nordic" superiority, and as his theories could be construed into a sort of Pangermanism, his work obtained a vogue in Germany which it has not yet obtained in any other country. The very same reason impaired his chances of appreciation in France and also — just before the war — in Britain. However, his first editions are now being collected in France, and new editions are being published and bought. America translated some of him during his lifetime.

He will probably live as the author of a few short stories. His eastern short stories were brought to my notice by the enlightened, in French, before the war. While I enjoyed them I managed to keep my head about them. But a few weeks ago, by some fortunate hazard of destiny, I met with *The Crimson Handkerchief and other stories* translated (not at all badly) by Henry Longan Stuart, with a short, good introduction by Ernest Boyd (published by Harpers in 1927). This little book, containing three stories, has given me to think — so much so that I cannot keep the knowledge of it to myself. It is assuredly on a higher plane than the volume called in English *Five Oriental Tales*, excellent though the oriental tales are.

The title-story passes in Cephalonia, an Ionian island, in the first third of the nineteenth century, in which French, Russian and English influences, mutually antagonistic, brought about repercussions of the most complicated nature. (There was, and perhaps still is, more international politics to the square mile in any sizeable Mediterranean isle than in any great European country.) The Count begins with a brilliantly arranged account of Cephalonian civilisation, and builds upon it a tale of murderous revenges which reminds you of (though it preceded them by decades) the stories and novels of Giovanni Verga, author of what is perhaps the best known of all short stories, *Cavalleria Rusticana*.

The character-drawing is excellent, the intrigue is exciting, the wit is continuous; and Gobineau writes as though he had lived all his life in the society of the capital of Cephalonia. He convinces you of his fidelity not merely to the facts of human nature, but to the facts of Cephalonian human nature. He makes you feel at home in the streets, houses and cafes of Argostoli. *The Crimson Handkerchief* is an admirable short story, a perfect model of a short story. It is not, however, striking enough to cause you to set the Count apart as an absolute master.

The Caribou Hunt is just this, the last story in the volume, starts in Paris and proceeds to Newfoundland. I know nothing about Newfoundland — or rather I know that I don't know even whether its name should be pronounced "New*found*land" or "*New*funlun" — and in particular I know nothing about Newfoundland in mid-nineteenth century. Nevertheless I feel sure that the Count's picture of the state of things in Newfoundland during the period of which he writes is completely accurate. He gives you the impression that he had lived all his life on the coasts of Newfoundland. Here again the character-drawing is excellent. It is more than excellent — it is superb. Mr. Anthony Harrison and the nine members of his family are as convincing as any portraits could be. And the reactions between them and the young French hero straight from the boulevarde are worked out with really astonishing verve and robust humour. It is natural that the Count should deeply understand the psychology of the young Frenchman; but it is not natural, it is unnatural, that he should deeply understand the psychology of the English-colonial Harrisons, as beyond question he does. *The Caribou Hunt* is an exceedingly rich affair. And it sets the Count apart as as absolute master.

A still finer story is *A Daughter of Priam*, the scene of which is Naxos. The Count is just as much at home in Naxos as in Cephalonia and Newfoundland. The plot arises out of the visit of a British corvette to the island. The hero is the vessel's captain, and the heroine is a Greek girl of unusual beauty and taciturnity. Hero relinquishes his naval career, marries heroine, and settles in Naxos as a husband — successfully. Impossible! Yes, but you just have to believe the impossible, and you do. The character-drawing is marvellous. The hero is a triumphant bit of work, and the two aged counsels are even more triumphant. Wit, humour and pathos are merged into a very rare triune whole.

The story in essence has a resemblance to Conrad's *Falk*; but it is more subtle. Falk was a rough creature. Norton is a man of brains, birth and considerable culture. Yet he convincingly falls a happy captive to a lovely, ignorant girl who is completely unsophisticated and as alien by every tradition to himself as a girl could be. She does nothing. She exclusively *is*. The story is profound, and the Count comes as near as probably any novelist ever did to explaining the fundamentals of inter-sexual attraction. It is a beautiful story.

Gobineau has been compared to Stendhal. I cannot see the likeness. I should agree more easily with those who compare him to Mérimée. More ought to be heard of the Count in this country. That appreciation of him is growing on the Continent is certain. I think that in due course he cannot fail to be highly appreciated in Britain. But Britain is never in a hurry.

30 May 1929

There's Joy — And Money — In Book Collecting

I have been reproached for writing in this column about rare editions, first editions, beautiful editions, the argument being that such matters have no real relation to literature itself, and that what counts in a book is the stuff in it, not the presentation of the stuff in it. To my mind the argument is ridiculous. A book is a physical object as well as a medium for the transmission of thought, emotion and information. And the attributes, including the historical attributes, of the physical object react upon the person to whom the thought, emotion or information is being transmitted.

Many people read Dickens with joy, still more people assert (without adducing proof) that they read Dickens with joy. But it is an absolute certainty that the first category, if not the second, would be tremendously diminished if Dickens were only published in folio volumes like pulpit Bibles — were the price per volume only sixpence, were even the volumes given away!

To take a contrary case. I believe that there exist people who read Shakespeare eagerly. Give them a perfect copy of the first folio. Say to them: "This physical object is worth £5000 in the market. But you mustn't sell it." Would they refuse it? They would not. They would prize it. And though they might prefer to peruse that sensational author in the Temple pocket edition, they would also peruse the folio — in patches — and would derive from the difficult perusal an intensified emotional pleasure.

But even were the argument not ridiculous, it would still be beside the point. The point is that our age is a collecting age. And why should it not be? Only rare, beautiful, historical, odd, or scandalous objects are collected. To collect them is a virtue — for which the next generation will thank us, and will financially reward our executors and trustees. One hears (with a sarcastic tone in the voice of the social critic) that to-day "everything is collected." It is hardly true. I am waiting to meet the man who collects specimens of the "dust-jackets" of novels — those covers which you throw into the fire after or before you have read the volumes which they sheltered. In forty years the curious would be travelling miles to see such a collection, and its dispersal by auction at Sothebys would draw dealers and dilettante from New York and Berlin, fill columns of the front pages of newspapers, and put much commission into the pockets of auctioneers.

Nevertheless almost everything *is* collected, and almost everything is more and more collected. Millions of schoolchildren collect autographs of celebrities, and thousands of celebrities are naive enough to send autographs to the knowing little brutes who purposely forget to enclose a stamped and addressed envelope. First and rare editions are more and more collected. Manuscripts are more and more collected. Prices are high, and they are rising. The bulls, in fact, have it. One is warned that there will be a break. There will never be a break — unless a complete collapse of civilisation occurs — in any market which keeps the approval of the educated. Just as the demand for great or good pictures will continue to grow, so will the demand for first and rare editions, and for manuscripts, of great or good authors.

Everybody knows what present prices are, but they are simply nothing compared to what prices will be. Within half a century our posterity will be referring to 1929 as an epoch when inestimable objects could be "picked up for a song." For it is inconceivable that the supply should not fall away further and further from the demand. I am in favour of anything and everything which helps to foster and maintain an interest in literature. Hence I regard with benevolence the entire ardent race of collectors of books and manuscripts. Were I a member of the jury at the trial I would acquit even a book-thief who had stolen a first edition of *Desperate Remedies* — not because I did not think him a rascal, but because the immense pother due to his heroical transgression would attract the attention of the multitude to the existence of a first-rate author.

And yet I have little doubt that when I was young copies of Hardy's first novel were to be found in the twopenny boxes of second-hand booksellers, and that the collectors of that age ignored them. The extreme difficulty of the collector is to foresee. As a rule those who foresee are not collectors — at least not consciously so. If collectors could but get in on the ground-floor . . .! Not long since a man with his parched tongue hanging out for first editions of Bernard Shaw told me that he had not been able to get hold of a copy of Bernard Shaw's first play. I showed him a perfect copy of the first edition of *Widowers' Houses*. I had not collected it. I had merely purchased it — about the year 1066 or 1814. He wanted to buy it. I wanted to give it to him. But I was not generous enough to give, and to ask him the price which I deem it to be worth I was ashamed. Thus he departed without it. But one day I shall sell it and buy the freehold of a talkie picture-palace.

How many collectors of George Moore are aware that a new George Moore item has recently been issued? Here it is, lying before me, mine: *Letters from George Moore to Edouard Dujardin, 1886-1922* (published in New York by Crosby Gaige, and sold in England by the Cayme Press). A volume *de luxe*. Limited edition. Signed. It has a very great literary interest as well as a physical. Already it is worth quite a lot. Soon, full soon, it will be worth quite a bit more. Of that I am sure.

The trouble is that you can't always be sure. I am not sure, but I think it quite possible, that a novel lying at the moment here by the side of George Moore's letters will one day be the cause of research, envy, covetousness, and other vices: *Brothers and Sisters*, by I. Compton-Burnett (Heath Cranton, 7s. 6d.). I had never heard of the author, who I am informed is a woman. The novel has incurred the laudation of select high-brows — which of course put me against it. But, though by no means easy to read, it seems to me to be an original work, strong, and incontestably true to life. I. Compton-Burnett may be a new star, low on the eastern horizon. I shall attend with a certain impatience her next novel; but I do not propose at present to "pontificate" concerning her future. I might guess wrong.

6 June 1929

Finest German Post-War Novel Yet Translated

The other day I received from a firm of publishers a circular in which, in order to extol the virtues of a certain English war-novel, they decried the general coarseness of German war-novels. In my heart I objected: first, because I think that one ought to be able to praise one thing without specifically disparaging another; and second, because I do not quite see how any true picture of the great war can be comprehensive without here and there being coarse. Nor can I agree that modern German fiction is coarser than modern English fiction, though it may be more outspoken.

Take *All Quiet on the Western Front*. In it are printed in full about half of the famous nine unprintable "Anglo-Saxon monosyllables" referred to in one of Sinclair Lewis's novels. In it also is one of the most outspoken sexual scenes to be found in any modern novel. But nobody with any sense of critical responsibility has protested. Neither have the police intervened, nor has the Morality Council; nor has any police-magistrate launched his twopenny thunders against its "obscenity." To do so would indeed have been absurd, for the author out of his German coarseness has created real beauty. Not that I reckon *All Quiet on the Western Front* very high as a "novel." As a novel it does not compare with *The Case of Sergeant Grischa*. But as factual reporting it simply cannot be beaten, and as intensely readable propaganda for the League of Nations it almost stands alone.

For about a century — since *Wilhelm Meister* — Germany produced no fiction comparable with ours, or with the French, or with the Italian, or with the Russian; but within the last few years a German school of fiction has arisen from which we in our self-complacency have something to learn; and I hope we are learning it. Therefore I am glad to see a new edition in one volume (790 pages, Allen and Unwin, 10s.) of Jacob Wassermann's *The World's Illusion*, unequally and sometimes exasperatingly translated by Ludwig Lewisohn, Wassermann seems to be the biggest of the modern German novelists. His short historical novel, *The Triumph of Youth*, is entitled to rank as a masterpiece.

When I laid hands on the fifth edition of Mr. Jonathan Nield's vast *Guide to the Best Historical Novels* (Elkin Mathews and Marrot, 30s., and worth the money), I at once looked to see if *The Triumph of Youth* had been included in it. It had — and with an asterisk to denote special excellence. I recommend this Guide. It has positive mistakes. It comprises a whole lot of novels which are for ever deceased, and rightly deceased. The author's definition of the term "historical novel" is bizarre, and has compelled him to include many novels which are assuredly not in the ordinary sense historical. For instance, Smollett's *Roderick Random*.

If *Roderick Random* is a historical novel, then any old novel is historical. I hold that the first thing about a historical novel is that the author re-creates in it an age in which he did *not* live. In *Roderick Random* Smollett described his own age and events which he himself saw. When it was first published it could not possibly have been called a historical novel. At what subsequent date, then, did it become historical? Nevertheless,

Mr. Nield's *Guide* is a good book. The new edition represents the labour of more than a quarter of a century. It is laid out on an original plan. It has two excellent indexes, and it can fairly be classed with those select works of reference which for convenience we label "indispensable" — though probably nothing, and nobody is indispensable, except of course the new edition of *The Concise Oxford Dictionary*, which Buckle would have perused with passionate zest.

To return to *The World's Illusion*. It has serious drawbacks. The hero, Christian Wahnschaffe, may be sublime, but he is a fool. I don't mind that, but his foolishness is not satisfactorily motivated. The same is to be said of the girl Ruth. The other and more gorgeous girl, Eva, is never directly described until the hour of her too-picturesque suicide. The whole story is too long, and as for the climax, it is like the climaxes of some of Schubert's larger works, you wonder whether it is ever coming at all, or whether the creating artist will ever be able to persuade himself to stop.

The conversations are immensely too verbose, and resemble dialogues less than a concatenation of enormous monologues. Many of the characters use the same idiom (which is absurd), and some of the uneducated characters are gifted with a power and felicity of protracted expression equal to the author's own (which is still more absurd).

But the major scenes are magnificent in heroic splendour. They are epical. And quite a number of the mere anecdotes related have a superlative intrinsic value. In them is material for about 101 terrific short stories. And what a sweep has the book! The sweep is from the Argentine to Moscow and from the topmost dog to the most bottom dog. The author is inspired by a profound feeling for the under-dog; yet the majority of his under-dogs are awful creatures. I thought much of the spirit of *The World's Illusion* the other night when, amid supra-opulent surroundings, I heard the ferocious booings of hundreds of top-dogs at the electoral successes of under-dogs. I wanted all the frizzed top-dogs to read the book, defrizzed.

In my opinion *The World's Illusion* is the finest post-war German novel yet translated into English. I must point out that though the dust-jacket of the book gives bibliographical information about it, there is nothing in the volume itself to show that it is a new edition of a work eight years old. The reason no doubt is that the book is printed in America, while the dust-jacket is printed in England.

Another German war-book (I refuse to call it a novel — though it may be fictional) in the manner of *All Quiet on the Western Front* is Ludwig Renn's *War* (Secker, 7s. 6d.), translated by Willa and Edwin Muir. The translation begins very clumsily, then improves. Some of the phrasing in the first fifty pages is indeed lamentable. The book itself gives an effect of a confusion of good little bits shovelled together. It reads like the truth: which is a virtue, but not the whole of virtue. It is terrible. It is ruthless and even savage in the description of horrors: which in a war-book is another virtue. As anti-war propaganda it ranks with *All Quiet on the Western Front*. But not otherwise — despite authoritative statements to the contrary. It ought to be read. The irony of some of it is utterly corrosive. For example, in the section entitled "The March Offensive, 1918." Here you are made to see what Ludendorff's final grandiose effort really amounted to for a few individual soldiers.

War, considered as literature, is on a far lower plane than, say, Edmund Blunden's *Undertones of War*, but considered as a bludgeon for smashing the ideals of the bellicose it comes an easy first when compared with anything that I have read by English novelists. And it is useful in that it plainly shows that among the anti-Teutonic allies the hunger of German soldiers played no small part.

13 June 1929

A Book on Writing for Readers

Books about writing are not usually interesting to the public. Plays about the stage are. That is because the public thinks that whereas writing is dull work, acting is jolly work. Writing is indeed dull work, but by no means so dull as acting. Also, writing makes writers interesting. As a rule writers see the world. Acting does not make actors interesting. Actors do not see the world; their vocation prevents them from doing so. There is nothing on earth more dull than a party of stage-celebrities — except a night-club at 2 a.m. I speak of what I know, and I have sworn never again to attend either the one or the other — save in the way of business.

Now and then there comes along a book on writing which should interest the public. There was one last year — E.M. Forster's *Aspects of the Novel*. There is one this year: *Creative Writing*, by William Webster Ellsworth (Funk and Wagnalls, 8s. 6d.). (I very much question whether Funk and Wagnalls ever issued a bad book. And their *New Standard Dictionary*, which in addition to being word-dictionaries are biographical dictionaries and gazetteers, must count among the most precious and reliable volumes in the western world.) Mr. Ellsworth used to be the editor of *The Century* when that magazine had just passed its apogee. His book is mainly made up of lectures to young persons, and he originally intended to call it *The Joy of Writing*. I am glad he changed his mind about the title, for there is little or no joy in writing, though, sometimes, there may be a certain joy in having written. Editors know a lot about things written, but little about the writing of them.

The book provides infinite material for controversy. Thus Mr. Ellsworth says: "The Bible and Bunyan remain the great models of English prose." These works may be great prose (though I have my doubts about the author of *Grace Abounding*). But great "models" they are not. Any young writer who obstinately modelled himself upon either of them would soon have to turn to some other method of earning a livelihood. I would far sooner recommend as models for young writers such men as T.H. Huxley, Matthew Arnold, Cardinal Newman, Hilaire Belloc, D.H. Lawrence, Max Beerbohm, Sterne.

The best advice Mr. Ellsworth gives to young writers is quoted from Mary Roberts Rinehart, an author whose abilities, I regret to say, are incommensurate with her immense circulations. Mrs. Rinehart said: "The only way to learn to write is to write — so much a day every day." The inmost kernel of literary wisdom is there.

Again, Mr. Ellsworth says: "Nothing corrects slovenly construction better than writing newspaper advertisements, where every word must be paid for and compactness is a fundamental necessity. After inviting the public to buy the piano of a lady sailing for Europe with carved legs you become wary — precise." I question it. Newspaper advertisements, though some are good, would be much better if they were written by people who had learnt to write other stuff before they began upon advertisements. A few days ago I saw an advertisement of a periodical which opened thus: "Dear Acquaintance. Clear, keen, clamorous, these special numbers crash old stereotypes in the backs of our minds and dramatize the world in which we live." To which the only effective answer is "Rats!" The composer of these remarkable lines, which comprise nearly all literary faults, including both imprecision and vagueness, evidently did not know the first thing about writing.

The fact is that people who have no natural feeling for literature can only meddle with literature on pain of being silly. I remember once sitting down to struggle with Beethoven's piano sonata, Opus III. A great pianist happened to enter the room. He said to me laconically: "If I were you I shouldn't meddle with that." I didn't meddle with it. I remember also that Mr. Ellsworth himself, when he came to see me many years ago, told a sublime story of a meddler with literature. The meddler was a very successful stock-breeder, who had bred a bull which was the king of all bulls. He had been reading Tennyson and had conceived a hot passion for *The Idylls of the King* (Tennyson's nearly worst work). In the ardour of his literariness he christened the king of bulls "Sir Galahad."

Mr. Ellsworth is wrong, at intervals, in his facts. He says that John Masefield, when he finished his long poem *Dauber*, had difficulty in finding a publisher therefor, for members of that craft reasoned that the day of long stories in verse had gone by. I do not believe it. Before *Dauber*, Mr. Masefield had had tremendous successes with the long poems entitled *The Everlasting Mercy* and *The Widow in the Bye-Street*, and I would lay 100 to 1 that he had not the slightest difficulty in finding a publisher for *Dauber*.

And the day of long stories in verse has not even yet gone by. Stephen Vincent Benét's poem *John Brown's Body* is as long as a novel, and it has had, quite recently, a very remarkable vogue in America. I have read a lot of it. I will not affirm that it is poetry, but I will affirm that it is a good and continuously interesting book.

I seem so far only to have differed from Mr. Ellsworth. Nevertheless I enjoyed reading *Creative Writing*. It is full of chunks of horse-sense about writing.

I could differ on many points with Mr. Grant Overton, the (American) author of *The Philosophy of Fiction* (Appleton, 10s. 6d.). Mr. Grant Overton is a novelist, and it is apparent that he is acquainted at first-hand with the methods of novel-writing. (He also has acquaintance with the greater and still more mysterious craft of publishing.) But he has selected the author of this article for too warm praise; and I cannot write critically while blushing. One section of his book is called "A Short History of Fiction" — in some sixty pages. It is a curious, original, and not unsuccessful effort in extreme condensation. He is wise about the relations which ought to exist between truth and fiction. The book is worthy to be examined by both professionals and the laity.

Touching the relations between fiction and truth, I would recommend Messrs. Hodge's series of *Notable British Trials*, of which the latest volume is the *Trial of John Donald Merrett*, edited (like many of the other volumes) by Mr. William Roughead (10s. 6d., illustrated). Mr. Roughead does not write with marked distinction, but his "Introduction" to the case is (as usual) very thorough and judicial. The case itself is not specially interesting, inasmuch as it is deficient in the element of mystery.

The value of all these verbatim reports of trials lies in their revelation of the daily detail of common lives — especially as developed through the mouths of domestic servants. It is impossible to read such reports without arriving at a better understanding of the existence of such people as are concerned in them. All novelists ought to read them, and therefore the public ought to read them. They give the raw material for just comparisons between fiction and truth. And even the least exciting of them has intense interest for everybody who is interested in his fellow-creatures.

20 June 1929

Recipe for a Classic Mystery-Novel

A few months ago I offered here some deleterious remarks about certain very popular detective fiction, and the dust of resentment raised thereby has not even yet subsided.

Detective novelists have indeed doughty champions; also they seem to be rather capable of defending themselves. Hence I propose to raise a little more dust. In *Menace to Mrs. Kershaw*, a mystery story by a new author, Austen Allen (Bles, 7s. 6d.), I came recently across a sentence which struck me as being a suitable text for a sermon. It ran thus: "Although Ord's visits were for professional purposes, Sabina did not let him remain a *mere crime-detecting organism* without a human back-ground." (Sabina is a lady with a strongly developed intuitional side and Ord makes use of her strange insights. The idea appears to be original. The book is very well written, and, notably by dialogue, well characterised; but I cannot discuss it, because my theme is general and not particular.)

The present tendency is to reduce the novel of crime-detection to a dry and inhuman jig-saw problem. Now a mere jig-saw problem may be an excellent jig-saw problem; but it cannot be a satisfactory novel. The reader rightly demands more than a problem; he demands human beings and their backgrounds. He can tolerate a naked detective problem to the length of a short story. Most of the best mystery fiction is in the form of short stories or novelettes. Witness the work of E.A. Poe, R.L. Stevenson, and Sir Arthur Conan Doyle. If the length is to be successfully extended to that of a full-sized novel, then the plot must be supported by, must spring out of, elaborate characterisation and environments. Witness Wilkie Collins and Gaboriau. The latter by instinct felt this necessity so powerfully that in his later work he allowed the purely human interest to run away with him, so that the important mere detective interest was seriously impaired. Here was the fault of his maturity.

Various rules have been laid down for the conduct of a mystery-novel — as that mis-statements of fact are barred, and that the reader, though he may justifiably be misled, can only be misled subject to definite conditions, etc. But so far as I know the chief rule has never been clearly laid down: namely, that the story must be about human beings in human environments, not exclusively about calculating machines, impossible seers, and outrageous fools, drawn in the flat, instead of in the round, on a background of plain cardboard. Good characterisation, amply enriched by environmental detail, is the basis of all sound fiction, including detective-fiction. All other sorts of novelists realise this as indispensable, but detective-novelists persuade themselves that they can dispense with it. They can't; and their productions suffer accordingly. There is no intrinsic reason why a detective-novel should not be as great as *Jude the Obscure* or *The Brothers Karamazov*. Perhaps when detective-novelists have learnt their lesson, one of them will write such a novel. But not till then. Meanwhile detective-novels will never be better than third-rate, and the majority of them will be thirtieth-rate.

Further I think that detective-novelists would be well advised to acquaint themselves at first hand with the types of individuals with whom by the nature of their special craft they have to deal. For example, detectives. I should like to know how many mystery-mongers (except Edgar Wallace) have ever talked familiarly with a detective, or watched a detective at work, or even seen a detective. If they have educated themselves in this respect, how comes it that the average detective in fiction (and in plays) is lacking in all human characteristics save the minor and comparatively rare characteristics of self-conceit, blindness to the obvious, and perfect idiocy. My own acquaintance with detectives has hitherto been limited, but I am ready to swear that the average detective is not by any means a prize ass.

Again, why, in detective fiction, is the amateur detective so frequently superior to the professional? Is this the true relation of amateurs and professionals in other walks of life? If not, why should it be true of the walks of life conveniently described by the words "Scotland Yard"?

And detective-novelists make a still worse mistake. Their average criminal, and especially their average murderer, usually has the brain of an Einstein joined to the prudence of a political leader and the prophetic vision of an H.G. Wells. It is a notorious fact, demonstrated times without number in the annals of crime, that there is something mentally queer in criminals and especially in great murderers. These star performers always in a crisis contrive to accomplish some act of marvellous undoing. If anybody wishes to know how utterly and incredibly foolish murderers can be let him read Sir Cecil Walshe's judicial account of a famous Indian crime, *The Agra Double Murder Case* (published by Benns in the early part of this year). I mention the book because I have just read it. But nearly all murder trials in which a conviction is obtained show that at some point the murderer behaved as no person in his senses could conceivably have behaved. I would suggest to detective-novelists that they read and devoutly and humbly study a couple of score volumes of criminal trials. Judging by the evidence of their books I should surmise that some of them have neither witnessed, nor read a full account of, any criminal trial.

Lastly, I venture to assert, with my customary diffidence, that detective-novelists are too much addicted to the crime of murder. The most renowned of modern American detective-novelists seems to confine himself exclusively to homicide. There have been great murder novels, and the greatest of all is Dostoevsky's *Crime and Punishment*. But other crimes are from time to time committed, and not less interestingly human crimes. Murderers, as I have already indicated, are abnormal: they are too rare for the human novelist's daily food. Of course all criminals are abnormal, but the non-murderers are less so. See the *Newgate Calendar*. There are also, in actual life, tremendous mysteries in which no sin, or at any rate no crime, is involved. Many of these latter are never solved. A detective-novelist who could get rid of the fatal desire to imitate all other detective-novelists might profitably employ his gifts in providing solutions for a few of these enigmas.

27 June 1929

The Best War Novel Has Yet To Be Written

War-novels continue to be written and published, and though people (quite irrationally, to my mind) exclaim against their profusion and swear never to read another, they do in fact read another and another — especially when the novels happen to be translations from the German.

The fact is that war-novels written now are beyond question on the average better than those written eight or ten years ago. There is a probability that the ultimate outstanding novel of the great war will not be written for twenty years yet. We are all, both writers and readers, still far too near to the great war. Up to now the best English novels of the war have been written by A.P. Herbert (*The Secret Battle*) and Ralph Hale Mottram (*The Spanish Farm Trilogy*). It will take a pretty fine book to beat either of them.

A third one to join the distinguished pair, Mr. W.F. Morris's *Bretherton*, was fully reviewed in this paper a week or two since. I refer to it here and now only because, in addition to being a war-novel, it is a mystery-novel, and because it so well illustrates the remarks which I made in my last article about the importance of mystery- or detective-novels having a full human background and environment. *Bretherton* indeed furnishes such a background and environment on a very generous scale, and the result is the salvation of a fantastic plot which otherwise might well have failed to convince the doubting Thomases whose numbers are ever growing among a more and more sophisticated public. Even so, opinions will differ about *Bretherton*. Eight experienced readers out of ten will enjoy it, as I did. The ninth will say that it is the finest English war-novel yet issued. The tenth will be rude about it. I understand that it is a first novel.

Another first novel is *Grand Manner*, by Louis Kronenberger (Gollancz, 7s. 6d.). The publisher specifically states that it is a first novel (on the evidence of the book itself I should have guessed that it was a young novel but not a first novel). The publisher says nothing else about the author. I have suggested to publishers before, and I suggest to them again, that they should vouchsafe to the average reader (who after all is not gifted with second-sight) some biographical information about unknown authors.

Mr. Kronenberger may be writing English as his native language, or he may not. Often he displays much skill in phrasing. But the book is full of really extraordinary locutions. Here is one: "They could fill their conversation with such double meanings as only Pollak and Fourblineau *were capable of filling it.*" Here is another: "When he had . . . *drank* a glass of claret-cup." And here is a third: "The Count died, somewhat straitened in circumstances by having made investments *concerning which* he did not understand." Is the author English or is he foreign? If English, he deserves grave censure. If foreign, one is entitled to say of him that, though his command of English is wonderful, it is not wonderful enough. Joseph Conrad, when in his earliest books he was obviously writing English as a foreigner, never floundered half so badly.

Grand Manner depicts the court life of a small Teutonic kingdom. It is immensely "knowing" and allusive, and far too clever. The author strives youthfully to give the impression that he knows everything about everything, that no vagary of human nature can shock him, and that the superb calm of his philosophic disdain is incapable of being ruffled. He has committed one serious error. Instead of writing a *novel* he has written a modern *history* of the aforesaid kingdom as it might have been written by Mr. Lytton Strachey at his loftiest and his most negligent. I should say that it has less dialogue even than *Waverley*.

But the thing shows some promise. It can be read. It lures you on from page to page. Occasionally it induces a smile of admiration. And it makes you think that if you knew half as much about life as the author brilliantly pretends that *he* knows, you would know a hundred times as much as you do.

And further as to German novelists, who if they go on at the present rate will soon owe "reparations" to British novelists as Germany owes them to much of the rest of the civilised world. Thomas Mann is well known to us as the author of *Buddenbrooks* and the desolating *Magic Mountain*. Few of us know, and I have only recently learnt, that Thomas has a brother, Heinrich, equally famous in Germany as a novelist. His novel *Berlin* (Gollancz, 7s. 6d.) has just been translated into English by Axton D.B. Clark.

This work (published in Germany nearly thirty years ago) is a fine specimen of fiction. There is nothing new-fangled about it. Heinrich Mann constructs and writes in the established manner, and he is certainly the peer of Thomas Mann. The picture drawn of journalistic, literary, theatrical, capitalistic and scandalous Berlin at the end of the nineteenth century is admirably sardonic. But I will not try to hide the fact that the book is not pleasant. In some respects it demonstrates that Berlin and London are, or were, as like as two peas. In other respects it demonstrates that they resemble one another as closely as a dachshund resembles a fox-terrier. The comparison is in favour of London.

Nobody in London could possibly exert the theatrical influence which Frau Türkheimer, through her husband's millions, exerts in Berlin. The hero, Andrew, has no genuine quality as a creative artist. Nor has he the industry, the power of conscientious sustained effort, which is the finest characteristic of German writers. His rise was as undeserved as his fall was deserved. He is obviously true enough to life, but he is not a fair specimen even of the self-seeking climber. His liaison with Adelheid Türkheimer is also obviously true enough to life; but this tawdry and sordid business has been done just as well before, and perhaps better — by, for instance, de Maupassant.

Still, *Berlin* is not in the least a book to miss. It impresses. And it has moments in which the sardonic is curiously mingled with the charming; as when Andrew undergoes a regular shower-bath of flatteries from a group of silly young girls.

I have been told by a German author that Heinrich Mann is better than Thomas Mann. It may be so; but I await the proof — in English. The (American) translation of *Berlin* appears to me to be far from satisfactory. More than one passage is beyond my comprehension. And the sharp edge of the phrasing is, to my mind, continually dulled by a sad clumsiness. I say nothing of the Americanisms which, although they may chafe an English sensitiveness, an American is certainly entitled to use.

According to my information, a better novel of Heinrich's has already been translated and still better await translation. Let them come.

4 July 1929

A New Light in a *Dark Star*

Nancy's parents were negligent enough not to marry. Her mother had been over-familiar with a groom and with an aristocrat. Nancy could not be sure which of them was her father. She wanted to be the daughter of an aristocrat, and feared she was the daughter of a groom. She encountered Harvey Brune, one of those musical geniuses who live only in novels written by young women. They parted and met again by one of those blatant coincidences which, though they may infrequently occur in life, occur very frequently in novels written by novelists who take insufficient trouble about their plots or who disdain plots. How Harvey developed in a few years from a whistling boy into a great musician is not described. Not a sentence in the book concerning this enormous phenomenon! Nancy loves Harvey. Harvey loves Nancy; but he loves music more. He leaves her for music when a decent man would have married her. He writes to her, protesting his passion for her, and offering her money. She commits suicide.

This true account of Miss Lorna Moon's first novel, *Dark Star* (Gollancz, 7s. 6d.), looks rather black. But I have said the worst of it. The novel shows promise; it is captivating to read for the author has both a gift for narrative and a style which is distinguished and original. Extremely few ready-made department-store phrases in *Dark Star*. Some of the scenes are admirable and have power, especially the suicide of the heroine, which is a little masterpiece of poetic felicity in ten lines. The last page persuades you to forgive many sins on previous pages, and particularly the innumerable sins of retrospective explanatory narrative. I am very tired of the still prevalent fictional habit of beginning a story and then going back to earlier episodes. When a tale has started, let it in heaven's name run on! Nevertheless I must insist that *Dark Star* is not quite an ordinary affair; for it is vitalised by one of the rarest of all qualities — passion. I could write two colums in depreciation of it; but I salute it and recommend it.

Another novel worthy of the attention (of the robust) is Mr. Claude McKay's *Banjo* (Harpers, 7s. 6d.). I believe that Mr. McKay is a negro. You could hardly guess it from his style, which, while American, is very good. Only in the dialogue, with which he is rather free-handed, he exaggerates the American tendency to quite needless phonetic spelling.

But from the more serious passages you would guess at once that the author is a negro, for the book is subtly impregnated with pro-negro propaganda — and to my mind, fair propaganda. Mr. McKay insists upon the invincible dignity of the negro. (But I have not observed that he insists also on the negro's invincible naive vanity.) Some of his psychology is deep and startling. Thus when Banjo, the chief character, "signs on" for a ship, and takes a full month's wages in advance and then skedaddles, the man defends himself as follows: "I know you're thinking it ain't right. But we kain't afford to choose, because we ain't born and growed up like the choosing people. All we can do is to grab our chance every time it comes our way." And this: "When the police inspector said to Ray that the strong arm of the law was against Negroes because they were all criminals . . . what he unconsciously meant was that the police were strong-armed against the happy irresponsibility of the Negro in the face of civilisation." And Mr. McKay successfully explains the cause of this irresponsibility.

Yes, the book has a very serious foundation. But it is a picturesque book too. The scene is the port of Marseilles, with its shifting population, its touts, its toughs, its wantons, and its police. Practically all the male personages are negroes of one sort or another. The main fault of *Banjo* is disclosed in the sub-title, *A Story Without a Plot*. How can you have a story without a plot? A plot connotes a story and vice versa. Call the book a novel without a plot if you please. But "story" it is not. It is a series of sketches in which certain characters recur. The general effect of it is slightly monotonous, because there is no climax, and it is all negro, all picturesqueness, all slang, all physical phenomena. But it is essentially dignified, being negro. And I should imagine that it is never untrue.

Another port; another clime. Sydney, Australia. The story of James Hyde, who leaves the Navy in order to take up ship-chandling in Sydney Harbour, begins in the eighteen-thirties and ends in the 'eighties. It begins in modesty and ends in splendour. James Hyde built the great business house of Hyde and Sons. The novel is called *A House is Built* (Harrap, 7s. 6d.). It is signed "M. Barnard Eldershaw," and is really the work of two women graduates of Sydney University, the Misses Eldershaw and Barnard. There are two curious and satisfactory things about this book. First, that it gives no external sign of collaboration; it is an entity and a unity. Second, that it won the First Prize (£1000) in the *Sydney Bulletin*'s competition for the best novel by an Australian author. For not often does a truly fine piece of work take first prize in such a competition. Fine pieces of work are only too apt to be passed over in favour of something smoother, more fashionable, more sentimental, without any sharp edges. And *A House is Built* is beyond question a very notable novel. It has deeply impressed me.

I have already dealt with two novels that are by no means to be disdained. *A House is Built* is incomparably superior to either of them. Although certain chapters are no doubt better than others, I find it hard to discover faults with this extraordinary book. Its quality is epical. Time marches through it in the grand manner. And the emotional power is maintained right to the end — which is rare in any book by any author. I know that after finishing, and being laid under the spell of, a good book, one is in danger of exaggerating its merits — indeed of thinking that it is the only good book ever written. Nevertheless I must have the courage of my opinion, and my opinion is that *A House is Built* is a major phenomenon of modern fiction. Not one scene, not three scenes, but many scenes in it are magnificent. If more is not heard of the Misses Eldershaw and Barnard I shall be surprised. Either of them alone may be a tyro; but the two together make a finished and resistless creative artist.

11 July 1929

What the English Novel Needs

The Royal Society of Literature, of which one vaguely hears from time to time, has at last gone over the top, with a book entitled *The Eighteen-Seventies*, by Fellows of the said Society, under the editorship of Harley Granville Barker, who is not old enough to remember the 'seventies and who, having become the best theatrical producer of the century, suddenly abandoned the theatre — an act for which, with all my benevolence, I find it hard to forgive him. (The Cambridge University Press publish the book at 12s. 6d.) The R.S.L. is still 50 years behind the times; but its book is on the whole a good book and full of meat.

Of course, like some other books, it has faults. I cannot understand why it treats of Novelists and "Women Novelists" separately; nor why it treats of Poets and "Women Poets" separately; nor why a second-rate (though good) author such as Andrew Lang should be the sole person to have a chapter (by George Saintsbury) all to himself; nor why Mr. Frederick Boas, in his essay on criticism, should be so forbearing to Leslie Stephen, who was immensely tedious as a critic, if fairish as an editor; nor why lots of other things. But the book is alive.

Sir Arthur Pinero is excellent on the theatre. And Hugh Walpole, as usual, is very vivacious and sound in the matter of fiction. (Mr. Walter de la Mare is a little too lengthy on the subject of women novelists.) Mr. Walpole amusingly and truly says that up to 1870 the English novel "had been consistently regarded as a happy accident rather than an Art." I should have added that it kept this characteristic until about 1883, when George Moore began fiction. Mr. Walpole quotes the marvellous story of the young lady who wrote to Thackeray while *Vanity Fair* was appearing serially and asked him to leave out Amelia and Dobbin for a number or two — and Thackeray complied! I sympathise with the young lady, but instead of humouring her Thackeray ought to have assassinated her.

Mr. Walpole states, and I agree, that the modern novel shows an improvement on its forbears in form, and also in psychology. Nearly all the "best" novelists nowadays have given up the strange old habit of dividing their personages into sheep and goats. To-day, happily, there are no sheep and no goats. I think, too, that the modern novel shows

284

much improvement in style. Mr. Walpole gives considerable praise to Henry Kingsley. Henry was certainly superior to his far more famous brother Charles. But I personally have failed to read either *Ravenshoe* or *The Hillyars and the Burtons,* simply because of their atrocious writing. I would almost as lief read Walter Pater as Henry Kingsley — and that is saying a great deal.

Whether fundamentally better novels are being written in the 1920's than in the 1870's I doubt. Or rather I don't doubt. I feel sure that better novels are not being written by this living generation. The average is better — in externals. But the average has no importance. The average never has importance. I feel more and more that something needs to be done to the novel — English, French and German. I felt this strongly while reading Susan Ertz's new novel *The Galaxy* (Hodder and Stoughton, 7s. 6d.). Miss Ertz is a capable writer, perhaps more than capable. She has received rather high praise, and has deserved it. She presents a steel breastplate to hostile criticism. You cannot say that her work is not true and not good. And yet I was conscious of impatience with *The Galaxy.* I had not "read it all before"; yet I seemed to have read it all before — or at any rate to have read it all before with a difference so small as not to be worth counting.

What the English novel wants, like the French and the German, is a more various observation, a fresher observation. Why do novelists keep on tilling the same old fields? Other and larger fields of life exist, and novelists continue to ignore them. I cannot describe just what those fields are, but at certain moments I can transiently descry them.

I suppose that no Fellow of the august Society of Literature is competent, or would deign, to deal with the advertising of books in the 'seventies. Nevertheless publishers' advertising had, and has, important reactions on the production of literature. Some weeks ago I criticised advertising, and a trade journal, the *Newspaper World,* astonished me by taking my side; for as a rule the trade journals handle my occasional remarks on trade aspects of literature with contumely and disdain. I saw recently in the "house-magazine" of a famous firm of publishers an article which was very critical of publishers' advertising. The writer objected to publishers imitating one another — as if all tradesmen, by a law of nature, do not and must not imitate one another!

It can be said with assurance that the advertising of books has greatly improved since the 'seventies. Also that the improvement has been largely due to the animadversions of critics. The majority of publishers do now describe their wares. In the 'seventies they would not stoop to description. Indeed the startling thing was that they stooped to advertising at all. Publishers to-day are being urged to describe not only their wares, but the authors of their wares. And they obstinately will not do it, or they will do it only rarely and with reluctance. To me the personality and the biographical history of an author — and especially of a new author — have an exciting interest. I desire more than a mere name, and I imagine that I am by no means alone in this desire.

Further, publishers do not always show a lot of gumption in the choice, for their advertisements, of extracts from reviews. I have seen space occupied by quotations quite as futile as the following concocted one: "Enthralling from cover to cover. *Ashby-de-la-Zouche Morning Star.*" But publishers do at times show an odd and to me hardly defensible ingenuity in choosing favourable sentences from unfavourable reviews. Thus: "This book is one of the worst we ever met with; but here and there occurs a page which is very readable." And the advertisement quotation consists of the last two words! This kind of thing has happened to critical comments of my own. Experienced reviewers will occasionally try to write a not wholly unfavourable review from which no excerpt can be detached for the uses of advertisement. The feat is impossible.

Finally, publishers who advertise lavishly will print in their advertisements the same quotations day after day, and week after week, without varying them. This is surely a mistake. All people really interested in books read publishers' advertisements, and many of them read all publishers' advertisements. Such people are easily irritated by excessive repetition, and when they are irritated the advertisement becomes a bit worse than useless.

18 July 1929

Books I Cannot Look At

The problem of "keeping abreast" of interesting new books is now, and for a long time has been, worse than difficult; it is impossible. Even if a man was fool enough, and rich enough, to give his whole time to the job, he could not accomplish it, nor the tenth part of it.

In the ancient days the thing was possible. Even a hundred years ago it was not quite impossible. Everyone who read read Harriette Wilson's *Memoirs* (just republished in full in one volume by Peter Davies, Limited, price 7s. 6d.). Harriette probably made more money out of the book than out of any single love affair; and the publisher had to stockade his shop in order to keep book-buyers from attempting to buy her chatter and backchat.

No bookseller's shop and no publisher's office will ever be stockaded again. At the apogee of Dickens' fame Chapman and Hall's offices were never in a state of siege.

Modern publishers and booksellers would welcome the exciting and inconvenient experience of a public assault; but they may long for it in vain. The output is too vast, competition too keen, and the public too sophisticated. *Naiveté* has ceased to be a characteristic of the lettered.

In the matter of reading there are giants in these days — such as Aldous Huxley, Logan Pearsall Smith, and Leif Jones, M.P., but none of them attempts to keep abreast generally. None of them attempts to keep abreast of the comparatively few books which are understood to be the cream of the milk of publications. None of them attempts to keep abreast even of the finest books in any particular line. They have all realised that the least of these feats cannot be achieved.

I suppose that I see and look at as many new books as anybody not a bookseller or the head of the reviewing department of a newspaper; but I do not and cannot read five per cent. of the pages that reach me.

How do I select? I have no system. And I have only one rule which I sometimes break: never to read, for journalistic purposes, any book by a friend who is famous and successful. I select more or less at random, and for reasons which could seldom be called rational. And neither I nor anybody else could devise a satisfactory system of selection.

The known good books are too numerous, and many good books remain unknown for years, though I am convinced that any first-rate book ultimately receives the recognition which it deserves. Justice, with a cynical wink, in the end triumphs. We may as well make up our minds to the perhaps grievous fact that we shall be lowered into the grave without having read some thousands of books each of which was worth reading and would have enlarged our outlook and therefore improved our characters!

No one should or need apologise for not having read a good new book. And no confirmed reader should promise to read a good new book brought to his notice by a good judge, for the odds are enormous that he would break such a promise.

The fault lies not with the productiveness of authors, not with the assimilativeness of readers. It lies with the absurd rapidity of the earth's revolution, whose rate ought to have been altered when printing was invented. The earth has somehow refused to keep pace with the times. It outdistances the times.

If there were a hundred and twenty-four hours in every day and three thousand three hundred and sixty-five days in every year, and we all lived to seventy years, bookmen might have a chance. But nature is implacable as usual. All that bookmen can usefully do is to drop a book the moment it has bored them for a score of pages, sell it, and pick up another. The golden maxim for bookmen is: Cut your losses.

With regard to old books of established prestige, the problem is difficult, but less difficult, because the number of them is definitely limited. I think that I have read every known first-rate French novel published during the last century and a half. Ditto translated Russian. And I wish I hadn't, partly because, within such limits, I am in the awkward position of Alexander, and partly because I have had to come to the conclusion that many of them are not first-rate after all.

In English fiction I have still in reserve quite a number for perusal in my older age. I leave them and leave them, while giving up the precious moments of eternity to books which I feel sure are their inferiors. This is human; but one should thank heaven daily that one is human, for to be inhuman is to be a pest of society.

Only three years ago I went, for the first time, to the Tower, and only three years ago I read *The Moonstone*, which is in my view the finest of all English mystery stories. I have not yet been to the Crystal Palace, and I shall never go. I have not yet read *The Antiquary*, and unless I am consigned to a nursing home in a foreign clime and *The Antiquary* is the only book within ten miles, I shall never read it. Enthusiasts tell me that it is very good, and I respect them, but my determination not to read it is absolute. Of such stuff are we made.

On the other hand, like other erring and sensible people, I spend hours in bed reading books which I have read again and again. Which habit has confirmed me in the conviction that no great book is truly read until it has been read at least three times. Some books are readable thirty times.

287

When I am overwhelmed with books I say to myself like the naughty child we all are: "I won't look at any of them. I'll read something I know something about." (Auld Lang Syne and so on!) And the earnest and admirable new authors who demand and deserve attention are shamefully cast aside.

And what do I turn to? Well, the short stories of de Maupassant, who Meredith said was the greatest of all imaginative prose writers. Or the short stories of Chekhov, who I say is greater than de Maupassant. Or Stendhal, whose *Lucien Leuwen*, whose *Le Rouge et le Noir*, and whose *Journals* (which he certainly in part faked for effectiveness) are a treasure inexhaustible. Or Dostoevsky — all Dostoevsky. Or certain poems of Matthew Arnold, who has not yet reached adequate appreciation. Or the songs in *The Princess*. A strange list. Possibly; but my list.

Further, like other abandoned readers, I begin lots of fine books (that I have mostly read before) and leave them for other fine books. At this present there lie on my night-table, besides the Bible (whose love-stories and lamentations and diatribes are incomparable), *The Decline and Fall*, Sydney Smith's *Peter Plymley's Letters*, the *Journal* of the brothers de Goncourt, Froude's *Elizabeth*, Harriette Wilson's *Memoirs* (only semi-fine) and Rousseau's *Confessions*.

I am in the middle of all of them, and I have been in the middle of all of them before (except Harriette). And I must incidentally remark that the *Confessions* is a masterpiece among masterpieces of sober veracity. And the other night I rejected the whole batch for André Gide's new novelette, *L'Ecole des Femmes*. And I did not regret having done so. For in its simplicity it has the "feel" of the classic.

25 July 1929

Holiday Book Dreams

Ordinary people, by which I mean people not specially interested in books, when they are going off for a holiday, do their packing and then think: "Oh by the way! Books!" But bookmen (and women) take pleasure in thinking what books they will pack, and what wonderful reading they will do while distant from their bookshelves. They dream upon books before they dream upon neckties — or even upon frocks. Their dreams seldom come true; but does that seriously matter? A dream is an end in itself.

My experience is that the more bookish people are the more ingenuous they are. And such is part of their charm. Not one in ten of them but is the victim, year after year, of the illusion that holiday means plenty of lovely, luscious leisure for reading.

The thing somehow works out differently. To be idle is an arduous occupation and holidays are usually arduous. Settling into your quarters means three restless days, getting out of your quarters means three more restless days; and the too brief interval of security during which you really know where you are, is apt to be filled up with activities not favourable to the delicate affair of perusal.

The notion that you have more time for reading from home than at home is a fallacious one. The great readers of the earth, I have found, are generally the busy people with not a moment to spare. If I want an opinion about a book which I think might interest me, I go to some bookish head of a vast organised business enterprise; he has always read it: his opinion may be wrong, but he has an opinion.

We all assert, honestly and not untruthfully, that we lack time for reading; but we have at home more time than we think. The proof: When an overworked person happens to get hold of a book which really interests him, he will miraculously discover hidden reserves of time for reading it.

I once knew a young woman, whose existence, like that of most young women, was one incessant rush. She was for ever complaining that she could only read in bed, and that as soon as she began to read in bed she went to sleep. I excited her by remarks about Tolstoy's *War and Peace*. I lent her the book. She read it in four days. *War and Peace* is one of the longest novels written in the nineteenth century. When I asked her how she managed the feat she could not reply, because she did not know the answer.

Similar cases are by no means uncommon. If you don't often read the explanation is that you don't often genuinely want to read. You fancy that you are ever hungry for intellectual or emotional literature; but you deceive yourself.

People read at home because minutes for reading are few, and therefore precious, and therefore eagerly seized. On holiday minutes are as plenteous as pebbles on the beach. People conceive that a day is eternity. No hurry! The morning drips away, but afternoon awaits illimitable. Afternoon drips away, but evening is in store. Evening connotes fatigue. Bed — with the happy prospect of another illimitable day, and an endless succession of them! . . . Then the approach of the end of the holiday. The terrible distracting thought of packing! All is over.

Which of us has not undergone this experience? Still, some of us, possibly the majority, do get through a certain amount of reading even in the leisure of a holiday; though for myself I have never yet on a holiday read what I had intended to read or as much as I desired to read.

In regard to the choice of holiday books, the first rule is to choose too many. A man once said to me: "When I go for a holiday, I absolutely must be free from material harassments. Hence I calculate what is the largest sum of money I can possibly require. I double it, and I take that. Then I don't care." An excellent device, but not all of us can follow it. All of us, however, can follow it in the matter of books if not of money.

The wise reader takes books not necessarily to read them but to have them handy for any accidents of mood. A woman knowingly takes more frocks than she can wear; a dandy takes more neckties, socks and suits than he can wear. A bookman takes more books than he is ever likely to read. They are his balance at the bank.

Nothing is more terrible than to be seized with a fever of reading and to finish the last of your stock. It is like the end of the world, the Day of Judgment, being thrown out of a situation, being cast on the streets. The heart horribly sinks. You look around in the lounge of the hotel. Everybody else is reading *The Chicago Tribune, The Iron-Foundry News, The Rosary*, or a detective novel. You cannot borrow, and there is naught worth stealing. The sensation is awful. I know, because I have suffered it.

Take an extravagant plenty of books, for you know not what a day may bring forth.

The second rule is to include in your selection a good proportion of old friends. You would not go for a holiday with a party consisting exclusively of total strangers, or if you did you would deserve the worst that might happen to you. One stranger; two or three strangers; but always an ample leaven of friends with whose character and idiosyncrasies you are familiar.

Surely it should be the same with books! A fine, strange book may enthrall you. But on the other hand it may exasperate you, and then you must have a refuge from it and from all other strange books. The sole refuge is a book that you know of old. It may not be a great book, but you know the thing. You need not be on your best behaviour with it. You can skip pages without accusing yourself of bad manners or fearing to miss a passage which might influence the curve of your whole life.

The third rule is to free yourself of the idea that on a holiday you should improve your mind and that therefore you should choose books which you ought to read rather than books which you enjoy reading. The idea is ridiculous. If you have not improved your mind in eleven months at home you had better leave your mind in its primeval imbecility. A holiday is for fun, and neither July, August nor September is a proper month for mental reform and advancement. Think only of the *pleasure* of reading. If your taste is low, which God forbid, let it be low.

There are no other rules for holiday reading.

1 August 1929

A Man Who Breaks Books

A book such as Mr. G.D. Hobson's *English Bindings before 1500* (published by the Cambridge University Press in an edition of 500 copies at three guineas each) may not at the first glance seem to be of tremendous interest to the average book-lover. And yet to me, who have no specialised knowledge on any subject on earth, it has proved extremely interesting.

To begin with there is the interest of finding a really learned man such as Mr. Hobson — no doubt the most learned man on his subject in Britain — writing like an angel, and wearing his immense erudition with the elegance of a well-cut and not-too-new suit. (Would that all specialists wrote as well, as clearly, as gracefully, as — indeed — perfectly! The general curse of specialism is bad writing.)

Then there is the historical interest of the bindings, displayed in numerous illustrations. The earliest example of binding (in leather, without "tools") is a Northumbrian seventh-century affair (St. John's Gospel) taken from the tomb of St. Cuthbert in 1104. Curious, the passion of mediaeval persons for opening holy tombs! St. Cuthbert's was opened four times, and only at the fourth opening was the unique volume removed from the coffin.

A gap of some five centuries exists between this rarissime survival and the next survival, which by comparison is quite modern, for the time-difference between them is about the same as that between the battle of Agincourt and the battle of the Marne.

Then there is the artistic interest of the designs, some of which are as beautiful as they are morbid! We see, in our cathedrals and elsewhere, mediaeval designs, and we assume that in the Middle Ages what to us is morbidity appeared quite natural and wholesome. But was it so? St. Bernard himself was inveighing nearly eight hundred years ago thus:

"What profit is there in those ridiculous monsters, in that marvellous and deformed comeliness, in that comely deformity? To what purpose are those unclean apes, those fierce lions, those monstrous centaurs, those half-men. . . . Many bodies are there seen under one head, or again many heads to a single body. . . . In short so many and so marvellous are the varieties of divers shapes on every hand that we are more tempted to read in the marble than in our books, and to spend the whole day in wondering at these things than in meditating the law of God. For God's sake, if men are not ashamed of these follies, *why at least do they not shrink from the expense?*"

What could be more modern and more sane, than these antique words? I wish I could quote them in full. They lead naturally to the sociological interest of the book, in which Mr. Hobson shows how the changes in binding were brought about largely through sociological or economic causes.

The one complaint I have against *English Bindings before 1500* is that the letterpress is too brief. The author might with advantage have expanded the original lectures to three times their length. The volume is one for collectors as well as for mere book-lovers. It is as large as a folio, but in fact it is a quarto. In these days one rarely sees a real folio, though there are not a few quartos which have the dimensions of folios.

Of course, I ought now to make a comparison between antique bindings and modern bindings, extolling the antique to the depreciation of the modern. But I will not do it. As regards bindings de luxe, my opinion, founded on my experience, is that an amateur who takes the trouble can obtain as fine bindings to-day as amateurs could obtain in any age without exception. But he must take the trouble and he must pay the price, as his predecessors took the trouble and paid the price.

As regards the customary cloth bindings of commerce, they are the inevitable outcome of new economic editions; and if many are bad, many are good. And English cloth bindings are probably on the whole better than either German or American. The French have few commercial bindings, and those few are of a surpassing ugliness.

The mischief with modern commercial cloth bindings is the stitchery and the paste. The mischief is also with the user of the book, who too often abuses it. He usually forces the book open anyhow, hears that formidable crack which means that the binding is ruined for ever, and utters diatribes against commercial binding.

The proper way to open any unread book is to hold it perpendicular with its back on a table and then put down flat the front cover and then the back cover, and then to press down a few of the first pages on to the front cover and then a few of the last pages on to the back cover, and so on till all the pages have been pressed down — half of them to the left and half to the right. In this manner and no other will the shape of the book be conserved. And be it remembered that the shape of a book once spoilt can never be restored.

And further be it remembered by collectors — and to-day we are all collectors! — that the integrity and cleanliness of the cloth binding has a very important influence on the monetary value of all first editions. Take, for instance, a copy of Shaw's *Widowers' Houses*, tear off the common cloth binding, and spend £25 on a fine calf binding, and the book will be worth less than it was before you began to meddle with it.

And surely this is right and just. If you wish to maintain the worth of a rare first edition of a modern author, you may have a case made to contain it, but you may not re-bind it. I saw only the other day a rare first edition of Darwin which had been elaborately bound in costly calf and fatally diminished in market value.

A few weeks ago, speaking of the collecting-habit (which is unquestionably growing at a great rate — especially in the matter of books and manuscripts) I suggested that somebody ought to begin collecting "dust jackets" of new books. I felt quite convinced that this notion was a novelty of my own invention. Soon afterwards I was stopped in Piccadilly by a stranger who asked me if I was I. The reply was, and had to be, in the affirmative.

"Well," said the accoster, "I should like to tell you that I have been collecting dust jackets for years, and that I already possess between four and five hundred of them." He further told me that he knew of another man who had been collecting them for some time.

I stood subdued. Nothing is new except bread, and not always that. The collecting of dust jackets puts the collector in a rather awkward position. Either he must remove the dust jacket at once, or he must risk the shop finish of the binding (so valuable at auction sales), or he must put on a dust jacket of plain paper.

Most dust jackets are ugly; but some are really beautiful; and the best show the excellent influence of Mr. McKnight Kauffer's old Underground posters. The average is far higher than it was five years ago.

8 August 1929

The Oddest Novel Ever Written

On the Continent, the most *discussed* English author is James Joyce. And perhaps rightly so. *The Dubliners* and *Portrait of the Artist as a Young Man* both show genius. *Ulysses* contains the grossest obscenity. It may not be a great whole. But it is a work distinguished by much greatness and still more originality. It has pages which no novelist in any country has ever surpassed. Its influence has been and is enormous.

And now after five years of hard labour, it has been integrally translated in French by Auguste Morel and Stuart Gilbert. That the translation has been revised from start to finish by Valéry Larbaud is a sufficient guarantee, not merely of the excellence of the translation but of the artistic value of the work. Edition of 1000 copies, the cheapest 200 francs. Each copy 2½ inches thick. Published by Madame Adrienne Monnier.

It is curious how James Joyce has been helped by women. Miss Margaret Anderson and Miss Jane Heap got themselves into the police-court in New York over the serial publication of *Ulysses*. Another lady tried and failed to publish the novel in Britain. And Miss Sylvia Beach is publisher-in-ordinary to James Joyce in France.

Miss Beach has just published (24 francs), in English, a book by a dozen more or less young authors about Joyce's new and still unfinished novel at present provisionally called *Work in Progress*. The title of the explanatory volume is too absurd to be quoted.* And some of the contents are absurd. On the other hand some of the contents are not. Mr. Stuart Gilbert and Mr. John Rodker write well enough about it to compel respect for it.

Work in Progress is understood to be a novel about heroes. It may be. I read (I should say, I examined) various excerpts from it when portions of the book appeared serially in *Transition*, and I must say that I haven't the least idea what the story is about.

For this James Joyce has invented, concocted, and conjured up a sort of super-portmanteau language of his own. He has obviously had a vision of the possible evolution of the English tongue. None but a man of very remarkable gifts of imagination and pure brain could have had such a vision. It does immense credit to his brain and his imagination. But little to his common sense.

The more you study his language (by the light of Stuart Gilbert's essay) the more you are impressed by the man's learning, ingenuity, and astounding capacity for multiple allusiveness.

Anyone who is prepared to make the reading of James Joyce's new, incomplete book a life's career, and who has the lexicographical skill to construct a James Joyce encyclopaedic dictionary might conceivably derive emotional benefit from *Work in Progress*, and might procure the same benefit for at most a dozen other bizarre human beings. Apart from such thirteen human beings, *Work in Progress* will not be read, because it cannot be read by any individual normally constituted. *Ulysses* has had many respectable imitators.

Work in Progress will never be respectably imitated. I think it ought to rank as the oddest novel written. It will probably be unique.

If James Joyce is content with a possible thirteen readers, that is his affair and his alone. But to me the entire business is queer in a high degree. Indeed I do not hesitate to give my opinion that James Joyce has been culpably wasting his time (and other people's), and his genius. Also I regard it as a bad sign that an unfinished work should be the subject of an exegetical volume (200 pages) by twelve ardent disciples. Of ardent disciples the sane person should always beware. I recommend the discipular book solely to those with a passion for the curiosities of literature.

In the interstices of reading, re-reading, and reading about, James Joyce, I read a short novel, if novel it can be called, which shows a mentality as different from the mentality of James Joyce as any sound mentality could be from another. Namely, Mr. G.F. Bradby's *Little George* (Constable, 6s.).

Our Exagmination round His Factification for Incamination of Work in Progress by Samuel Beckett, M. Brion & c. The title was Joyce's own.

Mr. Bradby is or was a schoolmaster, and his novel, *The Lanchester Tradition*, about schoolmasters and pedagogic politics, is so good that anything from the same pen and mind merits careful attention.

Little George is aged nine, and the story of him is concerned much less with school than with what George called "hols." It is a goodish book, and worth reading; but I was somewhat disappointed with it because it is on the "sweet" side, and because various aspects of what must have been the totality of George's character are simply not displayed. The contents of the story are truthful, but they are misleading by reason of the author's omissions.

I never yet met a boy, in intimacy, much less a girl, whose make-up had not quite a fair percentage of cruelty and general unscrupulousness. And I am still waiting for a realistic novel whose hero or heroine is a child. People not without discernment say that a novel mainly about a child cannot be first-rate in interest. I doubt it.

If no novel about children (within my restricted knowledge) has hitherto been of first-rate interest, the reason, I think, lies in the too kindly, sentimental attitude of authors of novels about children. A child, like a woman, is a realist. Vast quantities of nonsense are written about men, but still more about women and children.

There is a "cult" of women and a "cult" of children. Both cults do a disservice to truth, and truth alone makes the stuff of first-rate interest. Women do not in their hearts like to be told pretty untruths concerning themselves which they know to be untruths. Such treatment gives them a sense of inferiority.

A man will get on better with a woman by conveying to her, with cold, measured moderation, what he deems to be the truth about herself for, say, ten minutes every other day. (She will return the favour with high interest.) Children do as a rule hear this truth about themselves daily, and for more than ten minutes. Do they resent it? They do not. They respect the teller, as a realistic equal. They will even passionately embrace the teller.

Then why should the complete truth concerning children be withheld in a novel about children written for adults? Children would read it, for children read almost anything. It would be helpful to children, and it would be even more helpful to adults — and far more amusing and enthralling.

Too many children are treated by novelists as charming toys. They are charming toys, with moments, hours, of the tenderest enchanting witchery. But they are more than toys. Of all mammals in the universe the human child can be, and often is, the most terrible. Plenty of good novelists have an intimate acquaintance with children. Yet they either leave them out of their novels, or, if they put them in, they handle them with padded gloves. Why? I know not.

A realistic, aloof, judicial, fearless, ruthless novel about a child would assuredly raise a stir in the world of letters. The author would be vilified for six months. But what matter? The novel would survive. And it would do something to kill sentimentality in future novels about children. H.G. Wells could write such a novel. Aldous Huxley too.

15 August 1929

The Great Sham of a Pall Mall Club

In the Italian hotel was a row of forty-four books, almost entirely English. Now books ought to be on bookshelves. But these were on a sideboard, with a thick volume laid flat on either side — to keep them from slithering to the floor. So placed, they had an air as unnatural and forlorn as lions and tigers on a Mappin terrace. Nobody read them. Nobody even touched them. I alone took notice of them, and I only looked at their titles.

And yet they were an extraordinary collection of works. Dr. Moffatt's new and perhaps misguided translation of the New Testament stood next to Oscar Wilde's *A House of Pomegranates*, and next to that the two most popular volumes (about children) of the century — *When we were very Young* and *Winnie the Pooh*.

Ivanhoe was present of course, and equally of course *The Pickwick Papers* and *Cranford* and *A Child's Garden of Verse*. But there were two Conrads, an Anatole France, Ruskin's *Seven Lamps*, *The Hunting of the Snark*, *Diana of the Crossways*, Ernest Milton's *To Kiss the Crocodile*, a comparatively obscure Edgar Wallace, *Aylwin* (once so famous, now on the far side of the Styx), a Smollett, a P.G. Wodehouse, and two books of Louisa Alcott (who is a ten times better writer than most haughty moderns suppose, and who will be read long after *Beau Geste* — not absent from the sideboard — has joined *Aylwin* on the far side of the above-named dark river).

On the whole an excellent catholic, if limited, library. More than half of it was worth reading. And of how many hotel libraries can this be truthfully said? Assuredly not of the renowned Tremont Library of Boston, Mass., whose catalogues I once examined with too much care.

The majority of hotel libraries are astounding. And when the hotel is large enough to maintain a bookshop, the contents of the bookshop are usually still more astounding. At the "bookstand" of one of the most fashionable hotels in the world (London) the following conversation recently took place.

Customer: "Haven't you got anything else but Edgar Wallace?"

Salesman: "No, sir. We are scarcely ever asked for anything else."

Which shows the quaint result of luxury. Not that I have anything against Edgar Wallace, a man of singular ability and fecundity. Still, other authors do exist.

And there are worse phenomena than a collection consisting exclusively of Edgar Wallace. On an unforgettable day some years ago I was led into a large club in Pall Mall and there discovered a well-designed small bookcase full of marvellously attractive titles. Only the books were sham books — backs of books glued on to boards, as for a library scene on the stage.

I doubt whether, in the whole history of clubs and literature, this phenomenon has ever been surpassed. Withal, the sham books did give an atmosphere of letters to the magnificent palace.

I wanted books to read in the Italian hotel. Apart from the most reliable and informative author of all time — Karl Baedeker — I had only three books of my own: a volume of Chekhov's stories, a volume of the

Goncourt *Journal*, and Stendhal's *Abbess of Castro*; and I had read them all before, more than once. I could not, however, persuade myself to take up a single one of the admirable works on the sideboard. They wistfully appealed to be opened and read. But there was not an ounce of sentimentality in me.

Those books were somehow denaturalised for me. They were under a curse, and I would not lift it. At some period of their past life they must have committed a crime, been guilty of at least a nameless turpitude. And only the exploring hand of naive innocence could absolve them and release them from the sinister spell under which their sin had laid them. My hand, in the matter of books, is not naive and not innocent. I glanced again and again at their titles; and resumed contact with my familiars, Chekhov, Stendhal and the brothers de Goncourt.

And now I must make my annual complaint against Continental and British hotel-keepers. They — particularly the former — provide every kind of physical luxury for their clients. Some of them even provide machinery for bolting and unbolting doors from the bedside; a few of them even provide nocturnal silence, which is the rarest of all hotel commodities; a mere handful go so far as to provide the total absence of those third-rate orchestras which both impair digestion and destroy conversation.

But none of them, so far as my knowledge extends, provides in a reasonable manner for the literary needs of its customers, who for the most part are everywhere Anglo-Saxon. Never in any hotel have I seen the smallest supply of works of reference in the English tongue — or in any tongue. Yet people on their travels do frequently feel the need of works of reference. All sorts of people — not only lettered persons! How many British people, for instance, would make good use of *Ruff's Guide to the Turf* if it were available? Quite a lot. Similarly with the cricket, golf, and lawn-tennis annuals.

As to ordinary works of reference, I know nothing of the American. But of British works of reference, did anybody ever see a copy of the current issue of *Whitaker's Almanack* in a continental hotel? I never did. Nevertheless, if any book can be called indispensable to the daily life of hundreds of thousands of educated British people, *Whitaker* is that book.

A dictionary and a small encyclopaedia and a handy world-atlas could be obtained by hotel-directors for the price of a dish of caviare. There are at least a score of reference books in Dent's Everyman series the entire cost of which would be negligible in the installation of a hotel.

It cannot be any consideration of expense which deters hotel-directors from this form of catering. It can only be either a lack of imagination, or a deep disdain for the intelligence and the intellectual needs of their clientèles. Such disdain is in my opinion undeserved. Plain travellers are not cows; nor is education, even advanced education, aught but a spur to travel. Again and again have I met on my holidays individuals who knew ten times as much as I knew on forty different subjects.

The remedy for the present barbaric state of affairs lies in the active exercise of travelled public opinion. Hotel guests have got numerous physical conveniences by the simple method of making a fuss. They might get books by the same simple method.

I would not absolutely demand of hotel-directors a supply of good general literature, though I think they would find their reward in supplying it. And I think also that such a body as the National Book Council might do something to guide them. But I do absolutely demand a fairly efficient supply of reference books.

One day the demand will be satisfied. The date of that happy day, however, will depend on the degree to which travellers are prepared to make themselves vocal on the matter.

22 August 1929

This "Bosh" About Art For Art's Sake

Some short time ago I said that often, in reading even good novelists, you had the impression that you had read before all that you were reading. I said also that large fields of human interest, psychological and other, were left absolutely untouched by good novelists. In view of certain correspondence received by me, I wish now to make it clear that these observations were not intended to put blame upon our good novelists. For blame is not due. Novelists, like hotel-keepers and theatre-managers and street-hawkers, work under very difficult conditions. The public itself constitutes the most difficult condition of all. Fiction-writing would be easier if the public did not exist. The novelist, however, wants and needs a public more than anything. Novelists don't write for themselves. They write in order to share their sensations with, and to give pleasure to, the rest of the world. The rest of the world is the public.

Now the public does several things which are inconvenient to the novelist. In the first place, it establishes taboos. There are various enthralling matters of which it dislikes the mention. Some taboos have been lifted within the last ten years; and to-day the novelist actually enjoys about fifty per cent. of the freedom of talkers at an ordinary dinner-table. Nevertheless we are still victimised by powerful taboos. Shakespeare — and even writers as late as Balzac — could state and suggest ideas, both serious and comic, which are utterly forbidden by current taboos. Some of Shakespeare's finest jokes are his "coarsest." Ditto for Balzac.

If you would realise what a novelist might do, but what he mustn't do, examine, for instance, Freud's astonishing and superb article on "Dostoevsky and Parricide" in the July number of *The Realist.* Nobody has taken offence at this article, because it appeared in a scientific and philosophical periodical. It is full of brilliant material for novelists. But let a novelist begin to use the material, and see what would happen! An earthquake is naught compared to what would happen.

In the second place, the public shows an instinctive hostility to anything really *original.* The original disturbs and disconcerts, and who among us likes such an experience? Be good enough to note that in my opinion the public is fully entitled to its point of view. But this fact does nothing to ease the situation of the novelist who desires to be original.

In the third place — and here perhaps is the worst of the affair — the public hates to think that any artist works for money. It knows of course that almost every artist works for money. It knows, or ought to know, that the majority of the world's masterpieces, in all the arts, were commissioned by exacting patrons, done to order, and done for money. Yet let not the disgraceful truth be so much as whispered!

Men are praised for earning money by broking stocks and shares, by building houses, by manufacturing tobacco, artificial silk, soap, champagne, refuse-destructors. It is recognised that these men are subject to a given economic régime. But to the public the artist, though he lives under precisely the same economic régime, is in a different category, and unless he is a mercenary scoundrel he should toil without thought of money! The public does not trouble to explain to artists how they are economically to survive. The shortest proper word for this extraordinary notion is "Bosh." But the notion exists. I have been consistently frank about it in print for thirty years; and none of my assorted candours has incurred for me half so much odium as this candour.

I maintain that it is an essential part of the job of an artist to meet the demands of a market. He need not try to meet all of them, but he must meet some; because he must live, and if he has a family (as he should have) the family must live too. I have no use for artists who, determined to be original at any cost, are original at the cost of their friends and their tradesmen. I would call them spongers, harpies, and even thieves. If I procured potatoes from a greengrocer on credit, and then shuffled off the mortal coil of debt on the plea that I was engaged in the august enterprise of being an original artist, I would deem myself rather worse than a plain thief.

An artist should be a citizen before he is an artist. I esteem more highly a man who is an honest citizen at the expense of art than a man who is an honest artist at the expense of citizenship. Everything is relative; honesty is relative; so is art. And reasonable compromise is and always has been the basis of the artist's peace of mind in a naughty world.

One thing more has to be said of artists. As a rule they are by nature unbusinesslike. Often they fail in good citizenship chiefly because they do not understand finance and are incapable of keeping accounts. They cannot change their nature.

Thus it is seen that the obstacles to originality in the arts, and not less in the art of fiction than in the others, are of two kinds: moral and economic. Some novelists are not original because, at one with their public, they have no yearning after originality. What suits them suits their public, and there you are! Other novelists are not original because they are timid, prudent, chary of accepting risks. It takes a very big man indeed to confront and defy a whole generation, a whole system of taboos and prejudices. And those very big men who have achieved the feat successfully have always compromised, and I think that they have always been interested in money.

The supreme instance is Shakespeare, who compromised like anything, but who possessed the exceedingly rare gift of pleasing both himself and a considerable public. An ingenious fellow, Shakespeare! And he knew when to stop. Having acquired a sufficiency of money, and having the sense to see that he could never do better work than he had done already, he said to himself: "I am going to get out." And he got out.

There was startlingly little of art for art's sake in the greatest literary artist of the Christian era. I doubt if he complained much of the conditions in which he had to work. The greatest men don't so complain. It is the little men who are always at loggerheads with the public and maundering about martyrdoms. The greatest men have comprehended that obstacles are good for the soul. For myself, I should be inclined to be sorry if the desire to be original were suddenly to be untrammelled. A lot of dreadful printed nonsense would ensue.

29 August 1929

Always Read With An Open Mind

Spring and the New Year are about to begin. I mean the book Spring and New Year. The seasons of literature are different from the seasons of nature. They are shorter and more frequent. Indeed, for every revolution of the earth round the sun there are two literary years, one briefer than the other. The greater though briefer literary year starts with what is called in nature the Autumn. Its Spring coincides with September. Its Summer — always very hot indeed, for both readers and reviewers — coincides with November.

In December the literary Winter sets in. By mid-December those lusty plants the publishers have ceased to bear flowers and fruit, or even vegetables. And by the end of nature's year all is frozen hard in the literary domain. The ice gives sign of cracking and crumbling as early as mid-January, when the longer but lesser literary year opens. All which, though it may sound complicated, really is not complicated.

Now the literary New Year, like nature's, is the moment for good resolutions, and I wish to propose a good resolution. It has nothing to do with buying, borrowing, begging or stealing books. I care not how many or how few readers read books, nor by what means, fair or foul, they obtain them. I care not about programmes of reading, syllabuses, collecting, learning, nor any such trifles. What concerns me to-day is the judgment of readers on whatever books they do happen to read. My good resolution may be thus phrased: "I will form my own opinions of the books I read, and I will not accept in advance the opinions of other people."

This seems easy enough. Most readers will exclaim: "But I *do* form my own opinions." To which I would reply: "If you do form your own opinions, unprejudiced by what you have seen in print, or heard, you are a somewhat exceptional person, and I remove my hat to you as to a superior being." The truth is that very few readers form their own opinions about books. To do so is exceedingly difficult. As with politics, so with books, the majority of the citizens are far too inclined to believe what they are told, and to think what they think they ought to think.

The prestige of weighty or oft-repeated names is powerful. And the influence of fashion is equally powerful. Take the classics of English literature. Any nice-minded reader who picks up a classic is convinced beforehand that he ought to like it, and that if he does not like it he is a barbarian and a savage without taste. Therefore whether he truly likes it or not, he tries earnestly to persuade himself that he does like it. Why?

Snobbishness is by no means the whole of the explanation. A genuine

299

yearning after righteousness enters largely into it. But there can be no righteousness in an act of self-deceit, however well-intentioned. An honest individual opinion, though it may be bad or half-bad, is better, morally, and perhaps artistically too, than an insincere opinion which coincides with authoritative opinion. It assists the two great causes of honesty and personal freedom. Besides, the classics are not sacred. They are not fixed for ever and ever in the firmament. Authoritative opinions change from epoch to epoch. That which was held to be a classic a century ago may have lost its position to-day. And that which is totally neglected to-day may a century hence have ascended to the dignity of the classic.

What is the use of pretence? If you don't really enjoy a book you don't; and there's no more to be said. You may be wrong; but on the other hand you may be right. Classics are made and unmade by the expression of honest individual opinions and by nothing else.

For myself I have done, and still am doing, my best to destroy the classicality of Dickens. And a rare lot of trouble I have brought upon myself thereby! But I blandly suffer the trouble as being part of the fair price which has to be paid for honesty. Ninety per cent. of Dickens bores me. I can't help it. I won't hide it. And I have the satisfaction of perceiving that more and more people are siding with me.

But Dickens is a highly dangerous topic. Let us take a topic less dangerous: Sterne. I rejoice in the *Sentimental Journey*. I emphatically do not rejoice in that starry classic, *Tristram Shandy*. I find the bulk of *Tristram Shandy* tedious. But I should love to know what percentage of the readers or alleged readers of *Tristram Shandy* honestly revel in it as they are supposed to do. I met an ardent admirer of the book not long since. He said that he re-read it every year. I asked: "Do you read it all through?" He blenched. Yes, he blenched. "No," he said at length. "I read *in* it." I was satisfied with the admission. My belief is that *Tristram Shandy* is dropping out of the firmament. And a good thing too, if five experienced readers in every six now read it with difficulty and without pleasure! Let honesty reign, if the stars fall.

It is perhaps even harder to be uninfluenced in the judging of a modern book than of a classic. Fashion has a way of autocratically ruling over intelligences. When "everybody" is chattering about a book and saying what a wonderful book it is "everybody else" is moved not only to read it, but to believe that it must be good even before the first page has been perused. The prejudice in favour of the fashionable book exerts its dominion in such a manner that the reader unconsciously assumes the excellence of whose very existence he ought, for himself, to be the sole judge. The most glaring faults are condoned. The verdict indeed precedes the trial. This is a common phenomenon, and occurs half a dozen times during each literary season.

But you may proudly say: "I am not thus constituted. When a book becomes the rage I ignore it." Yet in saying this you show that you are the victim of another prejudice — the prejudice against. Why should a book be ignored because it happens to be fashionable? It may be a good book. And anyhow a book which has pleased a large number of one's fellow-creatures is meet to be glanced at as a matter of human curiosity. Further, a certain percentage of readers, even if they go so far as to read a very popular book, read it with a determination not to like it. And the natural result is that they generally succeed in not liking it. I am quite ready to admit in my own case that the praise of some critics, or the dispraise of some others, has the effect of prejudicing me against or for a book. I say to myself: "X has given frequent proof of bad taste. X likes this book. Therefore this book is bad." Or the reverse. In such grossly unfair mood do I sometimes begin.

The entire business is studded with pitfalls. It is necessary to examine one's reactions to a book with as much care as one examines the book. Totally to eliminate prejudice is out of the question. But by taking thought one can achieve more sincerity of judgment than can be achieved without taking thought. The final difficulty, when a sincere judgment has been arrived at, is to express that judgment fearlessly. Are we not all moral cowards?

5 September 1929

The Art of Writing Six Novels At Once

I was surprised the other day to find that the run of *Rose Marie* in Paris has now exceeded one thousand performances, and the end is by no means yet in sight.

I ought not to have been surprised at the French success of this apparently deathless work which marries music to literature, considering that I have spent about a quarter of a century in maintaining, contrary to the general view, that French dramatic taste is no better than English. (Nevertheless French dramatic technique is much better.)

I remember seeing, in the earliest nineteen-hundreds, an extraordinarily crude French farce called *Tire-au-flanc* (*The Shirker*). *Tire-au-flanc* is still succeeding, and will fill a Paris theatre in summer when almost nothing else will.

Then again: I observe on the bookstalls of every French railway station the detective-novels of which the illustrious American detective Nick Carter is the hero. I imagine that Nick Carter is as popular in France as in the United States, and more popular than in England.

I know not whether the Nick Carter novels are great, but their author, John Coryell, was certainly great — he died only a few years ago. Before he had written any Nick Carters he went into the office of a New York firm of publishers specialising in the detective species, and said: "I can write better detective stories than anything you publish."

Now an English firm would probably have asked such a man to leave the office instantly. The American firm characteristically answered: "Try."

Coryell tried, and won. His stories fabulously sent up circulations.

Coryell was the American Edgar Wallace — before Wallace. Possibly more so. He contracted to write a million words a year, was never late with his copy, never altered his copy, never corrected a proof. He could and did write six different novels at once, one for every weekday. He began work at 4 a.m. He out-Trolloped Trollope. He loved writing. He was never at a loss for a solution.

His son, in a very interesting article in *The New York Bookman*, relates that once, when Coryell had tossed Nick, bound hand and foot, over the side of an Atlantic liner in mid-ocean, his editor "shook a doubting head" and protested: "My God, Coryell, can't you curb that d——d imagination of yours?"

He couldn't. Nor was there need for him to curb it. He wrote under at least six different pseudonyms, several of them girlish, and under the latter he produced the sentimental-domestic, once beating even Louisa Alcott in a competition! There were no limits to John Coryell. He indulged freely in the moral-purpose; and, further, he wrote plays.

The above must be taken as a parenthesis. To return. I have been surprised, too, to find, in the French literary weekly *Les Nouvelles Littéraires*, publishers' advertisements larger than any in English papers (which is saying a lot), and as large as anything in New York papers.

Les Nouvelles Littéraires is printed in the spacious format of a daily paper, so that in reading it you have the illusion (not altogether an illusion) of reading the news of the day. It is "popular" in its demeanour, and has a large circulation; but at the same time it caters also for the elect. Last month it gave an entire page to the twenty-fifth anniversary of the death of Chekhov.

Its contributors include some of the best names in France. The most high-brow publishers advertise in it in letters a full inch high: which is truly astounding.

I mention this fact because of late months there has been a considerable subterranean pother about the alleged "blatancy" of publishers' advertising in London newspapers. (Provincial newspapers complain of neglect.)

I do not sympathise with the makers of the pother. I am so constituted that I can perceive nothing but good in the advertising of books on a scale similar to the advertising of alcoholic liquors, remedies for sloth in the alimentary tract, and lingerie.

If the book is good, and the type employed is beautiful (it rarely is), my slogan is, "The larger the type and the greater the space, the better." Many bookish persons prefer typographical discretion and timidity in literary advertising. I am a bookish person, but I do not agree with the objectors.

Advertising is and should be advertising, whether of a book or of a soap.

I must finish by stating that I have not read Nick Carter, and that, therefore, I do not recommend him even to detective fans. I say this plainly because I have been sharply corrected for recent alleged inconsistencies.

I gave the opinion not long ago in these columns that Leslie Stephen was a tedious critic, if a fairish editor. Desmond MacCarthy, perhaps the acutest and most broadminded literary critic now writing, took strong objection to this *obiter dictum*. His remarks, in *The New Statesman*, had the genuine accent of indignation.*

I do not propose to argue about Leslie Stephen, except to point out that, as regards his editing, he did not edit the whole of the *Dictionary of*

* MacCarthy's article was reprinted in the posthumous 1953 collection, *Humanities*.

National Biography, but less than half of it, and also that a number of editorially chosen contributors to the *D. N. B.* were merely tenth-rate critical biographers who produced tenth-rate articles that no editor ought to have passed. The *D. N. B.* has one quality in common with the Bible — it is an extremely unequal work.

I do not resent Desmond MacCarthy's attitude. But I do fail to see the sense of the attitude of certain correspondents who followed him. These correspondents pointed out that I had "recommended," in a little work published in 1912, not only a book of Leslie Stephen's but the books of two other authors whom I was rather rude about in the article above referred to — Henry Kingsley and Walter Pater.

Now the aforesaid little work of mine contained, by way of appendix, a selected list of books covering the whole of English literature, as a sort of guide to readers who wished to begin the formation of a library. I did not base this list on my own personal preferences; to do so would have been both ill-judged and egotistic. I based it on the general reputation of authors as then settled by the consensus of sound critics.

As to Henry Kingsley, the fact that the clumsy carelessness of his style renders him intensely repugnant to me would not have justified me in excluding him from my list; for he has fine qualities, and the majority of readers do not care a pin how a book is written. At worst he was a far better man than his more celebrated brother Charles.

As regards Walter Pater, I am convinced that he is pretty well done with and that his "masterpiece" of fiction, *Marius the Epicurean,* is a very poor book and to-day "unreadable" in the ordinary sense of the word.

I will say no more, lest I become tedious in my turn. To the majority of readers in 1929, Leslie Stephen, Henry Kingsley and Walter Pater are little more than names.

12 September 1929

What is the Right Length for a Novel?

The other day I was talking to one of the "omnivorous," a reader who has had vast experience in reading fiction, a fisherwoman whose net would catch whales and sharks, without letting whitebait slip through. She said that she preferred long novels to short. In this I think that she was with the majority of readers; but that is not the point. I replied that you could not classify novels according to their length. You can only classify them according to their length considered in relation to their material.

A long novel can be too short, though more often it is too long. And a short novel may be either too long or too short. Only masterpieces, and not always masterpieces, are of the right length. A novel is of the right length when, a certain "scale" of treatment having been established, that scale is maintained throughout, and at the end the material is exhausted, the problem solved, the reader's legitimate curiosity satisfied.

I have been reading Sarah Gertrude Millin's *The Fiddler* (Constable, 7s. 6d.). Mrs. Millin is usually called a "South African novelist." I am content to call her a novelist. (Her material is local. But then all material is local.) If you describe a poet as, for instance, "the Dorsetshire poet," you imply that he is not much of a poet after all. Mrs. Millin's treatment of her material is not local. She always raises the local to the universal. Nobody would describe John Galsworthy as the West End novelist. And similarly I refuse to call Mrs. Millin the South African novelist.

As for *The Fiddler*, I regard it as a clear example of the short novel which is too short. Mrs. Millin has always been terse. I do not object to terseness. Few novelists are terser than Turgenev. What I object to in *The Fiddler*, and in other books of Mrs. Millin, is the careless casting away of material deliberately chosen.

The narrative is exciting. It may be capricious, but having begun the book you will finish it. A first-rate novel, however, does much more than force you to finish it. It satisfies you page by page. Mrs. Millin's narrative leaps over obstacles. You take exception to the leaping. You say: "Here! Wait a moment! I want to know so and so." The author won't wait. She drops you. And the fact that she immediately seizes you again does not lessen your dissatisfaction at being dropped.

Mrs. Millin seems to get impatient, or even petulant, with the difficulties of her story. Like Thackeray, but from a different motive, she thinks that a difficulty ignored is a difficulty mastered. It isn't. She commits many minor sins of omission and two major ones.

The heroine of *The Fiddler* is a highly respectable woman (wife of a highly respectable man) who falls instantaneously in love with a morally worthless musician and runs off with him. Obvious difficulty of character here. Mrs. Millin hardly meets it. Instead of explaining the passion, she assumes it. She has the ability to explain, but not the patience.

Second major omission. The story is an episode, but an episode which does not and cannot stand alone. It is part of the larger theme of the married life of heroine and husband. The lover is got rid of. The episode is ended, but the material is not exhausted. In a very few words Mrs. Millin suggests that the husband forgives and resumes possession of the wife, who is now the expectant mother of another man's child.

This portion of the material is more interesting, and immensely more difficult to handle, than the episode itself. Mrs. Millin turns her back on it. Either she ought to have devised an episode which was entirely independent of any larger theme, or having introduced the larger theme, she ought to have worked it out to the stage of conjugal equilibrium. She has done neither. Hence *The Fiddler* is too short. But Mrs. Millin, if she could marshal and control her great natural gifts, might any day startle the reading world with an important novel which satisfied the reader by its completeness and overcame him by its power.

An example of a novel being too long is Mr. Graham Greene's original and considerably discussed *The Man Within* (Heinemann, 7s. 6d.). As this book has already been noticed, I will refer only to one aspect of it. The book in my view is good, and for a first book it is very good. But the opening third of it is unduly lengthened by the author's play of fancy on minor details.

As the narrative proceeds the author's absorption in it forces him to neglect his bright fancy and abandon to a large extent the elaborately fanciful decoration of the tale. The result is a lack of homogeneity of treatment.

On page 66 Mr. Greene takes eleven lines to explain the visual effect of a large fire in a room at night. We are told that the fire instead of "bearing light" "spilt pools of darkness." Then that the dark "pushed back" "formed a sombre and concentrated wall." Then that the flash of a girl's knitting needles was like sparks from a gaseous coal. Etc.

It is all ingenious and charming, if somewhat confused; but the story, being both psychological and melodramatic, will scarcely support the excessive ornament. The story stood in no need of it, and would indeed have been far better without it. There is a place for fancies and metaphor in fiction, but not in this sort of fiction; and certainly not in the opening chapters of this sort of fiction, where the author's first aim should be to capture the reader, not to tickle him.

Another error of proportion starts on page 271. Here the author takes a course which (I think) should always be avoided if avoidance is possible. He turns back in the tale. He relates at length a dialogue which occurred long before the incidents described on his first page. This passage ought in my opinion to have been compressed into a paragraph. Other excrescences big and little might be mentioned. The book has 354 pages. To cut it down to 300 would have improved it.

The above remarks are of a technical nature, but since everyone writes nowadays it is conceivable that they may interest everyone. The majority of novelists neglect technique. The majority always did; and this present is no worse than that past. Personally I could never bring myself to flout technique. I would prefer to flout posterity.

And as to the value of technique in the great enterprise of impressing posterity, I am very doubtful. Some English novels, and some Russian, have managed to impress several generations of posterity despite the most deplorable sins against good technique. The life of a novelist is exceedingly difficult.

19 September 1929

Three Modern Rebels

About Richard Aldington I know nothing except that he is an interesting poet, an unusually good translator, and probably something of a scholar. Now he has published a long novel, *Death of a Hero* (Chatto and Windus, 8s. 6d.).

This novel belongs to what is properly called "the literature of revolt." It is often annoying, sometimes exasperating, sometimes in my opinion bad (because it is sometimes tedious). It is, or was, so outspoken that the publishers, with the author's consent, have translated quite a number of words, sentences, and short passages into very black asterisks. It is bitter, one-sided, and unfair.

The author says in the dedication: "I believe in men." I think he should have added to this credo a qualifying clause: "Now and then." To my mind, if he had been Abou Ben Adhem chatting with the angel in the famous poem, he would have said:

"I pray thee then,
Write me as one who *hates* his fellow men."

The statement would have been incorrect, but in one of his fits of spleen he might have made it; and if the angel had taken him at his word . . . .

I think that the chief trouble with Mr. Aldington as a novelist is spiritual pride. He writes: "I disbelieve in bunk." Which somehow reminds me of the women who say: "I loathe cruelty to animals." As though nobody else did! As though they were in a tiny superior class apart!

I doubt whether *Death of a Hero* itself is entirely free from bunk. The best chapters in the novel are those in which the author deals with people whom he detests. (This is strange, for the first feeling of a novelist ought surely to be compassion. But it is so.) When he comes to characters whom he admires he is liable to fall into sentimentality, that is, bunk.

He is "out" against two kinds of cant, the cant about love and the cant about war; and on both of them he is extremely and convincingly destructive. But he would have got finer effects with less violence. First-rate novelists rarely indulge themselves in anger. The war-sections are better than the love-sections, which latter show the influence of earlier works of H.G. Wells. Wells was original in this field; Richard Aldington is imitative, whether he is aware of it or not.

On the other hand, the war-sections are on the whole superb. The opening of Part III, describing a parade of a draft of 120 men in full marching order, before departure for the Front, is just about as good as it could be. It ranks with any chapter in any war-novel, English, French, Russian or German. And the close of the book, culminating in the death of the hero, is very powerful indeed.

Nevertheless, I like best the Prologue, inspired by a perfectly homicidal detestation of the human beings therein displayed. These thirty pages are a majestic and thrilling diatribe. They will hold you, even against your will.

Unfortunately for his novel, the author, in addition to being "out" against cant, is "out" against form in art. He says in the dedication: "To me the excuse for the novel is that one can do any damn thing one pleases." To which the reply is twofold: (1) The novel needs no "excuse." (2) One can't, with impunity, do any damn thing one pleases in a novel. Many pages of *Death of a Hero* are ruined by naive preachments. As for form, this novel suffers throughout from the lack of it.

Withal, *Death of a Hero* is a book impossible to ignore. It may enrage you. It may here and there bore you so that you get "stuck" in it. It is frequently unjust to Richard Aldington's fellow-creatures. And frequently it is too strident. But it has genuine quality. The peaks of it are lofty. I will take the responsibility of advising everybody to have a try at it. And if I receive abuse from the disappointed I don't care. Lastly, the writing is excellent: which fact makes the grammatical slip in line 4 of the Prologue all the more regrettable.

For a dozen years I have been hearing, from the young, of the work of Ronald Firbank; and during all that time I refrained from reading him because of a suspicion in my wrong-head that he belonged to the confraternity of the precious. I gathered that he was in revolt against current ideals of imaginative literature, and I like and sympathise with literary rebels — but on the sole condition that they are not precious. I admit that I have listened to praise of him from young men who had done good things themselves and whose opinions, therefore, I valued.

A series of the Firbank stories is now in course of re-issue in an agreeable slim format by Duckworths, at 3s. 6d. each. I could not resist them. I read *Caprice*. The story, like its format, is agreeable and slim. It is strange, odd, clear, queer, humorous, unlike anything else, and not appreciably precious. The tale of a girl of ecclesiastical origin who left a cathedral Close in order to espouse the stage. She did espouse the stage, in quite impossible circumstances, and then died.

The whole thing is lit with the refracting light that never was on sea or land. It is a lark, a joke, a satire, accomplished in a manner rather distinguished, mainly by dialogue and in brief paragraphs. It is brief, but it is homogeneous. It can be read easily, and without shame or humiliation. Whether it is worth reading I cannot quite decide, even in the privacy of my wrong-head. I have a notion that it isn't.

At the same time, I should not be surprised if the Firbank cult grew. I can foresee young men and maidens at large in King's-road, Chelsea, stating plainly to the uninstructed that Firbank is the sole modern author worthy of attention from the elect. However, I am not of the elect, and never shall be. And I should regard Firbank more seriously if he showed strong imaginative power. He does not show it. To me his is an elegant weakling.

The last of my rebels is James Joyce, a man who has done great stuff. I have referred before in these columns to his "unfinished work," and to the fragment of it entitled *Anna Livia Plurabelle*. This fragment has been published by Crosby Gaige, of New York, in a beautifully printed and produced volume as thin as a biscuit. Edition of 800 signed copies. A collector's morsel. A genuine curiosity. I am charmed to have it. But I cannot comprehend a page of it. For it is written in James Joyce's new language, invented by himself. Here are a few words from one page: limpopo, sar, icis, seints, zezere, hamble, blackburry, dwyergray, meanam, meyne, draves, pharphar, uyar. It ought to be published with a Joyce dictionary.

Someone (I read somewhere) said to Joyce: "I don't understand it." Joyce replied: "But you will." Joyce is an optimist. Human language cannot be successfully handled with such violence as he has here used to English. And *Anna Livia Plurabelle* will never be anything but the wild caprice of a wonderful creative artist who has lost his way.

26 September 1929

"Comical Bunk" About Super-Realism

I have met one or two optimistic publishers. But the other day I met an optimistic bookseller. Unique event in my life! He said that business was good, and improving. He said also that of all reading publics the British was the best, the keenest, the most responsive to originality in new authors. I questioned: "Better than the German?" He said: "Yes, certainly. Better than either the German or the French public." He then with excellent candour upbraided me for certain alleged slighting references to the British reading public in these columns.

I was under the impression that I passed my time defending the British public against the taunts of British high-brows, mandarins and precious persons. Apparently a mistaken impression! About the German reading public I know too little to justify me in making a comparison between the Germans and ourselves. Nevertheless the multiplicity and the excellence of bookshops in Berlin incline me to think that the German reading public shows in books an interest at least as wide and keen as our own.

About the French reading public I have explicitly stated my view that it is inferior in these qualities to the British. Money talks, even in literature; and nobody, surely, with any knowledge of the two countries, can doubt that we spend more, and far more, on books than the French. I admit that, though most French literary criticism in the press is shamelessly venal, the finest French literary criticism is superlative — I would say rather better than the best English.

The late Paul Souday used to do a weekly book article in *Le Temps* (in other respects the dullest solemnity in Europe) which was magnificent in freshness, audacity, erudition, taste and sound anti-tosh common sense. He once rebuked myself, but I admired him too much not to sit quiet. Besides, he had imperfectly comprehended me.

The quality of its literary criticism, however, is not a satisfactory criterion of a nation's literary taste. There is only one satisfactory criterion. Can a serious author live modestly by his pen? Some serious French authors do so, but the great majority do not even hope to do so. In Britain the state of affairs is decidedly better. In Britain some serious authors can afford to take a taxi, now and then.

I have just read a translation (by Irving Babbitt — probably an American translation and not wholly evil) of Julien Benda's book about modern literary taste in France, *Belphegor* (Faber and Faber, 7s. 6d.). What an uninforming title! A title ought to be informing. Who among us knows that, according to Benda, there have always been two types of Jews — those who worshipped Jehovah and those who worshipped Belphegor, Belphegor being the Septuagint variation of the Baal-peor of our Authorised Version? I didn't. To Benda, the worship of Belphegor stands for decadence. Julien Benda is extremely destructive, and his book will infuriate fashionable literary tea-fighters in Paris.

A year or two ago a young apostle of the latest French school of *surréalism* (which I insist on translating "super-realism") came to lecture London on his creed. I attended one of the lectures. The admission was ten shillings. Feeling that such earnestness ought to be encouraged I put a pound into the collection plate on entering. Afterwards I regretted this splendid generosity. For I could make nothing but pretentious nonsense of the lecture, and I left the hushed drawing-room not a bit wiser than before concerning the tenets of super-realism.

Julien Benda has enlightened me. I am now aware that the super-realists do not describe phenomena from without, that they enter *into* phenomena feeling them from within, that they are at one with phenomena, that they practise unity, that they adore emotion, that they utterly despise intelligence and knowledge.

Tut-tut! Benda has no difficulty at all in smashing this comical bosh into a shapeless paste of ridiculousness. He attributes the declension of French taste largely to the influence of women.

308

The super-realist will tell you that he writes only for women, and that nowadays women alone read. I can only repeat, Tut-tut! And I can only say that if what Benda asserts is true, Frenchwomen and Frenchmen have startlingly changed since I lived in Paris. *Belphegor* is worth reading, for its author has a most pleasing gift of bland irony. But you need not begin to read it if you are not genuinely interested in new books. Super-realism as a cult could not survive for one week in London.

The above-mentioned London bookseller thought that the autumn season would be a busy one, more remarkable for quantity than for quality. He had inspected two hundred new and as yet unpublished books in the morning of the day on which we interviewed one another. He seemed to foresee little literature of consequence. But he firmly prophesied that J.B. Priestley's *The Good Companions* would be an autumnal bestseller, and he admired it tremendously.

I wish now to inform the keen public of a book which, whether it rises to be a bestseller or not, will undoubtedly give distinction to the season: *A High Wind in Jamaica*, by Richard Hughes (Chatto, 7s. 6d.).

Mr. Hughes has so far produced a few short plays, of which I have witnessed one, and a few (said-to-be) very original short stories. *A High Wind in Jamaica* (not a surpassingly good title) is a novel, shortish, but entitled to call itself "full-length." In an abbreviated form it lately appeared in *Life and Letters*, when it made an impression on many people, including me. The restoration of the omitted portions improves it considerably. It is a novel chiefly about children. It begins in Jamaica, and continues very romantically in a pirate ship on the Spanish Main, or, more accurately, on the Caribbean Sea.

There is no super-realism in *A High Wind in Jamaica*, but plenty of realism (in the decent sense). Richard Hughes makes no attempt to achieve "unity" with his youthful characters. He has emotion, but it is governed by intelligence and knowledge. And as his book has no super-realism, so it has no sentimentality. The author knows children for the callous, imperturbable, fatalistic, delightful, imaginative little animals they are. The style is brilliant, the ingenuity of narrative is brilliant, the characterisation is brilliant, and the total effect of the story completely satisfactory.

Some weeks or months since I was demanding a novel in which children were treated with the impartiality which marks their private judgments on their elders. Here it is. The Jamaican children are delicious, and dead-true to life. Yes, I have really enjoyed Richard Hughes. Further, he has played the ancient mariner to me. If he continues at the level of the present book, he is bound soon to rank with the best. And if the season provides a better novel I shall be somewhat astonished.

3 October 1929

No Original Writers Need Apply!

What is a literary prize? A literary prize is a sum of money — interest on a capital donated by some person more earnest than knowledgeable about literature and the wholesomeness, purity, and dignity thereof — to the end that it shall be bestowed annually upon the author of the best book of the year in a particular department of letters. The annual book is chosen by a committee of "experts" each of whom has different notions of excellence from the others. All of them are as sensitive as toy-dogs. All of them have theories concerning literature. All of them are sentimental and respectable, as the donor was sentimental and respectable. All of them object to the social structure being too rudely shaken. Their delicate susceptibilities have to be seriously considered. Hence no book with a really original anti-tradition bias has the least chance of winning the prize; no "spiky" book has the least chance; and few such books even get themselves submitted to the solemn séances of the high-minded committee. Ninety-nine times out of a hundred the prize goes to a shop-finished conventional work.

Original writers resent the institution of the literary prize — not because they don't like prizes; they do — but because they are well aware that a prize will never come their way. The original writers say that the institution does nothing or less than nothing for the advancement of literature, and that on the contrary it encourages the reactionaries of literature and their prim mediocrity. This is true.

But I am not antipathetic to the institution of literary prizes. (I once won one in the shape of an honoured cheque for £140 — perhaps that amazing fact has somewhat influenced my views; you never know.) As in politics, so in letters, there are, and ought to be, two opposing forces, the progressive and the conservative. Tradition is not a bad thing. Woe to the activity in which tradition is not the subject of an everlasting and violent scrap! And dignity, purity and wholesomeness are not bad things either. All four are worth fighting for and fighting against.

Further, I maintain that the main body of decent readers, always conservative, is entitled to consideration. Why should this body not be flattered by the semi-official "crowning" of a workmanlike book which pleases it? And why should it be hurt by the semi-official crowning of a book which it would regard as an outrage? A majority has its rights, though the minority won't admit them. The business of a literary prize is not to shove literature forward but to keep it steady. A legitimate business!

In France literary prizes have been numerous for over a century, but I doubt if one of them was ever given to a book which afterwards rose to be a classic. No matter. In Britain we have a few literary prizes, and occasionally one of them, by some extraordinary mischance, has gone to an original work. (Not mine — I am never original, and nearly always respectable.) No matter. What will be, will be.

I have recently learnt that there are literary prizes in Germany. Germany must be a wonderful country. It has established a monopoly of war-books; and now a German committee has awarded a prize to an original novel! The book is *The Revolt of the Fishermen*, by Anna Seghers, translated for backward Britain into English by Margaret Goldsmith (Elkin Mathews, 6s.). The publishers have listened to my incessant exhortation to provide biographical details about new authors. They announce that Anna Seghers is twenty-seven, married, retiring, and has "two charming children." (If they had left out the charming children, and told me whether the young author was dark or fair, plump or slim, I should have been better pleased.)

The Revolt of the Fishermen is the story of a strike. It is certainly beautiful; and certainly it has also a rather deep originality. Unfortunately it has in addition a superficial originality of mere technique, the result of which is quite unnecessarily to bewilder the reader. Too often, especially in the opening chapters, the reader doesn't know where he is; he knows only that he is in a mist or fog, where events and characters loom up vaguely at intervals. And says the translator: " The author occasionally enters the minds of her characters and describes their thoughts *without indicating* that she is no longer describing the immediate happenings." (My annoyed italics.) Why on earth should not the author give her readers the courtesy of an indication? And why should she be so horridly parsimonious of relevant detail of place, environment, and time? It may be great girlish fun to bewilder the reader; but it is bad manners — and worse than futile.

I can perceive that an appreciable percentage of the reading public will not get beyond the first fifty pages. Those, however, who continue will have a rich reward for their perseverance. The book is original, unsentimental, and true. The translation, by no means faultless, is far above the average.

I know one good reason why I enjoy reading criminal trials. Because the *whole* of the ascertained facts are succinctly placed before me. A thousand trifling material details help the large effect. Nothing is withheld. I have just read the best murder-trial book I have met with for years. *The Trial of Norman Thorne*, edited by Miss Helena Normanton (*Famous Trial Series*, Bles, 10s. 6d., illustrated). Thorne was a wicked young man and a frightful liar, and he admitted that he cut up Elsie Cameron, his mistress, and buried the pieces. Elsie Cameron was one of those neurotic, oversexed, intolerable, unhappy women who simply invite assassination. But whether she died by assassination or suicide has never been made clear. For myself, like thousands of others, I incline to the theory of suicide. In my view Thorne was unjustly treated — unless dismembering a dead mistress is a capital offence. The defect of most verbatim reports of trials is that the editorial introductions are otiose and tedious. Miss Normanton is a barrister. Her introduction, though not impeccably written, is masterly in content: a genuine constructive exegesis of the evidence.

Another book crowded with exciting detail is *When* —— by "the late J.L. Pole, with a foreword by Peter Grimstone, C.B." (Chapman and Hall, 15s.). A work of fiction, doubtless founded on fact, masquerading as an autobiography. (I question whether "J.L. Pole" or "Peter Grimstone" ever existed.) Pole was an author, among other things, and he died of G.P.I. The book is in effect a free, frank and outrageous survey of British manners and customs from 1877 down to recent years. It is thoroughly well done, therefore readable; and its pictures of life are romantic in addition to being veracious.

Now I have more or less described three good books. Not every week provides as many.

10 October 1929

The Short Story — With Kipling as Master

For many years now the short story has been in great demand. And recently the demand seems to have increased. One daily paper has taken to printing a short story every day. I am surprised that this scheme was not adopted earlier in England.

Serials have been known to raise circulations, but not very often. The serial, though it has its uses and undoubtedly gives pleasure, suffers from two disadvantages. First. Pressure of other matter usually makes the instalment too short. Second. The serial can hardly give pleasure unless it is read daily without fail. If the reader misses a day he is lost. The Paris *Journal* has for decades printed a short story every day (in addition to two serials). The *Journal's* type, however, is as a rule smaller than would be tolerated in Britain, and its stories are extremely brief — a thousand words or so. I have read hundreds and hundreds of them, and have not met with ten good ones in ten years.

Two thousand words is in my opinion the minimum space in which an author can be expected to create characters, seize hold of the reader, relate an episode and get a general narrative effect. Most editors expect impossibilities from most authors of fiction.

I should be prepared to maintain that two thousand words of short story will satisfy the reader better than two thousand words of serial. A short story read is done with. A reader can dismiss it from his mind. With a serial the editorial hope is that a reader should not dismiss it from his mind, that on the contrary the fellow should be preoccupied during twenty-four hours with curiosity concerning the next instalment. The trouble about the serial, however, is not the reader's condition at the end of the instalment, but his condition at the beginning of it. At the beginning he is bound to say to himself: "Let me see, now. Where were we? I must reflect a bit." Which unhappy necessity for preliminary cerebration does not occur with the short story.

Monthly magazines print more short stories than they used to do. You can frequently obtain six for a shilling — twopence apiece. Weekly papers also sometimes condescendingly publish short stories. I estimate that several thousand short stories are offered in print yearly to hungry British readers. (In the United States the figure must be astronomical: it might well express the mileage from the earth to the moon.) But one rather important thing must happen to the short story, as to all fiction, before it is read. Editors are more anxiously aware of this thing than readers. Before the story is read it has to be written.

One might imagine that a trifling island like ours could not produce several thousand short stories in a year. Nevertheless I would assert with confidence that out of every ten short stories written only one is printed. Demand will always bring supply — in plenteous quantity. But quality . . . ? That is different. All that may be said as to quality is that to-day's short stories are much superior to the short stories of forty years ago. If you doubt, and if you feel equal to the strain, examine the files of old magazines. I guarantee that you will start back therefrom in horror-stricken amaze. Modern British short stories are at worst workmanlike. We have learnt technique, if not veracity, from the adroit artificers of the United States, the artificers trained to a hair in the craft of "punch."

Still, our short stories might be better. The lettered élite say that they would be better if editors did not insist on the convention of the happy ending. I disagree. A genuine creative artist can and does fit his work into any convention. And a story with a happy ending can be just as true, and even just as sad, as a story with an unhappy ending. Also the unhappy ending can be just as sentimental and conventional as the happy.

Besides, it is not true that editors always insist on a happy ending. Two of the most melancholy and tragic short stories of the century have appeared in popular periodicals: Pauline Smith's *The Pain* and *Desolation*. The first is one of the very finest stories, and the second unquestionably the most distressing known to this generation.

One currently hears, and perhaps I have myself said, that the short story is not a characteristically English form, and that the two supreme masters of it are foreigners — de Maupassant and Chekhov. Well, I have read all de Maupassant and all Chekhov several times, with undiminished satisfaction. But in the depths of my conscience I think that neither of them has surpassed Kipling at his best. And I know Frenchmen who would concur. The fact is that though Britain took late to the short story, she has in thirty years borne a whole brilliant galaxy, school, and flying flock of short-story writers, both grave and humorous. To name British names would be imprudent. I will be content with the generalisation that twentieth-century British short-story writers are better than those of any other country. Assuredly better than the vaunted performers of America. I know of but two Americans whom it would not be absurd to put in the same class with half a dozen Britons: Joseph Hergesheimer and Ernest Hemingway.

Two collections of short stories have just been issued: *My Best Short Story* (Faber and Faber, 7s. 6d.) and *The Mercury Story Book* (Longmans, 7s. 6d.). For the first, a number of celebrities or notorieties have selected what they consider to be "my best." The result is pretty good, but the system of selection is not good. Few authors are capable of recognising their best when they see it. H.G. Wells has succeeded. And if you would properly appreciate Wells's pre-eminence in the vein of fantasy, read *The Man Who Could Work Miracles*, and compare it with the new stories of that world-renowned inventor, Carol Kapek. In this *My Best* volume are represented a sprinkling of writers who would be a liability, not an asset, to any such volume.

The second collection is made up of stories which have appeared in J.C. Squire's *London Mercury*. The volume is a striking testimonial to J.C. Squire's catholicity, courage and taste. It sets out with a very distinguished story by George Moore, *Wilfrid Holmes*, Wilfrid being a man who was incapable of earning money. There is not an overtly humorous line in this realistic, quiet tale, and yet it is charged everywhere with humour covert, subtle, darkly sardonic. It is the best item in the book. There are others not to be neglected.

17 October 1929

A Confession About Learning French

"He speaks French like a native." Phrase frequently heard, but hardly ever true. More romantic lies are told about the speaking of French than about even the catching of fish. Now here is a plain tale: I began to learn French at the age of nine. I learnt French for eight years and then could not read it at sight. At twenty-two I put myself to some trouble and learnt to read French currently. Soon I was regarded in Fleet-street as quite a fair minor authority on French literature. At the age of thirty-five I went to live in Paris, alone, and I discovered that I could neither understand ordinary French conversation nor make myself understood in the same. I had then been studying French for over a quarter of a century, and had been writing about French literature for over a decade. I decided that something must be done. I did it. End of plain tale.

The number of pure-blooded Englishmen who can "talk French like a native" is so small as to be negligible. I have never met one. I remember once, when I had acquired terrific volubility in colloquial French, and could teach French slang to Frenchmen, and fancied myself enormously, a Frenchman saying to me: "Whatever you do, don't lose your English accent. It is adorable." A blow! To this day I rarely read a page of French without coming across a phrase that I do not entirely comprehend, nor see a play without missing phrases. So much for speaking and understanding French.

Messrs. Dent have just published *A Glossary of Colloquial and Popular French*, by L.E. Kastner and J. Marks (12s. 6d.). Both authors belong to Manchester University. Their book of nearly 400 large, full pages is very good. It is by far the best thing of the kind I ever saw. There is no prim nonsense about it. I did not hope to find the slang word *"flanelle"* in any English work of reference. Very many phrases are explained. I was familiar with the phrase "Yell like a blind man," but I could not have explained it. The explanation is that it is an abbreviation of "Like a blind man who has lost his dog and his stick."

Being a critic, of course I must pick holes. For instance, *"Ne te fais pas de bile"* is given, meaning "Don't let it worry you." My experience is that of late years the phrase has shortened itself in ordinary use to *"Ne t'en fais pas,"* the word *"bile"* being assumed. Also I miss various specimens of really picturesque slang. For example, *"Il en bavait des tringles de rideau."* And *"Il ne se mouche pas avec des tessons de bouteille."* On the other hand, many of the colloquialisms are very up to date, and so are the illustrative quotations. All those who wish to know how little they know of *French* French should study this book, which is packed with fun for the discerning.

Incidentally I must mention, for those who are more interested in English than in French, another work of reference just published by Messrs. Dent: *English Proverbs and Proverbial Phrases*, by G.L. Apperson (31s. 6d., 720 pages). Mr. Apperson was editor of *The Antiquary* for sixteen years. He is erudite. He deals mainly with proverbs of the past, proverbs that have mostly passed out of general use. But every proverb is a light on national manners, customs, character. I recall my vivid sensations on first encountering, in a village, the obsolescent French proverbial phrase: "As dirty as a comb."

The majority of English translations from the French demonstrate two things about the translators. First, that they do not really understand

French, and particularly French idioms and proverbial phrases. Second, that they cannot write English. But fortunately there is a minority of translations which demonstrate the contrary. Among the latter I have received two. The first, and the better, is Mr. Vyvyan Holland's rendering of Julien Green's *Léviathan*, entitled *The Dark Journey* (Heinemann, 7s. 6d.). I commented on this novel when it originally appeared in French. It is very fine, and Mr. Vyvyan Holland has succeeded in mitigating the author's only stylistic fault — heaviness.

The other is Mrs. Winifred Stephens Whale's rendering of André Malraux's *Les Conquérants*, entitled *The Conquerors* (Cape, 7s. 6d.): a novel of the Chinese revolution. An excellent novel, and assuredly rather a terrifying novel. Those who read *The Conquerors* will not forget it next day.

Last week, discussing the question of the supply of short stories, I said that at most one short story in ten written reaches print. The editor of a very famous popular magazine writes me to say that, apart from stories commissioned from established writers, he printed last year only one story submitted, and that the odds against him accepting any story not definitely ordered by him are 3990 to 1! Matter for reflection, here, for unestablished concocters of short stories.

24 October 1929

Why Be A Learned Author?

A man climbed on to a rock by the sea and sat down and began to think about the nature of truth, spirit, goodness — in fact all the usual everlasting subjects; and the radiant sun declined over the sea, approaching the horizon; and there was a nip in the tonic maritime air; and the man felt a sudden chill in his toe; and he looked and beheld that the tide was rising faster than the sun was setting, and that he was surrounded by water, and that soon, full soon, the rock and he on it would be submerged beneath the uneasy surface of the waves; and he did not wake because he had not been asleep: his situation was real.

I am the man, and the tide is the rising tide of new and unique literary masterpieces. The autumn publishing season is sweeping on at a speed of at least five knots, as it sometimes sweeps past the entrance to Dover Harbour; and high tide is not yet. The Motor Show may not be quite as popular as it was; but the theatres are doing a great business in deep waters, and the autumn publishing season is a good one; so good that in six weeks' time, when the flood has receded, my drowned body will have to be reclaimed from the ocean's marge.

Far from being able to examine all the books which arrive unsolicited, or the tenth part of them, I find that I can hardly cope with publishers' advertisements. Quite a number of good books have already been issued; but still more bad ones. Often, to my mind, the advertisements are more interesting, more thrilling, more uplifting than the books which they describe.

I think that the names of the writers of certain book-advertisements ought to be divulged and placed among those of the successful authors of the year. The announcer of geniuses may himself be a genius — indeed he sometimes obviously is a genius, in addition to being a "best-seller" — in the only correct meaning of that phrase. Anyhow the success of the autumn publishing season is assured, barring earthquakes, changes of Government, and pestilence.

Withal, the literary outlook is not wholly bright. Monthly magazines, to put it nicely, are not enlarging their circulations. I had hitherto supposed that the disquieting condition of the magazines was to be attributed to the competition of daily papers, which give six times a week, at no increased price, all that the magazines give only twelve times a year. I am authoritatively told that this is not so. The damager of the magazine is the motorcar. People can read in a train, but they cannot read while driving a car, or even while sitting in a car that moves. Nor is this all. Fewer people travel by train than aforetime. Hence fewer people buy magazines at railway bookstalls. I am informed that at some of the big termini the sale of magazines has fallen by 50 per cent. Something must be done, and probably will be done.

And there is another dark spot. Impassioned students of book advertisements will have noticed a spacious advertisement by a well-known firm of publishers to the effect that the circulating libraries have practically banned all works whose price exceeds thirty shillings. Therefore the firm has been obliged to reduce the price of three important works by the sum of twelve shillings apiece, thus incurring inevitable loss. In future no doubt the circulating libraries will lengthen their prospectuses and add to the guarantee of a service of all new books the words: "provided the published price thereof is not more than thirty shillings." For is not honesty the best policy? (Different persons will give different answers to this question.)

Some publishers, and especially some of the younger firms, will request the libraries to go and bury themselves. I see, for instance, that the Cresset Press is offering an edition of *Gulliver's Travels*, illustrated by Rex Whistler, the young painter who a year or two ago illustrated the refreshment room of the Tate Gallery, at sixteen and a half guineas a copy. Further, the *edition de grand luxe* of this *edition de luxe* is priced at one hundred and fifty guineas, otherwise £157.10s. a copy. Still further, both editions have been sold out, to the booksellers! And under a Labour Government!

Since the booksellers have here taken a risk, at any rate a theoretical risk, I do not very strongly object to the profit (which they will probably make) of fifty guineas a copy on the *grand luxe* edition. I emphatically do object to the 33⅓ per cent. profit of the booksellers when they take no risk. The following example was recently brought before me. A large work of genuine importance in several volumes is published at six guineas. A bookseller refuses to stock it — naturally. He gets an order for a copy. Promising to supply the work the next day, he telephones to the publishers, procures the work and sells for six guineas what he gets for four guineas. The author's royalty is 13s. 6d. a copy. Why be a learned author — if you can be a bookseller?

So far I have done nothing to ameliorate my perilous position on the rapidly disappearing rocks amid the furious flood. And I fear that I shall continue to do almost nothing. I shall just blandly permit myself to drown. I will nevertheless mention one or two books. And, though I have no sympathy at all with the bookworm who said that whenever he heard of a new book he took down an old one and read it, the books I will mention are not new ones.

First, there is Dumas' *Story of My Yacht*, which I lauded on its (partial) appearance as a serial in *Blackwood's* and which is now published under the title *On Board the Emma* (Benns, one guinea, illustrated). This narrative is good Dumas, and good Dumas is extremely readable. Why the dimensions of the volume should be ten inches by six and a quarter inches, and the price one guinea, when the volume might better have been of the ordinary novel size and its price three half-crowns, I cannot imagine. You may say that it is not a novel. I should reply that a great deal of it is fiction — enchanting fiction, but fiction.

Two other not-new books are revised issues of Henry Williamson's *The Wet Plains of Flanders* (Faber, 5s.), an admirable account of an after-war visit to the Belgian battlefields, and *The Beautiful Years* (Faber, 7s. 6d.). This latter is an old novel, of childhood, re-dressed; not entirely free from sentimentality, but in the main very sound. Henry Williamson is the author of a most distinguished novel, *The Pathway*, published last year. *The Beautiful Years* and *The Pathway* are, I learn, respectively the first and the fourth parts of a tetralogy. The second and third parts have apparently yet to come. If they prove not to be exceedingly fine, I shall express grave disappointment.

After all, I must mention a new book, C.H.B. Kitchin's *Death of My Aunt* (Hogarth Press, 7s. 6d.). I do so because it is that rare thing a detective novel which I have read with pleasure and without tedium. (And it is something more than a detective story.) The author's narrative method is quite unusually satisfactory.

31 October 1929

Disclosure About the Idea that Brought Him Fame

About Mr. Geraint Goodwin I know nothing except that he is the author of *Conversations with George Moore* (Benn, 10s. 6d.). This volume interests me because I admire George Moore's work exceedingly — not all of it, but perhaps ninety per cent. of it. There are novelists of importance who differ from my estimate of George Moore. H.G. Wells differs. St. John Ervine differs. We three shall agree to differ. On the other hand Humbert Wolfe once wrote: "Almost alone in contemporary English literature Mr. Moore has brought to the writing of fiction the severity, the discipline, and the perfect control of art that the French had in their great periods. Mr. Moore has the violent literary integrity of Flaubert and the artistic rectitude of Anatole France. His work is a Greek statue beside the Flemish riot of life symbolised by such a writer as D.H. Lawrence."

Twenty-five years ago I wrote a complete study of George Moore's work up to that date. No review would publish it. At that date the name of George Moore had a sinister odour in the nostrils of the mandarins. I had at last to include the essay in a volume of literary criticism, which volume I believe is now out of print;* the rare specimens of it are the quarry of collectors. I adhere to the estimate of George Moore which I then made. I remain convinced that *A Mummer's Wife* and *Esther Waters* (in their original editions) count among the finest English novels of the last hundred years, and I have read each of them several times. They have form, they are original, they are true to life, they are honest, they are courageous, and they are beautiful — all in a very high degree.

I may be prejudiced. I admit that *A Mummer's Wife* was a revelation to me. In it I "first saw the light." It showed me the fictional potentialities of the Five Towns, which I had previously quite failed to discover for myself. *A Mummer's Wife* has influenced all my work — far more than any Russian novel ever influenced it. But even so I don't think that I am prejudiced.

Mr. Goodwin has had talks with George Moore, and I should say that he has rendered them fairly accurately. The conversations are not as good as those recorded by George Moore himself, but they are admirable and diverting specimens of that "school" of writing, and ought to be perused. They are studded with authentic Moorish pearls. Such as the following: "Does anyone know, or has everyone forgotten, that genius discovers itself? . . . Genius can be likened unto apples. This year you complain that the apples are not as red as they should be; maybe they are too red, or maybe they are too plentiful, but small. But the apples go on just the same. They alone are unconcerned as to what the world says or thinks of them."

Is this a pearl or isn't it?

George Moore avows that he came to Britain from France with the express intention of revolutionising the English novel. Apart from his own novels, did he succeed in the enterprise? I think that he did not. I can find little trace of his influence in the novels of any of his outstanding successors of two generations: Wells, Galsworthy, Kipling, Lawrence, Joyce, Swinnerton, Mottram, Aldous Huxley. The English novel went on just the same. It alone was unconcerned as to what the world and George Moore said or thought of it. George Moore has permanently enriched English literature, but he has failed to overthrow the dynasty and his revolution has therefore miscarried.

Even the newest authors ignore his influence. I have just been introduced to a new writer of fiction, Malachi Whitaker, author of a book of short stories entitled *Frost in April* (Cape, 7s. 6d.). One ought to be able to say from internal evidence whether the author of a volume is man or woman. In this case I cannot. I incline to the view that Malachi is a woman, but I am by no means sure. Twenty stories (though one or two of them, for instance *The Mother*, would more properly be called sketches). Made up of the common daily stuff or small beer of existence: just the sort of stuff that George Moore has so magnificently utilised; but there is no grain of George Moore in *Frost in April*. Withal, the book is very fine. (I am glad to observe that publishers are losing their hostility to short stories; we have

---

* *Fame and Fiction* (1901). The George Moore essay is reprinted in *The Author's Craft and Other Critical Writings of Arnold Bennett* edited by Samuel Hynes (University of Nebraska, 1968).

lately had other remarkable collections of them from new authors. Once publishers would turn down short stories without looking at them.)

These chiefly sad stories, in addition to being thoroughly well observed, and well done in the technical sense, have strong originality, much beauty, and much emotional power. Yet their tone is very quiet indeed. The first story in the book, *The Music Box*, and also the title-story, are masterly in impressive energy soberly handled. By the way both of them spring from the outrageous domestic tyranny of husbands and fathers. On the other hand, *Something Funny* is gloriously funny — the richest, juiciest comedy: and not a funny phrase in it! *The Journey Home* narrates a railway accident in a manner new to fiction. I reckon myself something of an authority on railway accidents and the narration of them, for I have both experienced and described them. Malachi Whitaker has quite unusual talent. And no habitual reader of fiction can afford to ignore him — or her.

In the matter of the common daily stuff of existence, I must mention a new book by Mr. and Mrs. Quennell, authors of *A History of Everyday Things in England*, and of four volumes dealing with everyday life in various ages from the Stone Age to the Norman. The new book is *Everyday Things in Homeric Greece* (Batsford, 7s. 6d., illustrated by the authors). The earlier Quennell volumes have been very popular, and with sound reason. The Greek affair is not planned in quite the same way, but it is as good. Apparently all these books have been aimed at young students. I am neither young nor a student, but they have hit me. The first two of them hit me years ago. I could wish that the latest had been available before I beheld the wonders of Mycenae and Tiryns. It would have made those wonders more wonderful to me. It supplies the Homeric background, and much besides.

The dailiness of life is as interesting in fiction as any heroical doings, and indeed heroical doings cannot be made really interesting without some picture of the dailiness behind them. Explain to me how Nausicaa went out to do the washing, and I am held. Similarly with the characters in the tragedy and the comedy of George Moore and Malachi Whitaker and any other modern or ancient imaginative author. "How they lived" should be as exciting as "What they did," perhaps more exciting. Deeds can be invented, but not backgrounds.

7 November 1929

Englishmen Do Not Read Enough

I happen not to be the chief Registrar, neither a statistician; but I am prepared to say that twenty millions is a low estimate of the adolescent and adult population of the U.K. On the other hand twenty thousand is a very large sale for a new novel. A circulation of that size constitutes a great popular success, a best-seller, and is held to justify the assertion, "Everyone is reading. . . ." Suppose that on the average ten people read each copy of the best-seller. (Probably an exaggeration.) This means that one grown-up person in every hundred reads the book that "everyone is reading." It means that if you form a queue of a hundred average persons and ask them one by one whether they have read a given best-seller, ninety-nine of them will reply No.

As for prose non-fiction, a sale of five thousand is called popularity. As for volumes of verse, a sale of one thousand is considered excellent. As for learned works — I forbear!

Note that I am leaving out of account the sale of old books, which is very large. I speak only of the latest literary phenomena, with which an average person ought surely to be acquainted if he wishes to know what year he is living in. To live solely in 1829 or 1529 is not to live.

Tell me not that average persons can't, in practice, read. They can. They read with earnestness and understanding, at certain hours of the day, the prophecies of gifted men about the relative speeds of horses at certain later hours of the day. Nor tell me that they can't afford to buy books. The average adolescent and adult person spends on alcohol at least £15 per annum, a sum which would enable him to buy forty new novels, or ten volumes of history or biography or philosophy.

Here is a general state of illiteracy which might, I think, advantageously be altered. Now the National Book Council, which is four years old, and which I mentioned here a year or so ago, is trying to alter this state of illiteracy. The Council is directed by authors (of whom by the way I am not one), publishers, booksellers, and "bookmen." Its aim is "the promotion of book reading and the wider distribution of books." Its directors work for nothing.

Of course, being mainly authors, publishers and booksellers, they may hope to get benefit from the wider distribution of books; and to that extent there is self-seeking in their toil. But as their aim comprises the national welfare and the advancement of civilisation, and as assuredly few but authors, publishers or booksellers would undertake the job, I think that their self-seeking is pardonable; it is even richly justifiable. The membership of the Council has grown from 471 to over 2000 in four years; and its income has more than doubled. Both its membership and its funds ought to be multiplied by about twenty.

You can become a member by simply filling in a form. You obtain, in return for almost nothing, extremely useful lists of good books, new and old, on all manner of subjects; about a hundred of these guiding lists have already been issued. You obtain also a monthly *News Sheet*, which will be more exciting than it is when it contains more matter than at present it does. The N.B.C. (3, Henrietta-street, Covent Garden) also gives lectures up and down the country; some of them really are exciting.

I am in favour of the increased reading not of books alone but of periodicals. The average person misses much that would interest him in periodicals, and even in newspapers. Periodicals have been giving pretty good stuff lately. As the recent "Printing" Supplement of *The Times* has already been admirably praised in the admirable newspaper now in front of you, I will content myself, concerning it, with the suggestion that such a wonderful collection of truly sound, informing articles and essays ought to be reprinted in book form — but of course without the grievous coloured illustrations. It would make a stout book, and the book would sell.

And I should like to mention a revolutionary and highly readable essay which appeared in last month's *The Realist*: namely J.B.S. Haldane's " The Place of Science in Western Civilisation." Anybody who reads this startling

320

essay will finish it with his brain thrilled and with a new perspective of government. And I should like to mention the reminiscences of French artists by Professor William Rothenstein, and the reminiscences of British artists by Muirhead Bone, both plenteously illustrated, and both appearing in the current quarterly number of *Artwork*.

And I should especially like to mention the correspondence between Erich Remarque (author of *All Quiet*, etc.) and General Sir Ian Hamilton printed in the current number of *Life and Letters*. *All Quiet*, etc., has had a world-sale of at least two million copies (not counting its immense serial circulation in the *Sunday Express*), and in addition it is an exceedingly fine book. I doubt if ever before a book so fine has achieved such a success of popularity in so short a time. Any disclosure by its author about his aims in writing it ought to interest a very large number of people. This disclosure certainly will. Further, it will strengthen one's admiration for the author. The contributions of both Erich Remarque and Sir Ian Hamilton have nobility.

The stream of German war books has not yet dried. The latest of them is Hans Carossa's *A Roumanian Diary* (Secker, 7s. 6d.). Carossa was an Army medical officer serving in the campaign in Roumania. The first fifty pages of the book appeared to me rather ordinary, dull, flat. Long before I reached the end I changed my view.

Carossa is without doubt a man of unusually broad culture. He is sensitive to other things than war. He can handle a pen as subtly as Edmund Blunden himself. And if you want the horrors of war — well, they are here, superbly and fearlessly set down. *A Roumanian Diary* is translated by Agnes Neill Scott. I know of no better translation from the German than hers. It is to be praised unreservedly. Carossa has a tremendous reputation in Germany as a stylist. Judging by the translation I can believe that this reputation is merited.

Short stories are still arriving. Some time since a new author, H.E. Bates, presented himself to a public rendered negligent by surfeit, with a beautiful novel entitled *Two Sisters*. He followed this by a volume of beautiful short stories entitled *Day's End*. His third book, just out, also consists of short stories: *Seven Tales and Alexander* (Scholartis Press, 7s. 6d.). This volume — edition limited to 1000 copies, and well produced — is an item for collectors, and should appreciate in value. Nevertheless I rank the book scarcely as high as its forerunners. It lacks vividness; its sobriety is a little excessive. But it unquestionably has distinction. The stories are rural. Three of them are about children; two are in the nature of fairy-tales. The longest story reminds one of Chekhov's *The Steppe*, without being in the same class.

14 November 1929

The Topmost Peaks of War Fiction

The war-novel is still more and more becoming a major phenomenon of current literature. A few years ago people were inclined to protest against the alleged surfeit of war-novels! I remember protesting against the protest. Yet since then war-novels have both increased in numbers and improved in quality. If you would realise the degree of improvement in quality read again Henri Barbusse's flushed and feverish *Le Feu*, which made a great impression in various countries including Britain. *Le Feu* was written too soon. It had too much resentful fury, too little form, and no detachment. Its effect depended on its subject. A great subject is the first essential of a great imaginative work, but it is not the sole essential, nor even the chief.

Since then, as far as I am aware, no really memorable war-novel has appeared in France. Within my knowledge no really memorable war-novel has at any time yet appeared in Britain, for Edmund Blunden's magnificent and delicate *Undertones of War* is not a novel. Germany has had a practical monopoly of memorable war-novels, perhaps because the war left a deeper impression in Germany than in any other country. It may be that the finest war-novels are the product of defeat, not of triumph. Sadness, not exhilaration, brings beauty. *All Quiet on the Western Front* and *The Case of Sergeant Grischa* have so far been the topmost peaks of war-fiction. (For myself I should put the last first.) In our enthusiasm we must guard against rating them too high.

It would be good for us to read again some of the classics of war-fiction. For example, Tolstoy's *War and Peace* and *Sebastopol*, and Zola's *La Débâcle*, and especially the sublimely ironic final pages of *Nana*. Will the modern successfully stand comparison with the classic? I doubt. . . . Indeed I would lay ten to one on Tolstoy outrunning any modern war-novelist on the immeasurable course of time. The definitive novel of the 1914-1918 war, however, has probably − nay, certainly − yet to be written. The author of it may not yet be born. Meanwhile the new generation has done very well, has done better than could have been expected.

And it is still doing well. Could one have reasonably hoped, at this stage, for another war-novel fit to rank with the two German novels above mentioned? Yet such a novel has come. And it is Anglo-Saxon. *A Farewell to Arms*, by Ernest Hemingway (Cape, 7s. 6d.). Ernest Hemingway is a youngish American, whose work, in short stories, to which I have referred once or twice in this column, began to impress me first about a couple of years ago.

A Farewell to Arms deals with the Italian front. Gorizia, Udine, Piave, Milan, are some of the place-names that occur prominently in it. Its detail is as marvellous as any yet given. The description of the wounding of the hero in a bombardment is as tremendously effective as anything current. In fact, I seriously question whether this description has been equalled. Its dialogue, possibly over-plenteous here and there, is masterly in reproductive realism. Short sentences, page after page, admirably marshalled and grouped. Its detachment is perfect. No flush and no fever in this novel; but the sane calmness of a spectator who combines deep sympathy with breadth and impartiality of vision.

The book is hard, almost metallic, glittering, blinding by the reflections of its bright surface, utterly free of any sentimentality. But imbued through and through with genuine sentiment. A strange and original book. Whatever it may not do to you, it will convince you of its honesty and veracity. You will never be able to say as you read: "This isn't true. This is exaggerated. This is forced."

The weakness of the novel, if it has one, springs from the author being in two minds about his purpose in writing it. He seems to me to be undecided whether he is writing a description of the war as his hero saw it, or the love-story of his hero. The heroine is a nurse, or a sort of nurse; a heroical character. The love-story is quite as fine as the war-story, but a divided aim is bound to have some deleterious influence. In *A Farewell to Arms*, either the military background should have been less, or there should have been more of the sexual passion, or the two should have been more cunningly intermingled. (I could not suggest how.) Alternate layers of war and of love are scarcely satisfactory.

Withal, the book is a superb performance. I have specified a striking scene of battle. But the escape of hero and heroine into Switzerland is equally striking. And the birth of the baby in a Swiss hospital is even more striking. I have read nothing in that line so graphic, so beautiful, so harrowing. It need not fear comparison with the coming into the world of Anna Karenina's child.

The author, while often tactful in his omissions, permits himself a freedom of expression hitherto unexampled in Anglo-Saxon fiction printed for general sale. Some readers will object to it. I don't.

And now I must offer to you a specimen of the older school of fiction: Thomas Mann's *Early Sorrow*, excellently translated by H.T. Lowe-Porter (Secker, 5s.). It is not a novel, but a short story, containing about one-sixth of the matter in a novel of average length, and really too short for even a little book. But it is a lovely thing. Not "graphic," nor staccato, nor rapid, nor heightened by any new-fangled narrative devices. An apparently trifling episode in a middle-class German household, happening before the mark had been stabilised. Reading it, one perceives that the Hemingway generation has not really advanced the art of fiction. Hemingway is good. But the veteran Thomas Mann is just as good, and as skilled, and as effective. Mann's humour — not English — is of the subtlest, the most delicate. There was subtle and delicate humour last week in Beachcomber's tale of the Zulu infant prodigy who fell into a trombone, and in the *Times* leader about skyscrapers for oysters: each of them a rare morsel. But Thomas Mann's humour is far more rare.

And lastly, in the way of fiction in the classical style, I will mention the new English translation of Goncharov's novel *Oblomov* (Allen and Unwin, 10s. 6d., 521 pages). The translator is Natalie A. Duddington; she has succeeded with distinction in her task. *Oblomov* is one of the best Russian novels, and as characteristically Russian as any. It was published over seventy years ago. This is the first complete English translation! Still, we have it! The earth does revolve! Let there be no error. *Oblomov* is a very great novel: it must count among the very greatest novels in the world. And it is permeated with humour as subtle as Thomas Mann's.

21 November 1929

Some Hard Blows at Cherished Beliefs

Britain is supposed by Britons to be supreme in biography, especially biography of politicians and writers. The legend (whose truth I am not prepared to deny) of British supremacy in biography is no doubt built upon Boswell's Johnson. And Boswell's Johnson is a supreme work, though it begins with formidable dullness. Indeed, I would say that until Johnson is over forty his biography makes very hard reading.

This criticism will be held by devout readers in bookish dogma to be as sacrilegious as the laying of profane hands on the ark of the covenant. Let it be so. No sooner do I see an ark of the covenant (there are many arks) than I feel a desire to lay on it my profane hand. I have my own arks, which I will fight sanguinarily to protect from sacrilege; but other people's arks I am frequently ready to desecrate in the great cause of straight thinking.

Boswell's Johnson is long, yet not too long — except at the beginning. Most English biographies are cursed by their excessive length. Take the Monypenny-Buckle life of Disraeli. Six enormous volumes! (Now reduced — not in length, only in format — to two volumes.) I have not read it all, and I never will. Why should I devote a laborious fortnight of my too brief span to the perusal of half a million or a million words narrating the performances of a great music-hall performer like Disraeli, or the performance of any mortal man? To do so would be to demonstrate a lack in one of the most precious of all qualities, the divine sense of proportion.

Of what I have read of Disraeli's biography some is very good, but some is marvellously and frightfully bad. Take Morley's Gladstone. It is an Egyptian pyramid, enormous, terrific. And somewhere within it lies the spirit of that excellent but verbose and generally tedious Pharaoh, W.E. Gladstone. But nobody has ever found the spirit of Gladstone in the pyramid. Nobody, after reading Morley, could construct for himself a portrait of the man Gladstone. The book is un-human.

I much prefer to read a simple, shortish biography such as Constance Collier's autobiography, which she entitled *Harlequinade*. The book is full of art in its omissions. Otherwise touchingly artless! It is not written, it is thrown on to the page. Its grammar is unique. But it does give a living portrait of Beerbohm Tree, and another of Miss Collier. I started it in the middle, and when I had reached the end I went back to the beginning.

In the early part, the picture of the epoch of the Gaiety Girl is admirably effective. But, of course, Miss Collier did not set out to build pyramids. She set out to be her simple, remarkable self, with the result that she produced a book which genuinely diverts the plain reader and which no student of the social history of the last forty years can safely ignore.

The most interesting biography — it also is an autobiography, but autobiography is a form of biography — I have read for years is Axel Munthe's *The Story of San Michele*. (A bad, because an undescriptive, title.) Mrs. Patrick Campbell was masterfully insistent that I should read the book. She lent me a copy of it, which I received with reluctance. After I had read it I returned it with reluctance.

It is not quite a new book, but I think less than a year old. Story of the surprising adventures of a fashionable doctor, who was also a lover of solitude, nature, dogs, landscapes, common people, and all manner of immortal souls. The chapters dealing with rich, hysterical female patients are of the highest and funniest picturesqueness, and obviously true. Some of the other stories I accept with reserve. Mrs. Campbell said to me: "There is something in this book for everybody."

There is. When I wrote the opening words of this article I intended to introduce two new biographies. The first is *Walther Rathenau, His Life and Work*, by Count Harry Kessler (Howe, 16s.). One handy volume. Less than 400 pages. But completely satisfying! A model for British political biographers. I do not mean to review it, politics and industry not lying within my field. But I mean to recommend it. For this life of the murdered great German statesman, a European figure of first-rate importance, is an ideal biography. It concerns itself with psychological essentials, not with anecdotes and such like. And it is immensely readable. Had Rathenau been an Englishman some thorough-going and ruthless Briton would have seized hold of him and buried him deep in three or six elephantine volumes of unselected detail.

The second book is Robert Graves's biography of Robert Graves, entitled *Good-bye to All That* (Cape, 10s. 6d.). I wonder whether this title indicates that Robert Graves has really turned over a new leaf, and if so, why? He is in the early thirties, and the volume contains 450 pages, of which more than half deal with the war and the war-period. Some of you have had enough of the war and don't want to read about it. Well, the author wants you to read about the war, and you will read about it, for *Good-bye to All That* is a very good book, both picturesque and honest, and excellently written. Robert Graves is a fine poet — none better to-day, in my view. All poets write good prose, and he does.

I should not call it a pleasant book, and I have no desire that it should be pleasant. It is the sincere and convincing expression of a distinguished individuality, which has not always, or often, been in accord with its environment, an individuality somewhat resentful and hypersensitive. As such I welcome it. Candour is a great quality, but not a common one in the English character. Withal, a serene harmoniousness is not yet among Robert Graves's mental possessions.

I should like to have had a lot more than he gives about the creative-literary side of his life. He is almost silent on this. Of authors, Siegfried Sassoon has his chief attention. He prints a remarkable and hitherto unpublished war-poem (in the form of a letter) of Sassoon's. Why Sassoon has not published the poem himself, and why it should appear first in Robert Graves's autobiography I do not understand. It is a very striking poem, of the sort known as free verse.

As for the war-chapters, they are the work of a young man who had no illusions about "the lordliest life on earth," but who made himself "a good soldier." Scratch the surface of these chapters, and you will see rich deposits of sane, harsh irony. One hears that the English detest irony. They don't. They appreciate it as well as any race, except the French. And I am gravely mistaken if they will not appreciate *Good-bye to All That*. Those who read it and enjoy it and are not acquainted with the author's collected *Poems (1914-1927)* should read that book too; and then the later *Poems*. There is very considerable achievement in these two volumes.

Queen of the High-Brows

"There are two elements in language — sound and significance; the particular noise made when a word is uttered, and the particular meaning suggested to our minds by the noise when it is heard." These are the striking first words of a little book by Mr. Henry Bett (a name strange to me) entitled: *How to Write Good English. Some Principles of Style* (Allen and Unwin, 2s.).

Now the average "intelligent reader" does not want to learn how to write good English. Why should he? Technical handbooks are usually a bore to the intelligent laity (a man who drives a car for pleasure need not study how to build a car. He need only study how to drive a car — and not often will he do even that with any thoroughness). But the title of Mr. Bett's book is inadequate. The booklet might just as well have been called *How to Read Good English.* Having such a title it would appeal to the majority of people seriously devoted to reading. And that Mr. Bett himself means it to appeal to that majority is shown by his closing words: "A study of the principles of literary style will save an apprentice writer from some errors, and — *what is more important* — it will help the intelligent reader to understand, and not merely to feel, the charm of our greatest literature." Therefore I suggest that the title should be altered.

The booklet is very, very good. Its account of the growth of the language to-day known as English is clear, accurate, picturesque, and positively exciting. It gives the reasons for our belief that English is the finest of all languages as a literary vehicle. The booklet is cheap, in terms not only of money but of time; it can be read twice in two hours, and it should be read twice. It is impeccably written. Every paragraph of it is interesting, many have the character of revelation. A technical handbook it is: but if it were not far more than a technical handbook I would not have mentioned it here, no matter how much I had liked it. For a craftsman (of any craft) who tries to force the problems of his craft upon a defenceless public might properly be accused of bad form.

I am less enthusiastic concerning another and larger book about literary technics, Dr. Agnes Mure Mackenzie's *The Process of Literature, an Essay towards Some Reconsiderations* (Allen and Unwin, 10s.). It is a donnish professional volume with "Prolegomena" (a couple of them) and Appendixes, and a somewhat pretentious terminology.

Dr. Mackenzie is a novelist herself, and hence doubtless has some firsthand acquaintance with the art of imaginative creation. Nevertheless I think that Shakespeare would be a bit startled to read her chapter on the composition of *Othello*, and I cannot accept her conjectural account of the facts of that affair — though she certainly does make one or two good remarks about *Othello* considered as a finished product. Her chapters on the psychology of the reader are, in my opinion, better than those on the psychology of the writer. Harmless, I should call this book, but not necessary. It resembles a detective novel; it will serve to pass an idle evening.

Another book about writing, but a far better one, is Virginia Woolf's *A Room of One's Own* (Hogarth Press, 5s.). I have often been informed by the elect that a feud exists between Virginia Woolf and myself, and I dare say that she has received the same tidings. Possibly she and I are the only two lettered persons unaware of this feud. True, she has written a book about me and a mythical Mrs. Brown. But I have not read the book (I don't know why). True, I always said, until she wrote *To the Lighthouse*, that she had not written a good novel. But I have said the same of lots of my novelist friends. True, she is the queen of the high-brows; and I am a low-brow. But it takes all sorts of brows to make a world, and without a large admixture of low-brows even Bloomsbury would be uninhabitable.

One thing I have said of her: she can write. *A Room of One's Own* is a further demonstration of this truth. (She has her private notions about grammar. See p. 50.) And I have said that you never know where you are in a book of hers. *A Room of One's Own* is a further demonstration of this truth also. It is stated to be based on two papers read to the Arts Society of Newnham and the One-Damned-Thing-After-Another Society at Girton. On p.6 she refers to herself as a lecturer. On p.6 she suggests that you may throw "it" into the waste-paper basket. Well you can't throw a lecture into the waste-paper basket. You can only walk out from a lecture, or treat your ears as Ulysses treated the ears of his fellow-mariners.

The book has a thesis: namely, that "it is necessary to have five hundred a year and a room with a lock on it if you are to write fiction or poetry." With the implied corollary that women, being usually without five hundred a year of their very own, and liable to everlasting interruption, are at a serious disadvantage as novelists and poets.

The thesis is disputable. Dostoevsky wrote some of the greatest novels in the world while he was continually distracted by terrible extra-artistic anxieties. And I beg to state that I have myself written long and formidable novels in bedrooms whose doors certainly had no locks, and in the full dreadful knowledge that I had not five hundred a year of my own — nor fifty. And I beg to state further that from the moment when I obtained possession of both money and a lockable door all the high-brows in London conspired together to assert that I could no longer write.

However Virginia Woolf's thesis is not apparently important to her, since she talks about everything but the thesis. If her mind was not what it is I should accuse her of wholesale padding. This would be unjust. She is not consciously guilty of padding. She is merely the victim of her extraordinary gift of fancy (not imagination). If I had to make one of those brilliant generalisations now so fashionable, defining the difference between men and women, I should say that whereas a woman cannot walk through a meadow in June without wandering all over the place to pick attractive blossoms, a man can. Virginia Woolf cannot resist the floral enticement.

Some will describe her book as a feminist tract. It is no such thing. It is a book a little about men and a great deal about women. But it is not "feminist." It is non-partisan. The author writes: "Women are hard on women. Women dislike women. Women — but are you not sick to death of the word? I can assure you that I am." Admirable attitude! And she comes to no satisfactory conclusion about the disparateness of men and women. Because nobody ever has and nobody could.

You may walk along Prince Consort Road, and through the open windows of the Royal College of Music hear the scrapings, the tinklings and the trillings of a thousand young people trying to make themselves professional musicians. And you may reflect that ten years hence nine-tenths of the girls among them will have abandoned all scraping, tinkling and trilling for love, domesticity and (perhaps) cradles. And you may think that you have discovered the origin and explanation of the disparateness of men and women. Not so! Great opera-singers have borne child after child, and remained great opera-singers.

5 December 1929

Ill-Planned Homes of the Wealthy

What is the use of reading books unless the result is to civilise you? And how can you be said to be civilised unless you have acquired a sense of proportion; that is, a sense of the relative values of things? Babies have no sense of proportion; they are not civilised; they are indeed savages to whom with much difficulty adults first impart a code of manners, and then, so far as adults know how, a sense of proportion. But what kind of a sense of proportion have adults themselves?

Take motorcars. Every brand of motorcar advertises on itself the name of the maker. The owner indeed is compelled by the maker to give to the latter a continuous free advertisement. Yet if makers of umbrellas and overcoats stuck their names on those important articles there would be an insurrection of owners of umbrellas and overcoats. One reason why motorcars are labelled so that he who runs across the street may read is that we are tremendously interested in motorcars. We love to know the names of the makers; and he who cannot distinguish the brand of any car half a mile off is regarded with scorn by the truly educated.

Now take architecture. A few buildings bear the name of their architects. But very few, and very unobtrusively. Consider the new Regent-street. How many lay persons could give the name of the architect of a single building in Regent-street? How many lay persons could give the names of more than two or three living architects? Or even of one, unless he happens to be President of the Royal Academy? Further, it is fashionable and proper to bewail and despise the architecture of Regent-street. But how many of the bewailers and despisers of Regent-street architecture know anything about it beyond the appearances of the frontages thereof.

I admit that the beautiful frontages of Regent-street could be numbered on the fingers of a man who lost both arms in the war. But frontages are not the chief part of buildings. Planning is the chief part. Planning has immensely improved in the last fifty years. Compare the planning of the impressive nineteenth-century Paris City Hall with the planning of Knott's twentieth-century County Hall on Thames-side.

Lay detractors of the modern ignore planning. Planning never occurs to us. Why? Because we simply are not interested in architecture. Which means that we have only an infantile sense of proportion. For architecture is the most important, the most influential, of all the arts, fine or applied. It embraces in fact all the other arts, except music. Architecture influences us all the time, night and day. And especially domestic architecture. But

328

who cares? Who notices?

The dreadful proof of the indifference of the moneyed classes to domestic architecture is to be seen in the most expensive residential streets and squares of this city. The houses are ill-planned, dark, too high, too low, unventilated, absurdly costly in labour, and intensely unpractical. Had these streets and squares been commercial instead of residential they would have been torn down years ago, and replaced by habitable structures. But the moneyed classes put in central heating, turn two bedrooms into two bathrooms, and then have the nerve to call a house "modernised." Visit the new suburbs whose architecture is cursed by the "élite" as horridly as that of Regent-street, and you will see thousands of cheap houses which for practical comfort of living infinitely surpass, for instance, Belgrave-square.

Is this a literary column? It still is. Have the foregoing remarks any connection with literature? They have. I have been reading an entirely new kind of fiction. A book entitled *The Honeywood File. An Adventure in Building*, by H.B. Creswell (Architectural Press, 7s. 6d.). It narrates the relations between an imaginary architect and his client, during the designing and construction of a country-house. It is not a great work. Jane Austen, Hardy, George Moore are not challenged. But, though its humour is sometimes rather rude and crude, it is often very funny. The letter in which Spinlove, the architect, ventures to criticise the amateur plan of the proposed habitation sent to him by Sir Leslie Brash, the client, is enlivened by true comedy: "Also I am afraid it will be impossible to enter the house by the front-door except, of course, by going up the front-stairs and down the back, which cannot be your intention. . . . Moreover, the front-stairs could be used to reach the bedrooms only by going out by the back-door, or by one of the windows, and in at the front-door. I mention these matters in order to make clear why it is impossible for me to adopt your plan. . . ." Etc.

Further, the novel — for the book is a novel, though dealing exclusively with architecture — is full of human nature; and full of useful information, lightly conveyed, for everybody concerned with domestic architecture. We are all without exception concerned with domestic architecture. We all want to buy, build, or rent a wigwam of some description, or to know how, why and where the wigwams in which we are already camping are wrong and might be bettered. Hence I am inclined to think that all citizens who are capable of the sustained effort of reading a short book might read *The Honeywood File* with some pleasure and more profit. Even architects might pick up a wrinkle or two from it. I repeat that as literature it is not great. But it is an original and ingenious essay in fiction, and I insist that it has a civilising value.

On the same day as I received Mr. Creswell's small volume I received another small volume, *The Architect*, by Clough Williams-Ellis (Bles, 5s.). This is the latest item in the publisher's *Life and Work* series. Other items have dealt or will deal with the army, the stage, surgery, the Bar, and so on. The notion of getting a professional man to write a little book about himself as a professional man is a good one. Whether on the whole it will be well executed has yet to be seen.

Mr. Williams-Ellis gives a sketch of his life, from which one learns that

329

at a very tender age he lisped architecturally. He is known, to the few to whom architecture means anything, as an architect with ideals and ideas. It is not easy to gather from the book just what his purely architectural ideals and ideas are. But his social-architectural ideals and ideas are plain enough and very sound.

He writes in his closing pages: "I feel that it is a damnable and a cruel thing that beauty should be so rare. For each of us that have enough there are a thousand who have too little or none at all and who mostly do not miss it. . . . Yet instead of feeling ashamed in this wilderness, artists, critics, art patrons, and the enlightened and appreciative generally seem to be proud of their singularity and to enjoy being part of a superior and high-sniffing little clique. . . ." This warms my breast.

12 December 1929

Thousands Argue About the Modern Novel

The appearance of an anthology of *Twentieth Century Poetry*, chosen by Harold Monro (Chatto & Windus, 3s. 6d.), makes you think. It will make a lot of people think that such a collection is not for them. But it makes me think afresh about the situation of modern poetry on the map of modern literature. I doubt a little if modern poetry is on the map at all. Thousands of people will furiously argue for and against the value of a modern novel. But only tens of people will argue, even mildly, for and against the merits of modern poetry. Which of course means that modern poetry is read only by the few. What is not widely read will never excite the passions of any average-intelligent dinner-table. When a book sells well, people begin to say to themselves: "If I don't read that book I shan't be up-to-date." They read it, and, having read it, they talk about it in order to show that they have read it. Herein is one of the principal factors in literary popularity. Nobody, however, is going to worry himself about not being up-to-date concerning modern poetry.

Nevertheless there have been periods when people desirous of being in the movement could not neglect their contemporary poetry. A new volume by Tennyson was quite a social incident. Tennyson received £300 for his poem in the first number of *The Nineteenth Century* (and maintained that he ought to have got £500). A new volume of verse by Kipling was more than an incident, it was a prodigious event. And conscientious persons, after accepting an invitation to dinner, if they had not read the latest, would run out and buy it. Masefield's first long narrative poems made people ignore the fish at dinner.

Since then, nothing! And yet far better poems than Masefield ever wrote have been published in the meantime. For example, the Poet Laureate's recent book.* Why the present fashionable neglect of the modern? The reason in my opinion is that modern poetry has been revolutionary. The thing can be explained crudely by a simple juxtaposition. In the early years of the century the intelligent evening papers, the Gazettes —

* Robert Bridges' *The Testament of Beauty*.

Westminster, Pall Mall, etc. — published every day what they called "Occasional Verse," familiarly referred to among poets as "Occ. Verse." These verses usually portrayed the feelings of a young man languishing in adoration in front of his young woman. They were nearly all the same, and most of them were nauseating molasses. Edison, had he not been a lover of humanity, might well have invented a machine to compose them. Now to-day, instead of sweet Occ. Verse you read:

> Thank goodness the moving is over,
> They've swept up the straw in the passage
> And life will begin . . . .

The new poets have grown absolutely sick of the old material, and their impatient verve chafed under the old forms. So the new poets scrapped the old material, and stretched the old forms till they snapped like elastic bands. That, roughly, was the revolution. The British public is not partial to revolutions. It believes that your revolutionary, be he a poet or a socialist, is most effectively dealt with by leaving him alone. Later, the mind of the British public gets used to these novelties and practises socialism, and will, in the end, read the new poetry, as though it had never shied at either of them. The day of the new poet will come.

Harold Monro is a sound poet, an excellent anthologist, and a good bookseller. When the new poetry gets itself on the map, he will be entitled to count among the chief cartographers. I like his short preface. In it he drily announces that his anthology has not been compiled from other anthologies, and that he has read or re-read 600 volumes for the compiling of it. He quotes some excellent sayings of the great Emerson: "The experience of each age requires a new confession." Cowley: "A war-like, various and tragical age is best to write of, but worst to write in." J.M. Synge (author of *The Playboy of the Western World*): "Before verse can become human again it must become brutal."

Monro says that the author of *A Shropshire Lad* was the chief new influence up to 1920, and that T.S. Eliot is and will be the chief influence between 1920 and 1940. Certainly the influence of Housman is apparent in this anthology. The recurrent and, to my mind, rather facile lament (perfectly achieved by Shakespeare) that lads and girls who once were golden and amorous now lie beneath the green grass! Housman was a fine but narrow poet. I regard his influence as bad.

As for T.S. Eliot, I have never been able to understand his influence, which is unquestionable, on the younger poets. I have read I don't know how many times his celebrated poem, *The Waste Land,* at the mention of which every younger poet bows the head in awe, and I simply cannot see its beauty. I don't say it has no beauty: I say merely that I can't see its beauty. I once asked Eliot whether his explanatory notes to "The Waste Land" were not a pulling of the public leg. I seriously thought they were. He seriously assured me that they were not. I bowed the head. There are a few excellent poems by Eliot in this anthology, but not more excellent than many poems by other hands.

Seventy and seven poets are represented in the volume, of whom about sixty are not even names to the novel-reading public. I think that Robert Graves is the best of the living poets represented. (I except the Poet Laureate, a greater than Graves, because I do not think of his poetry as now in any reasonable sense "modern." It is of the nineteenth century.) Monro utters no word about Kipling, nor gives him a place in his anthology. The assumption, plain enough from the preface, is that Monro has re-read Kipling and ruled him out. I would not rule Kipling out. He may have written a lot of spurious and tendencious eloquence, but I shall hold to the opinion that he is one of the fathers of modern poetry. His poem containing the memorable line, "Romance brought up the nine-fifteen," is modern, and lovely.

Well I could make many more comments. And I am very interested in the subject, for at one period I underwent a spell of verse-writing myself (it nearly killed me). But I will refrain. I will only say I have been much impressed by *Twentieth Century Poetry*. I read it with increasing respect and pleasure. It no doubt comprises some poor, and more doubtful, poems — but on the whole its contents are surprisingly beautiful. There are more good poets around than I had supposed. *Twentieth Century Poetry* is the best anthology of the moderns that I have seen. It ought to sell. If it sells it will be talked about. If it is talked about the cause of poetry will be advanced.

19 December 1929

A Christmas Lament of Some Bookish Men

Last week I listened with surprise and sadness to some bookish men who were complaining that just before Christmas no new books were published! In the first place this is not quite the fact. A certain number of new books are published almost right up to Christmas. True, no apparently important books are published within a fortnight of Christmas, but who can be sure that a book apparently unimportant will not in the end prove to be really important? Nobody. In the second place a lull in publishing is an excellent thing, in addition to being a necessary thing. Reviewers deserve consideration. Their task is terrible. I doubt whether it is not better to be a coal-miner than a popular reviewer. The miner's hours are shorter, and his work is less deleterious to the mind; and since the body depends on the mind, the mind should count for more than the body; and I wish that the majority of persons could grasp this great fact; they don't. A popular reviewer has little opportunity or none to invigorate his mind and to revive and establish his standards by reading masterpieces. The larger part of his days is spent in boredom and in the excruciating and vain effort to be fair. He needs a rest from mediocrity. Let him have it.

And don't despise the reviewer. Not the publisher is the midwife of new literature, but the reviewer. He may unwittingly mislead you; he may be cursed with (what seems to you to be) bad taste. He may be cranky, or bitter, or over-kind. But where would you be without him? For at worst he does give you some notion of what a new book is about. He does help you to form a preliminary opinion of your own. Imagine your newspaper if all reviewers went on strike! There are two classes of men in society whom I daily venerate. Bus-drivers and book-reviewers. Their tact, their self-possession and good judgment in the bright face of danger, the courageous, indomitable fight against the deadly influences of endless monotony on the soul, inspire me with admiration.

As for the bookish men whose morbid appetite demands to be titillated by an everlasting diet of new books, I regard them as cases for brain-specialists. Their malady is akin to alcoholism, which is the worst malady of the mind known to medical science. The morbid appetite for new books will drive the sufferer to strange caprices. One of my interlocutors told me that, despairing, he read some Kipling. With an air of astonishment he confessed that he had found Kipling very good! Indeed, he seemed to think that he had discovered Kipling. He had to be told that Kipling is still, after more than thirty years, the most popular serious English author alive. I am informed that the rumour of Kipling's readableness has at last reached even the hunting and cocktail classes. Anyhow, new editions of Kipling are continuously being issued. This plain fact is a very considerable tribute to the good sense and good taste of the average man. I would sooner see the average man fonder of Kipling than of Dickens. According to the testimony of leading London booksellers, he is.

Now, on the other hand, I am well acquainted with bookish men who day in day out protest that too many new books are published. They gloomily assert that the majority of new books are worthless and can do no good to anyone; that the system is monstrous by which publishers avowedly expect to recoup themselves by their profits from one successful book for their losses on half a dozen failures. Lastly they weep, in a manner of speaking, because this is a decadent age and things are not what they were.

I have a primitive desire to assassinate these men. But I refrain, for the reason that they are misguided rather than vicious. They sin in ignorance. They are merely persons who do not know what they are talking about. This is no more a decadent age, in a literary sense, than any other age. On the contrary, in no previous age have so large a proportion of the populace shown such discrimination among books, such intelligent interest in good books, as obtains to-day. Further the success of a book is not necessarily a criterion of its worth. Even to-day bad books occasionally achieve large sales.

Further, the system by which successes pay for failures is a sound and a just system. Because without many failures there would be no or few successes. The existing system alone provides the soil, the climate, the mechanical apparatus, which render possible both popular successes and genuine worth. Why?

Well, a publisher must accustom the public to the spectacle of many books. If a bookshop displayed only the few really good books that get published in a year, it would be nearly empty. It would not attract. The public would not enter it. The bookseller would expire, and his family would go on the dole. Further, though a publisher can usually decide with some certainty whether a book is good, he cannot always or often be sure that a book is *not* good. Many books now recognised as masterpieces "fell dead" on publication. Only they were not dead; they were in a trance, and in course of time they awoke out of the trance and ended by making a noise, a stir, a regular row in the world.

Since the publisher, despite all his professional "readers" and tasters, cannot either immediately judge the permanent value of a book, or foretell the numbers in which it will sell, he takes a chance and publishes lots of books, giving the doubtful ones the benefit of the doubt. The result is that an author, especially a new author, finds it comparatively easy to reach publication. Hence he is encouraged to write. One reason why there are so few good plays is the notorious fact that to reach actual stage-performance is extremely, tragically difficult. Authors don't write plays for fun. Nor do they write books for fun. They write because they wish to share their ideas and emotions with a public. When they see an unbridgeable chasm between themselves and a public, they cease to write. If only one book in a score published proves to be good, the present system is amply justified. The system favours the publisher, the bookseller and the author.

I will close by giving an example of a novel which, good or bad, was worth publishing, and which probably would not have been published under any severer system than the present one — *The Sound and the Fury,* by William Faulkner (Jonathan Cape and Harrison Smith, New York, 2½ dollars). This book is published in America by an English firm, but so far as I know it is not yet published in England. Having heard, from an Englishman of course, of the promise of William Faulkner, I sent to New York for all his works. But I could only get this one. The author is evidently young. He evidently has great and original talent. Influenced by James Joyce, he is exasperatingly, unimaginably difficult to read. He seems to take malicious pleasure in mystifying the reader. The first part of his novel is supposed to be written by a deaf-mute who is also a lunatic! But William Faulkner may emerge from this youthful stage of eccentricity. If he does, he will emerge into wide appreciation. Infuriated as I am by the book, I would not have missed it.

BOOKS AND PERSONS : 1930

Young Woman Who Tackles Big Subjects

At the end of the year even the wise man who in the holiday season deals with his mail at each delivery thereof discovers that some gift has not been acknowledged, or (more tragic) some gift has not been chosen and sent. Similarly with books published. I have reconciled myself to the fact that I cannot read everything, or ten per cent. of everything. I never begin a book unless I think it will interest me, and I never finish a book unless it actually does interest me. Such is my literary rule of life, and there is no exception to it unless I think that a book has been so much over-valued, or will so acutely exasperate me, that I am likely to be moved to invective and violent dispraise. This does not happen often. In fact many people say that frequently I am too kindly towards books. I do not agree, addicted though I certainly am to what Swinburne called "the noble pleasure of praising."

Two bookmen, one unknown to me, have directed my attention to two books which without their signalling I should have missed, and which I should have been sorry to miss. The first is Miss D.M. Ketelby's *A History of Modern Times from 1789 to the Present Day* (Harrap, 8s. 6d. — and cheap). Miss Ketelby is a Birmingham woman, in the young thirties of her life. She is apparently drawn towards big subjects. Already she has published a *European History from the Fall of Rome to the Eve of the French Revolution.* No trifle of a subject! The new book, like its forerunner, is a condensation and popularisation of history. Even historians do not fully know history in these days. They cannot, because history has grown too big. They can fully know only bits of history. Of the rest they must be content to know merely the outlines.

What chance then have ordinary readers of knowing history? (How many citizens have read even the dozen obese volumes of the *Cambridge Modern History,* and lived to tell the tale? But the *C.M.H.* is only a popular condensation of more or less ascertained historical facts.) Hence there has arisen a school of comprehensive popularisers, of whom one of the first and the chief was H.G. Wells, whose morsel concerning the entire earth from prehistoric times down to date has brilliantly survived many heated attacks from specialists, and has not yet been rivalled. I have for many years regarded the two short opening chapters of the *C.M.H.,* "The Age of Discovery" and "The New World" (less than 60 pages together), by E.J. Payne, as the finest example of popularisation in this epoch. Payne died. His death was a very grave loss to the great cause of popular history.

Miss Ketelby belongs to the Wells school. Her Introduction (less than ten pages) is really good. So is the section on Europe between 1815 and 1850 (less than 50 pages). And so particularly is her concluding chapter (just over 60 pages) on the United States. I have not read the whole book (over 600 pages); but I have read the abovementioned parts of it, and if heaven is kindly to me I shall read the remainder. Miss Ketelby possesses what seems to me an immensely wide sweep of knowledge, together with a rich talent for inductive generalisations, especially as to America, which persuade the reader of their justness. I mistrust generalisations, which of course are seldom more than half true; but without them all history would be futile, and they are the very life of popular condensation. Miss Ketelby's manner of writing is sound, if not blindingly brilliant. Her book cannot fail to be of use and interest to the common reader, old or young, learned or ignorant.

The other book is an American novel, *Bottom Dogs*, by Edward Dahlberg (Putnam, 15s.). I should have left this volume strictly unread had it not had a preface by D.H. Lawrence. Impossible to ignore a piece of critical work by such a penetrating and original critic as Lawrence, who, by the way, says little about the novel but makes, at some length, a rather impressive generalisation about America of to-day to explain why Americans are so sensitive in some respects and not in others.

The preface is handsomely worth reading. The novel too is worth reading: a novel, or more correctly a series of episodes, about the careers of under-dogs in provincial cities. It is a true book, one of the truest that I remember. But it made me think of a recent saying of a French author: "The truth is atrocious, and certainly it does not proclaim itself." The human intelligence cannot tolerate the truth in large doses. In *Bottom Dogs* there is a very large dose of truth. Lawrence says: "Nothing I have ever read has astonished me more than the Orphanage chapters." He says also: "That directness, that non-dramatised thoroughness of setting down the under-dog mind surpasses anything I know. I don't want to read any more books like this. But I am glad to have read this one, just to know what is the last word in repulsive consciousness, consciousness in a state of repulsiveness."

The book is extremely repulsive. It gives simply frightful pictures of the under-dog mentality. Says Lawrence: "It is not till you live in America and go a little under the surface that you begin to see how terrible and brutal is the mass of failure that nourishes the roots of the gigantic tree of dollars."

Lawrence approves the author's style, which is all American slang. But if you would realise the difference between distinguished style and the sort of literary condiment, all mustard and red pepper, which Edward Dahlberg has employed for *Bottom Dogs*, you only have to compare the sentence just quoted from Lawrence with any page in the novel itself. Dahlberg's style, like his matter, is very monotonous and "non-dramatised." The book, however, contains remarkable things. The last chapter, "Solomon's Dancepalace," is a dreadful piece of convincing realism.

Bottom Dogs is published in Britain in an edition limited to 500 copies, at which one might excusably infer that its realism is quite unusually sexual. This is not so. Sexual reactions are realistically treated in it, but not more so than in various recent novels which have been permitted general circulation. The repulsiveness of the book is not a particular repulsiveness. It is a general repulsiveness. It is strong meat for robust stomachs. My attitude towards the book is that of Lawrence. I am glad to have read it, but I do not want to read another like it. At the same time it is by no means negligible as a sign of tendencies.

9 January 1930

Books That Make One See

New books published in the recently deceased year numbered about nine and a half thousand, a falling-off which will make you sad or mad or glad, according to your temperament. For me, here, the most interesting and really awful fact is that all these books had to be reviewed, and indeed were reviewed. Beyond doubt more literary criticism is written to-day than ever before. And whole volumes of literary criticism are actually published! In the official table of 1929 publications, printed in the current *Publisher and Bookseller*, books are classified under forty-eight headings. Is there a heading for "Criticism"? There is not. There are headings for "Facetiae," "Calendars," "Occultism," "Philately," "Wireless," and suchlike ravishing topics; but none for Criticism.

The official list obstinately maintains its extraordinary classifications. It still lumps Poetry and Drama together, Art and Architecture together; it still has a heading "Essays *and* Belles-Lettres" — as if Essays were not a particular variety of Belles-Lettres. I presume that volumes of Literary Criticism are to be found under this last heading. But one never knows. They may well be under "Facetiae." I therefore make my annual protest against the official classifications, and this time I urge that the words "Literary Criticism" should at least appear as part of one of the headings, so that a plain man may know where he is in the horrible maze.

It is not as though literary criticism were a matter unimportant to publishers and booksellers themselves. I rarely scan a page of publishers' advertisements without seeing my name and my views on some book or books used as a bait to buyers: and I rarely enter a bookseller's shop without seeing the same on the dust-covers of some book or books. The compilers of the official list may contend that but few books of literary criticism are published. Nevertheless more books of literary criticism are published than books on "Philately" (5) or on "Wireless" (18). The compilers of the official list cannot successfully defend their position, which is absurd.

I have been reading two essays on Literary Criticism in a volume entitled *Tradition and Experiment in Present Day Literature* (Oxford University Press, 7s. 6d.). "Tradition" in criticism is handled by Rebecca West, and "Experiment" by T.S. Eliot, a formidable pair. Rebecca West skates brilliantly over literary criticism from Aristotle down to R.A. Scott-James. I agree in the main with her views, and in particular with her appreciations of Aristotle and R.A. Scott-James and her murderous depreciation of Johnson's *Lives of the Poets*. But I have discovered little that is new to me in her witty remarks. As for T.S. Eliot, he gives in my opinion too much attention to the past (he discusses several antique and fine critics already discussed by Rebecca West) and too little to present and future criticism. His chief point seems to me to be that criticism is and will be influenced by the master-idea of evolution. Well, of course! On the whole, for me, these two essays have a more striking resemblance to stone than to bread, of constructive criticism they contain very little.

But when, in the same book, I read C.K. Munro's essay on "Experiment in

Drama" I met with constructive criticism which applies as well to novels (my province) as to the drama. Munro quotes from one of the greatest critical minds of the age, Roger Fry (whose province is painting). Says Fry: "We learn to *see* only so much as is needful for our purposes: but this is in fact very little, just enough to recognise and identify each object or person; that done, they go into an entry in our mental catalogue and are no more really *seen.* In actual life the normal person *really only reads the labels* as it were on the objects around him, and troubles no further. . . . We were given our eyes to *see* things, not to look at them." (My italics.)

And upon these statements Munro proceeds: "Now as soon as we have got well into our minds that we normally never see the world at all, it becomes clear that if we could ever manage to do such an unusual thing as to see it, the result might be interesting. . . . We should find a *new way* of taking experience. To provide such a *new way* is the function of art." (Author's italics.) Munro illustrates the theory by pointing out that to a Londoner "London is a place of practical consequences and possesses few romantic associations; what happens in London affects him to the exclusion of his ever observing it for its own sake." When, however, he goes to Paris "his imagination becomes alive with anticipations of wonder." Yet the inhabitants of Paris see Paris "as drab a place" as London is to the Londoner.

The core of the business of all imaginative literature is here. And the duty of the literary critic is to insist all the time that that imaginative literature is negligible which does nothing to make the reader see people, places, and phenomena as freshly as though he had never set eyes on them before. And vice versa. A book or a play treating of London which causes a Londoner to see London as interestedly and romantically as he sees Paris, is a good book or play. A book or a play which doesn't, isn't.

But a first-class book or play must have something more even than this quality. It must give an effect of beauty. No matter how sordid, squalid, ugly, repulsive its raw material, it must give an effect of beauty. It must cause the reader or the listener to see beauty where he could not have seen it before. One of the supreme instances of such an achievement is Dostoevsky's *The House of the Dead,* where the horrors of prison life, while realistically rendered, are turned into beauty. Another is the closing chapters of Stendhal's *Red and Black.*

The aim of the newer forms of art — for instance, the "expressionist" drama — is to compel people to *see* and to *feel* what hitherto they have neither seen nor felt. An example is Toller's *The Adding Machine,* * which I think Munro places much higher than I would. *The Adding Machine* does make you see, but it certainly does not make you see beauty. The same is to be said of Edward Dahlberg's panorama of American mental and physical sordidness and squalor, *Bottom Dogs,* which I mentioned last week. It takes you by the scruff of the neck and violently forces you to see, and to see afresh; but there is no beauty in it that I can perceive. (I admit that what is one man's beauty may be another man's ugliness. But that raises another question, which I cannot now examine.) Anyhow a work of art, whether poem, novel, play, picture, ought to make you think that you are seeing the things portrayed for the first time in your life, and also seeing beauty, or

* See next 'Books and Persons' for correction.

338

new beauty, in them for the first time. The literary critic of the future will more and more firmly establish this test for works of imaginative art, and by it judge more and more ruthlessly every book submitted to his judgment.

16 January 1930

Antiquated *Westward Ho!*

Charles Kingsley preached sermons at the age of *four*. He was the son of a clergyman and became a clergyman. His first published work was a verse-drama on the subject of St. Elizabeth of Hungary. He could walk over fifty miles a day. He loved horses. He loved tobacco. He was a Tory who tried hard to be a Radical, and failed. He was a chaplain to Queen Victoria. He tutored the Prince of Wales and made a friend of him. He got himself into trouble with Cardinal Newman: for which trouble we are grateful, for it caused Newman to write the celebrated *Apologia pro Vita Sua*.

He was appointed to the Modern History Professorship at Cambridge. He made a mess of that because, though he knew enough history to write historical novels, he didn't know enough to teach it. He obtained a canonry of Chester, and later a canonry of Westminster. He had a passion for things military, and much enjoyed the society of Army officers. He was generally in poor health and generally hard up. Why he should have been so hard up so often is difficult to understand, considering that he was not a spend-thrift and that some of his books had vast circulations. I should like to know who made most money out of *Westward Ho!* he or his publishers, and by how much. He died at the age of fifty-five, worn out, and his funeral was attended by statesmen, high Army officials, peasants and a pack of hounds.

Westward Ho! has the reputation of being his best book, and I think it is. I have read it again, after perhaps thirty-five years. The first thing that struck me in the volume was the bibliography at the beginning. (Would that all publishers would imitate Macmillans in this matter of printing biblio-graphies.) There have been fifty-nine editions of *Westward Ho!* and sixteen of them in the present century. The second thing was its tremendous length, 591 close pages. I quailed as I set forth on the voyage. There were storms en route, and good ones; but there were also interminable doldrums. My obstinate courage in sticking to the ship until she finally dropped anchor at Appledore, has convinced me that in a previous incarnation I must have been at least Sir Francis Drake.

The tale is of the days of the Armada, and of English marine audacity, pugnacity, and procacity, conceived and executed on the heroic scale. Nearly all the characters are superhuman either in manly Protestant virtue or in Papistical villainy. As you read the description of the qualities and the achievements of Frank Leigh, you think: "This fellow must be the hero of the piece. Nobody could possibly be more heroic." You are wrong. Amyas is more heroic, and he is the hero. In any realistic sense the characterisation is exaggerated to the point of absurdity. But you must remember that this novel is not a realistic novel. It is a romance. It is lyrical. It leaves poor life far behind.

The worst shortcoming of the physically and morally gigantic Amyas was to refuse Communion one morning when he had got out of bed on the wrong side of the hammock. If ever a novel was "wholesome," this is. It might have been still more wholesome if its author, who was a propagandist and a sermoniser to the last, had not continually falsified it by letting too loose his passionate hatred of Popery and his passionate admiration for the British Protestant sailors of the mighty age of Elizabeth.

The book is well constructed: by which I mean simply that it consistently holds the attention — or would hold the attention but for its overwhelming wordiness. Wordiness is not a fault of construction: it is an artistic fault due to emotional instability. Kingsley must have been an impulsive, flyaway creature. Once fairly started he could not stop himself until the impulse was exhausted. This wordiness is a pity, because it bulges out the flesh of an organism whose bones are excellently shapen.

The man is too addicted to proverbial phrases. And of course he never uses two words if eight or ten will do. For instance, he will call a money transaction "payment of certain current coins of the realm." And when his heroes go to bed they don't merely sleep, they "sleep the sleep of the just." Withal he had taught himself to write; though, I regret to say, he afflicts the sublime Amyas with a flagrant bit of bad grammar at a supreme moment. Now bad grammar is inexcusable in the mouth of an idealistic, aristocratic hero.

Kingsley's landscape painting is really brilliant. Chapter VI opens with a landscape which is done about as well as any landscape could be done by a writer of talent, as distinguished from genius. People talk a lot about his brother Henry. I read recently a very interesting essay on Henry, in which Henry's style is extolled! Henry never learned to write. He was content to throw the stuff down on the paper anyhow. He was always clumsy, had no feeling for the rhythm of a sentence, and continually involved himself in the coils of those devilish serpents — present participles. He lacked the character which is indispensable to the making of a sustained work of art. He was one of your gifted amateurs.

Nothing of the amateur in the Reverend Charles! When he begins a big set-piece he immediately wins your confidence. He has the justified assurance of those terrific persons, the swell music-hall comedians, who appear on the stage absolutely certain that, unaided, they can and will dominate a packed audience of thousands. And when he thinks he can't perform a certain feat, or he doesn't want to perform it, he frankly says so. ("There, dear readers . . . I cannot tire you with any wire-drawn soul-dissections.") Charles was as adroit and effective in the description of sea-fights as of landscapes. A sea-fight is an extremely difficult thing to picture in words. There is a truly admirable sea-fight in Chapter XX. The big Armada fight in Chapter XXXI, though fine — especially at its climax — is less fine than the smaller affair.

Lastly, in the matter of sentimentality, while Charles is very sentimental in detail, he is not sentimental in his larger curves of narrative. In the early chapters an "experienced reader" reading *Westward Ho!* for the first time would lay a hundred to one that after frightful calamities Amyas will marry Her Loveliness, Rose Salterne, a passion for whom "consumes" him. Well, he just doesn't. And the story is a tragedy.

There is a great deal to be said for *Westward Ho!* I have said some of it.

But I must keep the balance. The book can be read, but only by a surrender on the part of the reader more abject than even a dead author has the right to demand of a living reader. It is old-fashioned. So is *Tom Jones*. But *Westward Ho!* is antiquated. *Tom Jones* remains fresh. The reason is that *Tom Jones* is sufficiently, and *Westward Ho!* is insufficiently, vitalised by original imaginative power. *Westward Ho!* is a confection. Honest enough, but a confection. I would not read it again for £100. No, I would not. "Good heavens forefend, Captain Raleigh."

A number of kindly and enlightened readers have written to me pointing out that I was wrong last week in attributing *The Adding Machine* to Ernst Toller. It is by Elmer Rice. Toller wrote *The Machine-Wreckers*. True, true! Impossible to excuse myself.

23 January 1930

A Tale of the Private's War

Prophets are rash fellows. They risk looking foolish, until they are forgotten. Most of them do look foolish and are forgotten. But those who prophesied that the output of war-books, and good war-books, would continue, despite the recent glittering procession of such books which have awakened the consciousness of all the western world, are being justified by the event. Every good new war-novel issued shows some new aspect of the tremendous and unique theme. If it did not, it would not be good. The grandeur of the theme compels creative writers who have first-hand knowledge of it to write about it. The theme is endless; it is as near the infinite as anything human can be, and the last word on it will never be written.

I have just read another war-novel: *The Middle Parts of Fortune*. For some reason the author neither divulges his name nor employs a pseudonym. He prefers to be strictly unknown. His identity, however, is certain sooner or later to emerge; for his book is one of the big novels of the war. So he might as well confess at once and save us from bad guessing. The title is explained by a well-known passage from *Hamlet*. It is not a satisfactorily descriptive title — save in a sense savagely ironic — and can only be attributed to the secondary effect of a poor pun. Never were men less in the favours of fortune than the heroes of this book.

But what an inspiring and beautiful book! Assuredly I have read no book which gives so complete, fine and true a picture of military life in the trenches before an attack, and of military life "over the top" and through the enemy's wire, than this book presents. The author knows what goes on in men's minds. And he knows all the smells, sounds, mud, and sights of warfare to the least particular. And he puts the whole thing down. So much and such various detail of the British soldier's life by day and by night has not before, to my knowledge, been got without crowding into one book.

The result is a quiet and utterly convincing glorification of the common soldier. The tale is full of horrors, cruelties, stupidities, grossnesses; but it is also full of nobility. It is a wreath laid on the innumerable tomb, known and unknown, visited and unvisited, of the war's victims. It compels in the reader a reluctant belief that war is glorious after all. The tale is of privates.

That is to say, the mind and sufferings of the private are described from the inside, whereas the mind and sufferings of the officer are described from the outside. The chief character, Bourne, is a gentleman-ranker, who lives philosophically in most intimate contact with the ordinary ranker — and profoundly understands and esteems him.

I would not mislead you. The book is not grandiose; it has no ingeniously calculated "effects"; it has indeed here and there a dull page or so; the best thing in it, after the culminating, futile, fatal attack (Somme and Ancre, 1916), is a long recital of an alcoholic and extremely earthy jollity. It has little or no "serial interest" in the usual significance of the term. Indeed to serialise it would be to ruin it. It depends for its moral magic on a continuous veracity, consistent, comprehending, merciful, and lovely. It is admirably written. *The Middle Parts of Fortune* will be remembered when *All Quiet on the Western Front*, with all its excellences, is forgotten. It goes deeper. It is bound to survive as a major document in war-literature.

The book is issued in a limited edition (published by the Piazza Press, distributed by Peter Davies, well printed by the Glasgow University Press), simply because all the language of the common soldier is displayed in full. You understand: all. You will find in it nothing whatever else to which even a Home Secretary could object; but the vocabulary renders general publication impossible. There is an edition partially expurgated for popular use.

Which reminds me of Mr. E.S. Jones's letter printed here (contrary to his expectation) yesterday. In that letter Mr. Jones said that he is "exceedingly irritated" by my "too frequent references to the works of James Joyce and D.H. Lawrence." Mr. Jones further says that Joyce's *Ulysses* is "darkly hinted at" by me! I have not been guilty of any "dark hints" about *Ulysses*. When it first appeared I wrote a signed review of *Ulysses* in a wholly respectable conservative weekly periodical, and my review has been quoted at intervals in the Press of two hemispheres ever since.

I have always publicly held that Joyce is among the most powerful influences in modern fiction, that he is a genius and recognised as such by a large number of experts well entitled to judge, and that while *Ulysses* is very unequal it contains some of the finest and most original pages in all fiction. On the other hand I have always held that a police-censorship is a necessity, that no British police-censorship could possibly pass *Ulysses*, and that therefore *Ulysses* cannot properly be offered for general sale in this country. As regards the merits and demerits of D.H. Lawrence I have been similarly outspoken.

I can see nothing in my comments which ought to "irritate" a wise man. I understand Mr. Jones's attitude, which is shared by multitudes of excellent citizens. I wish he could understand mine. I have no desire to compel him to read books which offend him; but I do not appreciate his desire to prevent me from reading books which, though they may in places offend me, in other places give me great and not ignoble pleasure. There is not one decent public; there are forty decent publics. The tastes of all those publics can be satisfied, if common sense and reasonable compromise in distribution are brought into play.

A famous British statesman said last year that he would like to forbid all literature which could harm the "little ones." He is entitled to his opinion. I disagree with him. I am as well entitled to my opinion as he is to his, and

I propose to stick to it. I should be interested to see the said statesman begin his censorship with Shakespeare, Aristophanes, Rabelais, Balzac, Swift, Fielding, Sterne, Hardy, and a few other similar immortal base traffickers in the alleged obscene. Per contra, I could name to Mr. Jones quite a batch of modern novels to which he might not object, but to which I do object, on the score of a pervading semi-disguised lewdness. These books would sail through any police-censorship.

I have room only to mention a novel which, when I had started it, forced me to finish it: *The Lost Child*, by Rahel Sanzara (Gollancz, 7s. 6d.). Rahel Sanzara is said to be the pseudonym of a famous German actress, who apparently suffers from an unnatural objection to publicity. It is the story of the murder of a little girl by a boy. The author has a considerable gift of narrative, and she has invented a plot which, while perhaps somewhat antipathetic to the normal mind (such as my own), is worked out very effectively indeed. The abnormal psychology is well done.

German critics call *The Lost Child* a masterpiece. I don't. I call it rather the brilliant outpouring of a highly emotional woman who was mastered by "a great notion for a story," and who freed herself from the obsession of it by writing it down at a temperature of 104deg. But the book is "enthralling," as people say; and it induces you to read it "from cover to cover," as people say. Certainly it is more enthralling than the majority of detective-novels. The translation, which seems to be American, is fair to middling.

30 January 1930

Laughter — And a Lobster Supper

Like most professional humorists, I rarely laugh, even at what I think is funny. There are two sorts of humour, the sort that makes you laugh audibly, and the sort that makes you laugh subterraneanly and noiselessly somewhere down in your solar plexus. Some people hold that the second is better than the first. I am not of this opinion. I would give the two sorts equal marks. And the first or loud sort holds a clear advantage over the second in that it has a positive ameliorating influence on the bodily health.

I shall never forget a supper, a long time ago in my dyspeptic days, at which Frederick Norton (whose name is musically connected with the stage) told stories. Mr. Norton is the finest and most elaborate raconteur I ever heard, with the possible exception of Lord Beaverbrook, whose style, however, is more dramatic than humorous. Now the supper consisted of lobster, beefsteak-and-kidney pudding and beer, any one of which items taken at night ought to have incapacitated me for at least three days. Yet the next morning I awoke in the sublime perfection of health. The reason was that throughout the meal and after it I had laughed, as they say, "consumedly" (I have no idea what this strange word *ought* to mean. All I know is that it is the only proper epithet to apply to my laughter, which was continuous for several hours). I laughed indeed more than I have ever laughed before or since. Now I maintain that a man who can by speech or writing make you laugh in this fashion is a doctor in addition to being a humorist.

He is a benefactor of mankind.

My thoughts have turned towards humour because I have been reading a new "omnibus" volume: *Humorous Stories* by Barry Pain (Werner Laurie, 8s. 6d., 754 pages). Barry Pain's humour, in either speech or writing, seldom or never made me laugh aloud. Nor does W.W. Jacobs's, nor Pett Ridge's. Like Pett Ridge, Barry Pain was an inveterate "tease" (which is another word for "teaser"). He teased incessantly, and as he grew older he grew more sardonic in his teasing. He teases human nature in his books. His first book, *In a Canadian Canoe* (published nearly forty years since), did make me laugh: but he was young then and I was young. He never, I think, wrote a satisfactory long book; and even his short books are usually divided into episodes each of which might well stand alone. His maturer stories are for the most part laid in an environment of the middle or lower-middle class. His method is to take a self-satisfied character (such as the husband of the famous Eliza, or Mr. Tamplin of the boot-shop), and while keeping grave to render the character utterly ridiculous, out of the character's own mouth.

All his humour is very quiet, astutely diminished; it appeals to you rather than knocks you down. His defects are two. He never allows a character to develop. And he often puts humorous remarks into the mouths of people who obviously are without humour. Thus in the tale of the false teeth which ultimately were utilised as a mouse-trap, Pain makes Tamplin say: "He had hopes that in another two or three months he might be able to make his mouth fit those teeth perfectly." Tamplin was incapable of a remark so bright.

I was already acquainted with the majority of the stories in the book, and I have re-read a lot of them with pleasure, though they were certainly not written to be read in large doses. The book may be recommended to all save the very young who were born old, weary, satiate, and disillusioned.

Have we any humorists now who can divert the whole town as Barry Pain did, and W.W. Jacobs and Pett Ridge in their heyday? We have, at any rate, one — P.G. Wodehouse, who has beneficially influenced my health on various occasions and agitated my solar plexus on hundreds of occasions. We have other admirable humorists — A.P. Herbert, for instance, creator of Topsy — but they have not yet gained the popular prestige of their elders.

We have also a few very young humorists, of whom the chief in my view is Evelyn Waugh. Mr. Waugh's first novel, *Decline and Fall*, provoked in me laughter of both sorts. Lord Brentford might not have unreservedly approved it. But it was really brilliantly funny about once a page. His new novel, *Vile Bodies* (Chapman and Hall, 7s. 6d.), is less successful. It has a few satirical sallies of the first order of merit, but the lack of a well-laid plot has resulted in a large number of pages which demand a certain obstinate and sustained effort of will for their perusal. Mr. Waugh's subject is the silly set, more commonly known as the smart set — social, pseudo-artistic, pseudo-literary, and genuinely alcoholic; the set which is always trying to run away from the shadow of its own fundamental stupidity. An easy subject. None of the satire in the book is unjust, but some of it is extremely, wildly farcical, and bits of it would not induce laughter in Lord Brentford. I began *Vile Bodies* with great expectations, and found hard times in the middle of it.

Evelyn Waugh has a brother, Alec. More correctly, Alec Waugh has a brother, Evelyn: for Alec began first, and probably has more to say. I think that Alec Waugh's *The Loom of Youth* was a pretty fine book for a youth of 17 or 18, better than for instance Disraeli's *Vivian Grey*, written at about the same age. The author of *The Loom of Youth* is weightier than his cadet. His new book, *The Coloured Countries* (Chapman and Hall, 18s., illustrated with photographs as good and as smooth and as shiny as such photographs can be), is full of the discernments and the pre-occupations of a weighty mind. A travel-book, mainly Oriental — Tahiti, Siam, Ceylon, New Hebrides, Hayti, etc.

Now a book of impressions of travel can be written in at least two ways: either as a *book*, with set chapters carefully constructed, or as a succession of vignettes each cursive, complete, rapid. I have tried both ways. I prefer the latter. Taine, an unsurpassable travel-diarist, used the vignette system. Alec Waugh has made a *book*, beginning formally with life on board ship and formally ending with the return to London. A good book, sound, wise, picturesque, and diverting; for if the matter is weighty the manner is not. The first rule in describing travel is to put down first what strikes you first, without fear of being trivial. The trivial is always interesting, and its interest increases with age. (This is a less fantastic generalisation than Mr. Waugh's generalisation, "Everything that can be put across is true.") Mr. Waugh is not afraid of being trivial. He is not afraid of anything. The writing is excellent: the proof-reading is not. There are misprints of which somebody ought to be ashamed.

6 February 1930

Why Not a *Novelist's* Detective Tale?

Somebody who really can write a novel ought to write a detective novel. The rage for detective fiction still continues. It is important therefore that at any rate one good model should be set. I see no reason why detective fiction should not reach the artistic level of other fiction. Recent specimens have been more or less unsatisfactory. One of the least unsatisfactory is Dr. Maynard Smith's *Inspector Frost in the City* (Benn, 7s. 6d.). I could find multitudinous faults therein; but relatively it is goodish. Opposite the title-page is a warning note: "All the characters in this book are fictitious." Well, they are. On the day when some real person brings a libel action against a detective novelist for putting him into a novel I shall take heart. Verisimilitude will have begun.

I have been somewhat enheartened by the perusal of what to me is a novelty in detective fiction: *Through the Eyes of the Judge*, by Bruce Graeme (Hutchinson, 7s. 6d.). The book has the form of an almost-verbatim report of a murder trial. Those who have appreciated the intense interestingness of verbatim reports of actual murder trials will at once perceive the possibilities of the scheme. Moreover, there are elements of grandeur in the ingenious plot. The judge falls in love with a beautiful girl sitting in court. An innocent man is convicted. The judge, who was about to retire, dies on the bench some time after delivering sentence. The innocent man is saved by the judge's dying notes.

The material of a terrific romantic tale is here. Handled consummately, it might have resulted in a novel which would have influenced the whole tribe of mystery-mongers and jigsaw-inventors for their own advantage and ours. Mr. Bruce Graeme does not handle his material consummately; but he handles it fairly well — better than he writes.

The main faults of the work are (1) The phrasing of the dialogue is frequently untrue to court-life; (2) Some of the witnesses are drawn farcically; (3) The author seems to me not to know enough about the details of daily existence. Thus he makes the famous advocate for the defence employ servant girl's English. Why? Ignorance? Thus he has named a Cunard transatlantic liner the "Kentucky and Devon," apparently unaware that the names of Cunard liners end in "ania" — Aquitania, Mauretania, Ascania, etc. Thus he makes a medical witness talk about "extravasion." No medical witness could possibly have talked about extravasion, because there isn't such a word. (4) Insufficient use is made of the judge and the judge's eyes. The judge-psychology ought to have been a thrilling as well as an original feature of the book. Only towards the end do we "effect an entrance" into the secret fastnesses of the judge's mind. Withal the book is not properly describable as a failure. It can be read; it does hold you. The author has chosen an extremely difficult form of narrative — dialogue — but he has the narrative gift, and his gift has just saved him.

I wish young novelists would understand that, just as the first business of a play is to be dramatic, so the first business of a novel is to "carry you on" from page to page, by the exercise of the narrative gift. If a novel fails in this first business, it may have all the other qualities in the world — it is a bad novel. I have just read Mr. Robert Herring's *Adam and Evelyn at Kew*, illustrated in colour by Edward Bawden (Elkin Mathews, limited edition, one guinea). This fiction in addition to being a fantasy is a preciosity. I don't object to it being a preciosity. A preciosity now and then makes a pleasant change. Mr. Herring is a film critic, and his story contains a lot of good satire about popular films. He has invention. He is a capable versifier (he includes quite a long poem in the story). He has taste. He writes with skill. He is probably a very diverting essayist and critic. But he is not a good novelist, by reason of a fatal lack of the narrative gift.

Now a possessor of the true narrative gift is Miss Helen Ashton, whose first novel, *Far Enough*, has stuck in my memory as being the genuine thing. Her new novel, *Dr. Serocold* (Benn, 7s. 6d.), is better. It takes the form of a day in the too-laborious life of a provincial doctor. Dr. Serocold pays eleven visits on the selected day, which begins with the death of an old man and ends with a birth. Each visit is described in full. All the characters in each visit are admirably drawn. The dailiness of existence — dramatic, tragic, comic — is rendered with unusual fidelity. Unassuming, but sure of her knowledge, her imagination and her powers, Helen Ashton must be classed among the novelists who count. To readers who like a quiet, veracious, dignified, broad-minded, humane story, I recommend her new novel without reserve.

Apropos of the above-discussed volumes I must mention a very short book, *The Craftsmanship of Books*, by J. Howard Whitehouse (Allen and Unwin, 3s. 6d.). It is full of suggestions to book-producers (and it contains also a few plain and unanswerable remarks to reviewers). All bookmen will be interested in it; and as for publishers, the Publishers' Association ought to issue a ukase compelling them to study it with humility.

I have space to refer to only one point, but it is not an unimportant point. Mr. Whitehouse says: "Nothing is more distressing than the custom of printing the title of the book at the head of each page." When I read that sentence I said: "Mr. Whitehouse, give me your hand. You are my brother in this affair." Now all the four books have the title of the book at the head of every page. In Mr. Bruce Graeme's book I was informed nearly three hundred times that the title of Mr. Graeme's book is *Through the Eyes of the Judge.*

What is the sense of this damnable iteration? Was I not fully aware of the title of Mr. Graeme's book before I began to read it? Did I forget it at the end of every page? The custom is silly. On the other hand, when I wanted to refer back to a passage (as one often does want in a complex narrative), could I find the infernal passage? Of course I could not, because the page-headings were no guide whatever to the contents. The book is divided into days. If the page-headings had been "First Day," "Second Day," etc., I should have had some guidance, though not enough.

Similarly with the other three books. Helen Ashton, who ought to know better, puts no titles to her chapters. Her publishers tell me 280 times that the title of her book is *Dr. Serocold.* To look for any given passage in *Dr. Serocold* is like looking — no, not for a needle in a haystack — for an empty taxi at 11 p.m. on a wet night in the West End. All chapters of all novels ought to have titles, so that the titles can be used as page-headings. I am of a meek and equable disposition, but there are occasions when I become dangerously infuriated. The present is one.

13 February 1930

Byron's Loves, As a Frenchman Sees Them

Even to-day Byron is better loved on the Continent than in Britain. Paris has not changed the name of a street christened after him in a fashionable quarter of the city. But do not go and imagine that we Britons have omitted to christen streets after him. There are quite a number of them — Avenues, Roads, Streets, Villas — in Poplar, Ealing, Walthamstow, Leyton, Bounds Green, and such districts! As for the W.1, W.C.1. and S.W.1 districts, they show no inclination to perpetuate the noble sinner's name. Lives of Byron all remind us we may with advantage order our careers differently from his. For ages past, however, lives of Byron have not excited the general public. They have been excellent and full of controversial matter, but they have only excited literary historians and critics.

Now in France the biggest literary event of the season, by far, is the publication of André Maurois' *Byron* (issued by Grasset, Paris, 2 volumes). The first edition for the general public consisted of some 90,000 copies. And this edition was preceded by various others, more or less special and all strictly limited, including at least five reserved for booksellers or private societies of bookmen in Paris, Nice, Normandy, Athens, and Brussels. Which phenomena alone are a truly remarkable proof of both popular and esoteric continental interest in the work. A further point. The price of the main edition is thirty francs for the two volumes: exchange value, less than five shillings, and the work can be had in London for six shillings. These details have nothing to do with the biographical and critical worth of the book. But they have a great deal to do with the relative conditions of taste in Britain and in France.

Still another point. I have discussed André Maurois' biographical books — Shelley, Disraeli, Goethe, Byron — with several English experts, and I find that they have a tendency, in my opinion utterly misguided, to disparage them. They say, in particular, that these books display little or no original research. But the books make no pretence of original research. Works of original research must be long; they are costly; and they are meant chiefly for specialists, who alone can judge them. They are of course indispensable; but they are not indispensable to the large public, which indeed ignores them.

No instructed person would deny the indispensableness of Monypenny and Buckle's gigantic performance on Disraeli. Without it, Maurois' *Disraeli* could hardly have been written. But it is not for the large public. The average intelligent reader could afford neither the money to buy it nor the time to read it. Should the average intelligent reader be depirved of an accurate and thrilling sketch of Disraeli simply because an expert is entitled to say: "I knew all that before"?

Then I have heard men of letters dismiss the Disraeli, and the Shelley too, with the one word: "Superficial!" Maurois is never superficial. On the contrary he is a most laborious toiler, with astonishing gifts of assimilation, order, proportion, clarity, impartiality, characterisation, graphic description, and *interestingness*. There is a sad, comic notion abroad among experts that what is enthralling to read cannot really be sound. Had Maurois been dull, he would have been better received by some of our high-brows of interminable biography. But the unfortunate man is incapable of being dull. What a pity! Anyhow he has taught several lessons to British biographers, and his example has already led to the birth of a new school of biography in Britain. He has not superseded the specialist. He has merely done what the specialist cannot do; he has done it almost to perfection, and he has marked every page of his books with his own individuality.

Byron is considerably longer than the Shelley and the Disraeli. But it is not inferior in sustained interest to either of them. Beautifully constructed, composed, and *done*! I sailed through it on a fair wind from start to finish. It reconstituted Byron for me and corrected all sorts of wrong ideas about him which no doubt I share with the man in the literary street. I was surprised to learn, for instance, that Byron was hostile to drinking and gambling, and that he had a decided preference for regular habits as opposed to irregular. Left to himself he would have done the same things at the same time every day. It pained me to learn that as a young man he had the low habit of scratching his name on public monuments.

To me the most startling item in the book is the quotation in which Disraeli says that Byron's chief characteristic was solid good sense! The proof of good sense is not in words but in acts. Byron had an extraordinary faculty of being foolish with ostentation. Imagine him setting forth on his first travels (which resulted in *Childe Harold*) with a hundred pens and two gallons of ink! Imagine him seeking relief from the funeral of his detested mother in a boxing-bout — on the day of the funeral!

No man of solid good sense is a sexual debauchee. Byron was. The catalogue of Napoleon's mistresses goes beyond a hundred. I should say that the catalogue of Byron's — if it could be compiled, which it can't — might almost rival that of Napoleon. Withal, he had apparently only one satisfactory mistress, Lady Oxford, who with Lady Melbourne contrived to carry on the traditional sexual freedoms of the eighteenth century well into the nineteenth. And he soon tired of Lady Oxford, and informed her that he was tired. Tedium always impaired his politeness. Maurois handles the affair with his half-sister in terms in which tact and irony exquisitely suffuse plain speaking. But then Maurois is French, and the French have comprehended, what has never been comprehended in Britain, that sex can be very funny at times. Lady Melbourne's attitude of mild protest against the extravagance of this Augusta episode was much funnier than she herself perceived. It might be described as the "Really, Byron, really!" attitude.

Byron, cursed with a mother whose character was rendered excrutiating by her frightful experiences with an ignoble husband, made a mess of his career. I would not cast stones at the unhappy victim; but solid good sense would have prevented the endless disaster. His work remains. That he was lovable is obvious. That he was a great poet in the big bow-wow style, and a great ironic poet, surely cannot be disputed. The thought of the permanence of his work redeems the melancholy of his history.

Maurois has had the ingenious and excellent idea of continuing the record of Byron's descendants and connections down to the year 1906. I prophesy that when the book appears in English it will not exactly fall dead from the press.

20 February 1930

Men Who Can Talk to the Barmaid

All my adult life I have had secret ambitions to be a dog — I mean a real dog, not the quadruped. Among them has been the ambition to lean up against a bar in the right negligent posture and say the right things to the barmaid. I have often, at a distance, seen other men do this feat apparently with complete success. In the war, when I was in Glasgow on a mission, I leaned up against the bar in a leading hotel there, and began. I had the moral support of a friend. Some pleasantry was addressed to the barmaid. I can remember only her reply, which was: "You can't tell me the tale. This is my second time on earth." We were beaten off with great loss, and the incident closed my career as a bar-frequenter.

Still, I do know something about public-houses. Although I have never been in a public-house at closing time, I know that the appointed official then cries out: "Time, gentlemen, *please*." He does not say: "Time, gentlemen, *time*." I have this detail on the authority of more than one absolutely first-class expert. And yet Miss Norah Hoult has entitled her new book *Time Gentlemen! Time!* (Heinemann, 7s. 6d.). Doubtless she corrected the typescript of her novel. Doubtless the publishers and their professional readers read the typescript. Doubtless a professional proof-reader corrected the proofs. And doubtless Miss Hoult corrected the proofs after him. Nevertheless the error has survived all these examinations. I note the slip, not because it is important, but because of its excessive oddness.

The novel is about a drunkard. Having regard to the slip, you might well say: "This lady doesn't know the first thing about drinking. Therefore her book must be bad." Evidently Miss Hoult does not know the first thing — more properly the last thing — about drunkenness. But she seems to know all the other things about it. And her book is not bad. It is very good. (It is far better than her book of stories: *Poor Women*, which was good — except for the two vague, unsatisfying ends of the stories.) In particular she knows exactly how male tipplers talk together when they are mellow. Her dialogues between addicts are most truly rendered; they accord with one's overhearing experiences; they convince. And the cruelty of their effect is desolating. The reading of them by tipplers when sober ought to be the finest cure for alcoholism ever invented.

Always, on the rare occasions when I have listened to such pitiful, pseudo-jolly pow-wows, I have pictured to myself the unseen domestic backgrounds of the roysterers. Miss Hoult gives the background of one roysterer. Carmichael is an Irish solicitor practising in a London suburb. His background is a wife, two small children, and a home lacking in food, light and heat through his fault; a background to which, after closing time, he returns half or wholly drunk and tries to play the man who will be master in his own house. The picture is relentless, excrutiating; and only about six pages out of over three hundred could possibly be described as tedious.

Personally I like a gloomy book, when it is well done, as this is. A gloomy book well done does not depress me. *Time Gentlemen! Time!* is exceedingly gloomy. Why did it not depress me? Because it is true and fair. Because Miss Hoult sees and renders the basic romance of the matter. Because she has a comprehending, explaining, forgiving attitude towards all her characters. And because romantic beauty does somehow disengage itself from the squalor of the tale. Several of the scenes in which the children figure are beautiful. The stolen afternoon-off when Carmichael pays a visit to his tippling friend Powell is romantic. And the evening excursion of these two into the sky-sign magic of the "West End" is very romantic. *Time Gentlemen! Time!* displays throughout the talent of a genuine-born novelist, and ought to be read by the courageous-discriminating. The end of the story, while not wholly unsatisfying, suffers a little from Miss Hoult's characteristic vagueness and instinctive dislike of a full close.

Those who read *Time Gentlemen! Time!* and find it a depressant, and in their dejection upbraid me for having recommended it, will find a powerful pick-me-up in *Archibald,* by Frederick Markham (Benn, 7s. 6d.). *Archibald* — a first book, I believe — is a novel chiefly of the advertising world, and it will probably make that world rather cross. Archibald Piper belongs to a familiar type of hero, the "card." In the advertising world, it is said, a man must get on or get out. Archibald gets on. Indeed, before the end, he becomes Lord Piper, and is punished for his sinister success by having an albino son. He is a rude, crude, shrewd, calculating fellow, with a few good points in his character.

Mr. Markham evidently knows the advertising world, and one would gather that *Archibald* is his reaction to certain unfavourable impressions. For myself I have personally known advertising agents and managers who were not in the least like Archibald, being infinitely more lovable, decent and modest.

The book has the vigorous breath of life. It diverts. It can be read with pleasure. A great deal of it is true; but not all. When Mr. Markham ventures into the theatrical world his truthfulness to life is very intermittent. His notion of what existence is in a theatre box-office is wild. He certainly has imagination. The trouble is that he often forgets to use it. With his mind's eye he does not see the entirety of an enviroment — perhaps from a hasty carelessness. Also his phrasing is frequently, in a literary sense, vulgar, Example: "Archibald was too obviously lacking *in inner refinement....*" A Theodore Dreiser might successfully carry off such an outworn, meaningless cliché. But nobody else could. And Mr. Markham doesn't. It grates. There are many others. Still, I found *Archibald* a quite considerable lark.

A specimen of the not-careless, immensely conscientious novel is Jacob Wassermann's latest (in English) *The Maurizius Case* (Allen and Unwin, 10s.). I hold to my original opinion that Wassermann is the best of the younger German novelists. His *The Triumph of Youth* is short and a masterpiece. His *The World's Illusion* is long and lyrical and full of wonders, but lacks the coherence of a masterpiece. *The Maurizius Case* is long. It shows, more clearly than the other two, the influence of the brothers Thomas and Heinrich Mann. I will not say that it is not a masterpiece. I think, however, that the psychological analysis is over-elaborate. If laborious conscientiousness can be a fault, Wassermann has that fault. The book is one of those to which, in order to get the full effect and beauty of them, you must surrender yourself without any conditions. Do that, and you will be justly rewarded. The impatient are hereby warned off these 516 large, close, clear pages. Translation good.

An English translation has just been published of Wassermann's biography of *Christopher Columbus* (Secker, 10s. 6d.). Tremendous learning, combined with the picturesqueness of a very expert narrator! Of Columbus the biographer says: "His fame is a collection of fragments; put them together carefully, and suddenly a spirit soars upward who looks at us with friendly eyes." There you glimpse the honest Teutonic sentimentality which sympathetically characterises the book. Wassermann has put the fragments together carefully, and reached the desired result. A "worthy" book.

27 February 1930

A Young Woman Who Knows All About the Circus

A good week. I have read Lady Eleanor Smith's *Red Wagon* (Gollancz, 7s. 6d.). A first novel. As such it is an unusual performance. The majority of first novels are in essence autobiographical. Beginners don't look outwards: they look inwards; it is easier, and to these mistaken neophytes it is more interesting. Again, the majority of first novels, though they may cost their authors "blood and tears," are clumsy and somewhat superficial affairs in so far as they are not based on personal experience. They are deficient in hard, fundamental brainwork. They are spotty, unequal, and misshapen. The authors can master neither their material nor their faculties.

These criticisms do not apply to *Red Wagon*. It is not autobiographical. Its subject is circus-life, both in Britain and in America, both ancient and modern. Lady Eleanor proves herself to be a serious person. She has collected her material with admirable conscientiousness. And instead of allowing the material to dominate her, she has dominated the material. Similarly with her quite considerable faculties of creation and form. Nothing has got the better of her intelligence. And her intelligence, which is high, has controlled her industry, which is beyond question quite extraordinary. The result is a mature, an impressive and on the whole a satisfactory book.

Clearly Lady Eleanor has a passion for circuses. She loves them as they are in their picturesqueness, their sordidness, their squalor, their brutality, their courage, and their charity. She has not shut her eyes to any aspect of them. Everybody likes circuses. Lady Eleanor understands them and knows *all* about them. She knows them in the middle of the inclement night, processional over the muddy roads of England and America. She knows them in a riot, when blood flows and souls leave bodies. She knows them when the big tents are empty and when they are full. She knows them in winter seclusion. She knows the minds on the trapezes and on the horses, the minds in the stable-tents, the minds in the swagger waggons of the proprietors, the minds in the tigers' cages. And she knows about a lot more things than circuses, for instance, orphan asylums, gipsy encampments, and the roads. Her pictures of road-travelling are exquisite.

The hero, Joe Prince, rises from naught to be a circus proprietor, with his name lettered in gold on fifty gaudy caravans. The book is the story of his rise and of his loves – all unfortunate. The story ought to be extremely picturesque, and believe me, it is. But it is better than picturesque. It accords with life. With every temptation to sentimentalise, the author is not sentimental. Again and again one is brought up with a jerk and reassured, by some unexpected truth concerning human nature.

Red Wagon has a defect, and a not unimportant defect. The writing. The author is intensely scrupulous about everything – except the writing. She is content to use the first ready-made phrase that offers itself to her pen. The book is full of ready-made phrases. A man "divests himself of his outer garments." A woman has "opulent charms." A man "grinds his teeth with rage." And so on continually. Now and then, even, the author by negligence fails to say what she means. Also she mixes her metaphors: "The dark pinions of death hovering over the house removed very completely the rigid barriers of circus etiquette." All this is bad. Useless to say that readers don't notice these trifles. They are not trifles. And readers, even if they do not notice them, are unconsciously estranged by their cumulative effect. In my opinion Lady Eleanor will not be appreciated at her potential worth by the small public which alone makes durable reputations unless she attends with more care, word by word, to her style. Happily the intelligence and the character which have made *Red Wagon* as good as it is should be well capable of curing the only grave defect in its author's equipment.

Next I read William Gerhardi's *Pending Heaven* (Duckworth, 7s. 6d.). Physically it is meagre: 272 small pages. But Gerhardi is so audacious in omitting the dull pieces from his narrative, he leaps so lightly from one place to another, that the novel probably contains about as much vital stuff as a more conventional novel twice its length. As usual with this author, the principal personages are a queer lot, silly, entirely without savoir vivre, un-moral, feckless — but not shiftless (for they are always full of shifts). They have no sense of money. The author may have, but if so he hides it, for he is continually making them perform impossible feats of finance. The un-heroical hero is a writer, apparently without the grit which makes an artist; just a dilettante among dilettantes. The novel is the story of his ridiculous and futile loves. Heavens! What a menagerie!

Last Sunday morning at six o'clock I was reading *Pending Heaven* in bed, hoping to get some more sleep. I got no more sleep, because every few pages I had to laugh. The tale is extremely funny. It is bitter, capricious, occasion-ally incoherent, and without any feeling for the existence of organised society. But extremely funny it is, and extremely original. No sentence in it can be foreseen. The man has genius. Whether he recognises that the possess-ion of genius involves artistic responsibilities I am by no means sure. In *Pending Heaven,* as in Gerhardi's previous novels, there seems to run a vein of autobiography. Real people who egotistically and perhaps wrongly fancy that they recognise humorous and acid travesties of themselves in the story may not be wholly delighted with certain pages. And now I expect to read in the publishers' advertisements those sole four words ripped out of what is above written: "The man has genius." I shall object. But he has.

Those who read *George Moore's Conversations in Ebury Street,* originally published in 1924, will not have forgotten that diverting series of stylised chats. It has since occurred to Mr. Moore that his interlocutors were all males. In a new edition (Heinemann, 10s. 6d.) he has repaired the sad and singular oversight by adding a conversation with a Mrs. Harley-Caton — who-ever she may be. Mrs. Harley-Caton, meeting George Moore for the first time, takes him in hand at once; indeed she rather masterfully takes charge of the conversation. Her speciality seems to be a strange attraction for priests, including a cardinal. The chat is brief, too brief for esoteric admirers of George Moore such as myself. But it justifies the new edition.

6 March 1930

Why Arnold Bennett Prefers Punch and Judy to the Theatre

Karsavina has written a book. Tamar Karsavina and Lydia Lopokova were the brightest stars of the Russian ballet, except of course for Nijinsky, who was unique and whose brief career was ended by a tragedy which did not end his life. And the Russian ballet was the greatest artistic phenomenon of this century. There have been other great artistic phenomena, individuals and groups, in the last thirty years: Debussy, Proust, Joyce, Picasso, Modigliani, Sibelius, Ravel, Chaliapine, Richard Strauss, Reinhardt, Schnabel, the Moscow Art Theatre; but in importance none could compare with, or give so much pleasure as, the ensemble of the Russian ballet. Never shall I forget the opening night of the Russian ballet at the Paris Opéra — that enormous home of State-aided, State-ruined art. Impossible to sleep after such a fête of moving beauty! (Some of the ballets have never been seen in their entirety in England. The censor mauled them as he mauled Strauss's *Rosenkavalier.* Both *Cleopatra* and *Scheherazade* were mauled.)

The most important person in the Russian ballet was Diaghileff. In the last two decades I frequently met Diaghileff, and I could not "get on" with him. But, manifestly, what a creator! He was as good an impresario as a producer. He had the finest taste in everything. He brought everything into the ballet, except words, which were unnecessary. All men, with eyes to see, who saw the Russian ballet, must feel intensely grateful to Diaghileff, a master. He was a bully; he was capable of enormities. The members of the ballet were his slaves. But they worshipped him, and rightly. Whenever I recall my sensations on Russian ballet nights, especially the earlier ones, I say to myself: "I lived, then!"

Well, Karsavina, idol of audiences, has written a book, and in English: her own correct, exotic English of a highly accomplished linguist — but a foreigner. It is called *Theatre Street* (a street in Petersburg), and it has a preface by Sir James Barrie (Heinemann, 25s., illustrated). This book has the enchantment of its author's personality. She has had quite first-rate material to handle, and she has handled it with distinction. *Theatre Street* subtly differentiates itself by the delicacy of its sensibilities from all other stage-reminiscences that I remember. I do not say that it is better than all others, but it is unlike every other, as Karsavina is unlike every other *prima ballerina assoluta.*

I could not recount it in less than ten columns. Very many episodes remain fixed in the mind. Karsavina's doll that had a habit of eloping. Chaliapine in a moment of acute exaltation suddenly and unexpectedly kneeling to the Tsar's box, and the Tsar weeping at this histrionic but genuine sign of devotion. Students throwing down their cloaks for the star to walk upon and the star refusing this pavement. The strictly cloistered life of the future stars in the Imperial school of ballet. The photograph of the pupils in the grotesque kitchen-maid aprons which they were forced to wear. The all-night theatre-queues in the arctic Petrograd winter. The woman who always made the sign of the cross on her mouth when she yawned. The last perilous escaping journey from Petrograd, a journey which was saved from disaster by Karsavina's tigerish courage in defence of her baby. . . . The stuff that our dreams of the fantastic, exquisite past are made on!

These dancers and their director were authentic Simon-Pure artists. They quarrelled; they wept; they sulked; they tore up contracts, they lived in hysteria, fever, haste, insomnia, and even penury. But what artists they were, and what artists some of them still are! After this lyricism, which startled my prosaic pen, I hope I need not further insist on the attractions of *Theatre Street.*

Another and quite a different sort of book of stage-reminiscences which I have just read and enjoyed is *Vagabonds and Puppets* by Walter Wilkinson, (Bles, 7s. 6d.). Punch-and-Judy is theatre, and perhaps the best. For myself I would sooner watch Punch-and-Judy for a quarter of an hour for twopence than a West End drawing-room comedy for two hours and a half for twelve shillings. It has one immense advantage. I can hear every word of the dialogue of Punch-and-Judy. Of a drawing-room comedy — in such manner is elocution taught among us to-day — I catch merely a phrase or two here and there. Punch-and-Judy has other advantages. Clear plots. Swift action. Satisfactory murders. Farce as broad as the Mall. Total absence of love-scenes.

Mr. Wilkinson is the vagabond with the puppets. He made his own puppets. He started off, short of fifteen shillings, in the garden city of Letchworth, and ended in a residential hotel, where his takings amounted to three pounds for a single performance. He has a few enraging mannerisms of style; but beneath these one discovers a good sound writer, with a communicative "sense" of the country, of roads, and of small towns. And he is vagabond-ishly cheerful, as becomes a Punch-and-Judy man. For rest on a chilly night I prefer the roof of even a residential hotel to any star-studded firmament. Mr. Wilkinson is different. He can perceive the humour of discomfort and hardship. I can't.

Still, he can be angry. He was really angered by a group of smart ladies with fat children who openly enjoyed his show till the final curtain fell, and then walked away without contributing a cent to his treasury. My heart beat as one with his over that affair. It reminded me of a newspaper critic whom I myself saw laughing like anything throughout one of my own drawing-room comedies and whose notice of the same the next morning varied from reluctant faint approval to envenomed vituperation. Never mind! I waited, and my turn came. *Vagabonds and Puppets* is a slight but endearing volume. One likes it, and one feels that one would like the author. I found it very succulent.

When I received tidings of a book entitled *C.B.C.'s Review of Revues* (Cape, 10s., illustrated with unusual excitingness) I demanded it. For I know a little about Mr. Cochran's revues. Among the few quite satisfactory episodes of my chequered theatrical life have been certain attendances at rehearsals of those revues. I was deceived in the volume. It is not by Charles Cochran, who only edits the concatenation of notions which it in fact is. Among the literary contributors are the chief dramatic critics of this city; also Constance Collier, Ronald Jeans, Quex, and Komisarjevsky. Among illustrating artists are William Nicholson, Fougasse, Oliver Messel, and Ceri Richards. The principal item is the replies of the chief dramatic critics to Charles Cochran's question: "What would you do with the theatre in England if you had a free hand and a full purse?" The replies are bright, but not very inspiring. They nobly if unconsciously show that one thing wrong with the British theatre is dramatic criticism. The best reply is Joseph Thorp's (of *Punch*). The book is worth possessing, and it might easily become a possession.

13 March 1930

A Hint to the "Superior" Author

Is the public interested in the work of a writer when he writes about writing? A question which has often been asked, and generally answered with an aggresive No! But personally I think that the reading public — the increasing public which reads regularly and reads a lot — might well be interested in the craft of writing, even without any practical experience of writing. If the stamp-collecting public, which never designed nor made a stamp, is interested to read all about stamps, I see no reason why the book-public should not be interested in book-making. Of course it may be argued that literature is not as exciting as philately. Still literature, in its humbler way, does undeniably possess a certain excitingness.

Among the major modern experts and virtuosi in writing must be counted the late C.E. Montague, a man with a passion for the proper use of words, a man who turned leading articles into literature (and whose best leading articles ought some time to be collected). A few years before the war, being acutely intrigued by the literary performances of this Manchester man, I went down or up to Manchester specially to make his acquaintance and that of the group of journalists with whom he worked; one or two of them hardly less brilliant than Montague himself. A temerarious excursion, rather like going over the top.

Prior to our meeting a journalist said to me: "Montague is surrounded by a good deal of unrequited affection." A *bon mot*; but I doubt its truth, though I admit that Montague carried his heart in a padlocked secret pocket, never on his sleeve. He was just about the most reserved man I ever met. He had the air of a secondary school teacher or a Wesleyan "local preacher"; but when he did talk, he talked; and I perceived that he knew a hundred times more than I knew, and had an infinitely more complex taste. He did not traffic in the simplicities. Assuredly he was inspiring; he lifted you to a higher plane.

And now is published a portly volume containing sixteen of his essays about the use of words, *A Writer's Notes on his Trade*, with an introduction by an equally accomplished artificer, H.M. Tomlinson (Chatto). Considering that nearly all writers, and nearly all persons interested in writing, are relatively poor, I cannot understand why this volume (edition limited to 700 copies) should be priced solely at three guineas. An edition de luxe I can indeed understand, and can treasure. But this edition ought surely to have been accompanied by a popular edition at, say, three half-crowns. I hope that a popular edition will come quickly. Without that hope I should not have drawn attention to the book at all; for to do so would have been naught but a self-indulgent exercise in the waste of both time and space.

It is a very good book. Some chapter-titles will give a fair notion of its contents: "Three ways of saying things," "Easy reading hard writing." "Too true to be good," "Doing without workmanship," "A living language." All professional writers, and the innumerable legion of amateur writers, will immediately be attracted by these subjects, which Montague treats with love, ingenuity, knowledge, and wisdom. And my conviction is that a large proportion of the non-writing public would be attracted by them. I have no sympathy with the too prevalent writers' tendency to despise the non-writing public.

Once upon a time the late Clement Shorter and the late Robertson Nicol and myself were talking together. Shorter said something rather good. I gave a start. Robertson Nicol said to me grimly, in front of Shorter: "Yes. Shorter is not such a simpleton as you think he is." Similarly I would say to writers, and with still more emphasis: "The non-writing public is not such a simpleton as you think it is." In *A Writer's Notes on his Trade* (I object to the last word) there is an essay on Matthew Arnold, which is really excellent, and ought to be studied by Edith Sitwell. But what it is doing in this volume I don't know. The book amply confirms Montague's high reputation. My one criticism of him is that he could not write novels but did write them.

I have mentioned Edith Sitwell. In addition to being one of the most original poets of this our day, she now stands forth as a literary biographer and critic. Her *Alexander Pope* (Faber and Faber, 15s., with illustrations, and a delightful "jacket" designed by Rex Whistler) has the qualities which one would expect from her. It is brilliantly written; it is challenging; and it is ruthless. She sets out to prove that Pope was a lovable and kindly man. (That he was a magnificent artist in words is more frequently admitted than *felt*.) I think that she proves her case without difficulty. And in doing so she has been wise enough to admit her hero's chief faults of character. As that he was as great and continuous a liar as a poet; as that he was highly quarrelsome or, if you prefer it, that he put his contemporaries into positions which rendered shindies inevitable; and that in the matter of unscrupulous literary manipulation for the advantage of his own repute, he was not surpassed by even Victor Hugo. Long before the end of the book is reached you are loving and keenly sympathising with the misshapen and fretful genius.

The final chapter is criticism of a very illuminating, unusual sort. If you would see what a virtuoso can see in a given collocation of words, read this chapter. It is revealing, and as fresh as the dawn. Edith Sitwell has a particular passion for that "flawless masterpiece," *The Rape of the Lock*. One has read, somewhere, that the supreme test of literary taste is a full appreciation of Milton's *Comus*. I agree. But it would be as true to say that the supreme test is a full appreciation of *The Rape of the Lock*, which by the way was written to order.

The plum of Edith Sitwell's book is the tirade in the opening chapter upon the "general blighting and withering of the poetic taste" during the first quarter of the twentieth century, by the "wish to reform," by the desire "to cure human ills," by sermon-preaching, by telling (like a photographer) "human nature to look pleasant," or by "other poetry-wrecking influences." It is deplorable that in the course of a fine, astringent philippic, she permits herself to get angry with Matthew Arnold, the "pre-eminent bore" in whose person was carried out the maleficent "substitution of scholar for poet, of school-inspector for artist"! This is very naughty of Edith Sitwell. Matthew Arnold is not even yet ranked as high as he deserves. If occasionally he preached, he preached in sublime verse. Hence I counsel Edith Sitwell to read Montague on Arnold. Not that she will. And not that her view would be altered if she did. I don't care. She is a powerful tonic, and she loves words as ardently as Montague did.

20 March 1930

The True-To-Life Novel is Not the Best

You might with advantage take out your map of modern literature and mark on it the name of Italo Svevo. (Italian of course; but the name seems to me to be a concocted pseudonym, and I have a vague recollection of having heard a year or two ago that the man is of Swedish origin, as indeed the pseudonym would indicate.*) For Svevo and his novel, *Confessions of Zeno*

*Italo Svevo was the pseudonym of Ettore Schmitz, born in Trieste in 1861 (d.1928).

357

(Putnam, 10s. 6d.), will henceforth be on other people's maps; and it is well that the atlases of the enlightened should agree. A translation of a book by Svevo was published not long since; but it was rather restricted in scope and thin in texture, and could hardly be called representative.

Confessions of Zeno is close-textured and it has scope. It rouses, however, an important question. In reading it one feels as if one were reading an account of something that really happened. Ought a novel to affect the reader this way? One's first impulse is to answer: "Yes. To say that a novel gives to the reader the illusion that it is a faithful report of actual occurrences is the highest praise."

Well, I doubt it. The business of fiction, as of poetry, is not to report life but to transform it, heighten it, make it more shapely, more beautiful, more harmonious in design, while avoiding the impossible and adhering to fundamental truth. If your verdict on a novel is: "That *couldn't* have happened," the novel, as such, is likely to be bad. If your verdict is, "It might have happened, had life been less haphazard and untidy than it is," there is a fair chance that the novel is good.

If you went to the Italian pictures — you saw a hundred times more people than pictures, but you may with luck have got a glimpse here and there, over the hats of a row of schoolgirls, of a great painting — you may have been able to gaze at one of the supreme works: some large magnificent group of Madonna, infant Jesus, angels, saints, magi, and donors. In real life did any group of people ever stand together so harmoniously in colour and arrangement? Were women ever so beautiful, babies so attractive, old men so majestic, so statuesque in pose? Were costumes ever so lovely, tints so accordant, architecture so stately, landscapes so perfectly complementary? No! Never! You were bound to say to yourself: "This thing didn't happen. But in an ideal world of good and evil it might have happened."

Similarly, did ever one of nature's birds sing as exquisitely as the bird in Wagner's *Siegfried*? Or did any shepherd ever go piping down the valleys wild with such celestial music as the shepherd makes on his reed in *Tristan*? Again, no! I might discuss this subject to the stop-press news on the last page of to-day's issue, and even then I should scarcely have begun it. I must be content to provoke thought. *Confessions of Zeno* appears to me to miss being a masterpiece because it lacks, not truth to life, but the deliberately-fashioned coherence, the satisfying form, and the intensifications of art. Withal it is a very remarkable book; I much enjoyed it; and I recommend it. Warning: I once started to read a novel by Svevo in French. I did not get on with it, and I gave it up. The reason, I think now, was that I did not yield myself to it with patience. Svevo's method demands a surrender from the reader. The surrender will be amply recompensed.

Confessions of Zeno consists of a series of episodes in the life of a young man of means. It is written in the first person, the person being the hero. The scene, by the way, is Trieste. The first episode deals with Zeno's vain effort to rid himself of the habit of excessive cigarette-smoking. It ends on p.33 and the pages are large and well nourished with type! The next relates the death of his father; the next the story of his marriage; the next the emotional oscillations between his wife and his mistress; and so on. The wife-and-mistress section is wonderful in its honest, shameless accuracy of detail of sentiment. And yet it is entirely dignified.

A large portion of the book simply must be autobiographical in essence. Nearly all good novels comprise a considerable admixture of autobiography, if not of fact, of feeling. They must be based upon the author's deepest, most intimate reactions to life. But *Confessions of Zeno* strikes me as autobiographical beyond the ordinary. There are in it numerous incidents which the author certainly did not invent, because, being what he is, he could have invented them better. The main interest of the book is psychological, not an interest of events. Svevo has been called the Italian Proust. Why, I cannot imagine. For he has none but superficial resemblances to the most serpentine and sesquipedalian of modern novelists. The translation, by Miss Beryl de Zoete, has some distinction, though its grammar is frequently at war with the usage of plain persons.

I said that nearly all good novels are autobiographical. An example of one that is not is Thornton Wilder's *The Woman of Andros* (Longmans, 6s.). Only it is a mere long-short story, not a novel: 105 pages. I am still waiting for Thornton Wilder to write another long novel. *The Cabala* was fairly long. *The Bridge of San Luis Rey* was not long. I am beginning now to doubt whether he ever will write a long novel. *The Woman of Andros* is a tale of ancient Greek life on a Greek island. Tale of two sisters in love with one man, and the death of the elder sister and the maternity of the younger. The elder, the heroine, is a hetaïra in Greek, a prostitute in English. The interest of the story is in the character of the heroine. A beautiful character, not sentimentalised. The whole thing is beautifully done, inspired by very delicate and subtle sensibility. And the writing is beautiful.

Usually I object to sententiousness in a novel, but this book is sententious and I do not object, because the sententiousness is original, true, and witty. For instance: "The loneliest associations are those which pretend to intimacy." Again: "It was Chrysis's reiterated theory of life that all human beings . . . merely endured the slow misery of existence, hiding as best they could their consternation that life had no wonderful surprises after all, and that *its most difficult burden was the incommunicability of love.*" (My italics.) Again: "She did not realise that this wasting of love in fretfulness was one of the principal activities on the planet." And again: "Of all forms of genius goodness has the longest awkward age." I was disappointed with *The Woman of Andros* because there was not enough of it. And yet the fair-minded judge in me was not disappointed. Is length a quality? The quiet book exalted me.

27 March 1930

Mistakes Detective-Novel Writers Make

Detective novelists and their impassioned admirers all seem to me to be as sensitive as a clan of Highlanders. My previous references here to this now important branch of fiction have brought me many vituperative epithets, many expressions of astonishment pained at my ignorance ("Do you mean to say that you have not read —— ! It is a masterpiece," etc.), and, what is worse, many actual volumes of detective-fiction which I have been ordered to read and to praise, or, in the alternative, to retire from business for ever.

Indeed I had almost given up my grandiose plan of campaign for purging, reforming and revivifying detective-fiction.

Then I received a detective-novel called *It Walks by Night*, by an American, John Dickson Carr (Harpers, 7s. 6d.). I doubt if I should have begun it had not the last 118 pages been sealed up by the publishers, who promise to take all copies back at full price if you will return them with the seal unbroken. Which means that the publishers count surely upon the reader's curiosity getting the better of him, for to take back a copy would involve them in a loss of at least half-a-crown, even if they re-sealed and re-sold it. I will not say whether or not my curiosity got the better of me. I had anyhow to break the seal and read on, in the pursuance of my business.

The scene of the book is Paris. The majority of the characters are French, Two murders — the most horrible sanguinary of my experience in fictional homicide — are brilliantly committed, and of course the criminal is at last found and forced to confess. Although John Dickson Carr is American the writing of the story is very bad; sometimes it is not even grammatical. The narrative is full of primeval clichés such as "wan smile." "She smiled wanly." "He gave a wan smile." The book is one incessant wan smile. (As a fact, I have never in half a century of reading understood how a smile can be wan.) Also the characters are incessantly making wry mouths, uttering strange sounds, or twisting their fingers in nervous emotion. Also the French characters never show a sign of French mentality. They are Broadway and Fifth through and through. Their Frenchness is confined to exclamations like *"Hein!"* and *"Tiens!"* There are about ten times more *"Heins"* in this novel than in any French novel I have read. Also the characterisation, such as it is, is conventional to the last degree, has no life in it at all.

I could have excused all these perhaps superficial defects if the story had not had two absolutely fundamental defects. What ought a detective-novel to do? It ought to state a crime. It ought to mystify the reader as to the identity of the criminal. And it ought to reveal the identity in a manner both ingenious and convincing. But it ought to do more. It ought to keep the story moving steadily forward in a given direction during the process of mystification. To tangle the reader up in a confused jungle of clues, some false, some true, is not enough. The story should be continuously dramatic. The majority of detective-novelists fail in this particular, as Mr. Carr has failed. Most detective-novels are a bog and a morass between the full statement of the enigma and the solution thereof. The reader submits to boredom chiefly in order to satisfy his curiosity. The reader ought never to have to submit to boredom. Mr. Carr does not really get going until p. 211.

Further, the detective-novelist ought to render the revelation convincing. Mr. Carr's mystery is very ingenious and, I imagine, original. But the solution of it is certainly not convincing. The criminal makes an interminable confessional speech exactly in the style of a bad purple-patched book. No human being ever did or could talk as this criminal talks. And the main difficulty — that of decapitating a man by a single stroke of a sword — is merely shirked. None but a highly experienced executioner could perform this feat, which demands both great skill and great strength. Mr. Carr's criminal has neither the skill of experience nor unusual strength. Consequently you just don't believe in the solution of the enigma. I have purposely refrained from giving any clue to the solution. Numbers of readers, the violence of whose curiosity surpasses even the delicacy of their taste in letters, may like to break the seal, and I do not care to run the publishers into the loss of even one half-crown.

Last week I was talking to a detective-novelist — and one of the best living. He said that he read quantities of mystery-novels. Therefore I asked him to name a few for my perusal. First of all he said that he couldn't remember any! Then he named three. Two by Miss I.R.G. Hart: *The Frontier of Fear* (1928) and *Forests of the Night* (recent), both published by Benn. And one by Francis Everton: *The Dalehouse Murder* (originally published, by Collins, in 1927, and recently reprinted). Miss Hart is certainly superior to the average. She can draw a character and she can be mysterious. But she is a long time in getting to work. And she lacks imaginative power. *The Frontier of Fear* is the better of the two books.

Francis Everton's *The Dalehouse Murder* stands on a very different plane. It has faults. Faults of writing which would not be tolerated in a serious non-detective-novel. Example: "They had dealt with several garments of the feminine gender which their maidenly modesty did not allow them to either mention or produce." The "knotted horrors" of this passage are as appalling as a murder. Second. Faults of invention. The hero, who tells the tale, himself says: "It seems to me up to this point in telling my story I must be constantly detailing trivial matters *which can have no possible interest taken by themselves* and yet which have a real bearing on the more important later events." (My italics.) This is an unconscious admission of ignorance of the job. Every incident related ought to be interesting in itself, and if it isn't the author is to be blamed. There is a trackless morass in the middle of *The Dalehouse Murder*. The reader steps out of it, a little bemired, on p.140. Third. Faults of revelation. The revelation is seriously deficient in direct drama. Nevertheless *The Dalehouse Murder* is at least as good as any modern detective-story I have read since Conan Doyle and Gaston Leroux. The mystery is original and ingenious. The character drawing is excellent. The mingling, in the house of crime, of the two atmospheres of tennis-playing domesticity and Scotland Yard detectivism is most piquantly and effectively done. And the whole affair coheres and convinces. I attend Mr. Everton's next work with considerable interest.

3 April 1930

Dying Author's Wish Ignored

It is certain that in Britain book reviews are on the whole too benevolent (though far less so than play-criticisms). That, however, is not because reviewers as a class are peculiarly benevolent, but because the British racial character is benevolent. Get back to Dover after some Continental travelling. The first thing that strikes you is the extraordinary "decency" of your railway porter. Yet you have not hit on an extraordinary railway porter. All the porters are the same. They are British. So are our book-reviewers British.

Of course if you examine publishers' advertisements in the mass, with their quotations from reviews, you receive the impression that in the opinion of reviewers nearly all new books are masterpieces of one kind or another, and you conclude that our book-reviewing carries Britishness to the extreme. This impression is fallacious. Reviewers may be benevolent, but they are not so benevolent as all that. As a rule the quoted extracts are misleading. They are bound to be misleading. A publisher can quote only a very brief extract (naturally and rightly he chooses a sentence which best suits his purpose), and rarely can a brief extract correctly render the general tone of a review. Again and again it has happened to me, when I have in the main disparaged a book, to see quoted from my criticism a remark from which the reader would be justified in assuming that I was enthusiastically in favour of the book. Which phenomenon has often won for me the vituperation of the discerning. I have tried, by my phrasing, to avoid the contretemps, but I have not succeeded.

Further, it is to be remembered, and forgiven, that a reviewer, terribly bored by nineteen books out of twenty, is deeply thankful to find the twentieth unboring, and hence he is apt to heap undue laudatory epithets upon it. Such is human nature. And, while authors would never believe it, reviewers are very human.

Withal, making every allowance for the humanity of reviewers and the too-saintly benevolence of the British character, I do honestly think that we live in a period of quite unusually good authorship, a period which will compare well with any previous period. I refer specially to fiction. Hardly a week passes but some new book arouses genuine admiration in this breast rendered fastidious, captious and hypercritical by the disillusioning hand of time. I can recall a dozen books in the last twelve months which have abashed the novelist in me by their originality and their excellence. And I know that I must have reviewed many others. War-books in particular have been wonderful.

Now this week, when I was in the mood to be harsh, a friend handed to me a novel together with a command to read it. I was determined to dislike it. I had no intention of finishing it. I said to myself that I would haughtily glance at it. Until last week had anybody ever heard the name of Myron Brinig? I hadn't. He is the American author of a novel about American Jewish life: *Singermann* (Cobden-Sanderson, 474 pages, 8s.6d.). The publisher, who ought to know better, naughtily refrains from issuing any biographical details concerning Brinig. *Singermann* cannot be his first book. It is conspicuously the work of a man who knows what he is doing, who knows life and knows how to write.

History of a family of Roumanian Jews who, scarcely able to speak English, settle in the provincial town of Silver Bow, U.S.A. Father, mother, a daughter, and half-a-dozen sons. Ups and downs of trading, and of family life. Rows in the home, where Yiddish is the native tongue. Loves. Marriages. Deaths. Strikes. Prizefights. Disaster. Tragedies. Comedies. The author gets into the skins of all his very various characters, with the possible exception of the younger, the boy Michael. In regard to Michael, the author seems to me to have allowed his method to deteriorate into a recipe, a formula. But the rest are almost perfectly done. The portrait of the neurotic mother is masterly. And the portrait of the chief non-Jewish character, Maxine, the courtesan who marries into the respectable family, is just as good. (Maxine had a pietistic stepmother. "It was bad enough to have to live on a farm; but to have your stepmother looking like the wrath of Jehovah, her long blue nose buried in Genesis, that was too much. Maxine just told her father where he could get off.")

Like all good realists the author is romantic, sees the whole of worldly existence romantically, but sticks to truth. "Plunge, rock through the night, my electric steed, my trolley-car operated by the Silver Bow Street Railway Company." There is a sentence which appealed to me. And this of the young man who left home too soon and landed himself in a mess: "He was thinking that no matter how bad home might be, it gave you a feeling of security that could be found nowhere else in the world. You sat down on the bed, and it was your bed. The sheets had a comfortable feel to them. They belonged to your skin somehow."

Singermann, strange to say, is not perfect. It is too loosely jointed; characters vanish for too long, reappearing when you have almost forgotten them; some of it is mannered, with the mannerism of D.H. Lawrence. It shows now and then an uncomfortable Jewish coarseness of perception. But in originality, creative power, honesty, beauty it is about a thousand miles ahead of the average novel. And it comes to you without warning, out of the blue, and lays you flat by its brilliance!

Do not imagine that *Singermann* is the only interesting novel for this week. By no means. *Sanatorium*, by Donald Stewart (Chatto, 7s. 6d.), is an interesting novel. *Singermann* is utterly American. *Sanatorium* is utterly English. The dust-jacket represents a patient's "chart" on which the thermometer degrees vary from 97.2 to 103.6, and the pulse varies from 70 to 116. From this chart and the title you can guess the subject — T.B. The leading character spends eight months in a Hampshire institution, then insists on leaving it — to die. The book has been called horrible, more horrible than any war-book. I do not agree. It is very painful, but less so than life. It is admirably done, with discretion and with taste. I never heard of the author before.

Speaking of T.B., I will mention — I have space only to mention — a third very remarkable novel, *The Castle*, by the late Franz Kafka (Secker, 7s. 6d.), finely translated from the German by Willa and Edwin Muir. There is more technical accomplishment, more conscious artistry, in *The Castle* than in either of the other two. A philosophical novel, an allegory of human existence, even more realistic than Bunyan's. The author died young, of T.B. He gave instructions that the book, and two others, should be destroyed because they were not finished. The instruction has been ignored, and properly so. Complex, and full of subtle implications, different from all other novels, *The Castle* (God's) is a notable affair.

10 April 1930

D.H. Lawrence's Delusion

The late D.H. Lawrence's * recent volume of verse, *Nettles*, gave me no pleasure. And when I beheld his posthumous collection of journalistic "fugitive pieces," with the obnoxious title, *Assorted Articles* (Secker, 6s.),

* Lawrence died on 2 March 1930.

363

I decided before I opened it that I should not like it. Which just shows how wrong one can be. For I like it very much. Twenty-three articles, some short and none long. Despite a certain occasional disdainful roughness in the writing of them, these articles might well serve as models for young journalists — also for old journalists.

Lawrence was a novelist, a dramatist, a poet, a critic, a descriptive writer, and often first-rate in every branch. And he was a first-rate journalist too. He chose his subjects well. He handled them well — clearly, succinctly, picturesquely, beautifully. He didn't flourish his pen before beginning, and when he had finished he knew he had finished, and stopped. Not a word wasted. The subjects chosen were important, elemental, fundamental, and he struck at once deep down into the core of them. Nothing could be more fundamental than "The 'jeune fille' wants to know," or "Sex versus Loveliness," or his "Autobiographical Sketch."

His remarks on sex are in the nature of an apologia. He is supposed to have been obsessed by sex. The fact is that at his best he was no more obsessed by sex than any normal human being. But he wrote more frankly and more cleanly about it than most. He tried to fish up sex from the mud into which it has been sunk for several hypocritical and timid English generations past. He had a philosophy of sex, which is more or less illustrated in all his novels. But he also had a philosophy of friendship, quite as profound and revealing as his philosophy of sex. As I have no space to discuss them I will not try even to state them.

I am a tremendous admirer of Lawrence. I should hesitate to go as far in admiration as that very distinguished critic E.M. Forster, who believes that he was "the greatest imaginative novelist of our time." In my opinion Lawrence lacked one quality — the power to discipline and control his faculties. Especially in his earlier books he let those superlative faculties — for instance his descriptive faculty — get the bit between their teeth and gallop around with a thunder of hoofs and a lightning of glances very exciting to hear and to see; but extravagant. Lawrence seemed to me sometimes to suffer from a delusion similar to the delusion of a sick man who thinks that if a given quantity of medicine will do him good, twice the quantity will do him twice the good. I wonder how Lawrence's description of seasickness, had he done one, would have compared with the classic description of that malady in the 107th Psalm! I think that David would have come out on top.

Still, I would say that no finer work has been done in our time than Lawrence's finest. He is not yet understood, even by the majority of his admirers. But he will be; and meanwhile his work must accept injustice. In the future no first editions of present-day writers will be more passionately and expensively sought for then Lawrence's, unless perhaps Joyce's. I regard this as certain.

I never met Lawrence; nor heard from him, nor wrote to him, though more than once I was tempted to do so. Accounts of his individuality vary greatly. I know well some of his intimate friends. They differ, not about his brilliance as a companion, but about the benevolence of his character. Once, many years ago, our paths crossed. My friend and business agent, the late James Brand Pinker, who was then also Lawrence's friend and business agent, came to me and said that Lawrence had said to him that my duty was to support such a writer as he was during the process of establishing himself. I thought there was something in this idea. Having reflected upon it, I told Pinker that I would give Lawrence three pounds a week if H.G. Wells and John Galsworthy would do the same. Pinker informed Lawrence, and returned with the report that Lawrence regarded the offer as an insult. So I confined my assistance to the preaching of Lawrence's dazzling merits.

A young author, Mr. Stephen Potter, has published a little book on Lawrence, *D.H. Lawrence. A First Study* (Cape, 5s.). It is an excellent book, subtle, lucid, enlightening, well written. It was finished before Lawrence's death. I enjoyed it, and learnt from it. It deals chiefly with the Laurentian philosophy. Mr. Potter ought to complete his survey with a book on Lawrence the creative artist. The man's philosophy will go the way of all philosophies. It will be outmoded. But his creative work cannot be outmoded. The creations of first-class emotional power never are.

As I am on the subject of writing men, I wish to announce that a truly delightful book is *The Poet's Progress*, by Walter D'Arcy Cresswell (Faber, 7s. 6d.). Mr. Cresswell is a young New Zealander, a poet, and a ceaseless adventurer before the Lord. He has a direct, Defoe-ish style, which he manages with the nicest aplomb. The adventures recounted are mental, spiritual, economic, and physical, and they occurred in various parts of this wide world. Here is a brief specimen of the style and of the adventures: "So I sold all I had, to an old Jew I brought up to my room from the Lillie-road, who quite charmed me, to see how well he could cheat, when never a word nor a look betrayed what a windfall he had. I kept nothing but one suit and the best of my books, *for my mind was loaded enough — "* (My italics.)

Now the flavour of the volume is very delicate. I do not recommend it to every palate, but I do recommend it to those palates which can distinguish between the taste of a winkle and the taste of an oyster. One of Mr. Cresswell's poetic adventures — I shall not particularise it, but will leave the reader to discover it — was certainly unique in our age; it must be read to be believed. Mr. Cresswell deliberately invited the experience, and he came through it heroically. Concerning his gifts as a poet I know little and I say naught. Concerning his gifts as a writer of an adventure story, I have no doubts whatever. The proof of my conviction on this point is the simple fact that I have read his book twice and liked it even better the second time than the first.

17 April 1930

"Snobs," Snags and Snares

The other day Sylvia Lynd said of a translated French book: "Had I read it in French it would probably have impressed me far more than it does in English. Perhaps because the satisfied vanity of understanding a foreign language intensifies the pleasure. It is certain that originals usually seem more admirable than translations." I always read Mrs. Lynd, because, the most courageous of reviewers, she rarely damns with faint praise and still more rarely praises with faint damns. No critic can more effectively influence the reader not to read a given book.

I agree that originals usually seem more admirable than translations. They seem because they are. No translations are or can be both first-rate and faithful. When they are first-rate they are not faithful. The late Scott Moncrieff's translations make marvellous reading; but faithful, no! Scott Moncrieff (who by the way once admitted to me that he could not speak French) translated the title of Proust's *A l'ombre des jeunes filles en fleurs* as *Within a Budding Grove*. Which is a brilliant rendering, but not in the least a translation. And compare Florio's wonderful *Essays of Montaigne* with the French original — you will be surprised, if not hurt!

Less defensible is Mrs. Lynd's contention that the ability to read a foreign language intensifies the pleasure of reading it. This is true of the early stages of foreign reading, but not of the later. The more you know of a foreign language the more you know you don't know: which is both annoying and depressing, and a grave weakener of pleasure. Not one in a thousand English readers of French can read a single page of French without meeting a snag. And not one in five hundred is conscientious enough to consult a dictionary about the snag. And even when consulted the dictionary nine times out of ten is useless. Bi-lingual dictionaries are apparently composed to the end of telling you what you know and not telling you what you don't know. Fortunately the French author with the fewest snags is also the best and most readable: Guy de Maupassant.

To me the most important French work recently issued or re-issued is the late Paul Souday's *Les Livres du Temps*, of which three volumes are out and more will follow (published by Emile Paul, 15 francs each). The work is made up of Souday's weekly critical articles from *Le Temps*, which before it employed Souday used to publish the worst literary criticism in Europe. Souday changed all that. Old-fashioned subscribers to the semi-official daily must have felt, in reading him, as if they had been dropped into a cold bath.

Like Emile Faguet and Ferdinand Brunetière, Souday knew everything, but he wrote better and more interestingly than either, and in my view he had a surer taste. Both Faguet and Brunetière were often ridiculous about really original new books. Souday never was. His range was as wide as the sky. In the first volume alone he wanders at large from St. Francis of Assisi to the detective-novel. Apropos of the latter, he has high praise for Tristan Bernard's crime-story, *Mathilde et ses mitaines*. Tristan Bernard is a quite first-rate sardonic writer; I think I would almost call him great. Souday says of the detective-novelist: "As a general rule he keeps outside literature." Devastating and horribly true. *Mathilde et ses mitaines* (published by Ollendorff) is richly worth reading. As for Souday, he is an extremely diverting guide to French literature new and old, and I unreservedly recommend the whole series of *Les Livres du Temps*. In addition to his distinguished positive qualities, he had the negative one of not being venal.

There are still big French newspapers in whose offices, if you want a book to be "noticed," you are editorially told to go first and see the cashier.

In the matter of French novels I have come across little or nothing of late that has genuinely moved me. J. Kessel's *La Rage au ventre* (published by La Nouvelle Société d'Edition) is a book of the moment, but I doubt if it will ever be anything more. Still, Kessel wrote that very fine Irish story, *Mary de Cork*, and he can be read without fatigue and without humiliation. Irène Némirovsky's *David Golder* (Grasset, 15 francs) has made a stir in Paris. . . . Yes, well, it has a certain glitter.

To either of these I prefer Drieu La Rochelle's *Une femme à sa Fenêtre* (Gallimard, 15½ francs). La Rochelle wrote a novel, *Blèche*, about the love of a girl-typist and her employer, which, though in places obscure and clumsy, was very original and had power. I discussed it in this column last year. The woman at her window is cleverer, far more skilful, but I doubt if it is as good, as authentic. La Rochelle seems to be on the way to being consciously fashionable. The story is chiefly laid in international circles in Greece, and concerns itself with the passion of a bourgeoise for a Bolshevist fugitive. It portrays the usual futile, semi-corrupt society of exiled and linguistic persons. International circles are a snare for good novelists, because, while they seem attractive, they lack reality. The book is exciting, and the interest is maintained.

Long ago I ought to have written of the Princess Bibesco, a French author, not the Princess Bibesco whom we know in London. Whatever she writes is worthy to be read, and especially her novel, *Catherine Paris*. Her latest book is a small one, *Portraits d'hommes* (Grasset, 12 francs). Her next will be about Egypt. *Quatre hommes* contains her souvenirs of four men, Ferdinand of Rumania, the Earl of Oxford, Anatole France, and a fourth whose name was previously unknown to me, Jean Lahovary, her father. The first and the last sketches are the best in the book, but the other two will better attract the English reader.

There is a pleasing page which depicts Asquith the scholar visiting Ravenna and demonstrating that he was more familiar with the gossip of the Byzantine court than with that of Windsor. And another page: Asquith gazing at a portrait of the youthful Disraeli covered with chains, lobs, buckles, etc. Asquith ejaculated these two sole words: "Incredible creature!" The author comments: "He was expressing once again the feelings of the thoroughbred English in front of that which is not English." The somewhat slighter sketch of visits to the aged *amie* of Anatole France, and to Anatole France himself, are impressive. This book has a tender charm which really touches.

Another good new book of souvenirs: *Oscar Wilde, La Tragédie Finale*, by Henry D. Davray (Mercure de France, 12 francs). M. Davray, one of the pillars of the historic French fortnightly, the *Mercure de France*, for thirty years, was a friend of Wilde's. I doubt whether anything that Wilde ever wrote was good enough to escape oblivion. The memory of his life will survive the memory of his books and plays. His career has been the cause of many reminiscences, some mediocre, some excellent; among the latter I should count Davray's.

Lastly I must mention Francis de Croisset's latest volume of travel, *Nous avons fait un beau voyage* (Grasset, 12 francs). I defy anyone to translate that title into current English. The book deals with India, and is as amusing as M. de Croisset's renowned boulevard plays. I will not, however, assert that it is as good as his previous travel-volume, *La Féerie Cinghalaise*, which, incidentally, had an immense sale.

24 April 1930

Is That Poetry?

A few weeks ago a politician offered to recite poetry to a few friends in my house, and we heard a piece of fifty or sixty lines. It was very subtle and very good and very carefully phrased. But at the end I asked: "Is that poetry?" The reciter said: "It is." And an acceptable literary critic present said: "*IT IS.*" So I modestly yielded to prestige. But I was not fully convinced that I had received the right answer to my perhaps naive question.

The poem was Robert Browning's 'A Light Woman.' Of course 'A Light Woman' (whose subject by the way is one such as would have well suited Thomas Hardy) is in the broadest sense poetry. "Poet," I am told, is Greek for "creator," and Browning here did create something, to wit, three characters and a situation. Also 'A Light Woman' has the attribute which alone differentiates poetry from prose: an intentional recurrent rhythm. I say "intentional" because some writers (for instance, Dickens) have written quite long passages of blank verse without being aware of the fact, and the result is certainly not poetry. Nevertheless the language of 'A Light Woman,' though it has fine qualities, is not in my opinion beautiful, shining, splendid. And in my poetry I demand these qualities, and if I do not get them I refuse the name of poetry to the composition and call it verse. It may be admirable verse, but I do not admit it to the class of poetry. For me poetry is an affair primarily of emotional words, not of thought. Much of the very greatest poetry has little or no basis of ideas — except conventional ideas. Of my schoolboy perusals of Virgil I remember one line as being great poetry:

> Infandum, regina, jubes renovare dolorem.

What a reply to a queen! (I object to classical quotations, but I cannot forbear to quote five words that I have lived with for nearly fifty years.)

And this too is my notion of poetry:

> Full many a glorious morning have I seen
> Flatter the mountain tops with sovereign eye.

And this:

> Brightness falls from the air,
> Queens have died young and fair,
> Dust hath closed Helen's eye.

And this:

> No man or woman has loved otherwise
> Than in brief longing and deceiving hope
> And bodily tenderness; and he who longs

For happier love but finds unhappiness
And falls among the dreams the drowsy gods
Breathe on the burnished mirror of the world
And then smooth out with ivory hands and sigh.

I am constantly citing these immortalities. Not much freshness of thought in them! But all the loveliness of words! Please note that I am not attempting to define poetry. I am merely stating a personal, possibly narrow and misguided desire to limit the sacred name of poetry to verse written with beauty in the grand manner. We have a number of excellent and refined poets whose work I can quietly enjoy. But they do not rouse me. They have not the grand manner.

Now two years ago I signalised here the appearance of the second volume of Frederick Irving Taylor's *Sacrifice, or Azal and Edras*. The work stands to-day complete, after ten years' work in the spare time of a journalist. (Published by Ingpen and Grant, 10s. 6d.) It did not need the illustrations by Frank Brangwyn. Too many novels have been issued about the Great War, and too few epics. *Sacrifice* is an epic, the only one that I have yet seen on this eminently epical theme. Further, it is a mystical epic, narrating the strife between the principles of good and evil. Still further, it is written, often with beauty, in the grand manner. Great single lines will not make a greap epic; but they will help to make it. What of this line?

Then with Hell's fury freighted, fell a star.

Or this?

Unfooted wastes and vast unfathomed glooms.

Milton might have written these lines, and there are scores as good in *Sacrifice*. I do not say that Irving Taylor is as fine a poet as Milton. Assuredly he is not. I have sharp reserves in my appreciation of his poetry. I do say that he has schemed a scheme noble and ambitious, that he has executed it in the grand manner, that he has achieved passages of very considerable beauty, and that as a war-writer he stands in a class by himself. Which is something to say! Mr. Taylor deserves to be congratulated. More, he deserves to be read. This is not a review; I am not qualified to criticise an epic. It is an announcement.

And the following is not a review either. It is a reference to Roy Campbell's new volume of poems, *Adamastor* (Faber, 5s.), made because Mr. Campbell writes verse beautifully and consistently in the grand manner. I read his previous volume, *The Flaming Terrapin*, and I did not fully share the enthusiasm with which it was welcomed by the initiate, for the reason that I deemed the work rather too flaming. *Adamastor* has had an even more enthusiastic welcome than *The Flaming Terrapin*. And rightly, in my opinion. It is a better book. I bow down to it.

Mr. Campbell is quite outrageously a poet. He has plenary inspiration. Emotions, crude and primeval, surge out of him in terrific waves. He is a prodigious master of words. He rides on them as on horses, loving them as violently as he whips them. His is indeed the grand manner. Nothing in him of the little master, the *petit maître*. He shows more vitality in a line than our excellent and refined poets can show in ten pages. He does not stretch out one fancy into a poem; he packs forty images and similes into a stanza — and sometimes they come near to bursting it. Here are a couple of lines for a sample:

The frost stings sweetly with a burning kiss
As intimate as love, as cold as death.

And here are lines from a satiric poem, entitled 'Poets in Africa' — one of the most powerful in the book:

We had no time for make-believe
So early each began
To wear his liver on his sleeve,
To snarl, and be an angry man.
Far in the desert we have been,
Where Nature, still to poets kind,
Admits no vegetable green,
To soften the determined mind.

Mr. Campbell is equally magnificent in different veins — the lyrical, the grandiose, the flaming, the sardonic, the ferociously ironic. He can be, and is, everything, except petty. The shaft of his satire is so deadly that it excites sympathy for its victims. He will compete, and not unsuccessfully, against Byron. He will be Miltonic, Keatsian, Swiftian. He has a mighty carelessness of ambition. His danger is that his ambition may overleap itself. In my view the Campbell muse needs watching, needs to feel the bit. To possess marvellous faculties is great; to be able to marshal and control them is greater. But at any rate we have in Roy Campbell a poet who will compel us to listen to his strain.

1 May 1930

Piquant Peeps Into the Past

Observers say that one of the most marked and widest-spread characteristics of human nature is love of the past. I doubt it. Instead of "love of the past" I would say "interest in the past": a different thing. People may hate the present, but they can't love the past unless they know a lot about it, and if they know a lot about it they certainly don't love it. Some of them talk terrible nonsense about the good old days. But if these persons were sent back into the good old days they would soon be ready to sell their shirts for a return ticket to the vile present.

Nevertheless the past is tremendously interesting to us: an unequalled museum. And the further off the past the more interesting it is, especially in the matter of small daily detail. Let a diarist describe how he saw Thomas Hardy use his first fountain-pen, and we should read the description with mild pleasure. Let a diarist describe how Wordsworth used his first steel pen, and our pleasure would be keener. If some contemporary record were discovered of Shakespeare's method of cutting a quill, the item would easily take precedence of earthquakes, revolutions, murder-trials, and the connubial adventures of film-stars, on the front pages of daily papers. And if a trifling document were unearthed relating how Homer used improper expletives because his amanuensis made mistakes, the rich tidings would simply turn the whole world upside down and nobody would talk about anything else for a week. China would hear of it. Scores of unreadable books would be written about it, though no modern past-praising author would be likely to abandon paper and a fountain-pen for papyrus and a reed.

At a distance of even fifty years, to say nothing of three thousand, the past acquires absorbing interest. Ralph Blumenfeld, benevolent dean of Fleet-street in general and of the *Daily Express* in particular, has published a book of daily details which goes back forty-three years. It is called *R.D.B.'s Diary, 1887-1914* (Heinemann, 8s. 6d., illustrated). I warn the public against this handsome volume. It is dangerous. Once begin it and you will have to finish it. Your house may be on fire, your children in the article of death — you will have to finish this book. It contains naught but jottings about trifles; it is utterly unassuming in both matter and manner, it is innocent of explicit philosophy; it is just journalism; but it will grip you more effectively than any ancient mariner gripped any wedding-guest.

Thus (1887): "I drove round London to-night in a curricle . . . inspecting fireworks. I have never seen so many people; certainly never so many drunken ones." "Had lunch with Sir William Pearce, who built the giant Oregon. He is a believer in big ships. He thinks . . . we may expect passenger ships of at least 20,000 tons, with a speed of 21 knots; electric light throughout, and even lifts to carry passengers between decks. *A visionary old gentleman.*" (My italics.) "Forbes [war-correspondent] was talking about Ku Klux Klan and essayed to compare them with the Irish Moon-lighters, but Parnell disagreed vehemently; said the Moonlighters were unorganised, sporadic, irresponsible, whereas the Ku Klux Klan were well led, and with a purpose." "Two are barmaids and two are shop-girls, and the combined weekly earnings of the four is £2.6s. The brother is a clerk in a shipping-office, and receives 21s. a week, out of which he has to buy his top-hats and black coats." "The police [London], by the way, are really wonder-ful, in spite of their ridiculous peg-top trousers and heavy frock-coats. How they can perform loyal service on £1.5s. a week goes beyond me."

All the foregoing entries occur in four days in June. The entire book is of similar piquancy. Its attractiveness to-day is extreme, and a century hence its attractiveness will be extreme. Indeed in 2030 it will have become a prime "source" for social historians.

Mr. Blumenfeld's volume ends where the war begins. He must positively publish a second volume, though it will necessarily refer to fewer persons by name. Documentary detail about the war is still thousands of miles from being complete. One might have assumed, for example, that everything had been said about conditions at the Front — until Miss Helen Zenna Smith published her affrighting book, *Not so Quiet* (Marriott, 5s.), which portrays minutely the daily existence of women-chauffeurs and other women workers just behind the Front. This work too may well become a prime source for historians. I am glad I read it. But no war-book has appalled me more. (Some of the English chapters are very inferior to the rest.)

Lastly, as a treasury of detail concerning mainly pre-war times, I will mention E.F. Spence's *Bar and Buskin* (Elkin Mathews, 15s.). The title is the worst part of this book, since it can convey nothing to the reader who is not a good guesser. Mr. Spence combined law-practice with theatrical criticism. I know little of his advocacy, but a great deal of his theatrical crit-icism. That he still healthily lives is proof enough that hard work does not kill. He made for many years a considerable income at the Bar, but no assured livelihood could keep him out of the theatre. He had a habit of doing theatrical criticism for three different papers simultaneously; the chief of them was *The Westminster Gazette.*

His description of an evening's theatrical toil after a heavy day in the Law Courts is impressive. He would go to bed at 3 a.m. and rise at 7.30 to receive and correct proofs. He brought into the theatre common sense and absolute sincerity. Which sincerity caused his dismissal by sundry editors, and his exclusion by managers from sundry theatres. (Times have not really changed; there is nothing new under the sun; Hannen Swaffer was not the first martyr; and clearly the blood of the martyrs is not always the seed of the Church.)

Mr. Spence's book is too kindly. There are too many charming women and brave men in it. Withal he is on the whole bluntly outspoken — about all manner of things. Honeymoons, for instance. I doubt whether any modern writer has been quite so outspoken about his own honeymoon. On the subject of the bar, his chapters are full of facts and figures highly useful for purposes of comparison between past and present. He candidly admits the existence of financial abuses in legal practice (which then as now tended to make litigation a luxury for millionaires only); and for some of the abuses he offers remedies which have a persuasive air. This book is a plain straight-from-the-shoulder affair for plain people. It is readable, because its author is a highly competent journalist. But, lacking elegance, it does not charm. Its strength is in its accuracy, honesty, fullness and wordly sagacity. Nobody will regret having read it.

8 May 1930

The War Story of the Ordinary Man

There have been so many war books, and so many good war books, and so many good English war books (none better), that on my soul I feel semi-apologetic about mentioning another. A characteristically English reaction has begun against the truthfulness of good war books, which are said to malign our armies. An effort is being made to maintain that our soldiers, in addition to being heroes, were archangels. For myself I prefer them to have been what they were: men. I have no use at all for archangels, but a lot of use for men.

Well, I must mention yet one more fine English war-book: Henry Williamson's *The Patriot's Progress,* illustrated by William Kermode (Geoffrey Bles, 10s. 6d.). It is short, and it is not a novel. It contains very little concerning the supposed-to-be chief military (and civil) diversions: beer and light women. It is the account of the war-career of a plain, ordinary man, John Bullock, who entered the army with a dogged sense of duty, and left it minus a leg. The author has not drawn John Bullock as an individual. John Bullock is Everysoldier, and *Everysoldier* would have been an excellent title for the book.

The account is simple, and awful, absolutely awful. Its power lies in the descriptions, which have not been surpassed in any other war-book within my knowledge. I began by marking pages of terrific description. But I had to mark so many that I ceased to mark. I said: "Nothing could beat *that,* or *that,* or *that.*" I was wrong. Henry Williamson was keeping resources in reserve for the supreme attack in which Everysoldier lost a leg. This description (p. 169), quite brief, is a marvel of inspired virtuosity. And it is as marvellous psychologically as physically. In fact when I had read it I said to myself: "I ought to retire from the craft of descriptive writing, for I am definitely outclassed." No overt satire, sarcasm, sardonic irony in the book. Yet it amounts to a tremendous, an overwhelming, an unanswerable indictment of the institution of war — "the lordliest life on earth."

A word as to Mr. Kermode's pictures. At first I resented them, for they are very numerous and they cut into the text, distracting the reader's attention. But in the end they justified themselves to me. For they are very good, and just as much a part of the book as the text itself. It would be as fair to say that the text illustrates the pictures as that the pictures illustrate the text. The two forms of expression are here, for once, evenly complementary. *The Patriot's Progress* ought to have a large sale.

Another example of effective satire by implication is Riccardo Bacchelli's *Love Town,* skilfully translated from the Italian by Orlo Williams (Duckworth, 7s. 6d.). It gives a glimpse or two of the war, very well done. But chiefly it deals with the United States. Now the author has never visited the United States. He has taken the modern legend of the United States, and employed it as the basis of a seeming-realistic novel. Such a scheme is interesting, and I can find no artistic reason why it should not be sound. It is the scheme on which all so-called historical novels are founded, and there have been a few excellent historical novels. The resultant pictures, though necessarily fanciful, have a certain convincingness, and they amount to a stiffish, subtle indictment of some recent aspects of existence in America.

The book is too loosely constructed, and it loses strength as it proceeds. The last part is the least satisfactory. Here Bacchelli has obviously revelled in a series of scenes of fantastic and outrageous debauchery. They may be faithful to some small section of American life — I don't know — but they are as tedious as a night-club at 2 a.m. In a novel truth is no excuse for tedium. Withal, *Love Town* is not unworthy of a skipping examination. Bacchelli shows a Latin skill in conveying impropriety of act with propriety of phrase. Some of his psychology is admirable. In fact it is sometimes probably better than any English psychology of a similar kind could be. For we are both timid and sentimental in our psychology as in other departments of our imaginative literature.

Bacchelli creates a youngish respectable woman who takes a bodily fancy to a young American soldier. She does not love him; she makes no pretence of loving him; she even dislikes him. But she yields to the fancy. True, the frail woman is French! But everyone knows that such respectable women yielding to such fancies do exist and flourish in this Anglo-Saxon isle. Yet I doubt if any English novelist would have the nerve to examine and portray the psychology of one of them as amusingly, ironically, unflinchingly and minutely (and decently) as Bacchelli does. Of course Tolstoy did the thing even better in the respectable, untemperamental feminine voluptuary who wanders through the pages of *War and Peace.*

There was a time when T.S. Eliot counted among our profane ironists and satirists in verse. He seems to have definitely abandoned this vein, in which he excelled. (Who that has read of him does not recall with joy Mr. Eliot's Mr. Prufrock?) I regret the deflection. Mr. Eliot's later vein is the mystical. I have no objection to the mystical. Quite the contrary. I love the mystical in the Bible. I am sympathetic to it even in Plotinus. But I do like to understand what I am reading, and, despite earnest effort, I cannot understand Mr. Eliot in his new manner. He has just issued a slim and physically-beautiful volume of six poems, entitled *Ash Wednesday* (Faber, 3s. 6d.). I approach this verse with respect, partly because of my admiration for some of the author's early poems, and partly because Mr. Eliot's work in general is most solemnly admired by men whose taste and judgment I could not flout. But my respect has a certain sardonic quality. I avow that I can make even less of *Ash Wednesday* than I could make of Mr. Eliot's *The Waste Lands* (which is said by some to mark an epoch in English literature). I cannot divine why *Ash Wednesday* is called *Ash Wednesday*. I have discovered one fine line in the little book:

Till the wind shake a thousand whispers from the yew.

And I think that the closing eleven lines have a pallid loveliness. But of the rest I comprehend nothing, naught, nothing! Were I flippant I would describe the work as Gertrude Stein for a super-intelligentsia. I felt while reading that if a magical open-sesame could be vouchsafed to me, I might suddenly enter into the secret conservatory of Mr. Eliot's meaning. It was not vouchsafed. I had to remain outside; and through frosted glass I could perceive only vowel-repetitions, word-repetitions, elusive assonances, and delicately-calculated discords. Yet I have a thrilling suspicion that there may be something valuable in *Ash Wednesday*. Only I was born too early to value it.

15 May 1930

Detective-Story Writers Hot on the Trail

Current fiction may be divided into two categories: (1) Masterpieces, (2) Also Rans. According to critical report, the Masterpieces easily out-number the Also Rans. Indeed I seldom open a new novel as to which I am not credibly informed that it is a masterpiece. I have expurgated my dictionary by cutting out "masterpiece." As applied to new novels the word needs a rest, which I shall give it. Current fiction may also be divided into three categories: (1) Good, (2) Half Good, (3) No Good. In this division the Goods easily outnumber the No Goods and the Half Goods. Current fiction may also be divided into four categories: (1) War-novels, (2) Detective-novels, (3) Daring novels (in which the authors skate over thin ice, occasionally falling through and disappearing for ever), (4) Miscellaneous. Number 4 of course outnumbers the others, but numbers 1, 2 and 3 are not far behind. No. 1 is numerous, No. 2 is more numerous. War-books will soon decrease. Certainly I can perceive no diminution in the output of detective fiction. Rather the contrary.

The latest sign of the vigour of detective fiction is the birth of an organisation entitled The Crime Club. The Crime Club has no entrance-fee, no annual subscription, no disclosed President, nor Committee of Selection. But it has an official firm of publishers. I therefore assume that the publishers have a certain commercial interest in its success. The Crime Club merely advises its members by post about the merits of new detective fiction. It would do well to advise itself to name its advisers by name.

They needn't be ashamed of their first selection — *The Noose*, by Philip Macdonald (published by the Crime Club, 7s. 6d.). It is good. The scheme of it runs thus: Bronson is condemned to death for murder on cast-iron circumstantial evidence. In less than a week he will swing. His wife asserts his innocence. Five detecting persons believe her. They set to work to find the real murderer. Naturally they do find him — otherwise there would not have been any novel. (In all detective-novels the criminal is and must be duly found.) The thrill of *The Noose* springs from the shortness of the time at their disposal.

The motivation is excellent; the revelation of the criminal's identity is as startling as it is convincing. The interest is continuous. The humour is terribly uneven. The writing saddened me. Mr. Macdonald has irritating mannerisms. He loves to invert the customary order of words in a sentence. And he has an infuriating trick of putting "apostrophes" after a common noun. He does this on nearly every page. A man who will say "the room's far corner" deserves to be prosecuted by the Royal Society for the Protection of Defenceless Readers. I could write a book about the remarkable peculiarities of Mr. Macdonald's style. I ought to write it. Nevertheless, *The Noose* is one of the best recent detective-novels I have read.

But not the best. The best is Gaston Leroux's *The Man of a Hundred Masks* (Cassells, 7s. 6d.). I wish I had read it in the original French, for the English translation is mediocre. Here you have Leroux's narrative gift, fresh invention, and light humour at their finest. You don't "plough through" this novel. You glide over it, as on a switchback railway. Leroux is still the most accomplished literary practitioner now detecting. His story in *The Best Detective Stories of the Year 1929* (Faber, 7s. 6d.) is by far the least unsatisfactory in a collection on the whole indifferent. Sir Arthur Conan Doyle still stands solitary on the highest peak of detective achievement. None of his English successors can compare with him. The anonymous author of an Introduction to the last-mentioned volume says: "The short story is as difficult a form of writing as the novel." Briefly, he is wrong. Other things being equal, a long fiction is always more difficult than a short fiction. Ability to stay the creative course is extremely rare.

I must turn from the too rank field of crime novels to that of verse. For this is a poetry week. It began with Humbert Wolfe's *The Uncelestial City* (Gollancz, 7s. 6d.), which the publishers regard as Mr. Wolfe's "most important work." I say abruptly and stoutly that it isn't. It cannot compare with *News of the Devil*. It is in verse. Over 250 pages of verse, with much rhyming therein. A specimen (and a fair specimen) of the rhyme:

> ... There's the little stone
> Terrace I was remembering at the place
> from which you hear the rivers white and brown pour,

. . . .

. . . . steady downpour.

I object to this kind of thing, and I object to Mr. Wolfe permitting himself to print it. I know that both Byron and Browning, and even Hardy, would go nearly as far, and Browning now and then quite as far. In those three cases, however, the content was good enough, the texture close enough, to excuse monstrous verbal vagaries. Mr. Wolfe's content is not. He has gifts, but he squanders them with an inglorious facility.

The structure of the book is too facile. The book is "all over the place." The satire is too facile. I will not call it cheap, but I will call it inexpensive, and I will assuredly call it obvious. There is poetry here and there in the work. "Swing dark, swing death!" has some lyrical virtue. I should not be surprised if *The Uncelestial City* makes a rather wide appeal to the public. (Mr. Wolfe's verse usually does.) But no popular success will convert me to liking it. I shall go on living in the expectation of something very much better from Mr. Wolfe.

Another volume of verse is to be noted: *First Poems*, by Philip Henderson (Dents, 3s. 6d.). Something wistful, touching, in that title, *First Poems*! The publishers give no biographical information as to the author. All that I know about him is the name of his native country, and the name of a street where he has lived. These facts I discovered for myself from the poems. But they do not suffice me.

I very much want to know the age of Mr. Henderson. If he is young he beyond question presents an interesting phenomenon. If he is not young, the phenomenon may or may not be interesting. At any rate, young or not, Mr. Henderson has cured in himself the customary faults of youth. He writes maturely and soberly. For the rest he is excellently unafraid of putting down with accuracy his real sensations and emotions. Little or no sentimental nonsense about him. What to me is the best piece in the book, 'Rhapsody on a windy night,' contains the line

Stepping out into Redcliffe Gardens as I said before.

And it does not destroy the mood of the poem. Which is something. I think that Mr. Henderson deserves some attention.

22 May 1930

Sex — What Would the Novelist Do Without It?

In spite of the "questionable" title of a recent humorous American book, *Is Sex Necessary?* (already reviewed in this paper), there seems to be no doubt that sex is positively still necessary — at any rate to novelists. Dramatists are apparently able to do practically without it, as has been three times demonstrated of late months on the London stage; but novelists never. Not even war-novelists. True, I recall Godwin's novel, *Caleb Williams*, from which, according to my recollection, love is beautifully absent; but *Caleb Williams* was published more than a hundred years ago, and it has been for more than a hundred years quite dead, though immortality was predicted for it.

I have read three rather remarkable fiction books this week, one dealing with eighteenth-century French history, another with the intimacies of modern domestic life, and the third with the Spanish-Moroccan war. They are all bursting their covers with love; and their plots all turn on the incalculable vagaries of women in making hay of the lives of men, or of men making hay of the lives of women. Serious persons may regard this as very strange; but they should address their complaints to nature, not to novelists. For over thirty years I have been trying to invent a plot from which the grossly miscalled "tender" passion of love should be absent; and I am no nearer my goal than I was in the late 'nineties.

The first and by far the longest of the three is Mr. F.L. Lucas's *Cécile* (Chatto, 8s. 6d.). Now Mr. Lucas is better known to those of us who are interested in the art of putting the right words in the right order, than he is to that large public which recks little of the right words and still less of their order. A few months ago I met with an essay of his, on "Silence," which showed, in addition to emotional power, an unusually sensitive feeling for words. So that I opened *Cécile* with anticipations of pleasure. My anticipations, while not wholly disappointed, were incompletely realised. The writing of the book is beautiful; I salute it. Also the excellence of the author's observation of, and insight into, the processes of the organism which from politeness we refer to as the "human *mind*," is equally unusual. That is to say, he is a psychologist of no common sort. But he is a novelist self-made, not born. He does not understand the business of narrative. He knows not when to stop either a scene or a conversation.

As for his conversations, they are often too good. They remind you of Landor's *Imaginary Conversations* in their delicious and witty neatness of phrase. But no human being ever talked as Cécile, Andrée, Gaston, Gabriel, and others eloquently orate in this novel. Of course Walter Scott's puppets are just as impossibly eloquent. Scott's convention of dialogue, however, has perished, to the general satisfaction. Mr. Lucas appears to have forgotten this important fact. He is behind his age. Further he drags in his history, and his own (admirable) sociological views, in a manner more ingenuous then ingenious. He inculcates: a sinful habit not to be forgiven in a novelist.

Lastly, I doubt whether the sentimental tergiversations of the sisters Cécile and Andrée were worth the elaborate and endless attention which Mr. Lucas lavishes on them. Cécile's particularly. In the above mentioned book *Is Sex Necessary?* there is a mocking "Case History" which begins thus: "George Smith, aged 32, real estate operator. Unmarried, lived with mother. No precocious mother fixation. Had freed his libido without difficulty from familial objects, and was eager to marry. Had formed an attachment in 1899, at the age of 29, with a young virgin. Her Protective Reactions had been immediate and lasted over a period of three years, during which he had never even held her hand" . . . . I fancy that many novels, including Mr. Lucas's, would be shorter and better if the characters were dealt with as "Case Histories." One page might then do the work of a hundred and do it more readably.

Perhaps I have been too airy in my treatment of *Cécile*. For it is a sound novel, much superior to the average. And it is interesting if you will yield yourself up to it, and read it with a slow patience, conscientiously sucking the honey from every sentence. But if you are in haste or have a train to catch, then *Cécile* is not your novel.

The second book is French, *Eva*, by Jacques Chardonne (Grasset, Paris, 15 francs). It came to me from the author, with an autograph inscription, "In witness of admiration." Wonderful, the numbers of French authors who in recent years have put themselves to the trouble of witnessing their admiration of me in a similar way! When I was a mere novelist not one of them would thus clasp my hand across the salt, estranging Channel. But since I resumed reviewing . . . ! Well, I open their books with caution, with reserve, with suspicion. And thuswise, having no acquaintance with M. Chardonne's previous novels, did I open *Eva*.

It is very short and very fine indeed. It takes the form of an episodic, quite fragmentary diary of a husband willingly victimised by a selfish, self-centred, unimaginative and neurotic wife. It is pathetic, tragic, true as any novel could be, original, subtle, and witty. Here is a specimen of the delicate wit, apropos of the tendency of honest fellows to blame before they praise: "The world is full of decent people who see everywhere nothing but rascals." I greatly enjoyed *Eva*, finishing it with regret. It is a sinister searchlight on conjugal existence. Here is a specimen of the author's views about that: "A man must stake his life on one love, and that is a great risk of the heart. Don Juan is only a little adventurer, too timid to love." The fault of the work is the inclusion of a small number of entries which, good in themselves, have no apparent relation to the main theme. *Eva* is nearly all sex, and quite all decorous.

My third book is Spanish, *The Blockhouse*, by José Diaz Fernandez, with an introduction by Walter B. Harris, and a special preface for England by the author (Hopkinson, 6s.). Its translation is smooth, and appears to be efficient. Adequate biographical note. Fernandez reaches the age of 31 this week. He has been office boy, clerk, postal official, lawyer, and soldier. He is now author — of short stories. If a trifle over curt, or bald, or terse, the stories in *The Blockhouse* are excellent, and well worth reading. They give a coherent, if partial, picture of the North African war. There must have been quite a lot of love in that war. Indeed, love seems to have been one of the major pre-occupations of the Spanish warriors. There is certainly quite a lot of love in *The Blockhouse*. The stories are chiefly horrible, and one of them has the distinction of being the most horrible story I ever read.

29 May 1930

Young Authors Should Shock

When I assisted, in spirit only, at the presentation of the Hawthornden Prize last Thursday to Lord David Cecil, author of *The Stricken Deer*, and saw the youthful, happy author and his happy and august relatives, and listened to the amiable banter of Mr. Stanley Baldwin in bestowing the Prize, I had revolutionary thoughts, which might have horrified the Hawthornden Selection Committee. Not that I objected to their choice this year. In the past they have "crowned" one or two books which in my opinion deserved no coronation. But this year none can cavil. *The Stricken Deer* is a praiseworthy performance, imitative without slavishness, brilliant without excessive originality, thoroughly conscientious, possessing a refined style, and saturated with correctness. In short, notwithstanding many laudatory reviews, it is a good book. True, I have not read it, I have merely run through it, in the decent somnolence of a club library. But with experience comes the power of divination. I have divined *The Stricken Deer* and in a year or so I shall honestly believe that I have read every page of it.

Now my revolutionary thoughts run thus. No selection committee of nice-minded authors and bookish persons can choose a really original work. Their intentions are excellent. They have a genuine desire to serve the Lord. But in their humanity and their righteousness they are apt to forget the warning of the writer of Ecclesiasticus: "My son, if thou come to serve the Lord, prepare thy soul for temptation."

Their temptations are frightful. The temptation to be correct; the temptation to stand well with a pernickety public; the temptation to favour an author whose ideals coincide with their own; the temptation to compromise in order not to have a hades of a row in committee; the general temptation to avoid friction and, above all, shock. The truth is that no book by a young author is or can be really original and strong unless it shocks nine people out of ten, and herein is the reason why no really original book has the least chance of acceptance by any properly constituted committee. Sad it is that this should be so. But it is so, and will be ever. The fault is human nature's, and incurable.

Hence, while leaving the Hawthornden Committee to continue in peace its mild and quite useful activity of advertising dignified literature, I would like to institute an entirely new organisation, complete with annual prize. Which organisation would have no committee, but a single autocrat of selection. Which autocrat would be changed yearly.

I am told that the Contemporary Art Society chooses a new autocrat every year, saying to him: "Here is money. Go away and buy what pictures and drawings appeal to you; but disdain fashion, and don't dare to return with anything that is not guaranteed artistically to shock us." The Contemporary Art Society has done, and is doing, admirable work for the encouragement of originality in the graphic arts. Doubtless it makes mistakes; but it does not often make the mistake of allowing itself to be influenced by those influential and energetic noodle-birds who settle down in flocks with equal earnestness upon what is good and upon what is bad, screaming in praise of the bad and polluting by their multitudinous patronage original and powerful works such as Epstein's *Madonna and Child* and Strauss's *Die Fledermaus*.

I want a Contemporary Literature Society with a short-lived autocrat determined not to care a tinker's curse for anybody or anything. We have original millionaires. Let one of them endow my society, and let him lay down a single condition, namely that the yearly autocrat shall be not less than thirty and not more than forty years of age. Between thirty and forty a man may have reached the height of discretion without having tumbled over the top into the feather-bed of correctitude which lies on the other side. On behalf of the Israelites the Psalmist moaned: "How shall we sing the Lord's song in a strange land?" The right autocrat will understand that it is precisely his job to sing the Lord's song in a strange land, and to sing it loud, though he be hung for his minstrelsy.

And I would have also a Book-of-the-Month Club devised on similar lines. Existing Book-of-the-Month Clubs usually send out to their subscribers books which their subscribers know a good deal about beforehand. My new club would send out books which as a rule only the keenly interested would have heard of. Subscribers would, of course, be warned in the prospectus that they must expect to be shocked by the monthly-arriving parcel. I do not mean shocked in the silly narrow sense of shock by audacity of sexual descriptions. Not at all. I use the word shock in a deeper, larger and nobler sense. These Book Clubs, I hear, are flourishing more and more mightily in the United States, and quite satisfactorily prospering, despite the myopic frowning of certain booksellers, in Britain. There is room for my new Club; indeed I think that there would be a fairly brisk demand for membership of it. The trouble would be to find the books.

I have recently heard of a French Book-of-the-Month Club which might interest English readers of French. From the number of grateful letters I receive on the rare occasions when I write about new French books, and of complaining letters when I don't write about new French books, I am convinced that English readers of French are pretty numerous. The club is called "Sequana" — I don't know why. It has been in existence for five years and its prosperity may be judged from the fact that it issues its own special editions (limited to the number of members) of its selections, printed on fine paper, and better stitched than the ordinary "odious mediocrity" of the *article de Paris*. Also in addition to the paper-cover edition it sells bound editions in three styles — two of them *de luxe*. Also it runs its own monthly illustrated review, called *Cahier*, which is perhaps the only literary periodical in France not controlled by a firm of publishers.

Its Selection Committee is formidable in size and in prestige; it includes too many Academicians; but I imagine that the working committee or sub-committee may be smaller. The latest selection is *Fez*, by the brothers Tharaud: a first-rate affair of picturesque and accurate sociology. (I have read it.) The price of the volumes, unbound, is the equivalent of less than 5s. The sooner "Sequana" sets up a British agency the better.

5 June 1930

"That's a Very Good Idea!"

Norman Douglas has a considerable reputation — as the author of *South Wind*. It is a book like no other. His more excitable admirers count Mr. Douglas among those few writers each of whom is in a class consisting of one person. For myself, I think that *South Wind* has the fault of monotony, and that the second half is much inferior to the first. But at worst it is a better book than *They Went*, which in half an hour dangerously lowered my temperature to sub-normal. *Old Calabria*, mainly descriptive, I prefer to either of the chief fictional works. Mr. Douglas's creative method is to get an idea, or to let an idea get him. He then says (I surmise): "That's an idea!" And it is. He then says: "That's a very good idea!" And it is. Finally he says: "I can make that idea into a book." And he does.

But in my opinion he is apt to be too content with his idea. When he says that he will make the idea into a book he does not give sufficient importance to the word *make*. An idea must be made; it will not make itself; it will only expand itself or nullify itself into a series of similar cells. The process of making an idea includes thrashing it, hammering it, tearing it to pieces, putting it together again, diluting it, draining it, shaping it, heating it, hardening it, chipping bits off it, adding bits to it, colouring it, and generally transforming it so that its own father wouldn't recognise it. There is more difference between an idea raw, and the finished, fashioned product than there is between a musical comedy star when she gets out of bed in the morning and a musical comedy star when she prances at night on to the stage in full, carefully-contrived glory of complexion, coiffure, and costume. Heaven does not do all, and artifice should assist nature, nature being a tenth-rate showman. A creative artist must play forty rôles. One of them is the rôle of showman. Mr. Douglas has somewhat neglected this rôle.

His new book (apparently his thirteenth), *How About Europe?* (Chatto, 7s. 6d.), is based on an idea, and it is a very good idea. Mr. Douglas read Katherine Mayo's *Mother India*, which is a tremendous and as yet unanswered indictment of a civilisation, and he said to himself, in substance: "Yes. This is all very striking. But what about Europe?" And proceeded to write down a lot of notes critical of the civilisation of the world's smallest and most conceited continent. These notes, comparing Europe with India, constitute his latest book. *How About Europe?* has no form, and needs none. It is a series of cells. At the same time, by reason of the nature of its material, it has a variety which may roughly be called infinite. Indeed the idea of it is the best idea that Mr. Douglas has yet met with, having regard to his talents and their limitations. The book is written with all Mr. Douglas's skill of phrase; it glitters with his malicious wit; it often shows perception; it is intensely readable; and "monotonous" is the very last adjective that can be applied to it. It compels you to think; it compels you to see the phenomena of European civilisation from what photographers term "a new angle"; and it compels you to laugh. You laugh and you laugh. You catch the author in the grossest unfairness. But you laugh. You reach page 200 before you know where you are and you exclaim: "Only sixty more pages! What a pity!"

Mr. Douglas is by temperament a rebel. He dislikes being governed, and still more does he dislike being reformed. His unfairness to reformers is merely monstrous. "Nine-tenths of the reformers of humanity have been mischief-makers or humbugs," says he. This is not true. We owe all our progress, and about 50 per cent. of our present happiness (such as it is), to reformers. But he has invented a perfect ironic phrase for reformers: "World-improvers." This phrase deserves to stick. Mr. Douglas is unfair to lots of other persons and things, but I will not enumerate them. I prefer to signalise his wit.

Thus: "Curry is India's gift to mankind. . . . Curry atones for all the fatuities of the 108 Upanishads." And on education: "American children, somehow or other, still come illiterate into the world." And this: "Hindus . . . know that men are not equal, and that a certain number by nature are unteachable . . . . The Western notion seems to be this: some dogs can learn tricks, therefore all dogs must learn them." And: "Once her children have grasped the binomial theorem, all will be well. Their future careers are assured." And on age-raising: "As we have a fit of age-raising just now, we might consider, I think, whether it would not be reasonable to raise the hanging age, which is at present fixed at sixteen." I have quoted, because the savour of the book can only be conveyed by quoting. The whole book is about the level (call it low or high as you please) of the above quotations. A few pages are very thin, but others are what the French call "dense" — not using the word in our colloquial sense.

If Norman Douglas were to read the latest volume of Routledge's truly admirable series, *The Broadway Library of Eighteenth Century French Literature*, he would probably say that in 150 years English civilisation has not perceptibly bettered itself. And he would be wrong. Still, a picture of an earlier century has this didactic usefulness: it does show a thousand traits and details in which we have certainly *not* improved. The Abbé Prévost is among the half-dozen French authors really familiar to the English public. He wrote *Manon Lescaut*, which has been translated into every language, including Choctaw and English, and whose story the operas founded upon it have carried into every city where opera is performed.

Prévost, like too many other gifted people, suffered from emotional instability, which in him took the popular form of mixing up religion with sexual passion. In addition to *Manon Lescaut* he wrote two hundred volumes. All the latter are generally supposed to be worthless. Which is absurd. No man who could write one great book could also write two hundred books all worthless. Talent will out, scribble you never so quickly.

The new Broadway volume is Prévost's *Adventures of a Man of Quality* (10s. 6d.), translated with an Introduction by Mysie Robertson, and illustrated. The Introduction has the air of being a University doctoral thesis. The story is very good, and I think that the best parts of it are the parts which deal, on a spacious scale, with refined and other sorts of life in England in the first half of the eighteenth century. The author knew England, the English, and the English language. And he loved all three, but with an impartial and discerning affection. *Adventures of a Man of Quality* is worth possessing and worth reading. And it diverts. The translation is sound.

12 June 1930

Back to Riceyman Steps

As I came down the hill into Clerkenwell I was reflecting in the back-parlour of my mind about those two books of Professor J.L. Lowes: *Convention and Revolt in Poetry* and *Of Reading Books* (Constable, 7s. 6d. and 5s. respectively). The first is a reissue. Despite a certain lack of distinction in the mere writing, it is a very good, provocative, judicial, readable book (as is its companion), and it contains more and better and brighter quotations than any book I can just now remember since Burton's *Anatomy of Melancholy*. The heart of one half of *Convention and Revolt* is in the following sentence: "Conventions die of being used to death." Personally,

382

in literature, though I preach revolt (and in doing so bring trouble on myself), I practise convention, as becomes my years. And I admit that I want more revolt — from others.

Well, as I came down from the Pentonville region into Clerkenwell, I saw Convention and Revolt all around me. Convention was on the slopes. He that knoweth not Percy Circus (distant view of the romantic towers of St. Pancras) should know it. It is a hundred times more conventional than Piccadilly-circus. Also Great Percy-street should be known. Also the Norman arches of Baker-street (W.C.1, not W.1). Also Helena-street, with its antique woodwork all painted verdant green, and its ruined chapel. Also Lloyd-square, the most withdrawn square in London. Also Riceyman Steps, formerly Plum Pudding Steps, where was performed a feat of transport surpassing anything ever done in that line in U.S.A., namely, the moving of an entire bookseller's shop with all its books and dust from a south coast port to the foot of the Steps. So I descended to King's Cross-road — a Rowton House, Mount Pleasant (whence the mail-bags used to appear), and the new factories and warehouses. It is the latter which represent Revolt. The latest industrial perpendicular style of architecture contrasts uncompromisingly with the conventional blocks of dark "dwellings" which it hems in. And so into Farringdon-road where the book-barrows are.

The object of my excursion was to visit and ransack the book-barrows. With a vengeance do they represent Convention. I have known them for over forty years, and instead of advancing they have receded. To begin with, the majority of them were shut up and sheeted down in their black tarpaulins. This at four o'clock on Saturday afternoon! Influence no doubt of the sinister week-end habit invented by the book-reading classes! And those that were still "open" might be divided into two classes: (1) Barrows stocked with too-excited literature such as *Notes on the Prayer Book, Transactions of the Hampstead Antiquarian Society*, publications of the Florentine Della Cruscan Academy, and works by the author of *The Schönberg-Cotta Family*. (2) Barrows heaped pell-mell with books in a disorder so acute that you could not possibly examine more than ten per cent. of them without employing a house-breaking and demolition firm.

Here indeed was the final, desperate example of the English mercantile Convention telling the customer plainly that your way of doing business is thus and thus, and that if the customer doesn't like it he can leave it, and be hanged to him. I did detect one or two pleasing items — a beautiful Plantin and a first edition of a Maurice Hewlett; but to prove the sincerity of my remarks to the barrow-man I refused to buy any of them. (He didn't care.) The book-barrow trade ought to look to itself, and if I do my duty I shall write to the secretary of the National Union of Associations of Book-barrow Dealers. Half an hour in Farringdon-road served to raise my opinion of (shop) booksellers, whom (with a noble disregard of my own immediate interests as an author) I have criticised on various occasions in this column.

And speaking of booksellers, I am glad to see that the enlightened Mr. J.G. Wilson's lectures on "The Business of Bookselling" are being printed in *The Publisher and Bookseller*, a periodical which has greeted my criticisms of the trade harshly and with a sad lack of respect.

The next revolt in the book-trade is coming from the United States.

Something has already been heard, but a lot more will soon be heard, of the revolutionary American scheme of reducing the price of novels from 2½ dollars to 1 dollar. It will not apply to all novels, but it will apply to most. The idea is to widen the market, by putting newly-published books into shops that are not book-shops. Drug-stores (of which there are sixty thousand in U.S.A.) and so on! I am told that even now the biggest bookseller in the world is Macy's Department-store in New York. The scheme will certainly be opposed by booksellers, who will certainly end by accepting it. And that it will have some repercussions on the British book-trade is beyond doubt. Authors may suffer at first, but in the end they will profit. And after all authors are nearly as important as booksellers, though not quite.

As to Revolt in literature itself, I have been reading quite a number of new novels lately (English and foreign), and I am very disappointed in the percentage of Revolt which they contain. It is about .001 per cent. Some of the novels have already been treated in this paper; hence I will only mention them. *Other Man's Saucer*, by J. Keith Winter (Heinemann, 7s. 6d.). Mr. Winter is an Oxford undergraduate. *Other Man's Saucer* is very good for a first book. But of Revolt in technique, not a sign in it, and of Revolt in matter very little. The story contains sundry and violent shocks; but the end is sentimental, and it is also far removed from life. Such incidents as the attempted murder by water simply don't happen. In manner the book struck me as somewhat Russian. *Diamonds to Sit On*, by Ilf and Petrov (Methuens, 7s. 6d.), is well translated from the Russian. Meant to be funny, it is more cruel than funny. Technique and attitude are thoroughly old-fashioned — more so than Gogol's.

A better Russian book is Michael Ossorgin's *A Quiet Street* (Secker, 7s. 6d.). Also well translated. Also thoroughly old-fashioned in technique and attitude. The author has fancy, which he overworks. But the pictures of life in the quiet street in Moscow in time of revolution and the Soviet are convincing. A still better book is *Coronet*, by Manuel Komroff, who is American by birth, Russian by origin (Harrap, 8s. 6d.). In technique and attitude old-fashioned; the plot with its coronet in the crimson-box might have come out of a museum. In moral substance, less old-fashioned. The book has nearly 600 pages, and is too short. If you are to sweep satisfactorily through the world and three centuries you need at least 1000 pages. *Tashkent*, by Alexander Neverov (Gollancz, 6s.). Fairly well Englished, but the style lacking in grace. A child-like story of a child. Thoroughly old-fashioned. But good.

No. I find recent post-revolutionary Russian and other imaginative literature singularly lacking in fundamental originality. The real originators are still Anglo-Saxon. William Faulkner in America. James Joyce, the Irishman, in Paris. And Edith Sitwell in London. Joyce's *Anna Livia Plurabelle* has been issued at 1s. (Faber). As a curiosity it is worth possessing; but it is utterly incomprehensible to me, and will be to you. Another fragment of Joyce's *Unfinished Work* (of which *Anna Livia* is a fragment) has just been published in a limited edition, and with much luxury: namely, *Haveth Childers Everywhere* (Babour and Kahane, Paris, price unknown to me). It is utterly incomprehensible, but sounds majestic when read aloud. I wish that Joyce had not set forth to out-Ulysses *Ulysses*. Lastly I must chronicle the appearance of Edith Sitwell's *Collected Poems* (Duckworth, 8s. 6d.). Fifteen years' harvest winnowed. As a revolutionary Miss Sitwell stands equal with Joyce. And it is something, it is a great deal, that she has come through very heavy fire to a collected edition.

19 June 1930

Beauties of the Barge

The tidings of a new novel by A.P. Herbert filled me with anxious expectancy. He wrote *The Secret Battle* (one of the earliest and best English war-novels), and though I was familiar with his *Topsy* narrations, his skittish essays, his admirable verse, his revue, his comic opera, and his destructive polemical letters, I had read no other novel of his. I have now read *The Water Gipsies* (Methuen, 7s. 6d.). The water gipsies are apparently the canal-boat population. But less than 50 pages (out of nearly 400) deal comprehensively with canal-boat life. True, these fifty pages are the most beautiful and sinister in the book. The *locus* of the greater part of the novel is a barge, lying eternally at Valentine Wharf, Hammersmith, and used as a permanent habitation by Mr. Bell, gambler, cornet-player and 'cellist, and his two motherless daughters, Jane and Lily: all lower middle-class.

The story, which deals with the loves of Mr. Bell, Jane and Lily, is mainly arranged in a series of scenes contrived against big descriptive backgrounds: the Derby, dog-racing, a Hyde Park demonstration, a night-club, a meeting of the League of Red Youth, a skittles match, a canal-journey, etc. All these backgrounds are wonderfully well done. They are accurate, they achieve picturesqueness without searching for it, they are imbued with the subtlest social satire and enlivened by humour as delicate as it is brilliant.

Rarely does Mr. Herbert slip down into farcical wit. But he does once or twice. I cannot believe that the mare Palfrey, walking backwards, brought the National Anthem to a premature conclusion by sticking her hind foot into the big drum. The coincidence is too enormous. And I do not think that the following is very funny: "Mrs. Raven admired his [modernist] paintings. She had been a wrangler at Cambridge, so perhaps had a tendency to triangles." But generally speaking Mr. Herbert's writing is impeccable in taste. (Withal, I should rather like to know why he writes your's, her's, it's, instead of yours, hers, its!)

As regards those two girls and their amours. Jane, the elder, is heroine-in-chief. She attracts three young men, Fred (canal-boatman), Ernest (Red agitator) and Mr. Bryan (the modernist painter). When she had a narrow escape of losing her honour to Fred, I said to myself: "If the author means to go on in this narrow-escaping style I shall despise him, for I simply cannot stand much of it." Then Lily does fairly and squarely lose her honour to a (splendidly drawn) rich Jew boy named Moss, whom she "picks up" at the "Dogs." Lily comes home next morning and relates the story of the fall in decent detail to Jane. And then Jane loses her honour to Ernest. You may argue that there is nothing in this. In the latest novels girls are always losing their honour. Some heroines, ignoring the great fundamental truth that a flower cannot be gathered more than once, lose their honour time after time.

Yes. But note the difference. The latest fictional seductions are always messy, and the authors are furtive and even unpleasant over them. Not so Mr. Herbert. I hate the word "healthy" and I hate the word "wholesome" applied to novels. These adjectives infuriate me, for they are almost invariably bestowed on novels which to my mind are neither healthy nor wholesome — very much the reverse. *The Water Gipsies*, however, is in the best sense both healthy and wholesome, really. No nonsense about Mr. Herbert's seductions. He tells you plainly (and beautifully) how such things happen. And they *do* happen as he tells you; and your susceptibilities are not excoriated. Here is an advance, and I salute it.

Jane is a fine girl, and she develops, and her marriage (to Fred) and her going-away to a canal-boat existence are lovely matters. (Nevertheless I think Mr. Herbert makes her a shade too callous about the drowning of Ernest.) All the characters are excellently drawn and they all develop. *The Water Gipsies*, like all very good novels, is both realistic and romantic. It is truly original. Also it is skilfully conducted save that there seems to be a certain lack of direction during and round about the skittles-match period.

Evelyn Scott's *Escapade* (Cape, 7s. 6d.), explicitly autobiographical, is the recital of the consequences of a highly respectable and serious seduction. The book has become the subject of conversation at the dinner-tables of the enlightened. The scene of it is South America — at its Portuguese worst: dirt, disease, foulness, sensuality, stupidity. But extreme picturesqueness. The story of the gestation of the narrator's child! An honest book, showing considerable talent and some originality, and not to be ignored. It adds to knowledge of human nature. I was on the point of saying that it was well written. But it isn't. It contains a lot of this kind of thing: "A stasis of life had created a vortex of intensity, a stillness into which life poured itself with the vividness of death." Which I call bad writing. I should more correctly say that it is written with ingenuity and skill which are too often misguided. To my mind the author's attitude towards humanity is all wrong, though perhaps inevitably so. She says: "If I could consider sex more factually and with less mystical solemnity I might find amusement. . . ." Very true. There is not a glint of humour in this strange and repellent book. If I were protestingly told that the ghastly history could not tolerate any humour, I should reply: Why not? I defer to the solid qualities of *Escapade*. But I did not enjoy it.

I appreciated more Josef Kallinikov's *Women and Monks* (Secker, 906 pages, 15s), which is all compact of seductions. The title points to a certain sort of book, and *Women and Monks* is precisely that sort of book. It is conceived on a grand scale and executed in the grand manner. It even has a dry, covert humour at intervals. It is indeed thoroughly well done. Yet, though it is grand in scale and manner, it lacks genuine grandeur. In order to justify itself it ought to reach the sublime, but in my opinion it fails to do so. I admit that I have not finished it. If I ever do finish it, which is doubtful, I would write about it at length; for it must certainly intrigue the experienced amateur of fiction. The pictures of Russian monkish existence between 1905 and 1917, crowded with living figures, is frightful, and the imperturbable blandness of the author intensifies its frightfulness. The translation, by Patrick Kirwan, seems to me to be good beyond the ordinary.

26 June 1930

American Authors "Made" in England

Last year I made some fuss in this column concerning the young American novelist, William Faulkner, who had been mentioned to me in conversation by Richard Hughes, author of *High Wind in Jamaica*. No American, and even no American publisher, whom I asked about Faulkner had ever heard of him. I sent to New York for his books, but could get only one, *The Sound and the Fury*, and that not without difficulty. Strange that Americans have frequently to be told by Englishmen of their new authors!

The first printed fuss made about Theodore Dreiser's first book was made by an Englishman. *Sister Carrie* fell flat in the United States until a review of it by myself was republished there. Then Americans said: "Who is this man Dreiser?" and *Sister Carrie* began to sell in America. That was thirty years ago. Yet American critics say that English critics sniff at American novels.

Now Faulkner is getting a show in England. His first book, *Soldiers' Pay*, has just been published here, with a preface by Richard Hughes (Chatto and Windus, 7s.6d.). His second and third will follow. *Soldiers' Pay* is labelled "Not a war-book." I call it a war-book. Its chief male characters are returned soldiers, and the whole story hinges on a terribly scarred aviator, who dies of war. Also war-scenes are directly described in the book, and very well described. Unless Faulkner runs off the rails, as some young men do, but as he probably will not, *Soldiers' Pay* will be an extremely valuable collectors' item in twenty years time. Faulkner is the coming man. He has inexhaustible invention, powerful imagination, a wondrous gift of characterisation, a finished skill in dialogue; and he writes, generally, like an angel. None of the arrived American stars can surpass him in style when he is at his best.

But praise of *Soldiers' Pay* must not be unreserved. It is a first book, and has the usual defects of a first book. It is clumsily constructed, being lopsided; the opening chapters, though admirable, are far too long. Faulkner is like Schubert was: he doesn't know when to stop. Further, the book is over-emphasised throughout. Also, some of the locutions are irritating: "His hands cupped her shoulder," "Jones released the fragile writing of her fingers." Etc. Faults of youth, minor and excusable.

A more serious fault, however, is that the book is difficult to read. Not as difficult as his second book, *The Sound and the Fury*, but still difficult. To read it demands an effort. (The effort is adequately rewarded.) There is no excuse for this. The great masters are not difficult to read. You know what they mean, and in their passages of dialogue you know who is saying what. In too many novels of young authors a mathematical calculation, a counting of speeches, is needed to find out who is talking. A novel ought to be easy to read; it ought to please immediately. But too many young novelists seem to be actuated by a determination not to please. They seem to say: "Whether you like it or not, there will be some rough going in our books. Kant's *Critique of Pure Reason* is difficult, and our books will be difficult. We will not smooth your path. Indeed we intend to make your path as hard as we know how."

In this matter, Faulkner is not guiltless. To get his full value involves some heavy work for the reader. But he is the most promising American novelist known to me; more promising than, for instance, Ernest Hemingway, author of the splendid *A Farewell to Arms*. He has in him the elements of real greatness, and *Soldiers' Pay* contains many quite marvellous pages.

William Faulkner writes no more like an American than like an Englishman: neither English English nor American English, but English. And in his novel are several very convincing full-length portraits of American women who seem to me to be not American women but women. Which demonstrates, I think, that he is interested in essentials, not in accidentals. I must say the same for W.J. Turner's 169-stanza poem, *Miss America* (Mandrake Press, 6s.), whose autobiographical heroine is officially stated to be American. She is just as English as American. Would that *Miss America* had been more carefully fashioned! It is disfigured by bad spelling, bad grammar, and bad rhyming. The rhyming is probably the worst committed by any modern poet of any pretensions. A versifier who will rhyme "pattern" with "hat on" ought to have his taste X-rayed, for that important organ must clearly be in a pathological condition. I could wish also that Mr. Turner had chosen for his heroine a name other than Altiora. Altiora is an amusing name for a lady who desires to rise on stepping-stones of her dead self to higher things. But it was used by H.G. Wells for such a lady before W.J. Turner began to write; and Wells's Altiora is an unforgettable creature.

As for the matter of the book, some of it is bad, and some not bad; I will not go further. Beauty glints transiently on the pages here and there; Mr. Turner is a poet, though "he hasn't been doing much at it" in his latest poem.

How different is the workmanship of Mr. Sturge Moore's *Mystery and Tragedy, Two Dramatic Poems* (Cayme Press, 7s. 6d.)! If you desire beauty and dignity and a craftsman's utter verbal conscientiousness, you will get this book, which by the way is printed and produced with genuine distinction, and which will certainly become a collectors' item. These two poems, within their antique classical garb, are full of original emotion, and are really far more "modern" than the loose colloquialism of W.J. Turner. Poetry means toil, and Sturge Moore has toiled.

Still another collectors' item is Robert Graves's *Ten Poems More* (The Hours Press, Paris; edition limited to 200 signed copies, 30s.). A large, slim, slight volume. I regard Robert Graves as on the whole our major poet, and I have said aforetime that his collected works are an impressive monument for a poet well under forty to have created. Since the issue of the collected works in 1927, Mr. Graves has apparently been living in a period of creative transition, from which he will doubtless in due course emerge. The ten new poems have value, but for me they have not quite the fine, close texture and the complete satisfactoriness of the poems of his earlier maturity. They strike me as experimental rather than definitive, wayward rather than straight-aimed.

388

3 July 1930

Thomas Hardy's "Sex-Psychology" As a Frenchman Sees It

Mrs. Thomas Hardy's biographical writings on her husband, so truthful, so tactful, so modest, and so well written, have really done much to draw new attention to the author of *The Dynasts* and *The Romantic Adventures of a Milkmaid.* When great authors die their names seem to slip for a time off the map. Hardy's is now beginning to reappear thereon. Another book whose mere publication will help the return is Pierre d'Exideuil's *The Human Pair in the Works of Thomas Hardy,* translated from the French by Felix W. Crosse, with an introduction by Havelock Ellis (Humphrey Toulmin, 10s. 6d.). To me the chief interest of this book is (1) the introduction, and (2) the bibliography at the end, which discloses that ten volumes of Hardy's novels and stories, in addition to two of verse, have been translated, and that a number of important articles on him were printed in Paris at his death. The French are becoming less insular.

M. d'Exideuil's work has been considerably praised in Britain. I do not understand why. He has apparently read all Hardy and all about Hardy, and a lot besides. But I think little of his literary criticism, which is written in a kind of pretentious jargon happily uncommon in France. For instance: "In its most rugged pages Hardy's work contains a vigorous study of the human pair. This study, at once solid and sombre, has all the character of a demonstration. As treated by our author it even assumes the mark of necessity." Have the last two sentences any meaning? Or are they just a pattern of ink on paper? I incline to the latter theory. There are furlongs of such sentences in the book.

Also the author, too, inadvertently betrays the real nature of his taste. In naming the names of several distinguished English writers, such as George Moore, George Gissing, and Arthur Morrison, he puts that of Lucas Malet amongst them! Now the daughter of Charles Kingsley was not a distinguished writer. Her novels quite properly are dead for ever. She could not hold a candle to her father or even to her Uncle Henry; she ranks about level with Mrs. Humphry Ward. Again, you can always judge a critic by his quotations, and the quotations cited by M. d'Exideuil are ninety per cent. clichés. Again, you can always judge an author by his chapter-titles. Here are some of the chapter-titles: "Conflict of the Sexes," "Passion and Necessity," "The Mystery of Attractions," "Towards a Twilight Hope." Incidentally, the titles might have been transposed, and nobody the wiser. Almost any title would fit almost any chapter. To read the titles was enough for me. Nevertheless, I read the book, so flattered was I to see a volume by a French writer about a modern English writer.

My answer to the book would be: "We knew all that before." It might also be: "You can't evolve a philosophical theory of mating out of the individual histories of the characters of any single novelist, though you might evolve forty theories all equally destructible." And my answer might also be: "The women and men in the Wessex novels are so like the women and men of other creative geniuses that you would want a microscrope to tell the difference." I feel sure I could prove that Hardy took his notions of women from Racine, and that all the Hardy 'sex psychology' is contained in Racine's famous line: *Vénus toute entière a sa proie attachée*. In fact I could prove anything if I chose to use the d'Exideuil jargon. The best thing in the book is Paul Souday's: "Nature in her malevolence, while seeming to have need of the couple, almost always extends its scope, so that it becomes a triad." But Souday never used jargon, and he was a wit.

Something appears to have gone wrong with the proof-reading of this book. Stendhal's name is misspelt throughout; and other names too are misspelt. And the title of one of Nietzsche's best known books is given in a language that I have not been able to identify (not German nor English).

M. d'Exideuil might concoct a book on the "sexual philosophy" implicit in a short novel which I have received, *Brother and Sister*, by Leonhard Frank, translated from the German by Cyrus Brooks (Peter Davies, edition limited to 500 signed copies, 30s.). And if Havelock Ellis wrote an Introduction to it, the Introduction would certainly be better than either the novel or the book about the novel. Leonhard Frank is the author of the highly successful and praised *Carl and Anna*. But *Brother and Sister* will not be highly praised, by me. The theme, to describe it in five words where one would do, is "marriage within the prohibited degrees." Now, under suitable and adequate treatment, the theme would be permissible. De Maupassant handled it very well in a short story. Shelley employed it. Byron lived it — or half-lived it.

Frank has handled the theme neither adequately nor suitably. As regards adequacy, he was sentimentally determined that the couple should sin in ignorance, but in my opinion he quite fails to convince on this, to him, crucial point. In the peculiar circumstances which he invents for them, the transgressors would assuredly have discovered their blood-connection in about a couple of days of friendship. As regards suitability of treatment, he has inserted scenes which in any story might offend many readers; these scenes are unnecessary to the development of the theme, and they are not well done.

Now the prohibited degrees are determined by conditions of time and place. The ancient Greeks might well have exclaimed upon the book: "Why all this fuss?" So might the Pharoahs. But the twentieth century is the twentieth century and Europe is Europe. And further, the susceptibilities of even the enlightened public (which is ourselves) are entitled to some consideration. Having unavoidably shocked us, a wise author who knows his business will not also shock us gratuitously. Scorpions should not be added to whips. Heaven knows that I am not Lord Brentford. Nevertheless, my attitude towards *Brother and Sister* is antipathetic.

I remember, a year or two ago, not liking a too vague German biography of Lenin. I have just read another (partial) biography which I do like: *Memories of Lenin,* by Nadezhda Krupskaya, translated from the Russian by Eric Verney (Martin Lawrence, 5s.). Krupskaya is Lenin's widow. Her book is, in its Russian way, nearly as readable as Mrs. Hardy's *Hardy*, or Edgar Wallace's *Edgar Wallace* (both wonderful).

Krupskaya gives you the man Lenin "intimate." You see him walking to and fro in a confined room, murmuring to himself the sentences which he is about to write. (He wrote at aeroplane speed.) You see him checking the additions of authoritatively *printed* figures which he used in his books and tracts. (He had the largest-sized conscience of any reformer who ever lived and wrote.) You see his propagandist classes of working men and women, and Party girls unpacking glass tumblers for the Party club. You see a Party house with its door always unlocked, and food always on the table ready for any pursued traveller who knew the ropes and arrived in the night. You see him enjoying *The Cricket on the Hearth* and Jack London — also not enjoying Jack London.

A portrait of a great and an honest man emerges. I read *Memories of Lenin* with a certain gusto, though there is in the book a little too much about his speeches and his writings. The Memories end in 1907. A second volume is to follow. The translation is vivacious, perhaps now and then too vivacious with outright colloquialisms. The book lacks a table of contents.

10 July 1930

I Am Not An Amateur Reviewer

Constantly I am receiving advice, chiefly by letter, as to the proper way to review books. My counsellors seem (1) to be young (2) to regard me as an amateur. A few weeks ago I got a whole circular of hints (unsigned). Every hint was quite silly, except one which ran thus: "Don't be too literary and devote columns to a memoir about some long-forgotten writer (like Leigh Hunt) whom no one has ever read or wants to read." I admit that I heartily agree with the hinter on this point. But then I have never done what he ordered me not to do; and to see precious space wasted weekly on authors who though unburied are shockingly dead, exasperates me at least as much as it could exasperate my caustic anonymous mentor. While granting the validity of his complaint against the too prevalent habit of mauling corpses, I wish to inform the complainant and indeed the entire review-reading world, that I am not an amateur reviewer. On the contrary if there is a born reviewer writing to-day I am he.

Forty years ago, when I was free-lancing, I wrote a review of a book by an obscure French author and sent it in to *The Illustrated London News.* Nothing more ignorantly foolish than such a journalistic proceeding could be conceived. As if editors of great papers accepted from outsiders reviews of books of no importance whatever! Still, the review was accepted. It did not appear for many weeks, and I spent a large part of my remuneration (15s.) in vainly buying issues of the paper week after week at sixpence a time; but it did at last appear.

Again, I wrote a review of Edward Carpenter's *Towards Democracy* and sent it to *The Weekly Star* (long dead). *Towards Democracy* was even then an old book. Nevertheless the review was accepted. Again I wrote stylistic news-paragraphs about forthcoming books, and sold dozens of them to *The Daily Chronicle* (at 3s. 6d. — or was it 2s. 6d. — apiece). But did *The Daily Chronicle*, then the Thunderer of literature, ever invite me to do reviews for it? Did *The Weekly Star?* Did *The Illustrated London News?* No, no and no.

Nevertheless I became a reviewer for another weekly paper, and I have found my reviews quoted in books about authors a quarter of a century later. How did I get the job? Very simply. By being assistant-editor, then editor, and always a debenture-holder, of the paper. I gave the job to myself, and by the easy device of being a shareholder of another paper, I obtained another reviewing job. I have reviewed a thousand books in three years. Even the most modern reviewers, in these efficient days of large-scale rationalisation of reviewing, can hardly beat that. But did any other papers invite me to do their reviews? They did not.

Then I asked *The Academy* for work: the only occasion in my life when I have lowered myself so far as to ask any editor for any job! *The Academy* answered my prayer. My reviews were the talk of the few hundred people who call themselves "the town," and I succeeded in raising *The Academy's* space rate from half-a-guinea to fifteen shillings a column. But something sinister happened, not to me but to the paper, and I wrote no more for it.

And then arrived the marvellous day when the editor of *The New Age* called on me and implored me to write reviews for him. It was too good to be true. I am bound to say that he said he couldn't pay me anything. Still, it was too good to be true. I consented. These reviews genuinely did flutter the dovecots. So much so that people might be observed reading them while crossing Fleet Street; and the editor, who was nothing if not munificent, began to shower on me weekly cheques of one pound one shilling each. Great days! Then something sinister happened to *The New Age* also. I ought to mention that years after I republished a selection of these reviews in volume-form, and the book sold like editions of evening papers containing the winner and s.p. of the 3.30.

But did any other editors invite me to do reviews? Certainly not. So I took seriously to writing novels and plays, and the mandarins of Fleet Street told me what a fool I was to try to write fiction when my obvious bent was criticism.

And now, when I have taken once more to reviewing, well-meaning persons tell me what a fool I am, and what impudence I display, to try to write criticism when my obvious bent is fiction. There is a saying that you can't please everybody. Well, I have always done all I honestly could do to please everybody: I have never succeeded; and I shall never cease this Christian endeavour. With one exception. If I displease anybody by denying that I am an amateur reviewer, I shall stoutly continue in the denial, and anybody can be as displeased as he chooses.

Reviewing has changed since the early 'nineties when I began. It has changed for the better. In those days it was on the whole as bad as it is to-day in most of the leading American papers. It is better informed and better written (because editors are more keen in their search for reviewers); it gets itself more talked about, is better paid, and is more punctual than of old. I can recall the spacious age when a review would appear six months or even twelve months after the publication of the book. And no one seemed to perceive anything odd in this majestic dilatoriness. The publication of a book was not news then. To-day it is news. Therein lies the literary difference between the twentieth and the nineteenth centuries. Why does the publication of a book constitute news now? Because the public is more interested — or less uninterested — in literature than it used to be. There cannot be any other reason.

I intended to write an article about the nature, scope, difficulties, influence, and general high importance of book-reviewing as a vocation.

Whereas I have written only the introduction to such an article. The explanation is that when writers start to write about themselves they are always long-winded. But later in the summer, when I have cleared off the new novel by H.G. Wells and a few other major items, I shall return to the subject.

17 *July 1930*

Too Many "Beats" to the Bar!

I had never heard of Michael Kelly until I received Mr. S.M. Ellis's *The Life of Michael Kelly, Musician, Actor and Bon Viveur, 1762-1826* (Gollancz, 25s.). (The title, by the way, intrigued me; for I had never heard, either, the phrase "bon viveur." It is not given in Kastner and Marks's *Glossary of Colloquial and Popular French*, nor in Clarke and Charpentier's *Manual Lexique*, two works very precious and humbling to those who think they know French; but the former gives "bon vivant," with which I was familiar.) Kelly was a musical prodigy, a great tippler, and a great simpleton. Gout killed him, and, because it also killed his forbears, he thought that gout was hereditary and unavoidable!

The *Reminiscences*, which appeared in 1826, and enjoyed the distinction of being spaciously reviewed by Sir Walter Scott, were in part dictated to that illiterate joker Theodore Hook, who seemingly made rather a mess of them. Mr. Ellis has made a very good job of them. I should estimate that much more than half of this *Life* is Kelly himself; the rest is Mr. Ellis, who thoroughly knows the period, and has the right attitude towards his subject. My sole criticism of Mr. Ellis refers to his style. I prefer Kelly's. Now here is a specimen of Mr. Ellis's: "He was the friend and fellow-player of Mrs. Siddons, Kemble, Mrs. Jordan, and scores of others *whose names are writ clear in the Roll of Thespis.*" Upon which my one comment is that we are in the year 1930. The illustrations are excellently chosen. There is a good index.

Apart from a few tedious passages — tedious because written without a feeling for narrative — this book is a very rich affair. It would be a bed-book, but for its size and its weight. Publishers ought to keep a pair of scales and a foot-rule in their offices, and before they decide on the format of a volume they should reflect upon the limitations of the physique of the average reader. The present book measures 9½ x 6¼ x 1⅝ inches. It would suit Carnera. Still, it will well repay a certain amount of muscular exhaustion.

From early youth Michael Kelly had a tremendous time. His motto was: "Pleasure to-day, business to-morrow." He knew everybody and drank everything, and had the luck to live till 64. His accounts of light vocal and roystering life in Naples, Rome, Florence and Venice are as spectacularly picturesque as such things could be. They appeal strongly to the wastrel-hedonist which happily resides somewhere in all of us, even the staidest.

The book is crammed with stories. Thus: the young and beautiful daughter of the richest nobleman in Naples was ordered by family council to take the veil. "All right," she said in effect, "I'll take the veil, but Cafferelli must sing at the ceremony." She was told that the supreme male

393

soprano singer had retired from his profession to Calabria, and could not be obtained. "Very well," she said. "No Cafferelli, no convent for me!" She won. Her father induced Cafferelli to sing at the ceremony, and the lovely girl became the bride of Christ.

Italy in those gorgeous times had the finest coloratura singers, and Italians knew how to treat them. Thus: the manager of the Palermo opera-house wanted the services for a season of La Gabrielli, who was singing and living in sin and splendour at Naples. She replied that if the manager would build a bridge from Naples to Palermo she would come; not else. The manager retorted: "Madame, if you can recollect and will give me a list of all those on whom you have bestowed favours I will build the bridge; not else." La Gabrielli went to Palermo, and the manager managed to add himself to her list of the favoured.

But the manners of Italians to singers whom they did not like would hardly have been approved at Covent Garden. Opera fans sat in the pit with the score and a candle to read it by, and at any mistake they shouted: "Bravo, you beast!" And when they detected similarity between one melody and an older one, they cried to the composer: "Bravo, you thief!" Or, "May the curse of God light on him who first put pen into hand to write music!"

Those were the days when opera did genuinely enter into the life of the people. One regrets them. When I have been bored, as I assuredly have, at Covent Garden or the Paris Opera or the San Carlos or the Fenice, how did I show my resentment? By going to sleep. A feeble substitute for eighteenth-century abuse!

To my mind Venice was the place of places for grandiosity and (what is called) pleasure. When the Pope attended High Mass at St. Mark's in Passion Week there were six orchestras. And the fête of the Ascension lasted for a fortnight. And Venice had a unique and comforting custom in its roystering: "The ladies particularly are fond of these banquets . . . but they make it a rule to pay their share of the bill. . . . Nothing would offend a Venetian lady more than any man of the party offering to pay for her." One could wish that English ladies of 1930 were capable of taking offence in the same way.

Venice enjoyed everything except sleep. Nobody ever went to bed. The shops were open till midnight and the restaurants nearly all night. D.O.R.A.* had not been invented. Kelly writes, in a justifiably lyrical mood: "Venice! Dear, beautiful Venice! Scene of harmony and love! Where *all* was gaiety and mirth, revelry and pleasure!" (My italics.) I have said that Kelly was a simpleton. The word I have italicised proves it. I did not see Venice until a century and a half after Kelly, but I assert that in Kelly's Venice *all* was not gaiety and mirth, etc.

Our roysterers only see what they wish to see; their pictures are child-ishly incomplete, and thereby are their reminiscences far less interesting than they might be. If Kelly had told us something about the existences of the shop-assistants who sold costumes till 4 a.m., and dishwashers who washed dishes till 6 a.m., if he had added a few trifles concerning water-supply, drainage, epidemics, and taxes, his book, like some other similar

* Defence of the Realm Act (August 1914), introduced to give wider restrictive powers to the war-time Government.

books, might have made an immortal document. But they won't do it; these darlings of self-indulgence, and they couldn't if they would. Well, perhaps it is asking too much of human nature that a Charles Booth cr a J.L. Hammond should inhabit the lively body of a globe-trotting opera-singer.

I have no room to discuss Kelly's memories of Vienna, Paris, and London. His book is profoundly moral — at the end. Dissipation is punished with due poetical justice, and, though the august patronage of George IV did much to soften the rigours of the hero's decline, it did not do enough. If I have not conveyed the impression that the reminiscences of Kelly make very savoury reading, this is a bad article.

24 July 1930

What Arnold Bennett Thinks of H.G.Wells

A new novel by H.G.Wells: *The Autocracy of Mr. Parham*, with illustrations by another genius not unknown to this paper, Low (Heinemann, 7s. 6d.)! H.G. has now published about sixty books, of which about forty are fiction, and of which one, *The Outline of History*, has probably had a wider and a more immediate educative influence on the public than any other work of the twentieth century in any language. These sixty books, I am told, are unequal; that is to say, some are better or worse than others. Strange! For is it not notorious that all the works of Shakespeare, of Hardy, of Dickens, of Thackerary, of Tennyson, of Kipling, of Meredith, are equally great? H.G. alone has been unequal.

And I am told, especially by the vanguard of the new generation, that H.G. is now a back number and "counts" no longer. In reply I wish to state (1) that I could do with a few more back numbers like H.G.; (2) that there is not an author alive, young or old, who could begin to write a novel with the scope and sweep of H.G.'s sociological novels, or with the tremendous verve and humour of his lighter novels, or with the imaginative invention of his "scientific romances," and (3) that no book of H.G.'s needs his name on the title-page, for his signature is written on every paragraph of every one of his books. (The same is true of Kipling.)

I know not whether H.G.'s books are immortal, nor whether the books of any living author are immortal. What I do know is that there is nobody like H.G. in variety and vivacity and plenteousness of gifts, and I don't care half a hoot whether all or any of his books are immortal or not, though I pleasantly entertain a sort of suspicion that some of them have in them the mysterious seed of longevity.

The attitude of certain persons and reviewers towards H.G. makes me laugh. I remember the year 1895, when *Select Conversations with an Uncle*, *The Stolen Bacillus*, *The Wonderful Visit* and *The Time Machine* all appeared in one dazzling constellation. Nothing like the last three had ever appeared before; and nothing like them not written by H.G. has ever appeared since, and let us in the sight of heaven make no mistake about it. No! And nothing like *The Undying Fire* and *The World of William Clissold*, perhaps my favourites in his catalogue, has appeared, or will appear, either.

H.G. is above all the novelist with a social and a sociological conscience. His supreme preoccupation has been and still is the imperfection of the world and of men, and their betterment. He is the apostle of justice and efficiency and right living. He has created quite half a dozen new and better worlds. His subject is worlds; not individuals, nor even nations, but worlds. His noble aim is the quickening of civilisation, the utter righteousness of worlds. Nothing less will satisfy him, and he can't sleep at nights for worrying about the best method of achieving his aim. And he has embodied his ideals and the search for them in a series of exciting and diverting and uplifting and absolutely serious fictions that can be read in the languages of the imperfect world now existing.

It may appear to you that I am getting a bit lyrical about the life-work of H.G.Wells. I am, and not for the first time. *The Autocracy of Mr. Parham* is a dream (or rather a nightmare) springing from a spiritualistic séance. ("But there was nothing in my nightmare that might not happen.") What happens in it is a *coup de'état* which puts Britain under the rule of a dictator, and a new world-war whose mere opening frightens the chief nations into an unacknowledged armistice. The book is an annihilating satire on dictatorships and a tremendous description of what "might happen," and what will happen if civilisation does not move along at a more rapid pace than now marks its progress. There is no love-interest in it worth mentioning. At the beginning there are individual interests, but soon these are lost in an all-embracing world-interest.

The book is lighted by all the chief facets of the H.G.Wells genius. Watch H.G. describe with wit a man's face: "One eye, because of that same accident, was of glass: it maintained an expression of implacable will, while its fellow, alert and bright brown, gathered information. His eyebrows were the fierce little brothers of his moustache." See him describe a political speech: "His discourse carried along platitudes as hosts carry time-honoured banners, and one familiar phrase followed another, like exiled leaders refreshed and renewed returning to their people."

Trollope would recount Cabinet-meetings. H.G. gives whole chapters to politics, and five and a half pages to an American Presidential Declaration; and these things can be read with gusto. And the same pen which sets them down can describe an unparalleled naval battle in the grand thrilling manner. And the same pen can wither up an ideal: "And then we will take Anarchy — which is Science the Destroyer — by the throat. . . . Essential to science is the repudiation of *all* foundations, her own included. She disdained philosophy. The past is a curiosity or waste paper. Anarchism! Nothing is, but everything is going to be. She redeems all her promises with fresh promissory notes."

Is this fresh? Is this illuminating? Is it disturbing?

And the same pen can put the unique, gleaming touch of symbolism into the immense disastrous explosion in the gas-factory: "The rotunda yawned open as though some mighty hand had wrenched it in two, and through the separating halves of the roof *appeared the warm glow of sunrise.*" Six words. But only H.G. could have written them.

There are defects of detail in this book. But they are H.G.'s defects.

A Famous Secret Police Service Loses Its Reputation

Ever since I was a boy the grandiose legend of the fiendish, impassive craft and general efficiency of the Tsarist Secret Police has romantically inhabited my mind. I could learn little that was authentic about this alleged-to-be marvellous organisation. Of course, innumerable books have dealt with it, but for obvious reasons they showed a certain anti-police bias! For reasons equally obvious the Force itself behaved like Brer Rabbit and said nothing, its ideal being grim silence.

More serious, the great Russian novelists took care not to bring the Force into their novels, for to do so would have meant suppression of their books and perhaps bodily exportation to Siberia. Hence even the finest Russian novels present somewhat incomplete pictures of the Russian social organism! What we do learn from the novels is that nearly every male character in them above the peasant and small tradesman class either was or had been in the Government service — usually in conditions that gave him plenty of leisure for pleasurable relaxations. Which left us with the impression that the whole of "intelligent" Russia was kept busy, at liberal salaries, in the vast executive job of governing the Empire!

Thus, despite various "revelations," we have had to imagine for ourselves what the Russian Secret Police was. I must say that when I visited the notorious fortress of SS. Peter and Paul at Leningrad last year I arrived at the conclusion that my imagined picture of the Russian Secret Police must be substantially correct. I now know that it wasn't. For I have read *The Ochrana*, being the memoirs of A.T. Vassilyev, once Chief of the Tsarist Police of all Russia (Harrap, 15s.), who escaped from the Bolshevists, became a railway porter, and died in complete penury. This book is an eye-opener. My imagined picture was all wrong, and I ought to have known that it was all wrong.

Before going further I should mention that *The Ochrana* has a very good introduction by Fülöp-Miller, author of *The Mind and Face of Bolshevism*. Fülöp-Miller insists on two points. First, the Russians have never, even to the present day, had any clear conception of the ideal either of a constitutional State or of individual legal rights. Bolshevism, the Russian adventure in Socialism, is based, exactly like Tsarism, on compulsion and the ruthless oppression of the individual. In which respect it shows no advance on the old régime. Secondly, that Russians are racially very cruel, in a mediaeval and indeed quite primitive way.

Fülöp-Miller gives the most ghastly examples of this Muscovite characteristic. He describes, briefly and horribly, the Museum of the Revolution in Moscow, full of refined instruments of torture, including lashes studded with screws, and of other devices which I should hesitate to mention here. These sinister ingenuities were in common use as late as 1906. But, he cynically adds, if Soviet rule were to be replaced by another system, the leaders of the new counter-revolution would "have no difficulty in bringing together a Museum of the Past with another Chamber of Horrors, the contemplation of which will leave the visitor equally convinced that the fall of the Communist dictatorship had been a necessity, if civilisation were to stand."

The interest of Vassilyev's book, however, is psychological, not physical. The great enigmatic chief seems to have been an honest official, without a glimmer of a gleam of a suspicion that all the activities of his Force were bound to fail, and that he and his merry men were engaged all day and every day in operations as silly as that of trying to cure small-pox by means of a skin-lotion. (The medical profession had, and has, no monopoly in the ancient art of confusing symptoms with causes.) And to this day the pathetic, tragic belief that violence can be exterminated by violence still survives intact in Russia.

In other respects Vassilyev apparently had few illusions. He certainly had no illusions as to the truly remarkable stupidity of his agents. One would have thought that these agents were chosen for their knowledge of and insight into human nature. Not a bit of it. They were simpletons compared to whom a Western boy of ten would count as a Machiavelli or a Francis Bacon. Their ingenuousness was hardly credible. And here for years and years I had been thinking of them as miracles of guile and deep cunning!

Who would credit that, having bribed an Anarchist to betray his comrades, they would believe him, trust him, and assume that he had told them all he knew? The tales of the simplicity of the Ochrana are merely fantastic. There was the case of the agent (a colonel!) who deliberately shared a flat with a renegade, and left the furnishing of the sweet home to his companion. The renegade stuffed the hollow leg of a table with dynamite and connected the ignition thereof with a switch at the street door. He then said to the confiding colonel, "Excuse me a moment," ran downstairs, pressed the button and blew the colonel to fragments. But the renegade also was an idiot. Not having allowed for the constabulary of the street, he was caught instantly, and executed. If you have the Russian sense of humour this story will make you laugh. The story of the murder of Stolypin in a theatre at Kiev in the presence of the Tsar is hardly less side-splitting!

Vassilyev makes a gallant attempt to prove that he did not encourage *agents provocateurs,* yet all the while he proves that an Ochrana policeman could not avoid being an *agent provocateur.* The lengthy account of Rasputin most convincingly puts the lecherous monk in a new light. It is the only satisfactory account of Rasputin that I can recall. Some of the illustrations of the book are revealing. Study with a magnifying glass the group-photograph of the chief officials of the St. Petersburg Ochrana, and you will understand the Ochrana mentality better than you did before. Then look at the photograph of the body of Plehve, Minister of the Interior, shattered by a bomb, and you will have a wholesome attack of the horrors.

The Ochrana has one defect: it is the work of a man whose natural freedom of style had been seriously cramped by many years spent in writing official minutes. Vassilyev had material in the highest degree picturesque, but he had grown to be incapable of writing picturesquely. Withal his book has first-rate interest.

Forgotten "Best Seller" With a 2,000,000 Circulation

Some little time ago Mrs. Amy Cruse published a book showing the reactions of English persons to books, and the consequent fashions in reading, from the earliest reading times to the end of the eighteenth century: *The Shaping of English Literature*. This book was good. She has now published a sequel to it: *The Englishman and his Books in the Early Nineteenth Century* (Harrap, 7s. 6d.). This book is better. Also, it is cheap. Mrs. Cruse writes well; she has knowledge, and carries it lightly. And she has a sense of humour which finds limitless scope in her subject. Many of her "revelations" are quite startling. And everyone who is interested in the evolution of reading, apart from reading itself, will enjoy the volume, not mildly, but with gusto.

Mrs. Cruse begins with the printed list of eleven hundred subscribers to Fanny Burney's *Camilla,* which list she dissects minutely. Here indeed, as in the other chapters, she descends to detail — more correctly, she ascends to detail. *Camilla* was in five volumes, price one guinea, perhaps the equivalent of three guineas to-day. Some subscribers took ten copies. Human nature does change after all. Fanny's human nature took her to Windsor Castle, bearing two presentation copies of *Camilla,* one for the Queen, the other for the King. The Queen was in her parlour, and gave her a "compliment" of fifty guineas. The King was summoned to the parlour, and gave her another "compliment" of fifty guineas. Such an event could not happen today. But if their Majesties had given Fanny five thousand instead of fifty guineas apiece, the compliment would hardly have repaid Fanny for the terrible years of bondage which, to the loss of English literature, she spent as a court official.

The most tragic chapter in the book is "The Schoolroom," which must be read to be believed, and even then . . . . A learned man told me, a few weeks ago, that the favourite oath of William the Conqueror was, "By the Splendour of God!" Only my strong instinct not to be imitative prevents me from using that magnificent oath upon the sufferings and servitudes of not-"out" girls in the Waterloo period. Still, they did naughtily subscribe to lending libraries and they did read the multitudinous shockers of the time in bed after their maids had retired for the night. As for their serious reading, some of the "questions set" in them were without price. Thus: "What is the difference of latitude between the places where Burns was born and Lazarus raised from the dead?" Even the examiners of London University in the 1880's never surpassed the dreadful and asinine stupidity of that question.

Two things have struck me in reading Mrs. Cruse. First. We simply don't know what popularity is in these latter days. Has anybody ever heard of the Rev. Legh Richmond's *The Dairyman's Daughter*? I hadn't. The story of an "unnaturally pious girl," it had a circulation of two million copies. And let us remember that the reading public then was perhaps about one-sixth of what it is to-day! Second. The really popular authors kept on writing the same book, and they nearly all wrote the same book. Which demonstrates that, however changeable human nature at large may be, the leading characteristic of *writing* human nature is the same now as it was then. I have not even indicated the contents of *The Englishman and his Books*, much less discussed them all. Every chapter is extremely succulent.

We know what we think of the ruck of novels of those days. It would be instructive to know what the admirers of Mrs. Radcliffe and the Minerva Library would have thought of the novels of these our days, could they have read them. Creative power has of course not increased; but technical skill and the field of vision have both increased. And just as there are sounds and odours which certain animals can detect and we can't, so there are certain sensations clearly enough observed and described by modern novelists which apparently eluded the notice of the novelists of a century ago.

I have recently read a very modern novel, *The Great Meadow*, by Elizabeth Madox Roberts (Cape, 7s. 6d.). Miss Roberts is a young American novelist, "discovered" by one of the surest and keenest critics of the present age, Edward Garnett. Those who encountered it will remember Miss Roberts's *The Time of Man*. To the new book Mr. Garnett writes a preface, which in my opinion is a trifle too enthusiastic. *The Great Meadow* has dull passages here and there. And it suffers, too, from the gradual absorption of individual interest into a general interest. Further, the closing, highly important passages, appear to me to move too rapidly in comparison with the leisurely opening chapters.

Nevertheless, what a novel! How original in feeling! How dignified and decorous in its extreme modernness! How charged with subtle emotion! How admirably written! It is a post-war product, and could not have been accomplished by anybody before 1914. The time is the second half of the eighteenth century. I imagine that the public which Mrs. Amy Cruse deals with would have been bewildered by it, and wondered whether the author was mad, or they themselves.

The story is that of the great trek of a young married pair from Virginia into what is now Kentucky. No railways. No hotels. No roads. No nothing, except love and endurance and natural wit. The 500-mile journey is rendered with consistent power and modest brilliance. Then the perils and scalpings of Indian warfare. The mere plot is a very old one — return of missing husband to a wife who believing him to be dead has married another man — but I should say that it has never before been treated as Miss Roberts treats it. To the discerning I can recommend this novel.

And I have read another very modern fiction: E.V. Lucas's *Down the Sky* (Methuens, 7s. 6d.). Mr. Lucas calls it an "entertainment." He is entitled to do so, for it is one. I call it a novel. It is modern by virtue of its technique and its range; not by virtue of its attitude towards human phenomena. It has more, and more diverting, common sense to the page than 99 per cent. of novels. As the book has already been reviewed in this paper I will say no more about it, though I could say a lot more.

Withal, the un-modern novel vigorously persists. The latest specimen of it to reach me is one of the fashionable French novels of the year, *David Golder*, by Irène Némirovsky (Grasset, 15 francs). Study of the international new very-rich: scenes, Paris, Biarritz, Soviet Russia. Exceedingly dramatic. Exceedingly well done. It held me throughout. With the softening of the crudity of a few episodes, it ought to have some success in English. But if there is a single original notation in the whole book, I missed it.

14 August 1930

A Country of Glorious Talkers and Writers

Ireland is a country of contrasts: this must be true, since every country is a country of contrasts. But Ireland, surely, in a special degree. I know almost nothing of Ireland. I have been there only twice. Still, I would sooner judge by the little I actually see and hear than by the much that I read and hear *of*. My first visit, in 1916, was semi-official, journalistic. I shall never forget the contrast between the magnificence of the domestic architecture of Dublin and the squalor of the poor people who inhabited it. But the chief of the impressions was the hospitality. What dinners! What lunches!

I remember one Sunday lunch which began shortly before two o'clock and had not quite finished at seven o'clock. The brilliance of the talking. Everyone (except myself) could talk brilliantly, and did. French talking was outclassed, in wit, humour, invention, and inexhaustibility. And the talking was also realistic — cruel, delicately malicious; and what would life's banquet be without the cruet of malice? I went to bed dazed. I thought: "These fellows by their intelligence ought to be ruling the world."

Yet the next morning I could recall hardly a single thing that had been said, not an idea, not a generalisation. The attempt to take hold of the import of that symposium was like trying to tie up a cloud in a parcel. Gradually, as the intoxication passed, I began to perceive what the talking had lacked: direction and common sense.

Of course I was interested chiefly in literature. And what puzzled me was the earnest effort, then just begun, and still being continued, to re-establish the old Irish language as a living tongue. Its futile wrongheadedness, its childish flouting of the lesson of history, positively shocked me. How could these intelligent Irish start such a scheme, or allow it to be started? Why had not public opinion killed it dead by laughter on the day of its inception? Could a country which permitted such a tragi-farce to be enacted have any genuine understanding of what literature is? Could literary genius spring from such a soil?

Well, it could. We relatively taciturn Anglo-Saxons are apt to ignore the fact that modern imaginative English literature is dominated by three Irishmen, all of whom, by the way, have in their time been wild and glorious talkers. W.B. Yeats is the greatest living poet. Shaw is the greatest literary world-force (with the possible exception of Wells). George Moore is — in my opinion — the greatest living novelist; many would deny this, but few would deny that he is one of the greatest. I might mention Synge, author of the greatest modern play, *The Playboy of The Western World*; but Synge is dead, and of late years the spirit of his masterpiece has been assassinated in performance, and he is being temporarily forgotten. Withal the sole vital renascence of the English drama in the present century has been purely Irish! One could name about five plays by Irishmen with which no play by a living Englishman can advantageously compare. No

401

mean record for a small country, and a country whose brains have been mainly devoted to politics and backchat.

The occasion of the above reflections is a book which I have just read: *Edward Martyn and the Irish Revival* by Denis Gwynn (Cape, 12s. 6d.). If anybody says to me: "And who was Edward Martyn?" I shall retort: "If you had read George Moore's *Hail and Farewell*, you would know." You will do well to read those invaluable reminiscences, so diverting, so individual, so *rosse*. Edward Martyn, like Synge temporarily forgotten, was a rich man, an Irish landlord, a hater of women, a lover of Ibsen, a student, and an extremely strict Catholic. Although he was entitled as a serious scholar to read books which are on the Papal Index, he formally applied for permission to do so; whether he ever got the permission does not seem to be quite clear. "He runs after his soul," said George Moore, "like a dog after his tail, and lets it go when he catches it." He was actively interested in, and helpful to, several arts, and a creator in one — literature.

Forty years ago he published a long and elaborate satirical romance, inspired by Rabelais and Swift, and entitled *Morgante the Lesser*. I have not read it and never shall, but Mr. Denis Gwynn in his biography prints considerable extracts from it which make good reading, and I imagine that the book merits perusal. Martyn's fame, however, will rest on his activities in the new Irish theatre. He laboured very hard for it, he paid for it, and one may doubt if without him the revival would ever have taken place.

Yeats in his chronicles of the time has not been conspicuously generous to Edward Martyn. He wrote, of Martyn: "My *Countess Cathleen* and a play of his own were our first performances." *A play of his own!* The great poet's gift of subtle, belittling sarcasm was never better exemplified than in those five words. You would infer: a play not worthy of notice. Who could guess that the unnamed "play of his own" was the celebrated *Heather Field*, which had a far more striking success than "my *Countess Cathleen*." Nor apparently are Lady Gregory's chronicles much fairer. *The Heather Field*, written under the strong influence of Ibsen, is certainly a good play and deserved its triumph; but I will not prophesy as to its longevity.

Martyn wrote another play, *Maeve*, which some assert is better than *The Heather Field*. I have not read it. These plays were offered to West End managers, including George Alexander, who lost not a moment in declining them. It would not be easy to conceive a spectacle more comically incredible than that of George Alexander producing *The Heather Field*.

In undue course Martyn withdrew from the Irish theatre enterprise. Which was a pity. He did not see eye to eye with Yeats. In particular he did not see that a play had any special value because it happened to be about Irish peasants. He wanted plays with ideas in them.

Mr. Denis Gwynn's book is agreeably done, and it is not too long. The best chapters in it are those which deal with Martyn's life and industry and woman-avoiding in his rather portentous Galway home, and with the establishment of what is now known as the Abbey Theatre. Martyn died only six years ago. He gave instructions that his body should be abandoned to medical students for dissection; it was afterwards taken to the cemetery in the workhouse van, and, to the music of Palestrina, was put into a common grave with the bodies of six paupers. Not on the whole a very gay book!

21 August 1930

It's the Mediocre Writers Who Make Money

Of all critics, literary critics are the most martyrised, except perhaps critics of the drama (which after all is a branch of literature). The musical critic attends a concert, or, oftener, part of a concert. He has to deal with more familiar music than unfamiliar, and with more good music than bad. At the longest his ordeal lasts an hour and a half. An art critic can glance at a picture and in nearly all cases can decide in a moment whether according to his standards it is good or bad. The critic of tea, called in the City a tea-taster — an expert the delicacy of whose palate is worthy of his princely remuneration — never swallows what he tastes.

Whereas the literary critic, especially if he is in large practice, lives a continuous martyrdom. He has to deal with vastly more new books than old, and with vastly more mediocre or bad books than good. It takes much longer to read a book than to listen to a symphony. In rare instances the critic can decide from a single paragraph that a book is bad, for the reason that no author of the bad paragraph could be capable of writing a good book. But if the critic has to give an account of the book he must read it all the same. And he is bound to swallow what he tastes. Willy-nilly it gets into his system, producing effects sinister and unavoidable. In this respect the literary critic is in the same box as the old lead-workers in earthenware manufactories. Critics have been known to contract mortal "occupational diseases" of the mind from a steady diet of bad books. All literary critics will agree with me as to the dangers of the craft.

Not that I am inveighing against mediocre books. They are a necessity of human nature. Mediocre means middling. Whatever else they may be, the majority of people in every section of life are and must be middling. The majority of authors are and must be middling. And it is well that they should be so. Middling people best appreciate middling books. And why not? Every man is entitled to gratify his personal taste. No sin is there. The man who likes an under-cooked book is no more a criminal than the man who likes over-cooked meat (as most British citizens do).

It is socially right that mediocre authors should prosper, and they do prosper. Indeed they flourish more luxuriantly than really good authors. The biggest circulations are not those which achieve even notoriety, to say nothing of renown. They are the quiet circulations of harmless, necessary mediocrity. When Sinclair Lewis is exalted he asserts that his books have the biggest circulations in America next to the Bible. But I doubt the statement. I imagine that the circulations of the books of that stupendous mediocrity Harold Bell Wright surpass those of the creator of *Babbitt*. I could give similar comparisons for Britain. But discretion and decency forbid. Britain is not three thousand miles off. I sometimes wish it was. I am often reproached for the vivacity of my remarks on books and persons. But in reality I restrain myself with extraordinary force. If Britain were three thousand miles off I believe my vivacity would rival that of H.L. Mencken and G.J. Nathan, for whom Britain *is* three thousand miles off.

Now the chief business and pleasure of the literary critic should be to uphold the highest standards of literature. In other words, he should be

403

the foe of mediocrity. There are a hundred reasons why he should treat honest mediocrity with the respect which it assuredly deserves; but one can fight a foe while respecting him, and the critic who wishes to find himself on the safe side on the Day of Judgment should fight the foe all the time. Does he?

The majority do not. They yield insensibly to the terrible, the insinuating, the enervating, the septic influences of the "pabulum" which they are daily compelled to swallow for a livelihood. They make more and more compromises, until they compromise themselves so far that in the end they actually prefer mediocrity to original excellence. They eat and drink mediocrity until they become mediocrity, with all mediocrity's detestation of original excellence. Thus mediocrity triumphs over them, and they cease bravely to bite the hand that feeds them. Ah! The sweet but cankerous ease of compromise! Herein is the reason why the bulk of book-reviewing is too benevolent. And, you know, almost all reviews really are too benevolent.

The small minority of critics who escape the dread infection of mediocrity have one great quality in common. They possess powerful individualities. Just as physically vigorous men throw off diseases of the body, so do these few critics resist the onset of moral contagion. It is essential that first-rate literary critics should have an enthusiasm for literature, and all critics over a certain age are in fact enthusiastic, for if they are not they abandon reviewing after a few years and go in for coal-mining or bus-driving or some such relatively lighter occupation. It is advisible that they should have knowledge, for knowledge fortifies. It is advisible that they should have taste, for taste guides. But above all, before all, they must have powerful individualities. It is not what a man knows that counts in literary criticism; not what he prefers; but what he *is*.

There are monstrously learned critics who are nincompoops. They lack individuality. There are refined critics who would run away from a rabbit. They lack individuality. Individuality comes first. Good taste is better than bad taste, but bad taste is better than no taste, and men without individuality have no taste — at any rate no taste that they can impose on their publics.

All the great critics have had great individualities. None has had perfect taste. Every one of them has committed outrageous errors of judgment, due either to the most deplorable ignorance or the most rampant prejudice. But they have had something to express: namely, themselves. Hence they have always been interesting and provocative of thought. Literary criticism is not merely a report on a book; it is a report of the reaction of an individuality *to* a book. Cushions, putty, mashed potatoes do not react.

I am well aware that I have been exaggerating and over-simplifying, but in order to put a truth across the footlights it is convenient, even necessary, to do this. And the reader knows what I mean.

28 August 1930

What I Call An Adventure

Adventures are to the adventurous (wrote Disraeli, who was an expert on

404

the subject). These things happened to me. I was in a small and modest English seaside resort, about as far from London as any English seaside could be. The most exciting thing in such a place is not the sea; it is the market-day interiors of the fashionable shops, where you can watch the ladies changing their minds ten times a minute about what they really wish to buy. Having surfeited myself with this spectacle, I went into a bookshop. You might walk many miles in London without seeing a bookshop to walk into, but the town possessed two. The shop I chose had outside the usual case of entirely negligible books, all one price — a shilling. For myself, I should have asked to be handsomely paid for taking any of them away.

I said to the bookseller: "I want an old Bible." (I did.) He said with pride: "I have a 'Breeches' Bible." I said: "No, thanks." It is very strange to me that there still exists among bookish people a demand for copies of the "Breeches" Bible. It is an ugly tome, difficult to decipher, usually in bad condition, and its special interest is confined to one word.

The bookseller had no other old Bibles, but he had stacks of new ones, and in default of the old I bought the least obnoxious new. (I know of only two modern Bibles which are not obnoxious to a person of taste in the craft of bookmaking: The *Tudor Translations* Bible, not meant for practical reading, and Macmillan's *Eversley* Bible in eight handy volumes.) The specimen I obtained (10s. 6d. marked down from 15s.) displayed the customary Biblical horrors: rounded corners; edges neither red nor gilt, but revoltingly both; bad lettering on the secure but deplorable binding; and semi-transparent paper. The page, however, was fairly well designed.

Something in the tenor of my remarks affected the bookseller's nose, which scented a bookman. He began to talk of interesting bargains upstairs, and offered me a superlative copy of a famous illustrated work. The price was a mere £150 — a sum probably equivalent to about a penny in the pound on the town's rates. (Nevertheless he was evidently a prosperous bookseller.) I searched everywhere for any book that I was prepared to pay money for. In vain. And yet, how could I leave the shop without demonstrating to his eager amiability that I was indeed a bookman.

At last I lit on a first edition of a novel of Anthony Trollope's that I had never seen and had only heard of through the report of Hugh Walpole: *He Knew He Was Right*, illustrated by the world's worst illustrator, Marcus Stone. I bought it for the wild unconscious humour of the captions under the drawings, and left the shop with forty shillings and sixpence less in my pocket, and three books under my arm. There is a doubtful chance that one day I may even read *He Knew He Was Right*. On the shop steps I was affronted by the awful tidings that though England had won the toss she had lost the Test. All which is what I call an adventure. Not wholly unmerited by my adventurousness.

And when I regained my transient summer home on the hill overlooking seven seas, I had a further reward. The postman had taken advantage of my absence to bestow upon me two books in separate packages from two different benefactors. New books follow me about, as young animals run after the magic attraction of a born animal trainer. I esteem them but lightly, for the majority of them prove to be miserable mongrels capable of arousing no sentiment save that of compassion. But by some caprice of destiny both the books turned out to be thoroughbreds.

The first was a volume of short stories by a Russian writer new to the English language — Romanof or Romanoff (one "f" on the title-page, two on the cover!), with an introduction by Stephen Graham: *Without Cherry Blossom* (Benn, 7s. 6d.). Most introductions are written on a note of ill-advised profuse-at-any-cost laudation which develops in me a mood the very opposite of what is desired. But Mr. Graham's introduction struck me as a model of impartial sobriety. Romanof is a peasant with a Tsar's name. He writes simply, without flightiness or modernness or any shock tactics. His manner is thoroughly old-fashioned. Those who "hate Russian fiction" may read Romanof with pleasure. His characters, of course, have Russian characteristics, but Romanof has not. The characters are, in fact, the new Russian intelligentsia — Dostoevsky would hardly have recognised them.

The general theme of the stories is love. Or rather, not love, but the physical commotion which under the Soviet régime has taken the place of love. Romanof gives a series of intimate pictures of Soviet life, untidy, dirty, disordered, squalid, and self-consciously fleshly-sad pictures, but painted without offence, and quite beautifully done. They are certain to interest everybody who is curious about domestic conditions in Russian cities to-day. The book convinces, and is well worth attention. Translation, middling.

The second book (or booklet) is by André Maurois: *Chelsea Way* (Elkin Mathews), a deliberate imitation of Marcel Proust. It is exceedingly brilliant and exceedingly funny, and just the right length for a skit. The author calls it a pastiche, but I should prefer to call it a skit. All the Proustian foibles and eccentricities are humorously rendered, together with a lot of his genuine analytic quality. The narrator, with a female companion, pays a visit to London, and enters the highest circles of smart-artistic society in this isle. M. Maurois ticks off, though admiringly, the national characteristics of all of us — from the Pullman agent on the boat, via a priceless lady's-maid, to the rich lord whose brother is a famous novelist. The novelist's luncheon-party, in Chelsea, is lifelike as well as side-splitting. Ditto the country-house tea-party. Read also the observations on the Turner pictures at the Tate. M. Maurois squanders his ironic wit like the millionaire he is. The translation, by Mr. Hamish Miles, is admirable. *Chelsea Way* will enchant a few, and particularly the recognisable individuals who are ticked off. It would delight many — I mean some thousands. The publishers have issued this great lark in a limited edition of 500 copies at 15s. It is now their duty to reissue it at a price suitable to the purses of those who, while gifted with a sharp sense of humour, cannot afford to pay at the rate of threepence a page for their laughter.

4 September 1930

Don't Grumble — Wait Your Chance

A few weeks ago I received a long letter from an author (personally unknown to me) conceived in the following terms: [In the last three years] "there have been published three English books of *original* style and subject-matter and you have not as much as mentioned one of them. I know because I wrote them. . . . I will make no bones about it: I am going to grumble at you. . . . As I grow older I am losing my sense of politeness. What matters it? You and I will presently be dead — and we shall be dead for millions of years. Why shouldn't I have my little grumble while there is yet time. My grumble with you is this: That instead of using so much space in noticing books which you condemn — the gibberish of Joyce's *Work in Progress* for example — the Russians and the Frenchmen, you might very well use such space . . . to bring to the notice of a reluctant public English books that really matter. *Mine for example*." (His italics.)

My correspondent goes on to assert that in one of his books a certain kind of life is "portrayed better than it has ever been done before"; and that in another he has written the first novel of its kind ever done, and that in a third, etc., etc.

While I do not accept his statement that we shall be dead for millions of years (for on this point I doubt whether his information is trustworthy), I am quite ready to accept his other statements. His books may be all that he claims for them. They have been praised by high authorities. I like an author to believe in himself. I sympathise with his resentment against the heedlessness of literary critics, including myself. I shall keep an eye open for his next masterpiece.

But I emphatically object to his objecting to the attention which occasionally I give to foreign books. (I do not habitually condemn foreign books. Quite the contrary.) If there were no public demand for news of foreign books, I would not write about them. My first aim is always to interest the public. But there is such a demand. Although many of my correspondents (chiefly exasperated authors) show impatience at my notices of foreign books, a far larger number of correspondents complain that I do not give sufficient space to foreign books. (I estimate that year in year out ninety-five per cent. of my space is given to English literature.)

And why should I entirely ignore foreign literature? The principal newspapers maintain a regular and costly service of news of foreign politics, economics, crimes, sport, music, art, disasters and frocks. Why should foreign literature alone be banned? What is sauce for the gander is sauce for the goose. Should we be content if foreign newspapers kept silence about English books? We should not. We should be rather cross. Has foreign literature been of no benefit to us? Should we not be poorer if critics, confining themselves exclusively to the discussion of English authors, had not told us about Dante, Goethe, Rabelais, Cervantes, Montaigne, Dumas, Stendhal, Flaubert, d'Annunzio, Hauptmann, Ibsen, Tolstoy, Dostoevsky, Chekhov, Thomas Mann, Knut Hamsun, and so on and so on?

The fact is that only those who know something of foreign literature can fully appreciate English literature; just as only those who have travelled abroad can fully appreciate the virtues of even an English railway-porter. If foreign literature had been banned in this island, English literature would be a very different and a very inferior thing from what it actually is. And if foreign literature is not to be banned it must be discussed publicly, space must be allotted to it in newspapers. The space thus allotted to it is necessarily withheld from English authors, and therefore English authors must suffer. (Similarly, ordinary English news suffers in order that foreign news may get a show.) The only question is: Does the public gain on balance? The clear answer to the question is, Yes.

Further, no individual critic can be expected to single out all really promising books and praise them. To do so the critic would have to examine carefully scores of volumes every week: a task beyond human endeavour even if the devoted fellow read all day and wrote all night. Even if forty critics were banded together and organised to perform the task they would assuredly fail in it.

I believe that the discovery of original excellence in a new or a comparatively new author is largely a matter of chance. And the appointed rôle of the new author is to grin and bear it — and wait philosophically for the arrival of the chance. In 999 cases out of 1000 the chance does arrive. Moreover, the new author is no worse off than the new painter, the new composer, the new architect, the new financier, the new manufacturer. In all biographies of those who have succeeded occurs the phrase: "His chance came." It may come soon; it may come late; but it comes. Nothing but incurable disease or untimely death can prevent the fruition and the appreciation of a genuine talent. Waiting for the chance is a very desolating business. I say this with the more sincerity in that I know something myself about waiting. Indeed in my private, conceited soul I reckon that I am still waiting. The philosophic author will wait with dignity, and work with incorrigible confident persistence.

A final point. It is in the nature of things that, other factors being equal, the author of false talent usually gets his chance earlier than the author of genuine talent. This has always been so and always will be. Why then complain? Why tear your hair and waste in anger energy which should be employed in creation? The meretricious author is as a rule a good starter and a bad stayer. Genuine talent is a bad starter and a good stayer. Only the few can have it both ways. Which way do you prefer to have it? I have asked several questions in this article. But the last is the most important.

11 September 1930

Many Women Know a Lot Too Much About the Technique of Words

I have received a challenging question from a distinguished medicine-man. The communication to me ran thus: "Dr. —— wants to know how it is that all the great war-books are written by amateurs, and not by professionals. Further, he asserts, most good books are written by amateurs. And he notices a tendency among professional authors to criticise the medical profession."

Short, with sharp points! The last point is quite unrelated to the other two. Nevertheless, though mine is not a medical column, I will press the point to my bosom, like Saint Sebastian. I do criticise the medical profession. There are many first-rate doctors in Britain, but I do not think that the average British doctor is as good as, for instance, the average French or German doctor. My criticism of the average British doctor is that, compared with Continentals, he is entirely too casual in his diagnoses, and his enquiries are very incomplete and cursory. And speaking of amateurs, I have known amateurs succeed in curing diseases which whole strings of professional doctors have failed to cure. So much for that.

To return to literature (which I admit is less interesting than curative medicine). The first thing is to define the difference between amateur and professional. If by the word "professional" my complainant means one who devotes his entire working life to writing, then I will not argue the question. My complainant can take the verdict. Such a definition would exclude authors like Wordsworth, Charles Lamb, Anthony Trollope and A.B. Walkley, every one of whom I should class as a professional author in the strictest sense, though each had a regular job which occupied at least as much of his time as the writing job.

For myself, I should define the amateur writer as one who writes spasmodically, when he has nothing better to do, who regards writing as merely "fun," who does not bother about technique, and who would not look upon the total abolition of printing as a disaster fatally affecting his whole life. I should define a professional writer as one who took writing seriously, who wrote as continually as circumstances allowed, who conscientiously tried to perfect his craftsmanship, and who had convinced himself that he simply must write, live stultified, or expire. To my mind the status of his professionalism would not be impaired by the fact that he was a part-time and not a whole-time author.

Assuming the justness of my definitions of the amateur and the professional author, I should wish to know the titles of our "great war-books" which have been written by amateurs. There are very few great war-books in English or in any other language. Indeed, I know of only one in English: the anonymous *Her Privates We*, whose author is Frederic Manning, with a literary career behind him of over 20 years. A really fine, if not a great, war-book is *Undertones of War*, by Edmund Blunden, who was professionally writing before the war. Both these men are very highly accomplished technicians, and what they don't know about the handling of words is negligible. Further, I should wish to know of even one fine English war-book written by an amateur without the help or revision of a professional. As for the foreign war-books, I could ask for similar information concerning them. It is inconceivable that *Sergeant Grischa* or *All Quiet* was the unaided performance of an amateur. These books bear all the marks of professionalism, of writers who were born to write.

And taking the distinguished doctor's larger generalisation that "most good books are written by amateurs," were or are Dickens, George Eliot, Walter Scott, Landor, George Moore, Thomas Hardy, George Meredith, Joseph Conrad, Wells, Galsworthy, Trollope, Tennyson, Browning, Swinburne, Robert Bridges, Yeats, Shaw, amateur authors? Is P.G. Wodehouse an amateur author, or Sinclair Lewis or Theodore Dreiser, or Ernest Hemingway, or W.W. Jacobs?

Possibly an amateur here and there has by chance produced a fine book; it may happen to anybody who is literate, and inspired by a tremendous experience, to produce one fine book; but how many have produced three? The war provided a unique opportunity for amateurs to demonstrate what amateurs can do under emotional stress to beat the professional; for millions of men had tremendous experiences. What has been the amateur literary reaction to that opportunity? I should describe it as inconsiderable.

And yet the amateur in literature has an important advantage over the amateur in other arts. An amateur in architecture who without expert help designed a house and then had to live in it, would probably within six months be calling himself a fool, and his wife might be applying to him even worse terms of abuse. An amateur in painting would either be ignored by people of taste or advised to go and take lessons. Likewise with musical composition. And an amateur who struck up on the fiddle in a public hall would stand in danger of a violent death. But an amateur in literature may write a book and get it published and make quite a respectable show.

Why is this? The reason is that whereas no untutored person knows anything about the technique of architecture, painting or music, everybody knows something about the use of words. Words are the sole medium of thought and the chief medium of emotion, and we are all using words all the time. We all possess in some degree the technique, for we have spent years in the laborious business of acquiring it. (Many women know a lot too much about the technique of words.) Without a certain equipment of literary technique it would be practically impossible for any individual to live in a civilised society.

Thus there is a sense in which nobody is a rank amateur in literature. The most stupid and the most ignorant have in them a tinge of the professional. And thus it may and does occasionally occur that an individual with a natural bent for creative literary composition accomplishes a good book at the first attempt. If he thinks clearly and feels strongly and has read good models he has but to organise his powers and he will succeed. But without this natural bent he can hardly succeed. Having this natural bent he will continue, and his later works will by contrast expose the weakness of his first. You may say that the author of a good first book is an amateur. I prefer to say that he is a professional in the making, for from the beginning his attitude towards the art of literature is professional.

18 September 1930

Too Much Love!

"Why are all novels about love?" a rather pert and peppery correspondent asked me the other day. "Is there nothing else for novelists to write about but this everlasting sex business?" The question has been put before. The replies vary with the decade or the century. As the subject-matter of fiction has of late been discussed by literary mandarins in the American press, I will take the opportunity to answer the question again.

To begin with, all novels are not about love. Many detective novels, for instance, ignore love. Nevertheless, nearly all novels are about love. And the reason is obvious. People — and even novelists are "people" — seem to be more interested in the relations of the sexes than in any other topic. Life without love might be calm, but it would be more dull than calm. Love leads to a fair amount of suicides. The total absence of love would probably lead to more.

In the race of human interests for popularity love is an easy first, for nature has made it fundamental. And this will always be so — as long as the earth continues to revolve at anything like its present rate of speed, and the sun to shine with anything like its present power. One day warmth will be the chief human interest. But that day is distant, and until it arrives novelists, who deal with life, will quite sensibly and inevitably keep love prominent in the foreground of their pictures of the activities of mankind.

Withal there are plenty of other things for novelists to write about — and novelists for the most part neglect to write about them. Which is very wrong of them. If novels show a certain monotony, and if captious readers of the school of Solomon cry out: "Stay me with flagons, comfort me with apples, for I am sick of love," and assert that the novel as a form of literary art is dead — the fault is the novelists' own. The tendency of the average novelist is to assume that kissing and quarrels are the whole of life. Whereas they just aren't, not by a long way. Everybody knows this, except apparently the average novelist. Love has always an enormous background, which background is too often ignored in fiction.

The novel needs a renascence, and my opinion is that such renascence will be brought about by creative work on the backgrounds of love. The author who recreates the novel will be he who, while maintaining the interest and importance of the characters in the foreground, gives exactly the right, realistic amount of interest and importance to the background. The interest of the foreground must be individual interest (largely springing from love); the interest of the background must be a general interest (which cannot be a love-interest).

Examples exist of novels in which the relative importance of fore-ground and background has been accurately and admirably displayed. Zola wrote several such novels. So did Balzac. Balzac wrote an enthralling novel of which the background is the French law of bankruptcy (but he alone could accomplish such a feat). In our day Wells has attached if anything slightly too much importance to backgrounds. So has Fowler Wright, whose canvases of world-disaster have been insufficiently appreciated in Britain. Moreover, world-backgrounds are dangerous matters, at once too easy and too difficult to depict. I see more hope for the future of the novel in group-backgrounds. The majority of novelists have been sadly blind to the dramatic interest of group-backgrounds, thereby depriving themselves of the use of the most effective antidote to that accursed, disgustful monotony of love of which so many critics now complain.

What about the management and corporate life of a trade union for a background? It is full of actuality and of drama, and the common reader knows almost nothing of its secrets and the motives which move it. Let me note in passing that one duty of the novelist is to enlighten the large public as to social facts. If he does not do this, it will not be done. The novelists may object that they are unfamiliar with working class existence. True. Not one novel in a hundred shows the slightest comprehension of any existence save that of the library-subscribing classes. The clear answer to the objection is that the business of novelists is to alter this deplorable state of things.

But I will point out that the most powerful and reactionary unions, the most ripe for reform, and therefore the most interesting to the creative writer and his readers, are the professional unions, such as the trades unions

411

of doctors and of lawyers. Why not a novel whose hero is a fighting member of the British Medical Council and whose heroine is a woman doctor? The action might comprise the main opposing forces now at work in the evolution of the profession and give a thrilling conspectus of the profession regarded as a whole. So far as I am aware such novels have yet to be attempted. They would be quite as interesting as novels about financial magnates or artists or adventurers.

And why not a novel about the House of Commons, the chief characters being M.P.s, male and female, and the background the living entity of the House itself? A House of Commons novel, if it was outspoken and fairly good, would healthily excite the passions of the reading public and cause quite an uproar in the world.

To my mind, however, the background of backgrounds is the Church — or the churches. There have been innumerable novels about religion, but how many about the organisms of the churches? Trollope toyed with the vast subject, as in *The Warden*; but he never seriously took hold of it and measured his tremendous talents against it. The churches are in an extremely dramatic condition of flux; everybody is either for or against them; nobody can be indifferent to them; their activities are crowded with fine plots for novels, plots in which love does and must play no mean part. Of course, the author of any realistic novel dealing on a large scale with organised religious life would beyond doubt get himself into dreadful trouble, but he would also have his great moral reward. Those who were not against him would be intensely for him. And he would have done something more than tell a good story — provided that he *did* tell a good story.

I might continue the catalogue of backgrounds for the novels of the future. But I think that I have said enough to indicate that the most splendid materials for fiction are lying around in heaps, in mounds, in mountains — untouched, hardly perceived. The lesson, for novelists, is plain.

25 September 1930

"Crime" Novels Fail To Thrill

On my return from a short holiday in the "dead" season of publishing, I found eight feet linear of new upright books awaiting my surgical attentions. And although most of them were in a sense review copies, they did not reach me through the *Evening Standard* literary department, but direct from publishers or authors. Did this formidable row of volumes intimidate me? Not at all. By ceaseless industry I might adequately review them in three months or so; but I take a sinister joy in looking facts in the face, and I instantly decided that the only practical course for me was to ignore them, drastically clean the slate, and make a new start in life. After all, I had not asked for the books; they came quite unsolicited.

I was, however, compelled by a strong natural inclination to except two authors from my unscrupulous decision. Namely, Mr. Freeman Wills Crofts — and Hazlitt. And, strangely, these two authors quickly connected themselves together in what remained of my mind after a holiday. Without formally reviewing either of them, I must show the connection between them.

Mr. Croft's new mystery novel is *Sir John Magill's Last Journey* (Collins, 7s. 6d.). Now Mr. Crofts has a very considerable reputation in detective fiction, and, I think, justifiably. By the more serious experts he is regarded as the chief of his exciting tribe. On the wireless, a perhaps high-brow critic of undeniable taste, erudition and prestige has recommended the new book in terms extremely warm.

Mr. Crofts established his name years ago with *The Cask*. I well remember *The Cask*. It is an example of good, very elaborate construction, of logic, and of honest methods, far surpassing about ninety-nine per cent. of detective novels. Impossible not to respect it, and him. And I can conceive that *Sir John Magill's Last Journey* is even better than *The Cask*.

Nevertheless I feel about *The Last Journey* as I felt about *The Cask*. It lacks liveliness. Mr. Crofts is terribly slow off the mark. He seems to disdain the common business of interesting his reader page by page. In other words, page by page, he is arid. No wit. No humour. No vivacity. He says, as it were: "You must take me as I am, and in the lump. I am a serious narrative detective, and nothing matters to me, and nothing ought to matter to you, but the deliberate, sure, logical, highly complicated unravelling of a mystery. When you have got to the end you will appreciate what an artistic whole my story is."

Quite. I admit it. But I maintain that the cost of getting to the end is somewhat excessive. I maintain that the first 86 pages of the book may fairly be described as dull. True, the reader has his rich reward on page 286 or thereabouts; but my contention is that he ought to have his reward by instalments, on every page. Mr. Crofts will not, or cannot, divert his reader. He refuses all compromises with the poor man. He does not even care twopence about his mere writing, which, if not repellent, is certainly not attractive. He will calmly and negligently commit incredible sins of composition. Hardly could I believe my eyes when I saw Mr. Crofts describing a meal as "fortifying the inner man"! Does not Mr. Crofts know better than this, or doesn't he care? If he doesn't know he ought to know, and if, knowing, he doesn't care, he ought to care.

Here Hazlitt intervenes. In the first volume of Mr. P.P. Howe's grand collected Centenary edition of Hazlitt's complete works (Dent, 21 volumes, 1000 sets, 15 guineas a set) I read the following words in Hazlitt's "Advertisement" to his "Reply to the Essay on Population by the Rev. T.R. Malthus": "I have indeed endeavoured to make my book as amusing as the costiveness of my genius would permit. If, however, these critics [of his liveliness] persist in their objection I will undertake to produce a work as dry and formal as they please, if they will undertake to find readers."

These remarks powerfully appeal to me. And the result of Hazlitt's philosophy is always apparent in his extraordinary readableness. He was, really, a grave writer, and a less diverting subject than the theories of Malthus could scarcely be found. Also Hazlitt's treatise on Malthus is very long. But it diverts. It can be perused without strain because "something is going on" on every page. Hazlitt is serious, but he does not take himself too seriously. He has the wisdom to be diverting also. I suggest that here is a lesson from which Mr. Crofts and many other detective novelists might well profit.

As to Mr. P.P. Howe's Centenary edition of our second-greatest English essayist, it is monumental. (The cliché cannot be avoided.) It is handsomely produced, and with dignity, and securely bound. Three volumes only are yet issued: I, IV, and V. The final volume will consist of pure index, which is good news. And the work is certainly cheap; the price works out at 15s. a volume, averaging about 400 large pages each. Comparatively few people can afford 15 guineas for a work of literature (though apparently everybody can afford a hundred and fifty for a motorcar). But I hope that a thousand people will find themselves able to afford 15 guineas for this work. Those who cannot may look forward to the approaching Nonesuch Press *Selected Essays*, edited by Mr. Geoffrey Keynes, at 12s. 6d. If the Nonesuch Hazlitt is equal to the Nonesuch Blake and Donne it will be value for money.

I cannot pass judgment upon Mr. Howe's labours on the majestic inclusive edition, but up to the moment of going to press I have not succeeded in finding fault with it. Mr. Howe has, of course, based his edition on that of Waller and Glover, now very rare, and costly to buy. I do not see how Mr. Howe's can ever be superseded. He has spent many years on it, and spent them well.

Some will put the crucial question: Was Hazlitt a great enough writer to merit this tremendous monument? I think that assuredly the answer must be Yes. He was a great stylist, in the difficult familiar vein. And nobody can be a great stylist, in any vein, without being a great man. And of him it is to be said: *He can be read.* There is a character in one of the lovely plays of Porto-Riche (who died recently) of whom another character remarks: "M. Fontanet will always be twenty years younger than anyone else." The remark applies to Hazlitt. He stays young because he is always fresh, honest, unpompous, direct; because, though he read little and hated to write, his thought and his writing have the best qualities of youth. Indeed, his pugnacious heart never grew up.

To-day, thanks to Waller and Glover and Mr. Howe, he is emerging, after a century, from a dark cloud of his own making. I would describe him as an "uncomfortable" man. He knew how to write, but he did not know how to live. He had too many and too sincere convictions. He wrote what he thought, and he wrote it with an inconvenient pointedness. He carried intellectual honesty and outspokenness to excess. Such a writer is inevitably the enemy of his generation, which rightly resents the ruthless egotism of his candour. Any individual who indulges himself in undiluted candour is apt while living to be a waspish nuisance to mankind. Hazlitt's intellectual honesty fortunately broke down at the end. Dying, he said: "Well, I have had a happy life." It was grossly untrue — a piece of bravado in the menacing face of death. I like him the more for saying it.

2 October 1930

A Grievance Against Somerset Maugham

A new novel on Monday last; a new play on Tuesday. Somerset Maugham's versatility! I cannot judge the play, as I write this just before the grand occasion of the first night. But I can judge the novel, which I read at a sitting. It is a story about novelists. In principle I am against authors as protagonists in a novel. Authors know so much about authors as such that they are apt to stress unduly the literary side of these fellows. Somerset Maugham has seen and avoided the danger. To the general public novelists are, rightly, more interesting on the uncreative practical side — as husbands, lovers, and ingenious exploiters of their own talents; and this is the side which Mr. Maugham deals with.

Besides the narrator, there are three principal characters in *Cakes and Ale* (Heinemann, 7s. 6d.): Alroy Kear, a novelist of little talent and miraculous skill in exploiting it; Edward Driffield, a great novelist; and his first wife, Rosie, beautiful, kindly, and innocently sensual. The portrait of Alroy Kear (called "Roy") will be commonly described as "deadly," "terrible," "devastating," and so on. But it is none of these things. Somerset Maugham, writing of one of Driffield's novels, says: "Not the most celebrated of his books, not the most popular . . . but the most interesting. *It has a cold ruthlessness that in all the sentimentality of English fiction strikes an original note.*" The sentence applies to much of Somerset Maugham's fiction. But the portrait of Roy is not ruthless. It is simply impartial, calm, true, and unmalicious. The author, benevolent towards human nature, really likes his creation. And no one could help liking Roy, despite his clever, crude, cunning way with critics, especially adverse critics.

Roy gave lectures around the world in praise of novelists younger than himself. "When you had heard his lecture you felt that you really knew all you wanted to know about them. . . . I suppose that is why when Roy had lectured in some provincial town not a single copy of the books of the authors he had spoken of was ever asked for, but there was always a run on his own."

The portrait of Roy is delicious. (If I had not forsworn the use of the word "masterly" I should employ that exhausted adjective here.) It will intimately amuse and exasperate the ten million authors of Great Britain, and the handful of adult, lettered British citizens who have contrived not to be authors will enjoy it not less well — and more judicially.

The portrait of Driffield is a very different affair. Driffield was a genuine bohemian, far more so than the late Odell or any of the unhatted quarrelsome pacers of the pavements of Chelsea and northern Bloomsbury. He was not a gentleman, and had no desire to be a gentleman. ("It is very hard to be a gentleman and a writer," says the narrator.) He was scarcely even straight. And he was quite capable of utilising his bohemianism for the furtherance of his career. Nevertheless Somerset Maugham has succeeded in giving him an air of greatness. Some of his peculiar qualities, good and evil, coincide closely with qualities which I have myself noticed in various first-rate writers.

As for his first wife, she was, in the ordinary sense, unmoral. She was artless. "She loved to make people happy. She loved love." Her performances as a bohemian make strong meat, right from the start. And the meat gets stronger, until in the final scenes it damands prodigious digestive powers, and the dyspeptic will probably protest. Withal, truth is on every page.

Driffield's second wife (once his nurse), a very respectable woman, took her husband in hand, and superficially reformed him. After his death she asked Roy to write his life. Roy agrees to write it. "It can't fail to do me a lot of good. People have so much respect for a novelist if he writes something serious now and then." Roy's difficulty in the biography was of course Rosie. He wanted to leave her out of it, but he couldn't.

Cakes and Ale is oddly constructed. Somerset Maugham jumps to and fro between "present day" and thirty years ago in a manner apparently, but not actually, capricious. I have no objection to the leaps. My objection, a grave one, to the book is that it stops too soon. We do not learn what kind of a sticky mess Roy made of the biography of Driffield nor what were his methods of preparing the book-market for it. I offer this objection with diffidence. For Somerset Maugham is a first-rate writer, and his earlier novel, *Of Human Bondage*, is in my view an absolutely first-rate work — indeed one of the half dozen major English novels of the century. And those who doubt the statement should read the affrighting book, or re-read it. I have read it twice.

Just as Somerset Maugham in *The Gentleman in the Parlour* mingled observation with reflection, so in *Cakes and Ale* he has mingled reflection with fictional narrative. The reflections, when they are not about life, deal with literature. And they are very amusing, particularly on the pages where with characteristic bland mischievousness he brings in real individuals. The narrator read an article in the *Evening Standard* by Evelyn Waugh which aroused in him a desire to study books on the art of fiction. Naturally he consulted the omniscient Roy on the matter. "On his advice I read *The Craft of Fiction*, by Mr. Percy Lubbock, from which I learned that the only way to write novels was like Henry James; after that I read *Aspects of the Novel*, by Mr. E.M. Forster, from which I learned that the only way to write novels was like Mr. E.M. Forster [I doubt this] ; then I read *The Structure of the Novel*, by Mr. Edwin Muir, from which I learnt nothing at all."

Driffield himself, who was genuinely ruthless, uttered a deep saying about Henry James. He remarked that James had "turned his back on one of the great events of the world's history, the rise of the United States, in order to report tittle-tattle at tea-parties in English country houses."

Cakes and Ale is not in the same class with *Of Human Bondage*. Though cleverer, and more adroitly written, it is slighter. Its theme calls for less emotional strength. But it is intensely original, and rigidly, audaciously, true to life. I have read no novel about authors which hits the nail plump on the head so many times, and none which is as consistently diverting. Reading it, I smiled as often as a few days earlier I had laughed at the wild and wayward fun of Noel Coward's brilliantly-phrased farce, *Private Lives*. Which is saying something! A smile is as good as a laugh any day. At the same time I shall bear a grievance against Somerset Maugham until he puts himself to the trouble of producing another book on the scale of *Of Human Bondage*.

416

Arnold Bennett Is Extremely Critical Towards the Stage

The stage this week. It is a subject which interests me as a woman interests a man whom he both loves and hates. And I reckon to know something about it. For, although when I go to a rehearsal the people concerned therein still say anxiously and kindly to me: "Please remember, Mr. Bennett, that this is only a rehearsal," I have been attending rehearsals for thirty years. Also for a number of years I occupied a highly responsible executive position in a theatre.* Also the censor alone knows (I don't) how many plays I have had produced — multitudinous failures and a few successes. Also for years I was a dramatic critic. Also . . . .

The fact is, I ought to write my stage reminiscences, which ought to be very funny, and very mordant too. My attitude towards the stage is extremely critical. My criticisms would come under four heads: (1) The badness of public taste, which cannot be helped. (2) The untruthfulness-to-life of plays, which might be helped. (3) The ignorance and the lethargy of managers, which now are somewhat less terrible than they were. (4) The astounding incompetence of young players. Often have I helped to rehearse youthful and self-satisfied players who, after several years of experience, have shown that they had not learned the mere elementary rules of acting, including the first rule of all — namely, that a player must make himself clearly heard to the end of every sentence. The other night I found myself at a première in the first row of the stalls. I murmured what Beethoven is falsely said to have murmured on his deathbed, "I shall hear!" . . . But perhaps after all I had better not write my stage reminiscences. If I did I should meet with opprobrium, and I detest opprobrium. Like everybody else, all I ask for is undiluted praise, which I never receive — and rarely give.

But I would almost give it to Mr. Robert Courtneidge, the author of *I was an Actor Once* (Hutchinson, 12s. 6d., illustrated). True, it has no table of contents, no chapter headings, and no dates: a serious fault in a book of reminiscences. I had not hoped to enjoy this book, for in my mind Mr. Courtneidge was associated exclusively with the production of musical comedy, and I have been more acutely bored by musical comedy than by any other form of theatrical entertainment. But I soon began to enjoy the work. It is the expression of a strong, wise, kindly, audacious, and upright individuality. And in an unassuming way it is well written. For instance: "In small, as in great problems, the answer frequently comes unexpectedly, and with the sudden sweep of a tropical sunrise." An enlightening comparison! I could quote numerous such instances from the volume.

Mr. Courtneidge had many small and many great problems to solve. His memories go back to the days of provincial repertory "legitimate," when players were refused admittance to respectable lodging-houses, and when Barry Sullivan and Charles Dillon were the provincial kings of the stage. I am glad that Mr. Courtneidge puts Charles Dillon above Barry Sullivan, who, when I saw him in the 'eighties in the Five Towns, came very

* Chairman of the Board of the Lyric Theatre, Hammersmith.

close to my notion of a bad actor. (But he could be heard. Oh, yes! He could have been heard in the next street.)

The acting of those days was different from the acting of to-day, though I doubt if it was any better. I doubt whether any actor of the great legitimate days ever gave a finer Hamlet than Martin Harvey's, or a more superb comedy performance than several of Fred Terry's.

Mr. Courtneidge's memoirs would be largely incredible if they were not beyond question true. The adventures of this adventurous man! The straits into which he was driven! When a company was disbanded through financial disaster on the road, Mr. Courtneidge would play in public-houses, and was glad to collect three shillings. And there was that night when he waited around the pay-box until the first patron of the drama appeared and paid threepence for a seat, and Mr. Courtneidge grabbed the threepence and, famished, ran off with it to get something to eat. Those were marvellous times, if regrettable. Yet even to-day, and in London, there may be — there probably are — numbers of young stage-girls (I hesitate to call them actresses) who are just as hard up for threepence as Mr. Courtneidge was then.

The first part of the book is provincial legitimate. The second part deals with the ups and downs (more ups than downs) of a star-impresario of musical comedy in London, Manchester, etc. It is good, but not so good as the first part. And although the author treats of some aspects of the present stage situation with sagacity and benevolence, he does not in my opinion really take hold of the more important modern problems. Nevertheless two-thirds of the book are really excellent, and all of it is both diverting and informing.

An extreme contrast to *I was an Actor Once* is Gordon Craig who is, I believe, a first-rate scenic and producing artist. He has all the refined, sophisticated sensitivity of a first-rate artist. His contentions about the stage appear to me to be unanswerable — in an ideal world. But I suspect that he has the fatal defect of being incapable of compromise. As a writer — and he has written much — he has always struck me as vague, formless, suffering from a mind as pathless as a butterfly's — and from an imperfect grasp of grammar.

I started his book with misgivings, which the opening chapters did not allay, but as I proceeded I observed gradually that he had something valuable to say and was saying it. He achieves a convincing, an adorable, portrait of a great man. The book should be read, and read with care, for you never know in what obscure corner of it you will not come across a truly profound remark.

It was in Glasgow about 1884 that I first saw Henry Irving, with Ellen Terry. The pit was 4s. a head, and it was packed, and I was very uncomfortable; but I have never enjoyed any theatrical performance so much, either before or since — not even excepting my first pantomime at the Hanley Theatre Royal! In the late 'nineties I had the inexpressible thrill of attending a Lyceum première as a dramatic critic. I think the play was *Ravenswood*. Whatever it may have been, it was a thoroughly bad play, and Irving's elocution was chiefly incomprehensible. As dramatic critics do to-day, I supported tedium in dignified reserve.

Gordon Craig ranks *The Bells* as Irving's masterpiece. When I saw Irving

418

in *The Bells* I was overwhelmed, not by Irving, but by the shocking mediocrity of the play, and the author's wonderful gift for ruining fine situations by feeble dialogue. Apart from Shakespeare, Irving rarely produced a good play. Nearly all great actors, and nearly all great producers — Reinhardt for example — prefer bad plays to good. They demand strong situations, and do not care a pin if the author mishandles the said situations. They handle them afresh. One can say what one chooses against Irving's acting — as against Tree's — his technique was of the very highest histronic brilliance. He carried it into private life. And he had worked for his technique. At Edinburgh once, in one sojourn there, he played 429 parts in 782 days. And in his composition there was absolutely no nonsense. "If anyone had shown inspiration in Irving's company . . . he would probably have been sacked." And quite right.

Both the above books deserve close attention.

16 October 1930

Is the Modern Novelist Going Too Far?

The experiment of Mr. Victor Gollancz (entitling himself for this occasion "Mundanus Ltd.") of publishing new full-length novels at 3s. is now in being. The first issue, Louis Marlow's *The Lion Took Fright*, in its yellow and red, has a very attractive, fruity appearance. It is well designed, well printed, and well stitched; also it is slim and pocketable and convenient for perusal in bed. The important point, however, is not what the paper-bound book looks like before perusal, but what it looks like afterwards. My copy has survived the ordeal with complete success — far better than any fifteen-franc French novel has ever done in my experience. Its shapeliness has not suffered, and the corners of its covers are not dog-eared.

Different opinions are held as to the future of the experiment. At present I have no opinion. The similar American experiment of publishing new novels at two-fifths of the old price (one dollar instead of two and a half) is so far at any rate not a failure. I have had figures. Whereas a circulation of four times the old price circulation had to be achieved if the scheme is to succeed, either for authors or for publishers, there have been instances in America in which the new circulation has risen to eight times. British book-buyers are perhaps more conservative. Two previous experiments of the same kind have disastrously failed. As an author I once took part in one of them — to my cost.

Success will depend (1) on advertising and (2) on the booksellers. I think that the booksellers, who buy for two shillings what they sell at three, ought to be able to persuade themselves to push the scheme. (The libraries, who get cloth-bound copies, certainly ought to push it.) But besides the booksellers, there are booksellers' assistants. In this connection I note with much satisfaction that the Associated Booksellers have instituted a Course of Instruction (with examination) for booksellers' assistants. I have seen the first syllabus, and it is judiciously comprehensive. It might have been even more comprehensive had it included an examination in the art of salesmanship. My ideal bookshop has assistants who will never admit ignorance of the book I want, and never fail to assure me that, if they haven't the volume in stock, they will instantly obtain it. Already the old, curt *non possumus* attitude ("Haven't got it. Never heard of it.") has changed.

The Lion Took Fright is the story of the infatuation of a very young girl for a man more than twice her age. It is most brilliantly written, and displays all Mr. Marlow's gifts of narrative, analysis, romance, and quiet, lethal satire. Assuredly it ought to be read. But I make reserves. The story in essence is a mere episode, hardly sufficient for a novel. And the hero, Mr. Brangdon, has no heroical quality. Now I maintain that all chief characters, be they good or evil people, ought to have some heroical quality. Consider the various bad men in *The Brothers Karamazov*. Everyone there is drawn on the heroic scale. Mr. Brangdon is not good, and only feebly evil. He is true enough, but inadequate to the rôle assigned him. He is simply a perfect conceited ass, in whom it is impossible to be interested. Further, the end of the story, being purely accidental, does not satisfy. The girls and women are superbly done.

Louis Marlow is a rising novelist. And so is John van Druten, whose second novel, *A Woman on Her Way* (Putnam, 7s. 6d.), has just appeared. In narrative skill and breadth of handling it is an advance on the excellent *Young Woodley*. But it lacks a central theme. And it suffers from the same defect as *The Lion Took Fright*. The heroine, Elinor, is not heroical. Nobody in the book is heroical. You never met with such a set of wasters: untidy, even dirty, living lives totally unorganised, capricious, idle, self-indulgent, tedious, adulterous, and rude. Their manners are appalling. In their conversation the adjective "bloody" abounds (as in numerous modern novels). The use of coarse words, like the practice of casual adultery, is steadily growing in the newest literature, if not in life.

John van Druten deals very faithfully with his personages, and, apart from an excess of dialogue (goodish dialogue), the book artistically justifies itself. But what a crew! I wish to point out that genuine dramatic quality cannot be got without serious clashes, and that in novels where the majority of the characters are as casual and careless as animals, a serious clash cannot convincingly be brought about. Some sustained force of character is necessary for a clash. I await calmly the next phase of this writer's progress.

Touching a central theme, Laurence Oliver's *The Secret Image* (Harrap, 7s. 6d.), has a very striking one. Exceedingly difficult to manipulate. The author has manipulated it fairly well; but he has not done the impossible, and the almost impossible was required, for the story is pivoted on the gradual return of a lost memory. The culminating scenes, however, descriptive of a murder and a conflagration on a Scilly island, are rendered with real power. And the heroine is truly heroical. All the characters are well drawn. The writing falls short of distinction. This tragic book has been "chosen" by one of the book-of-the-month clubs.

The culminating scene of the second book of another rising author, *Gay Agony*, by H.A. Manhood (Cape, 7s. 6d.) is the most ghastly I ever read. Assassinations and burnings are nothing to it. Mr. Manhood's book of short stories, *Nightseed*, was quite remarkable. And by its style *Gay Agony*, a rural tale, is remarkable. Mr. Manhood loves words, both singly and in picturesque and startling metaphors: he loves them not wisely but too well. The book, morbid, creatively vigorous, intensely original, is over-written. Reading it, one is too conscious of its wonders of style. Here again the plot is a mere episode (of seduction and infidelity) insufficient for a novel. Those who enjoy the novels and stories of T.F. Powys will probably enjoy *Gay Agony* more. I await the next phase of Mr. Manhood's talent with anxiety.

Lastly a new short posthumous novel of English provincial life by D.H. Lawrence: *The Virgin and the Gipsy* (Secker, 6s.). It shows some of Lawrence's characteristic defects, but it is a dazzling, first-rate affair. What style, and what a lesson in the bare style for Mr. Manhood! What strokes of characterisation! What synthetical felicities! What sheer power! And what breadth! Lawrence is as easily and perfectly at home in an English rectory as in a gipsy encampment. Short the book is; but it has in it fundamental stuff for a novel three times its length. This is a work to keep and to read thrice. Speaking of Lawrence, Miss Rebecca West has written a lively essay on him: *D.H. Lawrence* (Secker, 3s. 6d.). It is a passionate defence of Lawrence; it girds at the public attitude and the Press attitude towards the death of a great writer; it is reminiscent and largely personal; and it has all the author's brilliance, and less than usual of her waywardness.

23 October 1930

The Doom of Mankind

In the so-called feverish present, just as in past ages, the worst hindrance to full living is the groove. Grooves deepen. There are people half-alive in grooves so profound that you can hardly see them when you look over the edge. Yet they would deny that they are in a groove at all. It needs imagination to realise that you are in a groove. The other day I got from a refined and superior south-coast hotel a prospectus containing these words: "No charge for electric light"! The manager of that hotel has no suspicion that he is in a groove unfathomable.

Matthew Arnold wrote:

Calm, calm me more, nor let me die
Before I have begun to live.

To which I would reply: "By all means. But do beware of the groove, for it may be fatal." Readers and writers are specially apt to sink into grooves. Books may be good, and they may be bad, but in their several categories the good and the bad are terribly alike. You don't fully perceive how alike they are until a book that is unusual comes along and dispels the cataract from your eyes. Unusualness is a quality in itself.

Now recently I have read several books which appear to me to be unusual, some in essentials, some in inessentials; but all unusual. The first is Mr. W. Olaf Stapledon's *Last and First Men* (Methuens, 7s. 6d.). It is a "discovery of the future," as far forward as thousands of millions of years hence — even to the last man. There have been many visions of the future, and a few fine ones. But none in my experience as strange as *Last and First Men*. It is related by one of the last men, who has projected himself into the mind of a man of to-day. How does he accomplish this feat? And how can a man of the future influence what to him is the past? Well, here are questions of metaphysics which Mr. Stapledon explains as briefly and simply as he may. Enough to say that the men of the future have discovered that, Time being an illusion, all events, are simultaneous. An old idea, but here exploited with very ingenious originality.

A great people, these men of the future! When the sun cooled, they contrived to shift the earth's orbit nearer to the sun. When, previous to final disintegration, the sun grew hot again, they endeavoured to make the earth recede. The device failed, and mankind was doomed.

The book is serious, and written with a gravity proper to history. No fireworks or diversions in it. If you skim it, you may find it dull. If you read faithfully, you won't find it dull. Mr. Stapledon, whose name was unknown to me, possesses a tremendous and a beautiful imagination. He has attempted the impossible, but nobly. Sometimes the narrative vehicle proves unequal to the strain put upon it by the sublime matters to be narrated. That cannot be helped. *Last and First Men* will handsomely repay patient perusal. It is not a novel.

Next, *Monsieur Nicolas, or the Human Heart Unveiled*, by Restif de la Bretonne, translated from the French by R. Crowdy Mathers (Rodker, six volumes, 825 copies. 15 guineas the set, illustrated). Two volumes have appeared. Though octavos, they have the dimensions of quartos. They are a simply magnificent specimen of printing (Glasgow University Press). They are splendidly illustrated. The work is admirably translated. And the Introduction by Havelock Ellis is worthy of him. One unusualness of *Monsieur Nicolas* is that Restif, being a compositor as well as a great writer, did not *write* the work at all. He composed the whole of it straight off "at the case," in the compositors' room.

He says in his own Introduction: "I undertake to give you in its entirety the life of one of your fellows, without concealing anything of either his thoughts or actions." Of course he was asking for trouble, and he got it. Even Sainte-Beuve called him "ignoble." For more than a hundred years he was under a cloud, which cloud at the beginning of the present century dissipated itself. And to-day these prodigious pre-revolutionary Memoirs of the intimacies of middle and low class life in France have taken their just place in the panorama of European literature. Casanova and Laclos (author of *Les Liaisons Dangereuses*) are accepted in Britain. Restif is less licentious than either, and the sweep of his observation is far wider than that of either. He cannot *not* be accepted in Britain. The interest of him is intense. He has social theories, but his first concern is with individuals.

My previous acquaintance with Restif was limited to the volume of selections in the excellent series, *Les Plus Belles Pages*, published by the Mercure de France some twenty years ago. This latter volume is to be highly recommended to those who read French more easily than they can spare 15 guineas. Withal, Mr. Rodker's monument to Restif is cheap at the price.

Next, *Dumb Animal and Other Stories*, by Osbert Sitwell (Duckworth, 7s. 6d.). Eight stories, of which one, *Happy Endings*, occupies about a third of the book. I have space to refer only to *Happy Endings*, whose extreme unusualness lies in its combination of passionate and wounding Sitwellian satire with a sense of beauty and pity. The satire of the elaborate picture

422

of life in a military academy is absolutely ruthless. It is seriously as cruel as the famous humorous cruelty of Harry Graham, who has just published *More Ruthless Rhymes for Heartless Homes* (Arnold, 3s. 6d.). (This large little book, by the way, is also very unusual; for the foreword and index are together as long as the rest of the work, and — the index especially — quite as funny. Phenomenon perhaps unique in literature!) On the other hand, the beauty and the pity of Osbert Sitwell's eventless account of the life and death of an academy-hack-teacher are most moving. In my opinion this story shows a considerable advance on any of his earlier prose work. It is really remarkable. He will continue to excite opposition. But never mind! He is emphatically and indisputably "there."

Lastly, I hear news of a novel of the days of the Duma, by a Russian author: Nikolai Gubsky's *The Gladiator* (Elkin Mathews, 7s. 6d.). Decidedly unusual because it is written in English! But as the book will not be published till next week I cannot discuss its merits — except one merit, the merit of not being translated. A large section of the English-reading public is always interested in Russian fiction. No English author is better known in England than Tolstoy, and few English authors are better known than Dostoevsky. But 99.999 per cent. of English readers have never seen a Russian novel save through the more or less obscuring veil of a translation. So that they (I include myself, naturally) cannot be said to know what a Russian novel actually is. I suppose that *The Gladiator* is the first Russian novel to be written in English. Conrad was a Russian by birthplace, but not by birth, his parents being Polish; and the Polish mentality is more different from the Russian than the mentality of London from that of Connemara: which is saying a lot.

30 October 1930

Eve and the Lipstick

In the English language a word may mean anything. For instance, "valuable" and "invaluable" are continually used to convey the same idea. For another instance you might suppose that "small" could mean nothing but small. But those experienced in receiving hospitality know with certainty that the word "small" on a party invitation card invariably means large. And take the word "sensuality," which may mean non-intellectuality or non-spirituality, or self-indulgence, or general carnality, or sexual carnality in particular. The last two are the usually accepted meanings.

Now John Cowper Powys (author of *Wolf Solent* and other exceedingly long novels) has just published a book under the title *In Defence of Sensuality* (Gollancz, 7s. 6d.), and the title is wildly misleading. Mr. Powys tries to defend it and fails. A far more suitable title would have been *An Attack on Sensuality*. After all, words intended to be read by the public ought to be used in the sense in which the public uses them. Mr. Powys's book is as spiritual and as disdainful of nearly all that "sensuality" signifies for the public as any new book I have read for years. It is a really interesting book, provocative, challenging; and in order to make room for a new ideal it cuts right across the leading ideals which inspire the activities of the majority of mankind. (Not that the new ideal is really new; it has merely been forgotten.)

Mr. Powys would minimise the machinery of life, to the advantage of genuine "living." He thinks that most of us never fully "live." He says: "Life itself, the purpose . . . of life, does not even begin until both the tiresomeness of 'work' *and the tiresomeness of 'play'* are laid aside, and we obtain leisure to *enjoy* those dreamy, sensual, imaginative feelings out of which our inmost identity or interior 'ego' weaves its unique material-spiritual cocoon." (My italics.)

There is a great deal in this theory, for both men and women. Men wear themselves out to obtain the means of physical existence, and they wear themselves out in trying to "keep fit," by dint of games and sports; and they have no time to live till they are old and safe, and then they are too tired to use either their brains or their emotions for the purpose of living. Then they die at the age of three score and fifteen, having been not alive for seventy-five years.

As for women, their case is more complicated. I have never understood them; nobody has, not even themselves. All I know about them is that they are apparently actuated by the ideal of pleasing, the means to which seem to be chiefly physical and chiefly to concern the face. They "make up" before starting out on an evening of "living" — that is, pleasing. They ride with you for five minutes, then they vanish so that they may reconstruct the face again. Halfway through the meal they unfasten a bag of tools and reconstruct the face a third time, quite openly. It is as if they said: "Kindly note that there is no deception. My lips are not in fact vermilion. I tint them, and I am honest about it." (We knew it already.) At the end of the meal they reconstruct the face a fourth time. If a theatre is visited they reconstruct a fifth and a sixth time, in the entr'actes. If there is a supper or a snack later, they reconstruct a seventh and an eighth time. And their last act of the day is to prepare, with the aid of revolting unguents, for pleasing the next day.

But what about pleasing? If they gave to pleasing the tenth part of the trouble which they give to the preliminary mechanics of pleasing, there wouldn't be a bachelor left in the land.

To return to Mr. Powys. He divides the universe into the self and the not-self, and he defines full living as the pleasurable, sometimes ecstatic, contemplation of the latter by the former. In other words living is thought. "The real purpose of life is simply and solely the arrangement of thought." And it is! Mr. Powys advocates egotism. He is against utter devotion to "humanity" as an end. (And surely it is true that nearly all "lovers of humanity" are very hard on individuals!) He admits that we "owe" humanity for food, shelter, protection. We owe it daily labour, honesty and kindliness. But "what we do *not* owe it is the thoughts, feelings and sensations with which we contemplate the universe. These are our own. These are the raison d'être of our existence."

Mr. Powys has invented some telling phrases, such as "The bully-boys of the Status Quo." And he has some startling arguments, such as the argument against the disastrous effects of too much humour. (He points out that Jesus did not employ humour.) Finally, stating with correctness that every man is fundamentally lonely, he preaches the exploitation of this loneliness. "Alone, alone, alone! The grand secret of cosmic happiness lies in growing more and more deeply aware of this loneliness," and embracing it. I was reminded of that sentence when reading Mr. Louis Bromfield's new novel *Twenty-Four Hours* (Cassells, 7s. 6d.) in which the old hero has so completely missed life that he is afraid of loneliness, and to avoid it invites all manner of tenth-rate persons to share his table.

My account of *In Defence of Sensuality* is inadequate, necessarily. The book is full of original stimulation. It is a disturbing message to the age (which age, however, in the respects above indicated, is no worse than other ages), and it deserves to be read by those who possess any intellectual curiosity. The writing of it is a trifle over-elaborate, and hence the book is hardly one that "reads itself." Another disadvantage of it is that, in addition to being misnamed, it has neither table of contents, nor chapter-titles, nor page-headings. It is a sea shockingly uncharted.

I will briefly refer to the before-mentioned novel of Mr. Louis Bromfield's. The book is American, dealing mainly with New York plutocracy and its parasites and victims to-day. The whole of the action passes in twenty-four hours: which is neither to its credit nor to its discredit. The action might just as well have passed in twenty-four days. Though rather old-fashioned in conception and execution, *Twenty-Four Hours* is no ordinary affair. It has here and there a few pages of tedium, but its creative power is strong enough to carry you safely through them. I can recommend it. The characters have vitality; the ensemble pictures are very effective; and the big situations, if possibly melodramatic, are beyond question authentically dramatic also. I read the opening chapters with distrust. I continued to read from a sense of duty. I finished the book because I could not contentedly put it down: which means that I finished it with pleasure and praise.

Mr. Bromfield has a considerable name, and a very large circulation, in America. This is my first acquaintance with his work. To me it is remarkable how serious books, such as this, and serious plays, such as *The Green Pastures* and *Street Scene** achieve immense popular success in the United States.

6 November 1930

Long Novels — I Myself Am That Sinner

Something must be said about the "modern" fashion of very long novels, which has lately become a favourite topic of journalism. No modern long novel is as long as the longer novels of Dickens, Thackeray and George Eliot. Nor is any of them as long as the longest translated Russian novels. Nor is any great Russian novel as long as the more famous long French and English novels of the seventeenth and eighteenth centuries. Indeed the general tendency of the novel, seen broadly, is to get shorter. If any individual can be said to have reintroduced mere length into the twentieth-century

---

* *The Green Pastures*, by Marc Connelly, won the 1930 Pulitzer prize; *Street Scene*, by Elmer Rice, was produced the year before.

English novel, I myself am that sinner; my sin was committed over twenty years ago. Among my successors in crime were Herbert George Wells, Francis Brett Young, and John Boynton Priestley. The effort of writing a novel, assuming that facile padding is not indulged in, is roughly proportionate to the square of its length. Thus it is not twice but four times as exhausting to succeed with a novel of 200,000 words as with a novel of 100,000 words. To begin a long novel is as easy as to begin a short one. Any gifted babe-in-letters can begin it brilliantly. To finish it without disaster requires a man.

The above observations, which I might extend but won't, have been prompted by the new novel of Lion Feuchtwanger, author of *Jew Süss*. *Success* (Secker, 742 large, dense pages, 10s.) is longer than any modern English novel within my acquaintance. It may best be described as a revue of post-war Bavaria, with excursions into Prussia. The author loves the Bavarian, and chastens him. It is also a history of the fall of the mark and the domestic consequences thereof. When the book opens the mark stands at less than a hundred to the dollar. On page 677 the mark stands at 630,000 000,000 to the dollar. Long before this the resulting anomalies of price were astounding: for instance, fifteen pounds of apples equalled the monthly rent of a flat in Munich.

The book is also a history of the decline of order in Germany, to the point at which someone discovered that the simplest way of disposing of a political opponent was to murder him. Lastly and chiefly the book is a history of the gradual perversion of legal justice for political ends.

The tale of Martin Krüger, museum-director and European authority on art, is the thin thread that holds the immense book together. Because of the troublesome bent of his mind Krüger was indicted for perjury, and shamelessly condemned. The endless obstinate efforts of his wife Johanna (who married him in prison) to obtain his release were about to succeed when he died. The author's treatment of the trial is typical of his methods. He narrates the trial in minute detail for many pages, and then deliberately omits the final dramatic scene of it.

Throughout Feuchtwanger is apparently determined to avoid melodrama and even drama. He never stresses anything. The book is a tableland, with no hills and scarcely an eminence. He does not miss big single effects, he disdains them. His aim is a cumulative effect. And to reach it he continually interrupts the narrative in order to describe minutely the reactions of everybody to everything. He will, for instance, describe the reactions of all the different passengers in a railway-carriage compartment to a minor item of news in a newspaper. He illustrates the psychology of his characters by tremendous recitals of theatrical shows, film-shows, bull-fights. I have not attempted to calculate the number of characters, but it probably runs to several hundreds, nearly all fully set forth both physically and mentally. I could not decide even for myself, whether or not the monstrous masses of detail are well marshalled or not without reading the book again. And I shall not read the book again. To read it conscientiously means at least three hours' application a day for at least a week. To read it is almost a career.

Beneath Feuchtwanger's apparent cold imperturbability burns the fire of a passionate resentment against injustice and violence. And one is inclined to regard the fire as too fierce, until one comes across such casual trifles as this: "It was terrible to hear the record of these recklessly slain, their yellow faces and riddled breasts hastily thrust underground in some wood by night, unavenged, or shot down in a quarry by droves, as if for sport, and then thrown into a pit with lime on top, unavenged; terrible, the dead lying by the wall of a barrack courtyard after serving as targets for ten unconcerned rifle-barrels, guiltless, but shot in the name of the law. But still more terribly was her breath taken away by the dry, official hand which presented the mother with the bill for the bullets expended in slaying her son."

Why the book is called *Success* I do not know, unless the explanation is in the following words: "Germany had calmed down and settled itself. The attempt to separate the Rhineland from the Reich had failed; the struggle with France over the Ruhr had ended in an industrial agreement; and a commission of experts presided over by a certain General Dawes had been appointed by the Great Powers to draw up a reputable plan of reparations. The Reichsmark was stabilised again, and the dollar was worth 4.20 marks as in the days before the war." Withal Krüger, whose rehabilitation would have been the symbol of success, was dead in ignominy, and a whole worthy class had been ruined for ever by the antics of the mark.

Is the book itself a success? I doubt. But I do not doubt that if it is a failure it is a failure that one can warmly admire. It may and probably will be a very considerable popular success in Germany, where it will touch every heart, where countless incidents will be at once recognised and various important characters labelled with the names of real people, and where the vast lesson of the book will be comprehended and deeply felt.

But Britain has not been through a revolution, blood has not trickled in her streets, and justice rarely been smirched in her courts of law. The novel cannot possibly excite Britain as it will excite Germany. Nor in Britain are there as many readers as in Germany who are capable by training of the sustained intellectual effort which the reading of the book demands and should have. I might catalogue numerous small defects in the work — for example, the chapter-titles are really disconcerting in their wilful bizarrerie — but as in the space at my disposal I could not do so without destroying the true perspective of my estimate of the novel, I will refrain. *Success* did not bore me; it exhausted me. The translation by Willa and Edwin Muir is extremely good. I say "extremely" and I mean it.

13 November 1930

And They All Saw the Joke!

"Criticism of Burns is only permitted to Scotchmen of pure blood." So wrote Leslie Stephen, a critic nevertheless who seldom lacked courage. And even Scotsmen must walk delicately in this great matter. One of the most astonishing sentences in any encyclopaedia is the following: *"The history of most of his [Burns's] life is so well known . . . that a meagre sketch must here suffice."* Even in a Scottish encyclopaedia, even in a first-rate encyclopaedia, even in a work whose very purpose is to inform ignorance, information about Burns is withheld. Could prudence further go? Could fear of the sensitive Burns public have been more touchingly indicated?

But if Scotsmen are timorous, at least one Scotswoman is not. Mrs. Catherine Carswell (a novelist of repute) has audaciously published *The Life of Robert Burns* (Chatto, 15s., illustrated). Now I have read her book, and I could see nothing in it to which a reasonable and impartial person could seriously object. Yet the work, parts of which Mrs. Carswell still more audaciously permitted to appear in serial form in a Scottish daily of large circulation, has been received with storms, cascades, cyclones of howling and protesting fury. A couple of columns, mainly of abuse, were printed in the paper six times a week for goodness knows how long. The high priests of the reputation of Burns tried to get the book suppressed; then they tried to get it boycotted. Bullets were bestowed on the authoress by post. And so on. In my opinion both Mrs. Carswell and the editor of the paper deserved the V.C. Withal, I like the enormous rumpus, for it shows that Scotland "cares."

Mrs. Carswell has not "attacked" Burns. On the contrary she is everywhere warmly sympathetic towards him. But assuming for a moment that she had attacked Burns and that Burns were England's greatest poet, would England have turned a hair? Assuredly not. England knows how to keep its geniuses in what it deems to be their proper place. Scotland has another ideal.

The difference between Scotland and England is that Scotland is educated while England, relatively, is not. All creative artists, literary, dramatic, musical, graphic, are aware that Scotland is keener than England on the phenomena of art. The theatre and the concert audiences of Glasgow and Edinburgh are far more alert than any London audience. I remember once being present at a performance of one of my own plays in Glasgow. The audience was unique in my long experience. It took every point. It saw jokes which have never been seen either before or since by a living soul — except myself.

True, Scotland has but one great poet. And she has made the most of him. Whereas England has about forty great poets, including the greatest in the world, and she has made the least of them. There is no recipe for emptying a West End theatre more efficacious than the mere name of Shakespeare.

Nor is England strikingly interested in Burns, who after all, if not the greatest poet, was one of the greatest in all literature. Broadly speaking, England does not read Burns. She says to Scotland: "He is yours; you can have him." For myself, I had reached quite a mature age before the notion of casting a casual English eye upon Burns occurred to me. I confess that Burns bowled me completely over. For weeks I kept saying: "This man stands alone!"

And so he does — almost. What mighty inspiration, what free-flowing lyricism, what wit, what humour, what satire, what verve, what nerve, what reckless and abounding vivacity, what sheer resourceful skill. It is rather surprising that a poet so great should not have burst the borders of a country so small, and flooded England even unto Stratford-on-Avon. Hadrian must have built his Wall in a prophetic mood.

To come to Mrs. Carswell and her book. What exactly all the Scottish pother has been about I know not fully, and care not at all. I have not read the newspaper correspondence, nor shall I. The biography is very well done, and gives evidence of long and intimate research. Out of it arises gradually the portrait of a great man (not specially of a great poet, for Mrs. Carswell scarcely deals with his poetry), jolly, hard-living, generous, melancholy, unvenal, morbid, dyspeptic and triumphant, a man who loved both life and women, a ploughman who was also an aristocrat in his bones and who could be commandingly at home in any society: the very archetype of the supreme creative artist. The spectacle of his career makes English poets seem only half-alive. Matthew Arnold was a great poet, but in the master-enterprise of being alive he was a timid grey amateur compared to Burns.

Mrs. Carswell has made, I think, one mistake: that of quite unnecessarily and unsatisfactorily excusing herself. She says: "Where the incidents of the poet's life are obscure, I have felt obliged for the sake of a plain narrative to make my choice after prolonged study . . . to relate my finding as though it were the only one possible. This method . . . has the advantage of being the procedure of life itself and the way in which we all deal with the individual lives around us." Well, it is no part of the business of a formal biographer to use that method which "we all" use "with the individual lives around us." Nor does Mrs. Carswell herself unduly employ this method.

I approve her more when she caustically says, of the biographers of Burns, that "most of them would seem to be immune from experience alike of folly and of passion in themselves." Another shortcoming of the Burns biographers is shown in their inability or their unwillingness to relate the "manners" of Burns to the manners of his times. The times were barbaric. Witness the detail of the street bacon-seller who "allowed each customer to suck a piece of bacon for flavouring, but not to bite the piece or take it away, as it must serve for all who came." Thus for the populace, to which Burns belonged! And the manners of the mighty to whose heights he so easily ascended were startlingly uncouth.

Morality, in the narrow conventional sense, was better preached than practised in Scotland in Burns's day. The lips of excellent girls were, in George Moore's phrase, "liquid with invitation." Virginity was not prized. And if Burns ranged around begetting children, he followed the fashion. Still, when Mrs. Carswell points out that two of his children were born within a fortnight of each other she must have known that she was asking for trouble from the Burns priesthood. And when she prints, though with dashes, the certainly staggering letter from her hero which appears on p. 314, she must have known that a fair amount of trouble was absolutely unavoidable. It has come. Personally I should have omitted that letter. But I am not utterly sorry that Mrs. Carswell has printed it. In fine, I should say that when the tumult aroused by her loving candour has died down, the book will emerge as unscathed as makes no matter.

And now I await the thunderings of the Burns priesthood against a pure-blooded Englishman who has dared to offer a few remarks about their god, themselves, and the Scotswoman who defied them.

20 November 1930

The Book Of The Month

For men of science my respect and my admiration are great. They are noble devotees of their work. They are tirelessly industrious. They acquire some exact knowledge about something, and exact knowledge about anything is very rare. They are ill-remunerated in both money and prestige. But I do wish that, as a class, they would learn to write. I do not expect them to be star-performers with a pen, like an H.G. Wells. I do not much mind how they write for their own scientific public; let experts muddle about as they please among themselves. But when they write for the general public, when they write for me, when their avowed aim is to popularise scientific truths or theories, I maintain that they ought to show an adequate acquaintance with the vehicle of expression which they use, and to obey the rules of the craft — rules which common sense has made and long experience has justified.

Take the columns of *Nature*. Now I regard *Nature* as perhaps the most important weekly printed in English, far more important than any political weekly. My esteem for *Nature* is enormous, for I have learnt a tremendous lot from it. But the writing of it is considerably inferior to the matter of it. I was reading last week in *Nature* an article entitled "Scientific Workers in Government Employment," and I came across an error of writing very common among men of science, namely the use of the same word twice close together in two different senses. "*It* will be seen that it represents a very important stage of the development of those services." The first "it" refers to the whole of the sentence from the word "that." The second "it" refers to a certain Report. This is bad, for the reason that it is confusing.

Again, in the same article: "The recognition of the fact that the scientific workers in State employment are as a class performing a distinctive service will be more readily achieved now that, *like other distinctive classes of civil servants,* their conditions of employment have been closely assimilated." I simply don't know what this means. I have to guess at its meaning. And anyhow imagine comparing "distinctive classes" with "conditions of employment"! You merely can't. The writer did not write what he meant.

It may be argued that these mistakes are trifling. But think of what men of science would say if a similar slipshoddiness were displayed in the conduct of a laboratory experiment! The truth is that such slipshoddiness would not be excused in a writer of general, as distinguished from scientific, articles.

The foregoing remarks are one result of my perusal of Sir James Jeans' *The Mysterious Universe*, which has rightly reached the status of the book of the month. Its interest is absorbing, its scope immense, its courage admirable. But—— Well, I will not insist on its occasional clumsiness of expression, nor on its repetitions, nor on its, to me, frequent incomprehensibility. I will only say that the learned author has frequently forgotten, or seems to have forgotten, that he is writing for the general public.

For instance, he says: "Clearly we can only preserve our belief in the uniformity of nature by making the supposition that particles and waves are in essence the same thing." The general public will say: "A wave is due to the motion of something. It is not a something. It is the description of the motion of a something. A flag waves, but the wave is not the flag. The sea is not the waves of the sea. If you ask us to suppose that the sea and its waves are the same, our reply is that our mind is incapable of supposing this, because in our opinion a something and the movement of a something stand in two different categories." The general public may be wrong, and the man of science may be right. But surely the first business of the man of science is to explain how the supposition can be made.

Further, Sir James speaks of the "annihilation" of a proton and an electron, by radiation. The man of science may be able to picture the process of annihilation. The plain man cannot. Annihilation is complete destruction, the wiping out of existence of a something. The plain man can conceive the transformation of a something, the breaking up of a mass into its minutest particles. But can you who read this ever conceive that a something has utterly ceased to exist in any form? I can't.

Still further, Sir James theorises that the transformation "of matter into radiation is proceeding vigorously throughout the universe." My contention is that the plain man cannot conceive this process either. Matter is a thing: radiation is a function. Radiation assumes a something that radiates. How is any plain man to conceive the transformation of a thing into a function of the thing? My poor plain man ought to be told how to accomplish the conception.

Sir James ends this chapter (Chapter III) thus: "These concepts reduce the whole universe to a world of light, potential or existent, so that the whole story of its creation can be told with perfect accuracy and completeness in the six words: 'God said, "Let there be light." ' " Which summary I personally should characterise as a cheap play on words.

On the other hand Sir James's allusions to Einstein's theory of relativity are rather illuminating, and gave me more assistance than anything else I have read about relativity. Nevertheless the close of this chapter (Chapter IV) has little or no meaning for me. I am lost in the conceptions of space and time; for, though I can conceive "empty space," I have great difficulty in conceiving "empty time."

Nor do I comprehend what Sir James means when he speaks (in Chap. V) of "waves" not being located in space and time at all, but being "mere visualisations of a mathematical formula." Withal, he is persuasive enough in his advocacy of a mathematical explanation of the universe. And yet, while admitting that mathematics can describe only the behaviour of things and not their reality, he appears to shirk the difficulty that "behaviour" cannot exist by itself and that it connotes the existence of things which behave.

But presently we find him advancing a theory that the universe may be nothing but "thought." (Here he has quite removed himself and the universe from the physical to the metaphysical plane.) And why not? The theory has marked advantages over all other theories. But the very foundation of it is and must be a definition of thought. What is thought? To which crucial question Sir James offers no answer whatever.

I repeat that *The Mysterious Universe* is a book of absorbing interest, but more by its subject than by its treatment of the subject. It is written

431

for the plain man, and the plain man cannot possibly understand a great deal of it! The main difficulties of the subject are terrific, no doubt insuperable; but where they are too much for the author, the author ought to say so: "I don't know where I am, here." He ought not to state a theory and slur over some of the main difficulties of it. He knows as well as anyone, and better than most, that final reality will never be explained. Indeed, he does not deny this. But his ultimate theory has a (quite misleading) air of explaining the inexplicable.

Sir James is, I believe, a great man of science, but as a writer he is not even satisfactory. He has not seen the importance, in writing, of construction. The first chapter is not clearly related to the rest of the book. The second is a sad maze. The last, "In Deep Waters" (too deep, I fear), is at once the best and the worst. Had Thomas Henry Huxley been alive and active to-day, he might have written a better book than Sir James's. When Huxley wrote for the plain man, he remembered the plain man all the time, and the plain man could understand what he wrote.

27 November 1930

Shocking People: An Author's Duty To Go On Doing It

Aldous Huxley, who can never be neglected with safety, has published a booklet, *Vulgarity in Literature* (Chatto, 2s.). It is diversely instructive; it is also amusing, and the most amusing thing in it is praise, by means of faint damns, of vulgarity in literature. "For a self-conscious artist, there is a most extraordinary pleasure in . . . proceeding deliberately, and with all the skill at his command, to commit precisely those vulgarities against which his conscience warns him and which he knows he will afterwards regret. To the aristocratic pleasure of displeasing other people, the conscious offender against good taste can add the still more aristocratic pleasure of displeasing himself."

But Aldous Huxley, while at heart thoroughly condemning vulgarity, is thoroughly in favour of shocking persons of feeble taste. "The fact that many people should be shocked by what he writes practically imposes it as a duty upon the writer to go on shocking them. For those who are shocked by truth are not only stupid but are morally reprehensible as well." True! And I am glad to be able to say that he has never shocked me. His definitions of vulgarity in literature are all negative, except one: "It is vulgar, in literature, to make a display of emotions that you do not naturally have, but think you ought to have, because all the best people do have them. It is also vulgar . . . to have emotions, with so many *too many protestings*, that you seem to have no natural feelings, but to be merely fabricating emotions by a process of literary forgery. Sincerity in art . . . is mainly *a matter of talent*." (My italics.) Otherwise, the booklet is well described by the sub-title: *Digressions from a Theme*.

To my mind literary vulgarity consists in (1) insincerity, (2) exaggeration. The two vices are about equally prevalent. Neither of them is discoverable in acknowledged masterpieces. Both of them are plenteous in books which made a row in the world — and which are soon forgotten.

432

I have recently read two first novels which are free from literary vulgarity. One of them is American: *Sweet Man* by Gilmore Millen (Cassells, 7s. 6d.). *Sweet Man* (meaning "fancy" man) is the story of what is called a "buck-nigger," and I had the impression that it was the work of a negro. Then, much impressed by its sober excellence, I made enquiries, and found that the author is white, aged now 33, an owner of cotton plantations, who lived isolated among negroes for four years and afterwards turned journalist and novelist.

Sweet Man is a far finer book than the only other novel about negroes that has come my way since *Uncle Tom's Cabin*. Namely, Carl Van Vechten's famous *Nigger Heaven*, which has various vulgarities and which I did not and do not like. For a tenth novel *Sweet Man* would be very good, and for a first novel it is wonderful. I advise the discriminating to read it. Although it contains a lynching and one prime murder and one prime suicide, and although here and there it might startle the timid, it is always sincere and never violent. It does not flinch and it does not caterwaul. Its immense cumulative effect is got by steady sobriety in imaginative truthfulness. Its moderation and sanity produce beauty out of ugliness and even out of horror. They constitute a lesson to all of us in the quiet, confident exercise of sheer power. The book is short, because the author is a strange man — he never engages a hundred words to do the work of ten.

The other first novel is John Rothenstein's *Morning Sorrow* (Constable, 6s., 234 pages). A country story, of Diana, grand-daughter of a working gardener. She became companion to a lord's daughter and fell in love with the lord, who fell in love with her. The affair came to naught, chiefly because the lord's wife was very much alive. Diana then had an inclination for a nondescript vigorous man, also beyond her station; he felt an attraction towards her but he forgot her. Finally she married a social equal, Andrew, who was filled up with many political notions, to which he gave free vent.

A quiet novel, achieving considerable beauty without any strainings for effect. The descriptive passages are good; the character-drawing is frequently more than good, combining a rather original psychological vision with unusual clarity of expression. There are youthful clumsinesses, as when the lord's wife too theatrically surprises her lord and their daughter's companion in an embrace. But I give little importance to such defects of immaturity.

I hoped to be enthusiastic about *Morning Sorrow*, and I was enthusiastic till near the end. But towards the end John Rothenstein falls away. I will not say that Diana would not have married Andrew, despite his accent and his phrasing in conversation. I will say that the author fails to make her acceptance of him in the least convincing. My thoughts ran: "He's going to make her accept him, she will accept him, she has accepted him. . . . I simply don't believe it. It's a bit too sentimental." John Rothenstein has many of the qualities of a born novelist — especially in pure narrative. He will write a better book than *Morning Sorrow*. I shall be disappointed if he does not write that rare thing, a novel of which the end is as good as the beginning and the middle.

While there is no literary vulgarity in the above two books, do not go and imagine that absence of vulgarity suffices to make a novel good. There is no vulgarity in still another first novel, Henry Daniel-Rops' *The Misted Mirror* (Secker, 7s. 6d.), but it is not in my opinion a good novel, and a few touches of vulgarity might have rendered it, if not good, at any rate diverting. It is not diverting; it is not readable with pleasure. I read it; but then I am a sticker, and not often can I be shaken off. I should not have opened it, had it not been "translated with a preface by R.H. Mottram" — author of *The Spanish Farm* and other fine novels. There must be *something* in a novel that Mottram translated. I have looked anxiously for the something; it has been hidden from me.

Daniel-Rops has aroused some attention in Paris, and I know not why. His second novel, *Deux Hommes en Moi*, is just out, but though it is short I do not propose to myself to read it. *The Misted Mirror* (*L'Ame Obscure* in French) is very misted — by all manner of futile detail and by enormous conversations without apparent direction or purpose. The hero belongs to the type of youth (whom I am continually hearing of but never meeting) who was just young enough to miss active service, but not too young to be seriously unsettled by the effects of the war. My conviction is that Blaise Orlier would have been precisely as unsatisfactory and as not-nice had he lived fifty years earlier or fifty years later.

A difficult book and a difficult hero, both lacking interest and charm. "Forgive me, darling," said Blaise, "I'm talking like a character in fiction, and bad stuff at that." I should have disliked him less if he had talked like a character in fiction. But he didn't. Mr. Mottram is a better novelist than translator, much better. His translation is maladroit. "She snuggled her nose into the otter's fur that trimmed her coat with a kittenish gesture." This is not French. Is it English? Of course there is some truth in the book. But the truth is insufficiently trimmed.

4 December 1930

Real Romance of Publishing

The most striking sentence I have read for the better part of some time is: "I visited many bookshops in Leipzig." It was written for *The Publisher and Bookseller* by Maurice Marston, secretary of the National Book Council, who has just made a cross-examining excursion into Germany. (His collection of facts acquired ought to be published in full.) "Many bookshops!" The exact present population of Leipzig is perhaps unknown. But it is certainly under three-quarters of a million. I should like to hear of any city in Britain, outside London, where there are many bookshops for Maurice Marston to visit.

Not that I would exalt German literary taste at the expense of English. I don't think that German literary taste is better than English; and I am quite sure that, though as a rule more laborious, German literature is duller and coarser than English. I would not even say that there is less jealousy in the German book trade than in the English book trade. What I would say is that in Germany jealousies are allowed to impair good trade organisation less than they are in Britain. (Which remark will certainly cause the trade-papers here to comment caustically on my insolence in daring to say anything at all about the British book-trade.)

In the same number of the above-named interesting periodical I found an article entitled: "Is the real bookseller dying?" The contributor answered the question in the negative. I agree with the answer. But I would phrase it in my own way. I would say that whereas the "real bookseller" was till recently as near a corpse as makes no matter, he has lately given clear signs of restored vitality. For I have within the last few days encountered several bookshops in London which quite excited me by their manifestations of a new spirit — in stock, in display of stock, and also in advertising. If I had the power I would move certain sales-managers of frock-departments into book-departments, and I would instruct them: "Treat this book-business as you have treated your frock-business." I am convinced that some dramatic results would follow.

More than one publisher has said to me: "This is the worst book-season in the history of the world. It is awful." (Or similar words.) It may be, though I doubt it — for publishers are the finest persevering changeless pessimists on earth. I am inclined to think that the book-season in the United States is more awful than our own. At worst the book-trade is struggling on without a Government subsidy.

In the main, I am a conscientious objector to Government subsidies. And in particular I object to a Government subsidy for grand opera. Not because the tax-payer of Ashby-de-la-Zouche is thereby forced to contribute to the cost of spectacles which he will never see unless he leaves Ashby-de-la-Zouche. Not because I do not love and practically support grand opera. I do. But because so much grand opera is so bad and deserves no support, official or unofficial, and because much of it will remain bad for ever, and even get worse, if its badness is State-supported. At Covent Garden I have witnessed marvellously good performances, but also I have witnessed there performances so evil that Lisbon itself could not surpass their turpitude. Further — however, this is not a music column.

But a Government subsidy for books — yes. I can see something in such a phenomenon. Many are the valuable books unpublished, unwritten, un-compiled which might be brought into existence by means of a Government subsidy. I do not mean novels, or verse, or essays, or biographies, or treatises on the loves of Napoleon or the social eccentricities of deceased elder statesmen or living notorieties. I mean solid books of reference and re-search and collected learning, in science, economics, history, for the advantages of scholars and other earnest persons. His Majesty's Stationery Office has published a few excellent books which assuredly have not been financially remunerative. Nevertheless they have been highly useful — much more useful, and much less expensive, than for instance L.C.C. Theatre-inspectors. But His Majesty's Stationery Office has published nothing, within my knowledge, on a large scale of general utility — such as the *Dictionary of National Biography*.

Now the *D.N.B.* counts among the greatest and most interesting works of reference in the world. And yet what young man or woman to-day has heard of George Murray Smith? His name is not in the conciser encyclopaedias — except as the publisher of Thackeray, G.P.R. James, George Eliot, and so on. George Murray Smith was one of the supreme benefactors of scholars and British bookmen, and through them of the British public.

435

When he was nearing fifty he thought of the idea of a *D.N.B.*, and he thought it into existence. It was not then remunerative, though it may be remunerative to-day — I know not. At least it is indispensable. Can any bookman conceive a book-world without the *D.N.B.*? He cannot. George Murray Smith paid for the *D.N.B.* I have heard that he spent £150,000 on it. Was the money so royally dispersed made by publishing? It could not have been. It was made, chiefly, by the exploitation of a mineral water which Smith rendered famous. An excellent mineral water; I still drink it in cistern quantities. So that we owe our *D.N.B.*, and all that the *D.N.B.* implies and connotes, chiefly to a table-water! Here is what I call romance, compared to which the romances of our big department-stores are a bit prosaic.

A Government with a really large view of things might reorganise and enlarge the scope of His Majesty's Stationery Office, which has already done, and is doing, good work. The Government might spend £40,000 a year on it (not more than the owners will spend on the mere insurance of one of the new Cunarders), and perform wonders, and thereby earn a tremendous prestige. Such an enterprise would arouse less opposition than almost any enterprise that this or any other Government ever undertook. And it would have a better chance of success.

Music is not understood in Britain. Painting is not understood. Nor sculpture. Nor architecture. I shall not assert that literature is understood, but it is less deplorably misunderstood than any other art. Public opinion concerning literature is on the whole sound, and the citizens are more interested in books than in anything else except sport and politics.

The full literary machinery desirable for the production of good literature does not exist. (Our supply of it is always about fifty years behind the demand.) And in all probability it never will exist without Government aid. Governments live by their reputation, or because their disrepute is less affrighting than that of the Opposition. The grand opera scheme is simpleminded and wrong-headed, but it does amount to what is termed a gesture, and I rather admire the impulsive gesturing simpletons with all their pathetic ignorance of facts. The government's reputation will deservedly lose on balance by the grand opera scheme. But I am offering to the Government, or the next Government, an idea by whose execution they would undoubtedly "make." What more does any Government want?

11 December 1930

But Have They Read Them?

The spectacle of the Christmas shops (I refer of course to the Christmas bookshops) makes me think of a story of Zola. In 1882 or thereabouts, just before the publication of *Piping Hot*, the publisher's warehouse was piled right up to the ceiling with pyramids of that not very good novel, which a week or two later went off more quickly than penny buns ever went off. The exceedingly successful Zola was then, as usual, a harassed and nervously gloomy man. In the study of his country house he prominently exhibited the motto: "No day without a line." What he really meant was: "No day without a hundred and fifty lines." On a certain French classic being mentioned — one of the finest novels in the world — Zola said that he had not read it. Somebody said: "But look here, Zola, you really ought to read it." Zola retorted: "Read it! One has no time to read!" Signifying that nobody had time to read.

At this period he was employing twenty-five men on his estate. He used to say that he learned more from them about life than he could learn in any drawing-room. Though why more about human nature can be learned outside than inside a drawing-room I fail to see. But Zola was often a terrible sentimentalist, and, like most people who permit themselves to be bored, he generally managed to find the explanation of tedium outside himself rather than inside himself.

If people had no time to read in the eighteen-eighties what are we to say about the nineteen-thirties? A wide inquiry ought to be made as to the average time given to reading by the average person fond of books. And the time given to it by men is more important than the time given to it by women. Women read more, or at any rate longer, but it is the verdict of men that ultimately counts. Perhaps women can bestow a reputation on a writer for a year or two. But look through the history of literature and kindly tell me what woman-critic's influence has put a writer permanently on the map. We have had very fine women-novelists, some fine women-poets, some good women-historians, etc. Where have been the influential women-critics?

To say that women are not creative is manifestly absurd as regards imaginative literature. But it does not appear so absurd to me to say that they are not good critics. Women, through some decision of nature's, suffer as a sex from emotional instability. (I don't blame them; I keenly sympathise with them.) Emotional instability is not a sure foundation for good judgment in literature, or in anything else. Returning to men, I have reflected on the daily time given by our bookish or semi-bookish males to reading, and I estimate that on the average it cannot be more than an hour a day. And even that estimate is generous.

Now go into a bookshop and see the new books and new editions. Scan the literary pages of the press. Examine the multitudinous advertisements of publishers. Not only will you be intimidated by the mere mass — you will be compelled to admit that even if we had a hundred Christmases on end (which we don't), and ate and drank in strictest moderation (which we don't), and refrained from parties (which happily we don't), and read steadily all day and every day (which would be ridiculous), we could not read a quarter or an eighth of the books which may well be worth reading.

And yet there are marvellous persons, especially women, who make a serious effort to perform the feat of "keeping abreast" of modern literature. You ask these persons if they have read A, B, C, D, E, to the end of the alphabet. And they have read A, B, C, D, E, etc. At any rate they will deliver you a judgment on those books. But have they read them? A simple arithmetic calculation would confound the alleged readers, though you are too polite to suggest it.

I have been reading *in* Holbrook Jackson's *The Anatomy of Bibliomania* (Soncino Press, 28s.), of which only the first volume is yet issued. It is modelled on Burton's classic, *The Anatomy of Melancholy*, and gives nearly as many excellent quotations to the page as Burton does. To me it is more interesting than Burton, but I think that the author would not expect me to read it right through all at once. It is a pasture for browsing on.

Mr. Holbrook Jackson, in the section entitled "The Art of Reading," gives a number of quotations to show that certain great men indulged in "skipping," and thought that in that way the best could be extracted from books. While I agree that many books may deserve to be skipped through, I say (1) that "skipped" books ought nineteen times out of twenty to be afterwards ignored, and (2) that there are more new books worthy to be read carefully than any individual could by any possibility read carefully. On the other hand the judicial Holbrook Jackson gives various quotations from great and experienced bookmen who believed in reading little and reading it thoroughly. For myself, though I do not always practise what I preach — and who does? — I advocate the method of the latter school of thought. No one could seriously argue that it is not the better of the two. And further, I maintain that all those who attempt to "keep abreast" of the modern literary output are misguided and essentially flibbertigibbet persons whose real aim is not to get the best out of books but to shine at dinner-tables and in other places where jabber about literature is immoderately indulged in.

The output of books is enormous and growing. But the literary public also is enormous and growing. There is some sort of a public for nearly every good book, and the duty of the wise is to choose one book and totally to ignore another. All hurried reading is worse than futile; it is a waste of time. I admire a person who says when a certain book is mentioned: "It may be a masterpiece, but I haven't read it, and I shan't."

I can't finish without announcing what I deem to be a very wise little book about reading: M.R. Ridley's *Poetry and the Ordinary Reader* (Bell — I have not discovered the price, but it is no doubt low). I read this book with pleasure, and therefore with profit. Mr. Ridley is a Balliol man. His chapter on "The Study of Modern Poetry" is particularly wise. He speaks of the bookman's "duty" to read modern poetry. And he is right, though I confess that most modern poetry yields me neither pleasure nor profit. If I possessed the critical apparatus I could write such a diatribe against the bulk of modern poetry as would ruin me for ever in the esteem of poets thereof and their impassioned admirers. Withal, Mr. Ridley's remarks have affected me. I recommend all his plain wisdom to the attention of those who feel it to be a duty to read poetry, and especially modern poetry, but don't quite know how to set about the enterprise.

18 December 1930

So Embarrassing — This Christmas Book Buying

A number of people, all of them wanting information, most of them unwilling to make decisions, and many of them disinclined for mental initiative, have been asking me to tell them what books to buy for Christmas. This is apropos of my article last week. What they say amounts to the following: "You assert that we cannot read everything. Tell us, then, the right books to read." Some of them want to know what books to buy for Christmas presents.

438

I have refused to advise. Especially about books for Christmas presents. A book as a Christmas present is a dangerous matter. The recipient will quite probably not like it. He may even not read it. In which case his politeness will compel him to lie to you, or at best to prevaricate. Which will be bad for the very thing in him that you would wish to improve — his moral character! The one wise way of bestowing a book is to take the recipient with you into a bookshop, display to him the actual cash you are prepared to spend, and insist on his choosing a book for himself. All I would say positively about book-presents for Christmas is that they need not be Christmas books, nor books impregnated by what is termed "the Christmas spirit." There are excellent Christmas books, and I have read a few of them, but I should have enjoyed them equally well in a heat-wave. And I would absolutely decline to circumscribe Christmas reading by limiting its subject.

Unless you have set your mind feverishly on a particular book for yourself or for another person, your choice of a book must be to a large extent an affair of simple chance, because the stuff available for selection is too voluminous to sift. There are at least a hundred new volumes of fiction for sale, all worthy of some attention. And every English author in the list would be justifiably rather cross if you turned him down as negligible.

Take "omnibus" books, of which there are at least thirty on the counters, none of them at over 8s. 6d., and one of them at 5s. (more than 1200 pages). There are over thirty new anthologies of repute. There are over thirty cookery books of repute. As for children's books, they are as the sands of the sea. As for pocket editions, their other name is legion. As for books on natural history, I could name fifty. Similarly for books on religion. As for works of reference and reference-annuals, there are over thirty, and I should have no objection to possessing all of them. As for books on art, I have a current list of them which itself exceeds a hundred sizeable pages. As for "Standard Authors" (God save them!), there are dozens of different sets, meant to be ranged on shelves, and to be read — when you cannot think of anything else to do.

And so I might go on — for I have not mentioned such trifles as Science, History, Theatre, Humour and Sport. But I will not go on, except to give a hint for present-bestowers of the vast assortment of limited editions which appeal to collectors. These volumes ascend in price from half a guinea to a couple of hundred guineas apiece. They alone would fill a shop. Who am I, who is anybody, to choose among them on behalf of another?

You will now perhaps better appreciate the marvellous embarrassment of choice in which the prospective book-buyer finds himself at this season. He may be miserable, but he will also be happy — or the divine fire is not in him. I personally am both miserable and happy. I could readily name two hundred books in the Christmas lists that I should be glad to have or glad to present. Withal, I am writing in a room fortified by four thousand volumes — and five ashtrays.

And now I will briefly catalogue a few books which I have obtained, and which I think others may enjoy. Not the fashionable books, not the great names! I have nothing against fashionable books nor great names, as such. Indeed I am strongly in favour of some of them. But everyone knows them, and no one needs to be reminded of them. I have in mind books which have not, so far as I am aware, "captured the imagination" of a large public.

First, Elmer Rice's *A Voyage to Puerilia* (Gollancz, 7s. 6d.). I am surprised that this novel has not more or less monopolised conversation at dinner-tables. It is one of the most humorous — quietly, subtly, and richly humorous — fictions that have come my way for what are called "ages." In my opinion it is better than any of the author's plays. It is certainly the wittiest criticism of Hollywood films in existence. Either as a present or as a secret to be selfish about (like a good cheap restaurant), I can warmly recommend it.

Then a reprint: Frederic Manning's *Scenes and Portraits* (Davies, 7s. 6d.). This twenty-one-year-old book of seven sketches might never have been printed if the author had not written *Her Privates We*, perhaps the finest of all war-novels; but it was well worth reprinting, and for present-bestowers there is an opulent edition of 250 copies, signed by the author, at thirty shillings. Then a classic: McKnight Kauffer's illustrated *Don Quixote* in two magnificent bound volumes at five guineas (Nonesuch Press). I shall not say what I think of the illustrations, except that I know nothing like them, and that the deep spirit of Don Quixote is therein discovered. If I said what I thought I might be assassinated by enthusiasts for the Royal Academy, and I have no immediate desire to investigate the scenery of the Styx.

Next, another Nonesuch Press book: *Love Among the Haystacks*, by D. H. Lawrence, "with a Reminiscence by David Garnett" (15s.), beautifully produced. Mr. David Garnett's Reminiscence is several reminiscences — of the period in which both these sketches and *Sons and Lovers* were written. No publisher would entertain the wild notion of publishing these sketches at that time. One of the very best authors of the age was refused right and left. The reminiscences are excellent. Here is one, about *Sons and Lovers*: "It never occurred to me, or I think to Frieda [Mrs. Lawrence] not to interrupt him, and we spent all the day together in one room, while he scribbled away at odd moments in the corner, jumping up continually to look after the cooking."

And lastly Hans Carossa's *A Childhood* (Secker, 6s.). Carossa is the author of *A Roumanian Diary*, a war-book of quite exceptional distinction. *A Childhood* is autobiographical, and records the minute and lovely and sometimes silly sensations of infancy. It is very subtle, very quiet, and very readable. And it has been admirably translated from the German by Agnes Neil Scott. I had intended to mention some new French books, but I must leave them for the New Year.

BOOKS AND PERSONS : 1931

1 January 1931

New Year Resolution

When, a little over a week ago, I engaged myself in the perilous enterprise of Christmas shopping, I was impressed anew by the extraordinary relative cheapness, handiness and attractiveness of books.

In a big store where were collected together for my undoing the innumerable varied fruits of human activity, I could buy Gibbon for much less than the price of a new feminine hat which would lose its first charm after the first wearing; or a fine new novel for the price of three cocktails at a fashionable hotel — cocktails which could be drunk but once, and even so with sinister consequences; or all Froude for less than the price of a Christmas dinner to be eaten, but once, in a babel of explosions and formless chatter; or an explanation of the mysteries of the universe for the price of a pit-seat at a musical-comedy; or a history of the earth and the peoples of the earth from the earliest palaeolithic age to 1930 for the price of half a cigarette-case; or a Bible for the price of a handful of chestnuts; or an encyclopaedia comprising the sum of mundane knowledge to date for the price of a mediocre dessert service which a maid would irreparably impair by one negligent gesture of the hand; or a complete library for less than the price of a rickety drawing-room suite.

True, I was pleasantly amazed by the patronage given to the book-departments; but I thought that if people realised the cheapness of books, and their value for money in aesthetic and moral satisfactions, the book-departments would have been beseiged by determined fighters for the ownership of those inexpensive volumes, and authors and publishers would be depositing vast profits in banks until such time as it became safe to invest their savings in stocks and shares. The fact is that people do not realise the relative cheapness of books. Most people regard books as a luxury, to be indulged in only after every other luxury has been indulged in; while many people regard them merely as nuisances to be avoided. All which is no exaggeration, but perhaps less than the pitiful truth.

I returned home bearing sundry parcels (not one of which contained a book), and went into my too-small library and began to arrange my books. They were in need of rearrangement. They always are. I blew on some of the pathetic neglected things; I dusted others, and I moved some scores of them to and fro in the room. A few of them I could not remember having bought. Imagine forgetting the exact circumstances in which one has come to own a book! A few of them I did not even know that I possessed; and their inexplicable forlorn presence on my shelves shocked me with surprised joy — but also with shame.

And so I tended them as I might have tended a lost dog, and tried to convince them that they were not masterless, that they aroused my warm interest, and that they had a genuine mission in my life. I went so far as to read pages of some of them, here and there. How exciting! How disturbing to reflect that those now-printed words were put together with a pen or a reed by some earnest, bursting author, two thousand years ago, five hundred years ago, fifty years ago! Immortal — in our sense of the term! Giving glimpses into wonderful minds long since passed away.

I grew quite sentimental. At moments all of us are sentimental, and the experience is excellent for us. Good books are miracles; the history of their making is more wondrous than that of fur-coats; and we treat them worse than we treat common objects of the wayside.

This is New Year, traditionally the season for good resolutions. Few good resolutions are made; fewer are kept. One of the most influential of all resolutions is the resolution continually to freshen one's interest in one's books. This resolution should be made, and it should be kept. Therefore I am specially advocating it. The resolution ought to be seriously considered by budding bookmen, and still more seriously by bookmen of experience, accomplished bookmen, and most seriously of all by bookmen who have gathered together extensive libraries.

The majority of books in the majority of libraries lie utterly idle, like railway wagons in sidings. They await the reader, and the man who ought to be their reader never glances at them. What is the remedy for this deplorable state of affairs? Surely no man can read all his books all the time? Of course not. But every bookman can allot a certain regular amount of leisure — particularly between solid sustained perusals — to cultivating at least an acquaintance with books which he has not read and probably will never be able to read through. A lot of knowledge can be very pleasurably obtained by an hour's miscellaneous browsing twice or thrice a week. It may not be exact knowledge, but such as it is it enormously assists the formation of the mind and quickens every mental functioning.

Go to your books; pick one out at random, look into it, and so on. The process is rather like plucking flowers in an enamelled meadow. No higher praise of it is necessary. After an hour, or even half an hour, of the exercise, you will be conscious of stimulation. Let me add that I address this homily to myself as well as others. For I am a sinful neglecter of books, and compassion for them is not one of my major qualities. A man buys a book, rejoices in the purchase of it, sticks it on a shelf, and it vanishes from his memory. That vile man is myself.

A prime aid to the bookman in well-doing is the compiling of a catalogue. Everybody who has collected five hundred books ought to have a catalogue of them, and he ought to compile it himself. Index-cards can be bought for half nothing. Instructions for cataloguing can be bought for very little. The labour may stretch over a longish period of time, but it is agreeable. It teaches the owner about his books — not merely their titles and the names of their authors, but their dates and the details of their editions, and the names of their publishers and of the cities where they were printed. And it enables the owner by rapid reference to know exactly what he owns. How often have I been in the libraries of impassioned bookmen and asked after a given book, and the owner has not been entirely sure whether or not he possessed the book, or where it was if he did possess it, or what the date and the edition were, or even what the volume looked like. All this is highly regrettable. Lastly, the compiling of a catalogue, and the occasional study of it, always promotes the desire to make one's library more complete.

442

London Frankness Quite Disturbing

I have been reading some French books; and I have also read Mr. Philip Carr's *The French at Home* (Methuen, illustrated, 10s. 6d.). It is not my intention to review the latter; but merely to offer one or two observations about it. Mr. Carr has lived long in France, and he knows the country — far better than I do, though I lived there for eight years, both in Paris and the country. Still, he makes statements that puzzle me. On his first page he says, of the French, that "everyone goes home to lunch." My experience is that, especially in the provinces, the French use restaurants, and cheap restaurants, a great deal more than we do. All over France, in small towns ignored by tourists you will see good restaurants full at lunch time; full of people, chiefly local people, who know one another and talk about local affairs. I have listened to scores of such table-conversations. The talkers might have lunched at home; for various reasons they did not.

A little later he says that in France "there is a verbal frankness between the sexes which is *quite unknown* in England." (My italics.) This may have been true before the War. It is not true to-day. To-day there is a "verbal frankness" between the sexes as complete as any frankness in France. How often has an English hostess encouraged me: "You can say anything here"? The frankness of London — I cannot speak for the provinces — is often quite disturbing. Does Mr. Carr know modern London?

Then in the middle of the book he says: "French boys are never awkward and French girls never blush." Neither of these assertions is in accordance with my experience. I have seen French boys and young men very awkward. And I have frequently seen French girls blush — but not, let me add, at anything I myself have said!

Withal, *The French at Home* is a good book, well written with both knowledge and sympathy. If now and then it becomes a sort of apologia for the French, I see no harm in that. The illustrations are very happy. Mr. Carr deals with the nation as a whole, and with the fundamentals of its character and its habits; hence the book's value. I recommend it to English readers of French. To know the French language well is not enough. You may be able to comprehend such a phrase as *"Il est dans les huiles,"* and yet unless you comprehend the French mentality and outlook, and the climatic and historic explanations thereof, a large proportion of the significance and the allusiveness of a French novel will simply "go past" you; because you are not familiar with the novelist's raw material; you know what he is saying, but you don't know what he is talking about. Hence I suggest that a careful perusal of *The French at Home* must deepen one's appreciation of French literature.

Now for some French books. The author of the day is André Malraux, whose Chinese novel, *Les Conquérants*, I praised here — perhaps somewhat too highly — a year or so ago. (*Les Conquérants* has appeared in an English translation.) His second novel, and third book, *La Voie Royale* (Grasset, 15 francs), was the book of the autumn. Malraux is young, and he is a novelist of imagination. But he is not a novelist of invention. His preoccupation is Asia. First China, now Siam and its regions.

La Voie Royale relates the extraordinary journey of its hero, by the (almost pathless) "royal high road," through the jungle in search of "remains." Malraux has probably been influenced by both Kipling and Conrad, but he has not the invention of the one nor the bottomless imagination of the other. The book, however, is orientally impressive, and it is excellent in the portrayal of French officials in Asia. The author has two defects. Various aspects of the existence of Europeans in Asia merely do not interest him, so that he just omits them, with the result of leaving the reader in a state of confusion, of needing more bread and less cake. The confusion is increased by the second defect — the abrupt, eclectic, and yet overcharged style. The style assuredly has distinction and power, but it is often obscure. *La Voie Royale* is the opening novel of a trilogy; which fact ought not to prevent it from being a finished entity in itself. In the present instance it does somehow prevent this.

Apropos of French books of the autumn, one of the chief has been a German book, which I know only in French: *Dieu, est-il français?* by Friedrich Sieburg (Grasset, 15 francs). The title partially reveals the spirit of the book. You cannot possibly ask if God is French without irony, and Sieburg uses irony. But he shows a profound admiration for French ideals. Bernard Grasset, the publisher, who is also an author, has saved his face by adding to the volume a long critical letter of his own, for the soothing of the provinciality of the French mind. This letter is ironical too. "In sum, dear Monsieur Sieburg, you reproach France with having bad post-offices while professing to direct the world." The book is fine, provocative, stimulative reading.

Further as regards French books of the autumn, some English and American novels have had a cheering sale. *Babbitt* is in its thirty-eighth thousand.

Jean Giraudoux's *Aventures de Jérôme Bardini* (Emile-Paul, 15 francs) is a good Giraudoux: which is saying a lot, for he wrote *Les Provinciales,* and *Suzanne et le Pacifique,* and the astonishing *Siegfried et le Limousin. Bardini* is a leisurely affair, but it is not padded. The chapter "First Disappearance of Bardini" is worked out with a detailed and attractive psychology which no other French author could surpass.

If I mention André Billy's *Les Ecrivains de Combat* (published by "Les Oeuvres Representatives" — what a name for a firm! — 12 francs) I do so because, though the book is not startlingly good, the idea of it certainly is. M. Billy, after a long, flat preface, gives examples of the polemics and invectives of eighteen French writers, among whom are Henry Rochefort, Clemenceau, Jaurès, Octave Mirbeau and Maurice Barrès. (Why was not Voltaire included?) Of all of them I like best Rochefort. I shall never forget his leading article on the festal day of the announcement of the Franco-Russian Alliance: "It is brains, not cities, that need to be illuminated." Or his remark under the Third Empire: "The French Empire has thirty million subjects, not counting subjects of discontent." A book similar to *Ecrivains de Combat* about English bruisers would meet a felt want.

Finally, I will signalise Jean-Richard Bloch's *Destin du Théâtre* (Gallimard, 12 francs), a work which may open the eyes of amateurs of

444

the theatre in this country — where only one playwright has given something really new on the stage. (No, I shall not name him!) M. Bloch's vision is both broad and long; it embraces the cinema and broadcasting. M. Bloch has prejudices, and the tendency of them is shown in the dedication of the book to Gaston Baty. I have rarely been more painfully bored than in the pretentious little theatre of M. Baty, whose best attribute is his absolute belief in M. Baty. Still, he does try.

15 January 1931

Women's Novels of Wayward Love

The second novel of Lady Eleanor Smith, *Flamenco* (Gollancz, 7s. 6d.), seems to show, like the first, that the dearest ideal of this powerful and disciplined personality is the ideal of individual liberty. *Red Wagon* dealt with the waywardness of circus life. *Flamenco* begins with the freedoms of gipsy life in Andalusia in 1820 and ends on Dartmoor before the middle of the last century. There is, and there must be, something of the *pastiche* in these fictions, however brilliantly they may be done.

Novelists, I mean real novelists, do not choose their themes. Their themes choose them as unborn souls were once said to wander to and fro in the fourth dimension choosing their parents. Therefore I do not say that Lady Eleanor *ought* to write novels about the modern social London in which she lives and which she must intimately know. All I would express is the hope that one day a modern London theme will float along and choose *her*. No young novelist gives better promise of being able to handle such a theme with truth, force, picturesqueness and courage. Lady Eleanor is never afraid; and it is certain that a modern novel by her would, generally speaking, raise Cain.

The opening chapters of *Flamenco* — Seville, the fairs, the great gipsy trek of the outcast murderous father and his family across Spain and France into the New Forest, the roadside birth of the heroine Camila — all these things are admirably worked out, and as good as the best passages in *Red Wagon*. Then the scene definitely changes to the Dartmoor home of the cheating gentleman-gambler, Richard Lovell, who adopts Camila. The characters of Lovell and his moody, justifiably-resentful wife Harriet are very well drawn; for the authoress has a convincing skill in depicting parents. But the English country scenes are not as persuasive, nor as dramatic, as the Spanish and the French.

The story seems to lose itself like a river in a multiplicity of channels none of which has the air of a main channel. Camila is carried off by a gipsy into "twelve months hell" (not described), returns and marries the wrong one of the two young Lovells, and has a child by the right one, and ultimately she goes to live with the right one, with whom she will be deeply happy and superficially unhappy. And that's the end, arrived at somewhat by hazard. I know nothing of the composition of *Flamenco*, but it reads as if it were an early novel carefully re-written. Although certainly not as good as *Red Wagon*, considered as a whole, it is better written.

But even the writing is not always what it should be. Lady Eleanor is too often verbally old-fashioned. In 1930 or 1931 a young novelist ought not to be describing women, or men either, who move about "like snakes." Nor will outworn phrases like "land of faery" help, to-day, to create an atmosphere of mysterious romance. Nor should a sudden thunderstorm be employed as the machinery for keeping a girl under a roof where seduction threatens her. All these devices belong to a school that is dead.

The business of a young novelist is to be young, to keep abreast of the large general movement of letters. Of course a young artist must imitate — all the great artists have been imitative at first — but . . . well, the early imitativeness should be of the finest still-admired models.

Another novel of individual freedom, also by a woman, is Colette's *The Gentle Libertine* (Gollancz, 7s. 6d.). The "jacket" of this book gives a comparatively full account of Colette's career, but says nothing of the place of the particular work in that career. The anonymous translator (American, yet not obtrusively so) appears to have done his work passably well. The original French title is not given, but I assume that it must be *L'Ingénue Libertine,* which I have not read in French. The publisher says the book is "the most beautiful novel (with one exception) of this most versatile of great novelists." Versatile, yes. Great, yes. But I will not agree that *The Gentle Libertine* is even the second "most beautiful" of Colette's novels. It was written many years ago, and though undoubtedly beautiful, it is a bit thin in texture.

The opening scenes, of the home life of a girl of fourteen who had a secret passion for the genus *apache,* are the best; they are exquisite. The "freedom" is purely sexual. Several of the "lingerie" chapters are meet to be called "daring." They do not read comfortably in English. Which remark is less of a reproach than of a warning to the unwary. Colette, a truly first-rate artist, is French. Her own tongue suits her best. And there you are!

While reading the above realistic fantasies on individual freedom, I thought all the time of a book which I had just finished on the very negation of individual freedom: *The Methods of the Ogpu,* by Vladimir Brunovsky (Harpers, illustrated, 9s.). The Ogpu, as not everyone may know, is the new name for the Tcheka, and stands for the "Unified State Political Administration." The book is terrible and all who are interested in the development of the Soviet regime, and in liberty, ought to read it. Its terribleness is well documented and sounds authentic. But the book would have been much more terrible, and more influential, if it had been done with more skill.

Brunovsky says that he has "no pretensions to literary style," and that he feels he "will never be able to present sufficiently clearly and fully the sombre reality of what is going on." He is right. He has no narrative gift. His style is dry and unattractive, and he continually halts his tale by character-sketches of minor persons who have little importance in the events described. Also, the glossary at the beginning is incomplete. Also, there are no chapter-headings to guide the reader.

Brunovsky was imprisoned for four years, simply because he refused to accept high positions under an administration of which, though a strong socialist and anti-Tsarist, he did not approve. Three main things emerge from his book. First, the absolutely outrageous cruelty and injustice of Soviet "political" methods. Second, Brunovsky's utter lack of ordinary

446

diplomatic tact in his relations, as a prisoner, with the authorities. The miracle was that, after some of his plain-speaking, he was not shot in the back. (He admits that when in the early years he did occupy high positions he was exacting and severe with his subordinates.)

Third, the clumsy stupidity of Ogpu methods, which indeed are not a whit better than were those of the Tsarist police, as revealed in a recent book reviewed in this column. The prisoners were almost uniformly cleverer than their tyrants. Apparently Ogpu has no knowledge of human nature, and no interest in it. Brunovsky worsted Ogpu again and again. Ultimately he got away to Latvia by the method of exchange. And, sure enough, international cinema-operators were there when the exchange took place on the Soviet-Latvian border!

The Tsarist regime came to an end through fear and corruption. The Soviet regime will come to an end through fear (all dictatorships live in the shadow of death) and cruelty. Nothing can save it except a complete change of policy: which is impossible. There must be a lot of corruption in the Soviet regime, but probably much of it is indirect. (Thus the lowest grade of Soviet official earns twice as much as a school-teacher and is exempt from taxation.) Brunovsky says little about corruption. Indeed he states plainly that certain officials are quite incorruptible. You may read this book with difficulty, but when you have read it you will have something frightful to think about. Affrighting is the sole word for the general picture presented.

22 January 1931

Too Exciting! And It Was a History Book!

At the turn of the year one does extraordinary things — whether under the influence of the stars or from mere wild impulse I know not. I read some history. Always I am advising people to read history, and seldom reading it myself.

The value of reading history is fourfold. First, it teaches you that the good old times were the bad old times, and therefore that the world is improving, despite the jeremiads of disgruntled persons who, if they had lived a hundred years ago, would have wanted to live five hundred years ago, and if they had lived five hundred years ago would have wanted to live two thousand years ago, and if they had been contemporaries of Homer would have looked back with regret to the simplicities of the Stone Age. Secondly, it teaches you that the passion for cruelty has steadily decreased and respect for human life steadily increased.

Thirdly, it teaches you that human motives have been the same in all centuries; likewise the myopic vision of great men and their obstinacy in refusing to take advice. And fourthly, it teaches you that ignorance, stupidity, and lack of imagination are the root of all the ills mankind suffers from. I might add a fifthly: to wit, that nations will never get a fair chance on this earth until politicians and generals and Civil Service mandarins are compelled, before taking office, to pass a stiff examination in universal history.

I think it was Ranke who said: "No history can be written except universal history," meaning, of course, that all history is one and no part of it can be written without reference to all the rest. A large order, but things are what they are and the consequences of air-tight compartments will be what they will be. So why deceive ourselves?

Speaking of my history-reading. I doubt whether I have ever read a very long historical work right through, except H.G. Wells's *The Outline of History* and Gibbon. But I have made magnificent beginnings. I once started on a huge French work: *General History from the Fourth Century to the Present Time*, written and compiled under the direction of the great Ernest Lavisse and the lesser Yveling Rambaud. I read the first volume (800 terrific pages) and conscientiously made notes upon the same: which serried notes (amounting to thousands of words) still stand in proof of my industry. But the remaining eleven volumes I have not opened to this day.

Then I started the *Cambridge Modern History*. I was enthralled by the introduction and the two preliminary essays, which, however, were so brilliant and so enlightening that they rendered the rest of the first volume by comparison dull and hard reading. As for the succeeding volumes, I know them about as well as a traveller whose ship calls at Oporto for two hours knows Portugal. My other magnificent beginnings I will not trouble you with.

Well, at the turn of the year, I happened to pick up a volume of Froude. (Conceive the effrontery of "happening to pick up" an author of genius!) It was *The Reign of Mary Tudor*. People usually speak of only the commencement ("Henry VIII") and the close ("Elizabeth") of Froude's study of sixty years of sixteenth-century England. But I would maintain that the middle part of it is of tremendous interest. The smallish book on Mary's reign has held me as firmly as any novel I have read for years.

Few historians have been more severely criticised than Froude. In particular, he has been accused of a marked bias in favour of Protestantism as against the Papacy. I have not observed this bias in *Mary*, where there was plenty of room and excuse for it. Nor am I persuaded that Froude is more inaccurate than historians are apt to be. I would animadvert only upon the quality of Froude's writing, which is often as wild as was my sudden impulse to read him. But what descriptive power, what emotion of sympathy or antipathy, what breadth of view he has! And his raw material in the reign of Mary was not surpassed by that of the greater reigns. A virgin approaching the forties, badly advised and self-willed, who had hysterically convinced herself that she was in love with a man she had never seen! A Lady Jane Grey — the outstanding pathetic figure of English history — driven to the headsman's block at seventeen! The battle between Mary and Parliament, which Mary won and Parliament lost because she had the Tudor masculine courage and ability to stand up unaided to a situation! The all-pervading homicidal cruelty of the time, the victims only waiting a chance to be as cruel to their oppressors as their oppressors were to them! And the final tragedy of the appalling reign.

Yes *The Reign of Mary Tudor* can be read. And it is not a bed-book, because too exciting. Foreign critics have called Froude too English. He may have been — for foreigners, but nevertheless he had the world-vision. (And there is something to be said for Elizabethan England being the centre of the Western world.)

Not that I am an ardent partisan of English historians. I prefer foreign historians — for my own good and advancement in broad understanding. With the possible exception of Gibbon, I doubt whether we have had a historian on the level of the greatest foreign historians. And even Gibbon — well, if I had to guide a would-be student of Rome I would counsel him to read Ferrero before reading Gibbon. Ferrero's *Greatness and Decline of Rome* is not a better book than *The Decline and Fall*. It is not so good a book. But it is much shorter, and it "reads itself," which Gibbon certainly does not. And it is written — to the extreme of vividness — with modern problems always in mind. No one can read Ferrero without deriving from him a finer and wider comprehension of the age of Mr. Ramsay MacDonald, and a keener sense of the liveliness of life itself.

But who is Ferrero, and who is Gibbon, to compare with Mommsen? There are two absolutely great nineteenth-century historians. One is Mommsen, and the other is Ranke (*History of the Popes, History of England*, etc.). There may be others, but I know not of them. I have read a lot of Mommsen and not a quarter enough of Ranke. I have yet to meet the equals, anywhere of these two. They may be majestic — they are intensely readable. They have colour, picturesqueness, drama, solid wisdom, and very few prejudices.

Do not shy at the name, for instance, of Mommsen. You may obtain him in the reassuring Everyman Library, with a long Introduction by Freeman (the man who attempted and failed to slay Froude). Try Mommsen. And when you have recovered from the intoxication of him, try Ranke. You will then know what first-rate history is. If you ask why you, a Briton, should read about Rome and Italy, I should reply, "Why not?" The modern world is based on Rome. Besides, you can learn as much from the history of any one age as from the history of any other age. All history is one, because all history is human. And first-rate historical writing is exceedingly rare.

29 January 1931

The Most Sophisticated Man on Earth

George Jean Nathan ("America's foremost dramatic critic") rose into notoriety on the wings of an excellent periodical, *The American Mercury*, which is still directed by its founder, H.L. Mencken, a first-rate journalist. But Nathan parted from Mencken, and in what meadow he frisks to-day I know not. He has written a book, *Testament of a Critic* (Knopf, 7s. 6d.). Mr. Knopf has done Nathan a double disservice. He has published, as a photograph of his author, the photograph of some mother's unsophisticated darling of seventeen such as one can see in droves on a fine afternoon on the sacred Hill of Harrow. Now in his book George Nathan confesses to "forty odd," and I have calculated that he must be appreciably nearer fifty than forty — say forty-seven. Age may not be important, but by means of a photograph to accuse Nathan of lack of sophistication is merely monstrous. The whole of *Testament of a Critic* is a fervid effort to prove

449

that Nathan is the most sophisticated man on earth.

The second disservice of Mr. Knopf's is to state that Nathan has been proclaimed in Europe as "the greatest critical voice in the field of international drama." Who made the proclamation? That is the point.

The book is divided into four parts: "Revelation," "Proverbs," "Chronicles," and "Lamentations." Which sub-titles seem to me to be rather cheap. "Revelation" is Nathan's account of himself. The other three parts are his account of drama and the film. "Revelation" is the most interesting part of the work, and it is interesting in a way probably unsuspected by the author. Anyhow it is a very partial disclosure. We learn from it that he is not in favour of marriage before fifty, if then; and that he has no use for women save as beautiful conversational adjuncts in hours of ease. Still, Nathan's hours of ease must be plentiful; for he is against hard work. "Show me a man," says he, "who, as the phrase goes, works himself to death and I'll show you an unimaginative dolt." Well, I will show him Balzac.

Again, he is cautiously disdainful of money. "The best artists living to-day . . . are without exception men who have no need longer to worry about financial matters." To which the retort is monosyllabic: Rats! . . . What about D.H. Lawrence? Nathan scorns politics, which he calls "scurvy diversions of the rabble." (I was wrong — Nathan cannot after all be over seventeen.) His own notion of enjoyment is the diversion of "putting his inferiors in their places." (Say sixteen.)

The bulk of the alleged *Testament* is fairly bright chatter about stage and screen, with a few wholesome unwelcome truths scattered about therein. But it is no more. As for Nathan being "the greatest critical voice," etc., he says, truly: "*Behind* every great dramatic critic you will find one or more great dramatists." (My italics.) Nathan's chosen modern dramatist is Eugene O'Neill! He has no other!

There is some terrible maladroit writing in this slick book. "I suspect that what other men believe . . . may stand them in quite as sound service as my own beliefs stand me." One might write a column to expose the recondite vices of Nathan's style, so airy, negligent and tortuous.

I wonder what George Nathan, from the secret places of his lofty superiority complex, would find to berate in three novels by young women which I have just read. Cleverness is the lowest of good qualities: it cannot, however, fairly be called a bad quality. George Nathan has it, but all these three members of the sex which George Nathan derides have it in an immeasurably higher degree. Also they all three know far more about the job of writing than George Nathan does or ever will. The (merely) cleverest of the three books, *High Table* by Joanna Cannan, has already been noticed in this paper.

Lorna Rea's *Rachel Moon* (Heinemann, 7s. 6d.) has a somewhat original theme, with an elaborate study of a marked type of character — the born domestic martyr. The observation, the wit, the understanding, the invention and the imagination displayed in *Rachel Moon* add themselves up to an impressive amount. The management of the narrative, too, is excellent, except that some of the conversations, though truthful enough, are quite unnecessarily long.

Rachel is an awful girl, ruthless, heartless, selfish, cruel in the sweet determination to be a martyr at any cost — to other people. She quite calmly ruins lives (but never her own) with the Midas touch of her 22-carat sense of duty — actually a sense of pleasure. And she is conceited, vain-glorious, and a fool. She is all these things at the beginning of the book, at the age of eighteen, and she is much worse at the close. She cannot excite sympathy, except perhaps among the misguided, and I am sure that if Mrs. Rea followed her career to its end the end would prove to be a Scotland Yard-baffling assassination. The born female martyr is often the born murderer, and her "taking off" is usually an event which all her acquaintances and victims support with a noble fortitude.

But the case of Rachel Moon is essentially pathological. She has the unmistakable symptoms of chronic hysteria. Now chronic hysteria is just as definitely a disease as, say, elephantiasis: a fact which few realise. Mrs. Rea, in her attitude towards Rachel, does not sufficiently emphasise this important point; she hardly even refers to it; which is a pity. Further, I doubt whether a pathological specimen provides suitable material for a heroine. Rachel is the stuff of a minor character. For this reason I should not rank *Rachel Moon* as high as *Six Mrs. Greenes*. At the same time it has more accomplishment and more power; and it amply proves that Mrs. Rea can write a novel. *Six Mrs. Greenes*, while loosely described as a novel, was a collection of separate sketches.

My third novel, Winifred Holtby's *Poor Caroline* (Cape, 7s. 6d.), has a broader sweep than the other two. It relates the history of the totally wild-cat "Christian Cinema Company," in the hands of the aged poor Caroline, a woman whose sole outfit was her tremendous gift of self-deception. The egregious Christian Cinema Company never had the slightest chance of success; but Caroline believed absolutely in it, and died in the faith of it. The poor thing carried fatuity and blindness to the height of grandeur, especially at Board Meetings.

The ridiculous history is shown in different aspects (manner of *The Ring and the Book*), the aspects seen respectively by Caroline herself, by a financier, by an inventor, by a rascal, by a clergyman, etc., etc. The book is very readable, and of a various picturesqueness. And it is free from sentimentality. All the above-named novels are free from sentimentality. They are all strongly conceived, carefully planned, and admirably written. And they are all a shade too clever.

5 February 1931

People Who Want To Know You

Authors are strange people. I am one myself, and I probably know as many authors as any man living — except literary agents and income-tax surveyors. Authors are ticklish, sensitive people, and, more than most categories of persons, they are victims (generally willing enough) of the astounding and to me incomprehensible mania for "meeting" celebrities, notorieties and infamies.

So far as I am aware I have never had the desire to meet a celebrity because he was a celebrity. On the contrary I have had, and still have, the desire to avoid him. "But you are a great admirer of his books!" said an acquaintance to me once, when I had demurred to an encounter with genius. "Yes, I am," I said. "That's why I don't want to meet him. If I run across him by chance, all right! But deliberately to go out of my way to meet him — No!" And I never did meet him.

One has one's sense of dignity. Which sense of dignity works both ways. Once, in the historic past, when I was travelling in a special train of immense prestige, an acquaintance stepped into my compartment and said: "Forbes-Robertson is on this train and would like to come and see you." I was touched; I could hardly believe it. But I would not agree to the proposition, which seemed to me monstrous: my extremely illustrious senior approaching *me*! "No," I said. "I will go and see him." But Sir Johnston and I met in the corridor, he being on his way to me. I won, because it was in his compartment, not mine, that we sat and grew friendly.

Again, I was once sitting in a night-club or nightish-club when someone unknown to me came up and said: "Mr. Ralph Knott is at that table there. He would be so glad if you would go and talk to him. He wants to know you." (The late Ralph Knott — architect of the new London County Hall.) I didn't like this idea a bit. Authors are strange people. I held that if Mr. Knott wanted to know me he might at least have come forward and introduced himself. But then I recalled my own private proverb, which says: "Only men of short moral stature find it necessary to stand on their dignity." I rose and visited Mr. Knott.

Still, authors are strange people. On another occasion in a restaurant, a friend came up to my table and said with a superb histrionic modesty: "Steve Donoghue is dining with me. Do come and talk to him." My absurd sense of dignity was outraged. I thought: "A stop must positively be put to this kind of thing." And aloud I said: "No! Bring him along here. I'll be delighted." My friend was somewhat staggered, for at that time Steve was the first favourite in England. Nevertheless, Steve Donoghue did allow himself to be brought along, and he did delight me.

More than once this true story has been disbelieved. But it is less incredible than another true story. At a certain private dinner of male celebrities I was put on our host's right hand, and on his left was — Mr. Solly Joel. Then it was I first realised that somehow I had indeed "arrived."

I could continue about celebrities for columns, but if I am to write about individuals I prefer to deal with non-celebrities. Once I sold forty thousand words of reminiscences, in the dark, to the proprietor of a daily paper. When the copy was delivered the proprietor offered the objection that he had expected celebrities in my reminiscences, and there weren't any. So the reminiscences were removed from him and sold to another daily paper whose editor was less insistent on fame*.

The above remarks were begotten of my perusal of Mrs. C.N. Williamson's volume of literary reminiscences, *The Inky Way* (Chapman and Hall, 18s.), which has become a best-seller. My friendship with both Mrs. Williamson and her late husband "C.N." dates back full thirty years. C.N. had two foibles. He had a passion for tidiness, a virtue which he

---

* The reminiscences were actually Bennett's *Journal 1929*, serial rights in which were bought originally by the *Daily Telegraph*, but then re-sold to the *Daily Mail*, where they began appearing at the end of March 1930.

inculcated in others. Before leaving his editorial office he would "tidy" his desk — by shoving everything on it pell mell into a drawer. Then he would exclaim with pride: "There!" His second foible was a firm belief that he had perfected a system capable of beating the bank at Monte Carlo. His bland, confident assertion of this belief left me speechless outside the Casino.

Mrs. Williamson has a few benevolent souvenirs of myself. I have at least one of her. Once, when I was a young editor, and she was Alice Livingston, she came in to interview me on business, and said with a gentle timorous pride which I have never seen surpassed: "I have just sold a story to the *Strand Magazine* for thirteen pounds!" You may judge from the figure how long this was ago.

There are two schools of reminiscences, the kindly and the chatty. The latter is of course the more enthralling. Mrs. Williamson is an exponent of the former school. She is kindly about everybody, with one exception. That exception, I regret to say, is myself, as to whom she prints a most monstrous libel. (And me one of her first buying editors!) She says that I like split infinitives! Nothing worse was ever written of a self-respecting author. I have published over seventy books, and if she can show me a split infinitive in any one of them I will present her with a new hat of her own choosing. I hate split infinitives. An antique prejudice, but I belong to the Old Guard. I forgive her. I shall issue no writ.

What I like and envy in her is her unfailing natural gift for seeing the bright side of things. A supreme example is the following. She was one day strolling towards the Monte Carlo Casino with George Alexander, and their talk was not of roulette nor trente-et-quarante, but of what comes after death. Alexander said: "I believe that nothing comes after; just annihilation." Shortly afterwards Alexander died. Mrs. Williamson adds: *"Soon he must have learnt with joy how he had been mistaken."* (My italics.) This is faith. *The Inky Way* is written with all the skill in arrangement and diversity and serial interest which one would expect from a thoroughly practised novelist.

What I desiderate more than anything in the reminiscential line is a book of reminiscences by a known person about encounters with the admiring uncelebrated. Such a book might be marvellous. I would not write it myself, but I have heaped material for it. Example. Once on board ship a lady said to me suddenly: "Oh, Mr. Bennett, I do love your *Old Wives' Tale.*" I made no reply, because — well, what are you to reply that is not desolatingly banal? She thought I was displeased and went on: "But I love your *serious* books too!" "For instance?" I enquired. "Well, *How to Live on Twenty-Four Hours a Day.*"

AUTHOR INDEX

Achard, Marcel, 74
Achurch, Janet, 139
Acton, Harold, 204, 216
Adams, Francis, 97
Addison, Joseph, 11
Agate, James, 137-138, 145-146
Aguilar, Grace, 109
Aiken, Conrad, 64
Ainger, Canon, 156
Alcott, Louisa, 295, 302
Aldington, Richard, 205, 305-306
Allen, Austen, 278
Allen, Walter, xvi
"Alpha of the Plough" [A.G. Gardiner], 160, 162-163
Amiel, 53-55
Andersen, Hans Christian, 109
Anderson, Sherwood, 141
Apperson, G.L., 314
Applin, Arthur, 88
Archer, Frank, 8
Archer, William, 8, 139, 199-200
Aristophanes, 343
Aristotle, 119, 132, 207, 337
Arliss, George, 157
Arnold, Matthew, 53-54, 69, 118, 132, 145, 158, 207, 276, 288, 356, 357, 421, 429
Arthur, William, 109n
Ashton, Helen, 192, 346, 347
Asquith, Herbert, 261-263
Aubry, G. Jean, 96-97
Auriant, 155-156
Austen, Jane, 68, 157, 158, 161, 178, 215, 269, 329
Azevedo, Aluizio, 148

Babbitt, Irving, 308
Bacchelli, Riccardo, 373
Bacon, Francis, 84, 398
Baedeker, Karl, 198, 295
Baker, George, 199-200
Baldwin, Stanley, 153, 186, 378
Balzac, Honoré de, xxv, 5, 16, 17, 21, 23, 26, 31, 52, 60, 67, 102,
107, 122, 156, 186, 192, 211, 227, 230-232, 234, 237, 244, 259, 260-261, 297, 343, 450
Barbusse, Henri, 322
Baring, Maurice, 7, 23
Barker, Dudley, xxiv
Barker, Harley Granville, 284
Barrès, Maurice, 148, 444
Barrie, Sir James, 117, 162, 178, 201, 354
Barwick, G.F., 265-266
Bates, H.E., 321
Battúta, Ibn, 263
Baty, Gaston, 445
Bayle, Pierre, 115
"Beachcomber" [D.B. Wyndham Lewis and J.B. Morton], 44n, 267-268, 323
Beard, Charles and Mary, 69, 77, 144
Beaumarchais, 30
Beaverbrook, Lord, xvii-xxiii, xxvii, 106n, 147, 343
Beckett, Samuel, 293n
Becque, Henri, 29-30
Beer, Thomas, 159
Beerbohm, Max, 163, 222, 276
Bell, Clive, 51
Bell, Gertrude, 87
Belloc, Hilaire, 107, 162, 214, 222, 276
Benda, Julien, 183, 205, 308-309
Benefield, Barry, 140-141
Benét, Stephen Vincent, 277
Benjamin, René, 230-231
Bennett, Miss E.A., 196n
Bentley, Phyllis, 217
Beresford, John, 64
Beresford, J.D., 208
Bergson, Henri, 73
Bernard, St., 291
Bernard, Tristan, 366
Besant, Annie, 112
Bett, Henry, 326
Bibesco, Princess, 367
Bierce, Ambrose, 144

455

TITLE INDEX

TITLE INDEX

TITLE INDEX

TITLE INDEX